WORLD WAR II PACIFIC ISLAND GUIDE

WORLD WAR II PACIFIC ISLAND GUIDE

A Geo-Military Study

GORDON L. ROTTMAN

Foreword by Benis M. Frank

GREENWOOD PRESS
Westport, Connecticut • London

ISBN: 0–313–31395–4

Greenwood Press, 88 Post Road West, Westport, CT 06881
An imprint of Greenwood Publishing Group, Inc.

Printed in the United States of America

To all those Allied soldiers, marines, sailors, and airmen,
the civilians of those nations,
and the indigenous populations who endured the war in the Pacific.

Contents

CONTENTS

Maps

Foreword

Without a doubt, Gordon Rottman's *World War II Pacific Island Guide: A Geo-Military Study* is the most complete and comprehensive *vade mecum* I have ever read. Not only does he provide a complete survey of each Pacific islands on which a major battle was fought, but he also describes that action, and the units involved, and at the end of each chapter, he provides a succinct and valuable bibliography of important secondary source publications—including official histories—which detail the fighting that took place.

Equally as important as the island descriptions is the material in the front of the book: an expansive description of the Pacific itself; the geography, geology, and climatology of the Pacific islands; a listing of the discovery of the various islands and island groups; the differing nature and populations of the islands; and how each location figured in Japanese and Allied strategic planning in World War II. In addition, Mr. Rottman provides an interesting discussion of the political dynamics of what is now known as the "Pacific Rim." Almost equal in importance is his description of Allied and Japanese military organization, ranks, and order of battle for each combat action noted. It should be pointed out that while this book has worth of its own, it also serves as an excellent handbook to have immediately available as one reads a campaign narration or combat history. I would designate *World War II Pacific Island Guide* as a momentous standard reference which belongs in the library of every military historian and military history buff.

Benis M. Frank
Chief Historian of the Marine Corps, Retired

Acknowledgments

The greatest expenditure of effort in the preparation of this book was the collection of viable reference sources. Living in southwestern Louisiana, an area almost as remote as the islands examined in this book, poses many challenges to conducting serious research. Without the help of various libraries this would have been a most difficult task. The Beauregard Parish Library in DeRidder obtained scores of obscure books through inter-library loan, a truly invaluable service without which this book would have been almost impossible to research. The Vernon Parish Library in Leesville and the Allen Library on Fort Polk provided invaluable assistance in many research matters. David Bingham of the Fort Polk Military Museum made available its closed reference library, another valuable source of materials. The excellent military, history, and government collections of the Fondern Library at Rice University in Houston, Texas was of immeasurable value. A special thanks goes to Evyln Englander, Marine Corps Historical Branch Library, Washington Navy Yard, DC, and to the Service Historique de l'Armee de Terre.

Numerous individuals provided resources, information, and encouragement, including: Paul Lemmer, Jack McKillop, Tim Lanzendoerfer (Webmaster, The Pacific War: The U.S. Navy http://www.microworks.net/pacific), Michael Yared, and Marc Small. A very special thanks is deserved by the many participants of WWII@topica.com and WWII-L@LISTSERV.ACSU.BUFFALO.EDU, World War II discussion groups who unselfishly shared their wealth of knowledge and countless small details.

Introduction

While researching *U.S. Marine Corps World War II Order of Battle*, the companion to this volume, the author found it to be surprisingly difficult to find many facts and details regarding the islands of the Pacific on which military operations occurred or military bases were established. While every official military history of specific operations discusses the island objective to some degree, the coverage is uneven and frequently incomplete. In order to obtain complete geo-military and other pertinent information on a given island sometimes up to a dozen references need be consulted. This book is essentially a compilation of data and materials from a broad range of reference sources, both contemporary and modern. Its aim is to provide historians, researchers, academicians, veterans, wargamers, and those generally interested in World War II in the Pacific a single complete reference on each island. While the principal focus is on ground action, supporting and related naval and air operations are addressed as well.

The land area on which World War II in the Pacific theater was fought covers an area significantly less than that in the European-Mediterranean theater. In fact, the total land area of the Pacific islands will fit nicely into Western Europe. However, the Pacific Ocean spans almost a third of the earth's circumference covering more of the earth's surface than the total combined land surface, and stretches from the sub-Arctic Aleutian Islands south to Antarctica. The Pacific is almost eighteen times the size of the continental United States and abuts five continents. Colonial empires, ancient cultures, and modern world powers clashed in a region of greatly varied geographic, climatic, and political environments.

Any study of the Pacific War naturally focuses on the myriad of islands scattered across this immense ocean. While there were similarities between islands within specific regions, no two were exactly alike. There were vast differences between many providing a constantly changing combat environment as the Allies advanced across the Pacific. The Allies found that inshore waters, the beaches, the terrain ashore, vegetation, climate, and health hazards were varied and required a high degree of adaptability and flexibility of commanders and men.

The campaign histories, biographies, and memoirs of the war tell of battles and unforgettable experiences, but for one to fully analyze the operations ashore, in the air, and at sea, for the latter two were explicitly tied to island bases, a study of the islands is required. Also, an in-depth study of operations requires a detailed source of background material on each island as it appeared during the war.

Obviously not every one of the thousands of islands in the Pacific can be addressed, but those islands on which actions were fought or played other key roles in the Pacific War are examined. This is generally presented in the order the actions were fought and progressed across the Pacific on the two main axises of advance toward the ultimate island objective, Japan. Some islands served only as staging bases and no combat took place on them. The most important of these will be discussed as well because of their key role to the overall strategy of the Pacific War.

Most islands and atolls are arrayed in island groups or archipelagos and this part will be arranged accordingly. A brief overview and common aspects of each island group or archipelago begin the chapters followed by a detailed study of the key islands. This information includes:

Island or atoll name, alternative names, Allied code name(s), nickname.

Location (within the atoll or island group, its relation to the larger islands or land masses).

Physical description (type of island or atoll, shape).

Island or atoll dimensions (length, width, orientation of long axis).

Geographic characteristics (geophysical origin, soil, land forms, key terrain features, elevations, drainage, vegetation, offshore waters/bottom).

Environment (meteorology, health hazards).

Historical background (settlement, modern discovery, territorial claims).

Sovereignty, administration, and capital.

Indigenous populations (1941 ethnic groups, population).

Date of Japanese occupation and strategic intent.

Location of main Japanese defenses, installations, and airfields.

Japanese order of battle (list of units) at the time of the Allied assault.

Allied strategic intent for seizing the island.

Allied order of battle; ground force, naval task force, supporting air services, key commanders.

H-Hour, D-Day of the Allied assault; operation code name.

Landing beaches (code names and locations).

General flow of the land battle and any significant military "firsts."

Date and time island was declared secure.

Allied and Japanese casualties.

Development as an Allied base (military bases, airfields, naval stations).

Postwar sovereignty and political status and the island today.

The reading suggestions provided at the end of each chapter focus on the official service histories and readily available popular campaign histories. Most of those listed are those still in print.

A pointer to researchers. Further research on any Pacific island will bear a surprising variety and depth of material by a detailed search of the Internet. Without the aid of the Internet this would have been a much shallower effort to provide a viable research tool.

Abbreviations

ABDACOM	American-British-Dutch-Australian Command
aka	also known as
ANZAC	Australian-New Zealand Area Command
APO SF	Army Post Office, San Francisco
FPO SF	Fleet Post Office, San Francisco
IIIAC	III Amphibious Corps (USMC)
IJA	Imperial Japanese Army
IJN	Imperial Japanese Navy
IMAC	I Marine Amphibious Corps
KIA	Killed in Action
NEI	Netherlands East Indies
NGVR	New Guinea Volunteer Rifles
PI	Philippine Islands
PS	Philippine Scouts (component of the U.S. Army)
POW	Prisoner of War
RAA	Royal Australian Army
RAAF	Royal Australian Air Force
RNZAF	Royal New Zealand Air Force
Seabees	Naval Construction Battalions (derived from "CB")
SNLF	*Special Naval Landing Force* (Japanese)
TH	Territory of Hawaii
TF	Task Force
US	United States
USA	United States Army

USAAF	United States Army Air Forces*
US-Fil	United States-Filipino (combined forces)
USMC	United States Marine Corps
USN	United States Navy
USS	United States Ship (followed by ship's name)
VAC	V Amphibious Corps (USMC)
VOC	Vereenigde Ooslindische Compagnie (United [Dutch] East India Company)
V-J Day	Victory over Japan Day (2 September 1945)
WIA	Wounded in Action
(−)	Less (elements detached from parent unit)

U.S. NAVY SHIP TYPE CLASSIFICATIONS

The U.S. Navy has used warship classification codes since 1920 as an abbreviated means of identifying ships rather than using complete designations. Most ship types were designated by two letters, but up to four were used for specialized types. The ship classification code was followed by its hull number within its type, e.g., BB-35. Ship types should not be confused with ship classes, which was the designation given to ships of the same design. Classes were designated by the name of the lead ship built in that class. The following list is not exhaustive, but provides those mentioned in this book.

Code	Type Nomenclature
AG	Miscellaneous auxiliary
BB	Battleship
CA	Heavy cruiser
CL	Light cruiser
CV	Fleet aircraft carrier
CVE	Escort aircraft carrier†
DD	Destroyer
IX	Unclassified vessel
PG	Gunboat
PT	Patrol torpedo boat
SS	Submarine
YP	Harbor patrol boat

*The U.S. Army's air service was commonly called the U.S. Army Air Corps through World War II, but officially it was the U.S. Army Air Forces having been redesignated as such on 20 June 1941.

† Originally designated aircraft escort vessels (AVG) until 20 August 1942 when redesignated auxiliary aircraft carriers (ACV). Redesignated aircraft carrier, escort (CVE) on 15 July 1943.

PART ONE
GEO-MILITARY ASPECTS
OF THE PACIFIC THEATER

The Pacific theater in World War II, what the Japanese referred to as the *Dai Toa Senso Senkum* (Greater East Asia War), presented an extremely difficult strategic and tactical operating environment to all of the belligerents. The logistics effort alone posed difficulties not even imagined a few years earlier. Pre-war projections of the forces and supplies necessary for a protracted war in the Pacific were only a fraction of what was really required. Coupled with the vast distances, inhospitable climate, rugged terrain, the variables found on different islands, and the very nature of the reality of combat in the Pacific, it was one of the most difficult and challenging military theaters of operations experienced.

THE PACIFIC OCEAN

The Pacific Ocean was named by Portuguese explorer Fernão de Magalhães (aka Ferdinand Magellan), while leading a Spanish fleet around the world in 1520–23, *Mar Pacifico*—the "peaceful sea." The Japanese call it *Tai Heiyo*. The vastness of the Pacific Ocean cannot be understated (see Map 1). It stretches 9,600 miles (15,450 kilometers) from the Bering Strait between Alaska and Russia to Cape Adare, Antarctica. It is at its widest on latitude 8° north between Panama and the Malay Peninsula on mainland Southeast Asia, 15,000 miles (24,000 kilometers), about three-fifths the distance around the globe, almost three times the width of the United States. The Pacific and its marginal seas cover approximately 70 million square miles (181 million square kilometers), an area eighteen times larger than the United States, one-third of the world's surface and more than the earth's total land area. It spans thirteen time zones, 1 through 7 eastward from the International Date Line to South America and 19 through 24 eastward from the Indian Ocean to the International Date Line, longitude 180° west. The Pacific is bounded by five of the world's seven continents: North and South America, Asia, Australia, and Antarctica. It was truly a "war of distances," as the Pacific theater was described by Brigadier General Charles Willoughby, MacArthur's intelligence officer.

The Pacific is divided geographically into the North and South Pacific by the equator,

Map 1
Pacific Ocean

BERING SEA

GULF OF ALASKA

PRIBILOF IS.

ALASKA

KODIAK

Komandorski Is.

ALEUTIAN IS.

Attu   Kiska

NEAR IS.   RAT IS.   ANDREANOF IS.

UNIMAK

Dutch Harbor
UNALASKA

UMNAK

PACIFIC OCEAN

HAWAIIAN ISLANDS

Kure I.   MIDWAY I.

Lisianski I.

Laysan I.

Gardner I.

Necker I.

OAHU

HAWAII

WAKE I.

Johnston I.

Taongi

etok

MARSHALL ISLANDS

ape   Kwajalein

Jaluit

Kusaie I.

Palmyra I.

Fanning I.

Christmas I.

marang I.

GILBERT ISLANDS

HOWLAND I.
BAKER I.

NAURU

Ocean I.

PHOENIX IS.

Malden I.

Starbuck I.

MARQUESAS

TASMAN IS.

ELLICE IS.

Funafuti

UNION IS.

Tongareva

Vostok I.

TUAMOTU

SANTA CRUZ IS.

N IS.

NEW HEBRIDES

FIJI IS.

SAMOA IS.

PALMERSTON IS.

SOCIETY IS.

LOYALTY IS.

NEW CALEDONIA

TONGA IS.

Tongatabu

COOK IS.

but other terms are encountered such as the Southwest, Central, and Western Pacific to more closely define specific areas, especially in regard to military operations. The strategic military areas are discussed in the appropriate sections. There are dozens of named marginal seas defined by the islands and island groups surrounding them or sandwiched between large islands and mainland areas. Most geographers do not recognize the Antarctic Ocean, accepting rather that the Pacific laps the shores of Antarctica. Others define the southern edge of the Pacific as 50° south latitude with the waters surrounding Antarctica as the Antarctic or Southern Ocean. The Pacific's average depth is 12,900 feet (3,900 meters), but the world's deepest water is found in the Challenger Deep in the Marianas Trench off of Guam at 36,198 feet (11,033 meters). The narrow continental shelves off of North and South America are usually no more than 600 feet (183 meters); the continental shelves off of Asia and Australia are much broader.

The surface temperate of the water at the equator may be as high as 82°F (28°C), but cools as one travels north or south. Likewise the air temperature cools as one travels away from the equator, which remains consistently hot. Weather patterns over the Pacific vary greatly through the seasons because of the prevailing wind belts, although most areas experience moderate to high temperatures and high humidity year round. The tradewinds are caused by temperature differences in the lower latitudes. Heated air along the equator causes the hot air to rise and the tradewinds bring in cooler air to replace the hot. They blow from approximately the 30° north and south latitudes toward the equator coming out of the southeast in the Southern Hemisphere and from the northeast north of the equator. The prevailing westerly winds originate between 30 and 60° north and south of the equator frequently blowing at a steady 40 miles (64 kilometers) per hour. They bring stormy weather and rains along the 60° latitude, but provide little precipitation at 30°. The winds do not provide absolute weather conditions in most areas because of the effects of land masses and ocean currents, and the temperature changes they induce, on local wind patterns. In the North Pacific the ocean's surface currents are dominated by a warm-water, clockwise gyre (broad circular system current) and in the South Pacific by a cool, counterclockwise gyre. The proximity of islands to larger island land masses and mainland areas also affects temperatures, wind patterns, rain, and storms. Monsoons (from old Dutch *monssoen* and Portuguese *moncáo*—season) are encountered in the Southwest Pacific and elsewhere. These are winds that reverse themselves, bringing alternating wet and dry seasons. These winds are affected by the proximity of the Asian land mass with dry monsoon winds blowing from the mainland and wet monsoon winds from the ocean. Much of the rain in the Pacific region is caused by tropical cyclones accompanied by high winds. When cyclone winds reach 74 miles (119 kilometers) per hour they are called hurricanes in the southern and eastern Pacific and typhoons (a name derived from the Cantonese *tai fung*—great wind) in the western Pacific.

The Pacific Rim (a modern phrase, not used during World War II) is also known as the Rim of Fire (another modern phrase) because of the extensive volcanic activity found along much of its periphery, especially its western, southwestern, and northeastern edges where islands and land masses are on or near tectonic plates. This also makes the region earthquake- and tremor-prone. Submarine earthquakes can generate massive oceanic tidal waves called *tsunamis* (pronounced "tsoo-NAH-meez") capable of transiting thousands of miles of ocean unimpeded by significant land areas. Hurricanes and typhoons had little effect on military operations, although two typhoons in the western Pacific delayed operations. A 110-knot typhoon on 18 December 1944 sank three U.S. destroyers east of the Philippines with almost 800 men and caused significant damage to other ships to include the loss of 146 aircraft. Another on 3 October 1944 caused the 3d U.S. Fleet to suspend operations off of Formosa for two days. Minor earthquakes were experienced on Guadalcanal and Leyte, but had little impact and no *tsunamis* were noted.

Little was known of many of the Pacific islands. There were few accurate maps with many depicting only coastal terrain features. A landing force going ashore frequently found themselves encountering previously unknown swamps, hills, and ridges. Aerial photographs were essential in providing terrain data, but did not show the lay of the land beneath the multilayered jungle canopy. In the scramble to find information old sailing guides were consulted and former seamen, residents, traders, and travelers were sought out. Naval operations were guided by charts originating in the eighteenth century forcing extreme caution in navigating nearshore waters. The latitude and longitude of many islands were often misplotted. One ship, lying offshore of an island, reported she was one to one and one-half miles inland according to the chart. Naval engagements were sometimes terminated for fear of running aground in uncharted waters. Such was the operating environment.

THE ISLANDS

The islands of the Pacific Ocean are collectively known as Oceania (a term little used during the war). For all of the Pacific's massiveness, excluding Japan, New Zealand, New Guinea, Netherlands East Indies, and the Philippines, Oceania's land area totals only 42,000 square miles (109,000 square kilometers), just slightly less land area than Cuba, Bulgaria, or Newfoundland and a little more than the state of Ohio. Thousands of islands, islets, and reefs constitute this land area.

When one looks at a map of the Pacific and Oceania it is easy to diminish the vast distances involved. In reality the smaller islands appearing as pinpoints or pinheads would not even be visible if accurately depicted to scale. While a particular group of islands may appear to be in close proximity to one another they are actually so distant that it is no wonder it sometimes took hundreds of years for European explorers to discover all of the islands in a single group. For example, it took sixty years for all of the sixteen atolls and islands comprising the Gilbert Islands to be discovered, and they stretch in a line only some 600 miles (965 kilometers) in length. Some historians wonder at the "implausibility" of Portuguese explorer Ferdinand Magellan in 1521 to have crossed the entire Pacific from the tip of South America 9,000 miles (14,484 kilometers) to discover the Mariana Islands while missing dozens of other island groups through which his ships sailed. This becomes more understandable when one first considers that from a masthead the horizon is only twenty or so miles distant. Visibility is foreshortened by haze and sun glare, and shadowy, low-lying islands merge into clouds on the horizon.

In this study the Pacific islands are collected in "island groups," for which there is no fixed definition. An island group normally constitutes a chain or loose grouping of islands and atolls related by proximity to one another, even though they may sometimes be hundreds of miles apart, and separated from other groups by a relatively greater distance. They are often physically related by virtue of emerging from the ocean atop a common submarine mountain chain. Within some of the more densely distributed island groups will be found smaller island groups, perhaps two to six islands or atolls in comparatively close proximity, although they may or may not be in sight of one another. The larger island groups tend to be named after some discoverer or managed to retain a variation of an ancient native name, but the smaller integral island groups are usually named after the cluster's major island. The term "archipelago" (derived from the Greek/Italian *Ar-chipelago*—Aegean Sea, noted for its many small islands), describes a large island group spread over a comparatively vast area. While any large island group may be informally or geographically referred to as an archipelago, for example, the Philippine Archipelago, the only island group of note in the Pacific so identified is the Bismarck Archipelago. There are a number of remote, single islands dotted about the Pacific. Some geographers strive to include these with comparatively close island groups, but few are physically related. The single islands are merely the top of a usually high and segregated mountain surrounded by deep seas. The Japanese have their own terms for archipelagos, groups, and islands. These are discussed in the Western Pacific section.

Island groups are formerly named, for example, the Solomon Islands or Mariana Islands, but are informally known simply as the Solomons or Marianas. Individual islands and atolls, themselves comprised of from two to scores of islands and islets, may have borne European names in honor of the discoverer, a notable member of the expedition, of royalty or another benefactor, a physical attribute, or the day on which it was discovered, for example, Christmas or Thursday. It was not uncommon for a given island to have two to four European names (Spanish, Portuguese, English, French, Dutch, American, Russian) and one or two native names. The Japanese added their own names to the list. European names also changed as the island's sovereignty changed. Native names were commonly retained for many islands, although the accepted native names were often mispronounced and misspelled. Many of the islands today, which have been granted their independence from colonial or mandated powers, are known by corrected native spellings or have had ancient native names restored. The island names used in this work are those commonly accepted by the U.S. armed forces, but even here there were conflicts. Military code names were assigned to islands during World War II. These were sometimes changed if it was felt that they had been compromised (learned of by the enemy) or after combat operations were completed and the island was developed as a base.

Geographically there are four broad physical categories of islands in the Pacific: volcanic islands, reef islands, continental islands, and atolls.

Volcanic Islands

Many of the moderately larger islands were created by volcanic eruptions. Also referred to as shield volcanoes, the islands were built up out of the ocean by relatively thin layers of lava to form a roughly shield shape, generally oval or circular, but they may be of any irregular shape. The largest shield volcano island in the Pacific is Hawaii. Other examples are the Samoa Islands, Mariana Islands, and Nauru and Ocean Islands. Such islands are actually in stage 4 of the development of an atoll (see below). On smaller islands of this type the volcanic cone, which may or may not be dormant, is still distinguishable and there is little if any fringing coastal plain. The mountain sides are usually heavily eroded resulting in rugged terrain with streams flowing into the sea. Larger volcanic islands, such as found in the Marianas, were clusters of two or more volcanoes resulting in the multiple lava flows merging to form a single island. Erosion of the cones leveled the land between the extinct volcanoes to form plains. The soil is habitually fertile and the islands are covered with lush vegetation. The coastline is often lined with rocky cliffs, but small beaches are found. The islands are usually surrounded by barrier and fringing reefs. These types of islands are also referred to as oceanic islands as their bases are comprised of basaltic rock thrusting up from the ocean's bottom.

Reef Islands

Reef limestone islands were formed by the upheaval of the earth's crust through subtle tectonic plate movements and earthquakes. This explains why massive coral cliffs and ridges are found inland on some islands. The resulting exposed land is generally level, and soils well developed as vegetation, delivered by sea, wind, and birds, decomposed and the land became fertile. Most of the islands in the Tongas are raised reef islands, as are the Palaus. There are few if any streams. A variation of the reef island is the platform reef. The island's center, which may have once been an atoll's lagoon or a worn-down volcano's cone, is filled in with sand and coral debris. These islands are flat, or more commonly, slightly lower in the center with a raised rim-like shoreline. Baker and Howland Islands are examples of platform reef islands. Narrow fringing reefs often develop around these islands, although because of the customarily steep bottom slope of the nearshore waters, many lack notable reefs.

Continental Islands

The larger islands of the Southwest Pacific are classified as continental islands as their bases are comprised of andesitic rock (derived from the name of South America's Andes Mountains with similar rocks). They are usually a combination of massive uplifted rock and volcanic activity, which are frequently still active. Extremely mountainous and rugged, they are much higher than most Pacific islands. Fertile soil developed through the deterioration of their bountiful biomass coverings. Because of this region's heavy rainfall, contributing to the extensive vegetation, heavy erosion results on the steep mountain sides. Ridges, hills, gorges, and valleys cover much of these islands although coastal plains are common, but these too can be a series of low ridges and shallow valleys. Numerous streams and rivers course out of the mountains and across the plains. Movement over the plains parallel with the coast can be difficult because of the cross-compartmentation created by the rivers and ridges running perpendicular to the coast. Cross-compartmented terrain is difficult for the attacker as it requires repeated climbing and descent of ridges and ravines through dense vegetation and frequent river and stream crossings. It provides the defender with ready-made defensive lines and subsequent fallback positions. As with most other Pacific islands, continental islands usually have fringing reefs, although they are less common and often not as extensively developed as around the older atolls. Guadalcanal, New Georgia, New Britain, Bougainville, New Guinea, and most of the East Indies are examples of continental islands.

Atolls

The most distinctive and complex of the Pacific islands are atolls, a word derived from the Malaya word for reef, *atolu*. Atolls are indirectly volcanic in origin, but the part exposed above sea level was provided by the life and death cycle of coral. Atolls are generally circular or oval in shape, although some can be quite irregular in outline. They appear as a line of islets, or more accurately, as a string of scattered beads with frequent breaks between the islets. Many will appear to have extremely wide gaps or even entire sides devoid of islets. That is often misleading as the coral reef is submerged at a shallow depth barring entry into the lagoon, the atoll's enclosed waters. The submerged reef may be invisible or identified by lines of breakers. Entry by ships into the lagoon may be limited to just one or two passages. The lagoons themselves usually offer calm water and sheltered anchorages. They may be extremely deep or very shallow with countless coral heads and shoals (shallows) depending on the atoll's stage of development.

The development of a coral atoll requires millions of years. Stage 1 of the development is for a volcano to emerge from the sea and develop as a shield island being gradually built up into a mountain. Stage 2 begins when the external eruptions cease, the lava drains from the crater, and the summit collapses to form a caldera, a broad depression in the cone's center. During stage 3, internal volcanic activity continues with small pimple volcanoes emerging on the flanks of the cone. The caldera is filled with lava and ash to become a dome-topped mountain. By stage 4, volcanic activity has halted and the cone begins to diminish in size as erosion sets in. The soil is washed away, the exposed rock begins to deteriorate, and the coastline collapses to form cliffs. By stage 5, the island has largely been worn away by rain, wind, and wave action. Little of it may even break the sea's surface. The ancient volcano's core plug may protrude as a rocky pinnacle from the center of a mostly submerged island edged by the crumbled remains of the coastal cliffs and fringing coral reefs that formed during stages 3 and 4. Stage 5 also finds larger sunken islands with a number of islets and outcroppings protruding from the lagoon's waters. The island, or actually, the worn-away mountain top, is completely submerged by stage 6.

Rather than erosion, some mountains subsided into the sea. Coral reefs have continued to grow on the outer edge of the mountain's side with living coral growing upon its dead predecessors for millions of years. The dead coral solidifies into coral stone and wave action pounds it and seashells into sand. Sand, coral debris, and coral rocks heaped by waves build up atop the coral reef to form long narrow islands, short islands, and islets following the shape of the mountain's submerged edge. Most of the rim islands form on the windward side of the atoll, the upwind side, where waves and winds deposit materials. On the ocean, or outer, side, especially on the weather quarter, the portion of the atoll facing the prevailing winds, course materials accumulate by wave action. On the leeward side of the rim islands, the downwind side, finer wind-borne materials accumulate extending the shore outward into the lagoon. These islands may rise only a few feet to thirty feet or more, but a six-to-eighteen-feet elevation is common. There are seldom any sources of fresh surface water with rain catchment being one of the few means of collecting potable water. There is generally little if any fertile soil. Palms, salt brush, and low tough grasses are found on most atolls' islands. Fringing coral reefs develop on both the seaward and lagoon sides of the islands and between the islands. At low tide the reef between islands can often be crossed by wading. Fringing reefs, described below, continue to develop on both the seaward and lagoon sides of the atoll's rim. Charles Darwin was the first to advance the theory of the development of atolls and was later proven correct after further study and deep core drilling samples were acquired.

Coral

At the war's beginning little was known of the properties of coral and the impact that specific types of coral reefs would have on combat operations. Nor was the value of coral realized for construction purposes. The genus of coral that thrives in such abundance in the Pacific forming reefs and islands requires a seawater salt content between 2.7 and 3.8 percent, water temperature of 66–100°F, and a depth of less than 150 feet. Coral reproduces by the emission of free-floating larvae borne by current and winds to be deposited atop existing layers of dead coral skeletons, chemically similar to limestone: lithified coral debris. The coral embryo secretes a cement of calcium carbonate as it comes to rest and is permanently attached. The living one-eighth-inch spherical coral polyps are but a thin veneer growing and dying atop their predecessors. Coral feeds on waterborne plankton and this, along with well-aerated, clear waters, contributed to the more "rapid" development of reefs on the windward side of atolls. Millions of years pass to develop reefs, especially since the volcanic foundation on which they are built is often subsiding. An individual suffering from a coral cut or abrasion can receive a serious infection known as coral fever.

The use of coral as a construction material was little understood at the start of the war. Much was learned from early war military construction projects on Canton and Christmas Islands. Military engineers sometimes built coral rock causeways between an atoll's islands over the connecting reefs. Channels were dredged and blasted through barrier reefs where none existed and existing passages were widened or deepened by the same means. Shallow areas within lagoons were dredged to provide ship moorings and seaplane landing areas. The coral dredgings, spoil, was used for causeways, breakwaters, wharves, extensions to the islands to allow longer airfield runways to be built, and as landfill to make islands larger. Some islands were enlarged and changed drastically in shape such as Johnston and French Frigate Shoals. The lagoon side coral reefs around many atolls and adjacent to islands are still gouged and scarred from the rampant dredging, blasting, and drag-lining. Crushed and packed coral was used to cover low or muddy areas allowing camps and other facilities to be built on otherwise ill-suited ground. An extremely valuable use of crushed coral was for airfield runways, taxiways, and hand-stands as well as roads. Laid in layers, wet down with salt- or freshwater, and rolled, it hardened almost to the compactness of concrete, proving to be extremely durable. It requires daily rewetting, however, as it will easily rut, turn to dust, and blow away. This requirement was reduced when some runways were oiled. When the runways were cratered by bombing, repair materials were close at hand.

Coral reefs also proved to be an obstacle. On the windward side of islands and atolls the reefs proliferated and could be many yards to several miles wide. More often, though, the ocean side of an atoll or the windward side of an island has narrower reefs than the lagoon or leeward side, especially if the bottom slopes steeply. Coral heads and potholes are common on this side and wave action is heavier making the ocean side the less desirable on which to conduct an amphibious assault. The Japanese, however, assessed that the Americans would land on the ocean side as landing craft could disembark their troops closer to shore. On the lagoon side with its shallower waters, the coral reef is often wider, but it tends to provide a more even and level surface with fewer coral heads and potholes. There is also less wave action. The reef flat, on either side, may be exposed at low tide or covered by mere inches to a few feet of water. At high tide depth varies greatly from one to six feet. Often, though, the outer edge of the reef presents a lip and while high-tide water atop the reef may float landing craft, they may not be able to cross the lip unless a gap is found or blasted. For this reason the Japanese felt that the lagoon side would be avoided by landing craft. At Tarawa Marines were forced to disembark their landing craft because of an unexpected low tide and wade across hundreds of yards of reef under fire. The introduction of amphibian tractors and amphibian trucks[1] enabled troops and supplies to cross reefs regardless of water levels. Into early 1944, the Japanese oriented their defenses to the ocean side of atolls. Because of the advantage provided by amphibian vehicles, the Americans routinely assaulted from the less well-defended lagoon side ignoring its wider reefs.

The outflow of freshwater streams and rivers into the sea prevents coral from growing. This results in gaps in fringing reefs and nearshore barrier reefs. While these gaps may be used by landing craft, they are far from ideal approaches. Besides riptides and tricky currents, the streams are usually lined with swamps and/or dense vegetation making exit from the landing site difficult. The gaps are easily identifiable to the enemy and can be covered by fire.

Reefs

Two types of coral reefs are frequently mentioned in this study, fringing and barrier. Fringing reefs abut the shore extending outward from several yards to miles, although a few hundred yards to a couple of thousand is common. Fringing reefs are generally flat, although coral heads and potholes may be found. The outer edge may present a lip as described above. A barrier reef builds atop the edges of shallow submerged coastal shelves, a zone promoting favorable coral growth. The barrier builds up and may or may not break the surface at low tide. Eventually islets may develop atop the exposed portions of barrier reefs. The deeper water between the barrier reef and the island is known as a coastal lagoon. The lagoon may be only a few hundred feet or miles across. A fringing reef may develop inside the confines of the barrier adjacent to the island's shore. The distinction between barrier and fringing reefs is suppositional. A fringing reef may closely hug an island's shore, but a portion of it may curve out and away from the shore to form a barrier reef and create a lagoon. It could even curve back again to become a fringing reef and another part may bear off to form yet another barrier reef. Patch reefs, large coral outcropping and generally circular in shape, may be encountered within lagoons as their floors are covered with coral.

Health Hazards

A tropical environment by nature tends to be a breeding ground for disease and the hot, wet, humid conditions only enhance the health risks. The heat and humidity on many islands were considered enervating for Europeans. Numerous diseases indigenous to the region flourish. Their prevalence varies widely, however. A specific island may be considered a hotbed of tropical illnesses, but an adjacent island may be virtually disease free. Malaria, dysentery, yaws, filariasis, elephantiasis, blackwater fever, dengue fever, leprosy, and hookworm were common in many areas. Tuberculosis, smallpox, and plague were imported by Europeans, but were generally under control by the war. For an unexplained reason, the central Pacific islands west of the International Date Line and north of the equator, although the Gilberts and Ellices lying south of the equator apply, are generally free of malaria.

The horrid living conditions imposed by combat in such an environment only inflicted more suffering on combatants. High temperatures, humidity, rain, swamps and mud, brutal terrain conditions, physical exhaustion, sleep degradation, insufficient and irregular diet, dehydration, and mental stress, coupled with sometimes thousands of unburied bodies and the general filth of a combat zone, led to higher-than-normal incidence of combat fatigue, accidents, self-inflicted wounds, tropical ulcers, immersion foot, diarrhea, rashes, and unidentified fevers. It was an environment in which combatants suffered ceaselessly. Regardless of how well they were mentally prepared, physically conditioned, uniformed, equipped, and medically supported, they suffered. An April 1945 U.S. Joint Chiefs of Staff study found that the Allied casualty rate in the European theater was 2.16 per thousand troops per day while the Pacific theater saw 7.45 per day.

POPULATION AND POLITICAL DYNAMICS

To this point we have discussed the geography and related climate of the Pacific islands. Wars are caused and fought by people as an extension of politics, be it because of failed diplomacy, for economic gain, or because of ideological, cultural, or religious differences. All persons, whether combatants or noncombatants, are affected one way or another.

In 1941, the Pacific islands possessed a conservative estimate of seventy-eight million people (exclusive of Japan and New Zealand): natives, immigrants, and temporary residents. Of these just under two million were Asians (Chinese, Japanese, Indochinese, Indians) and 387,600 were Europeans (Australians, New Zealanders, British, Americans, Germans, etc.). The native population is categorized in three major groups, with each inhabiting an area of similar geography. Because of this their geographic and climatic environment has a major impact on their culture. Before discussing these groups it must first be mentioned that there are scores, even hundreds, of subgroups within any of these, including many of mixed blood. Hundreds of languages and dialects are spoken. It was common for neighboring villages not to be able to fully understand the other.

The largest of the regions, but with a moderate population, is Polynesia, a term meaning "many islands." This region is anchored on New Zealand in the south, the Hawaii Islands in the north, and Easter Island far to the east. Included within this vast triangle are the Phoenix, Line, Tokelau, Ellice, Samoa, Tonga, Cook, Austral, Tuamotus, and Marquesas Islands. Only those in the western-central part of the region played a role in the war. Polynesians are a tall, light-brown-skinned people who easily accepted Western ways and Christian religion.

Micronesia, the second smallest of the regions, is situated in the north-central Pacific to the north of the equator and Melanesia. Micronesia means "small islands." It includes the Gilbert, Marshall, Caroline, Palau, Mariana, and Nanpo Shoto Islands. Many of the islands in this region played important roles in the war. Micronesians are similar to Polynesians in appearance, but with more Malaya blood. They are subdivided into two groups. In the eastern and central Micronesian islands they are called Kanakas and those in the west are Chamorros. The latter tend to have more Malaya blood plus some Spanish blood. Christianity was accepted with Catholicism dominant in many areas.

Melanesia means "black islands" describing the dark-skinned peoples inhabiting Fiji, New Hebrides, New Caledonia, and Solomon Islands and New Guinea. This smallest area-wise of the three main regions is the most densely populated and has the most ethnically diverse populations. The region lies south of the equator and north of Australia.

Two subsidiary regions exist. The Philippines are populated by a Malaya race with heavy Spanish and some Chinese influence. The East Indies to the south of the Philippines has a Malaya population more directly related to its Indochina origins and is predominantly Islamic.

Oceania possesses vast natural resources in the form of agricultural products, marine products, timber, minerals, livestock, and others. The region's vast distances, its remoteness from markets, often harsh climate and weather conditions, health hazards, and overall underdeveloped infrastructure presented significant difficulties and high costs in developing, collecting, processing, and shipping the resources. Regardless, many nations sought to gain control over as much of the region as possible. Great Britain, Australia, New Zealand, France, the Netherlands, and the United States all possessed significant colonies, territories, and protectorates in the Pacific. Australia and Japan both held former German territories gained in World War I and mandated to their control by the League of Nations. Some former Spanish territories were under the control of the United States. The only independent nation in the Pacific, other than New Zealand and Japan, was the Kingdom of Tonga, but in reality it was a British protectorate.

The war changed the face of Oceania. The physical scars on the islands often remain. Some islands were literally transformed geographically, at least on the surface, by incredible feats of military engineering. Some may say that no good comes out of a war, but for Oceania benefits were realized. In many cases extensive infrastructures were developed to include airfields, docks and wharves, warehouses, harbors, and channels, much of which served island populations in developing their self-reliance and are still in use today. With that came independence in most instances. Virtually all of the former colonies and mandated territories are now independent nations, some more successful than others, participating in the world economy.

TERMINOLOGY

Much of a soldier's military education is designed to perfect his vocabulary, to provide standardized meanings for words, terms, phrases, and concepts. The goal is to provide him with a common vocabulary that reduces misunderstandings and clarifies the transmission of orders and reports in the confusion of combat. One often hears the phrase "military precision" when describing an action or event be it a raid on an enemy installation or a bank holdup. To many that is construed as an operation characterized by prior planning, rehearsals, precision timing, and rapid execution. Of equal importance to achieving military precision is a common vocabulary with precise definitions for words and phrases.

Distances and Dimensions

These figures are given in the contemporary feet, yards, and miles. Only statute miles are used, not nautical miles. Areas are given in square yards, square miles, and acres. To convert these contemporary figures to metric the following conversion formulas are provided:

feet to meters	multiply feet by 0.3048
yards to meters	multiply yards by 0.9114
miles to kilometers	multiply miles by 1.6093
square miles to square kilometers	multiply square miles by 2.590
acres to square meters	multiply acres by 4.047

Temperatures are provided in degrees Fahrenheit (°F).

Any two references, including military and authoritative geographic publications, seldom agree on distances between any given islands and can vary from a few miles to several hundred. In order to provide a degree of standardization, a U.S. Navy World War II chart, *Table of Distances, Pacific Ocean*, was used to the extent possible. Other distances were obtained from the 1942 *Rand McNally World Atlas, Premier Edition*.

Dimensions of a given island can vary as well in authoritative references. Without delving into a long explanation, the example of Saipan in the Mariana Islands provides an example:

Reference	Dimensions in Miles
The Pacific Islands Handbook 1944	9 × 18
U.S. Marine Operations in World War II	5½ × 14
U.S. Army in World War II	6 × 14

Times and Dates

It must be noted that time zones during World War II were often different from today's and this should be considered when consulting time zone maps. The nominal International Date Line is longitude 180°, but its stated track is much different. During World War II the International Date Line followed longitude 170° W from the North Pole to a point north of the Bering Strait through which it zigzagged to a point off the west end of Attu Island at the extreme west end of the Aleutian Islands. From there it angled southeast to 45°00' N 180°00' W. It followed 180°00' W, the accepted International Date Line, to latitude 5°00' S, a point just north of the Ellice Islands, where it angled to the southeast to 15°00' S 172°30' E, a point just south of Savi'i Island in the Samoa Islands, and then to the South Pole. The day west of the date line is one day later than that on the east side of the line, e.g., Sunday, 7 December 1941 in Hawaii was Monday, 8 December east of the date line, in the Philippines for example.

Military 24-hour clock times are used. Military times between 0001 and 1159 hours are the same as 12:01 A.M. and 11:59 A.M. Military times between 1200 hours and 2400 hours are the same as 12:00 P.M. and 12:00 A.M. To determine the equivalent civilian time (12-hour clock) for military times between 1300 and 2400 hours, subtract 12 hours, e.g., 1630 hours is 4:30 P.M.

The United States generally used local times in operations orders and reports while the Japanese used Tokyo Time, zone 21. At higher U.S. command levels Greenwich Mean Time (Zulu Time, time zone 12) was often used since operations frequently spanned a number of time zones. The Hawaiian Islands, from the big island of Hawaii northwest to tiny Kure Island, were within a modified time zone, 1:30. This zone stretched from the International Date Line (180° W) east halfway across zone 2 (150° E). It was situated between latitude 30° N to 17° N, just north of Johnston Island. Prior to 9 February 1942 Hawaii was 10½ hours ahead of Greenwich Mean Time and 5½ hours ahead of Washington, DC time. On that date Hawaii changed to "war" or "summer time," 4½ hours ahead of Washington and 9½ hours ahead of GMT.

D-Day is the day on which an amphibious assault operation or other operation commences. The Japanese usually used *X-Day* for the same purpose. H-Hour is the specific time on D-Day at which an assault commences—when the first landing wave comes ashore. The H-Hour times provided in this book are the actual landing time and not the planned time, which was often delayed for up to an hour, usually because of landing craft assembly problems, weather, and/or sea conditions, seldom by enemy action. As a planning aid dates and times of scheduled events were usually specified in relation to D-Day and H-Hour. This way, if D-Day or H-Hour was moved to an earlier or later date and time, the planned related events would conversely shift. By way of example, if D-Day was 20 June and the preliminary shore bombardment was scheduled to begin on the 18th it would be designated in plans to begin on D-2 (D-Day minus two days). If a certain objective ashore was to be secured by the 23rd it was specified as D+3 (D-Day plus three days). If D-Day was moved to the 21st, the bombardment would still begin on D-2, but on the 19th. From early 1944, to prevent confusion, other letters were often used to designate days and hours when multiple operations were conducted in the same area. The official date and time the island was declared secure does not mean all resistance had ceased, but that organized resistance had collapsed. Limited fighting and mop-up often continued for some time.

The Allies assigned code names to operations, islands, and places. In contemporary documents code names were shown in all capital letters. Small capital letters are used in this book as they are less intrusive. World War II code names were selected at random from the classified *Inter-Services Code-Word Index* issued in March 1942 by the U.S. Joint Chiefs of Staff. This included 10,000 adjectives and common nouns selected from an unabridged dictionary and de-conflicted with code words used by the British Inter-Service Security Board. The JCS Operations Division then assigned code word blocks to the different theaters of operation. Unlike today's operation nicknames, selected to inspire the troops and shape media and public perception, World War II code names were not widely disseminated. Usually, only planning staffs were aware of the often bland code names and they were frequently not declassified until after the war. For this reason they were seldom readily identified with by the public or even the troops. Code names were often changed if it was thought they were compromised or the original name was replaced by a new one when the island was developed as a base once it had been seized. Unfortunately, information was seldom available on the dates on which code names were changed.

As with distances, conflicts between dates are frequently found in first- and second-source references. This is especially true for dates of the arrival or departure of units. For example, often two or more different dates may be found for the arrival of a unit on an island. All may be correct; it is a matter of interpretation as the dates given may be the arrival date of the advance party, forward echelon, main body, headquarters, etc.).

Any errors in distances, dates, and times are the responsibility of the author as having made a choice of the source that appeared to be the most authoritative or those references that were in agreement with each other.

Military Organization

For the benefit of readers not completely familiar with the complexities and intricacies of military organization, this primer is presented to provide a basic understanding. While the basic hierarchy of military formations and units for United States, Commonwealth (Australia and New Zealand), and Japanese forces possessed similarities, there were distinct differences. It is not uncommon to find units bearing the same unit size designations that were actually of much different size. This hierarchy is briefly described from the largest to the smallest echelons.

In many military history books enemy units are identified by italicized letters. In this book Japanese units are so identified, not as the enemy, but to prevent confusion with Allied unit designations.

In the U.S. and Commonwealth forces an "army" consisted of two or three corps along with "army troops," that is, support and service units directly under army control. Support and service troops generally include engineer, signal, transportation, maintenance, supply, and medical units. Infantry, armor, field artillery, and antiaircraft artillery are classified as combat troops. In the Imperial Japanese Army (IJA) the equivalent command was an "area army" with two or three armies. The Japanese also employed a higher command echelon to control area armies within a region, the closest equivalent of the Allied "theater of operations." Of these only the *Southern Army* operated in the Pacific.

U.S. and Commonwealth "corps" consisted of two to four divisions plus "corps troops," elements of which might be attached to divisions. There was also a "corps artillery" controlling artillery units assigned to the corps. The term "corps" as a military unit should not be confused with the same term identifying a military organization such as the Marine Corps or Corps of Engineers. The equivalent formation to a corps in the IJA was the "army," comprised of two to four divisions and one or more independent mixed brigades. The actual mix of divisions and other units attached to armies and corps was highly variable to meet the tactical situation and frequently changed.

In all armies the "division" was the highest-echelon formation with a fixed internal organization, although units could be detached and attached between divisions. U.S. Army and Marine Corps divisions had three infantry regiments, a division artillery in the case of the Army and an artillery regiment in the Marines. Both of the artillery organizations generally had four battalions. There were also organic (permanently assigned) engineer, reconnaissance, signal, supply, maintenance, and medical units of battalion and company size. Commonwealth divisions were of a similar structure, but had three brigade groups rather than infantry regiments. IJA divisions too were organized not unlike a U.S. Army division with three infantry regiments, an artillery regiment, and engineer, reconnaissance, transport, signal, and medical units. Most possessed an "infantry group," a small headquarters for controlling the infantry regiments. These were often employed as a command element for a reinforced infantry regiment assigned a mission independent of the division. Some IJA divisions had two brigades rather than three regiments. Another type of IJA division was the "regimental combat team" division designed to fight on tropical islands. It had three infantry regiments, but no artillery or engineer regiments. The artillery and engineers were assigned to the infantry regiments and it had an organic sea transport unit with landing barges. How divisions were designated varied between the belligerents:

U.S. Army	6th Infantry Division
U.S. Marine Corps	6th Marine Division
Commonwealth	6th Australian Division
IJA	*6th Division*

In the U.S. Army the "brigade" was usually a controlling headquarters for units of the same branch such as field artillery or engineers and had several such battalions attached. In the Marine Corps it was a temporary tactical headquarters for one or two reinforced regiments. The Commonwealth used brigades or "brigade groups" in lieu of infantry regiments as the maneuver component of divisions. A brigade group included attached support units. The IJA used two basic types of brigades. Brigades comprising two-brigade divisions had four or five infantry battalions. The "independent mixed brigade" was a separate formation with three to six infantry battalions (four were normal) and assigned support units.

The meaning of the term "regiment" can be quite confusing as it often identified different sizes of units depending on the branch of service and nationality. In the U.S. Army and Marine Corps the infantry regiment had three battalions. Army cavalry regiments, fighting dismounted as infantry, had two battalion-size squadrons. The Army commonly called their regiments simply, for example, 147th Infantry or 112th Cavalry and the term "regiment" was not included. The Marine Corps did the same, but all regiments, regardless of type, were identified simply as 9th Marines or 10th Marines and the term "regiment" was never included. Only the initiated would known that the 9th was an infantry regiment and the 10th was artillery. In this book Marine artillery and engineer regiments are identified with their function following in brackets. In Commonwealth armies the regiment was a battalion-size unit in armor, artillery, engineers, signals, and service units. There were no infantry regiments as such other than battalions bearing traditional regimental titles. Infantry battalions were attached to brigade groups rather than regiments. In the IJA the organization was even more complex. Infantry and artillery regiments had three battalions, but all reconnaissance, cavalry, tank, engineer, signal, transport, and service regiments were of battalion size with three to five companies.

The structure of a "battalion" was generally similar in all armies. They normally consisted of three to five companies depending on the type. Artillery battalions were comprised of batteries rather than companies. Commonwealth battalion-size artillery regiments too were comprised of batteries. Batteries in most armies had four guns. In the U.S. Army battalion-size cavalry units were called squadrons and they were comprised of company-size troops.

The IJN employed a variety of land force units. The *Special Naval Landing Force (SNLF)* was roughly equivalent to the U.S. Marine Corps, though it is incorrect to refer to them as "Imperial Japanese Marines." They were combined arms units (self-contained infantry, artillery, antiaircraft, engineer, and service units) of approximately battalion size employed to seize and later defend naval bases and small islands. The name of the naval base (Kure, Maizuri, Sasebo, Yokosuka) in Japan at which they were organized was included in their designations. A "base force" provided command and service elements to operate a naval base. One or more "guard forces" of various sizes were assigned for base defense. Of widely different organization, they were armed with coast defense artillery, antiaircraft guns, and heavy infantry weapons.

A final organization unique to the U.S. Army bears discussion. "Engineer special brigades" had three engineer boat and shore regiments equipped with over 1,000 landing craft. These brigades supported shore-to-shore amphibious operations (as opposed to ship-to-shore, the Navy's prerogative) in MacArthur's Southwest Pacific Area due to limited Navy capabilities in that area.

Military Ranks

The ranks of the commanders of brigades, divisions, corps, and armies are included in the discussion of military operations as are the commanders of major naval forces. For those unfamiliar with the seniority of general and flag (admiral) officer ranks and the differences between national practices the below rank equivalent tables are provided along with the level of command they usually commanded. There ranks run from the lowest to the highest echelons.

U.S. Army/USMC	Commonwealth	Netherlands	Japan
Colonel	Colonel	Colonel	Colonel
Brigadier General	Brigadier	General Major	Major General
Major General	Major General	Lieutenant General	Lieutenant General
Lieutenant General	Lieutenant General	—	—
General	General	General	General
General of the Army	Field Marshall	—	Field Marshall

U.S. Navy	Commonwealth	Netherlands	Japan
Captain	Commodore 2nd Class	Captain	Captain
Commodore	Commodore 1st Class	Commodore	—
Rear Admiral	Rear Admiral	Vice Admiral	Rear Admiral
Vice Admiral	Vice Admiral	Lieutenant Admiral	Vice Admiral
Admiral	Admiral	Admiral	Admiral
Admiral of the Fleet	Admiral of the Fleet	—	—

Certain ranks were designated to command specific echelons of units and this too varied from country to country.

Unit	United States	Commonwealth	Japan
Regiment	Colonel	—	Colonel
Brigade	Brigadier General	Brigadier	Major General
Division	Major General	Major General	Lieutenant General
Corps*	Major General	Lieutenant General	Lieutenant General
Army*	Lieutenant General	Lieutenant General	General

*In the Imperial Japanese Army the equivalents to "corps" and "armies" were designated "armies" and "area armies," respectively.

Japanese names are shown in the traditional Japanese manner with the surname or family name first in all upper case and followed by the personal name, for example: Admiral YAMAMOTO Isoroku. In most Western references this name would be shown as: Admiral Isoroko Yamamoto. The practice of reversing the order of names in the Western style can be traced back to World War II. In early 1943 two Japanese documents listing all serving Imperial Japanese Army officers were captured. The *Register of Officers* and *Register of Reserve Officers on the Active List*, both dated 15 October 1942, were quickly translated and published in English as the *Alphabetical List of Japanese Army Officers* in May 1943 for use by Allied intelligence services. The names were listed in the correct Japanese manner, surname, personal name, but with a comma between the two names, for example: ABAIE, Shotaro. It was assumed by many that the "last" or surname was placed first along with the comma and the "first" name last in the normal Western practice when compiling rosters. Japanese names were thus often written in reports in the reversed manner and this practice was continued in most postwar histories and studies.

NOTE

1. The full-tracked amphibian tractor (Amtrak) or landing vehicle, tracked (LVT) was first viewed as a supply carrier to move materiel inland for delivery to front line troops. At Tarawa in November 1943, it was used to move assault troops across the reefs to deliver them to the first available cover. It continued to be used to deliver supplies and evacuate wounded. The amphibian truck, designated the DUKW (its General Motors designation meaning "D"—year model 1942, "U"—amphibian, "K"—all-wheel drive, and "W"—dual rear axles), hence its nickname "Duck," was used to deliver artillery and ammunition.

PART TWO
WORLD WAR II IN THE PACIFIC CHRONOLOGY

The following chronology of the war in the Pacific is not meant to be all-encompassing, but provides the sequence of island occupations and assaults by Allied and Japanese forces, significant key operational events, and sea battles. It is intended to be a helpful tool by providing the researcher with an understanding of the sequence and interrelation of strategic and tactical operations, especially since the island studies in this book cannot always be presented in the sequence they occurred. Allied operations in the Pacific theater were conducted by two major commands.

The U.S. Fleet was split into Atlantic and Pacific Fleets on 1 February 1941. The Pacific Fleet controlled all Operating Forces in the Pacific Ocean Area, itself divided into the North, Central, and South Pacific Areas (see Map 2; these areas are defined in the appropriate sections). Commander in Chief, Pacific Fleet and Pacific Ocean Area was Admiral Chester W. Nimitz. The Southwest Pacific Area was under General Douglas MacArthur.

The Allied strategy entailed three thrusts across the Pacific. In the North Pacific Area the Army and Navy, backed by Canadians, cleared the Japanese from the Aleutian Islands. The Southwest Pacific Area had at its disposal combined U.S. Army, U.S. Marine, Australian, and New Zealand forces with the Third and Seventh Fleets mainly supported by land-based aircraft. These forces first secured the line of communications between the United States and Australia. They then seized the Solomon Islands with the main objective being Rabaul on New Britain, thrust along New Guinea's north coast, and liberated the Philippines. In the Central Pacific Area the Fifth Fleet, supported by carrier-based aircraft, secured the Gilberts with the main objective being the Japanese base at Truk Atoll in the Carolines. Both Japanese bastions at Rabaul and Truk were neutralized by airpower and bypassed. The 5th Fleet went on to seize the Marshalls and Marianas. The 3rd Fleet then took Iwo Jima, after first liberating Guam, followed by the 5th Fleet seizing Okinawa. It was relieved by the 3rd Fleet just prior to the cessation of hostilities.

In order to most effectively depict the interrelation of operations between these two

Map 2
Pacific Ocean Areas

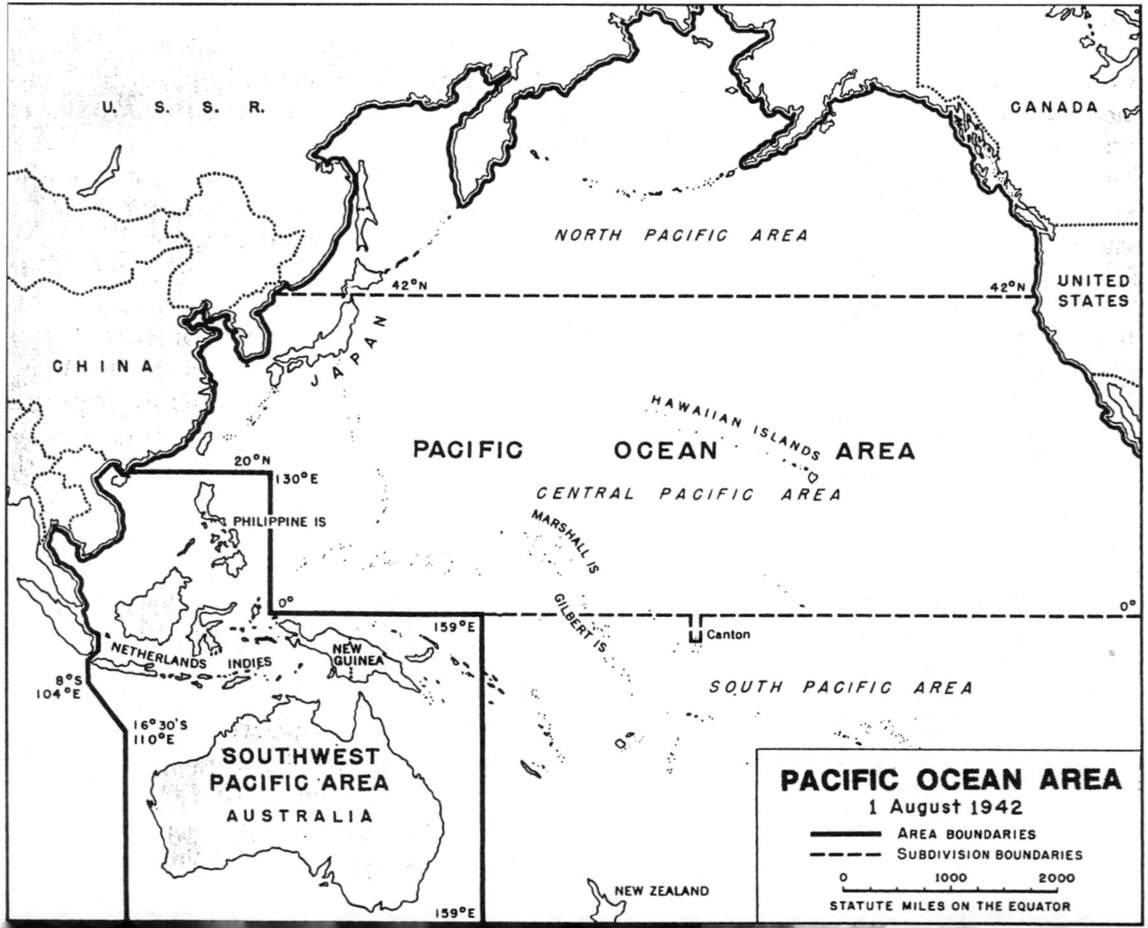

U. S. S. R.

CHINA

CANADA

UNITED STATES

42°N

NORTH PACIFIC AREA

JAPAN

42°N

20°N

PACIFIC OCEAN AREA

HAWAIIAN ISLANDS AREA

CENTRAL PACIFIC AREA

MARSHALL IS

GILBERT IS

Canton

SOUTH PACIFIC AREA

0°

NEW ZEALAND

PHILIPPINE IS

130°E

0°

NETHERLANDS INDIES

NEW GUINEA

159°E

SOUTHWEST PACIFIC AREA

AUSTRALIA

16°30'S 110°E

8°S 104°E

159°E

PACIFIC OCEAN AREA
1 August 1942

AREA BOUNDARIES
SUBDIVISION BOUNDARIES

0   1000   2000
STATUTE MILES ON THE EQUATOR

commands, the chronology is divided into parallel columns for Pacific Ocean Area and the Southwest Pacific Area.

Prior to the outbreak of the war in the Pacific, several events occurred leading up to 7 December 1941:

1 Sep 39   Germany invades Poland beginning World War II.

8 Sep 39   President Roosevelt declared a "limited emergency" directing measures for strengthening national defenses within peacetime limitations.

2 Jul 40   U.S. places an embargo on certain materials and oil shipped to Japan cutting off the source of 80 percent of Japan's oil.

11 Mar 41   U.S. passes Lend-Lease Bill to provide supplies, materiel, equipment, munitions, and armament to nations fighting the Axis.

27 May 41   President Roosevelt declares a "full emergency" authorizing the armed forces to be brought to a level of readiness capable of repelling any threat to the Western Hemisphere.

19 Jul 41   Japan demands that Vichy French government allow her to base troops in Indochina to protect the French colony.

26 Jul 41   Japanese assets in U.S. and U.K. frozen followed by same in NEI. NEI cuts off oil to Japan.

28 Jul 41   Japanese troops begin to occupy French Indochina with the intention of using it to launch the invasions of Malaya, East Indies, and the Philippines.

29 Nov 41   Japan decides that the U.S. will not lift its oil embargo, makes the decision to attack Pearl Harbor on 1 December.

2 Dec 41   The order is given to attack Pearl Harbor.

4 Dec 41   Japanese Malaya invasion forces depart Hainan Island, Indochina.

PACIFIC OCEAN AREA

1941

7 Dec	At 0755 hours IJN aircraft attack Pearl Harbor, TH. IJN shells Midway.
8 Dec	IJN aircraft attack Wake defended by USMC. IJN aircraft attack Guam defended by USMC. *SNLF* occupies Butaritari (Makin) Atoll.
9 Dec	*SNLF* temporarily occupies 3 atolls in the Gilberts.
10 Dec	IJA/*SNLF* assaults Guam.
15 Dec	IJN shells Johnston.

SOUTHWEST PACIFIC AREA

1941

8 Dec	In morning hours Japanese aircraft attacked U.S. air bases on Luzon, PI. IJA invades Malaya and Burma.
10 Dec	IJA assaults north Luzon (supporting landings).
12 Dec	IJA/*SNLF* assaults south Luzon.
16 Dec	*SNLF* assaults North Borneo. IJA/*SNLF* assaults Mindanao.

		17 Dec	Australians and Dutch reinforce Portuguese Timor.
		22 Dec	IJA assaults Sarawak. IJA assaults Lingayen Bay, Luzon (main landing).
23 Dec	*SNLF* assaults Wake.		
24 Dec	IJN shells Palmyra. *SNLF* occupies Tarawa Atoll, Gilberts.	24 Dec	IJA conducts additional landing on south Luzon.
		25 Dec	IJA assaults Jolo Is, Sulu Archipelago, PI.
		27 Dec	Manila declared open city.
1942		**1942**	
		3 Jan	*SNLF* seizes Labuan Is, British Borneo.
		6 Jan	US-Fil forces close on Bataan Peninsula, Luzon.
11 Jan	IJN shells Tutuila, Samoa.	11 Jan	*SNLF* assaults Tarakan Is, Dutch Borneo. *SNLF* assault Celebes, NEI.
		12 Jan	ABDACOM activated to coordinate defense of Burma, East Indies, and the Philippines.
		17 Jan	*SNLF* seizes Sandakan, North Borneo.
19 Jan	USMC defense force arrives at Tutuila.		
		20 Jan	IJN bombs Rabaul, New Britain, Bismarcks.
		23 Jan	*SNLF* assaults Rabaul and IJA seizes Kavieng, New Ireland. IJA/*SNLF* seizes Balikpapan, Dutch Borneo.
26 Jan	ANZAC established to coordinate defense of South Pacific Area.		
		31 Jan	IJA/*SNLF* assaults Ambonia Is, Moluccas, NEI.
		4 Feb	Battle of Makassar Strait, IJN wins.
		14 Feb	*SNLF* assaults Sumatra, NEI.
		15 Feb	Singapore falls to IJA.
		16 Feb	IJA assaults Sumatra.

17 Feb	USA garrison arrives at Borabora, Society Islands.		
		19 Feb	IJA assaults Bali Is, NEI. First Japanese air raid on Darwin, Australia. Battle of Badoeng Strait, IJN wins.
		20 Feb	IJA/*SNLF* assault Dutch and Portuguese Timor.
		25 Feb	ABDACOM dissolved.
		28 Feb	Battle of Sunda Strait, IJN wins. IJA assaults Java.
3 Mar	IJN bombs Pearl Harbor with 2 float planes using French Frigate Shoals as refueling point.		
		8 Mar	*SNLF*/IJA seizes Lae-Salamaua, New Guinea.
		4–8 Mar	Battle of the Coral Sea turns back IJN Port Moresby invasion force.
		11 Mar	*SNLF* seizes Finschhafen, New Guinea.
12 Mar	USA garrison arrives at New Caledonia.	12 Mar	MacArthur evacuated from Corregidor Is.
30 Mar	Pacific Ocean Area activated to coordinate operations. It is subdivided into South, Central, and North Pacific Areas. *SNLF* seizes Bougainville, Shortlands, and Buka Is.		
		2 Apr	*SNLF* occupies Babo, Dutch New Guinea and other sites through the month.
		7 Apr	*SNLF* occupies Hermit Is.
		8 Apr	*SNLF* occupies Manus Is, Admiralties.
		9 Apr	US-Fil forces on Bataan surrender.
		10 Apr	IJA assaults Celu, PI.
		16 Apr	IJA assaults Panay, PI.
18 Apr	Doolittle raid on Tokyo.		
22 Apr	ANZAC dissolved.		
1 May	IJN bombs Tulagi and Gavutu, Solomons.		
4 May	*SNLF* seizes Tulagi and Gavutu.		

		5 May	IJA assaults Corregidor.
		6 May	US-Fil forces on Corregidor surrender.
8 May	USMC defense force arrives at Upolu, Western Samoa.		
9 May	USA garrison arrives at Tongatagu, Tongas.		
		10 May	US-Fil forces in Visayas and southern PI surrender.
29 May	USMC defense force arrives at Wallis Is.		
30 May	USMC defense force arrives at Savai'i Is.		
4 Jun	Battle of Midway, USN wins.		
7 Jun	*SNLF* occupies Kiska and Attu Is, Aleutians.		
11 Jun	USA garrison arrives at Viti Levu, Fiji.		
		25 Jun	Australians land at Milne Bay, Papua.
4 Jul	IJN airfield construction discovered on Guadalcanal.		
8 Jul	USA garrison arrives at Espíritu Santo, New Hebrides.		
11 Jul	Japan cancels planned invasions of Samoas, Fiji, and New Caledonia due to Midway defeat.		
		22 Jul	IJA lands at Gona, Papua to conduct overland advance on the Kokoda Trail on Port Moresby.
7 Aug	USMC assaults Guadalcanal, Tulagi, and Gavutu.		
11 Aug	Battle of Savo Is, IJN wins.		
		13 Aug	IJA lands at Buna, Papua
17 Aug	USMC raids Butaritari (Makin) Atoll, Gilberts.		
24 Aug	Battle of the Eastern Solomons, USN wins.		
25 Aug	*SNLF* seizes Nauru Is.	25 Aug	*SNLF* assaults Milne Bay, New Guinea and fails.
26 Aug	*SNLF* seizes Ocean Is.	26 Aug	*SNLF* troops stranded on Goodenough Is.

31 Aug	*SNLF* occupies Apamama Atoll, Gilberts.		
		23 Sep	Additional Australian independent company reinforces company already on Timor for guerrilla operations.
		26 Sep	Australians begin advance over Kokoda Trail pushing the Japanese back to the coast.
2 Oct	USMC occupies Funafuti Atoll, Ellices.		
11 Oct	Battle of Cape Esperance, USN wins.		
13 Oct	First USA units arrive on Guadalcanal.		
		22 Oct	Australians assault Goodenough Is.
26 Oct	Battle of Santa Cruz, IJN wins.		
13 Nov	IJA/IJN occupies Munda Point, New Georgia.		
13–15 Nov	Naval Battle of Guadalcanal, draw.		
		16 Nov	Australians/USA attack begins on Buna-Gona. Area not cleared until 21 Jan 43.
18 Nov	Battle of Tassafaronga, USN wins.		
1943		**1943**	
21 Jan	US secures Russells.		
1–8 Feb	Japanese evacuate Guadalcanal and island is secured.		
		6 Mar	USMC assaults Willaumez Peninsula, New Britain.
23 Mar	Battle of Komandorski Is, draw.		
		23 Apr	USA relieves USMC on New Britain.
11 May	USA assaults Attu Is.		
21 Jun	USMC lands at Segi Point, New Georgia.		
30 Jun	USA secures Rendova Is, New Georgia Group.	30 Jun	USA occupies Kiriwina and Woodlark Is.
2 Jul	USA lands at Zanana, New Georgia.		

12 Jul	Battle of Kolombangara, USN wins.
27 Jul	Japanese evacuate Kiska Is.
11 Aug	USA occupies Howland Is.
13 Aug	USA assaults Baanga Is, New Georgia Group.
15 Aug	USA lands on Vella Lavella, New Georgia Group. USA and Canadian Army seizes Kiska Is.
18 Aug	USMC occupies Nanomea Atoll, Ellices.
27 Aug	USA assaults Arundel Is, New Georgia Group. USMC occupies Nukufetau Atoll, Ellices.
3 Sep	Australians assault Huon Peninsula, New Guinea.
22 Sep	Australians assault Finschhafen, New Guinea.
25 Sep	New Zealanders land on northern Vella Levella.
28 Sep–3 Oct	Japanese evacuate Kololbangara, New Georgia Group.
6 Oct	Battle of Vella Lavella, IJN wins. USA secures Kolombangara Is.
27 Oct	New Zealanders/USA lands on Treasury Is.
28 Oct	USMC raids Choiseul Is.
1 Nov	USMC assaults Cape Torokina, Bougainville.
7 Nov	USA units begin to arrive on Bougainville, Solomons.
20 Nov	USMC assaults Betio Is, Tarawa Atoll, Gilberts. USA assaults Butaritari (Makin) Atoll, Gilberts. USMC seizes Apamama Atoll, Gilberts.
27 Nov	Australians begin relieving USA on New Britain.
10 Dec	Australian units relieve USA units on Bougainville.

15 Dec	USA assaults Arawe/Cape Merkus, New Britain, Bismarcks.
26 Dec	USMC assaults Cape Gloucester, New Britain.

1944

1944

2 Jan	USA assaults Saidor, New Guinea.

30 Jan	USA seizes Majuro Atoll, Marshalls.

1 Feb	USMC assaults Roi-Namur Is, Kwajalein Atoll, Marshalls. USA assaults Kwajalein Is, Kwajalein Atoll, Marshalls.

15 Feb	New Zealanders assault Green Is, Bismarcks.

17 Feb	Carrier raid on Truk Atoll, Carolines.

29 Feb	USA assaults Los Negros and Manua Is, Admiralties.
20 Mar	USMC occupies Emirau Is, St. Matthias Group.
22 Apr	USA assaults Aitape, NE New Guinea. USA assaults Hollandia, Dutch New Guinea.

1 May	USMC/USA assaults Eniwetok Atoll, Marshalls

17 May	USA assaults Arare, Dutch New Guinea.
18 May	USA assaults Wakde Is, Dutch New Guinea.
27 May	USA assaults Biak Is, Dutch New Guinea.

15 Jun	USMC/USA assaults Saipan, Marianas
19 Jun	Battle of the Philippine Sea, USN wins.

2 Jul	USA assaults Noemfoor Is, Dutch New Guinea.

21 Jul	USMC/USA assaults Guam.
24 Jul	USMC assaults Tinian, Marianas.

30 Jul	USA seizes Sansapor-Cape Opmarai, Dutch New Guinea.

15 Sep	USMC assaults Peleliu, Palaus.		15 Sep	USA assaults Morotai Is, NEI.
17 Sep	USA assaults Angaur, Palaus.			
22 Sep	USA secures Ulithi Atoll, Carolines.			
20 Oct	USA relieves USMC on Peleliu.		20 Oct	USA assaults Leyte, PI.
			24 Oct	Battle of Leyte Gulf, USN wins.
			15 Dec	USA assaults Mindoro, PI.
1945			**1945**	
			3 Jan	USN conducts air attacks on Formosa and Ryukyus.
			9 Jan	USA assaults Luzon landing at Lingayen Gulf.
			31 Jan	USA makes second landing on Luzon at Nasugary Bay.
			16 Feb	USA assaults Corregidor.
19 Feb	USMC assaults Iwo Jima.			
			28 Feb	USA assaults Palawan, PI.
			4 Mar	Manila, Luzon is liberated.
			10 Mar	USA assaults Mindanao landing on Zamboanga Peninsula.
			18 Mar	USA assaults Panay, PI.
26 Mar	USA assaults Kerama Retto, Ryukyus.		26 Mar	USA assaults Cebu, PI.
			29 Mar	USA assaults Negros, PI.
1 Apr	USA/USMC assaults Okinawa, Ryukyus.			
7 Apr	IJN Battleship *Yamato* is sunk.			
			9 Apr	USA assaults Jolo Is, PI.
			11 Apr	USA assaults Bohol, PI.
			17 Apr	USA assaults Mindanao landing at Parang.
			1 May	Australians assault Tarakan Is, Dutch Borneo.
7 May	Germany surrenders.			
			10 Jun	Australians assault Brunei Bay and Labuan Is, British Borneo.
			1 Jul	Australians assault Balikpapan, Dutch Borneo.
			5 Jul	Philippines declared liberated.

6 Aug	Atomic bomb dropped on Hiro-shima.
9 Aug	Atomic bomb dropped on Naga-saki.
15 Aug	Japan declares its intent to surren-der.
2 Sep	Japan formally surrenders.

PART THREE
THE ISLANDS

1

Central and Southern Pacific U.S. Possessions

The islands discussed in this chapter played important roles early in the war when the Allies were on the defensive. Most continued to contribute to the war effort to varying degrees as the Allies assumed the offensive, but often the war had passed them by from after late 1942. Operationally these islands fell under the command of either the Central or South Pacific Areas, but are discussed separately because of their early war role of securing the Hawaiian Islands, other islands in the South Pacific, and the Southern Lifeline to Australia and New Zealand. Those outlying Hawaiian islands (Wake, Midway, Johnston, Palmyra) in the Central Pacific Area were subordinate to the Hawaiian Sea Frontier.

In 1899 the Navy proposed that its main Pacific Fleet base be located at Manila in the Philippines. The Army objected to this stationing as it felt that the proposed base was vulnerable to attack by Japan. The second option was to concentrate the Fleet in American waters as ordained by Mahan, but this positioned the Fleet too far (6,965 miles) from the Philippines to respond to the defense of an important possession in a timely manner. The Army did not possess the resources to establish a sufficient defense force in the Philippines capable of holding out until the Fleet arrived. Annexed at the request of the queen of the Republic of Hawaii at the same time the United States gained control of the Philippines, the Hawaiian Islands were an ideal location for a naval base to defend the west coast of the United States, protect America's far-flung possessions across the Pacific, to include the Philippines (5,300 miles), and allow the Fleet to redeploy to the Atlantic via a Panama Canal, once completed in 1914. The Navy withdrew its proposal to base the Fleet in the Philippines in 1909 and development of a base at Pearl Harbor (World War II code name DREAM) was soon begun.

The Hawaiian Islands consist of eight main islands covering 6,407 square miles located just over 2,000 miles east-southeast of San Francisco. They span an almost 400-mile arc between 155° to 160° longitude west just south of the Tropic of Cancer. The location, size, and well-developed support infrastructure made Hawaii strategically significant. Pearl Harbor's distance from key areas follow:

San Francisco	2,091	Tutuila, American Samoa	2,276
Panama Canal	4,683	Guam	3,330
Auckland, New Zealand	3,876	Tokyo, Japan	3,908
Sydney, Australia	4,420	Dutch Harbor, Aleutians	2,046

Massive expansion of the existing Navy Yard, Pearl Harbor, began in the fall of 1939. The base is located on the south coast of Oahu, the third largest island in the archipelago, and immediately west of Honolulu, the capital of the Territory of Hawaii (COPPER, TH). In January 1940 the U.S. Fleet, later to become the Pacific Fleet, moved from San Diego to Pearl Harbor. In October it was announced that the U.S. Fleet would permanently base at Pearl Harbor. Major U.S. Army, Navy, and Marine Corps installations and air bases were located on Oahu, Hawaii, Maui, and Kauai. (These islands are not a subject of this book. Researchers are directed to: Coletta, Paolo E. and Bauer, K. Jack (Editors). *United States Navy and Marine Bases, Overseas*, Westport, CT: Greenwood Publishing Co., 1985.)

In order to effectively support War Plan Orange, a war against Japan, the U.S. Navy established the Hepburn Board in May 1938. The Board, chaired by Admiral Arthur J. Hepburn, was authorized by Congress to conduct a strategic study of the Navy's need for additional bases "to defend the coast of the United States, its territories, and possessions." The potential utility of Midway, Wake, Johnston, Palmyra, and Canton Islands, spread in a wide, ragged arc from the east-northeast to the south of the Hawaiian Islands, was recognized when the Board presented its report to Congress in January 1939. These remote islands were to serve as land plane and seaplane bases to protect the Hawaiian Islands from attack. Plans were developed to construct bases on these islands in 1939–40. All were the responsibility of the Navy, with the exception of Canton far to the southwest, assigned to the Army. Maritime searches by patrol planes, defensive fighter and offensive bomber operations could be conducted from the islands. The USAAF's contribution to the defense of these islands was the formation of Task Force FIVE ISLANDS in January 1942 to provide pursuit squadrons for Canton, Christmas, Palmyra, Fiji, and New Caledonia.

These islands served an additional role as the war progressed. They proved to be invaluable as aircraft refueling way stations as the southern lifeline to Australia developed and the war moved into the Solomons and beyond. This route originated at Hamilton Field, California running to Hickham Field, Oahu, TH. From there aircraft could fly directly to Canton or to Canton via Christmas Island. The route then took them to Viti Levu in Fiji, New Caledonia, and then to Brisbane or Williamtown, Australia.

Besides their remoteness, these islands had other common characteristics. While habitually called an "island," most were actually small atolls, usually with two or three white coral sand-capped main islands and seldom with any adjacent islets. They were small and low, possessed no vegetation other than low desert magnolia, pisonia, scaevola scrub brush, and sometimes coconut palms, were populated only by countless sea and shore birds, and had no freshwater sources. In fact the size of the early defense forces and civilian construction crews was dictated by the production capabilities of seawater distillation units[1] on the islands. Fringing reefs were generally narrow and the lagoons' waters were very shallow, often just a few feet deep. Few had protected anchorages and extensive dredging of the lagoons and entry channels was required. The Hepburn Board's 1939 recommendations for the defense and development of these "outlying islands" served as guidelines for establishing their defenses in 1941–42.

Midway and Wake were considered by the Board to be the most important and land plane naval air stations were planned along with seaplane bases to allow patrol bombers to screen the most critical approaches to Hawaii. Small submarine bases were also planned from which protective patrols would be launched. The other islands would support tender-based patrol seaplanes. The replacement of War Plan Orange with Rainbow 5 in May 1941 did not lessen the importance of the outlying islands. All of the islands required piers to land supplies, dredged channels and turning basins within the lagoons to accommodate small ships and seaplane landing areas, defense troop quarters, hospitals, support facilities and shops, fuel storage tanks, and antiaircraft and seacoast defense gun positions. When the war broke out, civilian construction crews were working on all of the islands. They initially remained to complete their projects and improve island defenses, but most were soon withdrawn to Hawaii and employed there on defense projects.

WAKE ISLAND

Wake Atoll was code-named MOCCASIN during the battle. It was redesignated BERRY after the Japanese occupation and later still as JEROBOAM. Once it was captured, the Japanese renamed it Tori Jima (Bird Island).

Wake is located in one of the most remote regions of the North Pacific 2,004 miles due west of Pearl Harbor, 1,110 miles southwest of Midway, and 1,334 miles from Guam at 19°17' N 166°36' E. The nearest land was the then Japanese-controlled Marshall Islands 450 miles due south. Wake was in time zone 23. While east of the International Date Line, Hawaii time (zone 1:30) was used by the U.S. armed forces.

Wake Atoll consists of three islands arranged in a rough "V," or wishbone shape, oriented with the apex of the "V," Peacock Point, to the southeast and the lagoon's open end to the northwest (see Map 3). The atoll is approximately 4-½ miles long and 2-½ miles wide at the lagoon's open end. Total land area is 2,600 acres. Wake Island, the largest of the atoll's three islands, is "V" shaped with the northwest end forming a hook; the outer north corner is called Heel Point. Both arms of the "V" are some 5,300 yards long. The thick apex of the "V" provides sufficient land area for an airfield.

Peale Island, the atoll's second largest and on its north side, extends the atoll's "V" to the north-northwest of Wake Island. Roughly an elongated triangle, it is 2,600 yards long and 1,200 yards wide at the southeast end with a small peninsula, Flipper Point, jutting into the lagoon. It is separated from Wake Island by a 100-plus-yard-wide, bridge-spanned channel. The island's northeast end is called Toki Point.

Wilkes Island extends the atoll's "V" to the northwest from Wake Island on the atoll's south side. The two islands are separated by the 50-yard wide Wilkes Channel. The island measures 2,300 by 500–600 yards wide. Its northwest end is called Kuku Point. A small lagoon-side inlet, New Channel, almost cuts the island in two.

The lagoon is comprised of very shallow foul ground with numerous coral heads. It could not be entered by ships and was not sufficiently dredged for other than small craft and seaplanes.

All of the islands are flat or of slightly rolling coral sand dunes. They are low with the highest elevation on Wake Island being twenty-one feet. All are almost completely covered with up to ten-foot-high scrub trees; a few rise to twenty feet, and very dense underbrush, but the ocean-side beaches are wide and bare. The atoll's dense vegetation allowed the Japanese to infiltrate between Marine positions. The atoll has twenty-one miles of shoreline. The heavily surf-pounded reef edge is 30–1,000 yards offshore. The reef's edge drops steeply so deep that ships cannot anchor in most areas. The reef's

Map 3
Wake Island

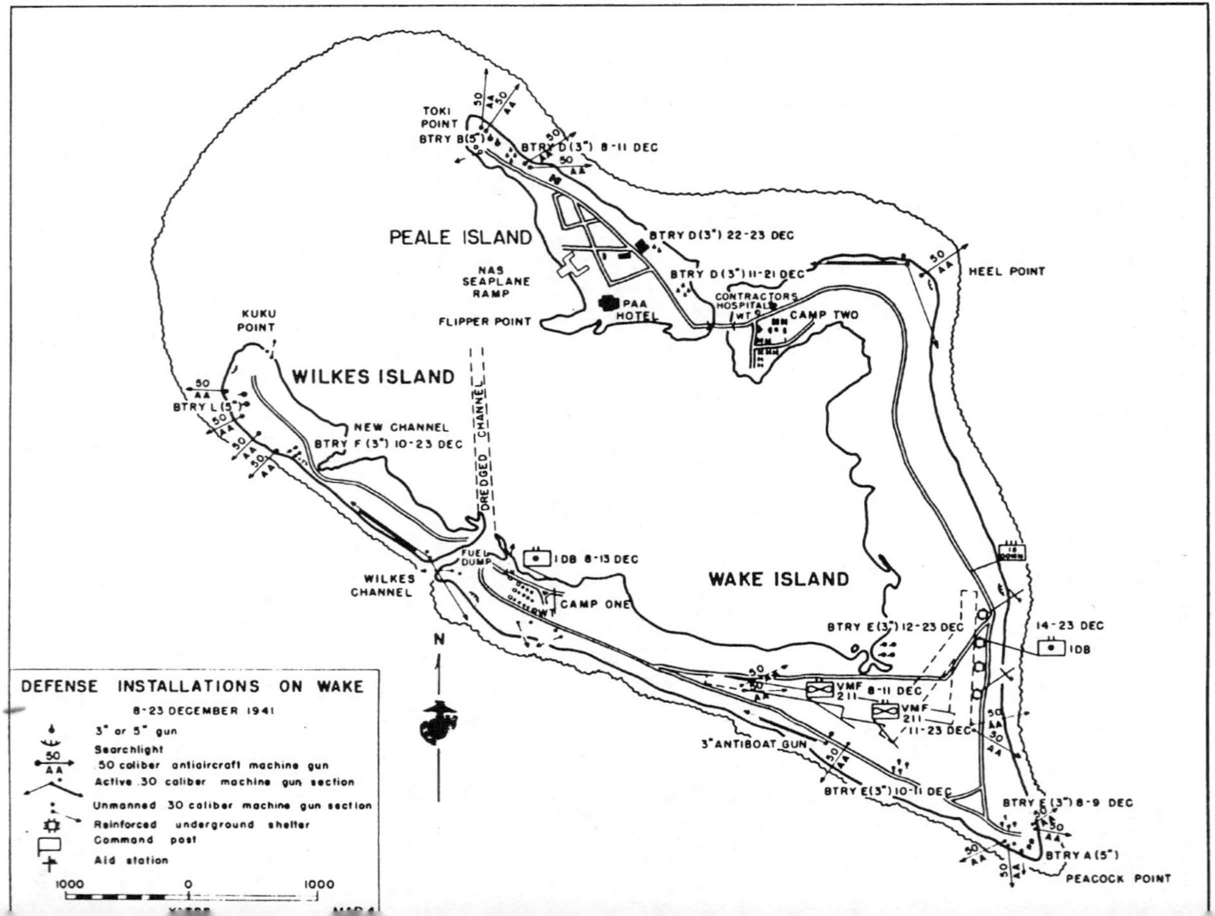

DEFENSE INSTALLATIONS ON WAKE
8-23 DECEMBER 1941

3" or 5" gun
Searchlight
50 caliber antiaircraft machine gun
Active 30 caliber machine gun section
Unmanned 30 caliber machine gun section
Reinforced underground shelter
Command post
Aid station

1000   0   1000

PEALE ISLAND

WILKES ISLAND

WAKE ISLAND

HEEL POINT

PEACOCK POINT

TOKI POINT
BTRY B (5")
BTRY D (3") 8-11 DEC
BTRY D (3") 11-20 DEC
BTRY D (3") 22-23 DEC

CONTRACTOR'S HOSPITAL
CAMP TWO
PAA HOTEL
NAS SEAPLANE RAMP
FLIPPER POINT

KUKU POINT
BTRY L (5")
BTRY F (3") 10-23 DEC
NEW CHANNEL
DREDGED CHANNEL
WILKES CHANNEL
FUEL DUMP
IDB 8-13 DEC
CAMP ONE

3" ANTIBOAT GUN
VMF 211
VMF 211 8-11 DEC
BTRY E (3") 12-23 DEC
BTRY E (3") 10-11 DEC
14-23 DEC IDB
IDB
BTRY J (3") 8-9 DEC
BTRY A (5")

N

widest portions are along Wake's Island's northwest hook, the northwest side of Peale Island, and across the lagoon's northwest opening. On the southeast sides of Wake and Wilkes Islands the reef edge lies close to shore allowing small craft to land. The atoll's northeast side offers unfavorable landing conditions. Besides birds, the only wildlife was hordes of small gray rats.

The climate is humid and tropical with a prevailing easterly wind. Most of the infrequent rain falls in the winter. The Japanese used rain squalls to screen their air attacks while the sound of their approach was covered by the constantly thundering surf.

A thirty-foot-wide crushed coral road ran the entire length of all of the islands generally following the oceanside shore. A 450-foot-long timber bridge, which survived the battle, connected Wake and Peale Islands. Wilkes Island was accessible only by a Navy-operated small boat ferry service. A connecting road spanned the lagoon-side of Wake Island. The airfield was built within this inverted "A"-shaped triangle of roads on the island's "V."

Uninhabited Wake Atoll was discovered by Spanish explorer Alvaro de Medaña in 1568. It was named after Samuel Wake, captain of a British schooner, who "rediscovered" it in 1796. The U.S. Exploring Expedition under Commander Charles Wilkes visited it in 1841. Wake's two smaller islands were named after Wilkes and Titian Peale, a naturalist. Wake was not annexed by the United States until 17 January 1899. While some recognized Wake's military value, the Navy felt it was strategically insignificant and it was not even marked as a U.S. possession on many government maps. It was placed under Navy jurisdiction in 1934. The following year Pan American World Airways established a Clipper seaplane way station on the central portion of Peale Island. This was later taken over by the Navy. The Pan Am Inn, surrounded by rainwater catchments and a garden centered around the anchor of the German ship *Libelle* wrecked on the reef in 1866, was built at the base of Flipper Point peninsula to receive the biweekly Clipper flights.

In 1939 the Hepburn Board recommended that Wake be developed as the second most important (to Midway) outlying island for the defense of Hawaii. It was envisioned as a patrol plane base and was later to be developed as a small submarine base. The atoll was of strategic value as it provided a site for an airfield between Guam to the southwest and Midway to the northeast. This provided a staggered line of way stations running from Hawaii to the Philippines. It did lose some of its strategic importance when it was decided not to fortify Guam.

The first contractors arrived in January 1941 to cut the Wilkes Channel into the lagoon. Work began on the first two of the three planned naval air station runways on the broad, pointed southeast end of Wake Island. The northwest portion of the lagoon was dredged to accommodate a seaplane field. Naval Air Station, Wake Island was commissioned in August. Contractors also began building Camp 1, where they first lived, on the northwest end of Wake Island near Wilkes Channel. They then built Camp 2 necessary for a larger construction staff on the hooked north-northeast end of Wake Island. By December 1941, there were 1,146 civilian construction workers and support personnel of Pacific Naval Air Base Contractors (combination of three construction firms), and 70 Pan American Airways employees (most PanAm employees were evacuated prior to the Japanese attack). Camp 1 was only 50 percent complete at the time of the attack and most Marines lived in tents. Other base projects, including the airfield, were 65 percent complete. One 5,000-foot runway was usable. Planned projects included a turning basin in the lagoon capable of accommodating a tender and a small submarine base, a dredged ship channel through the open northwest side of the lagoon's reef, and additional defense installations.

Marine Detachment, 1st Defense Battalion, Wake Island arrived from Oahu on 22

August 1941. They immediately began construction of their defenses while the contractors continued building base installations. An approximately ten-foot-high sand berm was bulldozed from the beach along the vegetation line on most of Wake Island's southwest ocean-side shore (never mentioned in references, but apparent in aerial photographs). The Marine defenders were reinforced at the beginning of November and at the beginning of December part of Marine Fighting Squadron 211 arrived. There were now 449 Marines, 69 sailors, and 5 USAAF signalmen on the atoll. The garrison worked frantically to prepare defenses as war warnings poured in. Most of the Marine defenses were concentrated on the point of Wake Island's "V" and Peale Island while Wilkes was lightly defended. The Navy Officer in Charge was Commander Winfield S. Cunningham while Major James P. S. Devereux commanded the Marine detachment.

When notified of the attack on Pearl Harbor on 7 December, Wake went immediately to full war alert. The *4th Fleet* in the Mandates had long planned to seize Wake. Bombers of its *24th Air Flotilla* flying from Roi Island 620 miles to the south attacked Wake at noon on the 8th destroying most of the Marine aircraft on the ground and causing significant damage to facilities. Casualties among Marine aviators were especially high. The Japanese bombers attacked again the next day destroying more of the naval air station, the hospital, and much of Camp 2. This was followed by a third attack on the 10th, which inflicted much damage on Wilkes Island. Almost 400 construction workers volunteered to construct defenses, man guns, treat wounded, cook and distribute rations, repair and clear bomb damage, stand watch, and even offered to join the Marines. However, most refused to work on defenses and hid in the brush. Some caused difficulties for the Marines and a number were arrested and confined in the brig.

The Japanese attempted to land a 450-man party of the *Maizaru 2d Special Naval Landing Force (SNLF)* on 11 December. Two destroyers were sunk and seven ships damaged by Marine coast defense guns and the remaining fighters. This force withdrew to Kwajalein. Rear Admiral Kimmel, commanding the Pacific Fleet, began to implement a plan to reinforce the island and engage the Japanese fleet if it again attempted to seize the island. He was relieved on 17 December, being held responsible for the Pearl Harbor attack, and his successor failed to implement an effective plan on a timely basis.

The 8–12, 14–17, and 19 December air attacks were conducted by the *24th Air Flotilla*. The now reinforced *Wake Occupation Force* again departed Kwajalein on 21 December arriving from the south the next night. The Japanese expedition was under the command of Rear Admiral KAJIOKA Sadamichi. From 21 December the air attacks were continued by the carriers *Soryu* and *Hiryu*. The 23 December landing was made by some 1,000 troops of the *Maizaru 2d SNLF*. The landings took place on the southwest shores of Wake and Wilkes Islands at approximately 0230 hours (all sources disagree on the exact time). The two patrol craft (destroyer-transports) landing troops on Wake Island were run aground and abandoned due to severe damage by Marine guns. Other troops were landed by up to six landing barges at various points. It is possible that small groups were landed by rubber boat within the lagoon. The 100 *2d Company, Maizaru 2d SNLF* troops landing on Wilkes Island near New Channel were wiped out, but the force on Wake far outnumbered the defenders. Before dawn cruisers and destroyers provided fire support and air attacks commenced after sunrise. In the early hours of the 23rd the Marine commander was informed by Pearl Harbor that the relief expedition would not arrive within the next twenty-four hours. The Japanese landing force was firmly established ashore, Marine defenders had suffered 40 percent casualties, most heavy weapons had been destroyed or captured, and organized resistance could not be sustained. At 0730 hours, 23 December, Commander Cummingham informed Major Devereux that the garrison would surrender to prevent needless loss of life. Once contact was made with the Japanese it took hours for the scattered defenders to be notified of the surrender, some of whom refused to believe it. Fire fights continued until all Marines had surrendered by approximately 1330 hours.

The Wake Relief Expedition (Task Force 14), assembled around the USS *Saratoga* (CV-3), had departed the Hawaii area on 15–16 December after much delay. A further delay was encountered as the force required refueling prior to making its final approach to the embattled island. A series of poor decisions and faulty intelligence doomed the relief effort and it was recalled at 0911 hours, 22 December (Hawaii time) with the lead ships 515 miles northeast of Wake.

The Marines lost 56 KIA and 44 WIA and the Navy 3 KIA and 5 WIA. All 12 Marine fighters were lost. A total of 349 Marines, 65 sailors, and 5 USAAF signalmen went into captivity. Seventy contractors were killed, twelve wounded, and most survivors were sent to labor camps in North China. Their internment emphasized the need for the Navy to organize naval construction battalions (Seabees), although the decision had been made previously to do so. Five civilians were beheaded aboard ship while en route to China to ensure order was maintained. Ninety-eight civilians were kept on Wake as forced labor.

Japanese landing force losses on Wake Island were estimated at 280 KIA and 333 WIA. Total losses for the operation were 820 KIA and 1,153 WIA. The Marines shot down 21 aircraft and damaged 51. Rear Admiral KAJIOKA was relieved from command on 24 December because of his failure to take the atoll on schedule. In May 1942 he commanded the aborted Port Moresby, Papua invasion force.

The *4th Fleet* was responsible for Wake Island and it was garrisoned by the *65th Guard Force* under the *6th Base Force* on Kwajelein Atoll in the Marshall Islands, 1,600 miles to the south, elements of the *24th Air Flotilla*, and the IJA's *13th Independent Mixed Regiment*. It was strongly fortified, but rather than provide the Japanese with a base from which to threaten Hawaii, Wake proved to be a deathtrap for many of its occupiers. It was bypassed as an objective by the Americans advancing through the South Pacific. A plan to recapture Wake, Operation BUZZER, was canceled in mid-1942. From 24 February 1942 to 1 August 1945, the United States routinely shelled and bombed Wake. This included seven carrier strikes and numerous land-based bomber raids. Wake's 4,100 troops were virtually cut off from outside support by 1943. Infrequent resupply and evacuation of wounded and sick was conducted by submarine.

The Wake Island Surrender Acceptance Unit arrived aboard the USS *Levy* (DD-162) on 4 September 1945 under Brigadier General Lawson H. M. Sanderson, Commanding General, 4th Marine Aircraft Wing. There were 653 IJN and 609 IJA personnel remaining on the island. Over 400 of these troops were wounded and ill. Some 600 others had been killed by U.S. attacks, 1,288 died of starvation and illness, and 974 wounded and ill had been evacuated. The first man to step ashore was Marine Colonel Walter L. J. Bayler, the last man to leave Wake (then a major) on 21 December 1941 by flying boat. At 1330 hours local, the American flag was again raised over Wake. On the same date Naval Air Facility, Wake was established.

After the surrender the Japanese claimed the ninety-eight civilian workers held on Wake had attempted to signal American aircraft and ships and they feared a "fifth column" if the United States attempted to retake the island. In actuality, ration shortages suffered by the beleaguered garrison was the reason behind their execution on 7 October 1943. They were taken to the northeast end of Wake Island and machine-gunned on the beach by order of the island commander. They were buried on the site, but disinterred prior to the surrender and reburied in the American cemetery. The Japanese explained their deaths by asserting a U.S. bomb had hit their shelter and the survivors killed their guard. The garrison was forced to destroy them after they refused to surrender. Two members of the garrison incriminated those responsible and they were tried on Kwajalein in November 1945. The island commander, Rear Admiral SAKAIBARA Shigemitsu, and his adjutant, Lieutenant Commander TACHIBABA Soichi, were tried and hanged for the murder of the civilians on Guam, 17 June 1947.

Island Command, Wake and Naval Air Base, Wake (FPO SF 1181) were established on 1 November 1945. The naval air base was refurbished and the runway extended. Improved quarters and support facilities were built. In 1947, the Navy turned Wake over to the Civil Aeronautics Authority. Wake again was in the world's eye when President Harry Truman and General of the Army Douglas MacArthur met there on 15 October 1950 to discuss the conduct of the Korean War. From 1962, Wake was the joint responsibility of the Departments of the Interior and Transportation. A trans-Pacific telephone relay station was established on Wake in 1964. Wake remained an important military and commercial air refueling stop until 1972 when it was turned over to the U.S. Air Force. In 1975, Wake was used as a temporary camp for 4,000 Vietnamese refuges. Since 1994, it has been administered by the Department of the Interior through the U.S. Army as an unincorporated territory. An automated National Oceanographic and Atmospheric Administration station to monitor *tsunamis* and global warming is located on the atoll. It is closed to the general public.

Wake has been altered so drastically by typhoons and construction that little is recognizable of the early war battleground. A few Japanese coast defense guns still dot the islands and various underground facilities have been unearthed, but recovered, during construction over the years. Among the guns is a British-made Vickers 8-inch on Peale Island's Toki Point rumored to have been brought from Hong Kong. It is actually one of eight guns purchased from Britain in 1905 and first emplaced in the Japanese Home Islands. In 1955, the Navy dedicated a memorial on the island using the cowling and prop of F4F-3 Wildcat fighter No. 9 destroyed during the battle. This was removed in 1965 and the parts used to restore an FM-1 Wildcat on display in the National Air and Space Museum. A Marine 3-inch antiaircraft gun is mounted beside the airport terminal. A chapel, dedicated to the defenders of Wake, and a modest stonewall-surrounded memorial are located near the former Marine command post near the terminal. A similar one, with a Shinto Torii gate, exists for the Japanese garrison. The ammunition bunker used as the Marine command post is still intact. The old American cemetery is underwater. The Japanese cemetery on Wake was disinterred by the Japanese government and the remains cremated. The Japanese cemetery on Peale could not be located because of changes in the terrain and dense underbrush. A coral head at the water's edge on Wilkes Island's lagoon-side lower northeast shore is emblazoned with a small bronze plate, added in the late 1980s, to commemorate the murdered contractors. The wording "98 US PW 5_10_43" had previously been hand-cut into the coral head (the date should read 7-10-43).

MIDWAY ISLAND

Midway Atoll was code-named VERB during the June 1942 battle. Later it was redesignated BALSA and later still BACKBITER. The Japanese designated it "AF." The discovery of the Japanese code identification for Midway was crucial in determining their plans for the June 1942 invasion attempt. This was accomplished by ordering the Midway radio station to transmit in the clear that its water distillation units were (falsely) malfunctioning. Intercepts of Japanese radio traffic picked up their report that "AF is short of water" thus confirming that Midway ("AF") was the target of future Japanese operations.

Midway lies in the almost geographic center of the North Pacific some 2,200 miles west of Tokyo and 1,225 miles northwest of Pearl Harbor at the end of a long chain of rocks extending from the Hawaiian Islands. It is situated at 28°13' N 177°22' W. It was in the same time zone, Zone 1:30, as Hawaii; two and one-half hours earlier than the U.S. Pacific Time Zone (Zone 4).

The atoll consists of only two islands on the south side of a roughly circular coral reef six miles across with a circumference of some fifteen miles (see Map 4). The narrow reef rises no more than three feet out of the water and is open on its northwest side. At the southern end of this open area is the approximately one-half-mile-wide Seward Roads (named after the 1876 U.S. Secretary of State) allowing access to Welles Harbor (named after the Secretary of the Navy), a small natural anchorage on the northwest side of Sand Island (ALCATRAZ). Seward Roads is defined by a hooked end of the main reef on its south side and a coral head known as North Breakers. Another passage, the manmade Brooks Channel, allows entry into the lagoon from the south and separates Sand and Eastern Islands. Two sandbars lie on either side the channel, Gooney Islet on the west side and Spit Islet on the east. Near the atoll's north edge is Sand Islet, another sandbar. Most of the twenty-eight-square-mile lagoon is too shallow for anything but small craft and was marked shoals and foul ground on charts. An oval central portion of the lagoon was suitably deep for seaplanes.

Both islands are comprised of coral sand and partly covered by low, scattered scrub brush. Small dense scrub-brush-covered areas were found in the center of Sand Island and along the south shore, and at the north corner of Eastern Island. The cable station grounds were planted with eucalyptus, ironwood, and shrubbery imported from Australia. Both islands were expanded somewhat in size by dredging spoil and leveling. The islands are edged with narrow beaches on all sides. Tiny Kure Island, a small atoll formerly known as Cure, lies some sixty miles to the northwest of Midway, but was unoccupied. The Navy did station three PT boats there during the Battle of Midway.

Sand Island measures 3,800 yards along its southwest (Frigate Point) to northeast axis and is 2,000 yards wide across the midsection at Picket Point, which juts into the lagoon. Prior to occupation the island was crowned by a 42-foot hill, a considerable elevation for a coral atoll island. This was leveled to 13 feet and used to expand the island and provide a 600-yard breakwater jutting from the east corner.

Triangular-shaped Eastern Island is just over 2,000 yards east of Sand Island. It is 2,200 yards long east to west and its east end is 1,300 yards wide. Its highest elevation is twelve feet. Eastern Island was unused until occupied by the defense force in February 1941.

The humid tropical climate is moderated between 70 and 80°F year-round by prevailing easterly winds. The atoll receives an average of forty-two inches of rain a year with most falling in the winter months. At the time of the battle the temperature averaged 75°F with 90 percent humidity.

Midway was considered the most strategically important of the outlying islands and special emphasis was given to its development as a base. It was to possess a naval air station, seaplane base, advanced submarine base, and be capable of refueling and repairing ships. By 1940, the Army had dredged the Brooks Channel, built the Sand Island breakwater, dredged a small submarine basin on the island's north side, and connected it to Wells Harbor. The Navy took over the rest of the development in March 1940 with

Map 4
Midway Island

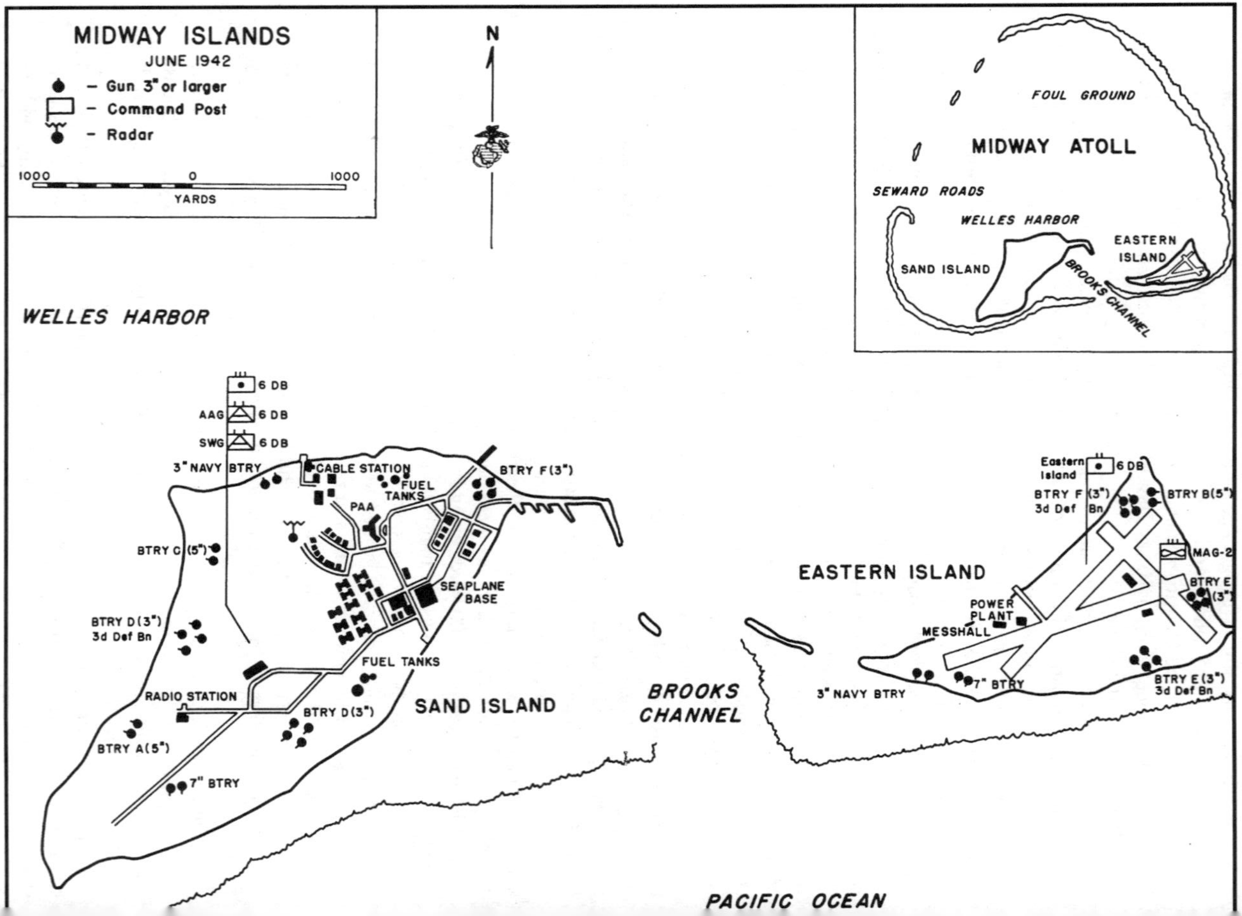

MIDWAY ISLANDS
JUNE 1942

● – Gun 3" or larger
▢ – Command Post
👁 – Radar

1000   0   1000
YARDS

N

MIDWAY ATOLL

FOUL GROUND

SEWARD ROADS

WELLES HARBOR

BROOKS CHANNEL

EASTERN ISLAND

SAND ISLAND

WELLES HARBOR

BTRY F (3")

CABLE STATION
FUEL TANKS
PAA
SEAPLANE BASE
FUEL TANKS

BTRY D (3")

6 DB
AAG 6 DB
SWG 6 DB
3" NAVY BTRY

BTRY C (5")

BTRY D (3")
3d Def Bn

RADIO STATION

BTRY A (5")

7" BTRY

SAND ISLAND

BROOKS CHANNEL

BTRY B (5")

MAG-2

BTRY E (3")

6 DB 6 DB
Eastern Island
BTRY F (3")
3d Def Bn

POWER PLANT
MESSHALL

7" BTRY

BTRY E (3")
3d Def Bn

3" NAVY BTRY

EASTERN ISLAND

PACIFIC OCEAN

additional dredging of the basin and channels. Naval Air Station, Midway Island (SINGS-ING) (FPO SF 1504) occupied most of Eastern Island with three runways (3,250, 4,500, and 5,300 feet long). It was commissioned on 18 August 1941. It was later named Henderson Field after Majar Loften R. Henderson lost during the Battle of Midway. (Another Henderson Field named after the same officer existed on Guadalcanal.) The island headquarters and seaplane base were on Sand Island. Low timber seawalls were built almost completely around both islands. Complete support facilities were built on both islands and were well developed by the time of the June 1942 Japanese attack.

Uninhabited Midway Atoll was discovered by Captain N.C. Brooks, the civilian master of a bark, who claimed it for the United States in 1859. He named it Middlebrooks Island after himself; it later became known as Brooks Island. Brooks kept its location secret, however, and planned to sell it to the North Pacific Mail and Steamship Company, which was searching for a mid-Pacific coaling station. The U.S. government sent the USS *Lukawana* to find the island and it was formally annexed in 1867, the first possession acquired by the United States in the Pacific. North Pacific Mail and Steamship soon established a coaling station on the island, which it renamed Midway owing to its central location. By 1903, Japanese bird poachers had occupied Midway to the extent that Theodore Roosevelt placed the island under Navy control fearing Japan might lay claim. The squatters were evicted in June 1903 and a Honolulu-Guam-Manila cable relay station was soon built by the Pacific Commercial Cable Company on Sand Island's north shore. A small Marine detachment garrisoned the island from 1904 to 1908 to prevent the squatters' return and maintain order among the construction workers, many of whom were Japanese. The Navy soon built a lighthouse on Sand Island. In 1935, Pan American World Airways established a way station and hotel, Gooneyville Lodge, for its Clipper seaplanes on Sand Island's north end.

The Marine Corps' 3d Defense Battalion occupied Midway in mid-February 1941, although reconnaissance details and advance parties had been preparing the island for the previous eight months. In mid-September the 3d was relieved by the 6th Defense Battalion. Midway was the only outlying island to be garrisoned by a full defense battalion prior to hostilities. Two Japanese destroyers, the *Midway Neutralization Unit*, shelled Sand Island on the night of 7 December from the southwest to prevent the island's patrol bombers from interfering with the retiring Pearl Harbor *Air Attack Force* carriers. Casualties were light (four KIA, ten WIA) and damage to installations was moderate. Submarines shelled or attempted to shell Midway on 25 January, 8 and 10 February 1942 inflicting no damage or casualties.

The Japanese effort to seize Midway, *MI Operation*, in June 1942 was to serve as a turning point of the war in their favor. Commander, Shore-Based Air, Midway (also Commander, Midway Local Defenses) was Navy Captain Cyril T. Simard while the 6th Defense Battalion, reinforced by elements of the 3d, was commanded by Colonel Harold D. Shannon. Part of the 2d Raider Battalion was also present. Marine Aircraft Group 22 and a 7th Air Force provisional bomber force provided Midway its air protection. The Midway garrison was informed at the beginning of May 1942 that the Japanese were expected to attempt to seize the island. The Japanese goal was to secure an airfield that threatened Hawaii reasoning it could be supported from their bastion in the Marshalls, some 1,400 miles to the south-southwest, via their newly acquired airfield on Wake 1,110 miles to the southwest. The coming battle was also an attempt to destroy the remainder of the U.S. Pacific Fleet using Midway as bait. At the same time another Japanese force would seize islands in the western Aleutians as a diversion. Admiral YAMAMOTO's plan was far too intricate and his forces too dispersed. Coupled with faulty intelligence, the Japanese plan was doomed.

The *Midway Occupation Force* sortied out of the *Yokosuka* and *Kure District Naval Stations* on 20 May for Saipan, which it departed on the 27th. The force consisted of the 5,000-man *2d Combined Special Landing Force* comprised of the 1,250-man *Yoko-suka 5th SNLF* (Sand Island) and the 1,200-man *Ichiki Force (28th Infantry Regiment [-], 7th Division)* (Eastern Island), plus the IJN *11th* and *12th Construction Battalions*. On the morning of 4 June 1942 the *Carrier Striking Force* launched 108 aircraft from four carriers some 180 miles north-northwest of Midway. Marine fighters intercepted the incoming raid, but most of the aircraft made it through and attacked Midway at 0630 hours. The garrison suffered significant, but not crippling, damage and light casualties (thirteen KIA, eighteen WIA). Follow-on attacks on the Japanese carriers were launched from Midway later in the morning. The next morning aircraft from Midway attacked the *Midway Occupation Force* transports discovered 125 miles west of the island. Both attacks achieved little. Thirty-five U.S. Marine, Navy, and USAAF aircraft based on Midway were shot down attacking Japanese aircraft and ships. Japanese aircraft losses in the attack have never been accurately determined, but that is a moot point as most were lost when the four Japanese carriers were sunk by U.S. carrier aircraft on 4 June. The American carriers of Task Forces 16 and 17 were over 100 miles to the east of the *Carrier Striking Force* and the two opposing fleets never directly engaged. The *Midway Occupation Force* never made its planned 7 June *N-Day* landing. A small IJN landing party was also to have secured Kure Island to the northwest. Japan lost four carriers, a cruiser, and 322 aircraft while the United States lost the USS *Yorktown* (CA-5), earlier damaged by air attack, to a submarine on 7 June, a destroyer, and 147 aircraft. *Yorktown*'s casualties were light. The Battle of Midway, coupled with its losses suffered in the 8 May Battle of the Coral Sea, inflicted a staggering defeat on the Japanese fleet from which it never recovered. As a result, in July 1942, the Japanese were forced to cancel their plans to invade the Samoas, Fiji, and New Caledonia.

The month following the battle saw heightened activity on Midway. It became an important base supporting Central Pacific offensive operations. A three-runway airfield (two 7,500-foot, one 8,600-foot) (ALCATRAZ) with extensive support facilities was built on Sand Island occupying the western three-quarters of the island. In the spring of 1943, a major submarine base was constructed on Eastern Island. Another breakwater with built to the south of the earlier one to provide a protected submarine basin on Sand Island's east end. This allowed submarines to use Midway for resupply, refitting, and rest without having to travel a further 1,225 miles to Pearl Harbor. This also reduced their patrol turnaround time. Additional channel and basin dredging was accomplished in 1943. In 1944, seven submarine and two tender piers were constructed in the submarine basin along with additional support facilities.

Midway remained an important Navy base after the war providing a mid-Pacific re-fueling stop, and navigation and weather stations. It was designated a wildlife refuge in 1988 and the cable station was closed in 1990. The Eastern Island airfield was closed after the war and the newer and larger Sand Island field became the atoll's only opera-tional airfield. Midway outlived its usefulness as longer-ranged commercial and military aircraft entered service. It was operationally closed in 1993 and jurisdiction was trans-ferred from the Navy to the Fish and Wildlife Service of the Department of the Interior in 1996. It is closed to the general public.

Map 5
Johnston Island

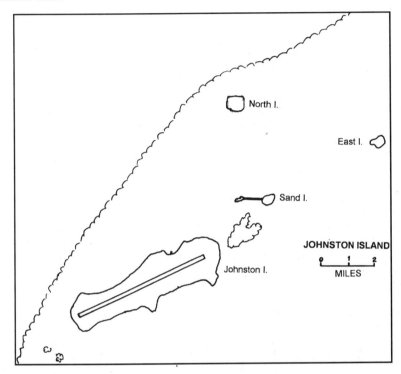

JOHNSTON ISLAND

Johnston Atoll was initially code-named JACKKNIFE, but was later redesignated GIFT.

Johnston is located at 16°45' N 169°30' W 720 miles southwest of Pearl Harbor. Even though relatively close to Hawaii, it is in time zone 1 and just to the south edge of Hawaii's zone 1:30.

The atoll is comparatively long and narrow, some 2½ by 9¼ miles with a 21-mile circumference and oriented southeast to northeast (see Map 5). Most of the reef is well submerged with only the northwest side breaking the surface 2 or 3 feet. Two islands are situated near the lagoon's southwest end. The larger Johnston Island was approximately 1,000 by 200 yards covering 64 acres with the long axis west-southwest to east-northeast. Roughly circular, 6-acre Sand Island was several hundred yards to the north-northeast of the main island. Both islands were low and flat covered with guano atop a coral sand and sandstone base reef. Between the northwest sides of the islands and the reef the lagoon was shallow and filled with coral heads. Small craft could approach only from the south. What little vegetation existed on the islands was widely scattered, low scrub brush. The size and shape of these islands would radically change during and after the war.

Johnston's temperature varies little seasonally, mid-70°F range from December to April while from June to October it rises to the mid-80°F range. The humidity averages 76 percent year around and the annual rainfall averages twenty-eight inches.

The atoll was discovered by British Captain Charles Johnston in 1807. The Kingdom of Hawaii claimed it in 1858, and by default, it became a U.S. possession in 1898. The atoll's guano deposits were worked until depleted in the 1890s. Franklin Roosevelt placed the atoll under Navy control in 1934. A ship channel was dredged into the lagoon and a seaplane runway cleared in 1935. In 1937, patrol plane units used it during a fleet exercise. The atoll's value was recognized as a tender-based seaplane base to guard the southwest approaches to Hawaii from the Japanese-controlled Marshalls and to aid in the long-range protection of the Panama Canal and the west coast of South America. Civilian contractors arrived on Sand Island in November 1939 to improve the ship channel, dredge a small turning basin, build seaplane base support facilities, and create a 300-by-800-foot manmade island of dredged spoil for a seaplane parking area. This unnamed island, considered part of Sand Island to its west, is connected to that island by a 2,000-foot-long spoil causeway. The barbell-shaped island covered twenty-two acres. Three extended seaplane runways were dredged in the lagoon.

An advance party of the 1st Defense Battalion arrived at the atoll in March 1941 and Naval Air Station, Johnston Island (FPO SF 311) was commissioned in August. In September, Johnston Island itself was enlarged by filling a 200-by-2,500-foot-wide area along the south shore. This provided space for a 4,000-foot runway. The facilities on Sand Island were occupied by the Navy when the contractors moved to Johnston Island. Marine Detachment, 1st Defense Battalion, Johnston Island arrived on the island on 24 July 1941.

At the time of the Pearl Harbor attack there were only 162 men of the Marine detachment on the atoll with very limited armament. A cruiser and five minesweepers were exercising off the atoll at the time of the attack, but they quickly departed for more exigent tasks. A Japanese submarine shelled the island on 15 December causing slight damage to a few buildings and inflicting no casualties. The contractors were not withdrawn and continued improvements until relieved by Seabees in July 1942. The seaplane runway was extended and the spoil from this effort was used to further expand Johnston Island allowing a 3,500-foot auxiliary runway to be built. Further air station facilities were built and the atoll became an important way point as the war expanded into the Gilberts in 1943 and even more so as the war moved into the Marshalls at the beginning of 1944. The year 1943 also saw the atoll being developed as a submarine support base. At the end of 1943, work began to further expand the runway to 6,000 feet by adding more spoil dredged from Johnston Island's north side. By the summer of 1944 the island had grown to 160 acres, four times its original size, and was roughly rectangular in shape.

No further combat action took place on the atoll. Marine Detachment, 1st Defense Battalion, Johnston Island was disbanded on 7 February 1942 and its assets used to form Marine Defense Force, NAS, Johnston Island. The Force was redesignated the 16th Defense Battalion in November. It moved to Kauai, TH in March 1944, but part of the unit remained and a new Marine Defense Force, NAS, Johnston Island was formed.

The Force was redesignated Marine Barracks, NAS, Johnston Island in 1946 and was deactivated in 1949. The naval air facility was inactivated on 1 July 1948 and the atoll's control was transferred to the Army. By the late 1950s the atoll was headquarters for high-altitude nuclear testing and was capable of test launching ICBMs. The Johnston Island Chemical Activity was established there in 1971 for the storage of chemical warfare munitions. The main island continued to be expanded by dredging with the last project in 1964 enlarging the island to 625 acres. North (aka Akau) and East (aka Hikina) Islands, approximately twenty-five acres and eighteen acres, respectively, were formed by dredge spoil during this period. North Island is 1-¼ miles north-northeast of Johnston and East Island is 2-¼ miles northeast. In 1990 the Johnston Atoll Chemical Agent Destruction System was built to demilitarize chemical warfare munitions transferred from Pacific and European depots. Today, Johnston Atoll is an incorporated U.S. territory jointly administered by the Defense Special Weapons Agency and the Department of the Interior's Fish and Wildlife Service. It is a National Wildlife Refuge intended to preserve the many sea and shore birds, Hawaiian monk seals, and green sea turtles, the latter two being endangered. It is closed to the public.

PALMYRA ISLAND AND KINGMAN REEF, LINE ISLANDS

Palmyra (pronounced "Pal-mi-ra") Atoll was code-named BRUSH. Palmyra is a term for palm tree derived from the Latin *palma*—palm.

Palmyra Atoll is situated at 5°52' N 162°06' W near the northwest end of the Line Islands. The atoll is 994 miles south-southwest of Pearl Harbor, 1,513 miles northeast of American Samoa, and 900 miles southeast of Johnston Island. Other islands comprising the uninhabited Line Islands (aka Equatorial Islands) run southwest from Palmyra Atoll. With the exception of Jarvis,[2] all were British possessions: Washington, Fanning, Christmas (which see), Jarvis, Malden, Starbuck, Caroline, Vostock, and Flint Islands. Kingman Reef, a U.S. possession, is located thirty-three miles north-northeast of Palmyra at the northwest end of the Line Islands (see Maps 6a and 6b). Palmyra and Kingman Reef are in time zone 1.

Palmyra is an elongated horseshoe-shaped atoll with over fifty small islands enclosed by the atoll's oval reef. The atoll covers 4.6 square miles. The long axis is oriented east to west and measures approximately six by two miles with a total land area of approximately 600 acres at high tide. The horseshoe's open end is to the west. The lagoon is very shallow. Shoals extend some 5 miles to the west of the atoll and two miles to the east. The main islands are Cooper, Menge, Engineer, Home, Sand, Eastern, and Straw. The islands are low and generally flat coral sandbars. The highest elevation is 7 feet. All are covered with dense scrub brush, coconut palms, and balsa-like trees up to 90 feet high. The year around temperature is in the mid-80s, humid, with heavy rains of 150–160 inches per year.

Palmyra was discovered by American Captain Edmond Fanning in 1798, who named it Samarang, but failed to properly report it. Another American, a Captain Sawle, aboard the *Palmyra*, rediscovered the atoll in 1802 and was given official credit for its discovery. It was annexed by the Kingdom of Hawaii in 1862, but Britain claimed the atoll in 1889. The United States included Palmyra in the annexation of Hawaii in 1898 and formally took possession in 1912. The atoll's islands were purchased by Judge Henry Cooper of Hawaii in 1911 to develop coconut plantations. Most of the islands were sold to the Fuller-Leo family in 1922. A legal battle regarding ownership followed with the U.S. government. The dispute was eventually settled in favor of the Fuller-Leo family. All have since been passed to heirs and are still privately owned (they are for sale for $49 million). In 1940 it had a civilian population of thirty-two, who were evacuated before the war.

Palmyra is just short of halfway between Hawaii and the Samoas making it an ideal air refueling way station. It is also midway between Hawaii and Canton Island, another U.S. outlying base to the southwest. Contractors arrived in January 1940 to begin work

Map 6a
Palmyra Island, Line Islands

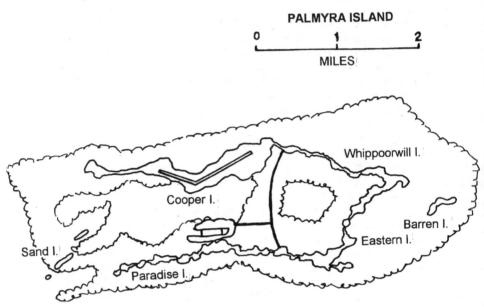

on a boat channel and a seaplane landing area in the lagoon near Cooper and Menge Islands. The two largest islands in the atoll, they are located on the lagoon's north-central side. Menge is less than one-half mile to the west of the larger Cooper Island. An anchorage, West Lagoon, was dredged. Later in 1940 it was decided a land plane base was required. No single island was of sufficient size. Dredge spoil was pumped between Cooper and Menge Islands as well as on the south side of Cooper. A 5,400-foot runway was built and later a 3,700-foot runway was extended on to Merge Island. Support facilities and quarters were built on Cooper. An advance party of Marine Detachment, 1st Defense Battalion, Palmyra arrived in the first week of March 1941. The remainder of the detachment arrived in the summer. NAS, Palmyra (FPO SF 309) was commissioned on 15 August.

The contractors' work on base facilities was redirected to constructing defenses after the Pearl Harbor attack. On 24 December, a Japanese submarine shelled the atoll slightly damaging a dredge without inflicting casualties. The Marine detachment was reinforced at the end of December and the Army's 12th Pursuit Squadron arrived in February 1942. To allow movement between the atoll's many islands a twelve-mile-long dredged coral causeway linked most of the islands from Straw on the northwest end around the "horse-shoe" to Home Island on the southwest end. On 1 March 1942, the Marine detachment was reorganized as the 1st Defense Battalion since its Wake Island detachment was lost and the Johnston detachment was reorganized as a separate defense force. Increasing air traffic to the Samoas in the summer of 1942 led to an expansion of base facilities. Army Task Force, Palmyra (APO SF 458) was based on the island from October 1943 and into 1944.

Kingman Reef, a U.S. possession, is situated at 6°24' N 162°24' W. It is thirty-three miles north-northeast of Palmyra and 1,075 miles southwest of Pearl Harbor on the northwest end of the Line Island chain. The shoals have been a U.S. possession since

Map 6b
Kingman Reef, Line Islands

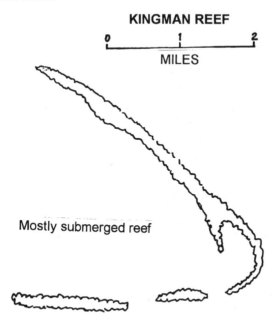

KINGMAN REEF

MILES

Mostly submerged reef

1922. Less than one square mile of the mostly submerged triangular atoll is exposed during low tide. The west side is open. It is approximately 9-½ miles long east to west and 5 miles wide. Kingman Reef is presently classified as a naval defensive sea area and airspace reservation. As such it is off-limits to the public.

NAS, Palmyra was closed on 15 February 1947 and turned over to the Civil Aeronautics Authority. It was administered by the County of Honolulu until 1959 when Hawaii was granted statehood. In 1961, the Department of the Interior's Office of Insular Affairs was given authority over the atoll. Cooper and Merge are still joined islands, but the airfield is overgrown with vegetation and eroded as are the connecting coral causeways. Rumors of the "Palmyra Curse" taint the still uninhabited islands today with stories of murders, shipwrecks, and unexplained disappearances. In May 2001, the Fullard-Leo family sold the atoll to the Nature Conservancy for $37 million. The private environmental preservation organization will develop it for ecotourism and scientific study.

CHRISTMAS AND FANNING ISLANDS, LINE ISLANDS

Christmas Island (often referred to as "Xmas Island" in official documents as a form of shorthand) was code-named BIRCH (Army) and GUMDROP (Navy). FPO SF 308, APO SF 915. Fanning Island, aka Tabuaeran, (PAGE, LAMPOON, RACKETEER), was used as an adjacent small base.

Christmas Island is situated at 1°59' N 157°30' W. It is 380 miles southeast of Palmyra Island. Christmas is the largest island among the five Line Islands and is on the southeast end of the island chain. Fanning is at 3°30' N 159°13' W 164 miles northwest of Christmas. Christmas is in time zone 2, but while Fanning lies within zone 1, it was the sole occupant of its own small time zone, 1:22. (Christmas Island, Line Islands should not

Map 7
Christmas Island, Line Islands

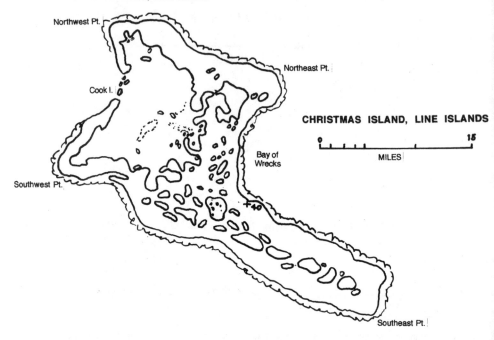

be confused with another Christmas Island in the Indian Ocean to the south of Java. It is an Australian possession occupied by Japan on 30 March 1942.)

Christmas Island is considered to be the geologically oldest atoll. It appears as an "L" laying on its back with hooked arms extending westward from the base of the "L" to enclose the shallow, coral-filled lagoon on the west end (see Map 7). The island is some seventeen miles wide and thirty-two miles long east to west covering about 60,000 acres total area. The inside of the "L" on the island's north side is known as Bay of Wrecks. Cook Island (not to be confused with Cook Island in the Society Islands far to the south), a sandbar, is situated in the lagoon's entrance providing two narrow passages. A number of islets and sandbars are scattered about the lagoon, especially on the east and north sides. Numerous shallow lakes are found on both arms of the "L" along with sand hills. Joe's Hill on the Bay of Wrecks side of the bend in the "L" is forty feet high. Scrub brush covers much of the island while the coconut groves are on the lagoon's arms. A coral mud road follows the coast on both sides of the east to west long arm of the "L" and around the inside edge of the lagoon.

Fanning Island is a kidney-shaped atoll thirty-four miles in circumference covering fifteen square miles (see Map 8). It is 9-½ miles long from northwest to southeast and 6-¼ miles wide across the southeast lobe. The atoll is rimed by an almost continuous low sand island no more than ½ mile wide with a maximum elevation of seventeen feet. Most of the shallow lagoon is coral-filled with parts of the southeast portion exposed at low tide. The lagoon's narrow entrance is on the central-southwest coast. Outside the entrance is English Harbour, an anchorage capable of sheltering small ships. Whaler's Anchorage, a calm-weather shelter, is off of the atoll's western corner, Bicknell Point.

Map 8
Fanning Island, Line Islands

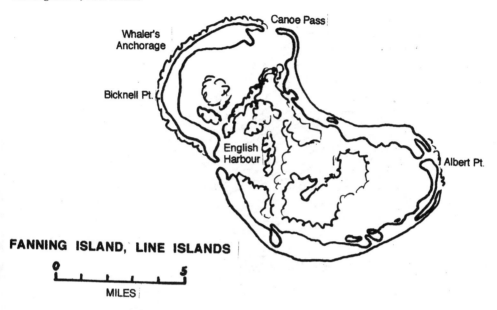

FANNING ISLAND, LINE ISLANDS

Just north of the point the British established a Canada-to-Fiji cable relay station in 1916. Fanning experiences about 100 inches of rain per year, but in 1940 it received more than that just in the first six months.

Christmas Island was discovered by Captain James Cook on Christmas Eve of 1777. Fanning was discovered by American Captain Edmund Fanning in 1798 along with Washington Island between Fanning and Palmyra. The British established the Gilbert and Ellice Islands Colony in 1915. While the Gilberts and Ellices are some 1,500 due west and 1,400 miles southwest of Christmas, respectively, Fanning was annexed the following year and Christmas in 1919. Regardless, Britain's claim to Christmas was disputed by the United States in 1936.

When the war broke out fewer than thirty civilians lived on Christmas, both natives and Europeans. Fanning was populated by 250 natives with 30 Europeans and a few Chinese. A British-operated radio station was located on Fanning with the cable station. Coconut plantations flourished on both islands. Pearl shell was harvested from Christmas Island's lagoon. A New Zealand rifle platoon had occupied the island shortly after the war broke out in Europe to protect it from German raiders. Additional infantry and a 6-inch gun crew reinforced the island in April 1940 to 105 troops.

Both Christmas and Fanning Islands were determined to be a usable as alternate air refueling stops, in lieu of Palmyra to the northwest, to Australia and South Pacific islands. While the Navy was responsible for the defense of most outlying islands, the Army was assigned Christmas, Canton, and Borabora. Christmas was secured by a 2,000-man task force with one each infantry, coast artillery, and antiaircraft battalions plus the 12th Pursuit Squadron on 10 February 1942 (APO SF 967). An airfield was built and is still operational. The New Zealand Fanning garrison was relieved by the 140-man Company

Map 9
Canton Island, Phoenix Group

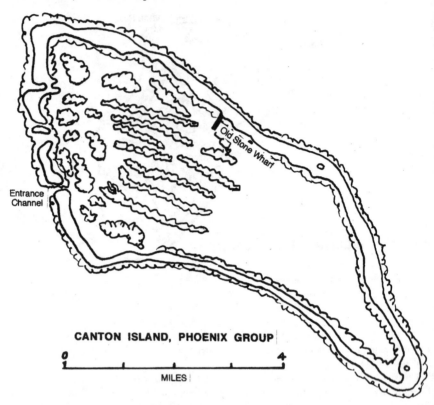

CANTON ISLAND, PHOENIX GROUP

L, 21st Infantry Regiment on 26 April 1942. The U.S. Fanning garrison was removed in July 1945 and the Christmas garrison force departed soon after the war's end.

Christmas, known as Kiritimati Island until recently, is now part of the Line Islands District of the Republic of Kiribati (see Gilbert Islands). On 10 August 1997 it was officially renamed Millennium Island when Kiribati unilaterally moved the International Date Line, which ran through the center of the republic's area, to its far eastern edge. This made the unpopulated island the first land area to greet the year 2000, even though Hilo, Hawaii to the north is two degrees further to the east.

CANTON ISLAND, PHOENIX GROUP

Canton Island, aka Mary or Swallow Island (both seldom used), was code-named HOLLY (Army) and MILD (Navy), later MYTHOLOGY.

The atoll is situated at 2°40' S 171°40' W approximately 1,600 miles southwest of Pearl Harbor, 800 miles south of Palmyra Island, and 960 miles from Japanese-held Makin in the Marshalls. Canton is in time zone 1.

Canton is an approximately 10-¾ miles long oriented northwest to southeast (see Map 9). The roughly parallelogram-shaped atoll's southeast end tapers to a point while the west side is five miles wide. While an atoll, most of the rim has formed into one long, almost continuous ribbon island following the reef's edge. The west ends of this thin, looped island hook inward. There are two small islands in the west end. An entrance to the lagoon is found between the south hook and the southern of the two small islands. The wider western half of the lagoon is choked with reefs and coralheads. The eastern portion is up to 66 feet deep allowing seaplanes to land. The island is of coral sand with only a few feet of elevation. The flat island varies from fifty to 400 feet in width with little vegetation other than a dense stand of low grasses, vines, scacvola bushes, and coconut trees on the southeast portion of the island's southern arm, and a few lone trees on the western hooks. Two brackish pools are found on the island. The offshore reef follows the island's outline and lies very close to the shore.

Canton is on the northeast edge of the widely scattered Phoenix Group, which includes Enderbury, Birnie, Phoenix, Sidney, Hull, Gardner, and McKern Islands. These islands contain approximately nineteen square miles of land. Annexed by Great Britain, they were of little economic value, but were leased to the Samoa Shipping and Trading Company in 1914, which worked them for guano and copra.

Canton Island was reported by a number of American whalers and British warships over the years, but it was not named until 1854 after an American whaler. The British claimed it in 1890 for a cable station site and the island was worked by guano diggers until depleted. The British established the Gilbert and Ellice Islands Colony in 1915. While the Ellices are almost 700 miles to the southwest of Canton, the uninhabited Phoenix Group was annexed in 1937. In the mid-1930s it was realized that Canton was an ideal location for a trans-Pacific seaplane way station. Between 1936 and 1938 the British and Americans occasionally landed naval personnel and civilians in an effort to confirm their claims. Occasionally the two groups simultaneously occupied the island, with both posting signs claiming the island's sovereignty, under amiable conditions. In April 1939, Britain and the United States agreed to jointly control Canton and Enderbury Islands as a condominium for fifty years, at which time the agreement could be modified or terminated by mutual consent. Enderbury, at 3°08' S 171°01' W, is approximately fifty miles east-southeast of Canton. The roughly rectangular island, an almost completely filled in atoll, measures some 1-¾ by 3 miles.

Pan American Airways developed a seaplane station on Canton's southern hook near the lagoon's entrance in 1938–39. Canton was assigned to the Army for development before the war, but the Navy took over the seaplane base when the war broke out. Well before the war, when plans were developed to reinforce the Philippines by sea and air, the Army Air Corps encouraged that an additional air route be developed that was less exposed to Japanese threats than Midway and Wake. The proposed route was via Christmas, Canton, Samoa, Fiji, and New Caledonia. Approval was given in August 1941 and work began in October. Canton was assigned to the Army for development and defense (APO SF 914). When war broke out the project was nearing completion and included a 5,000-foot bomber runway. Only seventy-eight Army engineers with no defensive capabilities "garrisoned" the island until February 1942.

A Japanese patrol-bomber reconnoitered Canton in mid-December 1941, dropped a few bombs, but caused no damage. The Army established a 1,100-man defense force of two rifle companies, a coast artillery battalion, and an antiaircraft battalion on 10 February 1942. A pursuit squadron followed, then a light bomber squadron. The infantry and coast artillery units were later withdrawn. It was redesignated a garrison force in June 1944. The Army built a three-runway airfield and the Navy improved the seaplane field (FPO SF 310). Canton's principal importance was as a refueling stop on the Hawaii to Australia route as well as flights to the Samoas, Fiji, New Caledonia, Espíritu Santo, and later, to the Solomon and Ellice Islands. The defense of Canton became a minor point of contention between the Army and Navy in the early months of the war. The Navy, fearing another Wake Island and the loss of a valuable way station, insisted that the Army strengthen the garrison. The Army felt it was sufficiently strongly defended with another pursuit squadron available on Christmas Island to the northeast. Even in the remote possibility that Canton was lost, Christmas Island offered an alternate refueling stop. The Army sent a few more men from Hawaii and the Navy was appeased. In October 1942, the B-17 bomber in which Eddie Rickenbacker, the top-scoring U.S. World War I ace, was serving as a civilian observer, was reported missing while en route to Canton from Hawaii. He and six of the crew were rescued after twenty-seven days in life rafts.

The Army removed its garrison force soon after the war and the naval air facility on Canton was closed on 14 October 1946. In the 1950s and early 1960s Christmas Island was used for above-surface nuclear testing by the United States and Britain. Through the 1960s and 1970s it served as the Air Force's Space and Missile Test Center. The United States dropped its claim on the island in 1979, at which time it was officially renamed Kanton and became part of the Rawaki Islands (formerly Line Islands) District of the Republic of Kiribati (see Gilbert Islands). The island today is known for its scuba diving. Guests stay at the Captain Cook Hotel.

FRENCH FRIGATE SHOAL, HAWAIIAN ISLANDS

The shoal is a mostly submerged coral atoll code-named PLUTOCRAT. It has been called French Frigates Shoal, and French Frigate Shoal, the official name since 1924, but French Frigate Shoals was widely used during World War II.

The atoll is located 530 miles west-northwest of Pearl Harbor on the direct air route to Midway Island and just short of the halfway point. It is located in Hawaii's time zone 1:30.

The crescent-shaped atoll is approximately 18 miles in diameter and consists of approximately 11 tiny sand islets and a basalt rock pinnacle on the north edge and scattered along the westward open of the atoll's crescent (see Map 10).The shoal rests on a platform averaging 100 feet in depth. The largest islet is Tern Island on the northwest corner, originally not much larger than a tennis court. The rock formation, La Perouse Pinnacle, from a distance appears as a pair of frigates under full sail. The Pinnacle, seven miles south of Tern Island and near the center of the crescent, is 122 feet above mean sea level, 500 feet long and 80 feet wide. Some 350 yards to its northwest is a 10-foot high, 100-foot long, 40-foot wide rock formation. No more than 4 feet of the islets are exposed at low tide. Over the years varying numbers of islets have been reported and the positions shift with tides and currents. This has resulted in the incorrect names being applied to some islets. The eastern portion of the lagoon varies from seven to over forty feet deep while the open western side is 60–100 feet deep, The shoal offer protection from the northerly and easterly winds and surf. The shoal is an extremely old atoll having mostly eroded away around the edges and the Pinnacle is believed to be all that remains of a once large rocky dome-shaped island.

French Frigate Shoal experiences year-round temperatures between mid-70°F and mid-80°F. The easterly trade winds blow at a steady twenty knots in normal weather. There was no vegetation, other than salt grass, but a clump of ironwood trees were planted on Tern after its enlargement.

Map 10
French Frigate Shoal, Hawaiian Islands

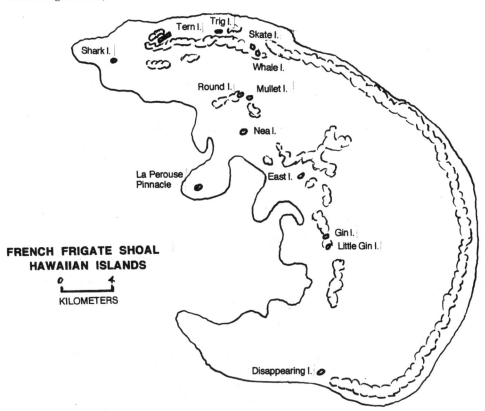

FRENCH FRIGATE SHOAL
HAWAIIAN ISLANDS

The shoal was discovered by a Frenchman, Jean Francis de Galaup, Comte de Pérouse (Count of Pérouse, namesake of the rock. Some sources state that it was named after his ship, the *Perouse*, but his ship was the *Broussole*). He named the reef Basse des Fregates Frangaises (Shoal of the French Frigates). It was first officially reported and claimed by Lieutenant John Brooke aboard the USS *Fenimore Cooper* in 1859. It was claimed by the Republic of Hawaii in 1895 leading it to again fall under U.S. control in 1898. In 1909, Theodore Roosevelt declared the Northwest Hawaiian Islands, except Midway, as the Hawaiian Island Reservation under the Department of Agriculture to prevent bird poachers from pillaging the islands. The Navy used the shoal as a seaplane anchorage and amphibious landing exercise site through the 1930s. The Navy determined that the shoal could equally as well serve as an enemy staging site for air attacks on the Hawaiian Islands. It desired to establish a refueling and emergency seaplane landing site in the shoal.

The first military use of the shoal during the war was by the Japanese *K Operation*. On the night of 3 March 1942, two long-range flying boat bombers flew in from Wotje Atoll in the Marshalls, rendezvoused with three submarines, and refueled. They then flew on to Pearl Harbor and dropped bombs in retaliation of the 1 February American carrier

Map 11
Tern Island, French Frigate Shoal

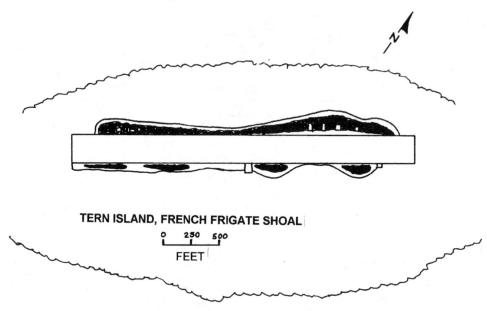

TERN ISLAND, FRENCH FRIGATE SHOAL

0   250   500

FEET

strike on the Marshalls. One bomber dropped its load on empty hills six miles east of Pearl Harbor and the other unloaded its bombs far offshore. In May 1942, as a prelude for the Battle of Midway, the Japanese attempted a repeat and sent two submarines to the shoal to again rendezvous with flying boats that were to reconnoiter Pearl Harbor to determine the U.S. Fleet's location. The submarines found the shoal occupied by a U.S. seaplane tender and the flying boats never arrived. No alternate rendezvous was provided for. The United States reinforced the shoal with a destroyer and second seaplane tender during the June Battle of Midway.

In July 1942, construction began on a small naval air facility at Tern Island (see Map 11). A seaplane landing area was dredged and spoil was used to expand Tern. Over 5,000 steel pilings were driven around the islet in a 400-by-3,300-foot roughly east-to-west-oriented rectangular, aircraft-carrier-shaped, manmade island. A 250-by-3,100-foot runway occupied most of the island, which was ringed with light antiaircraft guns. It was commissioned as Naval Air Facility, French Frigate Shoals (FPO SF 80) in March 1943 to serve as a way point between Hawaii and Midway through the war.

The facility was decommissioned in June 1946. The shoal was placed under the control of the Coast Guard, which maintained a Loran station, first on Sand, then Tern Island in 1948. From 1961 to 1983 a missile-tracking station operated on Tern in support of the Pacific Missile Range. It remains under Coast Guard control and is a Hawaiian wildlife refuge. The islands are heavily populated by protected sea birds and monk seals.

NOTES

1. The standard 250-gallon-per-hour distillation unit produced 5,000 gallons of potable water per day with a minimum of one unit required per 400 men. To operate it for 1,000 hours required

1,300 gallons of unleaded gasoline and 80 pounds of lubricants, thus increasing the logistics burden.

2. Jarvis Island, a U.S. possession since 1935, is located 460 miles south-southeast of Palmyra and 220 miles southwest of Christmas Island. The tiny island was not occupied by U.S. forces in World War II.

READING SUGGESTIONS

Bureau of Yards and Docks. *Building the Navy's Bases in World War II, Vol. II*. Washington, DC: U.S. Government Printing Office, 1947.

Coletta, Paolo E. and Bauer, K. Jack (Editors). *United States Navy and Marine Bases, Overseas*. Westport, CT: Greenwood, 1985.

Conn, Stetson; Engleman, Rose C.; and Fairchild, Byron. *The U.S. Army in World War II: The Western Hemisphere, Guarding the United States and its Outposts*. Washington, DC: Government Printing Office, 1964.

Craven, Wesley F. and Cate, James L. *The Army Air Forces in World War II, Plans and Early Operations-January 1939 to August 1942, Vol. 1*. Chicago: The University of Chicago Press, 1948.

Cressman, Robert J. *A Magnificent Fight: The Battle for Wake Island*. Washington Navy Yard: History and Museums Division, Marine Corps Historical Center, 1992.

Fuchida Mitsuo and Okumiya Masatake. *Midway: The Battle that Doomed Japan, The Japanese Navy's Story*. Annapolis, MD: Naval Institute Press, 1955, 1976.

Gillespie, Oliver A. *The Pacific: Official History of New Zealand in the Second World War 1939–45*. Wellington, NZ: Department of Internal Affairs, 1952.

Hough, Lt. Col. Frank O.; Ludwig, Maj. Verle E.; and Shaw, Henry I., Jr. *History of U.S. Marine Corps Operations in World War II: Pearl Harbor to Guadalcanal, Vol. I*. Washington, DC: Government Printing Office, 1958.

Morison, Samuel E. *History of U.S. Navy Operations in World War II: The Rising Sun in the Pacific, 1931–April 1942, Vol. III*. 1948.

Morison, Samuel E. *History of U.S. Navy Operations in World War II: The Coral Sea, Midway, and Submarine Actions, May 1942–August 1942, Vol. IV*. 1949.

Prange, Gordon W.; Goldstein, Donald M.; and Dillon, Katherine V. *Miracle at Midway*. New York: McGraw-Hill Book Co., 1982.

Smith, Myron J., Jr. *The Battles of the Coral Sea and Midway, 1942: A Selected Bibliography*. Westport, CT: Greenwood, 1991.

Urwin, Gregory J.W. *Facing Fearful Odds: The Siege of Wake Island*. Lincoln: University of Nebraska Press, 1998.

2

South Pacific Area

Prior to the war the South Pacific was an almost mythical region to most Americans, a source of adventure stories and exotic and romantic motion pictures. The Japanese call it the *Minamitai Heiyo*. The South Pacific Area as a zone of military operations was defined on its north side by the equator running from Ecuador to latitude 160° east, a point north of the Solomon Islands (see Map 12). West of the longitude was the Southwest Pacific Area. On 1 August 1942, this boundry was shifted one degree west to 159 degrees east to facilitate South Pacific Area operations in those islands. The area's east boundary was 110° west longitude, which separated it from the Southeast Pacific Area. That area was not subordinate to the Pacific Ocean Area, but answered directly to the Joint Chiefs of Staff.

The South Pacific Area was preceded by a short-lived combined command designated Australian-New Zealand Area Command (ANZAC). This command existed from 26 January to 22 April 1942 to coordinate the defense of the South Pacific Area. Its boundary ran from 140° E, a point on the equator north on New Guinea eastward to 170° E, then angled southeast to 20° S 185° W near Fiji, and then due south on 185° W. Its western boundary ran south from the equator on 141° E, the border between eastern and Dutch New Guinea. It then flowed the south coast of New Guinea eastward to 143° E and then south across the Torres Strait to Australia's Cape York. The ANZAC included the Australian territories on eastern New Guinea, the Bismarck Archipelago, Solomon Islands, Fiji, New Hebrides, New Caledonia, New Zealand, and the east coast of Australia. The command was dissolved after the Japanese occupied the northeast coast of New Guinea, the Bismarcks, and Solomons. The Pacific Ocean Area command was established 30 March 1942. The South Pacific Area was one of its three subcommands.

The South Pacific Area included a string of islands under American, British, and French control that were to prove vital to keeping sea routes to Australia and New Zealand open, the latter of which was within the area.

In the northwest quadrant of this area were the Solomon and Gilbert Islands, both of which were British possessions occupied by the Japanese. To the south of the Gilberts are the Ellice islands, also British possessions, but they were not occupied by the Japanese. The Ellices and Gilberts, however, are discussed in the Central Pacific Area section in order to maintain a more effectual continuity of operations.

THE ISLAND BASES AND THE SOUTHERN LIFELINE

With the Japanese sweeping through the Netherlands East Indies in December 1941 and May 1942, footholds established on New Guinea, the Philippines lost, and northern Australia threatened, it was imperative that the 3,425-mile-long shipping routes between the American West Coast and Australia be secured. It would be from Australia that these areas in the Southwest Pacific would be reconquered. South Pacific island bases were necessary to safeguard the "Southern Lifeline" with patrol aircraft and naval bases as well as ensure the Japanese were halted and that they were unable to seize additional islands in the South Pacific. The Southern Lifeline extended through Hawaii, Christmas and Canton Islands, the Samoas, Fiji, and New Caledonia. These islands were secured by defense forces and air forces in the early months of the war. Other islands, specifically in the Society, Tonga, and New Hebrides Islands, were secured as well to protect the supply line and to serve as bases for future operations into the Solomon Islands.

After their June 1942 defeat at Midway, the Japanese *Imperial General Headquarters* ordered the cancellation of the planned seizure of New Caledonia, Fiji, and the Samoas on 11 July 1942. The decision had been made to seize these islands in April. The execution of such a plan, which would have been launched from the Solomon Islands, would have necessitated seizing the New Hebrides or at least neutralizing Allied forces there through air and naval attacks and raids.

The buildup of bases in the South Pacific was extensive as the war moved into the Solomon Islands. In late January 1943, as the Guadalcanal campaign was winding down, Admiral Chester W. Nimitz stated his desire that only minimal construction be accomplished at the island bases and that they would be rolled up and moved forward as the war progressed northward. His wish was not realized. The funneling of massive naval, ground, and air forces into the South Pacific and beyond demanded an expansive network of supporting naval bases, aircraft way stations, supply depots, and troops staging bases. Construction continued on many bases after the war had passed through the region and in some cases into 1945. Many of the bases, however, began to be reduced and partially rolled up in 1944.

BORABORA ISLAND, SOCIETY ISLANDS

Borabora, the usual spelling in U.S. documents, was code-named BOBCAT as was the Navy construction force that developed the island's base. It was later designated BLUE-BERRY then CROMLECH as the base's status was reduced. The French referred to the atoll as *Ile Bora Bora*. It was also known as Pora Pora, Bola Bola, and Vavau.

Borabora is located at 16°30' S 151°45' W in the western portion of French Polynesia. It is the westernmost atoll in the Society Islands, which includes Tahiti 140 miles to the southeast, French Polynesia's center of government. The atoll lies 2,700 miles southsoutheast of Pearl Harbor and 1,420 miles east of American Samoa. New Zealand is some 2,500 miles to the southwest and Australia is 5,000 miles to the west-southwest. The Society Islands are located in time zone 2.

French Polynesia (*Polynesie Francaise*) covers a vast area and includes the Society Islands (*Iles de la Societe*) or Tahiti Archipelago (*Archipel de Tahiti*) or Leeward Islands (*Iles sous le Vert*) in the west, the colony's most important islands, which includes

Map 12
South Pacific Area

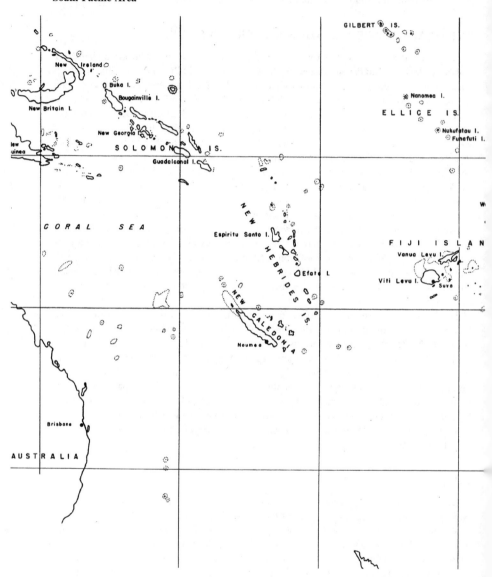

Borabora. It also includes the widely scattered Tuamotu Archipelago (*Iles Basses ou Touamotou*) with some seventy-four islands and atolls to the east of Tahiti; Marquesan Islands (*Iles Marquises*) in the northeast with eight islands; Tupuai Islands (*Iles Tubuai*) in the southwest with five islands; Gambier Islands (*Iles Gambier*) in the southeast with five islands; and other scattered small islands. The total land area of French Polynesia is 1,520 square miles populated by 29,500 natives, 5,000 French, and 4,500 Chinese at the beginning of World War II.

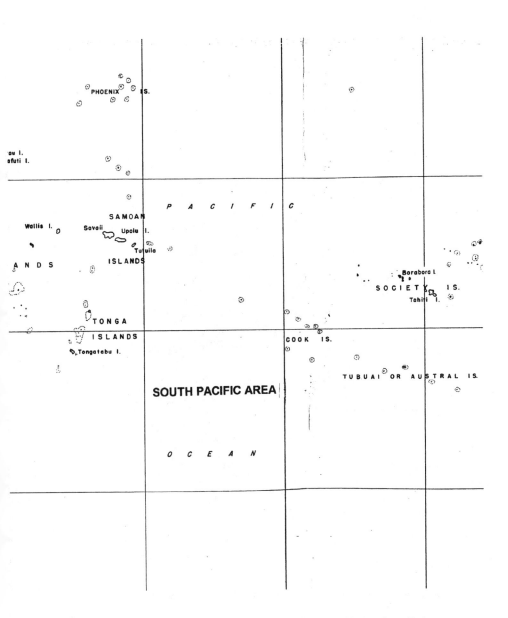

The Society Islands consist of two groups, the Leeward Islands with Borabora, Raiatea (largest), Tupai (second largest), Huahine, Maupiti, Tahaa, Scilly, and Bellingshausen Islands, and the Georgian Group with Tahiti, Moorea, Maiao, Makatea, Mehetia, and Tetiaroa. The total population of the Leeward Islands was approximately 9,500 and the Georgian Group was 20,000.

Borabora Atoll's outer reef measures approximately eight miles north to south and six

Map 13
Borabora Island, Society Islands

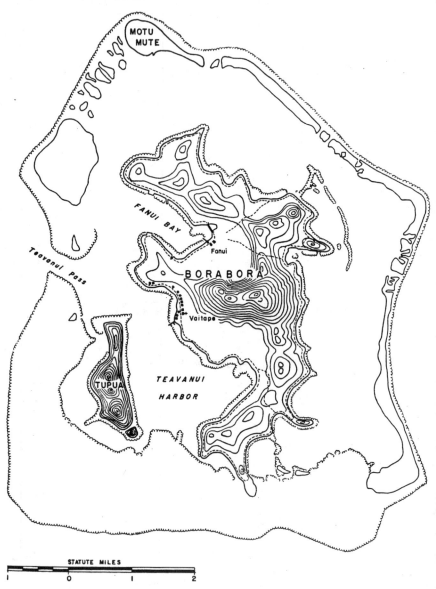

miles east to west (see Map 13). The east, north, and northwest portions of the reef are edged with narrow, low barrier islands. Most are covered with brush and palms as is the main island The southern and southwestern sides of the reef are devoid of islands, but here the shallow reef is 1–1-½ miles wide. Teava-nui (often spelled Teavanui) Pass, ⁵⁄₁₀-miles wide, is the only entrance to the lagoon and is on the atoll's west side. Irregular-shaped Borabora Island dominates the atoll's center. It is six miles long north to south and 2-½ miles at its widest. The island is hilly dominated by the central cone-shaped 2,380-foot volcanic Mount Taimanu. Vaitape Village, headquarters for the island's administrator and port with a population 1,400, sits adjacent to Teava-nui Harbor while the smaller Fanui Village is situated on Fanui Bay, both on the west shore. A one-lane, unimproved road followed the island's shore around its entire circumference. Covering over one square mile off of Borabora's southwest shore is the excellent Teava-nui Harbor. A secondary harbor lies off of the northwest shore, Fanui Bay.

Hilly Tupua Island protects the west side of Teava-nui Harbor. Edged by its own reef, it is 1-½ miles long north to south and ½ mile wide at its widest. Less than one mile north of Teava-nui Pass is an unnamed flat sand island covering approximately one square mile; 1-⅓ miles northeast of the unnamed island is chicken drumstick-shaped Motu Mute. It is 1-¼ miles long northwest to southeast and its northwest portion is ½ mile wide.

Borabora experiences mild mid-70°F to mid-80°F weather with light rains, but high humidity. There are no significant diseases or insect pests, but water shortages for the large garrison was a problem and reduced the base's value in that it could provide little to visiting ships.

The widely scattered islands of Polynesia were discovered by a number of different explorers ranging from 1595 to as late as 1824. Most were discovered in the late 1700s. Tahiti was discovered by Pedro Fernanez de Quiros in 1595, which he named *La Sagittara*. Captain Samuel Wallis rediscovered Tahiti in 1767 naming it King George Island. The Society Islands were discovered by Lieutenant (later Captain) James Cook in 1769 aboard the HMS *Endeavor*. They were named after the British Royal Society, which sponsored Cook's scientific expedition. In 1842, the French forced Queen Pomare IV, ruler of Tahiti and the neighboring islands, to accept France as its protector. The next year the French claimed the islands and the colony developed. There was some initial opposition by the natives, to include those on Borabora. The colony, the French Establishment of Oceania, was administered by a governor at Papeete, Tahiti who answered to the High Commissioner of the Pacific headquartered at Nouméa, New Caledonia. Prior to 1940, the colony was represented in France by a delegate to the Superior Council of the Colonies. The fall of France in June 1940 threw the islands into political and economic turmoil. While the vast majority of the population was pro-Free French, the colonial leadership answered to the Vichy government, which ordered trade with Japan. After much debate, political maneuvering, and a near revolt, the pro-Vichy faction abdicated and pro-De Gaulle leaders were appointed. Further political turmoil ensued through the summer and fall of 1941, but by the time of the December Japanese offensive across the Pacific, the situation in Polynesia had stabilized with a pro-Allied governor-general established.

In the closing days of December 1941, the Chief of Naval Operations directed that a refueling base be established on Borabora to support the Southern Lifeline to Australia. It was to be the first of a string of South Pacific bases. Task Force 5614 with the 102d Infantry Regiment (-3d Battalion), 198th Coast Artillery Regiment (Antiaircraft), and a naval construction battalion detachment, the BOBCAT Detachment, arrived at Borabora on 17 February 1942 with almost 5,000 men. This was the first operational deployment of the Seabees. Negotiations with the Free French on Borabora, assuring French sovereignty was maintained and U.S.-constructed facilities would revert to French control upon American departure, were concluded shortly after the force's arrival. With no fighting in French Polynesia, the war proved to be an economic boon for the islands although few islanders were directly employed by U.S. forces.

Refueling facilities, fuel storage tanks, piers, and support facilities were constructed on Teava-nui Harbor. Eight 155mm coast defense gun and numerous antiaircraft gun positions were built. Navy Air Station, Borabora (FPO SF 203), a seaplane facility, was quickly built and in early 1943 a 6,000-foot Army airfield and aircraft assembly depot were completed on Motu Maue occupying most of the small island. It was envisioned that fighters would be shipped to Borabora and assembled there to be ferried to forward areas. It served as a way point for landing ships and large landing craft convoying to the South and Southwest Pacific Areas. While Borabora served its original purpose as a refueling station, the war's rapid advance across the Pacific precluded its need as an aircraft forward assembly depot. On 1 April 1944, the base was placed in a reduced status and the defense force departed on 8 April. It still provided refueling services and an emergency landing field. By the war's end Naval Station, Borabora, Society Islands was of little use and was closed on 2 June 1946. Today Bora Bora, Iles du Vert remains part of the Territory of French Polynesia (*Territorie de la Polynesie Francaise*) and is one of the territory's main tourist attractions.

TONGATABU ISLAND, TONGA ISLANDS

Tongatabu ("Sacred South") Island is the largest in the Tonga, or Friendly, Islands. When discovered it was named Middelburgh by the Dutch, but its native name was soon accepted. Likewise, the Tonga Islands were christened the Friendly Islands by Captain Cook because of the natives' hospitality. The island, and American defense force, was code-named BLEACHER, and after the United States departed, EDIT and VERULAM.

Tongatabu is situated at 21°10' S 175°10' E at the southern end of the Tonga Islands. It is 490 miles southeast of Fiji and the same distance from American Samoa to the northeast. New Caledonia is 1,080 miles due west. Sydney, Australia is 2,000 miles to the southwest and Auckland, New Zealand 1,100 miles to the south-southwest. Pearl Harbor is 3,000 miles to the northeast. The Tonga Islands are in time zone 24, but were actually east of longitude 180°, the International Date Line (time zone 1), and in a small special time zone designated 24:19.

The Tonga Islands cover a land area of approximately 250 square miles with some 170 islands, most of which are uninhabited. The islands are divided into three main groups: The Vava'u, or Northern, Group is centered around its main island of Vava'u; the Ha'apai, or Middle, Group consisting of over 30 small islands; and the Tongatabu, or Southern, Group with Tongatabu and Eua Islands. The islands' total population was just over 35,000 with almost half of those residing in the Tongatabu Group. There were about 1,300 Europeans, half-castes, Chinese, and others while the majority were Tongans, a branch of Polynesians. Tonga means "South" referring to those who migrated south from Samoa many centuries ago.

Tongatabu's weather is mild with a December-to-May warm season followed by a cool season. The typhoon season is from October to April. There are few health problems.

The Tongatabu Group consists of the main Tongatabu Island (see Map 14) with the smaller Eua Island 11 miles to the southeast. The only other islands in the group are the very small islands of Eueiki, Ata, Tau, and Muihobohonga a few miles to the northeast and east, and Kalau just to the south of Eua. A few scattered islets lie off the northeast coast along an east to west barrier reef. Tongatabu is a low, flat island with a limestone base, topped with reddish-brown soil, formed from an uplifted coral reef formation, as are most of the Tonga Islands. The porkchop-shaped island is eighteen miles long northwest to southwest and nine miles wide across its southeast end. A fringing coral reef

Map 14
Tongatabu Island, Tonga Islands

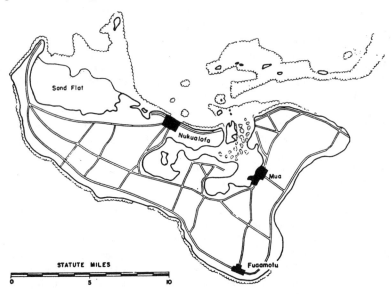

lines the southwest and northwest shores with a roughly triangular-shaped barrier reef
jutting north from the island's northwest end. This barrier reef cuts off a former 3- by
6-mile lagoon, which filled and became a huge sandflat. Another lagoon complex cuts
into the island from the north shore near the east-central portion. An islet and numerous
coral heads prevent all but small boats from entering. The town of Nuku'alofa, the capital
of the Kingdom of Tonga and the largest community in the Tonga Islands, is located on
the northeast-central coast and also adjacent to the lagoon. Nuku'alofa faces Maria Bay,
one of two excellent anchorages in the Tonga Islands with piers (the other being Neiafu
on Vava'u). The bay is protected by barrier reefs on its west and east sides, but is open
to the north. The town of Mua is located on the west side of the lagoon and Fuaamotu
is on the island's southeast corner. Numerous villages were scattered about the island's
many coconut, banana, orange, vanilla bean, and squash plantations. A well-developed
road system follows the entire coast and allows access to all of the interior. On the south
coast are the ruins of an ancient fortified town and blowholes generating 50- to 60-foot
waterspouts. Uncultivated areas are covered with palms, cedar-like avava trees, and brush.

The Tonga Islands were first visited by the Dutch, and then only the northernmost
islands, in 1616. The Englishman, Able Tasman, after discovering Tasmania and New
Zealand, discovered Tongatabu and other southern islands in the group in 1643. The
Englishman, Captain Samuel Wallis, visited in 1767 and Captain Cook in 1773 and 1777.
These early explorers found a well-established, orderly, industrious, and completely
peaceful kingdom over a thousand years old. A giant tortoise, presented by Captain Cook
in 1777, still lived on the palace grounds during World War II. English missionaries
arrived in 1797, but the effort failed because of misunderstandings with the natives and
a civil war resulted. The previously peaceful Tongans had learned the art of war while
earlier visiting Fiji and were involved in Fiji's wars and politics. Missionaries returned
in 1818 and by the mid-1800s the islanders had accepted Christianity. Further conflicts

evolved in the late 1800s, caused by competing churches. In the meantime Germany established a treaty of friendship with Tonga, but surrendered these rights in 1899 in exchange for British noninterference in the Samoas. The next year Britain established an agreement to serve as Tonga's protector (British Protectorate of Tonga), but the kingdom retained its independence. Queen Salote ascended the throne in 1924 and maintained an orderly kingdom. She reigned through World War II, the only remaining native monarch and kingdom in the Pacific. A British agent and consul advised the Queen on government matters and was instrumental in negotiating the kingdom's agreement to allow U.S. basing there during the war. The agent answered to the British High Commissioner of the Western Pacific. Tonga declared war on Germany when the war broke out in Europe and then on Japan. In 1939 the country raised the Tonga Defence Force, which grew to 2,000 regulars incorporated into the 16th New Zealand Brigade Group, plus a 2,000-man home guard trained and equipped by New Zealand. Coast-watching stations were established throughout the islands and some Tongan troops saw combat in the Fiji Regiment and the Fiji Guerrillas.

In early 1942, Tongatagu's value was recognized as a ship-fueling station, as an alternate staging point for aircraft en route to Australia and New Zealand, and as an air base supporting operations to the south of the Samoas and Fiji. An agreement was negotiated through the British consul and the American defense and construction forces arrived on 9 May 1942. The reinforced 147th Infantry Regiment, 77th Coast Artillery Regiment (Antiaircraft), and 68th Pursuit Squadron, 7,800 troops, and over 800 Navy base and construction troops garrisoned the island. U.S. planners felt that the Japanese would not land major forces in the Tongas. This defense force was deemed sufficent to deal with raids and perhaps dissuade the Japanese from landing in force during their expected move south on New Caledonia, Fiji, and the Samoas. The Navy built a seaplane base, refueling depot, and Army camps, support facilities, and gun emplacements. Contractors built a three-runway airfield for the Army near Fuaamotu. Natives were employed extensively as stevedores and laborers. The naval base (FPO SF 200) never operated at full capacity, but if the United States had lost the May 1942 Battle of the Coral Sea and the Japanese had subsequently moved on New Caledonia, Fiji, and the Samoas as planned after seizing Midway, it would have indeed become extremely important. The USS *Saratoga* (CV-3) and *North Carolina* (BB-55) undertook emergency repairs at Tongatabu after being torpedoed in August and September 1942. Most of the 147th Infantry departed for Guadalcanal in November 1942 with the 2d Battalion leaving at the end of January 1943. As the war moved on, Tongatabu was the first South Pacific base to be closed, ordered in November 1943. The fuel depot was dismantled and moved to Wallis Island. The airfield and other facilities were turned over to the New Zealand Army at the end of February 1943. The 77th Coast Artillery departed in early April. New Zealand troops departed before the end of the war, although the airfield remained in use. The Tonga Defence Force was disbanded after the end of the war.

The Kingdom of Tonga has retained its independence and was emancipated from British protection on 4 June 1970. It still relies on produce exports for income as well as tourism.

NEW CALEDONIA ISLAND

New Caledonia, or in French, *Nouvelle-Calèdonie*, was code-named CHEEKSTRAP and later IRET. The U.S. naval operating base at Nouméa was WHITE POPPY initially, LECTERN from February 1943, and then EPIC. The island is nicknamed the "Eternal Spring Island" and the main island is known locally as the *Grande Terre*.

New Caledonia is located at 21°30' S 165°30' E in the eastern Coral Sea making it the southernmost of the U.S. South Pacific bases (see Map 15). It was also the westernmost island base from all bases to its east and northeast on the air route to Australia. Brisbane is some 900 miles and Sydney 1,230 miles to the southwest. Auckland, New Zealand is 1,150 miles to the southeast. Pearl Harbor is 2,360 miles to the northeast. The Solomon Islands are 800 miles to the northwest. The nearest large island is Espíritu Santo in the New Hebrides Islands, another major U.S. base, 440 miles due north. The Fiji Islands are 700 miles to the northeast and serve as a link to the American Samoas 1,600 miles in the same direction. Both Fiji and the Samoas, along with New Caledonia, were planned to be seized by the Japanese after the June 1942 Battle of Midway. New Caledonia is in time zone 23.

Containing 8,453 square miles, after New Guinea and New Zealand, New Caledonia is the largest island in the South Pacific and extremely rich in natural resources. It is slightly smaller than the state of New Jersey. The cigar-shaped island's 248-mile length is oriented northwest to southeast and is 31 miles wide. Two parallel mountain chains run the length of the island, the main one being the *Chaine Centrale*. These are steep, razor-backed, broken, rugged, and heavily eroded in many areas. The most rugged mountains are found on the island's northwest third with 5,410-foot Mont Panié. The 5,340-foot Mont Humboldt is found in the southeast portion. Mont Dore is the dominating terrain feature southeast of Nouméa. Between the two mountain ranges, most over 4,000 feet, are secluded valleys and plateaus. Valleys, gorges, streams, and small rivers run toward the coast on both sides of the island cutting across the coastal plains. Water is abundant. Surprisingly, for a South Pacific island, much of New Caledonia is sparsely vegetated, often being compared to Australia. The southwest coast is dry with the northeast side being more tropical. Many interior areas are devoid of vegetation while others are covered with low grasses and the eucalyptus-like niaouli. However, many valleys and seaward-facing mountainsides are covered with kauri pines and there are substantial areas suitable for grazing livestock. Coconut palms dominate much of the coastal areas.

The coast is protected by a coral barrier reef broken by the freshwater outflow of the many streams and rivers. The 995-mile long barrier reef, the world's second largest after Australia's Great Barrier Reef, forms the world's largest lagoon. It forms a narrow, but deep, protected coastal channel around the island used by local boats and steamers. A number of islets are scattered along the southwest coast.

The Loyalty Islands (*Iles Loyauté*), sixty miles off the northeast coast, form a northwest to southeast line of three islands: Uvea or *Ouvea* (an atoll), Lifu or *Lifou* (the largest, twenty-five by fifty miles), and Mare. They total 800 square miles with a population of over 11,000. Thirty miles off the southeast end of New Caledonia is the Isle of Pines (*Ile des Pins*), aka Kunie. It covers fifty-eight square miles with a population of fewer than 600. Two parallel lines of coral reefs and several comparatively small islands, the Bèlep Islands (*Iles Bélep*), run northwest from New Caledonia. Other islands, lying further away, are administered by New Caledonia. The three islets comprising the Huon Islands are 65 miles northwest of New Caledonia while the uninhabited Chesterfield Islands are a further 285 miles beyond the Huons. Walpole, or Walpoole, Island is 155 miles southeast of Nouméa. Wallis and Futura Islands (which see), located between Fiji and Samoa, were administered from New Caledonia.

The climate is moderate with varied humidity and only forty inches of rain a year.

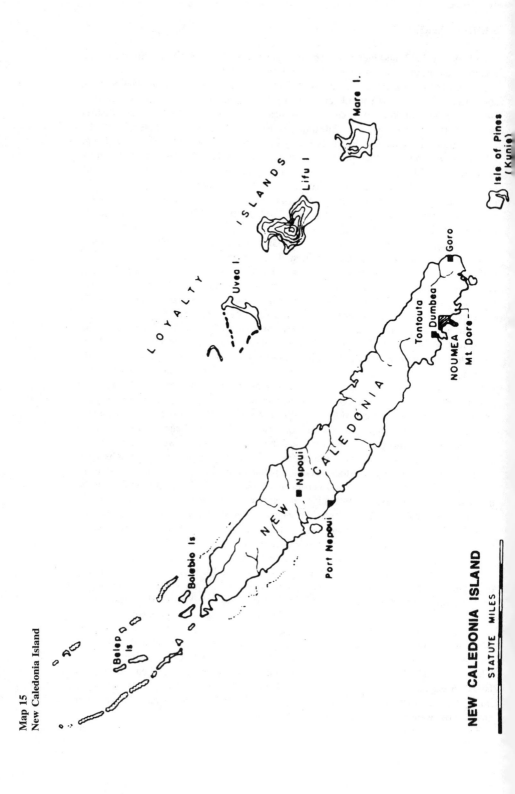

Map 15
New Caledonia Island

NEW CALEDONIA ISLAND

STATUTE MILES

Half of this falls in January through March, which is also the typhoon season. The warm season temperature, December to March, is in the upper-70°F to low-80°F range while the cool season has a mean temperature of 65°F. Prevailing tradewinds are from the southeast. Health problems are few and malaria is nonexistent.

The island was discovered by Captain James Cook in 1774. Since the pine-covered hillsides reminded him of Scotland, he named the huge island New Caledonia (the ancient name for part of Scotland). In 1792, a French expedition extensively explored the island. Others visited the island in the following years, including French Captain d'Entrecasteaux in 1791, but no claims were made. The then-estimated 70,000 natives were aggressive and cannibalistic; Melanesians derived from the Papuans. Languages were often dissimilar between even neighboring tribes. In 1840, British missionaries arrived and Crown planned to claim New Caledonia. A French survey ship crew was murdered by cannibals in 1850 and the French seized the opportunity to land in numbers. They claimed the island in September 1853. The colony was administered by an admiral until 1885 when a governor and local parliament (*conseil-général*) were appointed. Besides exploiting its abundant resources, New Caledonia served France as a penal colony from 1864. Some 40,000 prisoners were interned there under brutal conditions until transport ceased in 1894 (after which time convicts were incarcerated in French Guinea). Fewer than 100 prisoners remained in 1942. There were occasional native uprisings, suppressed by the French, as was cannibalism, for the most part. Certain tribes deep in the mountains were still watched by the French military during the war. The civilized natives were mostly landowners. While some laborers were available from the Loyalty Islands and the New Hebrides, the French were forced to import indentured labor from French Indochina, specifically Tonkin, and Java. Some 8,000 were on the island in 1942 and proved to be satisfactory for general labor.

Virtually the entire southwest coast was served by a well-developed road, Route Colonial No. 1, which continues around the northwest end and along about three-quarters of the northeast coast. Three cross-island roads in the central portion connect the two coasts. A twenty-mile-long narrow-gauge railroad connected Nouméa and Paita to the northwest. It was completely refurbished by the U.S. Army. Small coastal steamers served all towns and settlements. A government radio station operated in Nouméa. The capital boasted a telephone system, which was connected to the larger towns. Virtually every town and settlement was connected by telegraph.

New Caledonia was rich in resources and its agricultural industries well developed. Extensive mineral resources included 20 percent of the world's nickel and equally strategically important chromate plus cobalt, manganese, iron, lead, mercury, coal, copper, silver, and gold. Mines and blast furnaces are scattered about the island, but mostly in the northwest. The chrome mine at Tiebaghi was the world's largest. Since 1935, the Japanese were permitted to mine nickel and iron, but when the war began in December 1941, hundreds of Japanese at Goro near the southeast end were interned. Prior to the war Japan also purchased chrome as did Germany along with nickel. Copra, coffee, maize, tobacco, cotton, bananas, and other tropical fruits were the principal crops. Extensive cattle and sheep herds provided a large meat canning industry, a valuable resource for Allied armies. Animal hides, timber, and fish also provided local industries.

Over 17,000 French populated the island. About forty towns and villages were scattered along the island's coast. The island's capital, and the capital of French Oceania, is Nouméa with a population of 11,000. Hydroelectric power and natural gas works served the capital and nearby towns. Nouméa is situated at the base of a peninsula on the island's southwest coast thirty miles from the southeast end. The area around Nouméa was well served by a road network. The excellent deep-water port in Moselle Bay and its roads approaching through Anse Bay on the port's north side is protected by smaller peninsulas and Nou Island, aka Isle Nou (*Ile de Nou*). Barren and hilly, whale-shaped Nou Island, once the penal colony headquarters, is four miles long and one mile wide. A road ran around the small island. Pan American established a seaplane station there in early 1939 to service its California-to-New Zealand route. This included a moored ship serving as a floating hotel. The seaplane station was taken over by the Australians and later the U.S. Navy. The port, however, lacked adequate unloading, loading, and support facilities.

Soon after the fall of France in June 1940, the governor of New Caledonia reluctantly declared in favor of the Vichy government. The following month many citizens called for the governor to change his alliance to the Free French, but he continued to obey the Vichy government. A referendum found that the vast majority of the population was in favor of alliance with the Free French. In September the governor departed and left the colony in the hands of the pro-Vichy garrison commander. He ordered that trade be conducted with Japan, but his order was ignored. Martial law was declared and the pro-De Gaulle leader of an armed demonstration was arrested. A De Gaulle governor arrived from Efaté Island in the New Hebrides and was wildly greeted by New Caledonia's citizens. Pro-Vichy officials were deported to Indochina at the end of September. Confusion reigned through most of 1941 with disputes over the control of the government of French Oceania and the other main islands. The Japanese offensive in December 1941 solidified the colony and security concerns increased. The 800-man French garrison *Bataillon d'Infanterie coloniale de la Nouvelle-Calédonie*, an interior (security) company, two light coast defense batteries, and the Australian 2/3d Independent Company, a 300-man commando unit that arrived in December 1941, were insufficient to defend the vast island. A poorly armed 2,000-plus-man French Home Guard was rasied, but would be of little value. There was little doubt that New Caledonia was a Japanese objective because of its position to control the northern and eastern approaches to Australia and New Zealand plus its valuable strategic resources. French concerns of a Japanese invasion were strong and holding the realization that its defenses were completely inadequate, they were reluctant to allow the Australians to continue construction of a large airfield for fear that it would only make the island that much more desirable to the Japanese.

The United States recognized New Caledonia's value as an air refueling stop on the southern air route. The provision of a substantial defense force was critical to alleviate French fears and the very real threat that the Japanese might indeed launch an expedition (the *South Seas Detachment* with the *144th Infantry Regiment* was slated for this task). Australia and New Zealand were unable to reinforce the garrison and the United States agreed to assume New Caledonia's defense in late December 1941. This was left to the U.S. Army, already stretched to garrison existing bases and establishing offensive forces in Australia. The 16,800-man Army Task Force 6814 began to assemble in January 1942 being built around the 51st Infantry Brigade and 70th Coast Artillery Regiment (antiaircraft). A 2,000-man pursuit group, led by the 68th Pursuit Squadron, accompanied the task force. With the exception of forces sent to Australia, this was the largest U.S. Army overseas deployment to date. The American commander arrived on 6 March and began negotiations with the French High Commissioner of the Pacific. The task force arrived on the 12th and began to establish camps in and around Nouméa. A completed two-runway airfield was located at Tontouta thirty-three miles north of Nouméa and an uncompleted field was at Plaine de Gaics on the southeast coast 160 miles to the northwest of Nouméa. Another airfield was located at Oua Tom near the upper southern portion of the southwest coast. Seven auxiliary airstrips were built about the island. The U.S. Navy took over the small seaplane base at Isle Nou and began its expansion. Fleet Air Command, Nouméa was established in December 1942. On 23 May 1942, the 51st Infantry Brigade was reorganized as the Americal Division. Its title was a contraction of *"Americans on New Cale*donia." The division was phased to Guadalcanal in November and December 1943. Between November 1942 and February 1943, the 3d New Zealand Division staged to New Caledonia from Fiji. It remained until August when it deployed to Guadalcanal.

New Caledonia rated such a robust defense force because of its high value to the Japanese, but the United States considered it to be of little use other than as an air refueling station. A U.S. Navy task force operating in the Coral Sea considered basing at Nouméa, but it was decided to be too exposed to Japanese attack. By April 1942, it was preferred that Auckland be developed as the main South Pacific Fleet base. The Guadalcanal landing quickly changed this assessment of New Caledonia's value. Prior to the landing, Commander, South Pacific Area, established his headquarters at Nouméa (SCAVENGER). In early August the Marines successfully landed on Guadalcanal, but the following American naval defeat at Savo Island and insistent Japanese air attacks forced the supporting transports to withdraw to New Caledonia before unloading was completed. Nouméa was to serve as a logistics base to support the besieged Marines on Guadalcanal.

While Nouméa possessed an excellent harbor, sufficient unloading, warehousing, and support facilities were nonexistent. Scores of ships idled in the roads awaiting unloading. In October, the decision was made to relocate the main South Pacific Fleet base from Auckland to Nouméa (FPO SF 131). Unloading facilities were improved by February 1943 and construction immediately began on the naval operating base. Supply depots, a fuel tank farm, ship repair facilities, and many other facilities were built in the port area, on Ducos Peninsula north of Nouméa, and on Isle Nou. All 15,000 pontoons, used as barges and floating wharves, required in the Pacific Area for 1943 were shipped to Nouméa and assembled by a mobile plant on Isle Nou. A naval auxiliary airfield was built beside Magenta Bay 3 miles northeast of Nouméa (the island's other airfields were under Army control).

In December 1942, Headquarters, I Marine Amphibious Corps and its support units arrived at Nouméa. It controlled Marine units in the South Pacific and served as a planning staff for operations on Guadalcanal, Russell Islands, and New Georgia. Nouméa also served as a staging base and depot for Marine units in the South Pacific. Marine Aircraft Group 25 at Tontouta assisted with the island's air defense. Between September and October 1943 I Corps relocated to Guadalcanal; a rear echelon briefly remained on New Caledonia. A major Army staging area with several camps were built at Nepoui in the north-central portion of the island some 120 miles northwest of Nouméa in the fall of 1944. A large Army airfield was built at Koumac 38 miles from the island's north end on the west coast. This existing airfield had been destroyed to prevent its use by the Japanese. Naval Operating Base, Nouméa, served as the main supply and support depot for amphibious operations in the South Pacific, but it was Espíritu Santo that was developed as the main South Pacific Fleet base. Nouméa was also an important rehabilitation base for combat units. It continued to support amphibious operations as the war moved across the Pacific cumulating its service as a staging base for the April 1945 Okinawa assault.

The base began to be dismantled soon after and by June it was only a minor refueling and aircraft way station. Naval Operating Base, Nouméa was closed on 27 May 1947. While many of the base facilities had been dismantled, wharves and airfields were turned over to the French.

In 1956, the Colony of New Caledonia was made an overseas territory of France, *Territoire des Nouvelle-Caledonie et Dependances*. The dependencies are the Huon, Chesterfield, and Walpole Islands. New Caledonia still exports its rich resources and has added tourism as a main source of income. In 1988, a substantial degree of autonomy was granted. A referendum on independence was held in 1998, but the territory's status remains unchanged.

NORFOLK ISLAND

Norfolk Island lies just north of the midway point between New Caledonia 500 miles to its north and New Zealand 700 miles to the south. Sydney, Australia is 1,100 miles to the southwest and Brisbane is 900 miles to the east. The island is situated at 129°02' S 167°57' E in time zone 23:30, the same as New Zealand's.

The island measures three by five miles covering 8,538 acres (see Map 16). It is of volcanic origin with its shores faced by 200-foot cliffs offering few landing sites. Its plateau of fertile rolling plains is covered by scattered Norfolk pines up to 150 feet tall, light forests, scrub brush, and cleared pasture land. The highest elevation is Mount Bates at 1,085 feet on the northwest end. The climate is pleasant and mild with little seasonal change. It lacks a sheltered anchorage. Tiny Nepean Island lies about one mile off the south coast and larger Phillip Island is six miles to the south.

The unpopulated island was discovered and named by Captain James Cook in 1774, its namesake being the Duchess of Norfolk. In 1788, it began to be used as a British penal colony, considered to be the most brutal, but this was closed in 1856. That same year all 194 descendants of the HMS *Bounty* mutineers were relocated from overcrowded Pitcairn Island far to the east. Some later returned to Pitcairn. Norfolk's administrative center is Kingston on the south coast. It was administered by New South Wales until 1914 when it was placed under the control of the Australian Commonwealth. Its main export was fruit to Australia and there was subsistence farming, fishing, livestock, and dairies. The island was commercially important because of its cable station on the north-west corner. Its military value lay in its equidistant location between New Caledonia, New Zealand, and Australia. It would serve as a base for antisubmarine patrols and a way station for long flights between New Caledonia, New Zealand, and Australia. In 1942, there were 700 Europeans, most still being Bounty descendants. Besides English they speak the unique Norfolkese dialect, a mix of eighteenth-century English, *platt Deutsch*, and ancient Tahitian.

While Norfolk was the responsibility of Australia, that nation had little interest in providing for its defense and considered it a naval matter. They resisted the construction of an airfield proposed by the U.S. South Pacific command feeling that this would only make it attractive to the Japanese. Australia furnished only a fifty-seven-man defense detachment. In September 1942, the responsibility for the island's defense was assigned to New Zealand. Australia soon sent 200 civilian workers, under American engineer supervision, to build an airfield with two crossed runways near the island's center. The New Zealand "N" Force, the reinforced 36th Battalion, arrived in October and established defenses to protect the island from raiders. The airfield was operational on 28 December 1942. The original defense units were relieved in the spring and summer of 1943. A radar station was established on the island in May 1943 and remained operational until after the war guiding aircraft on the long overwater flights. The situation in the South Pacific had improved and in December 1943 the defense force was withdrawn and the

Map 16
Norfolk Island

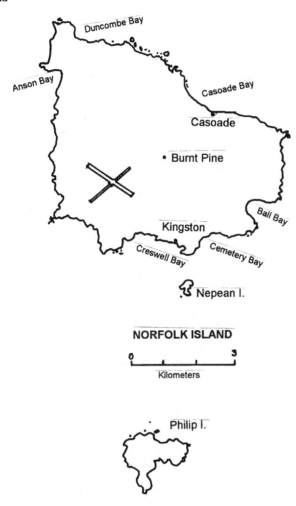

island became a RNZAF responsibility. The island is still administered today as a territory of Australia.

NEW HEBRIDES ISLANDS

The New Hebrides Islands, today's Vanuatu, are located to the north of New Caledonia and southeast of the Solomon Islands placing them in an ideal location to support offensive operations into the latter and serve as an intermediate base area for the main fleet base on New Caledonia (see Map 17). They are located on the northeast edge of the Coral Sea between 150°30' and 170°30' east longitude and 12°00' and 20°45' south latitude. The 550-mile-long northwest to southeast, "Y"-shaped archipelago covers an area of 5,700 square miles. It contains eighty-three islands and islets, most of which are

Map 17
New Hebrides Islands

Vanua Lava

Îles Banks

Gaua I.

Espiritu Santo I.

Maéwo I.

Aoba I.

Luganville

Pentecost I.

Ambrym I.

Malekula I.

Épi I.

NEW HEBRIDES ISLANDS

0 10 20 30 40 50

MILES

Efaté I.

Port Vila

Erromanga I.

Tanna I.

uninhabited. The volcanic islands are mostly mountainous with several active volcanoes present. The west arm of the archipelago's "Y" contains Espíritu Santo, the largest island, and Malakula. The east arm is comprised of Maèwo, Pentecôte (aka Pentecost), and Ambrym Islands. Ambae (aka Aoba) Island is centered between the arms of the "Y." The southern leg of the "Y" has Epi, Efaté, Erromanga, Tanna, and Aneityum Islands. Two small groups of islands lie to the northwest of the "Y," the Banks and Torres Islands. The New Hebrides are in time zone 23.

The New Hebrides' tropical climate is moderated by the southeast tradewind from May to October. Espíritu Santo receives some ninety inches of rain annually with most falling during the humid months of November through April. Typhoons may occur during that period. Malaria and other tropical diseases were similar to those found in the Solomons. It was here that American forces first suffered malaria with large numbers of troops inflicted.

The New Hebrides was found in 1606 by Pedro Fernandez de Quiros searching for the theorized Southern Continent. Believing he had discovered the long-sought continent, he named the group *Tierra Australis del Espíritu Santo* (Southern Land of the Holy Spirit). He was also responsible for naming St. Philippe and St. James Bay on Espírito Santo. Spanish efforts to settle the island soon failed. In 1768, French explorer Captain Louis Antoine de Bougainville sailed between Santos and Malekula Islands destroying De Quiros' claim of discovering the Southern Continent. His name was bestowed on the strait. It was Captain James Cook who charted most of the islands in detail in 1774 as well as discovering many of the group's southern islands. He named the archipelago after Scotland's Outer Hebrides Islands. Others explored the islands through the late 1700s. The island's were savagely exploited well into the 1800s by pirates, whalers, and slavers. The efforts of missionaries to protect the natives were futile. The islands had been populated since 500 B.C. by extremely primitive Melanesians without any form of organized rule. Savage and warlike, different dialects were spoken by neighboring tribes. No accurate estimates exist of their early population, but it was many more than the approximately 40,000 there in 1941. French, English, and Pidgin were widely spoken.

Both Britain and France were well established in the New Hebrides, but France had laid claim to the group in 1853, the same time it took possession of New Caledonia. In 1888, a declaration was signed by both nations to establish a joint commission to govern the islands. The effort was ineffective with no plan for government, courts, or law enforcement and the situation became even more confused. It was not until 1906 that the Condominium of New Hebrides was jointly established, modified in 1914. The dual heads of the Condominium were British and French resident commissioners. The French portion answered to the High Commissioner of the Pacific on New Caledonia while the British resident was responsible to the High Commissioner for the Western Pacific in Fiji.

While it was proven that the two nations could jointly govern a remote region, the dualism and triadism of the system necessitated excessive expenses and double standards including two court systems enforcing two sets of laws to confuse contract and land ownership issues, three police forces (British, French, Condominium for natives), three currencies (British, French, Australian), separate hospitals, French and British systems of weights and measures, and different traffic laws with the British driving on the left and the French on the right on the same roads. Standards of assistance to their respective citizens were uneven. When the copra market collapsed in the 1930s, the French government subsidized its planters, but no help was given to British and Australian planters by their governments. Few natives hired themselves out as labor, so the French imported indentured workers from Indochina, with some 1,000 Tonkinese working in the islands at the war's beginning. British and Australian planters were not allowed to import workers. By 1940, so many Anglos had given up and left the islands or had applied for and been granted French citizenship in order to stay afloat that there were almost as many British administrators as there were citizens they supported. Needless to say, it was a peculiar situation for U.S. forces stationed there.

After the June 1940 capitulation of France the Vichy government called for the administrators of the various French Pacific possessions to comply with its directives. In July, the New Hebrides French resident at Port Vila on Efatè declared in favor of the Free French and was immediately dismissed by the pro-Vichy High Commissioner of the Pacific, but he remained at his post. In September, after the French citizens voted overwhelmingly in favor of the Free French in a referendum, the Efatè resident went to New Caledonia and relieved the High Commissioner. He served as the acting High Commissioner until he was recalled in May 1942. The political situation in French Oceania was stabilized by the time American forces arrived in the islands.

The New Hebrides were in a key position to protect essential islands on the Southern Lifeline, namely New Caledonia and Fiji, and serve as a launch site for Allied offensive operations into the Solomons. The two major bases established in the New Hebrides proved extremely valuable to Allied operations into the outer Japanese perimeter.

The New Hebrides' cumbersome condominium arrangement was cast off in 1978. The Republic of Vanuatu, encompassing the New Hebrides in their entirety, was established on 30 July 1980 and was admitted to the Commonwealth of Nations. The republic's capital is Port Vila on Efatè. Vanuatu claims Matthew and Hunter Islands to the southeast, which are also claimed by France. Vanuatu's economy today relies on its agriculture, offshore financial services, and tourism.

Espíritu Santo Island, New Hebrides Islands

Espíritu Santo (often misspelled "Espiritu Santos" in military documents) means "Holy Spirit" in Spanish. It is simply called Santo locally, which was also its American serviceman's nickname. It was initially code-named AMPERSAND, from February 1943 BUTTON, and later EBON.

Espíritu Santo is located at 15°20' S 167°00' E in the northern portion of the New Hebrides Islands (see Map 18). Malakula Island (aka Malekula), the second largest in the New Hebrides, is ten miles to the south while Ambre Island (aka Aoba) is twenty-eight miles to the east. Santo is ideally located to serve as a hub for other U.S. bases and objectives in the South Pacific. Efatè Island, a smaller New Hebrides base, is 150 miles to the southeast while New Caledonia is 440 miles due south. Viti Levu Island in Fiji is 645 miles east-southeast. Guadalcanal is 540 miles to the northwest making Santo the northernmost U.S. South Pacific base and the closest to America's first objective. Sydney, Australia is 1,398 miles to the southwest and Pearl Harbor is 3,020 miles to the northeast.

Santo is a mountainous island with Mount Santo in the south being the highest point at 5,520 feet. The most rugged areas are in the west and south. Wide, fertile valleys in the mountains lend themselves to agriculture. Numerous streams, many navigable by small craft, flow out of the mountains and valleys across the narrow west and south coast plains and into St. Philippe and St. James Bay (aka Big Bay). This large bay, twelve by fifteen miles, on the north side is embraced by two peninsulas, the longer western one terminating at Cumberland Cape and the eastern one at Queiros Cape. Santo measures seventy-five miles north to south along its west side and forty-five miles wide across the

Map 18
Espíritu Santo Island

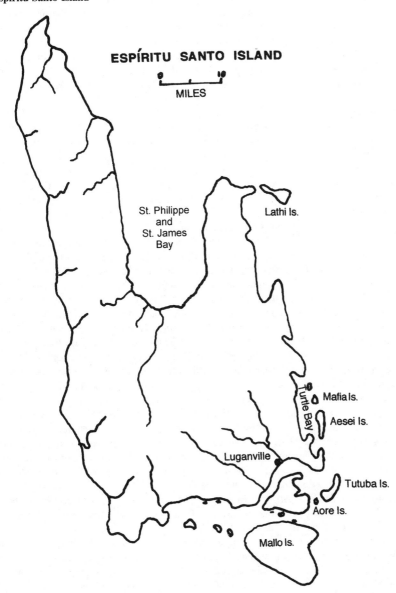

ESPÍRITU SANTO ISLAND

MILES

St. Philippe
and
St. James
Bay

Lathi Is.

Turtle Bay

Mafia Is.

Aesei Is.

Luganville

Tutuba Is.

Aore Is.

Mallo Is.

south encompassing 1,550 square miles. The island consists of uplifted volcanic rock and raised coral terraces. It is heavily forested with palm, sandalwood, hardwoods, and other tropical vegetation. Besides St. Philippe and St. James Bay, there are several smaller bays and natural harbors on the east coast and southeast end. The main settlements and plantations are in the southern portion of the island and some of the offshore islands.

Scattered small islands lie along the east coast and off the southeast end. Most of Santo's coast and the offshore islands have fringing coral reefs. The islands off of Santo's southeast end possessed important plantations. Aore Island is separated from the main island by the 1–1-½-mile-wide Segond Channel. The hilly island measures about five by seven miles. Much larger Malo Island is south of Aore separated by the 1-½-mile-wide Wawa Channel and measures nine by eleven miles. Malo is dominated by the 1,200-foot Mount Malo. Tutubu (aka Tutuba) Island, 1-½ by 4 miles, lies 2 miles to the west of Aore providing additional protection to the island's nearly landlocked harbor. While Santo is warmer than the more southern islands of the New Hebrides, it is milder than the Solomons to the northwest.

Soil, climate, and rainfall allowed a flourishing agriculture industry with coconuts, coffee, sugarcane, cotton, rice, and many tropical fruits. There was also a small cattle industry. A marked decline in production and exports hurt the island seriously just prior to the war, but a complete turnaround was made between 1940 and 1943 as the islands geared up to support the war effort. In 1940, there were just over 200 Britons and Australians, and almost 700 French citzens in the New Hebrides. Some 4,000 natives lived on Santo.

In June 1942, Santo was selected as a site for an air base to support the upcoming Guadalcanal operation as well as serve as a base for air patrols to detect any Japanese movement south from the Solomon Islands. Being some 150 miles further north than Efaté placed it closer to Guadalcanal. It was to become a hub for South Pacific bases with New Caledonia to the south, Fiji to the east-southeast, and the Samoas further to the east-northeast. A fighter field was begun on 8 July and located at Turtle Bay 12 miles north of Luganville, the island's administrative center and largest town at the mouth of the Sarakata River. Swamps and malaria slowed the task. At the end of the month B-17 bombers were launched from Fighter Field No. 1's 6,000-foot runway to attack Guadalcanal in an effort to delay completion of the new Japanese airfield there. Additional naval construction troops and Army engineers arrived in August immediately after the Marine landing on Guadalcanal. Fighter Field No. 2 with a 4,500-foot runway was completed near Fighter Field No. 1. On 16 October the Japanese ineffectively shelled Santo. The 6,000-foot Bomber Field No. 1 was built two miles west of Luganville and the 7,000-foot Bomber Field No. 2 at Pekoa four miles east of Luganville. Both bomber fields were completed in November. A seaplane base was built on Segond Channel. Extensive support facilities were also built and Santo was well on its way to becoming one of the largest air complexes in the South Pacific. The only action on the island was occasional shellings by submarines and a few air attacks launched from the Solomons, which had ceased by the year's end. The island was defended by the 54th Coast Artillery Regiment (155mm Gun) from October 1942 to February 1944. It was augmented by the Marine Corps' 10th and 11th Defense Battalions at different times (FPO SF 212, APO SF 708).

Additional construction troops arrived in the early months of 1943 and the 6,800-foot Bomber Field No. 3 was built outside Luganville and completed in May. Espíritu Santo became the largest Marine aviation complex in the South Pacific supporting operations into the Solomons and beyond. The 1st Marine Aircraft Wing operated there from September 1942 to February 1944. The 2d Marine Aircraft Wing arrived in May 1944 and remained until October. The Japanese began nuance air raids on Santo at the end of May 1943 lasting until June.

Espíritu Santo's military value was enhanced by the extremely well-protected harbor at Luganville in the Segond Channel. Along with the construction troops arriving in February was Lion-1, the largest of the different types of advance base units. Its mission was to construct the largest naval operating base in the South Pacific, Naval Operating Base, Espíritu Santo. The island's limited road network was improved and extended. These served only the eastern portion of the island and the south coast. Huge supply and ammunition depots, fuel storage, ship repair, aircraft engine and torpedo overhaul, pontoon assembly, and other support facilities were constructed east of Luganville stretching over two miles along Segond Channel and on Aore Island across the Channel. (Modern Luganville migrated west into the site of the former naval base after it was closed.) The island served as one of the main rest and rehabilitation bases in the South Pacific. As operations pushed into the Central Pacific, Espíritu Santo's importance did not diminish. It continued to serve as a key supply and repair base as well as a combat orientation center for Navy and Marine aviation units. The base refueled and resupplied many of the vessels involved in the Okinawa landing. While dismantling began in early 1945, the base remained in use to fuel and supply ships as U.S. forces withdrew from the Pacific. Tons of supplies and materiel and hundreds of vehicles were dumped into Segond Channel at Palilikulo Peninsula, known today as Million Dollar Point, a popular scuba-diving site. The base was disestablished on 12 June 1946 and its remaining facilities turned over to civilian authorities in November.

Over two million troops passed through or were based on Espíritu Santo during the course of the war with up to 100,000 stationed there at any one time. At the entrance of the anchorage are the sunken SSAT *President Coolidge*, luxury liner turned troopship with the 172d Infantry Regiment, 34th Infantry Division embarked, and the USS *Tucker* (DD-374), victims of U.S.-laid protective mines. These too are popular dive sites. The islands had such profound effect on a young Army lieutenant named James A. Michener that he was moved to write a novel, *Tales of the South Pacific*. From this came the musical *South Pacific*. It was set on Santo and the near mythical island of Bali-ha'i, hidden in the shadows of the equally fictitious Vanicoro, was influenced by the actual island of Ambae to the east.

Efaté Island, New Hebrides Islands

Efaté (pronounced E-fa-ta) was occasionally known as Sandwich Island (not to be confused with Captain Cook's early name for the Hawaiian Islands). Its code name was initially ROSES until February 1943 when it was renamed TRUCULENCE. It was later designated ACID, then SUXE.

Efaté Island is located at 17°42' S 168°23' E roughly in the center of the New Hebrides Islands chain (see Map 19). The nearest large islands are Epi some fifty miles to the north and Erromango 70 miles to the southeast. Espíritu Santo, a larger New Hebrides base, is 150 miles to the northwest while New Caledonia is 290 miles to the south-southeast. Fiji is 600 miles due east and Guadalcanal is 700 miles to the northwest.

Efaté is an irregular-shaped island, the third largest in the New Hebrides, and has varied terrain. It measures twenty-four miles from east to west and eighteen miles from north to south. A broad "Y"-shaped range of terraced coral atop uplifted volcanic mountains borders the northwest coast of the island. The southwest end of the range forms a plateau and a river valley running into the sea splits the northeast end range. The eastern arm of the "Y" provides the highest peak at 2,300 feet. It terminates at Quain Hill on the northeast coast, an area of hot springs. Southeast-running ridge fingers thrust into the southern half of the island's broad plain. Rivers and streams run southward from between the ridge fingers providing sufficient water year around. The flat southern plain provides space for any size of airfield desired. Most of the island is covered by dense tropical

Map 19
Efaté Island

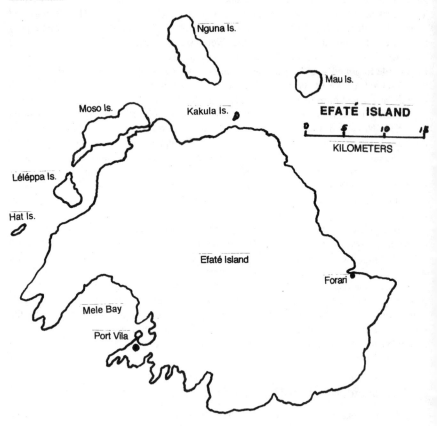

Nguna Is.

Mau Is.

Moso Is.   Kakula Is.   **EFATÉ ISLAND**

KILOMETERS

Léléppa Is.

Hat Is.

Efaté Island

Forari

Mele Bay

Port Vila

vegetation and crops as grown on Espíritu Santo. Manganese mining is conducted on the island. The weather is similar to Espíritu Santo's, but milder.

Meli Bay on the southwest coast covers an area of roughly six by six miles, but its wide oceanward side provides rough water conditions. However, the nearly landlocked Vila Harbor, covering just over one square mile is located on the bay's east side providing one of the best ports in the New Hebrides. The town of Port Vila (referred to only as Vila in most military documents), the Condominium of New Hebrides' capital and commercial center, sits at the harbor's northeast corner. Two islets occupy the harbor, Fila, inhabited by natives, and Iririki, occupied by the British residency of the Condominium government. The French residency was in Port Vila. Simple roads linked the town with several outlying settlements. The majority of the New Hebrides' French and British planters resided on the island along with several hundred Tonkinese workers and 1,700 natives. A second, but undeveloped harbor is on the island's northwest side. The lack of roads through the mountains was responsible for Havannah Harbor's remoteness. The harbor's large anchorage is protected from the open ocean by, from north to south, Moso, Léléppa, and Hat Islands. Nguna, Pele, and Mau (aka Emao) Islands lie off the north coast enclosing the large open Undine Bay with Moso Island on its west side.

Prior to the U.S. decision to develop Naval Operating Base, Efaté (FPO SF 156) there was only a small Australian garrison and a seaplane base. Vila Harbor, while an excellent natural harbor, lacked facilities other than simple commercial piers. In February and March 1942, Efaté was selected as an advanced naval base and a small Army detachment arrived on 25 March. The Marine 4th Defense Battalion and aviation units arrived two weeks later, but it was not until early May that the black 24th Infantry Regiment and naval construction troops arrived. Near the end of May a 6,000-foot fighter field was in operation near Port Vila (Bauer Field named after Lieutenant Colonel Harold W. Bauer, awarded a posthumous Medal of Honor in the South Pacific) and a seaplane base in Havannah Harbor. Vila Harbor was too small to support seaplane operations and Meli Bay too rough. Until a road was built in early 1943, Havannah Harbor could only be reached from Port Vila by boat. It was from this base that Navy patrol bombers launched the first attack on Tulgia and Gavutu Islands near Guadalcanal on 1 June. Various base support facilities were built around Port Vila. A 3,000-foot fighter field was built adjacent to Havannah Harbor in September and a 6,000-foot bomber field was completed near Quain Hill in January 1943. The airfields on Efaté were Finucane Field named after Lieutenant Arthur E. Finucane; Haring Field named after Lieutenant Richard Z. Haring; and Taylor Field named after Lieutenant Lawrence C. Taylor, all Marines. Fleet support facilities were minimal. In early 1944, the base began to be rolled up and recovered materials were deployed forward. It was relegated to a minor emergency airfield, ship refueling, and communications relay base until disestablished in February 1946.

TUTUILA ISLAND, AMERICAN SAMOA

The Samoa Islands, both the American and Western groups, were collectively code-named STRAW. They were later renamed PEON and then APOTHECARY. American Samoa, *Amerika Samoa* locally, was occasionally called Eastern Samoa. The name Samoa means *Sa* (sacred) and *Moa* (center)—"sacred center of the universe." They were named the Navigator Archipelago in 1768, but this name had generally fallen from use by the twentieth century. Tutuila Island, the main island in American Samoa, was code-named STRAWSTACK and it was later renamed HOST and then LOPSIDED.

The American Samoas include those islands of the Samoa Islands east of 171° W. Tutuila Island, the most important in the eastern (American) group, is also the western-most of the American Samoas (see Map 20). It is situated at 14°20' S 170°40' W. Tutuila is 2,276 miles southwest of Pearl Harbor, 1,580 miles northeast of Auckland, New Zealand, and 2,370 miles northeast of Sydney, Australia. Borabora is 1,420 miles to the west, Tongatabu is 490 miles to the south-southwest, and Suva, Fiji is 612 miles to the west-southwest. More importantly, the Ellice Islands are 600 miles to the northwest, a stepping stone to the Japanese-occupied Gilberts. Upolu Island in the Western Samoas is thirty-six miles to the west-northwest. The Samoa Islands are in time zone 1.

Tutuila Island is the largest island in American Samoa and the third largest in the Samoa Islands. It is twenty-one miles long east to west and varies from two to six miles wide. It is almost two islands being connected by a ¾-mile wide isthmus at Pago Pago (pronounced "pong-go pong-go") Harbor. The mountainous island, formed from a shield volcano, covers some forty-five square miles with the broken mountain chain running its length. The highest peak on the island's larger western portion is 2,141-foot Mount Matafao near the center with 1,700-foot Mount Piua to its east and the 1,600-foot Mounts Alava and Tuaolo to its west. All of the island is covered by lush tropical forests of

Map 20
Tutuila Island

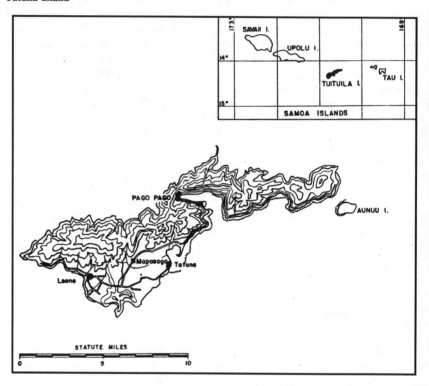

hardwoods, coconut palms, banana trees, and underbrush from the coast to the top of the tallest peaks. Numerous valleys run out of the mountains to the coast. There are no rivers; the considerable rains flow directly into the ocean. The north coast is very rugged and steep with few settlements, only eight villages of any size. The south and west coasts are more level and provide fertile land for cultivation. Most of the south and west coasts are fringed with coral reefs while the north is generally free of reefs. About twenty-four main villages are scattered along the south and west coasts. They are connected by a coastal road running from Amanave near Cape Taputapu on the west end to Tula near Cape Matatula on the east end. One mile south of the island's east end is Aunu'u Island, about 1-½ by one mile. There are several small bays scattered along the north coast and west coasts, some of which are used by fishing villages. The only bays suitable for large ships are Pago Pago Harbor, considered one of the best in the South Pacific, but not large enough for a fleet anchorage, and the undeveloped Leone Bay on the west end. Pago Pago Harbor on the south-central coast has a one-mile-wide entrance, bounded by Point Distress on the west side and Point Breaker on the east, and opens out into a two-mile-wide, three-mile-deep bay. The harbor is formed by an ancient volcano crater from thirty-six to 150 feet deep. Tutuila and all other islands in the group, with the exception of Rose Island, are of volcanic origin. The collective area of all islands is seventy-six square miles.

About 60 miles east of Tutuila is the Manu'a Group with three small islands. Táu is the largest island in the group with fourteen square miles and is dominated by a 2,000-foot peak. A Navy radio station was situated on Táu, FPO SF 69. Ofu and Olosega Islands, joined by a coral reef at low tide, are 6 miles to the northwest of Táu and contain four square miles together. The islands of the Manu'a Group are mountainous and had a population of 2,600 in scattered villages. Rose Island (aka Nu'uomanu Island), a very small, uninhabited coral atoll, is located some 170 miles east of Tutuila. It has two small islands, Rose and Sand. Most of the reef is awash at low tide. Swains Island is located 220 miles north of Tutuila. The densely vegetated island is three miles long and one mile wide. Enclosing a freshwater lagoon, its elevation varies from 15 to 25 feet. Swains Island, a small atoll, was previously regarded as in the Union Islands and claimed as part of the British Gilbert and Ellice Islands Colony. In 1926, it was scheduled for transfer to Western Samoa for administration by New Zealand. However, it was annexed by the United States on 4 March 1925 without challenge. It supported a population of 125 and a U.S. Navy radio station was located there, FPO SF 68.

In 1940, Tutuila had a native population of some 10,000 with another 2,500 living on the other islands. Pago Pago's population was 1,000. Indigenous animal life is limited to birds and lizards. The islands are free of most tropical diseases such as malaria and dysentery, but tuberculosis, yaws (an infectious skin disease), filariasis (a tissue infestation by parasite worms), and elephantiasis (also known by its native name of *mu-mu*) are suffered by the population. Unpreventable, mosquito-borne elephantiasis causes extreme enlargement and hardening of the legs and scrotum. It was as much responsible for the withdrawal of virtually all Marine Corps units from the Samoas at the end of December 1943 as the now negligible Japanese threat. Marine Barracks, Klamath Falls and its associated Naval Medical Unit, Klamath Falls, Oregon were established to study and treat the disease. Treatment requires a cool climate to suppress it. Some 3,000 Marine and Navy personnel were infected, and cured, through a comprehensive therapy program. Navy Department policy was to not return recovered personnel to the tropics.

Through December to February the high temperature is around 90°F with variable winds and occasional gales. In the other months the temperature can drop to 75°F, but is usually higher. Rainfall is 190 inches a year with most falling from November to April, although the island is sometimes inundated by up to 300 inches. While rainfall is heavy, there are water shortages in the summer months. Typhoons, though now more frequent, were rare during the 1930–40s. The islands are shook by occasional earthquakes.

Samoan tradition has it that the Samoa Islands were the original home of the Polynesian race. It is believed, however, that two migrations populated the islands from Southwest Asia beginning in about 450 B.C. and the Samoas were populated in about A.D. 400. There is little doubt though that Samoa was the source of seafarers who populated other islands of Polynesia hundreds of years ago. The Samoas lies roughly in the center of the great triangle populated by Polynesians (Hawaii, New Zealand, Easter Island). The islands were discovered, though inaccurately plotted, in 1722 by the Dutchman Jacob Roggeveen. Louis Antoine de Bougainville named them the Navigator Archipelago in 1768 after seeing numbers of canoes around the islands. Neither explorer landed. The Frenchman Jean Francis de Galaup (Count of Pèrouse) landed in 1787 and was attacked by natives. He did more accurately establish the main islands' locations. British, German, and American adventurers settled in the islands in the early 1800s to rule by force. British missionaries began to arrive in 1828 and by the mid-1830s Christianity was well established on the islands. One of the main benefits of the missionaries was that they developed a written Samoan language and within two generations many Samoans were literate and the islanders quickly accepted Christianity. The U.S. Wilkes Exploring Expedition visited the islands in 1839.

Through the late 1830s and 1840s various trade agreements, commercial agents, and consuls were established in the Samoas by the British, Americans, and Germans. While the Samoans continued self-rule, European and American settlement proceeded steadily as did trade rivalry. The Samoas was divided into five districts ruled by native families. The Atua District contained Tutuila and Eastern Upolu. Warfare between these districts and combined allied districts was unending, often encouraged by white commercial interests. If a given family or group was successful, a single king ruled. This was the case in 1830 when a king ruled until his death in 1841. This was followed by twenty-five years of wars and squabbles between the districts with two kings eventually emerging to control Upolu and Savai'i. This cumulated in 1869 in a series of battles raging into 1873. Samoan wars were extremely vicious and cannibalism of enemy dead and prisoners was practiced as a means of insulting their enemies. To finance their wars Samoans began to sell land to Europeans, something they had not previously practiced. Between 1860 and 1889, Samoa was essentially ruled by Samoan kings, but under the direction of British, German, and American consuls. In 1872, the chief ruling Tutuila sought U.S. protection in exchange for the right to establish a naval station, but it was rejected by the Senate. American and British consuls arranged a peace in 1873. Colonel A. B. Steinberger, an American special agent and one of the architects of the peace, severed his relations to the United States, drafted a constitution, and organized a government for the Samoans. The U.S. and British consuls distrusted Steinberger, but the Germans, who had plans to take over the islands as a colony, remained quiet. In 1876 it was found that Steinberger was actually working in German interests and he was arrested by the U.S. Navy and deported. The Samoan government disintegrated after Steinberger's departure and the islands reverted to ceaseless warfare for another twenty years.

A treaty with Tutuila was finally accepted by the United States in 1877, but the Tutuila Samoan's offer of annexation by the United States was refused. Tutuila's urgency to place itself under the protection of the United States was because of Germany's continued efforts to annex the island. The United States established a coaling station at Pago Pago on Tutuila in 1878 and the following year the United Kingdom and Germany established their own bases in the Western Samoas. At the same time an international municipality was setup at Apia, Upolu where Europeans were protected from native warfare. This protection was ensured by warships of the three powers, but rivalries between them were such that it is a wonder that they themselves did not battle one another. A series of treaties and agreements between the three powers and the various Samoan factions eventually resulted in the establishment of a single Samoan king in 1889 and the Berlin Treaty established Samoa as an independent nation. German intrigues were thought to have ended, the cause of much of the trouble, but in 1894 the fighting renewed. In 1899, an American and Englishman were murdered in Apia. A combined U.S. and U.K. landing party came ashore to attack organized resistance, believed to be aided by the Germans. Apia was shelled by the Anglo-American ships and the landing party suffered losses.

This forced a new treaty to be signed and the three principal powers were to divide up the islands. On 14 November 1899, Germany annexed Western Samoa as a colony and the United States took sovereignty of Eastern Samoa, i.e., Tutuila and other islands east of 171° W, on 2 December. This was named Territory of American Samoa, or simply AS. Britain dropped its claims for Western Samoa in exchange for exclusive rights to the Tonga and the Solomon Islands, previously claimed by Germany.

The U.S. Navy coaling station, established in 1878, was outside the village of Fagatoga on the south shore of Pago Pago Harbor. A severe typhoon sank several U.S. and British ships in the poorly protected harbor of Apia in 1889. The U.S. Navy began purchasing and east of Fagatoga and on Goat Island, actually a small peninsula adjacent to Fagatoga. Sufficient land was not obtained until 1898 and the modest Naval Station, Tutuila was completed in 1902.

The station commander, a captain or commander, from 1899 doubled as the informal governor of American Samoa. The official flag raising, after the naval governor persuaded the various chiefs to accept U.S. sovereignty, was on 17 April 1900. In 1905, the naval station commandant was formerly designated the Naval Governor of American Samoa. He was assisted by the secretary of native affairs, a civilian and executive officer to the governor. In addition to the station commandant, serving as governor and also commander of the station ship, other Navy officers assisted with governing of the islands. The captain of the yard doubled as the customs officer as well as the superintendent of roads and sheriff. The paymaster served as the treasurer and the medical officer as the health officer. American Samoa was divided into three administrative districts, Western and Eastern Districts of Tutuila and the Manua District containing the islands to the east. These paralleled traditional Samoan divisions and were governed by district governors appointed by the island governor. The districts were subdivided into counties and villages. A Samoan Council, the *Fono*, served only as an advisory council to the naval governor. Samoans were not American citizens, but did owe their allegiance to the American flag. Foreigners were not allowed to buy land and no outside commercial interests were permitted. The Navy's policy was Samoa for the Samoans. Samoan customs were preserved so long as they did not conflict with U.S. laws and their traditional district, country, and village councils were retained. Conditions were cordial and the islands were a pleasant assignment. This was the case until 1920 when a new naval governor created a climate that alienated the Samoans. The situation was so severe that most of the station's officers sided with the Samoan opposition. The offending commander was court marshaled.

In 1900, a fifty-eight-man naval militia was raised in lieu of a Marine barracks to secure the naval station, guard the prison, and perform law enforcement duties in the territory. The *Fiti Fiti* Guard and Band, Samoan for "Courageous" and their term for a soldier, was commanded by a Marine gunnery or first sergeant. He was also the prison warden. A small band was added in 1902 and the *Fiti Fiti* was eventually expanded to seventy men. The *Fiti Fiti* arguably wore the most unique uniform in the U.S. service consisting of a *lava lava* (red-trimmed, navy blue wraparound skirt), red sash, white undershirt, red turban, and no footwear.

In 1914, a German warship and liner requested to be interned by the U.S. Navy at Pago Pago to avoid capture by a British and New Zealand force, which seized Western Samoa at the end of the month. The ships were in turn seized by the United States when war was declared in September 1917. Between the wars American Samoa continued to serve as a small out-of-the way coaling station and was eventually converted to provide fuel oil. Pan American Airways established a seaplane station at Pago Pago, but the loss of a clipper there in December caused the route to be changed to Canton Island via New Caledonia.

The naval governor from 8 August 1940 was Captain Lawrence Wild. Because of the deteriorating international situation in the Pacific, from 15 May 1941 no unauthorized vessels or aircraft were permitted within three miles of Tutuila or Rose Islands. As on other U.S. Pacific possessions, limited construction was begun to improve Naval Station, Tululia (FPO SF 129) in the summer of 1940. This included a Marine airfield at Tafuna, four miles south of Pago Pago. It was partly ready in April 1942 and fully operational in June. It eventually had two runways, 6,000 and 3,000 feet. This initial construction was conducted by contractors. Most of the construction effort was intended to provide facilities for the coming Marine defense force. Later in the year a 6,000-foot bomber field was completed at Leone on the island's southwest plain seven miles from Pago Pago. A seaplane base was established in Pago Pago Harbor. Navy Radio Direction Finding Station, Vaitogi (FPO SF 70) was established on the southwest coast six miles from Pago Pago.

On 15 March 1941, the Marine Corps' 7th Defense Battalion arrived at Pago Pago to be the first Fleet Marine Force unit to serve in the South Pacific and the first such unit to be deployed to defend an island. Its guns were emplaced at Blunt's and Breakers Points covering Pago Pago Harbor. It trained another unique unit, the 1st Samoan Battalion, U.S. Marine Corps Reserve. This unit, the only Marine Reserve unit to serve on active duty in World War II, was uniformed in a khaki *lava lava*, white undershirt, and khaki garrison cap. Its officers and most NCOs were American Marines. The battalion was mobilized after the Pearl Harbor attack and remained active until absorbed into the new Marine Barracks, Naval Station, Tutuila, Samoa Islands in January 1944.

The Pearl Harbor attack redirected construction of station facilities to defensive works. The 2d Marine Division formed the 2d Marine Brigade, Reinforced, built around the 8th Marines, in California. This first wartime expeditionary brigade departed San Diego and arrived at Pago Pago on 19 January 1942 (Operation PICADOR). The only action experienced in the islands was a shelling of Pago Pago Harbor by a Japanese submarine on 11 January giving the en route Brigade an increased sense of urgency. No damage was inflicted and the only casualty was a slightly wounded Navy officer. The first elements of Marine Aircraft Group 13 arrived on 11 March to provide air support. A Navy patrol plane detachment was attached to the group making it the first instance in which a Navy aviation unit was subordinate to a Marine unit. The brigade commander, Brigadier General Henry L. Larsen, was designated Military Governor, American Samoa. The ships delivering the Brigade returned to the States bearing the naval station's and defense battalion's dependents. The Brigade's plan of defense for Tutuila scattered its units in small detachments around the island where they may have been defeated in detail had the Japanese not canceled their plans to invade New Caledonia, Fiji, and the Samoas in July 1942 (the *Kawaguchi Detachment* with the *41st* and *124th Infantry Regiments* were assigned this task). Doctrine called for early-warning outposts to be established around a large island and the bulk of the defense force positioned in a central location to defend critical installations, e.g., port and airfield, and allow it to counterattack in force.

The Brigade and MAG-13 were placed under Defense Force, Samoan Group on 29 April, a division-equivalent command under Major General Charles F.B. Price. This command also controlled Marine units in Western Samoa. Between August 1942 and September 1943 the Defense Force supported the occupation of the Ellice Islands some 600 miles to the northwest. The first Seabees arrived on Tutuila in July 1942 to relieve the contractors, but the Seabee unit was sent on to Espíritu Santo. Some contractors volunteered to remain and continue to work on projects augmented by native labor until another Seabee unit arrived in August. The 8th Marines departed for Guadalcanal in October 1942 and was replaced by the 3d Marines. The 2d Brigade was disbanded in March 1943, but the 3d Marines remained on Tutuila until May. Seven Marine replacement battalions, raised on the U.S. East Coast, were trained and acclimatized between December 1942 and July 1943 at the Replacement Training Center, Tutuila. Defense Force, Samoa Group was disbanded in December 1943.

Map 21
Upolu Island

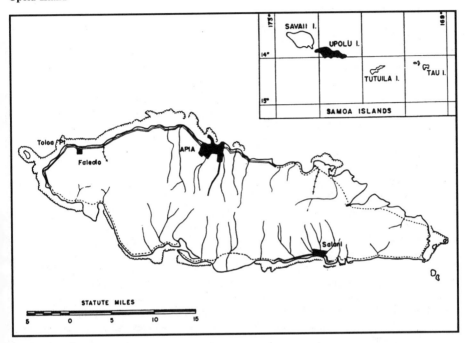

Tutuila's value diminished as the war moved beyond the Solomons and dismantling of certain facilities was ordered in February 1944. This operation was completed in August and by January 1945 only a small garrison remained securing a naval station used only for emergency aircraft landings and communications. The Marine Barracks was deactivated in August 1945.

The *Fiti Fiti* Guard was deactivated in June 1951 and the Navy administration was transferred to the Department of Interior on 1 July 1951. Copra was the island's major export, but this was a falling industry. In the 1950s tuna replaced copra as the major export. American Samoa remains an unincorporated and unorganized territory of the United States. The first Samoan governor was appointed in 1956 and the first election of a governor was in 1977. A military presence remains in the form of a detachment of a U.S. Army Reserve infantry company; its parent unit is on Hawaii. The ¼-square mile Fragatale Bay Marine Sanctuary, one of twelve such in American controlled waters, lies off the southwest coast of Tutuila.

UPOLU AND SAVAI'I ISLANDS, WESTERN SAMOA

Upolu Island was code-named STRAWHAT and later renamed HOUR, FPO SF 208. Savai'i Island was STRAWMAN and was later renamed TRAP, then LAPOVER.

The Western Samoas include those islands of the Samoa Islands west of 171° W. Upolu Island, the most important in Western Samoa, is situated at 13°85' S 171°40' W (see Map 21). Savai'i Island is at 13°30' S 172°24' W. The two islands are separated by the eight-mile-wide Apolima Strait with Upolu Island to the east of Savai'i Island. Tutuila Island in American Samoa is thirty-six miles to the east-southeast of Upolu. The Samoa Islands are in time zone 1.

The Western Samoas include the two large islands of Upolu and Savai'i, two much smaller islands, and five islets with a total of 1,133 square miles strung along a west-northwest to east-southeast line. All of the islands are ruggedly mountainous, rocky, and of volcanic origin with very fertile soil. Savai'i is the largest shield volcano island in the South Pacific. The islands are covered with dense tropical forests and underbrush. Co-conut palms are scattered about the islands with large plantations on both Upolu and Savai'i, mainly on the three-to-four-mile wide coastal plains. Water is plentiful on the two large islands, but scarce on the small ones. The islands' rainy season is from October to March and the dry season from March to October. March is the hottest month and July and August the mildest. Humidity is high year-round. The islands lie outside the normal track of typhoons, but one occasionally strikes.

Upolu Island is forty-seven miles long east to west and fifteen miles wide covering 431 square miles. The highest peak is 3,607 feet. On the western end is the 2,195-foot Mount Tofua, an extinct volcano crater. Numerous streams flow from the central mountain range into the sea with most on the south coast. Most of the coast is fringed with coral reefs. A number of villages are scattered along the coast with most on the northwest side. Apia, the capital of Western Samoa and the largest town, is located on the north-central coast around the small Apia Harbour. A devastating typhoon in March 1889 sank six warships in the harbor: the German SM *Adler, Eber*, and *Olga*; and the USS *Nipsic, Trenton*, and *Vandalia*. The largest village is Salani on the southeast coast. A road ran from Apia around the island's west end. A dirt track followed the rest of the coast around the island. A narrow gauge railroad ran inland some 4 miles from Saluafata Harbour, eleven miles east of Apia, to serve coconut plantations. A second rail line runs two miles inland from a point 2 miles east of Faleofo Village near the island's west end. No airfields existed on the islands prior to the war. Four islets lie off the island's east end: Fanuatapu, Namu'a, Nuutele, and Nuulua. Another islet, Nuusafee, lays off the south-central coast. Two islands lie in the Apolima Strait. The smaller Apolima is roughly midway between Upolu and Savai'i. Manono Island is about three miles off Upolu's west end.

Savai'i Island is forty-seven miles long east to west and twenty-seven miles wide covering 659 square miles. A mountain chain runs the island's length dominated by 6,097-foot Mauga Silisili in its center. Three extinct volcano craters are found on the north slope of the range. None have been active since 1911. A few streams flow off the mountains to the south coast with even fewer on the north coast. Coral reefs are found along the north coast, east end, and the southwest side. A few villages are scattered along the island's coasts. The main village is Fagamalo on the north-central coast near Matautu Bay and is home of the resident commissioner. A dirt track followed the island's coast.

The early history, discovery, and political developments in Western Samoa are discussed in the preceding section. There had been a German presence on Upolu since 1856 and they gradually expanded their influence over the subsequent years. Germany's annexation of Western Samoa on 8 November 1899 saw the end of the ceaseless Samoan warfare, although a disturbance erupted in 1908 and was quickly suppressed as was any other opposition, regardless of how peaceful. World War I saw the occupation of German possessions north of the equator by the Japanese and by Australia and New Zealand in the southern hemisphere. On 29 August 1914, New Zealand troops arrived aboard an Australian squadron and Western Samoa was surrendered by the German governor.

A New Zealand military government controlled the islands until 30 April 1920. On 1

May, the League of Nations granted New Zealand the right to govern Western Samoa under a Class C Mandate and the Samoan Constitution Order took effect establishing the Mandated Territory of Western Samoa. The administrator, subordinate to the New Zealand Minister of External Affairs, was assisted by a legislative council comprised of Samoans appointed by himself and locally elected Europeans. Local Western Samoan laws were essentially the same as New Zealand's. New Zealand's first fifteen years in Western Samoa were troublesome. Their comparatively indulgent rule, although unmindful of Samoan aspirations, lack of understanding of past Samoan conflicts, and the Samoan's traditionally combative temperament combined to almost cause the British Commonwealth to abandon the mandate. Samoans resented the Class C Mandate, i.e., the governing of a primitive people incapable of governing themselves. The Mau, a militant Samoan nationalistic organization, was soon established. From 1920 to 1935 the New Zealand administrators were military officers who typically responded to the belligerent Mau in a heavy-handed manner. At the end of 1929 a major riot erupted with death on both sides. New Zealand troops and police eventually arrested those held responsible. Between 1930 and 1935 the situation was dangerously close to open hostilities. In 1936, New Zealand's new Labour government completely revamped the administration of Western Samoa, effected major policy changes, and developed a more harmonious relationship with the Samoans. This remained the situation when U.S. forces arrived in 1942.

In 1940, Western Samoa had a population of 400 New Zealanders and Europeans, 3,000 Euronesians (mixed European and Polynesian), 61,000 Samoans, plus a few remaining Chinese and Melanesians. Since most Europeans and Samoans were landowners, the Germans were faced with a shortage of laborers. They imported Chinese and Melanesians from the Solomons. There were 2,100 Chinese and 1,000 Melanesians on the islands when New Zealand took control. New Zealand policies, even the Labour government, dictated that these two groups be repatriated. By World War II only 330 Chinese and 75 Melanesians remained. The island's bountiful plantations produced copra, cocoa, rubber, and bananas. The latter crops were introduced in the 1920s and 1930s because of the falling demand for copra.

After the 2d Marine Brigade arrived to defend American Samoa in January 1942, it coordinated with New Zealand authorities through February for the United States to assume the defense of Western Samoa and Wallis Island, a French possession. Only 157 New Zealander-led native troops of the New Zealand Defence Force secured Upolu. In March, the 7th Defense Battalion deployed from Tutuila to Upolu and the New Zealand Defence Force was attached to it. In the meantime the 3d Marine Brigade, Fleet Marine Force was formed around the 7th Marines by the 1st Marine Division in North Carolina. It arrived at Upolu on 8 May. Company G (Reinforced), 2d Battalion, 7th Marines was detached to occupy Savai'i on 30 May. The 7th Marines deployed to Guadalcanal in September and the Brigade was placed under Defense Force, Samoan Group. The 22d Marines arrived at the end of July 1942, was assigned to the 3d Brigade, and was based at Apia. The 22d Marines was relieved from the 3d Brigade in May 1943, but remained at Apia directly under Defense Force control until mid-November when it departed. The Army's 147th Infantry Regiment (Separate) was attached to the 3d Marine Brigade from May 1943, after completing operations on Guadalcanal and New Georgia, and remained so attached until the Brigade was disbanded on 8 November. Reinforcing Army units included two antiaircraft artillery battalions, one on Upolu and the other on Savai'i.

Seabees arrived on Upolu on 1 April 1942 to develop a naval air station and supporting port (FPO SF 209). By July, a 4,000-foot airfield was constructed at Faleolo near the island's northwest end and an adjacent seaplane base was soon established. By early 1943 the airfield had been lengthened to 6,000 feet. The air facilities on Upolu were mainly for local defensive purposes, but also served as a way station between Tutuila and Wallis Island to the west and Fiji to the southwest. Other than minimal facilities for the modest defense forces, no military installations were constructed on Savai'i. Rollup of the base was ordered in February 1944, but was not completed until November.

After the war Western Samoa gradually worked toward independence with a legislative assembly established in 1947. It was made a U.N. Trust Territory with New Zealand serving as a guide. Independence was voted on in 1961 and it was achieved on 1 January 1962 as the Independent State of Western Samoa. This made it the first Pacific colony or territory of a European power to be granted independence. It has maintained a treaty of friendship with New Zealand and joined the Commonwealth in 1970. In 1997, the government dropped "Western" from its title. American Samoa protested this change as it implies that the Independent State of Samoa governs all of the Samoa Islands.

WALLIS (UVÉA) ISLAND

What was commonly known as Wallis Island to U.S. forces is actually Uvéa Island (*Ile Uvéa* in French) or Uea Island. Uvéa Island is part of the Wallis Islands (*Iles Wallis*), which includes the Hoorn Islands. In the remainder of this section Uvéa Island will be referred to as Wallis Island. The phrase Wallis Islands refers to the group. Wallis Island was code-named STRAWBOARD.

The Wallis Islands are 250 miles to the west of Western Samoa and less than 490 miles northeast of Fiji. Wallis Island is situated at 13°20' S 176°10' W. The associated Horne Islands are 120 miles to the southwest of Wallis. The Wallis and Horne Islands are in time zone 1.

The Wallis Islands are comprised of the main Wallis Island (Uvéa) and eight islets enclosed by a roughly egg-shaped coral atoll with a total land area of twenty-three square miles (see Map 22). Wallis Island is eight miles long north to south and five miles wide. The hilly island's highest elevation is 476 feet. Small lakes are found in volcanic craters. The island is of volcanic origin providing fertile soil and is well forested. Most of the sixteen or so inches of rain per year falls between November and April. The cool, dry season is from May to October. Temperatures are generally mild and the humidity is around 80 percent.

The main island and the eight islets are enclosed within an outer barrier coral reef lying from one to three miles off Wallis Island's coast providing protected lagoon waters. The islets are low and insignificant. The two largest are Nukuaeta 1 mile off the south end of Wallis Island and Nukula 1-½ miles off the north end. Four passages allow entry into the lagoon. Honikulu Passage is at the reef's south end beside Nukuaeta Islet and allows access to Mua Harbor. Mata-Utu Passage is on the west side providing an entrance to the main harbor by the same name. Fatumanini and Fugauvea Passages are 1-½ miles apart on the northwest side of the reef. Mata-Utu Harbor is protected by the outer barrier reef and an inner belt of islets and large coral heads on the island's east-central coast. Undeveloped Mua Harbor is on the island's south end and is too protected by the outer reef, Nukuaeta Islet, and other smaller islets and coral heads.

The Horne Islands (*Iles de Horne*), aka Hoorn Islands, are 120 miles to the southwest of the Wallis Islands. They consist of Futuna Island (*Ile Futuna*), Alofi Island (*Ile Alofi*), and several islets. Horne is 8-¼ miles by five miles while Alofi, five miles to the south-east of Futuna, measures three by six miles. Both are hilly with the highest elevation on

Map 22
Wallis (Uvéa) Island

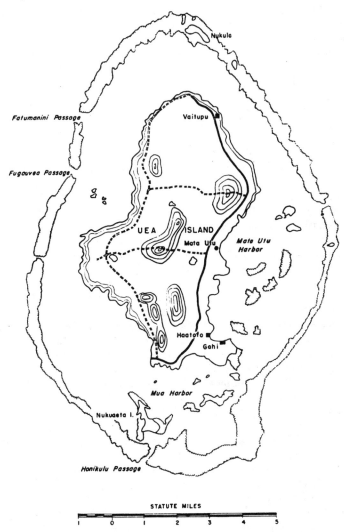

Futuna being the 2,509-foot Mount Singavi. Both were densely forested and possessed ample water. Some 300 French and 1,200 natives lived on the two islands. The Horne Islands' principal town is Sigave on Futuna. (Today the islands are heavily deforested, the more mountainous Futuna is seriously eroded, and Alofi is uninhabited owing to lack of fresh water.)

The Wallis Islands were discovered by the English Captain Samuel Wallis in 1767. The Horne Islands were discovered in 1615 by the Dutchmen Jacob Lemaire and William Schouten, who named it after one of their expedition's two ships, the *Hoorn*, which had been lost to fire while transiting Cape Horn. France occupied Wallis Islands in 1842 and administered them through Tahiti. The islands were declared a protectorate in 1887 and transferred to the administration of the Colony of New Caledonia. The Horne Islands were annexed by France in 1917 to establish the Territory of Wallis and Futuna (*Territoire des Wallis et Futuna*). The French resident and the native king reside at Mata-Uta (usually spelled Matauta in wartime documents) on the west-central coast of Wallis Island. In 1940, there were 300 French and 4,200 Polynesians on Wallis Island.

Coconut plantations, both French and native-owned, provided the island's main export. There were negligible resources and much was required to be imported to support the island. Mata-Uta Harbor provided only minimal facilities. An improved road followed the west coast from the south tip to the north. A dirt track followed the east coast and two more tracks crossed the central portion of the island connecting the east and west coastal roads.

The French resident declared in favor of the Vichy government at the beginning of the war in Europe. The turmoil on New Caledonia and in the New Hebrides from June 1940 to May 1942 had little effect on the backwater Territory of Wallis and Futuna. The United States occupied Western Samoa in May 1942 and it was soon realized that Wallis Island would make an excellent out-station for aircraft to patrol the western approaches to the Samoan Islands and the northern approaches to Fiji, both of which were considered Japanese objectives until July 1942. A defense force on Wallis Island would prevent the Japanese from occupying it as a base of operations to support attacks on the Samoas and Fiji. Defense Force, Samoan Group was assigned the mission of garrisoning Wallis Island.

Defense Force, Wallis Island was formed on Upolu to occupy and defend Wallis Island (FPO SF 207). On 26 May 1942, a Free French corvette from New Caledonia deposed the pro-Vichy resident on Wallis. The Force, arriving on Wallis on 29 May, was comprised of units detached from the 3d Marine Brigade and included the 8th Defense Battalion and 3d Battalion, 7th Marines. The latter was relieved by the 3d Battalion, 22d Marines in August and it in turn was replaced by the Army's 2d Battalion, 147th Infantry Regiment in May 1943. It remained on Wallis with an Army Provisional Antiaircraft Artillery Battalion until February 1944. The 8th Defense Battalion departed for the Gilberts in November 1943, but the defense force remained under Marine command until disbanded in February 1944. The Horne Islands were not occuiped by U.S. forces.

Seabees arrived in June 1942 and built a minimal port facility at Gahi Village on the southeast coast to support their main effort, the construction of a bomber field. The 6,000-foot airfield was not completed until October and was soon followed by a 5,000-foot fighter field. At the same time a seaplane base was completed on the lagoon as were support facilities for the defense force. The base was ordered to be dismantled in February 1944. This task was completed in July and the base was closed.

The Territory of Wallis and Futuna remain an overseas territory of France, which heavily subsidizes the islands. One of its few sources of income is the licensing of fishing rights to Japan and South Korea. Many Wallis and Futuna islanders have migrated to New Caledonia as laborers. The old bomber field today serves as Hihifo International Airport.

VITI LEVU ISLAND, FIJI ISLANDS

The Fiji Islands, the modernized pronunciation of "Viti" (Vee-tee), are known as the "crossroads of the South Pacific" owing to their central location in the region. The Fiji Islands are customarily referred to simply as "Fiji" rather than "the Fijis" as is common

Map 23
Viti Levu Island, Fiji Islands

for most island groups. Fiji was code-named FANTAN and later CHERVIL. Fiji is located between 177°00' and 175°00' west longitude and 15°00' and 22°00' south latitude. New Caledonia is 705 miles to the southwest, the New Hebrides are 600 miles due west, the Ellice Islands are 600 miles north, Wallis Island is 490 miles to the northeast, the Samoas are 500 miles to the northwest, and Tonga is 180 miles to the southwest. Sydney, Australia is some 1,700 miles to the southwest, Auckland, New Zealand is about 1,100 miles to the south-southeast, and Pearl Harbor is 2,740 miles to the northeast. The Fiji Islands as a whole were assigned FPO SF 305. Fiji is in time zone 24.

Fiji is comprised of from 250 to 330 islands, islets, and reefs (sources differ widely depending criteria for rating islets and reefs) with a total land area of 7,095 square miles (for the higher island/islet count). Approximately 80 of the islands were inhabited in 1940. The two largest islands are Viti Levu (pronounced Vee-tee Lay-vu) and Vanua Levu (pronounced Ve-new-ah Lay-vu), with U.S. bases established on the former (see Map 23). The next largest islands are Taveuni and Kandavu. There are only 24 other islands ranging in size from 90 square miles down to 5 square miles. All others are significantly smaller. The larger Viti Levu is located on the western edge of Fiji and

Vanua Levu on the northern edge. They are separated by a 40-mile-wide passage. Other islands are dispersed widely about the area with most scattered in a band stretching from the south to the northeast of the two main islands. With the exception of a few coral atolls found in the Lau Group, the Fiji Islands were formed by volcanic activity and rise sharply from the sea. Most islands are mountainous, rising over 4,000 feet on the largest islands, but with widely varied terrain and vegetation. The mountains are composed of volcanic lava and the coastal lowlands possess deep, rich soils excellent for cultivation. Numerous rivers and streams are found on the larger islands. All of the islands are fringed by coral reefs with gaps created by rivers allowing entry into the lagoons. Most islands have only a few small beaches with little surf because of the reefs, which also enhanced its defense. Geographers' grouping of Fiji's many islands sometimes differ, but the following breakdown of eight subgroups is generally accepted. The number of component islands and islets is general. These are listed from the southeast to the northwest:

Lakemba subgroup—thirty-three islands concentrated around Lakemba Island, the largest (twelve square miles) east-southeast of Viti Levu.

Exploring Islands (named after the Wilkes Exploring Expedition)—ten islands/islets clustered around the central Vanuambalavu (aka Vanua Balavu) (twenty-four square miles) due east of Viti Levu. (Note: The Lakemba Subgroup and the Exploring Islands comprise the Lau Group (aka Eastern Group) running from north to south.)

Vanua Levu ("Big Land"), Taveuni, and adjacent islands—over thirty islands concentrated around Fiji's second and third largest islands.

Lomai Viti (aka Inner Fiji)—twelve widely scattered islands located in the Koro Sea. The Koro Sea is an area enclosed by the Lau Group, Vanua Levu, Viti Levu, and Kandavu. Its many reefs, rocks, and shoals make it dangerous for navigation.

Viti Levu and adjacent islands—over sixteen islands/islets lying close offshore of the Fiji's largest island.

Ono subgroup—six islets clustered north of Kandavu.

Kandavu Island (aka Kadavu) and adjacent islands—the fourth largest island (165 square miles) in Fiji, south of Viti Levu, with about ten islands/islets nearby.

Yasawa Islands—a chain of about twenty islands/islets running north to south. The Mamanutha subgroup forms a southern extension of the Yasawas adjacent to Viti Levu.

The Rotuma Islands lie 250 miles due north of Fiji. This small group is administered by Fiji through a resident commissioner; the Rotumas were annexed by Fiji in 1881. The main island of Rotuma is 7-½ miles long and 3-½ miles wide. Eight small islands are scattered around Rotuma. The islands' population is 2,300, mostly Polynesians.

Fiji's climate is moderated by the southeast trade winds. Year-round average temperature varies from 62 to 91°F, but the humidity is high. Annual rainfall, however, differs greatly on the larger islands depending on the side. The east sides receives 100–120 inches a year with most falling during the November-to-March wet season, also the typhoon season, but some is received in the other months. On the west side of the islands, known locally as the "Burning West," only sixty-five to seventy inches is received during the same period and ceases during the April-to-October dry season. Tropical diseases are minimal and there is no malaria in Fiji.

Vegetation varies greatly between the east and west sides of the larger islands. On the more wet and tropical east and southeast sides the islands are heavily forested with hard and softwoods, dense underbrush, and tropical plants. Coconut palms and light woods are found on the narrow coastal plains and mangrove swamps dot the east coasts. Much of this land is under cultivation or used for livestock grazing. The islands' dry west sides are covered with grasslands and clumps of brush and reeds. Besides livestock, the predominant animal life are mongooses and iguanas.

The discovery of Fiji is credited to Abel Tasman in 1643, the discover of Tasmania, although it is believed that Spaniards may have visited the islands earlier. Tasman declined exploration due to the hostility of the natives. Captain James Cook surveyed some of the southern islands in 1774. Lieutenant William Bligh, after being set adrift by the HMS *Bounty*, passed through the islands in 1789 and was pursued by Fijians in war canoes. He explored the islands aboard the HMS *Providence* in 1792. Others briefly visited the islands and some inaccurate charts emerged, but it was not until the U.S. Wilkes Exploring Expedition's visit in 1840 that reliable charts were available.

These explorers found a warlike race of cannibals embroiled in a ceaseless state of war. The native Fijians, because of the islands' location, are a mix of Melanesian (predominate), Micronesian, and Polynesian. A series of wars were fought from 1830s as tribal factions attempted to gain and retain ascendancy. This resulted in two tribal groups, the Bau on Viti Levu and the Lauan Confederacy on Vanua Levu, gaining control. The Lauan were supported by Tongan Islanders. These two groups were on the verge of war to gain dominance of Fiji in its entirety when the first British consul arrived in 1858 and subsequently prevented a conflict. Acting on the belief that Britain would soon take possession of the islands, settlers and missionaries trickled in. After ten years of effort to form a government agreeable to all factions the Kingdom of Fiji was proclaimed in August 1871. The effort fell apart the following year and Britain considered annexation in order to maintain control of the local situation. The Fijian chiefs agreed to the cession of sovereignty to the Crown on 10 October 1874 and the Crown Colony of Fiji was established. The governor doubled as the High Commissioner for the Western Pacific, an office created in 1877, overseeing other British colonies and territories. He answered to the Colonial Office. The colonial capital was initially at Levuka on Ovalau Island off Viti Levu's east coast, but in 1877 it was moved to Suva on Viti Levu.

The British governor limited Fijian participation in politics and commercial enterprises, although they were allowed a system of indirect local rule based on their traditional political practices and served on the legislative council. The sale of Fijian lands to Europeans was prohibited. The acceptance of Christianity was an agonizingly slow progress, but it eventually took hold and the Fijians gave up the practice of war, cannibalism, and other unsavory social practices. To promote further economic development, the British imported indentured Indian laborers in large numbers to work the sugarcane, the islands' main export. The Colonial Sugar Company developed into a powerful force in the islands. Copra, tropical fruits, rubber, and timber were other important exports. Important too were the islands' livestock: cattle, goats, horses, donkeys, mules, and pigs. The indenture system was terminated in 1920, but the Indians did not receive full rights. This led to serious strikes and protests through the 1920s. A new constitution in 1937 gave Indians equal rights with Europeans and they eventually took over the sugar industry and many service industries. Gold was discovered on northern Viti Levu in 1932. Most of the islands' exports had long gone to New Zealand, but by 1939 over half were sold to Canada. The main shipping routes from the American and Canadian west coasts to Australia and New Zealand passed through Fiji making Suva, Viti Levu an important en route port of call. In November 1941, Pan Am established a station at Suva for its U.S.-to-New Zealand *Clipper* service.

Fiji has a diverse population. In 1940, this included 4,300 Europeans (mainly Australians, New Zealanders, British), 104,900 Fijians, 98,100 Indians, 5,100 half-castes, 2,100 Chinese, 3,100 Rotumans, 1,800 other South Pacific islanders, and 1,400 inhabitants classified as others for a total of 220,800. The official language was English, but Fijian and Hindustani were, and are, widely spoken.

Unlike most South Pacific islands, Fiji possessed modest military installations when the war began. This included airfields, seaplane bases, and minimal storage facilities constructed by New Zealand, virtually all on Viti Levu. New Zealand accepted responsibility for the defense of Fiji shortly after the World War II began and the 18th Army Troops Company arrived on Viti Levu in August 1940. This was followed by the brigade-sized "B" Force in November. "B" Force became the 8th Brigade Group and was the first armed force sent by a self-governing dominion to defend a Crown Colony. The Japanese fleet marshaling at Truk in mid-January 1942 to seize Rabaul were feared to be aimed at Suva, the capital of Fiji. In May 1942, the brigade group was enlarged to the 10,000-man, two-brigade 3d New Zealand Division, which established defense around Nandi Bay on the west side and Suva on the southeast. Between November 1942 and February 1943 the Division staged to New Caledonia. An RNZAF light bomber squadron was also initially based on Viti Levu and the USAAF 70th Pursuit Squadron arrived at the end of January 1941. The 1st Battalion, Fiji Regiment, a unit comprised of Fijians led by New Zealander officers and NCOs, was raised in early 1943 and two more battalions were later organized. It operated under XIV U.S. Corps on Guadalcanal, Kolombangara, Florida, and Bougainville from May 1943 to August 1944. Three small commando units, the Fiji Guerrillas comprised of Fijians and Tonganese, were formed in early 1942. They supported U.S. operations on Guadalcanal, New Georgia, Vella Lavella, and Bougainville until disbanded in May 1944. The Indian population refused to serve in the local armed forces because they were offered lower wages and conditions than Europeans.

On 13 May 1942, the United States agreed to assume responsibility for the defense of Fiji, although this was agreed on in late December 1941. The New Zealand force garrisoning Viti Levu would be free to conduct offensive operations in support of other American forces advancing through the Solomons. The 37th Infantry Division departed the States in late May 1942 and arrived at Suva on 11 June. Its mission was to establish defenses and train for future operations in the Solomons. All U.S. installations in Fiji were on Viti Levu with bases concentrated on opposite ends of the island at Suva and Nandi Bay.

Viti Levu ("Great Fiji") is situated at 18°00′ S 178°00′ E in the west-central portion of the Fiji Islands. The island, the largest in Fiji, is forty miles southwest of the second largest, Vanua Levu. Viti Levu is ninety-one miles long from east to west and 66 miles wide across its center. It covers 4,053 square miles being exceeded only by New Caledonia in the South Pacific. The island is mountainous with some twenty distinct peaks varying from 1,200 to 4,341 feet, the latter being Mount Victoria (now Mount Tomanivi) in the north-central portion and the highest peak in Fiji. Numerous rivers and streams flow out of the mountain emptying into the sea on all sides of the islands. The largest of these is the Rewa River flowing from the northeast portion to the island's southeast end and navigable by boats and small flat-bottom steamers up to 50 miles inland. The island's ancient native capital, Bau, was located in the Rewa River delta and connected to the Rewa by a manmade two-mile-long, sixty-foot-wide canal, truly an engineering marvel considering its origins. Other large rivers are the Navua, Sigatoka, and Ba.

Two groups of scattered small islands lie off the west and northwest coasts, the Mamanutha Group and the larger Yasawa Group, respectively. Ovalau Island (seven by eight miles) lies ten miles off the east coast with the smaller Levuka. Mbenga Island (aka Beqa), measuring eight miles across, is seven miles off the south coast.

The capital of Fiji and the seat of the High Commissioner for the Western Pacific, Sir Harry Luke, was at Suva with a population of 15,000. The majority of Fiji's population resided on Viti Levu. Other important towns included Lautoka, Nausori, Sigatoka, Ba, and Vatoukoula. A road, King's Road on the north side and Queen's Road on the south, circumscribed the island's coast and connected all towns and villages. A narrow-gauge railroad ran from Narawa on the west coast's Nandi Bay to Ellington on the north-central coast. There were no significant communities in the island's interior. A cable station was located at Suva.

The site selected for the main U.S. naval advance base (JAMPUFF) was Nandi Bay on the west coast. This area's sparsely settled coastal plain provided sites for support facilities, airfields, and an excellent, but undeveloped harbor. While open to the west, Nandi Bay's waters were tempered by the inshore reef and the outlying islands of the Mamanutha Group. The New Zealand-built Nandi Airfield was just to the south of Narawa on Nandi Bay. Taken over by the U.S. Navy and Marines, it had two 7,000-foot runways, one of which was an oddity in the South Pacific, concrete. The existing Narawa Airfield (aka Nandali), fifteen miles north of Suva on the Rewa River, had two 5,000-foot runways and was taken over by the U.S. Army. Seabees arrived in June 1942 to begin base improvements and expansion. Facilities were built at Lauaka eleven miles northeast of Narawa. A seaplane base was established at Saweni Beach on Nandi Bay just north of Nandi. A small port was established at Vundi Point on the north side of the bay. Facilities in the Nandi Bay area were collectively designated Fleet Air Base No. 1, Fiji, or FANTAN 1; FPO SF 201.

On the island's southeast coast at Suva the Navy established the smaller Fleet Air Base No. 2, Fiji, or FANTAN 2, FPO SF 130. Suva Harbour is almost three miles across and indented two miles deep inland. Suva and its adjacent towns are on the bay's east side. Protected by coral reef breakwaters, the harbor is entered through the narrow Levu Passage. Nausori Airfield was built ten miles to the northeast of Suva with a 3,600-foot runway. The Royal New Zealand Air Force had established a seaplane base in Lauthala Bay on the east side of Suva. It too was taken over by the U.S. Navy. An extensive Navy Fuel Depot was built there, FPO SF 516. It was there that chartered commercial tankers transferred their cargo to fleet oilers for delivery to the fleet.

By August 1944, the war had moved on and there was little need for the extensive FANTAN facilities. The Army and Navy airfields were abandoned. Only the Lauthala seaplane base remained in operation. On 1 July 1945, the remaining Navy facilities were turned over to the Army. These in turn were soon turned over to New Zealand control after the war.

Fiji received its independence from Great Britain on 10 October 1970. In April 1987 an Indian-dominated and Fijian coalition government was established. A military coup, with the aim of reestablishing Fijian control to protect their rights and traditions, on 14 May led to the declaration of the Sovereign Democratic Republic of the Fiji Islands on 8 October. Civilian rule was restored in May 1992. The Republic rejoined the Commonwealth on 30 September 1997.

SOLOMON ISLANDS

The Solomon Islands is the largest group in the South Pacific and is comprised of more large islands than any other group, although the Bismarck Archipelago contains more land area in its three main islands. The Solomons lie between 150°30' and 170°30' east longitude and 5°10' and 12°45' south latitude on the northeastern periphery of the Solomon Sea (see Map 24). The double chain of 992 islands stretches southeastward from the Bismarck Archipelago over 900 miles. The northwesternmost islands of the Solomons are in the small Shortland Islands group just eight miles from Bougainville in the Bismarcks. Geographically, Bougainville, and small Buka off its northwest end, are part of the Solomons, but they were administratively part of Mandated Territory of New Guinea and are addressed in the Bismarck Archipelago section. The islands furthest to the east are the remote Santa Cruz Islands separated from San Cristobal, the southernmost of the main group of islands, by approximately 230 miles. The Solomons cover an area of some 240,000 square miles. Its six large main islands and 992 smaller islands, atolls, islets, and reefs include a total of 10,938 square miles (18,670 square miles if Bougainville and Buka are included). The Allied code name for the Solomon Islands as a whole was ARTHRITIS and later WARD and SUSAN. The Solomon Islands and all related outlying islands, including Bougainville, are in time zone 23.

The islands run in two parallel chains separated by a twenty-to-forty-mile New Georgia Sound, dubbed "The Slot" by U.S. servicemen. The northeastern chain of islands, from northwest to southeast, includes the main islands of Choiseul, Santa Isabel, Florida, and Malaita. These islands were of little military value lacking suitable airfield sites and natural harbors, although Florida is an exception to the latter. The southwestern chain, edging the northeast side of the Solomon Sea (RIGHTHOOK), includes the main islands and key island groups of the Shortland Islands, Treasury Islands, New Georgia Group with the large islands of Vella Lavella, Kolombangara, New Georgia, Vangunu, and Rendova; the Russell Islands; Guadalcanal; and San Cristobal. Many of these islands and others in the Solomons played key roles in the war. The Solomons, for military purposes, was further divided into the Southern or Lower Solomons (Guadalcanal, Florida) and the Northern or Upper Solomons (New Georgia Group, Choiseul, Bougainville).

Henderson Field on north-central Guadalcanal is 1,905 miles north-northwest of Auckland, New Zealand; some 1,300 miles northeast of Townsville, Australia; 3,035 miles southwest of Pearl Harbor, and 800 miles due east of the southeast end of New Guinea. Prior to America's first offensive into the Solomons, the nearest U.S. bases were at Espíritu Santo 540 miles and Efaté 700 to the southeast, both in the New Hebrides; and New Caledonia 800 miles to the southeast. Bougainville and New Britain, the next Allied objectives after the Solomons were secured, are some 200 and 300 miles, respectively, to the northwest.

The Solomons' climate is characterized by moderate winds year-round. From April to October the southwest tradewinds bring gusting winds and moderate temperatures from the low 70s to the high 80s. From November to March the northwest monsoon brings hotter temperatures, up to 93°F, high humidity, and rain. Up to 200 inches of rain can fall in a year, but the yearly average on Tulagi was 164 inches. While most rain, delivered by the northwest tradewinds, falls in the November-to-March wet season, the southeast trades bring some rain during the "dry season." Since the larger islands are crested with central mountain ranges running their length, the northern coasts are in the rain shadow and hence "drier" than the southern coasts. Typhoons are infrequent being spawned in the Coral Sea to the south, but they usually steer southeast toward New Caledonia and the New Hebrides or down the Australian coast.

Tropical diseases are rampant throughout the Solomons. The fact that Americans, Europeans, and Japanese would contract malaria was a given. Endemic dysentery was

Solomon Islands

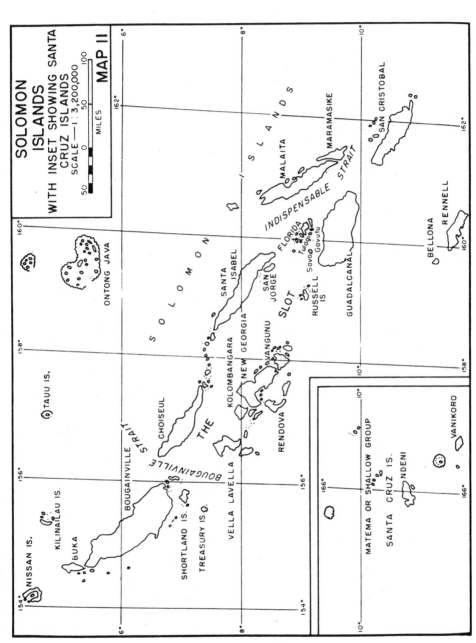

SOLOMON ISLANDS WITH INSET SHOWING SANTA CRUZ ISLANDS
SCALE—1:3,200,000
MAP II

MILES 50 0 50 100

NISSAN IS.
KILINALAU IS.
BUKA
TAUU IS.
ONTONG JAVA
BOUGAINVILLE
BOUGAINVILLE STRAIT
SHORTLAND IS.
TREASURY IS.
CHOISEUL
THE
VELLA LAVELLA
KOLOMBANGARA
NEW GEORGIA
VANGUNU
RENDOVA
SANTA ISABEL
SAN JORGE
SLOT
SOLOMON ISLANDS
FLORIDA
Tulagi
Savo
Govutu
RUSSELL IS.
GUADALCANAL
MALAITA
MARAMASIKE
INDISPENSABLE STRAIT
SAN CRISTOBAL
BELLONA
RENNELL

MATEMA OR SHALLOW GROUP
SANTA CRUZ IS.
NDENI
VANIKORO

another major problem as was dengue fever and fungus infections. Leprosy, yaws, and hookworms were particular problems for the native population.

The islands are volcanic in origin, mountainous, heavily forested, and abundant with water. The larger islands are comprised of igneous and metamorphic rocks overlaid with marine sediments. The many smaller islands around the larger ones are the edges of coral atolls or raised coral reefs. The mountain ranges are intersected by deep, narrow valleys. There is some volcanic activity and occasional earth tremors. Most volcanoes are dormant, but two are still active. The highest peak is Mount Makarakomburu, 7,520 feet, on Guadalcanal. Streams and small rivers flow out of the mountains and hills toward the coasts on most islands. None are navigable. Streams and rivers are of two types. The most common are long, swift, have low banks, and are usually shallow and easily forded in most areas. The less common are short rivers with wide, deep swampy deltas at their mouths. These often have steep, muddy banks. Often silt and coastal sandbars block river mouths making them deeper upstream. Stream and river mouths are usually fordable at low tide. The hills and ridges extend to the coast on most islands, but there are narrow coastal plains in some areas. Land travel parallel to the coast where there are no plains forces one to cross ridges and streams running perpendicular to the coast. The sand beaches are narrow or nonexistent with the jungle growing within a few yards of the sea strand, or, on the northern islands, at the water's edge. Swamps, just inland from the coast and coastal mangrove swamps, might be encountered anywhere.

Dense tropical forests of mahogany, teak, banyan, and acacia hardwood trees and thick underbrush cover most of the islands. Coastal plains are generally covered with kunai grass up to seven feet high. The hill and ridge sides are forested, but tops are often devoid of trees and covered only with shorter kunai grass. Mangrove swamps are scattered along many coastal areas. Coconut palm plantations were planted on the coastal plains of many of the islands. There are no coral barrier reefs and only a few scattered fringing reefs and offshore coral heads. The further north one travels through the Solomons the more densely vegetated, rugged, swampy, and inhospitable one finds the islands. Animal life includes wild pigs, wild dogs, and several species of rats swarmed in the vicinity of settlements. Crocodiles are found in rivers, streams, and mangrove swamps.

The islands on which combat actions were fought are discussed below, but a brief description of the main islands is provided here. Other than possibly lookouts and reconnaissance patrols, these islands were unoccupied by Japanese or U.S. forces.

In the northeastern chain of islands is Santa Isabel, fifty-eight miles northwest of Lunga Point on Guadalcanal's north-central coast where the U.S. Marines landed; it is 135 miles long, making it the longest in the Solomons, and thirty miles wide covering 2,500 square miles. A short chain of small islands runs northwest from the island's end. Small Saint Georges Island lies close to its southeast end. Today Santa Isabel is known as Santa Ysabel (aka Bogotu). Malaita (ECSTASY), fifty-six miles northeast on Lunga Point across the Indispensable Strait (DODGE), is 100 miles long and twenty miles wide. Maramasike Island lies off its east end. Of the islands of the southwestern chain only San Cristobal (EBONY, CHERRY) (also spelled San Cristoval and known today as Makira) was bypassed by the war. This ninety-mile-long, twenty-five-mile-wide island is forty miles to the southeast of Guadalcanal. The Santa Cruz Islands (CYANIDE), approximately 230 miles east of San Cristobal, consists of the main island, Ndeni (APRICOT, BRICABRAC) (misspelled "Ndini" in some contemporary U.S. documents; not to be confused with Ndeni Island north of Malaita), and a number of small scattered islands. Among these was Lord Howe Island, not to be confused with the Lord Howe Islands (aka Ontong Java) 170 miles north of Santa Isabel. The southernmost of the Solomons, 120 miles south of Guadalcanal, is Rennell Island (aka Mangana), fifty miles long, fifteen miles wide.

The Solomons was one of the first major island groups discovered in the South Pacific. In 1568, Alvaro de Mendaña de Neyra, acting on Inca legends, sought the fabled Southern Continent, *Terra Australis*, where it was said the inhabitants wore clothes woven of gold. He saw Ontong Java (Lord Howe Islands) 170 miles to the north of what would be called the Solomons and then found a large island in the northern chain. He named it Ysabel (old Spanish spelling for *Isabel*—Elizabeth) after his wife. This discovery was followed by Florida (from the Spanish *Pascua Florida*, Feast of the Flowers—the Easter season as it was found on Easter Sunday), Guadalcanal ("swampy canal," named after Mendaña's birthplace, a small town in southern Spain's Seville Province), Malaita, and San Cristobal (Spanish for Saint Christopher). Mendaña remained in the islands for half a year believing he had discovered the southern continent's outer islands. Believing too that the islands held gold and as an enticement to colonists from Peru, while ignoring the hostile natives, he optimistically named the island group the Solomon Islands (*Islas de Solomon*) alluding to the legendary King Solomon's mines. Mendaña was unable to raise support to colonize the Solomons until he attempted to return in 1595, but failed to locate them and found only the Santa Cruz Islands to the east. His colony, the first such European attempt in the Pacific, failed after his death. Attempts were made to find the main islands, but it would be almost 200 years before Europeans rediscovered the elusive Solomons. The Royal Navy, suspecting the islands were a myth, removed them from their charts.

The Santa Cruz Islands were rediscovered in 1767 by British Captain Philip Carteret, part of Wallis' expedition, and he subsequently found Malaita. In 1768, French Captain Louis Antoine de Bougainville, during his around the world voyage, passed through what he christened the Bougainville Strait between Choiseul Island and a much larger island later named Bougainville, to the northwest. Choiseul (pronounced "Choy-zil") he named after a minister of France and the larger island he named after himself. In 1788, Lieutenant Shortland of the Royal Navy named a small group of islands off the southeast end of Bougainville after himself. He also named the strait separating Bougainville and Choiseul after himself, but it would be known as the Bougainville Strait in the future. Further to the southeast he found a larger island group he named in honor of his king, New Georgia. At some point Ysabel Island was also named Santa Isabel (Saint Elizabeth—mother of John the Baptist). Both names remained in use, but Santa Isabel was used in U.S. documents while Ysabel was often used by the British.

The Solomons' inhospitable climate, dense jungles, and hostile natives made them less than a desirable possession. The islands remained unoccupied by Europeans other than a few bold missionaries, disappointed prospectors, whalers, and slavers from Australia and Fiji. Since about 1000 B.C. the islands were populated by Melanesians, warlike cannibals and headhunters lacking any form of government other than local tribes with no broader loyalties or common language; seventy-one languages and numerous dialects were spoken—five are now extinct. A Melanesian pidgin was widely spoken, but few spoke English during the war years. Intertribal warfare was vicious and unending. Polynesians populated the Ontang Java Atolls. The French unsuccessfully attempted to establish a mission in 1845. The first English mission was established in 1851, but it was not until after the turn of the century that progress was made in converting the natives and ending their ceaseless warfare.

Missionaries and traders were murdered by the natives as they attempted to establish a foothold in the islands. Nonetheless both nations increased their intrusions and the

British government began to intervene in the islands' disorganized affairs. In 1893, Britain declared the southern islands the British Protectorate of the Solomon Islands: Guadalcanal, Savo, New Georgia Group, Malaita, and San Cristobal. The islands of the Santa Cruz Group were annexed in 1898 and 1899. The German Solomon Islands (*deutschen Salomon Inseln*) Santa Isabel, Choiseul, Ontang Java Atolls, and the small islands in the Bougainville Strait (Shortland and Treasury Islands) were acquired from Germany in 1900 in exchange for Britain's withdrawal from Western Samoa. Germany retained control of Bougainville as part of its territories in New Guinea and the Bismarck Archipelago, a region it had claimed since 1884. In 1905, Leavers Pacific Plantations Ltd. began making large-scale land purchases and vast coconut plantations were cultivated. Other trading firms established themselves and the islands slowly began to prosper.

In 1897, a British resident commissioner's office, answering to the High Commissioner for the Western Pacific, was established on tiny Tulagi Island off of Florida Island's south-central coast. Selected for its healthy environment, it was to become the protectorate's main government center and port of entry. The resident commissioner was assisted by an advisory council. Additional government stations for deputy commissioners were established on Gizo in 1899 in the scattered New Georgia Group, at Faisi in Shortland Islands in 1906, and at Auki on Malaita Island in 1909. District administrative officers were stationed on Guadalcanal, Gizo, Malaita, Santa Cruz, Ysabel (Santa Isabel), Gela (Florida), Shortland, and Eastern Solomon Islands (Ontang Java), the eight districts bearing those names. An armed constabulary of 130 natives and five Chinese led by fifteen British officers were distributed in eight district detachments. Many of them joined the Coastwatching Service or served the Allies as guides after the Japanese invasion.

The Islands Coastwatching Service (Operation FERDINAND), established in 1919, was administered by the Directorate of Intelligence, Royal Australian Navy. It consisted of native-aided Australian, New Zealander, and British civil servants, missionaries, and planters who in wartime were to establish a system of lookouts spanning 2,500 miles from the west end of New Guinea through the Bismarcks, Solomons, and New Hebrides. After the war began they were granted Royal Australian Navy Volunteer Reserve officer commissions. The coastwatchers, hiding out on Japanese-held islands, reported enemy ship movements, aircraft flights, and activities ashore via short-wave radio to the Coastwatcher Headquarters in Townsville, Australia. Hunted by the Japanese and often living on the run, the coastwatchers' intelligence reports, recovery of downed airmen and marooned seamen, and small-scale guerrilla activities were invaluable to the war effort, especially in the Solomons.

A plantation economy developed in the Solomons with the main products being coconuts, copra, ivory nuts, and rubber. The largest coconut plantations were found on Santa Isabel, Gizo, and Guadalcanal. Cattle herds flourished regardless of the harsh climate. Kauri pine was timbered on Santa Cruz. As hoped so long ago by Mendaña, gold was discovered on Guadalcanal prior to the war, but was so difficult to extract that little mining was successfully accomplished. All labor required for these industries was provided by locally contracted Solomon Islanders whose employment was closely supervised by the protectorate government. It was not necessary to import indentured labor as was so often the case on other Pacific islands thus avoiding the many inherent problems. Regardless, the local labor was considered none too reliable. Plantation owners were required to provide for virtually all of the laborers' needs. Nonnatives could not purchase land and all plantation lands were leased by Europeans from native landowners.

Steamer lines provided scheduled service to the Solomons prior to the war and there were regular visits by Japanese trading ships. Smaller steamers, schooners, and other vessels operated by traders provided interisland services. There were no roads, other than a few native tracks, or railroads in the islands, until built by Japanese or U.S. forces. The islands were very poorly mapped with even the river courses and major terrain features seldom correctly plotted on what maps there were. Offshore waters were equally poorly charted.

In 1941, there were approximately 500 Europeans, 200 Chinese, and 97,700 natives in the Solomons. The most populous island was Malaita with 40,000. Except for the small government stations, plantations, and missions, there were no modern facilities. The out-of-the-way islands had only the barest necessities of civilization and lacked a developed infrastructure. Native villages were crude, desolate, and unsanitary. Tulagi Harbour, while providing an excellent anchorage for a large number of ships, had only a few small piers and warehouses with no repair or other support facilities. It was the only harbor of any significance in the Solomons. Admiral Earl Jellicoe, the British commander at the Battle of Jutland, recommended during a post-World War I tour that Tulagi be developed as a naval base.

Nothing significant took place in the Solomons when the war broke out in December 1941. The Japanese secured Rabaul on the north end of New Britain in late January 1942 and immediately began to develop it as a major base. It was from Rabaul that the new *8th Fleet* supporting operations to seize New Guinea and the Solomons, only 600 miles to the south, would be launched. (The importance of Rabaul to Japanese plans to dominate the South Pacific is discussed in the Bismarck Archipelago section.) Though there was little to oppose them, the Japanese moved cautiously southward into the Solomons. Only twenty Australian Imperial Force troops and a Royal Australian Air Force (RAAF) seaplane detachment were based on Tulagi and nearby Gavutu. W. S. Marchant was on-station serving as the resident commissioner. On 22 January, the Japanese bombed Tulagi as they moved on Rabaul. Most Europeans evacuated to other Commonwealth territories, but some administrators remained and continued to operate on a limited basis in the more remote areas. Little else occurred in the Solomons as the Japanese focused on securing the Netherlands East Indies through February and into March. Coastwatchers took up position and began reporting intelligence information while trying to survive their main enemy, the environment.

The Japanese first occupied Buka, Bougainville, and the Shortland Islands on 13 March 1942 and began building several airfields. Their plan was to develop a series of land and seaplane bases that would provide them with covering air support as they advanced through the islands. By securing the Solomons the Japanese would have additional bases to support operations in Eastern New Guinea and their planned push south to New Caledonia, Fiji, and the Samoas to block the Southern Lifeline to Australia. The execution of this plan depended on the successful Japanese effort to destroy the American fleet at Midway in early June. In the meantime they made their first effort to land on New Guinea in early May. This resulted in the 4–8 May Battle of the Coral Sea, Japan's first major defeat of the war. No landings were made on New Guinea. As part of the overall plan Tulagi and Gavutu were heavily bombed on 1 May. With coastwatchers reporting ships approaching, the islanders were evacuated to Port Vila, New Herbrides.

A *Kure 3d SNLF* detachment seized Tulagi and Gavutu landing on 4 May 1942 under Read Admiral SHIMA Kiyohide (he departed 10 May). It was from here that seaplanes were to attack Port Moresby on the southwest coast of New Guinea. The Japanese had no more than occupied Tulagi than the Allies bombed it for the first time while the Battle of the Coral Sea was raging. The Japanese soon established their own coastwatchers on Savo Island and Guadalcanal. The importance of Japanese bases in the southern Solomons did not die with the June Japanese defeat at Midway and the subsequent cancellation of their planned thrust to New Caledonia, Fiji, and the Samoas. The Solomon bases became even more critical as an outguard for the main base at Rabaul as efforts were focused on securing New Guinea. The bases also served to screen their southern flank as they moved westward to New Guinea. In mid-June, the Japanese landed a survey party on the north-central coastal plain of Guadalcanal to lay out an airfield. It was to supplement the seaplane base at Tulagi and construction began immediately on a grassland area behind a coconut plantation southeast of Lunga Point and the mouth of the Lunga River. American patrol planes reported the airfield's construction on 4 July and at the end of the month B-17 bombers from Espíritu Santo struck in an effort to delay its completion.

The first U.S. offensive, Operation WATCHTOWER, was directed on 2 July and scheduled to commence on 1 August with the occupation of the Santa Cruz Islands (Operation HUDDLE) followed by the seizure of Tulagi. This would provide a base for a slow push northward into the southern Solomons as cautiously as the Japanese had moved south. WATCHTOWER was Task No. 1 of a larger operation, CARTWHEEL, with the ultimate goal of seizing and occupying New Britain, New Ireland, and New Guinea and neutralizing the main base at Rabaul. The discovery of the airfield on Guadalcanal forced a change of plans. It would place Japanese bombers within striking range of Espíritu Santo and Efaté in the New Hebrides and Koumac, the northernmost airfield on New Caledonia. On 10 July, a revised order was issued to the 1st Marine Division mounting out of New Zealand to seize Guadalcanal and Tulagi as well as Santa Cruz. The changes made it impossible to execute the invasion by 1 August and a new date of no later than 7 August was issued.

A debate arose during the planning for WATCHTOWER questioning under whose command the operation should be, General MacArthur's Southwest Pacific Area or Admiral Nimitz's South Pacific command. The issue was based on the boundary separating the two commands, 160° E, which cut through Guadalcanal and the Florida Islands. MacArthur's forces were gearing up for operations on New Guinea and his nearest bomber base was almost 1,000 miles away. Nimitz's amphibious forces were uncommitted and sufficient naval forces were available after the Midway victory. Bomber fields and sufficient supporting naval bases were operational in the New Hebrides. The boundary between the two commands was shifted east to 159° E off the west edge of the Russell Islands on 1 August 1942. As the operation advanced into the Northern Solomons, MacArthur's command would take over.

The 1st Marine Division, under Major General Alexander A. Vandegrift, was arriving in Wellington, New Zealand and elements were still at sea when the order for WATCHTOWER was received. Other units assigned to the operation were in American Samoa, Hawaii, and San Diego. One-third of the Division, the 7th Marines, was detached to garrison American Samoa. It was replaced by the 2d Marine Division's 2d Marines, which sailed from San Diego on 1 July. As the forces assembled, ships loaded administratively for the trip to New Zealand. There they had to be unloaded, supplies and equipment reorganized, and reloaded for an amphibious assault. There was no space for many of the Division's vehicles. Supplies and ammunition reserves were scant, so much so that the troops began to refer to the effort as Operation SHOESTRING. Intelligence on the objective area and the enemy were equally sketchy. The Navy estimated up to 5,000 construction and service troops and a 2,100-man infantry regiment in the objective area. Maps of the objective area were completely inadequate. Task Force 62, the South Pacific Amphibious Force under Rear Admiral Richmond K. Turner, sailed on 22 July and rendezvoused with the other elements on 26 July 400 miles south of Fiji. Rehearsals

(Operation DOVETAIL) were conducted at Koro Island, Fiji from 28 to 30 July. Coincidentally, the Division had conducted amphibious training on Solomons Island in Maryland's Chesapeake Bay. America's first offensive task force departed Koro on 31 July heading northwest for the Solomons. The convoy passed northeast of the New Hebrides, from which aircraft screened its passage. Bad weather grounded Japanese patrol planes at Rabaul during the convoy's final approach to Guadalcanal. The Japanese were completely taken by surprise as the Marines executed America's first amphibious assault since 1898 on 7 August 1942.

Guadalcanal Island

Guadalcanal, known simply as "The Canal" or "Guadal" to servicemen, was code-named BEVY. The Japanese called it *Gadarukanaru*. This code name was little used with CACTUS being the accepted code name. CACTUS actually identified the objective area of Operation WATCHTOWER, Guadalcanal-Tulagi. In February 1943 it was redesignated MAINYARD.

Guadalcanal is located in the Southern Solomons' southwestern chain at 10°40' S 160°15' E (see Map 25). Lunga Point (DIAL), the Marine landing site, is situated at 09°25' S 160°05' E on the north-central coast. The New Georgia Group, the next objective after Guadalcanal was secured, is 146 miles to the northwest. The small Russell Islands are some thirty miles off of Guadalcanal's northwest end. The Florida Islands, with the operation's other main objective, Tulagi, are 20 miles across the Sealark Channel from Lunga Point.

Like most of the other large islands of the Solomons, Guadalcanal is comparatively long and narrow, but wider than most, covering 2,500 square miles. From Cape Esperance (Old French for Hope) (FERN) on the northwest end to Marau Bay on the southeast end Guadalcanal is 80 miles long. From Lunga Point on the north-central coast to Cape Hunter on the south the island is thirty-four miles wide. A mountain range runs the length of the island close to the south coast to which it drops steeply. The mountain range tapers out into broken hills on the northwest end. The elevations range from 5,000 to 7,500 feet. Contemporary maps showed Mount Popomanasiu as 8,005 feet, but this was later proven to be lower than the nearby 7,520-foot Mount Makarakomburu twelve miles inland from the south-central coast. Short streams and rivers, fewer than on the north coast, flow rapidly out of the mountains to the south coast. The more numerous and longer rivers and streams on the north coast flow more leisurely across the three-to-ten-mile-wide coastal plains. A dirt track ran along the north coast from Koli Point, eight miles east of Lunga, to Cape Esperance. A few native foot rails connected a small number of inland villages, but most settlements were scattered along the coast. Most of the island's estimated 8,000 to 10,000 natives moved to the south coast after the Japanese arrived and otherwise were little affected by the intense fighting. A small number were impressed by the Japanese for labor. The Japanese did not generally harass the natives, but an American and a French priest and a French and an Italian nun were tortured and murdered during the fighting.

From Point Cruz, a small bulbous peninsula where Mendaña first landed, and the Matankikau River about four miles west of Lunga Point to Cape Esperance some twenty-five miles to the northwest, the river and stream intervals are much closer than in other areas. Ridge fingers perpendicular to the coast rise between the rivers forced troops to traverse rugged cross-compartmented terrain as they advanced. The river bottoms and ridge sides are covered with forests and dense underbrush with the hill and ridge tops

Map 25
Guadalcanal Island, Solomon Islands

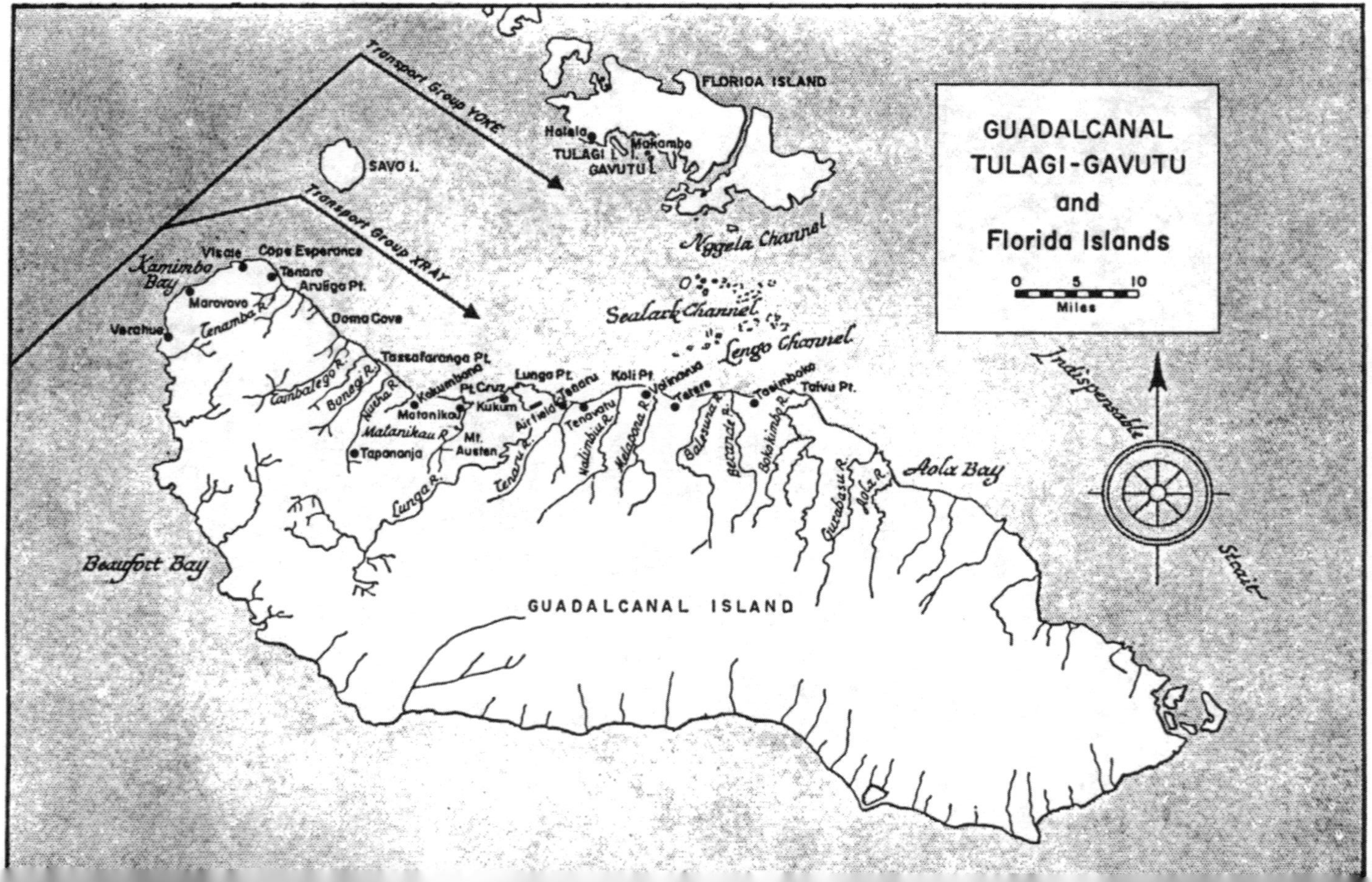

GUADALCANAL
TULAGI-GAVUTU
and
Florida Islands

0   5   10
Miles

open and grass-covered. They served the Japanese as strongpoints seized at a high cost. It was this area that the latter stages of the Guadalcanal campaign were fought north-westward to Cape Esperance.

The Lunga Point area, where the first bitter four months of the campaign were fought, deserves examination. Special effort had been undertaken by the Navy and Marines to collect information on the objective area. Much of this was obtained from planters and civil servants who had lived in the area. While many questions were answered, there were still data gaps and errors in plotting terrain features, some of which led to confusion.

The hard-packed tan sand beaches are flat and ten to twenty yards wide at high tide. The bottom gradient is very gently slopped and shallow, and there were no coral reefs. Beaches on the island's north end are covered with smooth stones and more reefs are encountered. Several slow-flowing rivers ran through the area. The names of two rivers on the east flank of the landing area were mistakenly transposed by a civilian intelligence source on a widely used sketch map. What was shown as the easternmost Ilu River was actually the Tenaru, a long river midway between Lunga and Koli Points. The short Ilu River, on which the initial Marine flank rested, was called the Tenaru, three miles east of Lunga Point. To this day the action fought on the Ilu is known as the Battle of the Tenaru. The correct names are used in this discussion. A backwater branch of the Tenaru stretched to the east. About 1,500 yards to the east of the Tenaru's mouth was the small Tenavatu River. Between the Tenaru and Ilu Rivers is the small Block 4 Creek. Alligator Creek is just to the west of the Ilu River. A wide L-shaped tidal lagoon, Lunga Lagoon, thrusts 800 yards inland on the east side on Lunga Point and a smaller lagoon is to the west of it. The largest river in the area, the Lunga, forms a swampy delta creating Lunga Point. Offshore is the Lunga Roads suitable as an open sea anchorage. On the west side of Lunga Point is the small Kukum Creek. The Marine's initial west flank was anchored on the Matanikau River, five miles west of Lunga Point and less than a mile from Point Cruz. Both the river and point would be scenes of intense combat.

An unimproved two-lane dirt government road followed the coast through the area just inside the palm tree line. One-way, three-ton-load-limit timber bridges crossed Block 4 Creek (2), Alligator Creek, both the Lunga Lagoons, Lunga River, and Kukum Creek. All bridges were captured intact. The Tenaru, Ilu, Lunga, and Matanikai Rivers were crossed by fords and were later bridged by the Marines and Seabees.

Four Levers Brothers coconut plantations were in the area: the Ilu east of the Tenaru River, which faced the main landing beach; Tenaru between the Tenaru and Ilu Rivers; Lunga between the Ilu and Lunga Rivers; and Kurum west of the Lunga River and straddling Kurum Creek. The plantations' thirty- to forty-foot palms were planted at fifteen- to twenty-foot intervals and the grounds devoid of underbrush. The Japanese began construction of their 3,778-foot airfield on a large cattle pasture 3,700 yards south-east of Lunga Point. The southern (inland) property line of the plantations and pasture was defined by five-strand barbed-wire fences, later pulled down and incorporated into Marine defenses.

Beyond the plantations the gently rising land was either wooded or open areas covered with thick four-to-six-foot high kunai grass. Low knolls, hills, and ridges dot the western portion of the area between the Lunga and Matanikai Rivers. Among these is a snaking 2,000-yard long, grass-covered, north-to-south ridge. Approximately 1,000 yards south of the airfield and 700 yards east of the Lunga River, it rose to only some 150 feet. In the middle of September it became known as Edson's Ridge or Bloody Ridge. This area rises toward the highest local promontory, the 1,514-foot Mount Aesten (called Mount Austen by the Americans and misspelled "Oseton" in some Army documents; the native name is Mambulo). This terrain feature, poorly annotated maps, and assumptions led to some confusion on D-Day.

A piece of high ground marked in the old tickmark-style on a sketch map prepared by a former resident was annotated, "Wooded Areas 'L' & 'TREE' Shaped on Grassy Knoll" (see Map 26). Beneath this was a horizontal line below which was marked "Mt AESTEN" with an "X" and "1514." The separating line and "X" indicating Mount Austen appear to have been ignored and it was assumed that the "Grassy Knoll" and Mount Austen were one and the same. The hill, clearly seen from the sea, was thought to be only six miles from the landing beach and was included in the first day's objectives. Mount Austen is actually eight miles distant through thick forests. Neither height could be seen once the Marines were ashore among the trees. Determined to be too far, occupation of either height was canceled. The Grassy Knoll is actually a 450-foot high ridge on the west side of the Lunga River some 3,000 yards southwest of the airfield.

Positioned nine miles northeast of Cape Esperance, and guarding the entrance to what would become Iron Bottom Sound, is Savo Island (LARKSPUR), a corruption of the native name, Sabo. A forested, craggy, 1,700-foot high volcano crater measuring four to five miles across, it has been inactive since 1850. In the crater are areas of boiling mud and ground tempatures of up to 215°F.

Japanese in the objective area consisted of only 430 IJN *11th Air Fleet* ground service personnel, detachments of the *Kure 3d SNLF* and *81st Guard Force*; and 2,570 laborers of the *11th* and *13th Construction Units*, far fewer than estimated. Captain MONZEN Kanae of the *11th Construction Unit* was the senior officer on Guadalcanal.

Florida Island Group

Florida Island was code-named RUNABOUT. Nggela is its native name, but is usually Anglicized as Gila.

The Florida Island Group lies twenty-three miles north-northeast of Guadalcanal across the Slot and is situated at 09°05' S 160°15' E (see Map 27). The Sealark Channel separates Guadalcanal and Florida at the Slot's narrowest point, twenty miles wide. Actually there are three named channels defined by two parallel east-to-west lines of coral heads and reefs with Nggela Channel to the north of Sealark and Lengo Channel to the south; the entire passage is generally called Sealark.

Florida (LANTANA) is actually two islands separated by the few-hundred-feet-wide Utaha Passage, but was refered to as a single island by U.S. forces; the native names, Nggela Sule and Nggela Pile, were never used. Together, the islands are twenty-three miles long and average five miles wide. Florida is ruggedly mountainous with elevations of over 2,000 feet. It is heavily forested to the water's edge. The few beaches are narrow backed by steep hills. A number of small villages were scattered along the coasts with most connected by foot trails. Less than 2 miles off Florida's northwest end across Sandfly Passage is Olevuga Island with Vatilau Island (PALM) 3 miles beyond it. A number of small islands and islets are scattered around these two islands.

Despite its size Florida Island was relatively unimportant to the Guadalcanal campaign. Of greater importance was a cluster of small islands off of Florida's south-central coast. These were the first objectives of Operation WATCHTOWER. Tulagi Island (RINGBOLT, later HIBISCUS and LUNGSAIL) is ¼-mile off of Florida. It is 1-¾ miles long oriented northwest to southeast, ½-mile wide, and some three miles in circumference. The island is a 200-to-330-foot-high, steep-sided coral ridge covered with trees, scattered brush, and

Map 26
Matanikai River-Koli Point, North Coast, Guadalcanal Island

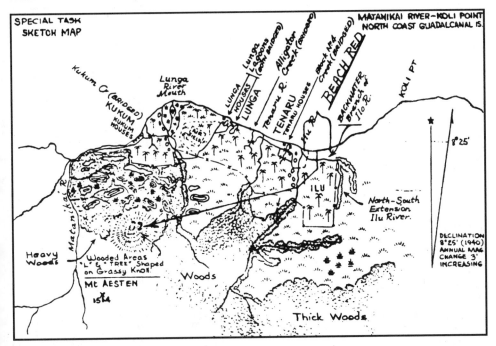

From a Marine Corps sketch map.

landscaped areas around the built-up sites. Hills, knolls, ravines, and caves are scattered over the rugged island. The government residency and facilities were located near and on the southeast end on low ground between Hills 330 and 230. The government wharves were located there on the northeast coast. Residences were scattered over the island. Sesapi, a native village, was located on the northeast coast near the island's northwest end. A small Chinese village was on this same side, just north of the residency. Coral reefs lie on the southwest side of the island with a ¼-mile wide gap on the central coast. This was the landing beach, Beach BLUE. Three islets stretch in a line to the south of Tulagi. The closest is Mbangai only 100 yards offshore, then Kokomtumbu, and Songonangona (nicknamed "Singsong") 1,400 yards from Tulagi. A slightly larger island, Makambo, lies 700 yards to the northeast between Tulagi and Florida—Tulagi Harbour.

Due east 3,000 yards from Tulagi are Gavutu (ACIDITY, later HEMLOCK, nicknamed "U2") and Tanambogo (ALMOND, nicknamed "Bogo") Islands connected by a 300-yard-long concrete causeway, which survived the battle, although the Japanese had removed a thirty-yard section. Palm-covered flat and tiny Gaomi Island (nicknamed "Palm") lies 300 yards east of Tanambogo, the northernmost of the two main islands. Gavutu is about 250 by 500 yards with a 175-foot central peak. This island was the main headquarters for Levers Pacific Plantations Limited. Tanambogo is 250 yards across with a 148-foot-high peak. Both islands are brush-covered with scattered palms, rugged, and honeycombed with caves. Small wharves are located on both islands' northeast and east sides.

Map 27
Florida Island Group, Solomon Islands

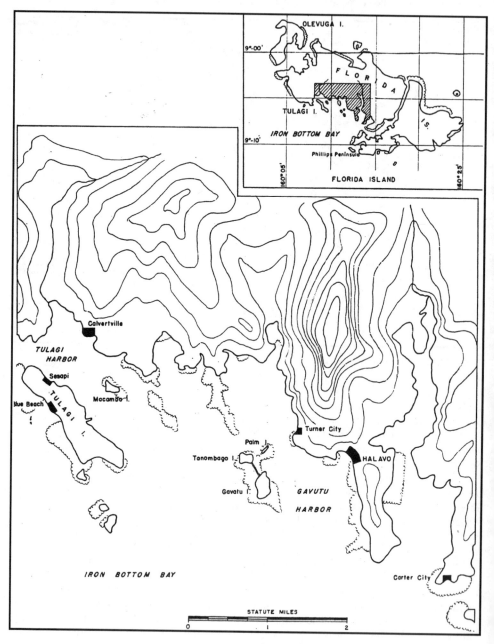

The three islands are surrounded by coral reefs. One mile to the east is Florida's Halavo Peninsula (CLOVER). Gavutu Harbour lies between Gavutu Island and the peninsula.

Tulagi and Gavutu-Tanambogo Islands were defended by detachments of the *Kure 3d SNLF, 14th Construction Unit*, 18 *25th Air Flotilla* float planes (*Yokosuka Air Unit*), and *Tulagi Communication Base*. There were 350 troops on Tulagi under Commander SUZUKI Masaaki, which served as the local Japanese defense headquarters and 550 on Gavutu-Tanambogo with Captain MIYAZAKI Shigetoshi of the air unit the senior officer in command of the Guadalcanal-Tulagi area.

The portion of the Slot bounded by Guadalcanal, Florida, and Savo Islands is known as Iron Bottom Sound, so named because of the one Australian, twenty-one American, and eighteen Japanese ships sunk there in the course of four battles. After Guadalcanal was secured and developed as a major base, American ships entering the Slot from the northwest and after passing Savo Island executed a zigzag turn over Iron Bottom Sound as a show of respect to the ships and crews resting on the bottom.

The Tulagi and Gavutu-Tanambogo landings were executed before the main landings on Guadalcanal by the 1st Marine Division's 3,900-man Northern Landing Force under Brigadier General William H. Rupertus, the assistant division commander. Task Force 62 split into two groups off of the northwest end of Guadalcanal at 0240 hours, 7 August 1942. The three supporting carriers took up position south of Guadalcanal. The Japanese sighted and reported the American ships off of Lunga Point at 0425 hours. The Americans first opened fire at 0614 hours on suspected targets on Guadalcanal with no response. Transport Group YOKE arrived at its debarkation area at 0637 hours south of Florida Island. Aircraft from the USS *Wasp* (CV-7) struck Tulagi destroying the moored float planes. At 0740 hours elements of 2d Battalion, 2d Marines landed on Florida near Haleta Village, west of Tulagi, and on Halavo Peninsula at 0845 hours to secure the flanks of the small island landings. Florida was found to be unoccupied.

The 2d Marines was assigned as the Division Reserve and the Ndeni Landing Force. Much of the regiment was committed to reinforce the Northern Landing Force and was never sent to occupy Ndeni (Operation HUDDLE) in the Santa Cruz Islands. The Navy still desired the occupation of Ndeni as late as November, but the Army did not deem it necessary for the operation's success feeling it would divert troops from the main effort and that the Japanese were unable to secure it. Nor was it needed as a staging base for aircraft flying from bases to the south. A U.S. Navy seaplane tender did eventually base there conducting area patrols, FPO SF 706.

The 1st Raider Battalion landed at 0800, H-Hour on Beach BLUE on the west-central coast of Tulagi with little opposition. The Raiders crossed the island while the 2d Battalion, 5th Marines, landing an hour later, moved to the northwest end. The Raiders then moved toward the southeast end meeting stiff resistance in the afternoon. The well-dug-in enemy was destroyed the next day and the island was declared secure at nightfall on 8 August.

At 1200 hours the 1st Parachute Battalion's landing craft landed under fire on the northeast corner of Gavutu. Resistance was extremely stout as the paratroopers pushed south. At nightfall the enemy still held out on the west-southwest side of the island's hill covered by fire from Tanambogo. Company B, 2d Marines attempted to land on the northeast end of Tanambogo after dark, but was driven off. The 3d Battalion, 2d Marines landed on Gavutu in the late morning on 8 August. Battalion elements assaulted Tanambogo across the causeway and by landing craft in the afternoon. Tanambogo was not secured until nightfall on 9 August. Marines occupied the islets around Tulagi that same day meeting slight resistance and Marine observation posts were established on most of these.

The Japanese lost 200 on Tulagi and almost 500 on Gavutu-Tanambogo. A total of 23 prisoners were taken on the three islands and an estimated 70 escaped to Florida Island. Marine losses on Tulagi were 36 KIA and 54 WIA and on Gavutu-Tanambogo they suffered 108 KIA and MIA, and 140 WIA.

Across the Slot, Transport Group X-RAY arrived in its assigned area at 0645 hours, 7 August, 9,000 yards off of Guadalcanal's Beach RED. The beach was 9,000 yards southeast of Lunga Point and flanked by the Tenavatu and Tenaru Rivers. The airfield was 6,000 yards due east of the beach. A west to east backwater branch of the Tenaru ran parallel with the beach 500 to 700 yards inland to define the beachhead. Naval gunfire softened up the beachhead along with aircraft from the USS *Saratoga* (CV-3).

The sky was mostly clear with a few low, scattered clouds. A moderate southwest breeze caused only very light surf. Subsequent days would be overcast with occasional squalls. H-Hour was set at 0910 hours. The 5th Marines (2d Battalion) landed at 0910 hours without encountering resistance and established a beach defense line. The 1st Marines began landing twenty minutes later and advanced southwest toward Mount Austen. The 1st Battalion, 5th Marines moved west along the beach. By late afternoon the units had moved only a mile and they dug in for the night. Some 10,000 troops were ashore and supplies piled up on Beach RED with insufficient means to move it. To make room for supplies still being landed, the beachhead was extended west to Block 4 Creek. The first Japanese air attacks, aimed at the transports, were launched from Rabaul.

On the morning of the 8th the 1st Battalion, 5th Marines moved west along the beach, passed north of the airfield discovering two abandoned Japanese camps where they engaged stragglers, crossed the Lunga River, and secured the flank on the Kukum Creek. Light resistance was encountered there and two more abandoned camps were found. The 1st Marines, with Mount Austen realized to be too distant and large to defend with the available force, crossed the Tenaru River and moved 5,000 yards to the northwest to seize the airfield and establish defenses on the Lunga. It was at this time realized how far the Japanese support facilities and airfield had progressed. The enemy garrison had fled to the west failing to destroy facilities, equipment, and supplies, which soon proved invaluable to the Marines. Work began immediately on the almost complete airfield and it was operational on 12 August.

In the evening of 8 August the three covering aircraft carriers withdrew having lost almost a quarter of their fighters to persistent Japanese air attacks. Having lost two carriers during the Coral Sea and Midway battles, the American commander desired not to endanger them as Japanese air attacks intensified. With the carrier air cover gone, plans were made to withdraw the transports on the 11th and efforts were made to unload as much supplies as possible. In the early-morning hours of 9 August a Japanese cruiser force slipped pass Savo Island and the American picket ships. The resulting Battle of Savo Island saw the loss of an Australian and three U.S. cruisers plus a cruiser and a destroyer badly damaged. The Japanese suffered only a damaged destroyer, although a retiring cruiser was sunk by a U.S. submarine the following day. Next to Pearl Harbor, it was the worst defeat suffered by the U.S. Navy. The only partly unloaded transports, with air cover withdrawn and fearing another Japanese naval attack, withdrew in the evening of the 9th taking part of the 2d Marines with them. The 16,075 marines and sailors of the 1st Marine Division left in the Guadalcanal-Tulagi area were on their own.

The Marines established beach defenses to prevent an expected Japanese counterlanding and tied into positions turning inland just west of Kukum Creek and along the Ilu

River on the east flank. The inland side of the perimeter was held by scattered units and outposts as it was thought the jungles were too dense for the enemy to penetrate. Japanese air attacks mounted concentrating on the airfield and, when supply ships sneaked through, on them. Japanese warships, dubbed the Tokyo Express, routinely ran down the Slot to shell the airfield at night. Nightly harassing air attacks kept the Marines on edge. Through August and September the Marines manned the perimeter and pushed combat patrols to the west and east. Marine and USAAF fighters arrived on 20 August at what was now christened Henderson Field, named after Major Loften E. Henderson, USMC, a pilot killed during the Battle of Midway. Dubbed the "Cactus Air Force," the one USAAF, twelve Marine, and five Navy squadrons were the core of the Marine defense.

Japanese *17th Army* forces from Rabaul did not land on Guadalcanal until the night of 18 August to begin *Operation KA* intended to eject the Marines. The *Ichiki Force* (originally intended for the Midway landing under Colonel ICHIKI Kiyonao—surname given as Kiyono in many documents) consisted of some 2,000 troops built around the *2d Battalion, 28th Infantry Regiment, 7th Division* reinforced with artillery and engineers. It landed far to the east of the beachhead at Taivu Point. Some 500 troops of the *Yokosuka 5th SNLF* (most were lost when its transport was sunk by Navy scout bombers) and 100 men of the *Kure 3d SNLF* landed to the west. The Japanese believed there were only 3,000 marines on the island. The *Ichiki Force* was destroyed at the mouth of the Tenaru River (actually the Ilu) resulting in about 800 Japanese dead on 21 August.

The Japanese dispatched another 1,500 troops on 19 August. A substantial Japanese carrier, battleship, and cruiser force covered the troop transports. A much smaller American force was operating some 100 miles southeast of Guadalcanal. On 24 August, U.S. and Japanese carrier aircraft discovered each other's task forces. The Battle of the Eastern Solomons, with the opposing fleets engaging each other with only aircraft, ensued resulting in the lost of a Japanese carrier, cruiser, and destroyer. The Japanese convoy pressed on to Guadalcanal, but were turned back by air attacks on the 25th. The American force lost no ships during the battle, but over the next three weeks lost a carrier with two more damaged along with a battleship by submarine attacks. The U.S. forces now had only one carrier in the region, the USS *Hornet* (CV-8). British Colonel O. C. Noel was appointed the new Resident Commissioner of Guadalcanal on 31 August 1943.

The 6,000-man *Kawaguchi Force*, under Major General KAWAGUCHI Ktyotake and built around the *124th Infantry Regiment, 18th Division*, arrived next from the Palau Islands between 27 August and 4 September and absorbed the shattered remnants of the *Ichiki Force*. A consolidated Marine raider and paratrooper force executed an amphibious raid at Tasimboko eight miles east of Lunga Point disrupting the *Kawaguchi Force's* rear echelon. The *Force* engaged the Marines on 12–14 September during the Battle for Edson's Ridge (Bloody Ridge). This small ridge 1,000 yards south of the airfield was the focus of resistance on the south-center perimeter. The Japanese assault against the raider-and-paratrooper-defended ridge, supported by flanking attacks on the ends of the marine perimeter, was an epic battle and destroyed the *Kawaguchi Force*.

The defeated remnants of the *Kawaguchi Force* were not reinforced until October. The 1st Marine Division received its first reinforcements on 18 September when its 7th Marines rejoined it from American Samoa. There were now 23,000 Americans on the island and they were adequately supplied. Late September saw intense fighting as the marines pushed west to the Matanikau River and Point Cruz five miles from Lunga Point. Substantial Japanese forces did not arrive from Rabaul landing at Tassafaronga Point twelve miles west of Lunga Point on 10 and 14 October in the form of the 25,000-man reinforced *2d*, or *Sendai, Division*, under Lieutenant General MARUYAMA Masao, with the *4th, 16th, 29th*, and *230th (-)* (detached from *38th Division*) *Infantry Regiments*, and *4th Artillery* and *10th Mountain Artillery Regiments*. This force, directly under the commander of the *17th Army*, Lieutenant General HYAKUTAKE Seikichi (most official histories list his surname as Harukichi), was defeated on the Matanikau River west of the beachhead and in attacks south of the main perimeter on 22–26 October. Throughout this period and into November U.S. ships delivering reinforcements and supplies withdrew before nightfall prior to the Tokyo Express' forays into the Sealark Channel to shell U.S. positions and cover the landing of reinforcements. Japanese forces fared badly because of poor intelligence and assessment, lack of coordination between units, piecemeal attacks, and difficult terrain.

The Battle of Cape Esperance (originally called the Second Battle of Savo) occurred on the night of 11 October between Savo Island and the north end of Guadalcanal. Each side lost only a destroyer and the Japanese a cruiser forcing them to retire. Two Japanese destroyers were sunk by aircraft the next day. The first U.S. Army unit arrived on 13 October in the form of the American Division's 164th Infantry Regiment. The next night two Japanese battleships inflicted heavy damage on Henderson Field and these attacks continued for two more nights augmented by day air attacks and long-range artillery fire from west of the Matanikau River. The Battle of Henderson Field put the airfield out of action for several days. The 4,600-foot Fighter Field No. 1, Sailer Field, named after Major Joseph Sailer lost at Guadalcanal, was built less than a ¼ of a mile to the east of Henderson. Fighter Fields No. 2 and 3, named Carney No. 1 and 2 after Captain James V. Carney lost at Guadalcanal, were constructed parallel to each other in October and December just over ¼ mile west of Henderson and south of Kukum. On 16 October, U.S. carrier aircraft attacked Japanese supply bases on Santa Isabel.

In late October the U.S. Navy assembled a task force to execute a counteroffensive intended to meet a renewed Japanese effort to eject the marines from Guadalcanal. While the battle raged ashore the American task force engaged the supporting Japanese fleet north of Santa Cruz on 26 October. The fleets engaged each other by air attacks only. The outnumbered Americans lost a carrier and a destroyer. Their other carrier, a battleship, and a number of other ships were damaged. The Japanese lost no ships, but three carriers and two destroyers were damaged plus they suffered significant aircraft losses. The Japanese withdrew to Rabaul, not because of a defeat at sea, but because of the *17th Army's* defeat ashore.

The *228th Infantry Regiment, 38th Division* landed on northwest Guadalcanal between 28 October and 8 November to join up with other *17th Army* forces. The 182d Infantry Regiment, Americal Division arrived from New Caledonia on 11–12 November.

Early November saw much activity ashore. On 1 November Army and Marine units began a push west across the Matanikau River toward Kokumbona. By the 4th they had wiped out a Japanese pocket at Point Cruz and dug in while a new threat from the east was dealt with. Elements of the *230th Infantry* were landed at Tetere Village (PACKARD), 10 miles east of the Lunga Perimeter, on 2/3 November and detected by a Marine battalion sent east for such an eventuality. Army and Marine units moved cross-country and executed landings on the Japanese flanks at the mouth of the Gavaga Creek. This action was called Koli Point (PLUM, UVIS), eight miles east of Lunga Point, although most fighting took place a couple of miles further east. This threat was wiped out by 9 November. In the meantime the separate 147th Infantry arrived from Togatabu, accompanied by the Marine's 2d Raider Battalion, landing unopposed on 4–5 November at Aola Bay thirty-one miles east of Henderson Field. There an attempt was made to construct an airfield, which proved impossible. The 2d Raider Battalion conducted its famous "Long Patrol" jumping off from Aloa Bay on 6 November. It harassed the Japanese and closed on the Henderson Field perimeter on 4 December. The 147th Infantry moved twenty-two miles west to Koli Point completing the move on 3 December where an airfield was built at Volinauna.

The push west to Kokumbona resumed on 10 November with Marine and Army units advancing into the coastal hills where they met stiff resistance. When intelligence was received that the Japanese were again mounting a major reinforcement effort, the offensive was halted and the units disengaged and withdrew into the Lunga Perimeter. From 13 to 15 November the Naval Battle of Guadalcanal (originally called the Third and Fourth Battles of Savo or Battle of the Solomons) took place off Guadalcanal's northeast coast around Savo Island with separate engagements on two nights. Japanese task forces attempted to land the remainder of the *38th Division*, under Lieutenant General SANO Tadayoshi, the *229th Infantry*, and the rest of the *230th Infantry*, and *38th Mountain Artillery Regiments*, and again bombard Henderson Field. The battle resulted in the Japanese loosing two battleships, a cruiser, three destroyers, and all eleven transports plus three cruisers and six destroyers damaged. U.S. losses were two cruisers and eight destroyers and a number of ships damaged. The engagement on the night of 14/15 November was to be the first gun action for the new U.S. 16-inch gun-armed fast battleships, the USS *Washington* (BB-56) and *South Dakota* (BB-57). The Japanese withdrew, but four transports managed to beach themselves at Tassafaronga within sight of Lunga Point and land 4,000 troops, but 6,000 had gone down in the other transports. This was the last major Japanese attempt to reinforce Guadalcanal. The *17th Army* was essentially cut off from its rear bases.

On 18 November the advance west again resumed and by the 23d the high ground on the west side of the Matanikau was secured. The last naval action in Iron Bottom Sound, the Battle of Tassafaronga (originally called the Fourth, Fith, and Sixth Battles of Savo or Battle of Lunga Point) took place on 30 November. The Japanese attempted to land supplies for their hard-pressed troops that night. The Japanese destroyers were intercepted by an American cruiser force, which scattered the destroyers, one of which sank and one was damaged, but a U.S. cruiser was lost and three damaged. The Imperial Navy was now incapable of mounting a substantial challenge to U.S. naval forces in the area.

The Americal Division Headquarters and its 132d Infantry arrived on 8 December to assume command of U.S. forces in the Lunga Perimeter, not much larger than it had been in September. At the same time the 1st Marine Division Headquarters and its 5th Marines departed. The Americal commander, Major General Alexander M. Patch, was designated Commanding General, Guadalcanal (known unofficially as "CACTUS Corps"). On 2 January 1943, this command was redesignated XIV Corps. The Japanese were now concentrated west of the Perimeter near Kokumbona and to the south on the north slopes of Mount Austen. On 17 December 1942, Americal Division units moved to secure Mount Austen, which dominated the Lunga Perimeter. Two artillery-supported Japanese regiments were dug in on the slopes in the Gifu strongpoint (named after a prefecture on Honshu, Japan). After twenty-two days of brutal combat the Gifu remained in Japanese hands. On the day the Mount Austen offensive began the 35th Infantry arrived followed by its 25th Infantry Division Headquarters on 23 December, under Major General J. Lawton Collins. At this time there were almost 40,000 U.S. troops on this island and only 25,000 Japanese, but the Americans were exhausted and waited for reinforcements to arrive.

On 1 January, the 27th Infantry arrived with the 161st Infantry following on the 4th.

On the same date the Advance Echelon, Headquarters, 2d Marine Division landed with its 6th Marines. The 2d Marine Division was under Brigadier General Alphonse de Carre, the assistant division commander. Its commanding general remained in New Zealand as he outranked Major General Patch. With 10,000 additional troops on Guadalcanal, a new offensive was planned for 10 January to seize the Gifu and another fortified hill mass on the Matanikau and inland from Point Cruz, the Galloping Horse, so named because of its shape. It was defended by two regiments of the *38th Division* and was seized by the 25th Infantry Division on 13 January. A smaller strongpoint to the south, the Sea Horse, was seized on the 11th. On the 13th the 2d Marine Division continued the attack westward along the coast into the defenses of the *2d Division*. The Gifu was not taken until 23 January. The 2d Marine and Americal Divisions pushing west along the coast were exhausted. The units in better shape were consolidated in the Combined Army-Marine (CAM) Division under Marine Brigadier General de Carre. The CAM Division attacked along the coast while the 25th Infantry Division moved west over the inland hills pushing off on 22 January. By the 25th Kokumbona, the area's main Japanese base, was taken and the Poha River crossed ten miles west of Lunga Point. An extensive logistical road network was built to support the westward operations.

In the first week of February the U.S. forces expected a major Japanese effort to land up to a division and send in a fleet to take on the American task forces in the area. American units were prepared to defend in anticipation of a landing, but continued to pursue the Japanese remnants withdrawing to Cape Esperance on the island's northwest end. On 1 February a reinforced Army battalion landed at Verahue Village on the northwest end of Guadalcanal to prevent Japanese reinforcement from that quadrant. American forces pressed on against light resistance securing Tassafaronga Point on 3 February. On the 9th the two forces linked up at Tenara Village just south of Cape Esperance. Only a few Japanese stragglers were found. While the Army units edged toward Cape Esperance opposed by rear guards, the Japanese managed to evacuate 13,000 troops to the Shortlands. *KE Operation*, ordered at the beginning of January, was accomplished on the nights of 1/2, 4/5, and 7/8 February by destroyers. The U.S. Navy was able to sink only three of these destroyers while damaging four. America's first offensive action was over inflicting the first defeat suffered by the Japanese at the hands of a foreign force since 1598.

The U.S. Army and Marine Corps ashore lost approximately 1,600 KIA (over 1,000 were Marines), almost 500 MIA, and over 4,200 WIA. Some 19,200 IJA and IJN troops ashore died in combat or of disease or starvation and about 1,000 were taken prisoner (mostly laborers). The Allies lost twenty-four warships and the Japanese sixty-five to include a significant number of transports and cargo ships. Japanese aircraft losses were close to 1,000 while the United States lost only a quarter of that.

Once secure Guadalcanal immediately began development as a major base (FPO SF 145) to support the drive into the northern Solomons, even though it was originally planned not to build a significant base there. The Japanese had built a pier at Kukum and this was pressed into use by the Navy. Piers were built at Lunga Point and at other sites along the beachhead. Point Cruz was developed as a port after the island was secured. A road system was begun during the fighting to supply the frontline troops as well as connect the airfields, camps, and port facilities. This was expanded after the island was secured and numerous Army and Marine camps were built. Commander, Aircraft, Solomons (ComAirSol) was established on 15 February 1943 to control all services' aircraft based in the area. A major Marine staging base was built at Tassafaronga

Point, the former main Japanese landing site. The base was largely shut down by May 1945. Naval Air Base, Guadalcanal remained operational until 12 June 1946.

Tulagi Island and its adjacent islands became the Navy's main small-craft base since it was secure from ground action on Guadalcanal. PT boat bases were built at Sesapi Village on Tulagi (FPO SF 152), on nearby Macambo, and on Gavutu (FPO SF 705). Tulagi and its attendant islands were unmolested during the fighting on Guadalcanal, but in February the Japanese executed their first air raid on the islands with several more to follow as the action moved into the Northern Solomons. A major attack in April, as part of *I Operation*, an effort to delay the American buildup in the Solomons and Papua areas, resulted in the loss of a U.S. destroyer and fleet oiler and a New Zealand corvette near Tulagi. Other attacks took place in May. Base facilities were built at Calvertville across Tulagi Harbour on Florida Island. Havavo Seaplane Base (CLOVER) was constructed at the base of the Halavo Peninsula. Landing craft repair bases were built at Carter City and Turner City on Florida. Advanced Naval Base, Tulagi and Naval Air Station, Guadalcanal facilites began to be dismantled in early 1945, but the bases were not completely closed until 12 June 1946.

After the war the Solomons soon returned to a rustic, out-of-the-way plantation colony. Rather than rebuild its colonial headquarters on Tulagi, the British established a new community on the site of the American depot at Point Cruz and named it Honiara (derived from its native name, *Nahoniara*—facing the tradewinds). The Point Cruz peninsula was reshaped and dredged into a wharf and seaport complex. In 1975, the British Solomon Islands Protectorate was renamed simply the Solomon Islands. In January 1976, the islands became self-governing and on 7 July 1978 was granted independence. The Solomons' capital is Honiara. Honiara International Airport was built on the site of Henderson Field. Little was done after the war to preserve artifacts and many deteriorated. A small collection of surviving relics are displayed outdoors at the Vilu War Museum and Cemetery on the northwest coast between Cape Esperance and Tassafaronga. The Honiara Botanical Garden is located in the valley and on the ridge where the November 1942 Battle for the Matanikau River was fought. The Solomons today remain largely a subsistence agriculture economy supplemented by fishing, forestry, and tourism. Its mineral resources have yet to be fully developed.

Russell Islands

The Russell Islands consist of two main islands, Pavuvu and Banika, and a number of scattered outlying islets (see Map 28). Many official documents refer to the small group simply as Russell Island (singular). It was infrequently known as Cape Marsh. The group was code-named CLEANSLATE and later EMERITUS, FILBERT, and JUMP.

The Russells are some thirty-five miles off of Guadalcanal's northwest end at 09°06' S 159°11' E. Approximately fifty miles northeast across the Slot is Santa Isabel Island and about 125 miles to the northwest is New Georgia.

Banika Island. Banika is the smaller of the two main islands and the easternmost. Irregularly shaped, it is roughly seven miles long from northeast to southwest and three miles wide. A flat peninsula projects from the northeast end and a smaller one from the southwest end, which encloses Wernham Cove. Long, narrow Renard Sound deeply penetrates the island's northeast coast. Smaller Tillotson Cove indents the northwest coast on Sunlight Channel. This is a ½-mile-wide, seven-mile-long channel separating the two main islands. The channel and coves provide excellent deep water anchorages. Banika's

Map 28
Russell Islands, Solomon Islands

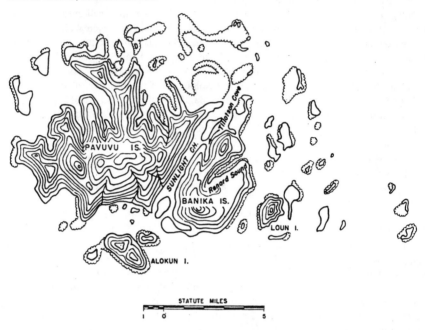

west side and south end have gently sloping hills, the highest elevation being 400 feet on the south end. The northeast portion of the island is relatively flat allowing airfields to be constructed.

Pavuvu Island. The larger Pavuvu measures some eight miles across east to west and nine miles north to south. Its much indented coast is especially pocketed with coves and inlets along the north side. Tidal swamps are found in many of these northern inlets. A large peninsula, Pepesala Point, juts from the north-central coast. About midway up the peninsula is an indented elbow enclosing Paddy Bay on the northeast side. The island is steep and hilly with an elevation of approximately 500 feet in the center.

Numerous islets are scattered around the main islands with most on the north and east sides. The three largest of these are flat Baisen Island off of the north side of Pepesala Point, twin-hilled Alokun Island protecting the southwest entrance to Sunlight Channel, and hilly Loun Island (aka Lona) off of the southeast side of Banika.

The flat coastal edges of both islands are covered with dense coconut palms devoid of underbrush. The large Leavers-owned Yandina Plantation, established in the 1920s, is based on Pavuvu. The islands' hilly interior is covered by dense jungle and underbrush. The soil is well drained and there is a coral subsoil providing stability. The climate is similar to Guadalcanal's, but the islands are free of malaria, an oddity in the Solomons. Fresh water is in limited supply. Much of the northern coasts of both islands are fringed by coral reefs as is the east coast of Banika. Numerous offshore reefs are also found off of the north and east coasts.

The Russells were administered as part of the British Solomon Islands Protectorate from Guadalcanal. They were named after Lord John Russell, Prime Minister of Britain from 1846 to 1852. The native population was small being largely employed by the plantations. The islands remained bypassed by the war until late January 1943 when some 300 IJN personnel established a barge-staging base on Baisen Island to support the evacuation of Guadalcanal. A coastwatcher reported their departure on 11 February when the evacuation was completed.

Admiral William F. Halsey issued a directive for the occupation of the Russells two days before Guadalcanal was declared secure, both to prevent the enemy from reoccupying it and to employ it as a supporting base for the coming New Georgia operation. The assembly of the Russells Occupation Force for Operation CLEANSLATE was rushed in the event the Japanese moved to reoccupy it after loosing Guadalcanal. The 43d Infantry Division (-) under Major General John H. Hester, which had arrived at Guadalcanal on 16 February from New Caledonia, provided the core of the landing force backed by Marines. Only destroyers and large landing craft were marshaled at Guadalcanal to move the landing force in an effort to prevent the Japanese from detecting the assembly of larger transports and assessing the objective. The amphibious force departed Koli Point, Guadalcanal on the night of 20 February. Extensive reconnaissance of the Russells had begun on 17 February to verify the absence of the Japanese. The scouts selected landing beaches, dumps, camps, and gun positions. They would meet the landing force and guide them to the selected positions.

Approaching from the east the amphibious force divided and landed on three beaches at 0600 hours, 21 February. The 43d Infantry Division Headquarters, 103d Infantry (-), and Marine defense battalion elements landed on Beach YELLOW in Wernham Cove on Banika's southwest coast. A battalion of the 103d Infantry landed on Beaches BLUE 1 and 2 on the south and north shoulders of the entrance to Renard Sound on Banika's northeast coast. The Marine 3d Raider Battalion landed on Beach RED on the east side of Pavuvu's Pepesala Point at Paddy Bay. They cleared the peninsula and then Baisen Island, the former Japanese barge-staging base. The islands were declared secured at 1200 hours and the landing force was established by nightfall well prepared to resist a Japanese counterlanding. The 169th Infantry landed the next morning at Beaches YELLOW and RED and before long some 9,000 troops were ashore.

The base developed quietly with the entire 43d Infantry Division assembled there by mid-March. The Japanese discovered that the Russells were occupied and conducted their first air attack on 6 March with irregular air raids lasting though July 1943 while the New Georgia operation was underway. Airfield No. 1 was immediately begun on the southeast portion of Banika, but the 3,100-foot runway was not ready until May. The 4,500-foot Airfield No. 2 was built nearby and No. 1 was extended to 6,000 feet. Landing craft bases were constructed at Beaches BLUE and YELLOW. An advanced base construction depot and other support facilities were built on Banika adjacent to the Sunlight Channel. Abundant coral and local timber were used in the construction projects.

Naval Advanced Base, Russell Islands (FPO SF 60) played a key role in supporting the June to October 1943 New Georgia operation. The 43d Infantry Division departed in mid-June for New Georgia (APO SF 709–2). The Army Air Force used the two airfields as an intermediate staging base for attacks on New Georgia and air patrols to protect the bases on Guadalcanal. Landing craft, landing ships, and patrol craft used it as a way station and repair base while en route to New Georgia. The base continued to support later operations in the Northern Solomons and the Bismarcks.

Pavuvu was employed as a rest and retraining base for the 1st Marine Division from

April to July 1944 and November 1944 to May 1945. The untended plantation's rotting coconuts and vegetation, rats and land crabs, mud, humidity, and crude facilities made it immensely unpopular. It was selected, however, to avoid stationing the division on Guadalcanal where the troops would have been overutilized for work details and security at the massive developing base complex.

In early 1945 dismantling began, even though the base was a staging area for the Okinawa assault. Most of the facilities were dismantled by the summer of 1945, but the base was not officially closed until 12 June 1946.

After the war the Russells reverted to a Levers-owned coconut plantation and has remained largely undeveloped as part of the Solomon Islands. There is currently much controversy over the extensive logging undertaken on the islands. Its principal town is Yandina on Pavuvu.

New Georgia Group

The scattered New Georgia Group is located in the Solomon's southwestern chain of islands and is situated at 08°15' S 157°30' E. Guadalcanal is 180 miles to the southeast and Bougainville is 110 miles to the northwest. The code name APERIENT was generally applied to both the New Georgia Group and the main island of New Georgia. It was later designated CELERY. In the following text the phrase "New Georgia Group" refers to the group of islands while "New Georgia" refers to the main, central island.

Eleven main islands comprise the New Georgia Group (see Map 29), many of which played an important role in the battle for New Georgia. There are scores of smaller islands and islets spread throughout the group. The New Georgia Group stretches from east to west approximately 150 miles and about forty miles across with the Slot bordering the north side and the Solomon Sea the south. For the most part the islands are hilly, rugged, and covered with dense jungle and underbrush. Slow moving, mangrove-lined rivers flow out of the hills into the sea on the larger islands. The climate is warmer and more humid than Guadalcanal's. It rained steadily for the first eleven days of the operation turning trails into a quagmire. Malaria and other tropical diseases are just as much a problem as on the former island.

Centrally located New Georgia Island is the largest island in the group and the sixth largest in the Solomons. It measures approximately forty-five miles northwest to southeast and forms two lobes, the western being about thirty-five miles across southwest (Munda Point) to northeast (Visuvisu Point) and the eastern 20 miles across. They are linked by a six-mile-wide central isthmus. Grassi Lagoon, fringed by long, narrow islets linked by submerged coral reefs, borders the north coast. Roviana Lagoon on the south-central coast possesses a similar barrier separating the island from Blanche Channel (COCONUT). Landing beaches are few with the dense jungle fringing almost the entire low cliff-faced coast. Roads were nonexistent, but numerous native trails linked the villages. The main means of travel between villages was by boat and canoe. Munda Point, on the southwest coast, is one of the most difficult areas to approach because of the reefs and shoals to the south—Munda Bar. An islet, Baanga Island, blocks the western approach through the narrow, twisting Hathorn Strait from the north. This strait separates New Georgia and Arundel Islands. Only small craft can pass through Hathorn Strait's south end, the 224–432-foot-wide Diamond Narrows. The west end of New Georgia is separated from Kolombangara Island by Kula Bay north of the Hathorn Strait. On this shore are found three jungle-lined, deep-water anchorages formed by river inlets. From north to south

Map 29
New Georgia Group, Solomon Islands

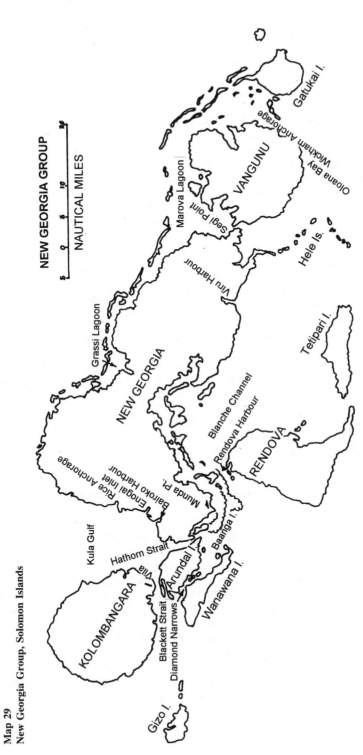

NEW GEORGIA GROUP

NAUTICAL MILES

5 0 5 10 20

KOLOMBANGARA

Gizo I.

Kula Gulf

Hathorn Strait

Villa

Blackett Strait

Diamond Narrows

Arundal I.

Wanawana I.

Baanga I.

Rice Anchorage

Enogai Inlet

Bairoko Harbour

Munda Pt.

NEW GEORGIA

Grassi Lagoon

Marova Lagoon

Segi Point

Viru Harbour

VANGUNU

Gatukai I.

Oloana Bay

Wickham Anchorage

Hele Is.

Tetipari I.

Blanche Channel

Rendova Harbour

RENDOVA

these were Rice Anchorage (Wharton River), Enogai Inlet (BLACKBERRY, PYRITES) (Enogai River), and Bairoko Harbour. On the southeast end of the island were two more, Segi Point (BLACKBOY) and Viru Harbour (CATSMEAT). All of these would play important roles in the coming battle.

Immediately off the southeast end of New Georgia, and separated by Njal Passage, is Vangunu Island. Roughly circular, eighteen to twenty miles across, its northern half is indented by numerous inlets. The better anchorages are Wickham Anchorage (ARMCHAIR) on the east coast and Oloana Cove on the southeast. The island's north coast and the cleft separating it from New Georgia is the ninety-three-mile-long Marovo Lagoon, the world's largest island-enclosed lagoon. The lagoon is edged with long, narrow islets off the north and northeast coast. Five miles off the east side of Vangunu is Gatukai Island. The six-miles-across island is separated from Vangunu by Kola Lagoon.

South of New Georgia five miles across the Blanche Channel are Rendova (DOWSER, later GLOW, WALNUT, PLATTSBURG) and Tetipari (aka Montgomery) Islands. Rendova is a rough rectangle measuring ten by twenty miles with a peninsula jutting off the southeast corner. Rendova Harbour on the northwest side, a small partly enclosed lagoon entry to which is gained through Renard Entrance between Bau and Kokorana Islands, is the best natural harbor in the group. Dominating Rendova's northeast end is a 3,448-foot twin peak. A lower mountain covers the southwest end. Off the end of the peninsula is Tatipari, about thirteen miles long and four miles wide.

Arundel Island, six by ten miles, is just offshore to the southwest of New Georgia separated by the Hathorn Strait. Kolombangara is to the north separated by Blackett Strait. Wanawana (sometimes shown as two words) lies off the southwest coast of Arundel. Off the northwest side of Arundel, separated by Blacket Strait, is large, circular Kolombangara Island (PLUMLINE, TUCKAHOE) (also spelled Kol*u*mbangara). The eighteen-mile diameter island is the peak of a massive extinct volcano jutting 5,450 feet out of the sea.

The first Australian settlement was the Lambeti coconut plantation, established at Munda Point at the turn of the century. Coconuts were just about the islands' only export. The native population was scattered about the island, but most were centered around Roviana Lagoon on the central-southwest coast. The New Georgia Group district was administered from Gizo Island (aka Ghizo)[1], like Tulagi, selected for its healthy environment. Regardless, the islands were very undeveloped and little was known of the interior.

The Japanese first reconnoitered New Georgia in October 1942 in search of airfields south of Rabaul to support the defense of Guadalcanal. A landing force of two IJA rifle companies and two antiaircraft battalions arrived at Munda Point on the southwest end of New Georgia Island on 13 November. Patrols moved to Rendova, Vangunu, Kolombangara, and other islands informing the natives that they were now under authority of the Empire. IJN construction troops landed on the 21st and work was begun on an airfield. Reported by coastwatchers, the Allies photographed the site, but initially found no evidence of construction. This was to change in the coming weeks when construction was detected, but well camouflaged.[2] Bombing raids followed, but the 4,700-foot airstrip was completed by 17 December. At about that time the Japanese began construction on an airfield at Vila on the south end of Kolombangara. No Japanese air units were based at Munda, but it was used as a refueling way station to support attacks on Guadalcanal-Tulagi and later the Russells. American attacks were relentless, but the Japanese kept the airfield operational in hopes of using it as a staging base for the reconquest of the Southern Solomons. The Allies planned to use it as a stepping stone to isolate Rabaul and move into the Northern Solomons. At that time it was decided that New Georgia would be the next major Allied objective.

Between February and May 1943 the Japanese reinforced the *New Georgia Sector* with a joint IJN and IJA force with both services contributing equal strengths. The *8th Combined Special Naval Landing Force (CSNLF)*, under the command of Rear Admiral OTA Minoru (commanded the Midway Landing Force transports in May 1942) consisted of the *Kure 6th* and *Yokosuka 7th SNLFs*. The *Yokosuka 7th SNLF* arrived on 23 February with almost 2,000 men to garrison Kolombangara. The *Kure 6th SNLF* established defenses with over 2,000 troops on New Georgia on 9 March around Munda and at Bairoko Harbour and Enogai Inlet on the west coast north of Munda. A battalion of the *51st Division* also garrisoned Kolombangara in February. It was relieved by a battalion of the *6th Division* in late April and the *229th Infantry Regiment, 38th Division* reinforced the Munda defenses. The Japanese expected the Allies to first attack Kolombangara and then land north on Munda on New Georgia's west coast and attack the airfield to the south. On Kolombangara the Japanese concentrated at Vila (PHARMACY), the largest town on the southeast coast, and built an airfield there. On 31 May, the joint forces were placed under the commander of the *38th Division*, Major General SASAKI Noboru as the *Southeast Detachment* and headquartered at Vila. It was administratively under the *17th Army* at Rabaul and under the operational control of the *8th Fleet*. This joint command arrangement was carried to the lowest levels with even small IJA and *SNLF* elements jointly defending remote landing sites. The IJA and IJN units on New Georgia and Kolombangara were reinforced with artillery, antiaircraft, and engineer units with joint detachments sent to Viru Harbour and Wickham Anchorage on the southeast end of New Georgia and to Rendova Harbour on the north end of Rendova and Kaeruka and Vura Villages on the southeast coast of Vangunu Island. Before the end of the Guadalcanal campaign the IJN established a seaplane base, defended by the *7th Combined Special Naval Landing Force* and an IJA battalion (3,100 troops), at Rekata Bay (SCROUNGER) on the north coast of Santa Isabel near its northwest end. This served as a patrol plane base to keep the Slot and Guadalcanal under surveillance until it was evacuated in late September 1943 before the fall of Vella Lavella.

The Allies set the preliminary invasion date for mid-April 1943, but the need to construct additional supporting airfields on the Russells, Woodlark, and Kiriwina (see New Guinea) and to marshal additional ground, air, and naval forces delayed it until late June. To fill the many intelligence shortfalls scouting of the Munda area began in late February and continued until Operation ELKTON was executed. Several coastwatchers operated in the New Georgia Group conducting the usual activities, aiding the many scouts probing the islands, plus small-scale guerrilla operations to harass the Japanese. The invasion took place with the Allies possessing much more intelligence on the area than they had had on Guadalcanal, but the severe terrain, especially the lack of beaches, offshore reefs, and dense, trackless jungles, restricted the landing force in other ways.

Reconnaissance showed that a direct assault on Munda Point (JACONET) was impractical because of Munda Bar (HUDSON) and the restricted channels leading to the objective. The final phased plan saw the early securing of anchorages on New Georgia's east end, seizing Vangunu and Rendova Islands, a supporting airfield constructed at Segi Point, a buildup of troops on New Georgia near the objective, and an all-out overland assault on Munda Point.

The six miles of chaotic terrain between Zanana Beach and Munda Point is cross-compartmented by streams, 200–300-foot ridges, valleys, ravines, rocky knolls and out-croppings, and dense tangled jungle. While basically cross-compartmented perpendicular to the sea, the terrain was patternless with ridges and draws running in all directions. From the air the densely forested terrain has a distinct washboard pattern. Land navigation was extremely difficult. The meandering Munda Trail following a twisting, muddy path between the point and Zanana Beach was of little aid.

Supply stocks were built up on Guadalcanal and the Russells and ground, air, and sea units assembled. Final plans were approved in early June 1943. The core of the New Georgia Occupation Force was the 43d Infantry Division under Major General John H. Hester reinforced by Marine units assembling on Guadalcanal. The first phase of the operation was to begin on 30 June, D-Day, when lodgments were to be secured by the Eastern Landing Force at Segi Point and Viru Harbour on the southeast end of New Georgia and Wickham Anchorage on the southeast side of Vangunu. An emergency airfield would be built at Segi to support the later main landing. The other inlets would serve as landing-craft staging sites. At the same time the Western Landing Force would land on the north end of Rendova to establish supporting artillery positions and concentrate the Munda assault force and supplies. These troops would assault the Zanana Beach as the Southern Landing Group on/or about D+4 and move west to take Munda Point. The Northern Landing Group would land near Rice Anchorage on the west of end New Georgia on/or about D+6 and move south to attack Japanese positions in the Dragons Peninsula north of Munda.

The operation was scheduled to commence with an Army battalion securing Segi Point and Lambeti Village. On 17 June, information was received that part of a Japanese battalion was moving toward Segi Point from Viru Harbour to subjugate the natives. Fearing that Segi Point would be occupied resulting in the loss of the essential airfield site, half of the Marine 4th Raider Battalion was sent immediately to seize and hold Segi until Army troops could be sent. The raiders landed at 0550 hours, 21 June and were met by coastwatchers. The Japanese were at nearby Lambeti. The raiders paddled rubber boats to Regi Plantation on 27 June, and moved overland to seize Viru Harbor on 1 July. There they forced the surviving Japanese to withdraw. On 30 June the Viru Occupation Force, a reinforced Army company, arrived off of Viru, twelve miles west of Segi Point, to await the raiders' capture of Viru. Because of the delay the company was landed at Segi Point and it followed the raiders overland to relieve them at Viru on 4 July. Work on the Segi Airfield began on 30 June and it was operational on 11 July. On the day work started the Japanese began air attacks on the field.

The remainder of the Eastern Landing Force departed from the Russells on 29 June as planned to land at Oleana Bay on the southeast side of Vangunu at 0630 hours, 30 June. The Army battalion and half of the Marine 4th Raider Battalion moved north two miles to Kaeruka and Vura Villages. The small Japanese force was virtually wiped out after four days of fighting with light U.S. casualties.

The Western Landing Force departed Guadalcanal on 29 June where it had laid over after sailing up from Efaté and headed for Rendova (see Map 30). Loaded with 6,000 troops of the 43d Infantry Division, it ran up the Blanche Channel from the southeast passing to the north of Tetipari and hoving to off of the north end of Rendova. Before sunrise on 30 June two rifle companies landed unopposed on little Sasavele and Baraulu Islands flanking Onaiavisi Entrance to New Georgia's Rovoana Lagoon. It was through this narrow twisting passage that the main landing group would make its run to Zanana Beach. The Rendova landing force, the 172d Infantry Regiment, first secured two tiny islands, Bau (ASTER) and Kokorana Islands edging Rendova Harbour (YONKERS) and guarding the Renard Entrance (WATERTOWN) on the northwest coast of the island. The main body landed unopposed on the East and West Beaches of Rendova Harbour at 0700 hours and the entire force was soon landed. The small Japanese force was mostly destroyed by the end of the day. Supply and troops buildup and artillery positioning on Rendova were hampered by rain and seemingly bottomless mud. Japanese air attacks soon followed inflicting moderate damage followed by a night shelling by destroyers causing no damage. Otherwise, the Japanese were unable to oppose the landings.

On the afternoon of 2 July the 1st Battalion, 172d Infantry departed Rendova for the eight-mile move to Zanana Beach passing through Onaiavisi Entrance and established a perimeter without meeting opposition. The 43d Infantry Division headquarters was set up. The rest of the 172d and 169th Infantry were completely assembled in the beachhead by 6 July. Artillery on Rendova could provide fire support from the beachhead to Munda Point. Preparations were made to advance westward toward the main objective.

In the meantime the 1st Raider Battalion and two Army infantry battalions, the Northern Landing Group, landed at Rice Anchorage on the northwest end of New Georgia sixteen miles northeast of Munda. This group departed Guadalcanal on 4 July running up the Slot and rounding the northwest end of New Georgia to land unopposed at 0200 hours, 5 July although a Japanese battery at Enogai Inlet to the southwest shelled the transports. Cruisers and destroyers shelled Japanese positions at Vila and Bairoko Harbour to cover the landing. This force moved southeast six miles to the Dragons Peninsula to secure the flanking Enogai Inlet and Bairoko Harbour on 5 July. By 11 July the peninsula was cleared. A roadblock was established on the trail to Munda on 8 July and held until the 17th to block Japanese reinforcements from the south and the enemy on the Dragons Peninsula from fleeing south. U.S. casualties were light, but the Japanese lost some 500 men. The Marines refer to this action as Dragons Peninsula and the Army as Bairoko Harbor.

Between 4 and 8 July the 172d and 169th Infantry moved west to the Barike River to launch a coordinated attack toward Munda, but the Japanese were alerted and disrupted the movement. The attack was finally launched on the 9th and immediately ran into heavy enemy resistance and terrain difficulties. By 13 July the regiments had covered less than 2,000 yards. The next day another battalion was landed at Laiana Beach (BRAIR) to the east of Munda Point to reinforce the attack. Munda was defended by the *229th Infantry Regiment (−)* reinforced by artillery. In mid-July the *13th Infantry Regiment* arrived.

A U.S. task group of three cruisers and four destroyers was running southeast down the Slot on the afternoon of 5 July after shelling of Vila and Bairoko in the early morning. The group received word that a Japanese force was heading in their direction. The group reversed course and steamed back northwest. On the night of 6 July the group engaged ten Japanese destroyers loaded with troops bound for Vila off the northeast coast of Kolombangara. Preparing to land their troops, they were detected by the 1st Commando, Fiji Guerrillas. The 27th Infantry, 25th Infantry Division arrived on 2 August. Munda Point was finally secured after taking the dominating Bibilo Hill at 1410 hours, 4 August and reconstruction of the airfield began immediately. Surviving Japanese forces withdrew to the north. The 27th and 161st Infantry Regiments spent most of the rest of the month clearing the western portion of New Georgia north on Munda and linking up with forces at Bairoko Harbour by 24 August.

The 169th Infantry assaulted Baanga Island to the west of Munda on 13 August, was reinforced by the 172d Infantry, and secured the island on the 20th. On 27 August, the 172d Infantry landed on Arundel Island's southwest end to the northwest of Munda. The 27th Infantry was committed on 5 September and the island was secured on 21 September. Most of the defending *13th Infantry Regiment* was evacuated to Kolombangara on

Map 30
Western New Georgia and Rendova Islands, New Georgia Group

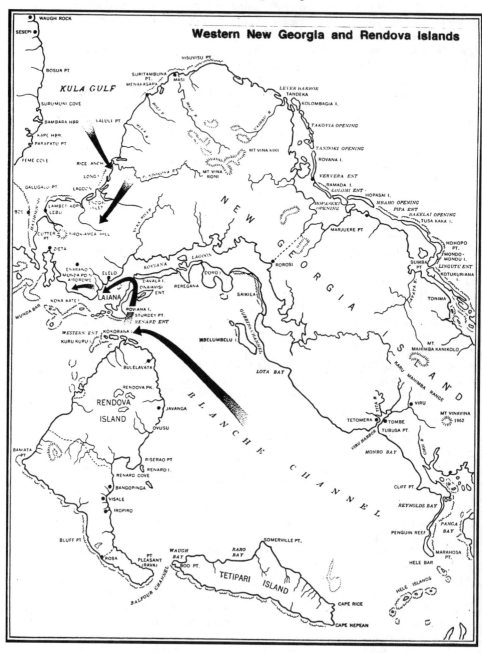

20 September. That strongly defended island was bypassed and the next Allied target was Vella Lavella to the northwest. In early October the Japanese began evacuating troops from Kolombangara losing several ships in the process. On 6 October the 27th Infantry landed unopposed on the island and occupied Vila on the 10th. The Vila Airfield (FLATBUSH) was used by U.S. forces (FPO SF 627).

The original occupation plan called for 15,000 U.S. troops to defeat 9,000 Japanese and for Munda Point to be secured in ten days. Over 50,000 U.S. combat and support troops were eventually committed and it took thirty-five days of hard fighting. U.S. losses were 1,100 KIA and almost 4,000 WIA. The Japanese lost approximately 2,500 dead.

The Munda Airfield (08°0' S 157°15' E) was soon extended to 6,000 feet and then 8,000 feet in December and redesignated BINGHAMPTON. It was to serve an important role in supporting operations on Bougainville and later into the Bismarcks. Landing craft bases were established at Segi Point (FPO SF 252), Viru Harbour (FPO SF 254), Munda Point (FPO SF 250), Wickham Anchorage (APO SF 253), Sasavele Island, New Georgia (FPO SF 529), and Bau Island, Rendova (FPO SF 251). Another airfield, 4,500 feet long, was built on Ondonga Island six miles north-northwest of Munda. A PT boat base was built on Bau Island (08°50' S 157°3' E) off the north end of Rendova in October 1943. This became the area's main naval base. Advanced Naval Base, New Georgia was closed in January 1945 and the other facilities on New Georgia were closed in March 1945.

New Georgia today is sparsely inhabited and remains underdeveloped. Logging, limited agriculture, and fishing support its economy. The airfield at Segi Point, today known as Seghe, is the second busiest in the Solomons next to Honiara (former Henderson Field). The island group is part of the Solomon Islands' Western Province and administered from Gizo, the old colonial district office.

Vella Lavella Island

Vella Lavella (also spelled Vella LaVella) is also known by its native name, Mbilua. It was known to servicemen simply as Vella and was code-named ASH and later as DOGEARED.

Vella is approximately forty miles northwest of Munda Point, New Georgia and fourteen miles northwest of Kolombangara Island separated by the Vella Gulf. It is situated at 07°55' S 156°42' E.

The hilly, forested island is twenty-six miles long northwest to southeast and twelve miles wide across the center. It is volcanic in origin with some raised coral with a maximum elevation of 2,651 feet. Small rivers and streams flowed from the hills into the sea. The southern portion of the island was well drained and suitable for airfield construction. Prior to the war the island was completely undeveloped and lacked roads, although a native trail followed the coast. The main settlement, Barakoma (ARTICHOKE), was near the island's southeast end. Most of the coast is fringed with a narrow coral reef with wider reefs and a lagoon on the northwest side and a barrier reef on the northeast. Some five miles to the southwest is Ganongga Island twenty miles long north to south and six miles wide. Baga Island, four miles across, is three miles off of Vella's west side. The island was part of the British Protectorate of the Solomon Islands' Gizo District.

On 12 July 1943, it was decided that once Munda Point was secured, and considering the 10,000 Japanese troops then dug in on Kolombangara, it would be bypassed and undefended Vella would be the next target in the Northern Solomons. Information on the island was extremely limited and a reconnaissance was conducted in late July. Landing beaches were selected as was an airfield site. It was discovered there was no garrison, only 250 marooned Japanese sailors in scattered groups. On 13 August an advance party landed to mark the beaches and collect prisoners. The Northern Landing Force, under Brigadier General Robert B. McClure, Assistant Commander, 25th Infantry Division, was assembled on Guadalcanal and the Russells built around the 35th Infantry Regiment with substantial Army and Marine reinforcing units. The 6,600 troops departed aboard Task Group 31, a part of Task Force 31, the Northern Force, for Vella on 14 August.

The first echelon landed unopposed at 0624 hours, 15 August, D-Day, on the south side of the Barakoma River near the island's southeast end (see Map 31). The second wave was attacked by Japanese aircraft. The air attacks increased through the operation with over 100 air attacks launched on Vella, but U.S. casualties were light. The Japanese considered a counterlanding, but transports were unavailable to ship the required two brigades. Instead they established a barge staging base at Horaniu Village on Kokolope Bay on Vella's northeast corner on 18 August and a small outpost on Ganongga. They also sent a reinforced battalion to defend Gizo as an outer defend for Kolombangara. The Horaniu barge staging base was defended by two rifle companies and a *SNLF* platoon, some 400 troops augmented by collected stragglers. The American buildup continued at a slow pace. It was not until 28 August that a U.S. battalion moved north along the coast toward Horaniu, but it was not secured until 14 September. The Japanese withdrew to Warambari Bay on the northwest end of the island. Work had begun immediately on the fighter field at Barakoma and the 4,000-foot strip was operational by 27 September (FPO SF 338). Aircraft from this field and Munda battered at the southern defenses of Kolombangara along with artillery firing from northeast New Georgia and Arundel.

On the 18th Major General H. E. Barrowclough, General Officer Commanding, 3d New Zealand Division assumed command of operations on Vella. The division's 14th Brigade Group, departing from Guadalcanal, landed on the northeast and northwest coasts of Vella on 25 September, L-Day, and leapfrogged up both coasts toward Warambari Bay and the Japanese. On the same date 900 Marines of I Marine Amphibious Corps landed on the east-central coast at the mouths of the Juno and Ruravai Rivers. This base force was designated Corps Forward Staging Area, Vella Lavella and had deployed from Guadalcanal to establish a base to support future operations on Bougainville. Air attacks on this base force resulted in almost as many casualties as suffered by the Army. The New Zealanders closed in on the Japanese on the island's northeast end, but almost 600 were evacuated on the night of 6/7 October. Of the ten Japanese destroyers and twelve destroyer-transports, only one destroyer was lost during the brief Battle of Vella Lavella northwest of the island while the United States lost a destroyer and two were damaged. The Vella Lavella operation was not costly for either side. The United States lost 58 KIA and 166 WIA, the New Zealanders 32 KIA and 32 WIA, and the Japanese about 250 dead.

Vella Lavella was not the only Japanese evacuation during that period. In mid-August it was directed that the central Solomons were to hold out while Bougainville was reinforced. The New Georgia area and adjacent islands were to be evacuated at the end of September or early October. The senior Japanese commander of their forces in the central Solomons, Major General SASAKI Noboru on Kolombangara, was not then told of this decision and he continued to fight. After Munda fell, the evacuation of all remaining Japanese forces in the central Solomons was ordered on 15 September. The battalion on Gizo, the remaining troops on Arundel, and the seaplane base at Rekata Bay, Santa Isabel were evacuated around 21 September. Most of the 12,000 IJA and IJN personnel on Kolombangara were evacuated to Choiseul and Bougainville on the nights of 28/29 Sep-

Map 31
Vella Lavella Island, Solomon Islands

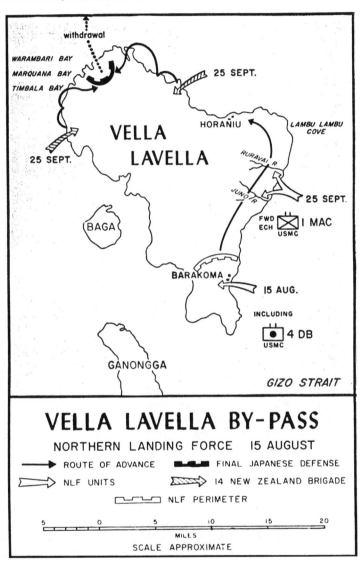

WARAMBARI BAY
MARQUANA BAY
TIMBALA BAY

withdrawal

25 SEPT.

25 SEPT.

VELLA

LAVELLA

HORANIU

LAMBU LAMBU COVE

RURAVAI R

JUNO R

25 SEPT.

FWD ECH | I MAC
USMC

BAGA

BARAKOMA

15 AUG.

INCLUDING

4 DB
USMC

GANONGGA

GIZO STRAIT

VELLA LAVELLA BY-PASS

NORTHERN LANDING FORCE   15 AUGUST

ROUTE OF ADVANCE   FINAL JAPANESE DEFENSE

NLF UNITS   14 NEW ZEALAND BRIGADE

NLF PERIMETER

5   0   5   10   15   20
MILES
SCALE APPROXIMATE

tember and 1/2 and 2/3 October even though there were high losses inflicted by U.S. destroyers and PT boats on the barges and small craft involved in the operation.

All of the central Solomons was now in Allied hands. The next target in the tightening ring around Rabaul was Bougainville. A string of troop staging bases, supply depots, naval bases, and airfields were developing on Guadalcanal, the Russells, New Georgia, and Vella Lavella.

A small Naval Advance Base, Vella Lavella was established at Barakoma on 8 October taking over from the Marine Corps Forward Staging Base, but the Marines still used it as a staging base. A PT boat base operated temporarily from Lambu Lambu Cove on the northeast coast of the island between September and December 1943. The naval base and airfield supported the Treasury Islands operation in October and the Bougainville operation from November 1943 to June 1944. Airfield operations ceased on 15 June 1944 and the naval base was closed in September.

Like New Georgia, Vella Lavella remains today a part of the Solomon Islands' Western Province and is largely undeveloped. Timber, subsistence agriculture, and fishing are the main economic activities.

Treasury Islands

The small group known as the Treasury Islands, code-named GOODTIME, is located 28 miles off the south end of Bougainville in the Northern Solomons. The Shortland Islands, clustered off Bougainville's south end, are eighteen miles to the northeast and Vella Lavella, the northernmost island of the New Georgia Group, lies sixty miles to the southeast. The group, often referred to as Treasury Island (singular), is situated at 07°20' S 155°35' E.

The group consists of only two islands of significance (see Map 32). Roughly oval Mono Island measures 6-½ miles east to west and four miles north to south. It is dominated by three volcanically formed peaks 1,053 feet high. The island is rugged and covered by dense mahogany and banyan forests. Streams flow from the central hill mass into the sea on all coasts providing good drainage; there were very few swamps. The shore is level with few fringing coral reefs. Only four small villages dotted the coast with Falamae on a south coast promontory being the main village. The only suitable landing beaches were at these villages. To the south of Mono, separated by the ½-mile-wide Blanche Harbour, is Stirling Island. Stirling is four miles long east to west and 300 yards to one mile wide. The harbor is dotted with a few palm-covered islets, the largest being Watson (aka Treasury), Wilson (RASPBERRY), and Savo (not to be confused with Savo in the Slot). The lightly forested, coral island is low and basically flat making it ideal for an airfield site. Coupled with the deep protected anchorage of Blanche Harbour, the Treasury Islands would make an ideal supporting base for the coming Bougainville operation. It was only seventy-five miles from Cape Torokina, the main landing site on Bougainville. Stirling was well drained and already had a simple road system to support the coconut plantation. A brackish pond, Soala Lake, is situated on the east portion of the island.

The islands were part of the British Protectorate of the Solomon Islands' Shortland District administered from Faisi Island beside Shortland Island. They were sparsely populated by extremely friendly natives who habitually gave sanctuary to downed airmen. The Japanese occupied Mono with 213 IJA troops armed with mortars and a light artillery piece at Falamae. They maintained a radio station and several lookout posts plus an outpost on Stirling, although intelligence indicated it was unoccupied. The initial reconnaissance was conducted in early August and in late September the 8th Brigade Group, 3d New Zealand Division was ordered to prepare for the mission, Operation GOODTIME. Besides providing a supporting base for the Bougainville operation, the securing of the islands was to serve as a diversion coupled with the Choiseul raid executed at the same time.

Brigadier R. A. Row commanding the brigade group was to head a combined force

Map 32
Treasury Islands, Solomon Islands

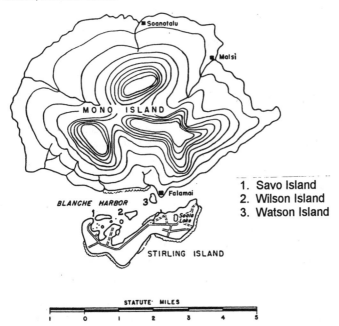

1. Savo Island
2. Wilson Island
3. Watson Island

STATUTE· MILES

augmented by U.S. Army antiaircraft units, Navy Seabees and base elements, and small Marine communications and air liaison detachments (5,700 New Zealanders, 2,000 U.S. troops). The initial landing force was 3,795 men. The GOODTIME Force conducted a practice landing on Florida Island and departed Guadalcanal and the Russells between 23 and 26 October 1943.

The Task Force 31's (III Amphibious Force) Southern Force (Task Unit 31.1) arrived at the eastern entrance of Blanche Harbour at dawn on 27 October, D-Day, with heavy rain and overcast, a condition that would last through the occupation phase. A Japanese patrol plane detected the force as it approached the islands, but still the Japanese were completely surprised. Divided into the Northern (Mono) and Southern (Stirling) Landing Forces, the landing craft entered the harbor with uncoordinated fire support provided by destroyers, landing craft, infantry gunboats (LCI[G], their first use), and air cover. The destroyers were required to remain outside the harbor because of the lack of maneuver room. Automatic weapons fire was received from Falamai Village on Moro and Stirling Island. Two battalions of New Zealanders landed east of the mouth of the Saveke River on Beaches ORANGE 1 and 2 less than ½ mile west of Falamai at 0626 hours. The Japanese were dug in at the river mouth and the village. Another battalion landed on Stirling's north-central coast on Beaches PURPLE 1 and 2 without opposition at the same time. On Mono the beachhead soon came under artillery and mortar fire as the two battalions cleared the high ground around Falamai and established a perimeter for the night. Air attacks began in the afternoon. Much of the Japanese garrison was destroyed in the first day and Allied casualties were very light. A third landing took place on Beach

EMERALD at Soanotalu Village on Mono's north-central coast at the same time as the main landings. This was conducted by Loganforce, a New Zealand rifle company escorting a U.S. Navy air warning radar unit. Landing without opposition the radar was soon operational to provide warning of air raids from Bougainville and further north. It was later used to keep the air space over southern Bougainville under surveillance during the landings there.

Most of the surviving Japanese fled into the hills and headed for the north coast hoping to be rescued. The Japanese had 25,000 troops and substantial landing craft on Shortland and at Buin on the south end of Bougainville, just twenty-two miles northeast of Mono, but they made no effort at a counterlanding. On the 28th a New Zealand company moved cross-country to secure Malsi Village on the east coast. Japanese stragglers soon began harassing the radar site on the north coast. On 31 October Malsi was secured. On 1 November the New Zealanders, after the follow-on echelons had arrived, began sweeps of the Mono's rugged interior to hunt down the stragglers. On the same date an estimated eighty Japanese struck Soanotalu in an effort to capture landing craft and flee. A smaller attack took place the next night. The attacks were beat back and the survivors hunted down. The island sweep was completed on 5 November and on the 12th it was declared secure with 305 Japanese KIA and eight prisoners taken. Allied losses ashore were forty New Zealander KIA and 145 WIA, twelve U.S. KIA and twenty-nine WIA. Air raids ceased after the main landing on Bougainville on 1 November.

Work on supply dumps, a PT boat base, and the fighter field on Stirling began immediately after the landing. The 5,600-foot runway was ready in late November and extended to 7,000 feet in December to accept bombers. Docking facilities were built and Naval Advance Base, Treasury Islands (FPO SF 811) supported the Northern Solomons and Bismarcks campaigns into 1944. By late 1944 much of the base had been dismantled and it was disestablished in March 1945, although maintenance elements remained until June. Today the Treasury Islands are part of the Solomon Islands' Choiseul Province and are largely undeveloped.

Choiseul Island

Choiseul Island, pronounced "Choy-zil," was code-named BLISSFUL. Its native name is Lauru. It is the northernmost of the central Solomons located approximately sixty miles north of Munda Point, New Georgia and thirty miles east of Bougainville. It is situated at 07°10' S 156°95' E in the northeastern string of islands.

Choiseul is approximately twenty miles long northwest to southeast and twenty miles at its widest (see Map 33). While not as mountainous as Bougainville, rocky ridges and spurs run from its central volcanic mountain range to the coast, often to the water's edge, making cross-country movement along the coast difficult over the cross-compartmented terrain. The highest elevation is Mount Maitanbe at 3,300 feet. Native tracks were few. The entire island is forested by dense jungles, often with vegetation growing to the water's edge. The shoreline is varied with few useful beaches. What beaches there are may be wide and sandy or narrow and rocky. Low cliffs front much of the coast. Rivers and streams flow out of the mountains into the sea. The higher elevations lie closer to the southwest coast than the northeast and thus the latter coastline is crossed by more streams and rivers. Swamps often edge the rivers near their mouths. Fringing coral reefs edge much of the coast with some barrier reefs along the northeast coast. Coral reefs run from the island's southeast end with a scattered twenty-mile long chain of islets and small islands, the largest being Rob Roy (Vealaviru) and Wagina (Veghena). In Choiseul Bay on the main island's northwest end are a half-dozen islets.

The undeveloped island was part of the British Protectorate of the Solomon Islands' Shortland District administered from Faisi Island. Most villages were along the northeast coast with few on the opposite side. The native population was only less than 5,000 with little European presence other than missionaries. The natives remained loyal to Australia and assisted the few coastwatchers on the island. Choiseul played a relatively minor role in the war. The Japanese used it only for supply dumps, troop transient camps, and barge staging bases to supply operations in the central Solomons and then to support their evacuation to Bougainville. No airfields were built by either side.

Choiseul was initially considered as a main target for the move into the Northern Solomons. It was envisioned that a staging base, airfields, and a PT boat base would be established there to support operations on Bougainville. This plan was canceled in September 1943 when the decision was made to focus operations on Bougainville. As with all other islands in the Solomons, intelligence was scanty. Three reconnaissance patrols were sent to the island in September and early October 1943. Choiseul Bay on the northwest end was considered the best site for airfields and a naval base. The patrols and coastwatchers reported that the Japanese operated barge staging bases at Choiseul Bay and Kakasa on the central-southwest coast. Almost 1,000 service troops and 2,000–3,000 troops in transit from New Georgia were located at Kakasa on the island's central-southwest side, 300 at Sangigai Village twenty miles southeast of Choiseul Bay, and a couple of hundred at Choiseul Bay. The Japanese were considered edgy and on high alert. In mid-October it was decided to land a small force on Choiseul to create a division for the 1 November Bougainville landing.

The 2d Battalion, 1st Marine Parachute Regiment on Vella Lavella was alerted for Operation BLISSFUL. The 725-man battalion, supported by 100 native porters, was landed by destroyer-transports at 0030, 28 October, which withdrew leaving four landing craft for local waterborne mobility. The landing took place at Voza Village on the southwest coast near the island's northwest end. The weather was extremely hot and humid during the operation with occasional rain squalls. Japanese aircraft discovered and attacked the landing force, but the dense jungle protected the paratroopers from further air attack even though the Japanese made a major effort to locate them. The battalion moved southeast along the coast to Sangigai Village and destroyed a barge staging-replenishment base. A company, which had remained at Voza, moved by landing craft on 1 November toward the island's northwest end and attacked enemy installations. It was withdrawn by two landing craft, one of which foundered and was rescued by PT-59 (commanded by Lieutenant [jg] John F. Kennedy) and returned to Voza on 3 November. Other small overland and waterborne patrols were launched from Voza completely misleading the enemy as to the force's true size as it operated over a twenty-five-mile-wide front. The Japanese made several attempts to locate the Marines resulting in minor engagements before the diversionary force was withdrawn at 0130, 5 November. Over 140 Japanese were killed and an undetermined number wounded in Marine raids. The Marines lost nine KIA, five MIA, and twelve WIA.

The diversion had little effect on the Japanese. They had expected an attack on Choiseul, albeit, a larger operation, and it was executed too close in timing to the Bougainville landing for it to have any impact on Japanese troop dispositions on the main target island. It was readily apparent to the Japanese that the Bougainville landing was in fact the Allies' main effort. The Japanese largely evacuated Choiseul after the start of the Bougainville campaign and the island played no further role in the war.

Map 33
Northwestern Choiseul Island, Solomon Islands

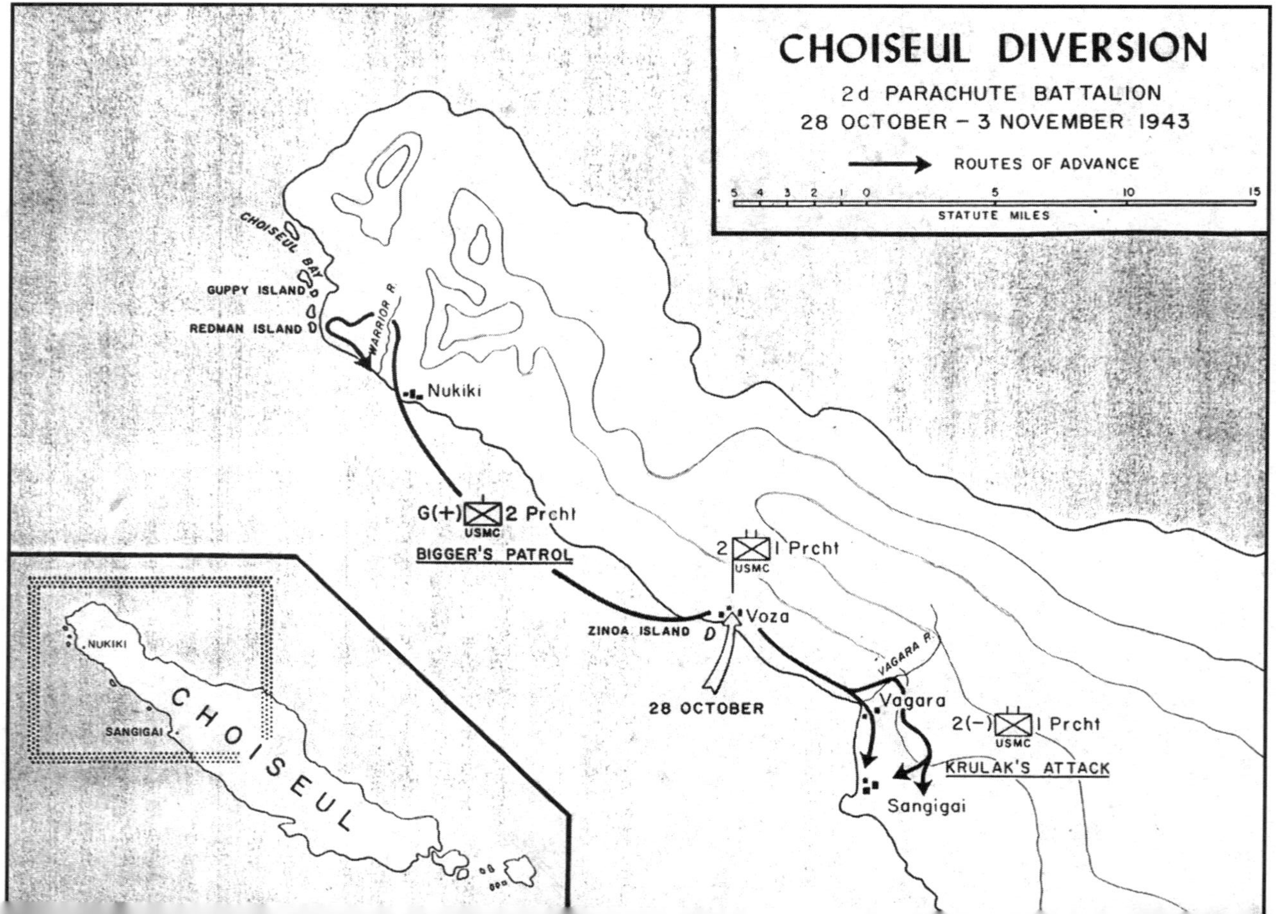
CHOISEUL DIVERSION
2d PARACHUTE BATTALION
28 OCTOBER – 3 NOVEMBER 1943
ROUTES OF ADVANCE
5 4 3 2 1 0 5 10 15
STATUTE MILES
CHOISEUL BAY
GUPPY ISLAND
REDMAN ISLAND
WARRIOR R.
Nukiki
G(+) 2 Prcht
USMC
BIGGER'S PATROL
2 1 Prcht
USMC
ZINOA ISLAND
Voza
28 OCTOBER
VAGARA R.
Vagara
2(–) 1 Prcht
USMC
KRULAK'S ATTACK
Sangigai
NUKIKI
SANGIGAI
CHOISEUL

Choiseul was part of the Solomon Islands' Western Province until 1992 when it was given separate provincial status bearing its name. It is still undeveloped and little of its interior has been explored. Coconut plantations are now found at Choiseul Bay. Timber, subsistence agriculture, and fishing are the island's main economic activities.

Bougainville Island, Solomon Islands/New Guinea

Bougainville Island, along with Buka Island off its northwest end (see Map 34), is the northwestern most of the Solomon Islands, but administratively was part of the Australian Mandated Territory of New Guinea to the west and northwest, which included the Bismarck Archipelago. A cluster of small associated islands off the southeast end of Bougainville, the Shortland Islands, administratively belonged to the British Protectorate of the Solomon Islands (discussed at the end of this section). Bougainville is discussed in the Solomon Islands section rather than under New Guinea as its occupation was an extension of the Solomons campaign.

Bougainville Island, code-named DIPPER and later FRIGIDAIRE, is west of Choiseul, the nearest large island, separated by the thirty-mile-wide Bougainville Strait. It is approximately 120 miles southeast of New Ireland in the Bismarck Archipelago and 190 miles from Rabaul on New Georgia. It is situated at 06°20' S 153°36' E. Even though Bougainville and Buka were part of the Mandated Territory of New Guinea, which was in time zone 22, they were in the same time zone as the rest of the Solomons, time zone 23.

Bougainville is 125 miles in length from northwest to southeast and almost 38 miles wide across the southeastern portion and 30 across the northwestern. It covers an area of 3,800 square miles. Two mountain ranges dominate the island's central spine. The Emperor Range covers most of the northwestern and central portions of the island. The 10,171-foot Mount Balbi in the northwest and the 8,560-foot Mount Bagana in the central portion are active smoking volcanoes. The less rugged Crown Prince Range, highest elevation 7,743 feet, in the broader southeast portion covers an area closer to the northeast coast providing broad plains along the southwest and south coasts. The rugged mountainous interior is densely forested and mostly unexplored. There are few areas covered with kunai grass as encountered on Guadalcanal. Steep-banked streams and rivers flow out of the mountains into the sea. Those on the northwest end are shorter than those in the southeast. Streams and small rivers are often fringed with crocodile-frequented mangrove swamps, but larger rivers have bare banks swept clean by flooding. The two sides of the island are markedly different. The northeast side has a narrow coastal plain crossed by fewer streams. The numerous beaches are good, but there are many coral reefs. The southwest side is more rugged and densely vegetated.

Many streams rush out of mountain gouges, but then meander slowly across a low coastal plain. Inland from the coast the streams form large swamps up to six feet deep with vast clumps of bamboo, marsh grass, mangroves, and nipa palms. The stream mouths are usually blocked by sandbars formed by silt at low water, which may be washed away during heavy rains, but will build back up. The gray-black volcanic beaches are very narrow and pounded by a hard surf unrestrained by shallow waters or reefs with a 3-½-foot tidal differance. Broad, shallow Empress Augusta Bay, twenty-two miles across, indents the central-southwest coast, its northwest side defined by Cape Torokina and the southwest by Mutupina Point. This would be the American landing site. The climate is hot and humid with a wet or "northwest" season in the summer months and a dry or "southeast" season in the "winter" months, but the 100-inch average annual

Map 34
Bougainville Island, Solomon Islands/New Guinea

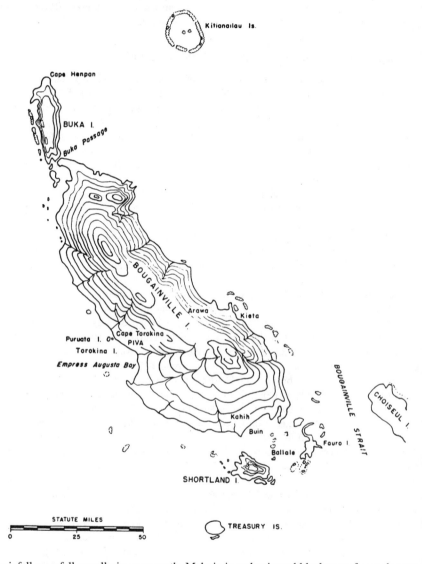

rainfall may fall equally in any month. Malaria is endemic and blackwater fever, dengue fever, and dysentery are prevalent. The natives suffered from tuberculosis, yaws, and hookworm.

A native track generally followed the coast and two trails crossed the central portion of the island skirting Mount Bagana and originated at Cape Torokina as the Piva Trail. It connected with the Nuna Nuna Trail, which ran to the northwest of Mount Bagana and connected with the coastal trail. Nuna Numa would be an important Japanese route to the Allied perimeter in coming months. The coastal track was reported to be drivable by motor vehicles along the northeast coast. Coconut plantations, worked by native labor, were scattered along the coast. Gold and copper were discovered on the island, but little effort was made to mine it. The natives inhabited the many small villages scattered along the coast, mainly around the southeastern end beginning at Empress Augusta Bay and along the northeast coast. There are few good harbors with the best being Kieta and Tonolai on the southern portion of the northeast coast, Buka on the northwest end, and Gazelle Harbour at Empress Augusta Bay. On the southeast end at Buin (INGRAIN), a large anchorage protected by the Shortland Islands was used by the Japanese to stage ships running down the Slot to the Solomons.

Buka Island. Buka (ENAMEL, SORDID) is separated from the northwest end of Bougainville's Bonis Peninsula by the two-thirds-mile wide Buka Passage. It is situated at 05°30' S 154°70' E. Buka is thirty miles long north to south and eleven miles wide across the center covering 220 square miles. A portion of the volcanic island's southwest is hilly with the highest elevation being 1,197 feet, but most of the interior is level and undulating. It is covered by dense forests interspersed with grasslands. Many coastal areas are covered with mangroves. It has a population of over 8,000 natives, known as hard workers, with most villages on the west coast. The main village is Buka on the south end. A motor vehicle road follows the coastline. Numerous coral islets lie off the west and south coasts. Coconut plantations are found on many of these. The west and north coasts are fringed with a barrier reef. Rain is abundant.

The following brief history of Bougainville concerns only the aspects pertaining to that island. Regional history of the Mandated Territory of New Guinea and the Bismarcks are discussed in more detail in those sections. Buka was the first to be discovered by British Captain Philip Carteret in 1767, which he named Winchelsea. The main island was discovered the next year by French Captain Louis Antoine de Bougainville and the Shortlands in 1788 by British Lieutenant Shortland. When discovered the warlike Melanesian natives had no organized government. German trading companies began to operate in the area in 1860s and by the 1880s the Bismarcks were completely under their control. Australia was alarmed at German intrusions, which included the annexation of northeast New Guinea and the Bismarcks in 1885. In 1900, Bougainville and Buka, claimed by Britain, were turned over to German control in exchange for Western Samoa and Santa Isabel, Choiseul, and the Shortlands in the Solomons. In 1905, the Germans established the Bougainville District headquartered at Kieta, but had done little to develop Bougainville by 1914. That year Australian forces took control of the German Protectorate of New Guinea, which included the Bismarcks, Admiralty Islands, and Bougainville. In 1920, the League of Nations mandated Australian control of the former German possessions, which was established on 9 May 1921. Prior to 1933 the Australian administration verged on dictatorial, but that year Europeans were given a slight degree of self-government. The natives were treated well in an effort to win their favor and local government administration was placed in tribal chiefs' control to some degree.

Kieta, on the southern portion of the northeast coast, was the district government center. There was also a government station on Sohana Island in Buka Passage and a police post at Buin. Kieta District, Bougainville and Buka, was one of the ten districts comprising the Mandated Territory of New Guinea and answered to the administrator at Rabaul, New Britain. Before the war Bougainville was populated by approximately 54,000 natives and only 100 Europeans and 100 Asians. By the time of the U.S. landing the native population was estimated at 40,000 as some had fled to other islands. Most Europeans had left before the Japanese arrived, but German missionaries remained. They had long encouraged the natives not to cooperate with Australian officials and there was a certain degree of hostility. Many natives supported the Japanese and helped hunt coastwatchers and downed airmen. Prior to the war tribal disputes were common and mountain tribes sometimes raided coastal villages. Some eighteen different languages were spoken along with Pidgin.

The Japanese occupied Bougainville, the Shortlands, and Buka on 30 March 1942, over two months after they seized New Britain and New Ireland. Bougainville became an important outguard for Rabaul. The Japanese concentrated their forces at Buin on the southeast end, on the nearby Shortland Islands, and on both sides of Buka Passage on the northeast end. Over 38,000 personnel garrisoned the Bougainville area by 1943 with 15,000 at Buin, headquarters for the *17th Army*, 5,000 of the *38th Independent Mixed Brigade* at Buka, 5,000 at Kieta on the lower northeast coast with an airfield nearby, and 1,000 at Mosigetta inland from the southwest coast. This latter group were mainly laborers planting rice for the garrison. Another airfield was located at Tenekow on the upper northeast coast. The *17th Army*, subordinate to the *8th Area Army* on Rabaul, was still under the command of Lieutenant General HYAKUTAKE Seikichi, the defender of Guadalcanal and New Georgia. His main combat force was the *6th Division* under Lieutenant General KANDA Masatane, shipped in from Truk, plus the remnants of units evacuated from the lower Solomons. The *8th Fleet* headquarters and the *1st Base Force* were on Faisi Island with a seaplane base, off the east coast of Shortland, with 5,000 men. Another 6,800 IJN personnel, mainly detachments of various *Special Naval Landing Forces*, were defending the Kara and Kahil Airfields near Buin. Another IJN airfield was on Ballale Island east of Shortland. Bonis Airfield was on the extreme northwest end of Bougainville and Buka Airfield was just across from it on Buka Island along with a seaplane base. The IJN still possessed adequate warships and aircraft in the area to defend Bougainville. These were backed by additional *Southeast Area Fleet* and *11th Air Fleet* forces at Rabaul. Two IJA brigade-sized forces, one provided by the *17th Division* on New Britain and the other the *4th South Seas Garrison Unit*, would arrive in November after the Allied landing.

Initial Allied plans for Bougainville called for attacking the Buin/Shortlands area with the 3d Marine and 25th Infantry Divisions. Planning for Bougainville began in July 1943, but it was soon determined that the area was too strongly defended and would require four divisions to be successful. The 25th was depleted from the New Georgia campaign and only four divisions altogether were available to the South Pacific command. If committed to Bougainville they would be tied up for months, depleted, and further offensive operations would be delayed. Because of the success on Vella Lavella, hitting the enemy where they were weak, it was decided to undertake a less direct approach on Bougainville. The Japanese air and naval forces at Buin/Shortlands and Buka would be neutralized by U.S. air and naval attacks.

The actual landing was to take place on a part of the island remote from Japanese forces. No effort would be made initially to take the entire island. Instead, airfields would be built in the lodgment area to support the defense and attack Buin/Shortland and Buka. It was hoped that the Japanese would expend themselves by attacking the Allied perimeter far distant from their main base.

The landing site selected was the remote Empress Augusta Bay on the central southwest coast. D-Day for Operation DIPPER[3] was set for 1 November 1943. To support the landing the Treasury Islands would be seized on D-5 and a diversionary raid would be executed on Choiseul. The Japanese had conducted a careful analysis of possible landing sites and established defenses on those most likely to be assaulted by the Americans. The Japanese considered the northeast side the most likely to be assaulted with its better beaches and sloping inland plains. While Empress Augusta Bay was not considered a likely landing site, light defenses were established at Cape Torokina.

Lieutenant General Alexandria A. Vandegrift's I Marine Amphibious Corps (IMAC) was assigned to command the operation with the 3d Marine Division (3d, 9th, 12th [artillery], and 23d Marines, 1st Parachute and 2d Raider Regiments) under Major General Allen H. Turnage conducting the initial assault. Task Force 31's (III Amphibious Force) Northern Force (Task Unit 31.5) would land the division. The 37th Infantry Division on Guadalcanal was the IMAC Reserve and would soon come ashore to strengthen the perimeter. The Americal Division in Fiji was the Area Reserve.

The actual landing site was not on Empress Augusta Bay (CHERRYBLOSSOM), but on the northwest side of Cape Torokina (AZALEA), the bay's northwest delineation (see Map 35). The cape is situated at 06°15' S 155°02' E. It juts approximately 350 yards into the bay. It is about 200 yards across at its neck where it joins the mainland and bulges out to almost 300 yards at its widest point some 150 yards from its rounded southwest end. The peninsula and adjacent mainland are low, flat, and sandy. It was covered with palms, handwoods, and moderately dense underbrush. Uncharted swamps were hidden behind the beaches extending as much as two miles inland. Because of dense overhead vegetation, aerial reconnaissance failed to reveal their presence. The swamps proved to be from ankle to waist deep with quicksand-like volcanic ash bottoms. The narrow, surf-pounded beaches stretches all along the shore in both directions from the cape. The Koromokina River lies about 2,500 yards northwest of the cape. About 1,300 yards southwest of the cape is low, palm-covered Puruata Island. Little Torokina Island is situated midway between the cape and Puruata. A company of the *2d Battalion, 23d Infantry Regiment, 6th Division* was assigned to defend the cape. The 270 troops were well dug-in on both sides of the cape with a platoon on Puruata Island and few men on Torokina Island.

The much reinforced 3d Marine Division on Guadalcanal embarked aboard its Task Force 31 transports and proceeded to Efaté, New Hebrides where they conducted rehearsals, although part of the reinforcements remained on Guadalcanal to rehearse. The units rendezvoused on 30–31 October and set sail for Bougainville. Approaching the island from the southeast after passing the now secured Treasury Islands, the transports took up station 3,000 yards off the beach before dawn on 1 November 1943. They opened fire on the cape in a rare instance when transports conducted the prelanding bombardment in support of their own landing force.

The skies were clear with a light southwesterly breeze, gentle offshore sea state, and initally a moderate inshore surf. The initial landing was conducted west of the cape with the 3d Marines landing at 0730 hours under moderate fire to the west of the Koromokina River on Beaches RED 1, 2, and 3. The 9th Marines landed on BLUE 2 and 3, GREEN 2, and BLUE 1. The 3d Raider Battalion landed on GREEN 1 on the north shore of Puruata Island. It went on to secure Torokina Island. By 1100 hours the Marines had secured the cape and the two islands. Surf conditions worsened broaching many landing craft on the beach. By dusk they had secured an 8,000-yard-long, 2,000-yard-deep beachhead by dusk. A raider blocking force was dug-in on the Mission Trail 1,000 yards east of the beachhead. The Marines had lost 78 KIA and 104 WIA. The Japanese suffered 192 dead with the survivors escaping east to rejoin their unit.

The *17th Army* had expected a landing within three days, but not at Cape Torokina.

Map 35
Cape Torokina Area, Bougainville Island

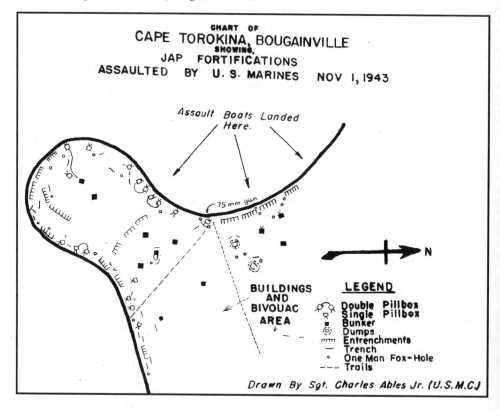

On hearing of the American landing at Torokina, the *Southeast Area Fleet* at Rabaul dispatched four cruisers and six destroyers on the 1st to attack the American transports. A U.S. Navy force of four cruisers and eight destroyers near Vella Lavella, resting after shelling the Shortlands and Buka to cover the landing, was ordered to intercept the Japanese force. In the early morning hours of 2 November the two forces engaged in the Battle of Empress Augusta Bay. The Japanese failed to intercept the withdrawing American transports and lost a cruiser and a destroyer before being forced to withdraw. An American cruiser and destroyer were damaged.

The perimeter was consolidated and expanded, the 21st Marines landed on 4 November, and the Marines waited for the Japanese to make their first move. This occurred before dawn on 7 November when 850 *17th Division* troops ferried from Rabaul conducted a counterlanding on the Marines' west flank. They then executed an unorganized attack and were forced to withdraw. The Marines counterattacked and by the 9th this force had been wiped out. The Allies controlled the air over Bougainville, but Japanese air attacks on the perimeter increased after the initial air neutralization operations on the fifteen known enemy airfields within 250 miles of Cape Torokina. All of the airfields on Bougainville were knocked out, but some were repaired and night attacks were launched at the perimeter for the first three and a half months of occupation.

Work on the fighter field on Cape Torokina began immediately after the landing. The 5,150-foot strip was operational on 10 December. It was later extended. Construction on two more airfields soon began three miles north of Torokina. The 8,000-foot Piva Bomber Field (aka Piva North or Piva Uncle) was operational on 30 December and extended to 10,000 feet in January. The shorter Piva Fighter Field (aka Piva South or Piva Yoke) was completed on 21 January. The Piva fields were named after the nearby village and river. These fields were used not only for local defense and strikes elsewhere on Bougainville, but served as staging bases for attacks flow into the Bismarcks, especially Rabaul 220 miles away. A PT boat base and landing craft repair facility were built on Puruata Island (HAIRBRUSH).

Over the next two weeks Japanese action shifted to the Marine's east flank and several engagements were fought along the trails and for the control of the 500–1,000-foot-high jungled hills and ridges as the Japanese sent *23d Infantry Regiment, 6th Division* into the area. One of the most notable battles was fought from 12 to 18 December to seize Hellzapoppin Ridge (Hill 1000). Rain, mud, coastal swamps, especially dense jungle, and unexpectedly high and rugged inland hills proved to be an enemy to both sides. The 37th Infantry Division (129th, 145th, 148th Infantry) under Major General Robert S. Beightler arrived between 7 and 19 November and was assigned to defend the western sector of the expanding perimeter, referred to as the Inland Defense Line, while the 3d Marine Division advanced in the east. IMAC, now under Major General Roy S. Geiger (Lieutenant General Vandegrift became Commandant of the Marine Corps), took command of the perimeter on 8 November and all IMAC units were ashore by the 15th.

In late November the Japanese dispatched a reinforcement force aboard five destroyers to Buka. The destroyers were intercepted in the Saint George Channel between Buka and off of Cape Saint George on the south end of New Ireland in the early morning of the 25th by an American force of the same composition. Three Japanese destroyers were sunk and the other two forced to withdraw without landing the reinforcements. The United States suffered no losses during the Battle of Saint George.

On 29 November the 1st Parachute Battalion mounted an amphibious raid on Koiari Beach ten miles east of Cape Torokina on the west side of Empress Augusta Bay. It was intended to harass Japanese reinforcements destined for the Cape Torokina area, but was to avoid decisive engagement. The 600-man force landed at 0400 hours, but due to unexpected Japanese strength, over 1,000 enemy were encountered; the force was withdrawn after defending the small beachhead by 2040 hours on the same day.

XIV Corps under Major General Oscar W. Griswold relieved IMAC on 15 December. The Americal Division (132d, 164th, 182d Infantry), under Major General John R. Hodge, began to relieve the 3d Marine Division on 25 December and the relief was completed by the end of the month. XIV Corps now controlled the Americal and 37th Infantry Divisions. While 15 December was the official end of the Marine defensive phase, some units continued to fight until later in the month and others remained with the Army until June 1944.

In mid-January 1944, the *17th Army* commenced efforts to eject the Allies from Torokina, *Ta Operation*. The reinforced *6th Division (13th, 23d, 45th, 53d, 81st Infantry Regiments*; the latter two detached from *17th Division; 6th Field, 10th Mountain Artillery Regiments)* began training for the offensive as roads were built northwestward and supplies built up. The road construction effort was attacked by air and most Japanese barges were destroyed forcing them to move everything overland. At the time of the attack, XIV Corps' perimeter had a beach frontage of 11,000 yards and a depth of 8,000 yards inland. On 8 March (*Y-Day*) the attack was launched at the perimeter from the east and north by 11,700 assault troops backed by 3,700 support troops. The 37th Infantry and Americal Divisions, backed by a tank battalion, substantial artillery, and air support, held and after six major attacks, the *17th Army* began withdrawing on the 25th, some to the north, most to the south. The final pockets of resistance around the perimeter were eliminated by 1 April. The Japanese had underestimated the 62,000-man American strength in the perimeter by half. Japanese losses, including those on the rest of the island lost to air attacks, were 5,400 KIA and 7,000 WIA. The Americans lost only 263 dead. Elements of the 93d Infantry Division (Colored) began to arrive at this time. While participating in some small-scale opereations, the troops were mainly used as stevedores.

In April Major General Robert B. McClure took command of the Americal Division and its commander, Hodge, assumed command of XIV Corps. For the remainder of 1944 the Torokina perimeter was generally quiet. The Japanese dug in on the southeast and northwest ends of the island and American forces conducted no major offensive operations, only aggressive patrols and limited objective attacks to expand the outpost line. Most contacts were made to the northeast of the perimeter. An apparent gentleman's agreement resulted and a "no man's land" developed with the belligerents generally keeping their distance, although patrols did engage each other. Besides perimeter security and patrols, the two divisions undertook combat training to include amphibious exercises to prepare for future operations.

In mid-July 1944 it was decided to withdraw XIV Corps for commitment to the up-coming Philippine campaign. The advance party of the 3d Australian Division arrived at Empress Augusta Bay in October. Between November and December the 30,000-man II Australian Corps, under Lieutenant General Sir Stanley Savige, with the 3d Division (7th, 15th, 29th Brigades), commanded by Major General William Bridgeford, and the 11th and 23d Independent Brigades arrived and relieved the 37th Infantry and Americal Divisions. XIV Corps was relieved by II Corps on 10 December. The Australians opted to conduct a more aggressive campaign to harry the Japanese and chip away at their defenses. A total effort to eliminate the Japanese could not be accomplished because of limited supporting air and naval forces. Between January and June 1945 the Australians concentrated their combat patrols and sweeps in three areas: the Numa Numa Trail and the northern northeast coastal area, the northwest coast to the Bonis Peninsula, and the coast southeast of Empress Augusta Bay, but short of the heavily defended Buin area on the southeast end. In February 1945, the commander of the *17th Army* suffered a stroke and was replaced by Lieutenant General KANDA Masatane, former commander of the *6th Division*, which was taken over by Lieutenant General AKINAGA Tsutomi (aka Tsutomu). A native guerrilla force, led by coastwatchers, evolved in 1945 operating mainly on the southern portion of the northeast coast. Australian losses on Bougainville were 516 KIA and 1,572 WIA.

Shortland Island. The *17th Army* ordered the evacuation of the Shortland and Fauro Islands in December with those forces withdrawn to southern Bougainville. Shortland Island (CHEMIST) eight miles off the southeast end of Bougainville in the Bougainville Strait was part of the British Protectorate of the Solomon Islands' Shortland District administered from Faisi, a small island on the east coast of Shortland. It is eighteen miles northeast of the Treasury Islands. Shortland is thirteen miles east to west and ten miles wide. The nearly level, undulating island has a maximum elevation of 777 feet. It is forested and the foreshore islets along the northwest, northeast, and east coasts are covered with palms. Much of the island is fringed by coral reefs. Faisi Island was made the headquarters of the *8th Fleet* and had a seaplane base. On Ballale Island, a couple of miles off the northeast coast, an IJN airfield had been built. Fauro Island, the second largest in the area and thirteen miles to the northeast of Shortland, was also defended by the Japanese. The Japanese expected the Allies to seize the Shortlands and large troop concentrations were stationed on the islands and the southeast end of Bougainville in the Buin area. The islands formed a sheltered anchorage at the northwest end of the Slot making the area a natural staging site for runs down the Slot into the lower Solomons. Allied plans to seize the Shortlands and the Buin area were canceled in August 1943 because of the extent of the defenses, poor landing beaches, and lack of airfield sites. Japanese installations in the Shortlands/Buin area had been under attack since late 1942 and during the Cape Torokina landing they were hit hard and often. It was from the Buin area that *17th Army* mounted its ill-fated May offensive on the Torokina perimeter and the area was heavy pounded at that time. U.S. radio-intercept operators intercepted and decoded a message that Admiral YAMAMOTO Isoroku, Commander-in-Chief of the *Combined Fleet*, would arrive at Ballele Island on 18 April 1943 from Rabaul. A flight of American fighters was dispatched from Guadalcanal to intercept his aircraft near Buin and downed it killing all aboard. Today the Shortland District of the Solomon Islands' Western Province is administered from the town of Korovou on the island's southeast end having been moved from Faisi Island.

On 15 August all hostilities ceased and the senior IJA and IJN commanders on Bougainville signed surrender documents on 21 August at Torokina. Japan formerly surrendered on 2 September, but the Japanese troops on Bougainville did not formerly surrender until 8 September at Torokina and on the 18th at Numa Numa. Only 21,000 Japanese remained at the time of the surrender.

Most of the American installations on Bougainville were rolled up or turned over to Australian forces in early 1945 along with the airfields and disestablished in March with the last U.S. base elements departing in June. Today Bougainville is one of twenty provinces of the Independent State of Papua New Guinea. Little development has taken place on Bougainville. Coconut plantations, subsistence agriculture, and a copper mine are the main sources of income. When Papua New Guinea was granted independence in 1975, Bougainville desired its own independence. In 1988 an insurgency movement, the Bougainville Resistance Army, emerged on the island and fighting broke out against the Papua New Guinea Defence Force. In 1990 Bougainville proclaimed its independence and Papua New Guinea blockaded the island economically leading to the death of many civilians. A cease-fire was implemented in 1994, but peace talks dissolved and fighting was renewed in 1996. The Papua New Guinea Defence Force relied chiefly on mercenaries to end the revolt and an unsettled truth was announced in 1997. Papua New Guinea is reluctant to grant the island independence as the copper mine and developing oil fields are the nation's richest resources.

NOTES

1. Lieutenant (jg) John F. Kennedy's PT-109 was rammed by a Japanese destroyer and the survivors were marooned on Olasana Island (aka Plum Pudding Island) just off of Gizo.

2. It was rumored that the Japanese strung cables under the treetops, cut away the trunks, built the strip under the suspended tree canopies, and cut them down when it was completed. No evidence has been found to substantiate this story.

3. Initially, from 15 October 1943, Operation DIPPER included Bougainville and related Northern Solomons operations, but from 22 October it designated the Bougainville Island operation only. Because of the austerity of supplies and equipment, not dissimilar to that experienced on Guadalcanal, the operation was popularly known as "SHOESTRING No. 2."

READING SUGGESTIONS

Averill, Gerald P. *Mustang: A Combat Marine.* Novato, CA: Presido Press, 1987.

Bergerud, Eric M. *Touched by Fire: The Land War in the South Pacific.* New York: Penguin Books USA, 1996.

Bureau of Yards and Docks. *Building the Navy's Bases in World War II, Vol. II.* Washington, DC: Government Printing Office, 1947.

Chapin, Capt. John C. *Top of the Ladder: Marine Operations in the Northern Solomons.* Washington Navy Yard: History and Museums Division, Marine Corps Historical Center, 1997.

Coggins, Jack. *The Campaign for Guadacanal.* Garden City, NY: Doubleday and Co., 1972.

Coletta, Paolo E. and Bauer, K. Jack (Editors). *United States Navy and Marine Bases, Overseas.* Westport, CT: Greenwood Publishing Co., 1985.

Conn, Stetson; Engleman, Rose C.; and Fairchild, Byron. *The US Army in World War II: The Western Hemisphere, Guarding the United States and Its Outposts,* Washington, DC: Government Printing Office, 1964.

Frank, Richard B. *Guadalcanal: The Definitive Account of the Landmark Battle.* London: Penguin Books, 1992.

Gailey, Harry A. *Bougainville: The Forgotten Campaign, 1943–1945.* Lexington: The University Press of Kentucky, 1991.

Gillespie, Oliver A. *The Pacific: Official History of New Zealand in the Second World War 1939–45.* Wellington, NZ: Department of Internal Affairs, 1952.

Hammel, Eric M. *Guadalcanal: Starvation Island.* Pacifica, CA: Pacifica Press, 1992.

Hammel Eric. *Munda Trail: The New Georgia Campaign.* New York: Orion Books, 1989.

Hixon, Carl K. *Guadalcanal: An American Story.* Annapolis, MD: Naval Institute Press, 1999.

Hough, Lt. Col. Frank O.; Ludwig, Maj. Verle E.; and Shaw, Henry I., Jr. *History of US Marine Corps Operations in World War II: Pearl Harbor to Guadalcanal. Vol. I.* Washington, DC: Government Printing Office, 1958.

Hoyt, Edwin P. *Guadalcanal.* New York: Stein & Day, 1982.

Leckie, Robert. *Challenge for the Pacific: The Bloody Six-Month Battle for Guadalcanal.* Cambridge, MA: Da Capo Press, 1999.

Livingston, Willaim S. and Louis, William R. (Editors). *Australia, New Zealand, and the Pacific Islands since the First World War.* Austin: University of Texas Press, 1979.

Long, Gavin M. *The Six Years War: A Concise History of Australia in the 1939–1945 War.* Canberra: The Australian War Memorial and the Australian Government Publishing Service, 1973.

Melson, Maj. Charles D. *Up the Slot: Marines in the Central Solomons.* Washington, DC: Marine Corps Historical Center, 1993.

Miller, John, Jr. *United States Army in World War II: Cartwheel: The Reduction of Rabaul.* Washington, DC: Government Printing Office, 1959.

Miller, John, Jr. *United States Army in World War II: Guadalcanal: The First Offensive.* Washington, DC: Government Printing Office, 1949.

Morison, Samuel E. *History of US Navy Operations in World War II: Breaking the Bismarcks Barrier, 22 July 1942–1 May 1944, Vol. VI.* Boston: Little, Brown and Co., 1950.

Morison, Samuel E. *History of US Navy Operations in World War II: The Struggle for Guadalcanal, August 1942–February 1943, Vol. V.* Boston: Little, Brown and Co., 1949.

Rasor, Eugene L. *The Solomon Islands Campaign, Guadalcanal to Rabaul: Historiography and Anointed Bibliography.* Westport, CT: Greenwood Publishing Co., 1997.

Rentz, John R. *Bougainville and the Northern Solomons*. Washington, DC: HQ, Marine Corps, 1948.
Shaw, Henry I., Jr. and Kane, Maj. Douglas T. *History of US Marine Corps Operations in World War II: Isolation of Rabaul, Vol. II*. Washington, DC: US Government Printing Office, 1963.

3

Southwest Pacific Area

The Southwest Pacific Area was under the command of General Douglas MacArthur's U.S. Far East Forces. It encompassed the largest land masses in the Pacific region. These include Australia (not a topic of this book), New Guinea, Bismarck Archipelago, Netherlands East Indies, and the Philippines. Besides U.S. involvement, Australian forces played a major role in this theater. The area's boundary trace began at longitude 160° east on the equator, a point north of the Solomon Islands. To the east was the Southwest Pacific Area. On 1 August 1942, this boundary was shifted 1° west to 159° east to facilitate South Pacific Area operations in the Solomons. Just off the northwest end of Dutch New Guinea the boundary made a 90° turn north at longitude 130° east to 20° north latitude where it turned back to the west, south of Formosa, and clipped the north end of Hainan Island in the Gulf of Tonkin off the south coast of China and the northeast coast of French Indochina. From the northeast coast of French Indochina the boundary followed the coastline south along Thailand and then the Malay States, edged the east end of Sumatra (within the China-Burma-India theater), and the west end of Java (both part of the Netherlands East Indies). At longitude 08° south, latitude 104° north it angled southeast toward the northwest coast of Australia and at longitude 16° 30' S 110° 00' E headed south. To the west of the Southwest Pacific Area was the China-Burma-India theater, which encompassed the Indian Ocean.

The Southwest Pacific Area was preceded by the short-lived American-British-Dutch-Australian Command (ABDACOM) established on 22 January 1942 under British command. This combined command was intended to defend the participating Allied countries' possessions in the Southwest Pacific. For the most part the national forces operated under their own command to defend their areas, but there were some combined operations conducted with naval and air forces placed under other nations' command. The ABDA Area's boundary ran east from the South China coast on latitude 30° north south of Japan to longitude 140° east, then ran south to just north of New Guinea where it made a 1° jog to the east and then continued south across New Guinea on longitude 141° east, the border between Dutch New Guinea and the Australian New Guinea territories. On New Guinea's south coast it ran east to longitude 144° east where it crossed the Torres Strait to Cape York, Australia. The boundary then followed the north coast of Australia west-ward to Northwest Cape and angled northwest to 15° S 92° E, a point in the eastern Indian Ocean, from where it went north to the India-Burma border. Burma and the Malay States were included in the ABDA Area; Thailand and Indochina were already occupied by the Japanese at this time. Within the ABDA Area were the Netherlands East Indies, the Philippines, a few British possessions, and, rather ambitiously, Formosa and Japan's Ryukyu Islands. ABDACOM was dissolved on 22 April 1942 when most of the area was conquered by the Japanese.

NEW GUINEA (PAPUA AND NORTH-EAST NEW GUINEA)

The interpretation of the name "New Guinea" and use of the word "Papua" (pro-nounced "Pap-yoo") can be confusing as they have been used to define several different geographic areas and political divisions.

1. "New Guinea" (*Niyu Ginia* in Japanese, *Neu Guinea* in German) is the second largest island in the world (next to Greenland) and was divided into three political divisions prior to the turn of the century.

2. "Papua," or Territory of Papua (formerly British New Guinea), covered roughly the southeast quarter of the island and was administered by Australia.

3. "North-East New Guinea" covered the northeastern quarter of the island and was part of the Australian-run Mandated Territory of New Guinea (formerly German New Guinea). It included the Bismarck Islands, Bougainville, and smaller islands off the northeast coast of New Guinea. North-East New Guinea was often referred to as "mainland New Guinea" when describing its relation with the islands of the Mandated Territory of New Guinea, i.e., the Bismarcks. The Germans called this mainland area *Kaiser Wilhelmsland*.

4. After the Japanese invasion and Australian civil administration ended, Papua and North-East New Guinea were together generally referred to simply as "New Guinea," code-named CENTRAL, or sometimes "eastern New Guinea," especially by the Japanese (*Higashi Niyu Ginia*). To confuse matters more, the Americans often referred to the eastern end of New Guinea as "Papua," where most of the fighting of the Papua Campaign unfolded, but this generalization included the southeastern portion of North-West New Guinea where action also occurred.

5. "Netherlands or Dutch New Guinea," the third political division, covered the western half of the island and was politically part of the Netherlands East Indies. It is also referred to as "western New Guinea." This territory is discussed in the following Netherlands East Indies section.

6. The term "Papua New Guinea" is used today as the name of the former Territory of Papua and Mandated Territory of New Guinea when consolidated into a single country in 1975. (On 1 January 2000, western New Guinea, formerly known as Irian Jaya within Indonesia, was re-named "Papua" as well.)
    The following section covers Papua and North-East New Guinea—eastern New Guinea.

The island of New Guinea lies at the east end of the vast East Indies Archipelago, the largest archipelago in the world, and north of Australia. Australia's Cape York, the continent's northernmost point, is only 100 miles from the south coast of Papua across the Torres Strait (GUNSMITH), which contains Thursday Island. This strait separates the Coral Sea, lapping Papua's south coast, from the Arafura Sea (BREAKFAST) along the Dutch New Guinea's southeast coast. New Guinea lies between the equator and 10° south and stretches from the 100° to the 150° east latitudes. The island covers 308,486 square miles and measures 1,306 miles from northwest to southeast and is 500 miles wide across the center, the border between Papua/North-West New Guinea and Dutch New Guinea, longitude 141° east. The border between Papua and North-West New Guinea follows a straight line southeastward through the Bismarck Mountains to turn east to the coast just to the north of Cape Ward Hunt on the northeast coast roughly midway between Buna and Salamaua.

The following discussion of New Guinea's physical characteristics is general in that there are many variances over such a large area. This discussion also focuses on eastern New Guinea (Papua and North-West New Guinea) and the island's long tail jutting to the southeast, the Papuan Peninsula, where most of the action took place (see Map 36). Papua, mainland North-East New Guinea, and the Bismarck Islands are in time zone 22 (Dutch New Guinea is in time zone 21).

The length of the island is dominated by a tangled maze of jagged and steep-sided, multinamed mountain ranges, which taper into the Owen Stanley Mountains (named after Captain Owen Stanley, a Royal Navy explorer in the mid-1800s) running spine-like to the end of the Papuan Peninsula. Numerous smaller named ranges comprise the Bismarck and Owen Stanley Mountains. The highest elevation on North-East New Guinea is Mount Wilhelm at 14,108 feet. In Papua the highest peak is 13,200-foot Mount Victoria. Every peak and ridge side is creased with sharp ridge fingers, draws, and gorges. The mountains are covered with dense rain forests, often shrouded in clouds at the higher elevations. Open areas are very rare. Much of the forest is choked with vines and moss that block the sunlight. Little of the island's interior was explored, and much is still unexplored to this day. On the north side of the mountains rugged foothills slope to the sea. A broad swampy valley is found in the western portion of North-East New Guinea through which the twisting 600-mile-long Sepik River (NECROMANCER, later shortened to ROMANCER) flows from the west originating in the Owen Stanleys near the Dutch New Guinea border. This largest river in North-West New Guinea runs roughly parallel with the north coast, bounded by the Owen Stanleys on the south and the coastal Victor Emanuel Mountains on the north, and then bends gradually to the northeast to flow into the sea. The Sepik is navigable for almost 300 miles. Scores of smaller rivers and streams flow out of the mountains and hills, often turning sluggish as they approach the north coast. The narrow coastal plain is forested with interspersed open areas. Open areas may be covered by marshes or four to seven-foot high kunai grass. Many of the forested areas cover swamps, but dry forested areas have dense underbrush. Much of the north coast is bounded by mangrove swamps. Sand beaches are narrow with coral outcroppings and fringing reefs. There are numerous bays and inlets that do provide landing sites, the most notable being Milne Bay on the end of the Papuan Peninsula, Goodenough Bay, Collingwood Bay, and Huron Gulf at the peninsula's northwest base.

The south side of the mountains, the area occupied mainly by Papua, is drastically different from the north. Patternless, sharp, steep ridges drop out of the mountains abruptly terminating at the coast. The terrain is cross-compartmented regardless of the direction of travel. The frequency of streams rushing out of the mountains increases as one moves westward. At the Gulf of Papua on the south coast the shoreline turns south away from the foothills of the Owen Stanleys. The land levels out into a broad undulating and hilly, forest-covered plain. Over this flows the 650-mile-long Fly River, navigable for 500 miles. Its source is high in the Owen Stanley Mountains near the Dutch New Guinea border. Rushing southwest out of the mountains the longest river on Papua hooks sharply to the southeast with its elbow jutting into Dutch New Guinea comprising a portion of the border. It flows across the plains and coastal lowlands into the Gulf of

Papua with its mouth forming a large bird-foot delta. The lowlands between the river and the south coast are inundated by one of the world's largest swamps. Beaches are scarce along the whole of the south coast.

New Guinea experiences some of the harshest tropical weather extremes in the world. Torrential rains vary from 150 to 300 inches a year depending on the area. During the rainy season, the northwest monsoon, it can rain up to ten inches a day. There are two seasons, the northwest monsoon from October to April with heavy rains, heat, high humidity, and low clouds; and the southeast monsoon from April to September, which is slightly milder and drier. Regardless of the season, rain is encountered year-round, although there are periodic droughts. The temperature varies little year-round remaining hot and humid along the coasts to quite cold in the mountains, even during the day. The further east one travels on to the Papuan Peninsula, the comparatively milder the climate. The western areas, especially along the coasts, are quite harsh with the "Gulf and Delta" area (Papua Gulf and Fly River Delta) of southwest Papua considered especially unhealthy.

Tropical diseases abound and, when coupled to the harsh climate, make New Guinea one of the world's most inhospitable regions. Malaria, respiratory diseases, dysentery, frambesia, yaws, tropical ulcer, hookworm, and filariasis are common. Both dry and water leeches are found in all areas regardless of elevation. Little had been done by any of the region's changing masters prior to the war to improve the health conditions of the natives.

In 1940 the total population of the entire island was estimated at approximately one million, of which only perhaps 10,000 were nonindigenous (Europeans, Asians, etc.). In 1940, Papua reported a native population of 275,000–300,000 and 1,800 Europeans (no Asians were permitted) while North-East New Guinea (mainland) reported a probable 553,500 natives (including an estimated 120,000 uncounted), 3,900 Europeans, and 2,200 Asians. The total estimated native population for the Territory of New Guinea, including the Bismarcks and other islands, was 797,600. Both territories admitted that accurate censuses were taken only in "patrolled areas." No generic term can describe the natives, although the terms Melanesian and Papuan have been used. There were estimated to be some 700 tribes. The natives of New Guinea vary greatly in physical appearance from area to area. For the most part they were considered among the most fierce and warlike in the Pacific, at least until civil authorities and missionaries were able to instill some degree of control in the patrolled areas just prior to the turn of the century. Cannibalism, headhunting, slave raids, and tribal warfare were ceaseless. During World War II, and even after, there were still areas in which white men never ventured and as late as the 1930s there were occasional attacks on whites. Too, even before the war, there were known to be "lost primitive tribes" deep in the mountains that had never seen a white man, some of these being "discovered" in the 1960s and 1970s amid great fanfare. For the most part though, the coastal tribes and the inland tribes in the patrolled areas conformed to Australian law and remained peaceful. There were hundreds of languages and dialects with few neighboring tribes able to communicate. The teaching of English to the natives was encouraged in both territories and required of any native in government employ, the police, and convicts. The use of Pidgin was permitted in the Mandated Territory before the war, but not in Papua. Nor was the employment of Mandated Territory natives allowed in Papua. In Papua, rather than Pidgin, the most common local dialect, Motuam, was required. This changed during the war when large numbers of Mandated natives were employed in Papua by the military administration. The use of Pidgin came into wide use in Papua during the war because of the passage of Allied troops through different areas and the movement of native laborers, porters, and guides

Map 36
Eastern New Guinea (Territory of Papua and North-East New Guinea) and Bismarck Archipelago

throughout the two territories. This led to some degree of the "standardization" of Pidgin in much of eastern New Guinea.

The island of New Guinea, or at least different parts of it, were discovered by numerous explorers between the sixteenth and nineteenth centuries. It was not until the 1870s that most of the island's coast was accurately charted. The Portuguese Antonio d'Abreu was the first to discover the north coast in 1512. In 1526, another Portuguese, Jorge de Menezes, discovered the west coast and named it *Ilhas dos Papuas* (meaning frizzle-haired to describe the inhabitants) (another source states that Papua was derived from *Papuwa*, Malay for frizzy or woolly, again describing the inhabitants.). In 1528 the Spaniard, Alvaro de Saavedra explored the north coast and named it the Island of Gold (*Isla del Oro*). Another Spaniard, Ynigo Ortez de Retes, exploring the northwest coast in 1545, named the land New Guinea (*Nuevo Guinea*) possibly because of its resemblance to the Guinea coast of west Africa or because its inhabitants appeared similar to those in west Africa. Other Spaniards, Englishmen, and Dutchmen explored and surveyed the coasts in the 1600s and 1700s. In 1793 the British East India Company claimed possession of part of eastern New Guinea, but the Crown did not recognize the claim. In 1828, the Dutch annexed the western half of the island (see Netherlands East Indies). Another British explorer claimed the southeast coast for Britain, but that claim too was ignored. It was not until 1883 that H.M. Chester, a British magistrate from Thursday Island, claimed Port Moresby and southeast New Guinea for the Crown because of German interest in the area. In 1888, British New Guinea was formerly annexed and 1902 it was transferred as a territory to the newly established Commonwealth of Australia and named the Australian Territory of Papua. On 1 September 1906, after the transfer took full effect, it was renamed the Territory of Papua. In the meantime Germany claimed protectorate status over North-East New Guinea, the Bismarcks, and Northern Solomons in 1884 formerly annexing the region as German New Guinea (*deutschen Neu Guinea*) in 1885. In 1914, German New Guinea was occupied by Australian troops after a few minor engagements. The League of Nations granted Australia control of German New Guinea under a Class "C" mandate in 1920, which took effect on 9 May 1921. The region was designated the Mandated Territory of New Guinea and included the Bismarcks, Bougainville, and other small islands east of New Guinea (see Bismarck Archipelago for additional information). Australia was now responsible for two separate political territories on New Guinea. The following discussions address the specific administrative and economic details of the two territories just prior to the war.

Territory of Papua

This territory covered a mainland area of 87,786 square miles. The islands off to the east of the Papuan Peninsula, discussed below, totaled another 2,754 square miles. The territorial capital is Port Moresby (named after Captain John Moresby, who discovered the site on landlocked Fairfax Harbour in 1873) on the south coast with a European population of 800. It had two small airdromes (U.S. forces generally continued the use of the British term "airdrome" or simply "drome" to identify airfields in this region, although if built and named by the United States "airfield" was used.) Small towns and villages were spread along both coasts and the islands. Papua was divided into eight districts administered by district administrators who doubled as magistrates. Papua was poorly developed with Australia, itself still a developing industrial nation, investing little in the territory. Settlement by planters was encouraged though, with liberal tax assessment of lands as a form of subsidy. The harsh climate and poorly developed infrastructure discouraged settlement, however. Regardless, coconut, rubber, and coffee plantations grew. Gold and copper mining was undertaken, but was not entirely successful, except for a lucrative gold mine on Misima Island. Oil exploration was underway when the war broke out and this resource remained untapped. At the time of the Japanese invasion the Honorable Leonard Murray was the territorial administrator.

Areas of importance in Papua during the upcoming campaign were Milne Bay on the east end of the Papuan Peninsula, the Buna-Gona area (two villages near Cape Endaiadere on the north-central coast), and the Kokoda Trial spanning the Owen Stanleys connecting Buna-Gona with Port Moresby on the south coast, itself the main Japanese objective.

Papua's islands' are scattered off the east coast of the Papuan Peninsula in the Solomon Sea. The D'Entrecasteaux Islands (pronounced "Dan-tre-kas-tow") lie about fifty miles north of Milne Bay (on the end of the Papuan Peninsula). They include, from northwest to southeast, Goodenough, Fergusson, and Normanby. Some fifty miles north of Fergusson is Kiriwina Island (Trobriand Group) while Woodlark Island is 120 miles east of Fergusson. Goodenough, Kiriwina, and Woodlark played a role in the war and are discussed later in this section. Scores of smaller islands and islets are dispersed among these islands or off the east end of the peninsula. The widely scattered Louisiade Archipelago is centered approximately 150 miles east of Milne Bay. The Louisiades and the other seven small island groups played no part in the war.

Mandated Territory of New Guinea

Mainland North-East New Guinea covered 69,700 square miles. The Bismarcks and other islands added another 26,300 square miles of land. The Schouten Islands (not to be confused with the larger Schouten Eilanden off the north coast of Dutch New Guinea) are a chain of small islands scattered off the northeast coast from the mouth of the Sepik River to Altape. The territorial capital was Rabaul on New Britain. The three principal towns on the mainland are the three district government centers: Wewak, Sepik District in the northwest, Madang, Madang District in the central area, and Lae, Morobe District in the southeast. Lae had the first airdrome (PICKUP) to be built on New Guinea in 1928. In 1939, Lae was selected to become the territory's capital, but this did not take place before the war. Numerous towns and villages dotted the coast, and, unlike Papua, there were a number of small inland communities, mainly because of the gold fields. Gold was discovered in 1921 inland from Lae in Morobe District. A minor gold rush developed and the gold fields proved to be very lucrative bringing in £3,000,000 per year. They were being mined by 1,500 Europeans and 10,000 natives right up to evacuation in January 1941. Besides the Morobe gold fields, some coconut, coffee, and cocoa plantains were established, but these are considered minor industries. As with Papua, the Mandated Territory was underdeveloped by the time of the war; limited oil exploration was underway at the time of the invasion. The territorial administrator was Brigadier Sir Walter McNicoll, who narrowly escaped the Japanese invasion. The islands of the Mandate, Bismarck Archipelago, and the Admiralty Islands are discussed following this section. Bougainville is addressed in the Solomon Islands section.

The key battle areas in the Mandated Territory were the Huon Gulf area's towns of Lae, Salamaua, Wau, and Nadzab; and above that the Markham River Valley and Finschhafen on the east end of the Huon Peninsula enclosing the gulf's north side. Wewak and Madang, the district centers on the northeast coast, became involved as well.

Both territories possessed their own Australian-led, native-manned constabularies. The New Guinea Volunteer Rifles (NGVR) was a local militia recruited from Europeans in both territories in 1939 and organized into companies. The Australian-led, native-manned Papuan Infantry Battalion was a light reconnaissance unit raised in 1940. In early 1944, another unit, the 1st New Guinea Battalion, was raised. Two more battalions followed and they were assigned to the Royal Pacific Islands Regiment along with the Papuan Battalion. In the 1941 the Torres Strait Infantry Battalion was raised on Thursday Island. When civil administration evaporated in early 1942 (Mandated Territory 23 January, Papua 12 February), the Australian government formed a military government organization known as the Australian Territories of Papua and New Guinea, which included the Papuan Administrative Unit and New Guinea Administrative Unit. They in turn were combined into the Australia-New Guinea Administrative Unit (ANGAU) on 10 April under Major General Basil Morris, who also doubled as Administrator of New Guinea. Both territories were a single component under martial law. The ANGAU managed thousands of native laborers, porters, and guides who supported Allied forces in the Southwest and South Pacific. Prior to this the two territories were within the 8th Military District, which was reorganized as the corps-level New Guinea Force (NATIVE initially, PHOSPHOROUS in May 1942) also under Morris. On 9 August, Lieutenant General Sydney Powell, commanding I Australian Corps, also took command of New Guinea Force leaving Morris in his administrative posts. The two territorial police forces, the Royal Papaun Constabulary and the New Guinea Police Force, remained active through the war.

A small U.S. Navy advance base (FPO SF 1403) was established on Thursday Island (10°40' S 142°15' E) in the Torres Strait north of the Australian mainland's Cape York. PT boats operated from there from May to July 1943. A fighter strip was constructed there and used until July 1944. Horn Island, immediately adjacent to the tip of Cape York, hosted an RAAF field.

Seaports were few and generally consisted of a pier or two with few if any support facilities. Roads were virtually nonexistent, except in the more developed towns, but an ancient, torturous native trail network connected the villages along the coast. On the Papuan Peninsula several trails spanned the Owen Stanleys and one of these would become a long, linear battleground. There were numerous crude airstrips scattered over the island, mainly near towns, plantations, and the gold fields. A few were suitable for transport aircraft. The only military airfield was Kila Kila less than three miles east of Port Moresby. While there was a naval docking facility at Port Moresby, there were no naval installations on New Guinea. Just to the northeast of Port Moresby was a barracks at Granville East. Two 6-inch guns were positioned on Ela Hill covering Basilisk Passage.

The complex New Guinea Campaign began within four weeks of the war's beginning and essentially lasted to V-J Day. For that reason only the campaign's key points are discussed. The campaign spanned both the Territory of Papua and the Mandated Territory of New Guinea.

The military value of eastern New Guinea to the Japanese was to provide a barrier to protect their southern flank, serve as a base to threaten Australia, and a position from which to block the Torres Strait in order to cut communication between the South Pacific and the Dutch East Indies as well as the Indian Ocean. Enemy fleets and merchant shipping would be forced to detour around the southern coast of Australia.

When the Japanese landed at Sarawak in the Dutch East Indies the evacuation of all European women and children from New Guinea and Papua was ordered on 17 December 1941. The Japanese bombed Lae, Salamaua, and Madang on the north coast on 21 January 1942 forcing the abandonment of the first two. On the 23rd the Japanese occupied

Rabaul. A few days later all able-bodied men in both territories were called to the colors. Wau, 30 miles inland from the north coast, was bombed on 1 February. The only defense force on the north coast was there, a few hundred NGVR troops. The only other troops on the mainland were a reinforced Australian battalion at Port Moresby (CARAMEL, MAPLE, SCARAMOUCH, TEAK) (09°20' S 147°09' E). It was soon reinforced by the 30th Brigade. On 3 March the Japanese executed their first air raid on Australia bombing Wyndham. Planned by the *4th Fleet* since early February, and delayed because of American carrier activity near Rabaul, a landing at Lae-Salamaua was conducted on the 8th with the *2d Battalion, 144th Infantry Regiment* seizing Salamaua as the *Maizuru 2d SNLF* took Lae. A base force and construction units followed and the infantry battalion was soon withdrawn with the IJN troops left to garrison the first foothold on New Guinea. On 11 March another force took Finschhafen on the Huon Peninsula to the northwest. Air attacks failed to dislodge the force and they built an airfield. On 31 March the first USAAF units began arriving at Port Moresby to reinforce its defense and U.S. Army antiaircraft units began arriving; eventually the entire U.S. 40th Antiaircraft Artillery Brigade defended the town. In April the *4th Fleet* prepared to seize Port Moresby in *MO Operation* to be executed just prior to the Midway assault. Units of the *Kure 3d SNLF* and *1st Battalion, 144th Infantry Regiment* would land on beaches flanking the port and assault the town overland on 10 May. The invasion force departed Rabaul on 4 May while the carrier striking force left Truk just prior to that to cover the invasion force. Anticipating the operation, the Allies were prepared, dispatching a carrier force to intercept the Japanese forces. The Battle of the Coral Sea lasted from 4 to 8 May with the invasion force and carrier strike force turned back. The battle was fought from the air with both sides losing a carrier and having a carrier damaged. The Japanese, however, lost a cruiser and nine other ships sank and six were damaged. The 14th Australian Brigade arrived at Port Moresby on the heels of the battle. The Battle of the Coral Sea, coupled with worse losses suffered by the Japanese at Midway, sealed their fate and they were never able to recover.

Port Moresby was the Royal Australian Navy's main operating base in the New Guinea area. The U.S. Navy operated an advance naval base at Port Moresby from June 1943 to October 1944.

To construct three airdromes to support future operations along the north coast, the Australians landed a small force at Milne Bay (FALLRIVER [changed because supplies sent there were often shipped to Fall River, Massachusetts], PEMMICAN, BENEVOLENT) on 25 June 1942. Within a couple of weeks the 7th Australian Brigade (Milne Force) arrived there for defensive duty. The small Australian force at Wau, known as Kanga Force, had been reinforced, and launched an unsuccessful attack on Salamaua (DOUBLELET) and Lae (BINOCULAR, PRIME, SCHOOLBOY, STILS) as a diversion for the Milne Bay landing. Operation PROVIDENCE, the occupation of Buna (CHIVALRY, NONCONFORMIST) on the north coast by a U.S. engineer force to build an airfield in support of future operation against Lae-Salamaua, was scheduled for 10 August. In the meantime the *4th Fleet* sent a convoy from Rabaul to do the same thing. On 22 July the *1st Battalion, 144th Infantry Regiment, 15th Engineer Regiment*, and numerous support units (1,900 troops, 1,200 Rabaul native porters and laborers) landed at Gona, ten miles to the northwest of Buna. Unable to seize Port Moresby from the sea, the Japanese planned to use the Kokoda Trail running from Buna to the objective. The 145-mile-long trail climbed though gorges, mountain valleys, along ridge crests, crossed countless creeks, crawled up and down mountain sides adding, some say, half again its map length to its actual length. It was a perpetually muddy track wide enough for one man. Some of the rises, such as the "Golden Stairs," consisted of log steps hacked into the mud. It crossed the thickly forested Owen Stanleys though a low pass at an altitude of 7,500 feet 20 miles south of Kokoda (50 miles south of Buna), a small outpost with an airstrip on a 1,200-foot plateau. The climate was rainy and cold. It was an impossible task for a heavily equipped force, relying on external logistical support, in face of determined opposition. Both sides would suffer immeasurably in an extremely hostile environment. The 900-man *Yazawa Detachment*, the reinforced *1st Battalion, 144th Infantry*, moved up the trail the night they landed. The Australians had only a small detachment, the Maroubra Force, at Kokoda. It was frantically attempting to reinforce Kokoda, but the defenders were overwhelmed on 26 July. On 28–29 July the Australians retook Kokoda without resistance, but lost it again on 10 August.

At Buna construction troops were landed on 13 August followed a few days later by the rest of the *144th Infantry*, artillery, antiaircraft, support units, and more porters. There were now 8,000 IJA troops, 3,000 IJN construction troops, and 450 *SNLF* troops in the Buna-Gona beachhead under Major General HORII Tomitaro, commander of the *South Seas Detachment*. Airfield construction began at Cape Endaiadere (GRACE) and the force dug in. The battle for the Kokoda Trail seesawed back and fourth through August and September. The 7th Australian Division arrived at Port Moresby in mid-August and the 21st Brigade was committed up the trail. Seven airfields around Port Moresby were nearing completion and a major advanced supply base was established as troops poured in making it impossible for the Japanese to obtain their objective even if they were able to reach it.

Milne Bay

The 7th and 18th Brigades, with 9,500 Australian troops and U.S. support troops, were at Milne Bay (10°45' S 151°30' E) when it was determined that the Japanese were planning a landing there (see Map 37). Fatally underestimating the Milne Force to be only a battalion, the Japanese committed 1,200 *SNLF* troops from New Ireland. Landing several miles to the east of the Milne Force near the head of the bay on the night of 25/26 August, the *SNLF* troops advanced to meet the Australians the next day and initially succeeded in pushing them back to the airdrome, the Japanese objective. Even though 770 reinforcements were landing on the 29th, by the 30th the Japanese had spent themselves and were in retreat. Most of the survivors were evacuated from the original landing beach on the nights of 4–5 September. After this failure, the Japanese pushing south on the Kokodo Trail were told to switch to the defensive after they crossed the Owen Stanleys and to remain so until Milne Bay could be secured. They continued to advance, but their supply situation was perilous.

Naval Advance Base, Milne Bay began as a PT boat base in December 1942. The 7th U.S. Fleet began developing it as a staging base in the spring of 1943 and major construction began in the summer. A supply depot was built on the south shore of the 20-mile deep, 5–10-mile wide bay at Gamadodo. The Army established a troop staging base there as well. Ship repair facilities were built at Gohora Bay on the west side. An amphibious training center was moved from Brisbane, Australia to Swinger Bay (FPO SF 818) on the northwest shore of Milne in late 1943. Seaplane stations were established on Samarai (BEADSMAN) and Sariba Islands. The headquarters of the 7th Amphibious Force was established at Milne in December 1943, but the base was not commissioned until 1 March 1944. The amphibious training center was relocated to Subic Bay in the

Milne Bay, Territory of Papua, New Guinea

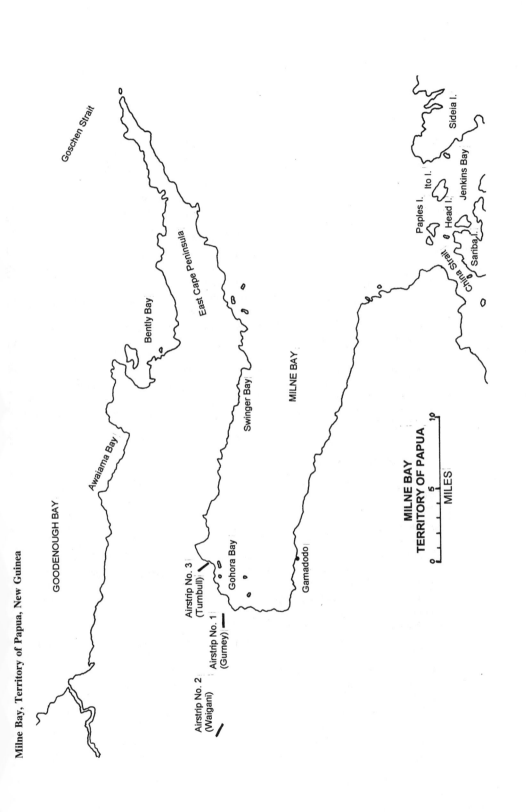

Goschen Strait

GOODENOUGH BAY

Awaiama Bay

Bently Bay

East Cape Peninsula

Swinger Bay

MILNE BAY

Airstrip No. 3
(Turnbull)

Gohora Bay

Airstrip No. 1
(Gurney)

Airstrip No. 2
(Waigani)

Gamadodo

Paples I.

Ito I.

Sideia I.

Jenkins Bay

Head I.

China Strait

Sariba I.

MILNE BAY
TERRITORY OF PAPUA

0   5   10

MILES

Philippines in March 1945 soon followed by the supply facilities. The base was disestablished on 21 June 1946.

Kokodo Trail

On 9 September the 25th Brigade was ordered up the Kokodo Trail behind the 21st
Brigade and the 16th Brigade soon arrived at Port Moresby (see Map 38). American
antiaircraft units were defending Port Moresby and its airfields. On the 15th the U.S.
126th Infantry, 32d Infantry Division began to arrive at Port Moresby and the 128th
Infantry followed on the 28th. The Japanese received new orders that all resources were
being funneled to retain Guadalcanal and the forces on the trail would withdraw back to
Buna-Gona, which could be better defended. The withdrawal began on 24 September;
they had reached a point twenty-seven air miles from Port Moresby; they could see the
searchlights around the port. The lead elements of the *41st Infantry* began landing near
Buna. The Australians began to advance up the trail on the 26th; the clearing of the trail
was a slow process taking through October to regain Kokodo on 2 November. An effort
was made to march the 128th Infantry overland toward Buna in mid-October after flying
them to the north coast, but this failed and they were moved closer by boat. At the same
time the 2d Battalion, 126th Infantry marched over the Owen Stanleys on a trail to the
east of the Kokodo, but this virtually wasted the unit. The rest of the regiment was flown
over the mountains' crest to a usable clearing, from which they marched to the coast.
These moves placed two U.S. regiments in a position to attack Buna. Savage fighting
continued on the Kokodo as the Japanese slowly withdrew to the prepared defenses of
their eleven-mile-wide beachhead, its depth varying from one mile to a few hundred
yards. The 5,500 Japanese concentrated in three pockets at Gona, Giruwa-Sanananda,
and Buna.

Goodenough Island

This island is the westernmost of the three main islands in the D'Entrecasteaux Islands
fifty-five miles north of Milne Bay and situated at 09°50" S 150°15" E. The other two
islands are the larger Fergusson (38 by 16 miles) and the reversed J-shaped Normanby
(45 miles long). Goodenough Island (Morata, native name) (code-named AMOEBA, GIN-
GER) is a forest-covered peak 8,500 feet high (Mount Goodenough), the highest of the
Papuan islands. The roughly oval island is twenty miles long northwest to southeast and
ten miles wide. A coastal plain, where coconut plantations were established, through
which streams course, surrounds the central peak. The island was named after a Commodore Goodenough of the Royal Navy who was murdered by natives on Santa Cruz
in the Solomons in 1875. The group was administered by Papua's Eastern District headquartered in Abau on the mainland.

On 26 August 1942, seven barges bearing 353 *Sasebo 5th SNLF* troops from Buna
landed on the island for a rest while en route to participate in the Milne Bay assault
(discussed above). Discovered by U.S. fighters, the barges were destroyed and the Japanese stranded. In September, sixty were evacuated by submarine, but the others remained. As part of the Allied effort to secure the Papuan Peninsula's north coast in
support of the effort to reduce Buna-Gona, Goodenough Island was to be cleared. The
2/12th Infantry Battalion,[1] 18th Australian Brigade embarked on two destroyers at Milne
Bay and landed on both sides of the island's southeast tip on the night of 22/23 October.
The 290 *SNLF* troops resisted throughout the day, but on the night of the 23rd were

Buna-Gona, Kokoda Trail, and Port Moresby, Territory of Papua, New Guinea

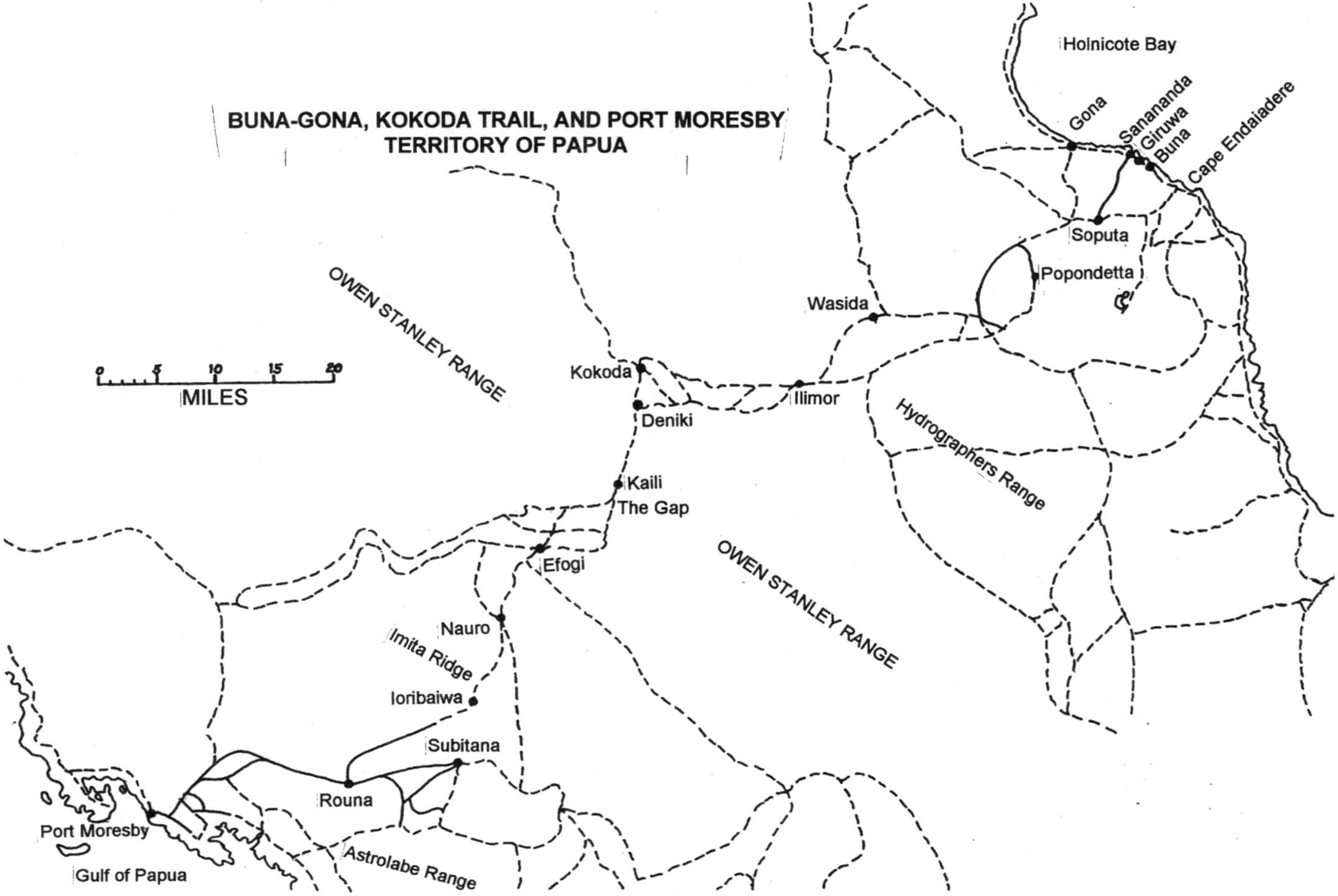

BUNA-GONA, KOKODA TRAIL, AND PORT MORESBY
TERRITORY OF PAPUA

Holnicote Bay

Cape Endaiadere
Buna
Giruwa
Sananda
Gona

Soputa
Popondetta

Hydrographers Range

Wasida

Ilimor

OWEN STANLEY RANGE

Kokoda
Deniki
Kaili
The Gap
Efogi

OWEN STANLEY RANGE

Nauro
Imita Ridge
Ioribaiwa
Subitana

Rouna

Astrolabe Range

Port Moresby

Gulf of Papua

MILES
0   5   10   15   20

shuttled by submarine to Fergusson Island from where they were evacuated by a cruiser. The forty-man rear guard was wiped out and the island secured on the 24th. The 18th Brigade secured the island and was relieved by the 7th Brigade in December. An airfield was soon built on the south side of the island. Goodenough Island served as the headquarters for the 1st Marine Division's rear echelon between September and December 1943 as it staged for the New Britain assault, FPO SF 724, APO SF 724.

Buna-Gona

By mid-November the 25th and 16th Brigades, 7th Division, with the 21st Brigade in reserve, were prepared to assault the Gona-Giruwa area. The U.S. 126th and 128th Infantry would attack the Buna area. On 16 November all Japanese forces on New Guinea came under the control of the *18th Army*. The terrain was flat and swampy with intermixed patches of palms, dense brush, swamps, and kunai grass. It was hot, humid, and rainy. The Japanese were dug-in in well-prepared bunkers and fighting positions in depth. The attack began on 16 November and immediately bogged down because of the terrain, inadequate supplies, already exhausted troops, the strength of the defenses, and the determination of the defenders. The Japanese were able to land parts of the *170th Infantry* and other elements of the *21st Independent Mixed Brigade* from Rabaul on 2, 14, and 29 December. Fresh U.S. and Australian units were poured into what the Australians called the Battle of the Beaches. Gona fell on 9 December to the 14th Brigade. Buna did not fall to the Americans until 2 January 1943 and Giruwa-Sanananda did not succumb to a combined U.S. (127th and 163d Infantry Regiments) and Australian (18th and 30th Brigades) assault until 21 January. Over 2,500 Japanese had died on the coast. Survivors from the coastal strongholds assembled at Holnicote Bay northwest of Gona and Buna. Some 3,400 were evacuated by sea between 11 February and 10 March and taken to the Lae-Salamaua area.

For the entire campaign the Australians committed seven brigades and 18,000 troops who suffered over 2,000 KIA and over 3,500 WIA. The Americans had over 800 KIA and 2,000 WIA in four regiments. Thousands of Allied troops suffered illness. The Japanese committed up to 17,000 troops. About 4,500 able-bodied, wounded, and ill troops were evacuated or recovered from various operations (Milne Bay, Buna-Gona, Goodenough Island), almost 12,000 were killed, and 350 prisoners were taken.

Reinforcement of North-Eastern New Guinea

The Japanese began planning to strengthen their position on New Guinea in November 1942. Finschhafen on the east end of the Huon Peninsula was to be occupied by a company of the *Sasebo 5th SNLF* from New Britain, Madang by two infantry battalions, and Wewak (PIPSQUEAK) by a single battalion, all detached from the *5th Division* in the Dutch East Indies and detailed to *18th Army*. This army, under Lieutenant General ADACHI Hatazo at Rabaul, would move to New Guinea to command all forces there. The convoys departed Rabaul on 16 December and all forces were successfully landed between the 17th and 19th. In late December 1942 the decision was made to transfer the *20th Division (62d, 82d, 83d Infantry)*, under Lieutenant General HIRATA Masachika, from Korea and the *41st Division (237th, 238th, 239th Infantry)*, commanded by Lieutenant General MANO Goro, from North China to reinforce Madang and Wewak, respectively. The *41st Division* landed at Wewak on 19 January followed by the *20th Division* between 20 and 28 February. It then moved to Madang. The rest of the *20th*

Division was landed at Hansa Bay (ABSTRACT), between Madang and Wewak, between March and May 1943. The *20th Division* at Madang began building a road to supply Lae, 135 miles to the southwest, considered absolutely essential by *18th Army* in order to retain control of that area. It would take four to five months to complete, but work did not begin until April. Once the road was completed troops and supplies moved by barge from Rabaul to Madang would be transported overland to Lae. Destroyers and barges moving directly to Lae were increasingly falling prey to Allied air attacks. The *18th Army* at Rabaul deployed to Madang on 19 April.

Wau-Lae-Salamaua

The Japanese force at Lae-Salamaua on the Huon Gulf (CONVICTION) and Finschhafen (DIMINISH, RED HERRING, WASHSTAND) on the Huon Peninsula (BILLSTICKING) faced the Australian Kanga Force at Wau (see Map 39). The Kanga Force had been entrenched at Wau in the 3,500-foot hills of the Wau-Bulolo Valley (PALLIASSE) thirty miles from the coast since May 1942 with virtually no action. Regardless of the defeat at Buna-Gona, the Japanese had not given up on their quest for Port Moresby; Wau is 145 miles north-west of Port Moresby. The recently landed *102d Infantry Regiment, 51st Division* attacked Wau on 28 January 1943. The Australian 17th Brigade was flown in, counter-attacked, and forced the Japanese to retreat. The Australians continued the attack on 3 February and gradually pushed the enemy back. By the end of February the Japanese were back at their start point at Mubo.

Having been defeated on Guadalcanal, which they had evacuated by 7 February, the Japanese were determined to prevail on New Guinea. The Japanese force engaged inland at Wau withdrew to the coast beginning on 14 February and assembled at Mubo south of Salaam in late March. To reinforce Lae-Salaam the Japanese attempted to ship the rest of the *51st Division (66th, 115th Infantry)* there from Rabaul on 28 February. Skirting the north coast of New Britain, the convoy rounded the island's west end and ran south for Huon Bay. On 3–5 March it was intercepted by Allied bombers and in repeated attacks, along with PT boats, all eight transports and four of the eight destroyers were sunk. Half of the 6,900 troops aboard were lost and most of the survivors returned to Rabaul. Other attempts were made to land *51st Division* units, but most failed. The Battle of the Bismarck Sea (actually taking place to the south in the Solomon Sea) denied the Japanese at Lae-Salamaua the reinforcements they needed to turn the balance in their favor. The *51st Division Headquarters* with Lieutenant General NAKANO Hidemitau was landed and took control of operations in the area. By late March the survivors of the Buna-Gona battles had been assembled in the area.

By mid-April the opposing sides were stalemated while the Japanese executed a series of air attacks on Allied positions on New Guinea including Port Moresby and Milne Bay. On 23 April the Australian 3d Division (11th, 17th Brigades) took over operations at Wau-Lae-Salamaua. Little more took place in the Lae-Salamaua area, other than skir-mishing and air attacks on Japanese installations, but in June most of the remainder of the *51st Division* was assembled in the Salamaua area with 7,200 troops.

In late April the Navy established a PT boat base at Morobe (PORTICO, STRAIGHT-FLUSH) near the south end of the Huon Gulf. It was used as a landing craft staging base by both the Army and the Navy until May 1944.

The 6th US Army (ALAMO Force), under Lieutenant General Walter Kruger, planned a major operation commenced in September to secure the Markham River Valley and the Huon Peninsula. Preliminary operations began on 30 June when the 3d Australian

Map 39
Wau-Lae-Salamaua, North-East New Guinea

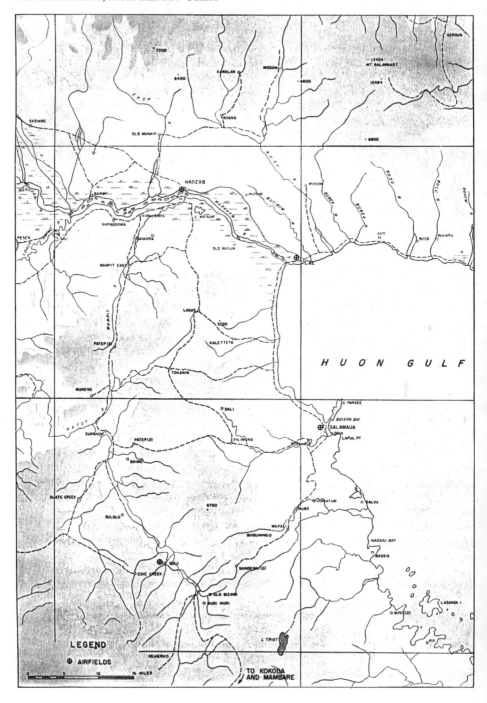

Division, now augmented by the 15th Brigade and the U.S. 162d Infantry, attacked toward Salamaua from Wau. In a flanking effort a battalion of the 162d was landed at Nassau Bay south of Salamaua on the night of 29/30 June. The Salamaua offensive was timed to coincide with the occupation of Kiriwina and Woodlark Islands (see below). The difficult terrain, a stern Japanese defense, and the wide front led to slow progress through July and into August. The Japanese funneled in reinforcements from Wewak. On 24 August the 5th Australian Division Headquarters, under Major General E. J. Milford, relieved the 3d and the 17th Brigade was relieved by that division's 29th Brigade. Two airfields were constructed in the hills at Marilinan and Tsili Tsili to the southwest of Lae to support future operations. Early September saw Japanese resistance crumbling as the Allies closed in on Salamaua.

Huon Peninsula

Dominating the north side of the Huon Gulf is the mountainous Huon Peninsula (see Map 40). It is an oval-shaped piece of land running northwest along the coast and terminating at Astroabe Bay on which Madang lies. The densely forested, thirty- to sixty-mile-wide, 120-mile-long mass contains the Finisterre, Saruwaged, and Rawlingson Ranges, up to 13,000 feet high, occupying the western, central, and eastern portions of the area, respectively. It is defined on its southwest side by the five- to twenty-five-mile-broad, level Markham and Ruma River Valleys. Both rivers originate at the central portion of the 380-mile-long trough with the 80-mile long Markham flowing southeast into the Huon Gulf and the Ruma to the northwest parallel with the coast until it enters the Sepik River south of Wewak. The flat valleys consist of vast grass-covered sand and gravel areas ideal for airfields. Several prewar Australian emergency airstrips were located in the valleys. The Kratke Range borders the south side of the Markham and the Bismarck Range the Ruma River. A trail followed the northeast sides of the rivers from Lae to Bogadjim (WINDOWBOX) on Astroabe Bay and there connected to a road to Wewak.

The 20th and 26th Brigades of the 9th Australian Division under Major General Sir George F. Wootten, loaded aboard Task Force 26 ships at Milne Bay, linked up with 2d U.S. Engineer Special Brigade landing craft, and proceeded toward Lae on the night of 3/4 September. The 20th Brigade landed unopposed on Beaches RED and YELLOW at 0631 hours, 4 September eighteen miles east of Lae. The 26th Brigade followed later in the day as the 20th Brigade pressed west toward Lae. The Division's 24th Brigade landed on the night of 5/6 September. The advance was held up on the 8th by a stout Japanese defense reinforced by the swiftly flowing, rain-swollen Bunga River. Crossings were forced and the advance continued on the 14th.

In the meantime the U.S. 503d Parachute Infantry Regiment enplaned at Port Moresby and flew over the Owen Stanleys to parachute on to Nadzab Airdrome at 1020 hours, on the north shore of the Markham River twelve miles west of Lae. The airfield was secured without opposition. Between 7 and 10 September the entire 7th Australian Division (18th, 21st, 25th Brigades), under Major General G. A. Vasey, was flown into Nadzab from Port Moresby. Construction began on two new 6,000-foot airfields at Nadzab and six more would be built there. On the 10th the 25th Brigade began advancing down the Markham River Valley toward Lae and the 4th Brigade arrived to secure the beachhead on the same date. Between the 11th and 14th the Japanese abandoned Salamaua and moved the troops there to Lae by withdrawing overland along the coast and by barge across Huon Gulf. The Allies occupied Salamaua on the 12th. With the remnants

Map 40
Huon Peninsula, North-East New Guinea

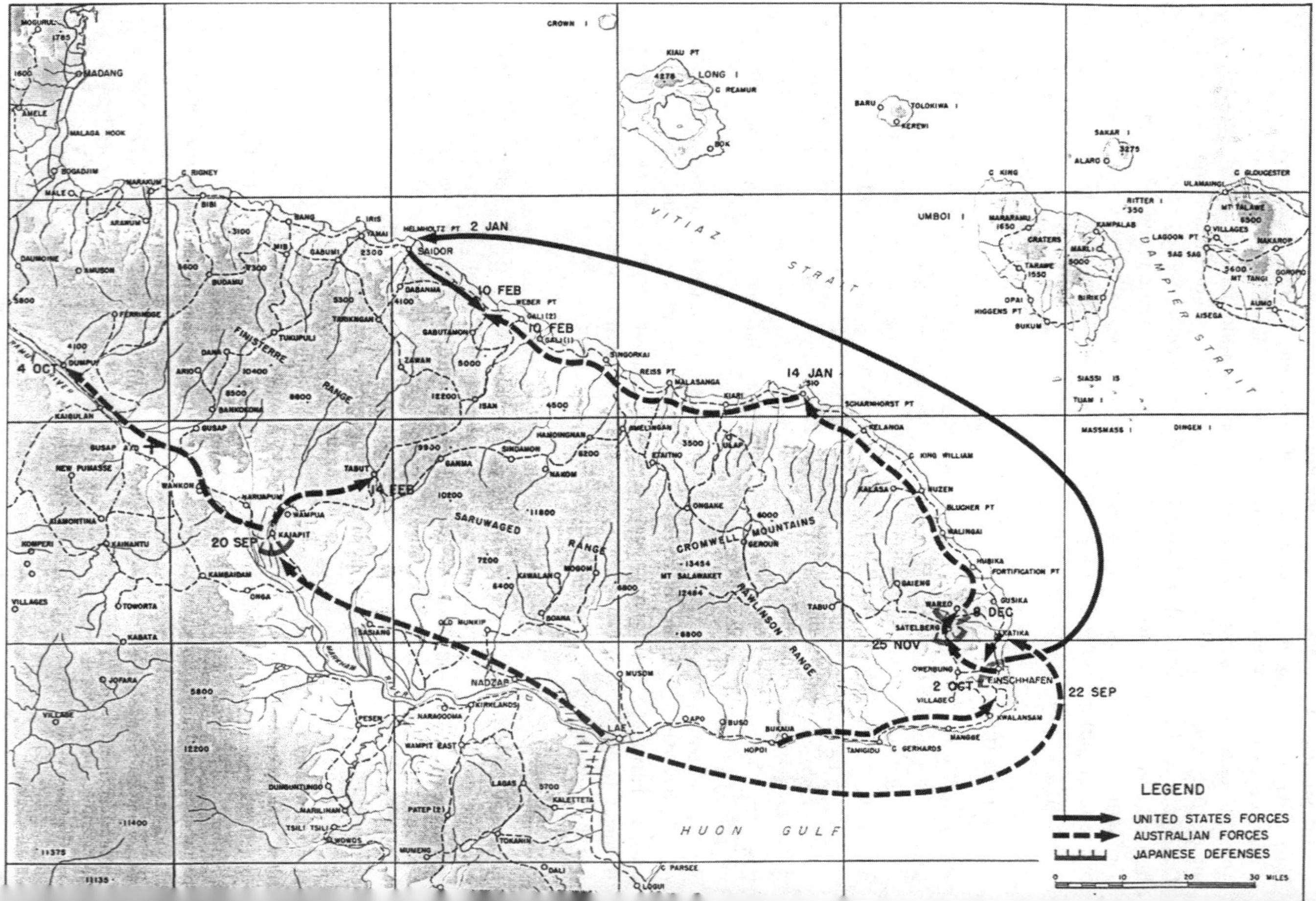

LEGEND

UNITED STATES FORCES
AUSTRALIAN FORCES
JAPANESE DEFENSES

0   10   20   30 MILES

of the *51st Division* concentrated at Lae, the Allies expected a hard fight as the Japanese closed in from the east and west. Malahand Airdrome four miles to the northeast of Lae was secured on the 15th by the 24th Brigade and Lae and its airfield were seized by the 25th Brigade on the 16th. Over 9,000 IJA and IJN troops had withdrawn northward between 12 and 15 September. The Allies attempted to trap the withdrawing *51st Division* in the Markham and Ruma River Valleys, but they retreated north over the Huon Peninsula's mountains. They left behind most of their heavy equipment, but most made it to the north coast of the Huon Peninsula in mid-October and took up positions there. The *78th Infantry Regiment* had moved up the Ruma Valley from Bogadjim to cover the withdrawal, but since the *51st Division* retreated north over the mountains rather than up the Markham Valley as originally planned, it did little good and was withdrawn after engaging Australian troops that had been flown into the valley. The defense of Lae-Salamaua and the withdrawal had cost the Japanese 2,600 troops.

The *20th Division* started from Bogadjim on 10 September and began moving along the coast 200 miles to Finschhafen where it was to arrive on 10 October. Finschhafen is located on the east end of the Huon Peninsula just north of Cape Cretin. It possesses two good harbors and an airfield. It was a key barge-staging site for barge traffic between Lae and New Britain. In August the reinforced *80th Infantry, 20th Division* was sent there and placed under the *1st Shipping Group* to total 5,000 troops. The 7th Australian Division moved up the Markham and into the Ruma Valley and secured Dumpu near its northwest end on 6 October and were prepared to advance on Madang to the north. Allied airfields were prepared in the two valleys.

In September 1943 the *Imperial General Headquarters* designated a new *National Defense Zone* anchored in the Marianas, Carolines, running through the eastern portion of Dutch New Guinea, and in the Dutch East Indies to the south facing Australia. This was forced by the loss of the Solomons and the Aleutians. The Japanese forces in the Bismarcks and eastern New Guinea were no longer a part of the perimeter defense of the empire, but were fighting a delaying action while new defenses were established to the north and west.

The decision to take Finschhafen (06°34' S 147°0' E) was made in mid-September and preparations soon began. Task Force 76 loaded the 20th Brigade at Lae on the 21st and sailed east to round Cape Cretin on the east end of Huon Peninsula. At the same time an Australian battalion left Lae on foot following the coast to threaten Finschhafen from the south. The *20th Division* was still 100 miles from Finschhafen. At 0445 hours, 22 September the assault troops landed unopposed on Beach SCARLET 5-½ miles north of Finschhafen. The *Yamada Force* was defending on the east slopes of 3,240-foot Mount Satelberg (Sattelberg in Australian documents) west of the beachhead and north of the main objective. Moving south the Australians attacked on the 23rd capturing the airfield north of Finschhafen and crossed the Bumi River the next day. There was a lull as reinforcements arrived to secure the beachhead from the Japanese forces on Mount Satelberg, from which they attacked on the 26th, only to be beaten back. Finschhafen was taken on 1 October and the next day the landing force linked up with the battalion moving from the south at Langemark Bay at the mouth of the Mape River. Besides the beachhead, this became the second main Australian lodgment. The Australians then attacked toward Mount Satelberg, but were halted. Intelligence indicated a major Japanese counterattack from the Satelberg and the lead elements of the *20th Division*. The Australians asked for reinforcements, but MacArthur refused the necessary shipping and air support feeling the Japanese threat was weak. As more intelligence was gained the Americans finally released the shipping and the 9th Division Headquarters and 24th Brigade arrived on 11 October. On the 16th the Japanese attacked the beachhead and action continued until 25 October, but all efforts failed to dislodge the Australians. The 26th Brigade arrived on 20 October and was thrown into the battle. There were several air attacks during this period. Two airfields were constructed, Finschhafen and Schneider Harbour south of Langemark Bay, and an advance naval base established as supplies built up. The Australians went on the offensive on 17 November, the day the 4th Brigade arrived. The Satelberg was taken on 8 December and the battered *20th Division* and survivors of the *Yamada Force* began retreating north, their strength cut in half. The Australians pursued along the coast and on 15 January 1944 they secured Sio sixty miles to the north of Finschhafen. The 8th Brigade continued the pursuit toward Saidor.

While it was proposed to next land at Madang, it was too strongly defended and an alternate objective, Saidor (MICHAELMAS, WHITEFLAG) (05°35' S 146°35' E), was selected. Saidor is on western portion of the Huon Peninsula's north coast seventy miles west of Sio and fifty-two miles east of Madang. It had a small harbor and a prewar airstrip. The Japanese used it as a supply and barge base. In mid-December it was directed that Saidor be seized to establish an airfield (DAYFLY) and advance naval base. The mission was assigned to ALAMO Force, the first operation on New Guinea directly under U.S. command rather than the Australian New Guinea Force. Most Australian forces were committed elsewhere and this was in preparation for ALAMO Force assuming control of operations farther to the west on New Guinea.

The much reinforced 126th Infantry, 32d Infantry Division on Goodenough Island assembled as the MICHAELMAS Task Force under Brigadier General Clarence A. Martin. There was no time for rehearsals and the force departed Goodenough on 31 December. Stopping over at Oro Bay, the attack force moved through the Vitiaz Strait and arrived in Dakays Bay before a rainy dawn on 2 January. The landing troops hit Beaches RED, WHITE, and BLUE, just east of Saidor, at 0725 hours with no opposition. Almost 6,800 troops were ashore the first day, which saw only limited air attacks. Saidor was secured and only a few Japanese were found. Within days the garrison was warned to expect the Japanese withdrawing westward from Sio to attack Saidor. Defensive preparations were made while the Australians urged the garrison to be more aggressive and intercept the Japanese that they suspected would bypass Saidor and make good their escape. The 128th Infantry arrived on 16–18 January and base development commenced. The 10,000 survivors of the *20th* and *51st Divisions* did in fact bypass Saidor and made it to Madang along with the *18th Army Headquarters*. They were covered by *78th Infantry Regiment* in the Finisterre Range from the 7th Australian Division in the Ruma Valley. The Australians, with fresh brigades in the line, cleared the Finisterres though January under difficult circumstances and forced the *78th Infantry* to join in the general retreat of the *18th Army* from the Huon Peninsula. The 5th Australian Division relieved the 9th after Sio was secured and continued the push up the coast. The Australians linked up with the Americans fourteen miles southeast of Saidor on 10 February. ALAMO Force declared that Operation DEXTERITY was completed on that date. On the 18th the 32d Infantry Division Headquarters, under Major General William H. Gill, arrived at Saidor and it took up the chase to the west. The 7th Australian Division had pushed north out of the Ruma Valley and linked up with the Americans at Kul on the east shoulder of Astroabe Bay on 21 March. The Australians pushed on to Bogadjim securing it on 13 April. The Japanese were in full retreat and abandoned Madang and the Australians entered it on 24 April. On 24 April the command of the *18th Army* in eastern New Guinea was changed from the *8th Area Army* on Rabaul to the *2d Area Army* at Davao, Mindanao, Philippines. The *2d Area Army* was also made responsible for eastern New Guinea as far east as the Huon Peninsula. The remnants of the *18th Army* were withdrawing west through Wewak and Aitape to Hollandia just on the Dutch New Guinea side of the border. The Huon

Peninsula was clear, the battered *18th Army* was retreating westward, and new U.S. operations were soon underway.

Construction on Naval Advance Base, Finschhafen (FPO SF 722) began in December 1943, although an Army airfield and PT boat base had already been built by the Navy. The base was commissioned on 1 February 1944 and it became an important amphibious staging and supply base. Further projects were canceled in November and the remaining base facilities were turned over to the Army on 1 April 1945, which continued to operate it until after the war.

Naval Advance Base, Madang-Alexishafen (FPO SF 928) was built on Sostrem Bay at Alexishafen (05°10' S 145°45' E) just north of Madang as a landing craft staging and repair base. Construction began in June 1944, it was commissioned 17 August, and closed in January 1945. A small naval advance base was opened at Saidao in March 1944 and operated there until June as a PT boat base and supplies landing site.

Aitape

One last major U.S. operation was to take place in eastern New Guinea at Aitape and was executed on the same date and in conjunction with the larger Hollandia operation (discussed in the Dutch New Guinea section). Aitape (PERSECUTION), is about ninety-four miles northwest of Wewak and 125 miles southwest of Hollandia. The operation's main objective was the three Japanese airfields at Tadji, 1,000 yards inland from the coast and eight miles east-southeast of Aitape. The fighter strip was the closest to the coast and the bomber strip was to its south. An uncompleted strip, because of drainage problems, was to the west of the bomber strip. Aitape is situated on Rohm Point on a coastal plain five to twelve miles deep edged by the foothills of the Torricelli Mountains. There are numerous rivers and streams, many bordered by large coastal and inland swamps. The best landing beaches were adjacent to the airfields. A few miles offshore and opposite of the beaches are four small islands. The Japanese had occupied the area in December 1942 and built the airfields for staging aircraft between Wewak and Hollandia and as a dispersal site when airfields in the east were attacked. The Allies estimated that there were 3,500 Japanese troops in the area, but only 2,000 construction and service troops, and replacements for the *20th Division* were located around Aitape. Japanese forces at Wewak to the east were considered a possible threat and might counterattack the landing force.

The PERSECUTION Task Force was provided by the 41st Infantry Division, which had arrived at Finschhafen on 20 March. The task force consisted of the 41st Division's 163d Infantry Regiment and the 127th Infantry detached from the 32d Infantry Division, under Brigadier General Jens A. Doe, assistant commander of the 41st. The reinforced 163d Infantry embarked aboard the Eastern Attack Group (Task Group 77.3) at Finschhafen and the 163d at Milne Bay to link up at the former. On 18 April they departed for the Admiralties where they rendezvoused on the 20th with the groups headed to Hollandia. The massed convoys sailed west and about eighty miles from New Guinea's north coast then separated and headed for their assigned landing sites.

On the morning of 22 April the Eastern Attack Group arrived off of Aitape. After a brief naval gun fire barrage by the destroyer-transports (APD), the first time they were used for this purpose in the Southwest Pacific, the 163d Infantry landed unopposed on Beach BLUE at 0645 hours. The landing was actually 1,200 yards east of the intended beach, but it proved to be a better beach. The Japanese had withdrawn and the fighter and bomber strips were secured before nightfall. RAAF engineers had the fighter strip operational by D+2 and an RAAF fighter squadron landed there to provide support to the Hollandia operation to the west. The bomber strip suffered from drainage problems and was not readied by American engineers for fighters and transports until 27 May. Bombers were able to use it in early July. Naval Advance Base, Aitape (FPO SF 927) (03°50' S 143°0' E) was developed as a PT boat base and used as an amphibious supply and assembly point from April 1944 to March 1945.

Between the 23d and 25th the four offshore islands were secured by the task force reserve. The 127th Infantry landed on 23 April. Small patrols had been sent to the west to establish outposts to protect that flank from any threat originating from Wewak, which would take at least two weeks to arrive. The 163d Infantry focused on pushing west, but its commander was overly cautious. Only stragglers were encountered. On 4 May the 32d Infantry Division Headquarters landed with the 126th Infantry. Two days later the 32d Division staff assumed command of Task Force PERSECUTION and the 163d Infantry departed on the 11th for another operation. The 128th Infantry arrived on 15 May, but remained the ALAMO Force Reserve until June 10 June when it reverted to 32d Division control. During this period the beachhead was expanded with the 127th Infantry deployed to the east. The first solid contact with Japanese elements was made on 11 May some twenty-five miles east of the beachhead. Lead elements of the *78th Infantry, 20th Division*, sent by *18th Army* from Wewak, were moving toward the beachhead.

With Huon Peninsula and eastern New Guinea secured by the Allies and now with U.S. forces ashore at Aitape and Hollandia, the 55,000-man *18th Army* found itself cut off from *2d Area Army* forces in the west. Faced with the choice of starvation (only two months' rations were on hand) and fighting their way through the intervening Americans, *18th Army* decided to move west, without orders from higher command. Within days after the American landing the *20th, 41st*, and *51st Divisions* made preparations to move. Some 20,000 troops remained behind to defend Wewak while another 20,000 moved west backed by 15,000 support troops. Through the rest of May there was much sparring as the opposing sides probed each other, but the Americans gradually fell back to the Driniumor River about fifteen miles east of the beachhead and began preparing defenses there in early June. The river was wide, but very shallow and presented no real obstacle other than providing a clear field of fire. By mid-June it had become apparent that the *18th Army* was preparing to launch a major attack in early July and reinforcements were rushed to the beachhead. The 112th Cavalry Regiment (an infantry unit) arrived on 27 June followed by the 124th Infantry, 31st Infantry Division on 2 July. Arrangements were made to speed up the deployment of the 43d Infantry Division to Aitape from New Zealand. On 10 July a reconnaissance in force was executed eastward on the coastal and inland flanks, but failed to locate the *78th* and *80th Infantry, 20th Division* and *237th Infantry, 41st Division*, which were preparing to attack center of the American line. They attacked on the night of 10/11 July penetrating the American line and creating a wide gap. The Americans fell back to a second defensive line, but the gap was sealed by the 14th during a counterattack. The line was restored by the 18th, but fighting continued on the American south (inland) flank for the rest of the month. The Japanese again attacked the south flank on 1 August in an effort to get behind the American positions and roll up the line. American counterattacks again restored the line within days. The much battered *20th* and *41st Divisions* withdrew to Wewak after loosing 8,000 men to combat and illness. U.S. losses were 450 KIA and 2,550 WIA. The operation was declared completed on 25 August. The 43d Infantry Division arrived between July and August and took over the defense from the 32d Division. Aitape was turned over to the Australians in November, who were responsible for containing the spent *18th Army*. The U.S. 32d Infantry Division departed Aitape on 1 October and the 43d on 28 December 1944.

Wewak

The ordeal of the *18th Army* was not yet over. Down to 35,000 troops, it was deployed at But on the coast twenty-five miles west of Wewak, around Wewak, and Baliffilahop in the Torricelli Range twenty-five miles inland southwest of But. Many Japanese were deployed in small scattered groups in an effort to live off the land and were tending gardens. The coastal plain in this area was very narrow and cut by numerous rivers and streams, which were often rain-swollen. The crests of the Torricelli and Prince Alexander Ranges paralleled the coast about ten to fifteen miles inland. The narrow spurs running off of these mountains provided excellent defensive positions. A track, the Old German Road, followed the coast.

The 6th Australian Division (16th, 17th, 19th Brigades), under Major General Sir Jack Stevens, arrived at Aitape between November and December 1944. The Australians began aggressive patrolling to the east upon arrival and numerous small actions were fought through January 1945. That same month saw stronger advances along the coast and in the mountains as the Japanese began to reinforce their positions in the west. Heavy rains damaged trails and washed-out bridges hampered both sides. By mid-March the Australians were twenty miles from Wewak and the following month the offensive was renewed. The advance was slow, but steady. The final effort to take Wewak began on 10 May as units attacked directly and others circled to the south. On the 11th a small landing force departed But and landed east of Wewak at 0834 hours to cut the road. By the end of May the Japanese had been forced into a confined mountain area away from the coast dashing any hope of resupply or evacuation. They could not retreat to the east as the 11th Australian Division blocked that route. To the south were only hundreds of miles of disease-ridden mountains and jungles. The Australians still pressed the *18th Army*, its three "divisions" now each mustering less strength than a regiment, to the end of the war. The Japanese had lost 7,200 dead since Aitape. The Australians lost 450 KIA and 1,160 WIA. In the end *18th Army* contained 13,500 starved, ill, battered survivors, all that was left of the over 60,000 troops it numbered in June 1943. It had actually lost more men when the late reinforcing units and replacements are counted.

Lieutenant General ADACHI Hatazo surrendered the *18th Army* on 13 September 1945. He was tried for war crimes at Rabaul by Australia and sentenced to life imprisonment, but committed suicide in 1947.

In all, 100,000 Japanese personnel were estimated to have died on eastern New Guinea. A total of 300,000 Japanese, including 20,000 civilian laborers, had been committed to the Solomons, eastern New Guinea, and the Bismarcks. Some 60,000 had died in combat and 110,000 by disease and starvation leaving 127,000 survivors to surrender.

The Territory of Papua and New Guinea was gradually returned to civilian administration in June 1946. From October 1945 the Provisional Administration of the Territory of Papua and New Guinea remained in effect until the Papua and New Guinea Act came into force in 1949. During this period Papua retained its status as a U.N.-sanctioned trusteeship of Australia. In 1971 Australia changed the title to Papua New Guinea. On 16 September 1975 Papua New Guinea was granted independence as the Independent State of Papua New Guinea. Divided into twenty provinces, the country includes the Bismarck Islands giving it 626 islands. The capital is Port Moresby. The nation's exports include coconut and wood products, gold, silver, copper, and oil. Development is slow because of the rugged terrain and limited support infrastructure, but a road now links Port Moresby and Giruwa (Girua today) generally following the route of the Kokoda Trail. Tourism is growing. A stunning monument to the resolute coastwachers provides a vigil of the sea and sky at Madang on New Guinea's north coast.

Map 41
Kiriwina and Woodlark Islands

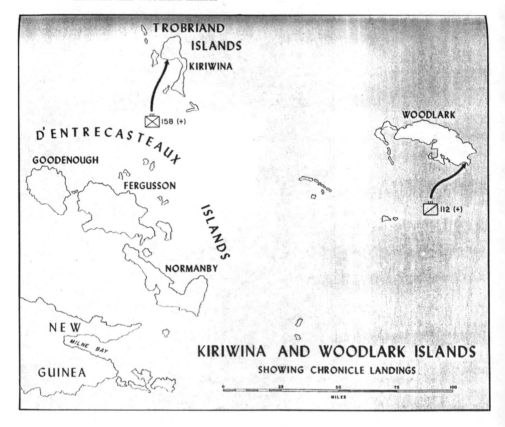

KIRIWINA AND WOODLARK ISLANDS, TERRITORY OF PAPUA

Off the southeast end of the Papuan Peninsula in the Solomon Sea are the D'Entrecasteaux Islands and beyond those is the Trobriand Group with its main island, Kiriwina, and eighty-five miles to its southeast is Woodlark Island (see Map 41). Kiriwina Island is sixty miles northeast of Goodenough Island, in the D'Entrecasteaux Islands, the nearest Allied airfield. Some references place the islands in the Bismarck Archipelago, but they are merely offshore islands of Papua. Kiriwina is 100 miles north of the Allied base at Milne Bay and 125 miles south of New Britain. Woodlark Island is 160 miles northeast of Milne Bay and 200 miles southwest of New Georgia. Both islands were within bombing range of Japanese bombers at Lae, Rabaul, and Buin (Bougainville). Nether island was occupied by the Japanese. They were assessed as ideally located to provide fighter airfields from which to escort bomber attacks on New Guinea, the Bismarcks, and the Northern Solomons. Operation CHRONICLE was planned by the 6th Army in early May 1943 for 1 June. The newly formed VII Amphibious Force would not be ready, this was to be its first operation, and it was postponed to 15 June, then 30 June. Task Force 76 departed Milne Bay on 25 June and headed north. Small advance parties were landed ahead of the main bodies. The occupation of these islands took place at the same time the Australian Salamaura offensive began.

Kiriwina Island

Kiriwina (aka Trobriand), code-named BY-PRODUCT, is situated at 08°30' S 151°03' E. The only island of significant size in the Trobriand Group (BIRTHDAY), it is approximately twenty-five miles long from north to south and seven miles across at it northern bulbous end; its twisted southern stem averages two miles in width. The group was administered by Papua's South Eastern District headquartered in Bwagaoia in Misima Island, as were most of the other islands off the east end of the Papuan Peninsula. The densely forested, raised coral island has an elevation of 180 feet on its north end. It is ringed with coral reefs with few openings and there were no good landing beaches. A long reef line stretches thirty miles from its south end. Most of the group's islets are scattered up to fifty miles to the west. The climate is wet and tropical. It had a population of 7,500 natives with the principal village of Losuia on the southwest coast of the protruding north end. Losuia could only be approached through a winding five-mile-long, 200-yard-wide channel from the south. The island had a well-developed trail system and was suitable for building an airfield.

An RAAF radar station had been established on the island in May. An advance engineer party landed at midnight on 24 June and began preparations for the arrival of the main body. A 300-yard-long coral causeway was built on Kiriwina's north coast because of the poor beach landing sites. The main BY-PRODUCT Landing Force, the separate 158th Infantry Regiment, reinforced but lacking a battalion, arrived before dawn on 30 June. The landing craft were grounded 200–300 yards from shore forcing men and equipment to wade across the shallow reef. Word of the north shore causeway had not reached them. Regardless, the 0630 hour landing put 2,250 troops ashore on Beach RED just west of Losuia. Base development efforts were plagued by heavy rain, but a 5,000-foot fighter field, later extended to 6,000 feet, was ready by the end of July and its facilities were completed in October. The field was bombed by the Japanese a few times during its construction causing only limited damage. The RAAF began flying strike missions to New Guinea from there in August. Even though the Japanese knew of the force's presence, Kiriwina was not attacked. The small Navy Advance Base, Kiriwina was established in October for PT boats to conduct barge interdiction missions along the south coast of New Britain. They had little success and the base was closed in February 1944. The airfield, though, remained in operation by the USAAF into 1945 and the Army used the island as a supply base from September 1943 (APO SF 928–2).

Woodlark Island

Woodlark, also known by its native name, Muyua, was code-named LEATHERBACK (later MANTELSHELF). It is situated at 09°10' S 152°80' E. Woodlark is a forty-four-mile-long crescent with a number of good anchorages along the convex south coast. It varies from ten to twenty miles wide. The wide beaches on the south coast are fronted by high cliffs 200–400 yards from the water's edge. Its highest elevation is 738 feet being hilly and covered with coral outcroppings. The island is densely vegetated by jungle. There was only a small native population. Most of the island is edged with coral reefs and there are a few islets off the west end. The best landing site is Guasopa Harbour on the southeast end approachable only through two channels.

An advance landing party of the LEATHERBACK Landing Force had arrived at 0032 hours, 23 June. The main landing force began coming ashore at Guasopa Harbour at 1600 hours, 30 June. The separate 112th Cavalry Regiment, 134th Field Artillery Battalion, and the Marine 12th Defense Battalion landed 2,600 troops. Only two feeble bombings were conducted by the Japanese beginning on 27 July. A 3,000-foot fighter field was ready on 14 July. It was extended to 6,500 feet in September and the base facilities were completed the following month. The USAAF fighters stationed on Woodlark ended up serving only as a defense force and never flew any strikes. Woodlark too was used as an Army supply base (APO SF 928–3). The Navy established a small advance base (FPO SF 528) there to repair PT boats and landing craft from November 1943 to March 1944.

BISMARCK ARCHIPELAGO

The Bismarck Archipelago (RATTRAP), known earlier as the New Britain Archipelago, stretches across the Bismarck Sea (WHIMSICAL) from the coast of North-East (mainland) New Guinea approximately 500 miles eastward to the northernmost of the Solomon Islands, Bougainville. The Japanese called it *Bisumaku Shoto*. From the south coast of New Britain to the north edge of the Admiralty Islands the area measures 300 miles. Besides New Britain and the Admiralty Islands, the other major land mass in the Bismarcks is New Ireland near the group's western periphery. The land area of the Bismarcks and Admiralties is 26,300 square miles. The Bismarcks were politically part of the Australian Mandated Territory of New Guinea, which administratively includes Bougainville, but that island is geographically part of the Northern Solomons and is discussed in that section. The Bismarcks and Admiralties were in time zone 22, the same as mainland Papua and New Guinea.

An Englishman, Able Tasman discovered New Britain and New Ireland in 1642. In 1686, another Englishman, William Dampier, rediscovered New Britain, which he named, and saw the Admiralty Islands for the first time. He revisited New Britain and New Ireland in 1700. Captain Philip Carteret visited and named New Ireland and discovered the Duke of York Group between New Ireland and New Britain. English Captain Simpson explored Blanche Bay (named after his ship) and Simpson Harbour, now Rabaul Harbour, on the northeast end of New Britain. In the early 1860s the Germans began trading and establishing some plantations on New Britain and New Ireland, the Northern Solomons, and North-East New Guinea. Little of this was known to the outside world. They found an ally of a most unusual type, Mrs. Emma Forsyth, a half-Samoan, half-American woman, the daughter of an American consular in Samoa. She established herself and her large extended family on the Duke of York Islands in the late 1870s. Battling the local natives, they established coconut plantations on New Britain around today's Rabaul. She had so much influence and local power that the Germans referred to her as "Queen Emma." She convinced the Germans to move their colonial headquarters from Finschhafen on the north coast of New Guinea to Kokopo on Blanche Bay and then built the town of Rabual at Simpson Harbour moving their headquarters there in 1910. Queen Emma sold out her trading and planting firm, Forsayth and Company, to a German trading firm in 1912 upon retirement. Germany had claimed protectorate status over North-East New Guinea, the Bismarcks (*Bismarck Archipel*), and Northern Solomons in 1884 and formerly annexed the region as German New Guinea the next year. The existing German South Sea Syndicate, a group of trading and planter firms, was granted virtual sovereignty over the "protectorate" by the German government and chartered as the New Guinea Company. The organization's overly ambitious development plan and climate led to its demise. Dissatisfied with the organization's poor performance, the German government bought out the firm in 1899. Relieved of governmental responsibilities, the New Guinea Company, Hamburg South Sea Company, and other firms grew and the economic situation improved. In 1910, the Mariana, Marshall, and Caroline Islands were added to the German protectorate. On 11 September 1914, German New Guinea was occupied by Australian troops after a few minor engagements. There were 1,005 Germans, 112 British, 131 Japanese, and 368 Chinese living in German New Guinea at the time. The Mariana, Marshall, and Caroline Islands were occupied by Japan and later mandated to her. The League of Nations granted Australia control of German New Guinea under a Class C mandate in 1920, which took effect on 9 May 1921. The region was designated the Mandated Territory of New Guinea and included the Bismarcks, Bougainville, and other small islands east of New Guinea. Australian development in the Bismarcks was slow. The principal source of income in the Bismarcks was coconuts, timber, and turtle shells. The principal trading firm in the islands was the W. R. Carpenter and Company Limited, which was given many government contracts to aid the civil administration to include operating an air mail route and shipping services.

The capital of the Mandated Territory was Rabaul on the northeast end of New Britain. In 1939, Lae, on North-East New Guinea, was selected to become the territory's capital, but the war prevented this. This was because of the danger posed by the volcanoes surrounding Rabaul and the desire to expedite development of the mainland. Besides the three mainland administrative districts, there were seven districts on the islands: Rabaul, Talase, and Gasmata on New Britain; Kavieng on northern New Ireland and New Hanover Island, Lavongai on southern New Ireland, Manus in the Admiralty Islands (and Kieta on Bougainville and Buka).

The natives of the Bismarcks are Melanesians with some Polynesian blood. There was no form of indigenous government beyond the tribal level. They were warlike and practiced cannibalism into the 1890s, with those on New Ireland being among the most notorious. By the time of the war those in patrolled areas had embraced Christianity and were turning to planting and fishing. There were still reports of headhunting and slave raids between tribes in the interior of New Britain though. Thousands of natives were employed as laborers. Plantation owners were required to provide for all their needs while in their employ. Indentured or contracted Asiatic laborers were prohibited. Tropical diseases were rampant and generally the same as found on mainland New Guinea and the Solomons. In particular, the natives of New Britain were wreaked by tropical diseases.

Weather conditions in the Bismarcks are regulated by the same meteorological events as on the mainland, the northwest monsoon from October to April with heavy rains and the southeast monsoon from April to September. Regardless of the season, rain is encountered year-round as is high heat and humidity as found in the Solomons.

The war came to the Bismarcks on 20 January 1942 when for two days all important towns and ports in the islands and mainland New Guinea were bombed by IJN carrier-based aircraft. Serious damage was inflicted on Rabaul, but only light damage on Kavieng; both were attacked the next day. Evacuation of European women and children had just been completed, ordered on 17 January, but all European men were still in the islands, mainly concentrated at Rabaul and Kavieng. Many of those who were fit joined the NGVR. The Australian government opted to neither reinforce nor evacuate the meager defense force at Rabaul prior to the Japanese invasion. The *4th Fleet's South Seas*

Detachment (144th Infantry Regiment), under Major General HORII Tomitaro, departed Truk on 16 January to occupy Rabaul, the *R Operation*. Rabaul, with two airdromes and a few old aircraft, was defended by a 1,400-man garrison, Lark Force: a coast defense battery, destroyed by the air attack on the 21st, 2/22d Infantry Battalion, an NGVR company, and No. 24 Squadron, RAAF. An approaching Japanese invasion fleet was detected on the 22nd and the remaining civilians were evacuated into the jungle. The Japanese landed at 0100 hours, 23 January and by late morning had routed the defenders. Many died fighting, others fled into the hills and were hunted down. Some 200 surrendered and on 4 March 150 were massacred at the Tol and Waitavalo Plantations on the south coast. Some 400 made it to the north and south coasts and were evacuated to the mainland by civilian boats searching for them into April. The territorial administrator, Brigadier Sir Walter McNicoll, narrowly escaped. Undefended Kavieng was occupied on the 23rd by an element of the *South Seas Detachment*. All remaining Europeans were interned. Surumi and Gasnata on the south coast of New Britain was occupied on 9 February by *special naval landing forces*. There were small detachments of the 1st Independent Company scattered as coastwachers all through the Bismarcks on New Britain, New Ireland, the Admiralties, Buka, Bougainville, and the Solomons, but many of these were hunted down with a few becoming coastwachers. The Japanese soon consolidated and began improving existing airfields and building new ones; the first aircraft arrived on 30 January. Rabaul became the headquarters for the *Southeastern Fleet, 11th Air Fleet*, and *8th Area Army*. These three headquarters jointly controlled all naval, air, and ground forces in the vast region covering eastern New Guinea, the Bismarcks, and the Solomons with up to 94,000 IJA and IJN personnel. It was the region's staging and logistical center. It was to become the focal point of all Allied operations in the region and had to be seized or neutralized before the Philippines could be liberated.

   The long and involved planning process for Rabaul began in July 1942 when the U.S. Joint Chiefs of Staff directed the commanders in chief of the Pacific Fleet and the Southwest Pacific to accomplish three tasks: (1) seize Tulagi and Guadalcanal, (2) capture the remainder of the Solomons and clear the enemy from the Lae-Salamanua area in Papua, and (3) seize Rabaul. With Task 1 accomplished in February 1943, a new plan, ELKTON II, was issued that same month directing that airfields on New Guinea's Huon Peninsula be seized to support operations against New Britain, Munda Point on New Georgia be seized for airfields to support operations against the Northern Solomons and New Ireland, the west end of New Britain and Bougainville be seized for airfields to support operations against Rabaul and Kavieng, and finally, Rabaul be recaptured. As operations were accomplished the plan evolved into ELKTON III issued in April 1943 resulting in Operation CARTWHEEL with the ultimate goal of seizing Rabaul and Kavieng by the spring of 1944. The operation to secure the Bismarcks and Admiralties was designated FISHNET. By July 1943 consideration was being given to bypassing Rabaul altogether rather than enduring an outright assault of the stronghold. After the success of the island-hopping strategy, reinforced by the late 1943 experience on Bougainville when the Japanese strongholds on the island's north and south ends were neutralized by air and sea actions negating the need for direct assault, it was decided to neutralize Rabaul in the same manner. No direct assault would be necessary. This was accomplished by pounding the Japanese stronghold by air and sea, and cutting off its supply routes to the Carolines and Marinas. A ring of islands around Rabaul would be seized for airfields and small naval bases from which to support this effort. These bases would be established on Kiriwina and Woodlark Islands to the south of Rabaul, Bougainville and Green Islands to the southeast, Emirau

Island and Admiralty Islands to the northeast of New Britain itself, and along the north coast of eastern New Guinea stretching from the west to the south of Rabaul.

While there are hundreds of islands large and small in the Bismarcks, only a small number were directly involved in the war. These are addressed in the order in which they were secured by the Allies: Green Islands, Emirau Island, Admiralty Islands, New Britain, and New Ireland. (Bougainville, eastern New Guinea, and Kiriwina and Woodlark Islands have been previously addressed.)

Green Islands, Bismarck Archipelago

The Green Islands, also known as Nissan Islands after its dominating island (see Map 42), was coded-named SQUAREPEG. It was originally named Sir Charles Hardy Islands, but the name fell from use. After it was secured by the Allies both the atoll and its main island, Nissan, were collectively known simply as "Green Island." The atoll is situated at 04°38' S 154°15' E approximately thirty-seven miles north-northwest of Buka on the north end of Bougainville and fifty-five miles east of the southeast end of New Britain. It is mildly disputed whether the Green Islands are considered part of the Solomons or the Bismarcks; they lie slightly closer to Buka than New Ireland, but appear to be an extension of four other small atolls lying along New Ireland's northeast coast. The islands were administered from New Ireland and were in time zone 22 (Bismarcks) rather than 23 (Solomons).

The Japanese had only a barge-staging base there to support Buka and northern Bougainville. Even after the Allies were well established on Bougainville they did not reinforce it as an out guard post for the protection of Rabaul and Kavieng, a position for which it was eminently suited. Rabaul is 117 miles to the west and Kavieng is 220 miles to the northwest. The Allies found it desirable to secure some foothold east of Rabaul from which to interdict barge traffic on the Rabaul-Buka-Bougainville run and to attack Kavieng and other bases on New Ireland. The proposed Tanga Islands, twenty-five miles east of New Ireland and some seventy miles north of the Green Islands, was too far for fighters from Bougainville to remain on station a sufficient time. The establishment of beachheads at one or both of the two Japanese airfields on New Ireland's east coast would require large landing forces and carrier air support. The Green Islands were within land-based fighter range and weakly defended. In late December 1943 it was decided to seize both the Green Islands and the Admiralties in February 1944.

The Green Islands' main coral atoll is nine miles across from north to south and five miles from east to west. The main island is Nissan, which constitutes virtually the entire atoll. Nissan is basically an oval with its northwest side open allowing entry into the lagoon forming a rough reversed "C." It varies from 300 to 1,800 yards in width with an average of about 1,000 yards. The gap on the northwest side is partly filled by two small islands, Sirot and Barahun, forming three entrances to the lagoon, North, Middle, and South Channels. The latter is only sixteen feet deep and forty to fifty feet wide and is the best. The south and north ends of Nissan are edged with coral reefs. The lagoon's shore is likewise edged with reefs around its south end, up the west side, and to the north. Most of the lagoon's east shore is free of reefs. In the center of the lagoon is the remnants of a volcanic cone, tiny Hon Island. Most of Nissan rises only a few feet above sea level, but there are two areas of raised ground on the east side, flanking the future landing beaches, and another on the south end. Most of the islands are covered with thick forest and brush, but there were coconut plantations on both ends of the reversed

Map 42
Green Islands

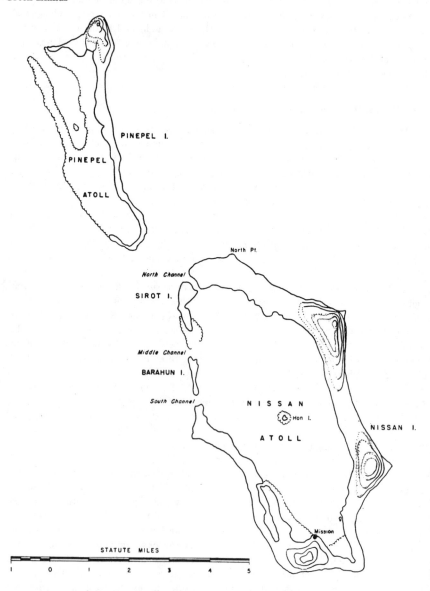

"C" and on the middle portion. There were 1,147 Melanesian natives living in small villages scattered over the island where they tended the coconut plantations and taro gardens. A mile and a half to the north is the small Pinepel Atoll, the other part of the Green Islands. Its main island, Pinepel, is shaped like an elongated "J" almost six miles in length north to south.

Little was known about the atoll and the South Pacific command planned two bold reconnaissance missions to answer intelligence shortfalls. On 10/11 January 1944 four PT boats from Torokina examined the lagoon channels finding the South Channel to be seventeen feet deep at low tide, sufficient to accommodate tank-landing ships. The next step was a reconnaissance in force executed on the night of 30/31 January, close enough to D-Day that it was hoped the Japanese would not be able to reinforce the garrison. Three destroyer-transports delivered 322 troops of the 30th New Zealand Infantry Battalion and a twenty-seven-man American survey team to Nissan at midnight. The transports withdrew and the force scouted the island selecting landing beaches and an airfield site, verified lagoon water depths (in most cases it is over fifty feet deep), and interviewed the natives finding them friendly, but hostile toward the Japanese. The seventy-two Japanese defenders, who had withdrawn to the south end of the island, fired on one of the landing craft killing four men. They were of no further trouble and the reconnaissance force did not pursue them. A single air attack was launched from Rabaul, but inflicted no damage. The operation's naval commander found that the island could have been secured at the time, but since there were no plans for immediate follow-on reinforcement and the threat of more air attacks from Rabaul, they withdrew the next day as planned. D-Day was set for 15 February with the 3d New Zealand Division's 14th Brigade Group, reinforced with U.S. antiaircraft and Seabee units, assigned the mission with the division commander in charge.

The Green Islands Attack Group departed Vella Lavella and the Treasury Islands on 12–13 February. The attack group was harassed by air attacks during the transit, but arrived off of Nissan's west side and sent landing craft though South Channel after first light. Two battalions landed without opposition on the excellent Beaches RED and GREEN on the lagoon's east side at 0700 hours. The battalions turned north and south to sweep the island's length. Another battalion landed at 0655 hours on Beach BLUE at the end of the lower arm of the reversed "C" and secured the lagoon's entrance. Allied aircraft had been pounding Rabaul and Kavieng for two weeks, but the Japanese were able to launch significant air strikes. Little was accomplished by these and no other air attacks followed other than a few night bomber harassing raids. The original seventy-two Japanese soldiers and sailors had fled to Feni Island thirty-five miles to the north on 1 February. A third of them returned on the 5th and were reinforced by a seventy-seven-man naval guard detachment delivered from Rabaul by submarine. There were 102 Japanese on the island. Some forty of them dug in around the Catholic mission on Nissan's south end and were wiped out between 16 and 19 February. A 5,800-man force was now established ashore and work began on an airfield on the central portion of the "C." On the 17th, a small landing party was placed on Sirot Island astride the North and Middle Channels and killed twenty-nine enemy there. A boat patrol visiting Pinepel Atoll to the north killed fourteen Japanese on Sau Island. Total Allied losses were thirteen KIA and twenty-four WIA. The natives were temporarily relocated to Guadalcanal by the Navy.

The bomber field was begun immediately and was 5,000 feet long in early March and 6,000 by the end of the month, even though there were terrain and weather difficulties. On 7 March, the first air strike on Kavieng to stage though Green Island came in from Piva, Bougainville. The runway was later lengthened to 7,300 feet. A PT boat base was built and began operations along the coasts of New Ireland and New Britain in February. A small seaplane base was built in June and support facilities for Naval Advance Base, Green Island (FPO SF 3202) were completed in July. The Army established Provisional Green Island Command (APO 293). Late in 1944 roll-up began and most facilities were dismantled by January 1945. The base was closed in August and the island turned over to its original inhabitants.

Admiralty Islands, Bismarck Archipelago

The Admiralty Islands were code-named BREWER and are spread around the large dominating island, Manus Island, code-named MERCANTILE. The islands were discovered by William Schouten, a Dutchman, in 1615. Captain Philip Carteret visited and named the islands in 1767. They were claimed as part of German New Guinea in 1884 and eventually passed to Australia.

The Admiralties, while not the northernmost of the Bismarcks, do define the archipelago's northwest edge being situated at 02°00' S 145°00' E (the northernmost island of the Bismarcks and the Southwest Pacific is Sae Island on the northeast edge of the scattered Western Islands to the northwest of the Admiralties). A small Japanese detachment occupied the Hermit Islands in the Western Islands, 120 miles to the west-northwest of Manus, but no action took place there. To the southeast are Kavieng at 260 miles and Rabaul at 390. New Guinea is 200 miles to the southwest. Due north are the Caroline Islands, across some 700 miles of empty sea.

The group's main island is Manus (see Map 43). Most of the other 160 small atolls, islands, and islets comprising the group are scattered up to fifty miles to the south, southeast, and east. The group's second largest island is Rambutyo about forty miles to the east-southeast. To the east are Pak and Tong Islands at eighteen and thirty-eight miles, respectively. Lou Island is about sixteen miles to the southeast. The islands contain a total of 800 square miles of land. Only Manus and a small island immediately adjacent to its east end, Los Negros, were to be the scene of significant action.

Manus Island (TEACUP) is forty-nine miles long from east to west and sixteen miles wide across the center. The island is of volcanic origin with a rugged 2,355-foot-high mountain range extending over its length. Most of the soil is a reddish clay. Numerous small streams flow into the sea on all sides of the island. Most of these are easily forded, but prone to flash flooding from mountain rains. The entire island is blanketed with dense forest with palms covering many areas of the coastal plains, often with underbrush. Small and large swamps are often encountered immediately inland and many coastal areas are lined with mangrove swamps. Most of the coast is fringed with close-in coral reefs. Beaches are few and those are very narrow with vegetation often growing to the water's edge on most of the shore. Hot and humid, the islands experience frequent rain, which, when combined with the clay soil, creates a gumbo-like mud.

The main settlement is Lorengau on the northeast coast on Seeadler Harbour (German for "sea eagle") (BICARBONATE, OREX). There were other small villages on the coasts, with most on the northeast, but the only other two of any size were Bundials on the north-central coast and Sopa Sopa on the west end. A native track followed the island's north coast from end to end and three trails crossed laterally over the mountains to the south coast. Only in the immediate vicinity of Lorengau were there any roads on which motor vehicles could be driven. Known for their canoeing skills, the 13,000 natives, Melanesians with some Micronesian blood, lived mostly on Manus' east end and adjacent Los Negros. The coconut plantations, turtle shells, and pearl diving were the island's source of income. Before the war the islands' abundant shell beds were plundered by the Japanese from the Carolines.

Most of the fighting took place on Los Negros Island and Manus' east end. Los Negros (UNDERDOG) is roughly horseshoe-shaped with its open side to the west enclosing Seeadler Harbour. It is an uplifted coral island. Los Negros' seaward northwest end tapers to a blunt point while the southwest end is over two miles wide in places. Both shores of the island's south and central portion are ragged and deeply indented by irregularly

Map 43
Eastern Manus and Los Negros Islands, Admiralty Islands, Bismarck Archipelago

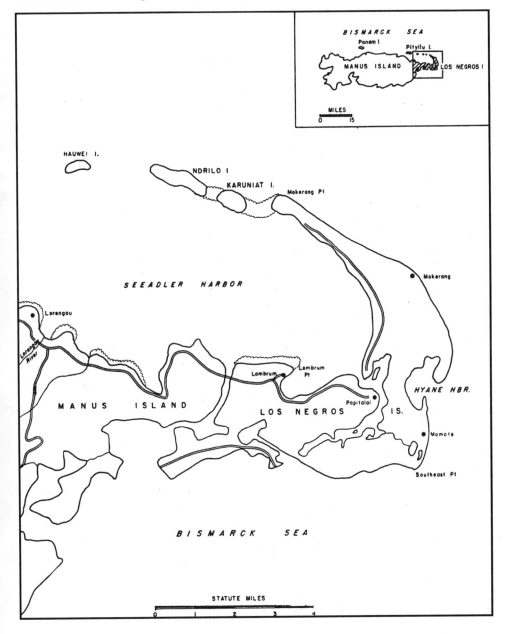

shaped inlets. Two of these, Papitalai Harbour on the west side and Hyane Harbour on the east, almost cut the island in two across the center, which is low and swampy. The northwest and southwest portions of the island are connected by a fifty-yard-wide spit. The portion of the island to the northwest is flat and low covered with swamps and the Salami palm plantation. The broader southwest portion is covered by forest interspersed with swamps and hills up to 200 feet high. Los Negros is separated from the east end of Manus by the 100-yard-wide Loniu Passage.

The east end of Manus Island serves as the south shore of Seeadler Harbour (02°1' S 147°25' E) while Los Negros wraps around the east end. The north edge of the harbor is protected by a line of low coconut palm-covered islets running west from the northwest end of Los Negros, Mokerang Point. These islands are, from east to west, Koruniat, Ndrilo, Houwei, and Pityilu, the largest. The harbor is six miles across, twenty miles long, and 120 feet deep, making it capable of sheltering a fleet. Northeast Manus is comprised of rolling hills gradually rising to almost 300 feet before they upsurge into the mountains further west. The coastal plain, broader than on the south coast, is cut by a number of streams, but is generally level. Lorengau Village is about 5-½ miles from the island's east end beside a small river bearing the same name.

The Japanese occupied Manus on 8 April 1942 after first securing New Britain and New Ireland. The Hermit Islands to the west-northwest were occupied on 7 April. Lorengau had been bombed on 21 January at the same time as Kavieng and locations on New Guinea. The occupation force was the battalion-size *51st Transport Regiment*, detached from the *51st Division*, dispatched from Rabaul. In the process they rounded up the small 1st Independent Company coastwatcher detachment. A 4,000-foot airfield was first built at Monote Point (STRAIGHTLEFT) on Los Negros just to the south of the fifty-yard-wide spit and in 1943 a 3,300-foot strip was built just to the northwest of Lorengau Village. Late in 1943 when the Japanese decided to reinforce Kavieng, it was directed that the Admiralties also be reinforced. A detachment of the *14th Base Force* was sent from Kavieng. The *2d Battalion, 1st Independent Mixed Regiment* and *1st Battalion, 229th Infantry Regiment* was sent from Kavieng in late January and early February, respectively. The senior officer was Colonel EZAKI Yoshio.

As part of the plan to cut off Rabaul, the Admiralties were selected for seizure. The USAAF hoped that by taking the Admiralties it might preclude the need to assault Kavieng and Hansa Bay on the New Guinea mainland as their airfields were needed by the Allies. In January and February 1944 numerous air raids hit the Los Negros from New Guinea. The intent was to encourage the garrison to abandon Los Negros and withdraw to Manus, but cause minimal damage to the airfield runways. Later low-altitude overflights received no fire and detected no enemy activity. Los Negros appeared abandoned. It was proposed that a reconnaissance in force be conducted immediately. If there was little or no resistance they would be followed by reinforcements standing by, but if they met strong resistance they could withdraw and a stronger landing force would be marshaled. A debate soon developed by the different involved headquarters over the Japanese strength. MacArthur's staff estimated 4,050 enemy troops and the 1st Cavalry Division (the landing force) assessed 4,900 while the Fifth Air Force said no more than 300. This was a serious concern as the reconnaissance in force would number only 1,000 men because of shipping limitations. The 6th Army sent a scout team to Los Negros in late February and they reported heavy concentrations of enemy troops. Natives confirmed the islands had not been evacuated. The Fifth Air Force discounted the reports. Another development occurred at that time, late February. U.S. destroyers venturing into the Rabaul and Kavieng areas were unmolested by Japanese aircraft or surface forces, once areas dominated by the Japanese. Encouraged by this and regardless of the disparity in the enemy strength estimates, MacArthur ordered that the reconnaissance in force be executed on 29 February. They were to land on Los Negros, seize the airfield, and prepare it to receive reinforcement by air as well as by sea.

The BREWER Task Force was drawn from the 1st Brigade, 1st Cavalry Division, then at Oro Bay, New Guinea. The landing force commander was Brigadier General William C. Chase, the brigade commander. The core of the force was the 2d Squadron, 5th Cavalry Regiment.[2]

The task force departed from Cape Sudest near Oro Bay on 27 February. The follow-on support force would depart from the closer Cape Cretin two days after the landing if the reconnaissance force did not withdraw. Rain and fog covered the task force as it proceeded north to arrive off the east end on Los Negros on the morning of the 29th. Little air support arrived because of the weather. The 4,450 Japanese troops were deployed to meet a landing from the north into Seeadler Harbour. They had taken convincing camouflage measures and refrained from firing on U.S. aircraft during the preceding month. The landing was made into Hyane Harbour on the east-center of Los Negros. The Japanese were completely taken by surprise even though they had been alerted of the American approach. Their strength advantage and deception efforts were lost. The mouth of the bay is only 750 yards wide and then opens into a 2,500-yard-wide semicircle. The north and west shores are lined with dense mangroves, but on the south shore is a 1,200-yard-wide sand beach with three piers. The first wave came ashore at 0817 hours receiving only a spattering of small-arms fire. The abandoned airfield was soon overrun and the entire force was ashore. General MacArthur, who accompanied the force as an observer, came ashore to assess whether the cavalrymen could hold until reinforcements arrived. Assured they could, he departed ordering the follow-on forces to deploy early. The cavalrymen pulled back behind the airfield and established a tight defensive line to await the enemy and reinforcement. The Japanese attacked that night making no gains. Japanese attacks continued, but another cavalry squadron was landed at Hyane Harbour on the morning of 4 March followed by the 1st Cavalry Division Headquarters the next day, under Major General Innis P. Swift. The 12th Cavalry Regiment landed on 6 March as the reconnaissance force began clearing the rest of Los Negros. Two cavalry squadrons were ferried across Seeadler Harbour on the 6th and 8th to land on the harbor's south side, Los Negros' southwest arm's north shore. The northern arm of the island was secured by 9 March allowing the 2d Cavalry Brigade (-) to land on the east end of Seeadler Harbour, on Los Negros. On the 10th an RAAF squadron landed at Momote Airdrome and began operations from there. The Japanese managed to launch in a few air harassing attacks from Wewak, New Guinea early in the campaign.

As the 1st Cavalry Brigade consolidated Los Negros, the 2d Brigade (7th and 8th Cavalry) was assigned to secure Manus by landing near Lorengau on the northeast coast. To support the landing, islands in Seeadler Harbour were selected on which to emplace artillery. One of these was Butjo Mokou near Bear Point on the east end of Manus (the northernmost of the two tiny islands of the Butjo Islands). The other was Hauwei on the north edge of the harbor five miles northeast of the landing beaches. The reconnaissance platoon was driven off of Hauwei on 11 March. A cavalry squadron was landed the next day and secured the island on the 13th destroying a platoon of sailors and coastal defense guns. Pityilu was cleared on 30 March. The 2d Brigade landed on either side of the mouth of the Liei River 3,000 yards west of the Lorengau Airdrome on the morning of 15 March. The airfield and Lorengau Village were secured by the 18th. Many of the Japanese fled west on Manus while small pockets held out on Los Negros. It was not until 25 March that Los Negros was completely cleared when the Japanese remnants made a last stand on the central portion of the island's southwest arm. The north coastal area on Manus was secured in May and it was not until 1 April that Ndrilo and Koruniat Islands were cleared. The 1st Cavalry Division lost 330 KIA and almost 2,200 WIA. The Japanese lost 4,380 KIA and seventy-five prisoners.

Momote Fighter Field was extended to 7,800 feet by mid-May. The Lorengau Air-drome, with both of its ends resting on the water's edge, could not be improved and was abandoned. A new 8,000-foot bomber field was built at Mokerang Plantation on the northwest arm of Los Negros in April and a second runway was added later. Both Lorengau and Mokerang were used by the USAAF. The Navy built a 5,000-foot fighter field with aircraft repair and overhaul facilities on Ponam Island three miles off of Manus' north coast and twenty-five miles west of Seeadler Harbour. A 4,500-foot airfield was built on Pityilu Island, the westernmost of the islands on the north edge of Seeadler Harbour, along with a fleet recreation center. A seaplane base was built at Lombrum Point on the harbor side on Los Negro's southwest arm. Seeadler Harbour was developed as Naval Advance Base, Manus, Admiralty Islands (FPO SF 3205) being commissioned on 18 May 1944. It was to serve as a main fleet base to support operations on the north coast of New Guinea, the Marianas, Carolines, and the Philippines. Major repair facilities, boat and landing craft repair facilities, fuel, ships' stores, and other materiel depots were established. The base continued to grow into 1945, but early that year some fleet support activities were moved forward to Ulithi, Guam, and Leyte. After assisting with the roll-up of other Southwest Pacific bases it was closed on 1 September 1945.

Even with the benefit of the ample port and airfield facilities built on Manus and Los Negros, the islands have undergone little development today. Manus Province, which includes the whole of the Admiralties, is the smallest of Papua New Guinea's twenty provinces.

Emirau Island, St. Matthias Group

The small St. Matthias Group (CARPETBAG) consists of the three main Mussau, Emirau, and Emananus Islands. Emirau Island, also known as Emira or Squally, was code-named BEEFSTEAK. The group lies some seventy-five miles northwest of New Hanover Island off the northeast end of New Ireland, 100 miles northwest of Kavieng, 150 miles east-northeast of the Admiralty Islands, and 250 miles northwest of Rabaul. Mussau Island is the largest in the group located is at 01°50" S 149°00" and measures some fifteen by thirty miles.

Emirau Island, which was secured by the Allies and a base constructed, is situated at 01°38" S 150°00" E (see Map 44). It is 12-½ miles to the southeast of Mussau. Emirau is the southernmost island in the group. Shaped like a disfigured shark, it is eight miles long east to west and 4-½ miles across the center at its shark's fin, a peninsula jutting to the north. The island's average width is two miles. The west end of the misshapen "head" has a large pond in the center; the east end tapers to a point. The coast is bordered by a flatland several hundred feet wide. A fairly level plateau occupies most of the island atop 75- to 185-foot high inland cliffs. The island is covered with a mix of light vegetation and dense forest. A number of coconut palm plantations are scattered along the coastal flatlands. Much of the south coast is edged with mangrove swamps. Virtually the entire shore is fringed by a reef and a few islets. Among these are Elomusad off the east end, Lucile and Weeze off the south-central coast, and Eanusau (aka Inusau) and Sanilu off the west end. Good anchorages are found on the north and south-central sides

Emirau Island, Saint Matthias Group

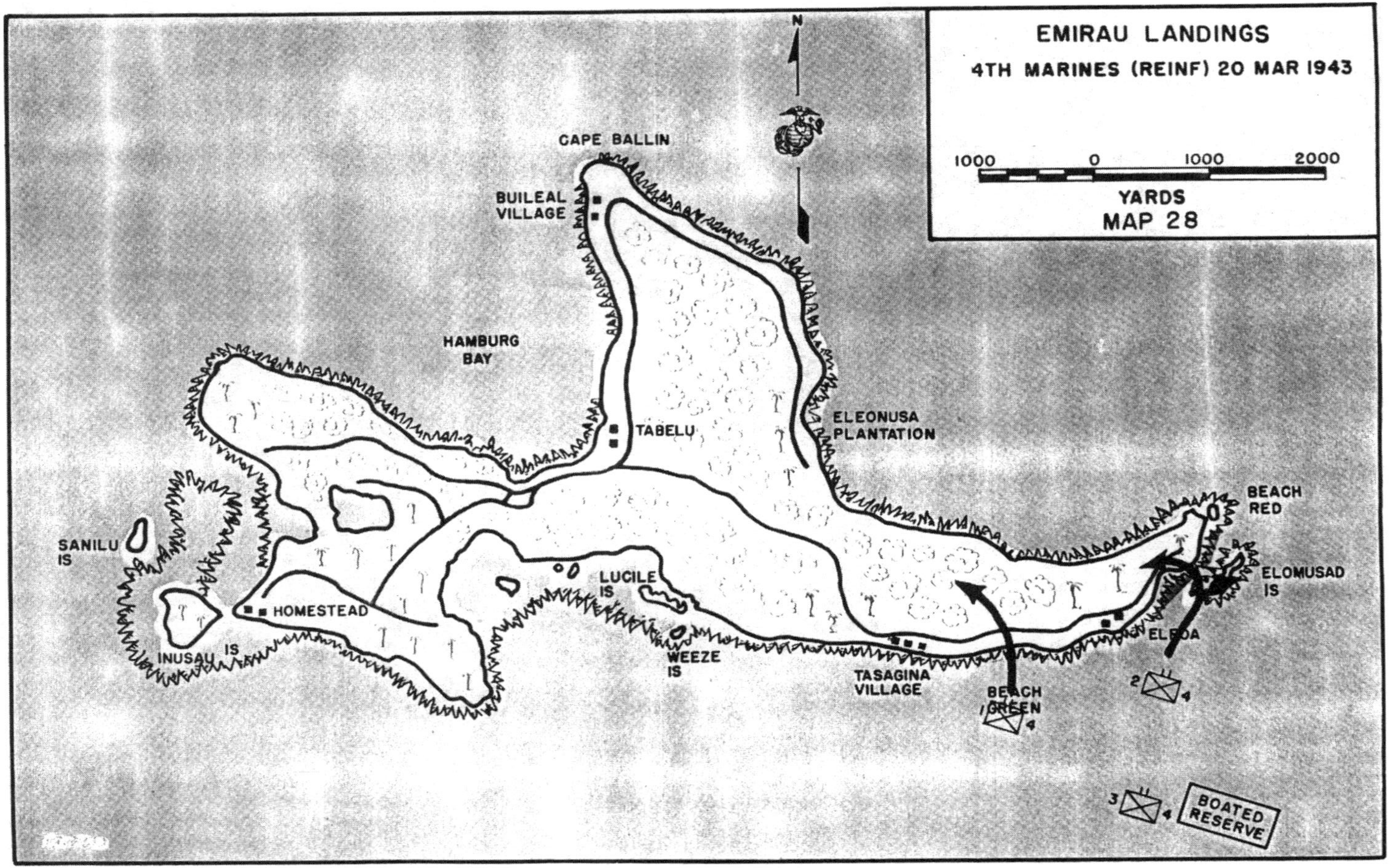

EMIRAU LANDINGS
4TH MARINES (REINF) 20 MAR 1943

YARDS
MAP 28

1000   0   1000   2000

N

CAPE BALLIN

BUILEAL VILLAGE

TABELU

HAMBURG BAY

ELEONUSA PLANTATION

LUCILE IS

WEEZE IS

TASAGINA VILLAGE

HOMESTEAD

INUSAY IS

SANILU IS

BEACH RED

ELOMUSAD IS

ELPOA

BEACH GREEN

BOATED RESERVE

of the island, Hamburg Bay, the largest, and Eulolou, respectively. Approximately 320 natives lived on Emirau. A native track ran the length of the island with a branch trail following the shore of the shark's fin, while on the west end there was a maze of trails. The climate is hot and humid with heavy rainfall.

The St. Matthias Group was part of the Mandated Territory of New Guinea and was administered as part of the Kavieng District on New Ireland. The Japanese had only occupied the island with lookouts, but by January 1944 they had departed. A group of forty-six IJN personnel operated a small seaplane base and radio station on Eloaue Islet just off the southwest coast of Mussau.

To close the ring around Rabaul it was decided in February 1944 that Emirau was to be secured to close off the approaches to Kavieng from the north in the direction of the Carolines. The Emirau occupation was preferred to a direct assault of Kavieng, which was subsequently canceled. Emirau would provide a base from which to patrol Kavieng across the Ysabel Channel and serve as an outguard for the Admiralties, on which Army forces had already landed. The newly reactivated 4th Marines, formed from the four existing raider battalions, was assigned the task. The Emirau Landing Force was formed by IMAC on Guadalcanal and organized into the brigade-sized Task Group A. The Emirau Attack Group sailed from Guadalcanal on 17 March and arrived off of the island's southeast end at dawn on the 20th. Two battalions landed unopposed on beaches GREEN and RED at the southeast end as well as on nearby Elomusad Islet. The island was swept, found unoccupied by the Japanese, all 3,727 troops landed, and was declared secured by night. As the landing took place a battleship force shelled Kavieng and nearby airfields giving the Japanese the impression that a landing on New Ireland was taking place. On 23 March the IJN seaplane base on Eloaue Islet was shelled by destroyers and the garrison fled for Kavieng in two large native canoes. One of these was interdicted the next day and destroyed.

Seabees arrived within days after the landing and construction on two airfields and small naval base began. The 4th Marines was relieved by the 147th Infantry on 11 April and Emirau Island Command was established. Naval Advance Base, Emirau, New Britain (FPO SF 3220) was commissioned on 28 April at Hamburg Bay. The PT boat base was on Eanusau Islet and conducted patrols off of New Ireland. The two 7,000-foot-long bomber fields, Inshore and North Cape, were built. With Rabaul and Kavieng neutralized, roll-up of the base began in December 1944 and the base was disestablished in March 1945.

New Britain Island, Bismarck Archipelago

New Britain Island, known as *Neu Pommern* (New Pomerania) to the Germans, is the largest island in the Bismarcks. It was code-named ARABIC.

New Britain forms a connecting span between New Guinea's Huon Peninsula fifty miles off the west end of New Britain to the south end of New Ireland only eighteen miles off the east end of New Britain. Bougainville is 190 miles to the southeast of Rabaul on the northeast end. New Britain is situated at 05°00' S 151°00' E on the north edge of the Solomon Sea appearing as a barrier to the Bismarck Sea.

The island is a rugged crescent spanning 370 miles east to west varying from twenty to sixty miles in width. A volcanic mountain range runs almost the entire length of New Britain with elevations just over 6,000 feet along much of its length. There is a break in the range near the northeast end where the coast is indented by Open and Wide Bays creating a forty-mile wide isthmus. The highest point on the main range is the Father, a

7,546-foot-high active volcano flanked by the North and the South Sons, near the shoulder of south Open Bay. The highest point in the mountains on the northeast end of the island, the Gazelle Peninsula, is 4,496 feet. The mountains are rugged and covered with rain forest of trees up to 150 feet in height. Beneath the canopy were twenty- to thirty-foot-tall trees and brush plus a common ground cover of ferns and light vegetation interspersed with clumps of bamboo and rattan palms. Rough terrain aside, the understory vegetation is light in many areas and allowed comparatively easy foot movement. Most of the island is ringed by a nearly level coastal plain between the mountain's foothills and the shoreline. The plains are covered by dense forests with thick underbrush. In many areas where natives had cleared dry land for crops and later abandoned it, there was extremely thick and tangled secondary growth that was almost impassable by foot. Much of the coast is backed by forested swamps with 100-foot-tall trees. The soil is reddish-brown volcanic soil that congealed into a thick, sticky mud in wet areas. The swamps are immediately behind the beaches separated by a low red clay embankment. Numerous rivers and streams flow across the coastal plains out of the mountains. On the plains these have low banks, but in the foothills and mountains they are steeply banked. There too, manifold tributaries flow into each river and stream making cross-country movement difficult.

The coastline is varied with black sand beaches ranging from eight to sixty feet in width, with the former the more common. Immediate offshore water may be shallow dropping off gradually or plunging steeply. Most of the 1,000-mile-long coastline is fringed by reefs with infrequent breaks. Barrier reefs and coral heads are found offshore with islets with the larger ones steeply peaked and jungled. Most of these islets lie close to the shore along the western portion of the south coast and central portion of the north coast. The largest nearby island is Rooke (aka Umboi) (BARNYARD) fourteen miles off New Britain's west end measuring some fifteen by forty-eight miles. It divides the gap between New Britain and New Guinea into two straits, Dampier (FEDERATION, TRAJECTORY) between New Guinea and Rooke Island and Vitiaz between Rooke and the Huon Peninsula. The Allies tended to refer to both straits as the Vitiaz, although they sometimes defined the two, and the Japanese used only Dampier without distinction. About forty miles to the west-northwest of Rooke is Long Island, the second largest of the offshore islands, and between the two lies little Tolokiwa Island. Two the north of New Britain were the scattered Vitu Islands (NORTHPOLE) comprised of islets and reefs. A number of bays indent the coast with the most notable being Blanche Bay on the northeast end with Rabaul, Open Bay on the north side and Wide Bay on the south creating the Gazelle Peninsula, Jacquinot Bay to the southwest of Wide Bay, Commodore (CANITE, WECOME) and Kimbe (MARDIGRAS) Bays on the north-central coast, the latter bounded by the Willaumez Peninsula on its west side, and Borgen Bay (GREYHOUND) near the island's west end on the north side.

Four specific areas are of key military interest on New Britain and each of these, since they are much different, is addressed separately. The town of Rabaul, the largest community in the Bismarcks, is situated on the northeast end of the Gazelle Peninsula.

Cape Gloucester. The extreme west end of New Britain is defined by shallow Borgen Bay and the small Natamo River of the north coast and the larger Itni River on the south emptying into the Solomon Sea at Cape Bushing (see Map 45). Cape Gloucester (BACKHANDER, DOVETAIL) itself is a improminent bulge on the island's northwest end. Patches of scattered grasslands are found south of Cape Gloucester suitable for airfields. The coastal plain varies from two to four miles in width around the west end and is dominated by two peaks. The twin volcanic peaks of 6,600-foot Mount Talawe (GOLDBRICK) lie seven miles southeast of Cape Gloucester. A ridge of three peaks, to include

Map 45
Western New Britain Island, Bismarck Archipelago

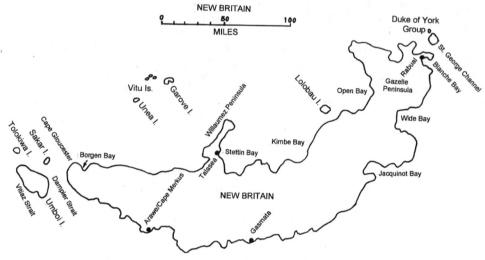

See Map 46 for Eastern New Britain Island.

the 3,800-foot-high Mount Langila (GOLDBERG), a dormant volcano, runs east from Mount Talawe. Ten miles to the south is 5,600-foot Mount Tangi (DAPPERDAN). The west end of the island possessed a web of native trails connecting both coastal and inland villages, the latter being more common than found in the interior of most islands. Between Silimati Point on the west shoulder of Borgen Bay and Cape Gloucester eight miles to the northwest there are numerous breaks in the fringing reef with suitable landing beaches backed by a five- to ten-foot-high red clay embankment. The boulder-strewn black sand beaches are thirty to sixty feet wide at low tide and at high tide the water laps the embankment. Nearshore waters are deep.

Arawe/Cape Merkus. The Cape Merkus (aka Mulas) (ABSCONDER) area bulges out of the western portion of the south coast some 100 miles from the island's west end and four miles to the west of the Pulle River. Thrusting out of the bulged cape's west side is the distinctly L-shaped Arawe Peninsula (DIRECTOR) protecting a small bay cluttered with islets and reefs, the Arawe Islands (QUININE). The heel of the "L" itself is Cape Merkus. Two of the islands, Arawe and Pilelo, are over a mile long and lie off the southwest end of the peninsula. Most of the south shore of the peninsula and the coast of Cape Merkus is faced with limestone cliffs up to 200 feet high. Virtually all of the bay's shore north of the peninsula and its islands are covered with mangrove swamps. The coast and much of the bay has fringing coral reefs, but there is a usable beach on the foot of the "L" of the peninsula known as House Fireman's Beach (FASHION). The peninsula's arm was covered by the Amalut Plantation. Inland the ground slopes up sharply through a wide break in the cliffs.

Willaumez Peninsula. The hilly and forest-covered Willaumez Peninsula (SHARE-CROPPER) thrusts abruptly north from New Britain's central coast some thirty-five miles into the Bismarck Sea. At its base it is approximately eleven miles across, narrows to two miles about halfway up its length, and then bulges out to ten miles across at its end, on which C-shaped, volcanic-formed Lake Dakataua is situated. On the peninsula's east side is Kimbe Bay. At the narrow isthmus on the bay side is Garua Island protecting Garua Harbour (BAGASSE). The island, largely covered by the Garua Plantation, is about two miles across. On the south side of the harbor is Talasea Village, the administrative center for the Talasea District. Both sides of the peninsula are fringed with reefs and the narrow coastal plain is mostly covered by forested swamps and dense secondary growth coursed by streams. Landing beaches were limited. The isthmus at Garua Harbour is dominated by hills and ridges up to 1,660 feet in height.

Rabaul. The largest town in the Bismarcks and the Australian government center for the Mandated Territory of New Guinea is situated on New Britain's north end. The island's roughly square-appearing north end is the Gazelle Peninsula, defined by the isthmus formed by Wide and Open Bays. The mountainous peninsula's highest elevation is 4,496 feet near its southeast corner. The northeast corner of the peninsula is pierced by Blanche Bay. The bay's entrance, flanked by Praed Point on the north and Raluana Point on the south, is four miles across and opens to the east into the Saint George Channel separating New Britain from New Ireland. On the south side of Blanche Bay is Karavia Bay and on the north are Matupi and Simpson Harbours. Simpson was named after a Royal Navy officer and the Bay after his ship, HMS *Blance*. Horseshoe-shaped Simpson is edged on its three landward sides by Rabaul. Blanche Bay and its harbors provided deep, well-protected anchorages sufficient for an entire fleet. Two tiny islands called the Beehives are centered in the entrance to Simpson Harbour. Rabaul (MEMSAHIB) itself is on a hook-shaped peninsula on which are three peaks: Mother (Mount Komvur) (2,247 feet), North Daughter (Mount Tovanurdatir) (1,768 feet), and South Daughter (Mount Taranguna) (1,620 feet), the latter being an active volcano. Other active volcanoes are Matupi, beside the harbor bearing that name, and Vulcan Island, on the west side of Blanche Bay. Vulcan burst from the bay's floor in May 1937 and in 1941 covered 193 acres and was 600 feet high. Laval flows connected it to the mainland. Several coconut plantations dot the coastal areas west of Rabaul. Much of the northeast corner of the Gazelle Peninsula is covered by coconut plantations. Watom Island, about two miles in diameter, lies six miles to the northwest of Rabaul. The Duke of York Group, which the Germans called *Neu Lauenburg*, is sixteen miles east of Rabaul in the Saint George Channel. It consists of twelve small islands centered around the largest, providing its name to the group.

Rabaul was established by the Germans in 1910 to become their administrative center. In 1920 it became the capital of the Mandated Territory of New Guinea, but with volcano eruptions in 1937 forcing the evacuation of 8,000 people, it was decided to relocate the capital to Lae on North-East New Guinea. The eruptions and earthquakes subsided, the population returned, and the capital's relocation was postponed. From July to October 1941, Matupi again erupted coating much of the countryside with black ash, and permanent relocation efforts were underway when the war broke out. Rabaul was a well-developed community with a motor road network serving the north end of the Gazelle Peninsula, but none crossed the mountains to connect to the south. Two small airdromes were near Rabaul. The main field, Vunakanau, was nine miles south-southwest of the town on the far side of Blanche Bay and Lakunai was on the south edge of the town. Small grass airstrips had been hacked out of the jungle prior to the war at Talasea, Gasmata, and Cape Merkus (Lupin) for local use. Only Gasmata was used by the Japanese and the others grew over.

New Britain was divided into three administrative districts: Rabaul on the north end,

Talasea on the north side, and Gasmata on the south side. The native population in 1940 was estimated at 101,000 in the patrolled areas and 4,674 Europeans and Asians.

For the Japanese Rabaul provided an ideal location to base a fleet, air assets, and command and control centers from which to direct, launch, and support the conquest of New Guinea and the South Pacific region. It was centrally located, and initially at least, far enough from Allied bases to protect it from air and sea attack. It possesses one of the best anchorages in the region and held abundant sites for airfields. The Japanese occupation of Rabaul on 23 January 1942 and the subsequent fighting was discussed previously. The Japanese quickly began to develop Rabaul into a major base complex, which was completed in late 1942. The Japanese did not possess a true joint command as practiced by the Allies, but the *Imperial General Staff* had directed the *8th Area Army* and *Southeastern Area Fleet* headquartered at Rabaul to closely coordinate, which they generally did on a more effective basis than experienced in other areas. The *8th Area Army*, under General IMAMURA Hitoshi, controlled the *18th Army* and *6th Air Division* on eastern New Guinea, *17th Army* on Bougainville, and the *38th* and *51st Divisions* and *65th Brigade* on New Britain. The *Southeastern Area Fleet*, under Vice Admiral KU-SAKA Jinichi, consisted of the *8th Fleet* based in the Shortlands and the *11th Air Fleet* at Rabaul. The *51st Division* was shipped to New Guinea in March 1943.

The Japanese airfield-building program was extensive with the existing Vunakanau and Lakunai being refurbished, the former becoming the main Japanese air base. Others were built to include: Keravat on Ataliklikun Bay six miles east of Vunakanau, Rapopo thirteen miles east of Vunakanau on the north shore of Cape Gazelle, and Tobera seven miles southwest of Rapopo. Two airfields were built on Cape Gloucester, which the Japanese referred to as Tuluvu after a village, another at Cape Hoskins (PICKUP) on the north-central coast and Gasmata (COWBOY, previously ROOSTER) on the south-central coast. Another small field was built on the north coast south of Open Bay at Ubili. A total of nine airfields were built. Significant naval base facilities were built at Rabaul to include a submarine base on Tallili Bay.

As the Allies closed in on Rabaul securing a ring of islands around it to effect its isolation, the Japanese began preparations for its defense. With the complete loss of the Solomons and much of eastern New Guinea, the Japanese began preparations for the Dampier Strait defense in October 1943, which focused on western New Britain. The *65th Brigade* had been sent from Rabaul in May to take control of the shipping engineer units on western New Britain and ensure the barge route to New Guinea across the Dampier Strait was kept open. In September the brigade was consolidated with the *4th Shipping Command* and elements of the *17th* and *51st Divisions* as the *Matsuda Force* with 10,500 troops and was made subordinate to the *17th Division*. Now commanded by Major General MATSUDA Iwao, the brigade had fought on Bataan in 1942. It garrisoned the Cape Gloucester area, the Willaumez Peninsula, Umboi Island off the west end of New Britain and deployed two detachments on the southwestern coast at Cape Merkus and Cape Busching. The *17th Division (53d, 54th, 81st Infantry Regiments*, but minus numerous battalions deployed to other islands), under Lieutenant General SAKAI Yashushi, had deployed from China between October and November. It established its command post at Gavuvu east of the Willaumez Peninsula. The *38th Division (228th, 229th, 230th Infantry Regiments)*, under Lieutenant General KAGESA Sadakki, with *8th Area Army* and detachments from other units, garrisoned Rabaul.

By the late summer of 1943 it had been decided to neutralize Rabaul by sea and air attacks and that a direct assault was unnecessary. With most of North-East New Guinea, Bougainville, Goodenough, Kiriwina, Woodlark, Green, Admiralties, and Emirau Islands secured, a ring of Allied bases surrounded Rabaul. It had been planned to use the 2d Marine and 3d New Zealand Divisions for the assault of Rabaul, but this operation (TOWPATH) was canceled. Marine and Army units would land on the west end of New Britain in December 1943 to destroy the Japanese garrisons there and establish additional airfields from which to continue pounding Rabaul and Kevieng.

Beginning in October reconnaissance patrols began scouting landing sites and enemy positions. It was discovered that the Japanese had forced the evacuation of coastal villages into the interior. The enemy was on short rations and had resorted to raiding inland village gardens. In August five coastwatcher teams were landed to establish air watch stations across the base of the Gazelle Peninsula. Four survived to send warnings of Japanese flights from the Rabaul fields to Woodlark Island and airfields on mainland New Guinea from which interceptors were launched.

Operation DEXTERITY, the seizure of western New Britain, was scheduled for December 1943. The operation had to await the completion of airfields on New Guinea, Bougainville, and other islands as well as the availability of shipping. U.S. ground forces committed to New Britain were under the operational control of ALAMO Force (6th U.S. Army) under Lieutenant General Walter Kruger, which was tasked with the mission in May 1943. With such a long lead time numerous plans and changes were developed for DEXTERITY to include a parachute assault by the 503d Parachute Infantry Regiment. A proposed landing at Gasmata, Operation LAZARETTO, was scrapped and replaced by a landing at Arawe, Operation DIRECTOR. Between August and October the 1st Marine Division (1st, 5th, 7th, 11th [artillery] Marines) deployed from Australia to staging areas at Dobodura, Milne Bay, and Finschhafen on New Guinea and on Goodenough Island. Landing rehearsals were conducted at Taupota Bay and Cape Sudest. The Arawe landing was to be conducted by the 112th Cavalry Regiment, commanded by Colonel Alexander M. Miller, eleven days prior to the main Marine landing at Cape Gloucester. Rehearsals were conducted at Goodenough Island and the DIRECTOR Task Force, under Brigadier General Julian W. Cunningham, departed on 14 December.

The Cape Merkus area was defended by a provisional, combined force of 120 Japanese soldiers and sailors. The *1st Battalion, 81st Infantry* was located at inland Didmop Village on the Pulie River eleven miles northeast of Cape Merkus. Its commander, Major MASA-MITSU Komori, would control all future operations in the Cape Merkus area. In the predawn hours of 15 December (Z-Day) Troops A and B, 1st Squadron, 112th Cavalry embarked aboard rubber boats to land at Umtingalu Village east of Arawe Peninsula and Paligmete Village on the northeast shore of Pilelo Island due south of Cape Merkus, respectively. Troop A's boats were destroyed by automatic weapons fire at 0600 hours with most troops being recovered. Troop B landed instead at Wabmete Village on the northwest shore of Pilelo at 0530 hours. They moved to Winguru Village on the island's north end and destroyed the Japanese squad there by 1130 hours. In the meantime the 2d Squadron and the regimental main body entered Arawe Harbour through Pilelo Passage between Pilelo Island and Cape Merkus. They landed on Beach ORANGE aboard Marine amphibious tractors on the base of the Arawe Peninsula's "L" at 0730 hours meeting light resistance. The peninsula was cleared by 1500 hours and 1,600 men were ashore. The surviving enemy withdrew to the east. The Japanese launched a number of largely unsuccessful air attacks against Arawe over the next weeks. The *1st Battalion, 81st Infantry* and the *1st Battalion, 141st Infantry* both began closing on the beachhead. The Japanese found the terrain and rain-swollen streams so difficult to traverse that the *1st Battalion, 81st* did not arrive until the 26th and the *1st Battalion, 141st* the 29th. By this time there were 4,750 U.S. troops ashore and their patrols pushed out well to the east; the defensive perimeter was maintained at the base of the peninsula presenting only a 1,700-yard-wide front to the Japanese. The Japanese resolutely dug in on the abandoned Lupin Airstrip (ABROGATE) east of the U.S. perimeter, which the Americans had no desire to seize (they did hack out a small liaison aircraft strip). The Arawe landing was successful in that it tied down two enemy battalions that could have been used against the main Cape Gloucester landing as well as attracted aircraft that were destroyed.

While the Arawe landing distracted the Japanese the 1st Marine Division (BACKHANDER Task Force), under Major General William F. Rupertus, embarked aboard Task Force 76 (BACKHANDER Attack Force) ships at Milne Bay, Cape Sudest, and Cape Cretin to depart on 25 December and headed north to the Dampier Strait. Aerial bombardment of the Cape Gloucester area had been continuous for one month prior to the landing. The Japanese detected the attack force, but deducted that it was bound for the Army lodgment at Cape Merkus and planned to launch massive air attacks there on the 27th.

The attack force split into the Western and Eastern Attack Groups before dawn on the 26th (D-Day). The former, carrying 2d Battalion, 1st Marines (STONEFACE Group) headed for Beach GREEN north of Tauali Village on the west end of New Britain and eight miles southwest of Cape Gloucester. It was to block the coastal trail to prevent *65th Brigade* units to the south and at Borgen Bay to the east of the main landing from cutting across on an inland trail skirting south of Mount Talawe to the west end of the island and then moving north to Cape Gloucester. The 1,500-man STONEFACE Group landed without opposition at 0748 hours finding only abandoned positions and soon established its trail block on the slopes of the ridges facing the sea.

The Eastern Attack Group continued on to Cape Gloucester. The morning provided a southeasterly breeze, haze, and a four-foot surf; heavy rains soon followed. After heavy naval shelling the 7th Marines (GREYHOUND Group) came ashore on Beach YELLOW 1 and 2 on the northwest flank of Borgen Bay at 0746 hours without opposition. The 1st Marines (WILD DUCK Group) soon followed them ashore. The division reserve, the 5th Marines, came ashore on the 28th. On the same day the 7th Marines were task-organized into the Assistant Division Commander Group to secure the beachhead's east flank from enemy attacks from that direction while the rest of the division pushed west toward the airfields. Light opposition was encountered during the day as the Marines consolidated the beachhead, severely hampered by the inland swamps, and 11,000 troops were put ashore the first day. Air attacks began that afternoon, and while they inflicted damage on the attack force's ships, they in turn suffered enough to make no further daylight attacks on the beachhead. U.S. Army engineers and an Australian radar station were established on unoccupied Long Island, eighty miles west of Cape Gloucester, on D-Day.

The *17th Division* immediately ordered the *Matsuda Force* to counterattack. All of its scattered units began to converge on the beachhead to include the *51st Reconnaissance Regiment (−)* garrisoning Rooke Island, which evacuated it and sailed for the mainland. The Marines fought westward against increasing resistance and at noon on 31 December they secured the two airfields. At the STONEFACE Group's trail block the Japanese conducted a counterattack on the 30th, which was easily defeated. On 2 January 1944, a company from the Cape Gloucester perimeter reached the trail block and reported no significant enemy activity. The STONEFACE Group was ordered to be withdrawn by landing craft on the 5th and rejoined the division.

On 2 January the Marines on the east flank made their first attack toward Borgen Bay only to run into extremely stiff resistance reinforced by rugged terrain along Suicide Creek. The Japanese counterattacked toward Target Hill on the Marine's extreme east flank the following morning, but they gained no ground in their weak piecemeal attacks. The Marines continued the push east, but the terrain, weather, and resilient enemy resistance slowed the advance to a crawl. It took over two weeks to advance just over three miles. By now the Japanese realized that the Cape Gloucester force was too strong to defeat; only air attacks could now slow the construction of enemy airfields. The *Matsuda Force* was ordered to withdraw to the east on 21 January. Work on Airfield No. 2 progressed, but the smaller Airfield No. 1 to the west was abandoned as it was not worth the effort to continue its construction in a sea of mud. No. 2 was not operational with a 4,200-foot runway until 31 January. A longer parallel runway was never completed.

At Arawe the Americans and Japanese continued to probe each other until on 16 January an American attack dislodged the Japanese dug in on the U.S. perimeter. They withdrew to the Lupin Airstrip, which they believed to be the American objective, but they now thought that the Americans were building a major airfield within their perimeter and felt they served no purpose. Both sides continued to spar until the Japanese were ordered to join the general withdrawal to the east on 24 February, even though the United States declared the Arawe area secure on the 10th and ALAMO Force officially terminated Operation DEXTERITY. A Marine patrol from Cape Gloucester and an Army patrol from Arawe linked up at Gilnit Village (DISCUS) on 16 February. A Marine company landed on no-longer-occupied Rooke Island on 12 February. During this same period increasingly heavier air attacks on Rabaul itself weakened its defenses further.

Marine patrols pushed south and east from the perimeter through February as the Japanese conducted an orderly withdrawal leaving behind covering forces. The *17th Division* planned to establish defensive positions west of the Willaumez Peninsula on the north coast and Gasmata on the south. The *8th Area Army* and *Southeast Area Fleet* decided that they would be better served by withdrawing the *17th Division* east to establish a strong perimeter around Rabaul rather than expending it in a futile attempt to halt the Americans in the jungle from a position they could not supply. On 23 February the *17th Division* was ordered to withdraw east. The remnants of the *Matsuda Force* were still staggering eastward and were two weeks from Willaumez Peninsula. The survivors might make it out if an escape route was kept open. The *51st Reconnaissance Regiment* served as a rear guard to slow the advancing Americans while the battalion-sized *Terunuma Force*, organized by the *54th Infantry*, was to defend the Willaumez Peninsula area as the remnants continued their retreat to Rabaul.

On the same date that the lead elements of the *Matsuda Force* reached the base of the Willaumez Peninsula, the Marines landed midway up the peninsula's length. Operation APPEASE was planned as a means to cut off withdrawing Japanese forces. The reinforced 5th Marines embarked aboard landing craft at Iboki Village for the fifty-seven-mile trip to Beach RED near Volupai Village on the west side of the peninsula's narrow isthmus. The APPEASE Attack Group landed at 0835 hours, 6 March being resisted by only a platoon. Just under 5,000 troops were soon landed and the Marines swept across the isthmus securing Garua Harbour and its namesake island with the area declared secure on the 9th as was the abandoned Takasea Airstrip (MATCHWOOD). Most of the *Terunuma Force* was located to the south, but some of it moved to face the invaders. After losing about 150 men, it withdrew to dig in at Ggarilli Village leaving a small rear guard. With the Marines at Talasea the *17th Division* was finally given permission to evacuate its 1,200-man garrison on Garove Island to the northwest of the Willaumez Peninsula, which they accomplished. The Marines had planned to assault the island, but canceled the operation as not worth the casualties. Most of the *17th Division* managed to close on Rabaul by the end of March. The last rear guard element was wiped out on 30 March, but the Japanese overall rear guard action and retirement had been largely successful. On 26 March a PT boat base was established at Garua Harbour and the north coast was swept clean of Japanese barges as far east as the Gazelle Peninsula. Australian-led native scouts harassed Japanese patrols venturing out of the Rabaul perimeter.

The 40th Infantry Division (108th, 160th, 185th Infantry), under Major General Rapp Brush, began the relief of the 1st Marine Division at Cape Gloucester on 23 April. The Marines had departed by 4 May. The 40th saw little action as it patrolled western New Britain. On 7 May the division occupied the Cape Hoskins Airdrome on the north-central coast without opposition. It relieved the 112th Cavalry at Cape Merkus in June and occupied Gasmata in October. In the summer of 1944 the Japanese activated the *39th Independent Mixed Brigade* on New Ireland from replacements and remnants of other units.

On 27 November the 5th Australian Division (4th, 6th, 13th Brigades), under Major General Sir Alan Ramsay, began relieving the 40th Infantry Division. The entire 5th Division was not assembled on New Britain until February 1945. The division continued to harass the Japanese and moved its bases further east. Division elements were soon deployed as far east as the Open and Wide Bays isthmus seeing light action in that area through the early months of 1945. There were only limited patrolling actions by both sides for the remainder of the war.

Lieutenant General Vernon Sturdee, commanding the 1st Australian Army, accepted the Japanese surrender at Rabaul on 6 September. Allied estimates of the Japanese at Rabaul were between 32,000 and 38,000 men with only a few surviving aircraft and no ships other than barges. After the surrender the Allies were stunned to discover there were 53,000 soldiers, 16,000 sailors, and 1,200 laborers in the strongly fortified sixteen by twenty-eight-mile Rabaul perimeter.

The New Britain campaign was not as strategically important as the securing of other islands in the Bismarcks and the Allies never developed the island as a major troop-staging, naval, or air base. The Admiralties to the north offered a better harbor and was closer to objectives in the Marshalls and Carolines. A small temporary PT boat base was briefly established at Talasea (FPO SF 941). The Marines had lost only 300 men and just over 1,000 wounded. U.S. Army and Australian Army losses were very light. The Japanese are estimated to have lost about 4,000 dead and 420 prisoners.

New Britain today is a part of Papua New Guinea and is divided into two of the nation's twenty provinces, East (capital Rabaul) and West (capital Kimbe) New Britain. Forestry and coconuts are the main products. In 1994 two volcano eruptions outside Rabaul destroyed almost half of the town, but it remains inhabited. Rabaul has become a scuba diver attraction because of the sixty-four Japanese wrecks in Simpson Harbour and Blanche Bay found at depths ranging from fifteen to 160 feet. Some of the many miles of Japanese tunnels are still open. The Allied War Memorial Cemetery is located at Bitapaka and there is a war museum at Ralum near Kokopo.

New Ireland Island, Bismarck Archipelago

New Ireland, the second largest island in the Bismarcks, was code-named FOSDICK and later FOREARM. The Germans knew it as *Neu Mecklenburg* (New Mecklenburg). Lavongai Island, off the northwest end of New Britain, was known at *Neu Hannover* to the Germans and was still commonly called New Hanover during World War II. It was code-named INTERLOCK.

New Ireland forms the eastern enclosure of the Bismarck Sea (see Map 46). It stretches

Map 46
New Ireland Island (and eastern New Britain Island), Bismarck Archipelago

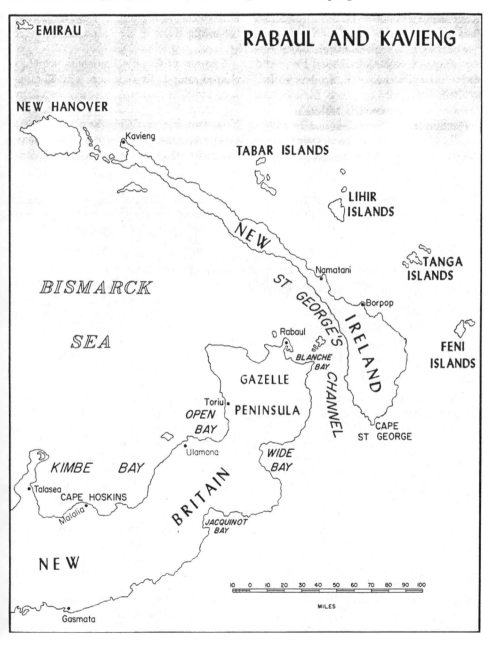

EMIRAU

RABAUL AND KAVIENG

NEW HANOVER

Kavieng

TABAR ISLANDS

LIHIR
ISLANDS

NEW

ST GEORGE'S

Namatani

TANGA
ISLANDS

Borpop

BISMARCK

IRELAND

SEA

Rabaul

FENI
ISLANDS

BLANCHE
BAY

GAZELLE

Toriu

OPEN
BAY

PENINSULA

CHANNEL

CAPE
ST GEORGE

Ulamona

WIDE
BAY

KIMBE   BAY

Talasea

CAPE HOSKINS

BRITAIN

Malalia

JACQUINOT
BAY

NEW

10   0   10   20   30   40   50   60   70   80   90   100

MILES

Gasmata

northwest from the east end of New Britain, which is only eighteen miles off its southeast end separated by the Saint George's Channel. Bougainville is approximately 120 miles to the southeast of New Ireland. The principal town is Kavieng on the northwest end, which is 162 miles to the northeast of Rabaul on the east end of New Britain. New Ireland is situated at 03°01' S 151°48' E and is in time zone 22.

New Ireland is 200 miles long from the northwest (North Cape) to the southeast (Cape Saint George) with an average width of twenty miles, as little as eight miles wide in some areas, and fifty miles across at its southeast end. It covers 3,340 square miles. Geographically older than New Britain, New Ireland is mountainous, but lacks the volcanic activity so prevalent on New Britain. The mountain chain extends most of the island's length closely following the southwest coast. The highest peak is 7,053 feet near the southeast end. There is a low break in the mountain chain just southeast of the central portion, but the chain continues northwest with its highest elevation being 4,962 feet in that portion. While the mountains drop steeply into the sea on the southwest side, their northeast side slopes gradually to that coast with a comparatively wide, fertile coastal plain. The mountain chain tapers out near the northwest end and that portion of the island is low and rolling. There are no rivers and few streams. The island is densely forested, but many northeast coastal areas were cultivated with coconut palms. Coastlines are rugged with the northeast side being more indented with bays and inlets. Kavieng on the northwest end of the island was the New Ireland District administrative center for the northwest portion of the island and Lovogai Island. It has a deep-water anchorage. The Germans developed Kavieng as an administrative center in 1900. A German-built motor road extended 150 miles from Kavieng along the northeast coast with a number of cross-island roads allowing access to the opposite side. On the southern portion of the northeast coast is a small anchorage at Namatanai. The wide southern end is rugged and lacks roads. There were an estimated 54,000 natives on the island speaking over forty-five languages and dialects. Like the rest of the Bismarcks, New Ireland is hot and humid with 120 to 160 inches of rain annually.

Lovongai Island (New Hanover) is twenty miles off the northwest end of New Britain at 02°30' S 150°15' E. It measures approximately forty miles northwest to southeast, is twenty miles wide, and covers 460 square miles. The forested and hilly island has an elevation of 3,140 feet. Well watered, much of the coastal area was planted with coconut palms. It had a population of about 5,000 natives and, before the war, twenty-five Europeans. The main town was Nugima near the northwest end. A motor road extends most of the way around the island. A barrier reef encircles most of the island and between it and New Ireland are numerous small islands, islets, and reefs. Lying at fifteen to fifty-five miles along the northeast coast of New Ireland are five atolls and island groups, from northwest to southeast: Tabar, Lihir, Tanga, Feni, and Green Islands (the latter which see).

The only Australian defense force available for New Ireland was part of the 1st Independent Company located at Kavieng. The Japanese launched a large air attack on Kavieng on 21 January 1942 and the Australian unit withdrew into the forest. Two companies, 500 men, of the *Maizuru 2d SNLF* from Guam occupied Kavieng on 23 January. On 30 January the Australian unit evacuated New Ireland aboard its station ship. It was damaged by a Japanese air attack and escorted to Rabaul where the troops and crew surrendered. The estimated 200 Europeans remaining on the island were interned.

The Japanese established the *14th Base Force* and elements of both the *Kure 5th* and *Sasebo 5th SNLFs* at Kavieng. The harbor was developed as a secondary fleet base to support Rabaul. Detachments of the *SNLFs* played a more active role when they were committed to the ill-fated August 1942 Milne Bay assault on eastern New Guinea. Elements of the *11th Air Fleet* were stationed on New Ireland with airfields at Kavieng, Panapai just to the southeast, and Namatanai and Borpop on the lower northeast coast. The naval commander at Kavieng was Rear Admiral TAMURA Ryukichi.

The Allies had decided to seize New Ireland in July 1942 scheduling the invasion for April 1944. A minor fleet base and six airfields were envisioned from which to place more pressure on Rabaul and later to support operations into the Marshalls and Carolines. The Allies periodically bombed Kavieng and this increased in frequency and intensity as the ring closed around Rabaul. The Japanese strengthened Kavieng to help protect Rabaul between late 1943 and early 1944 and at the same time the Allied air attacks increased. The *230th Infantry Regiment, 38th Division* from Rabaul arrived in October 1943 followed by the *1st Independent Mixed Regiment* from Japan between late 1943 and early 1944. Both units were under Major General ITO Takeo commanding the infantry group of the *38th Division*. These units were formed into the *40th Independent Mixed Brigade* at Namatanai in May 1944 directly subordinate to the *8th Area Army* at Rabaul. A total of 10,000 IJA and IJN personnel were on New Ireland.

The planned April 1944 Kavieng assault, Operation LOCKJAW, by the 3d Marine and 40th Infantry Divisions was canceled on 12 March. It had been decided that the assault would not be worth the casualties as both Rabaul and Kavieng had been effectively neutralized by air and naval power. The Allied-controlled islands that had been secured around Rabaul also served to isolate New Ireland and the Japanese forces there sat out the remainder of the war. On 19 September 1945, Lieutenant General K. W. Eather, commanding the 11th Australian Division, accepted the Japanese surrender. After the war a very small U.S. Navy installation was established for a short time at Kavieng (FPO SF 3217).

Today New Ireland is one of the twenty provinces of Papua New Guinea. It still produces coconut products, but forestry, subsistence farming, and gold mining supplement the traditional plantations. The Lihir gold mine is reported to be the largest in the Southern Hemisphere.

NETHERLANDS EAST INDIES (AND BRITISH AND PORTUGUESE EAST INDIES POSSESSIONS)

What was loosely known as the East Indies or Indonesia (not to be confused with today's nation) comprise the world's largest archipelago (see Map 47). It was mainly occupied by the Netherlands East Indies (NEI), today's Republic of Indonesia, but Britain and Portugal also possessed territories in the area (discussed separately herein). Geographically the region, referred to in this work as the East Indies, is divided into three areas. The Greater Sunda Islands in the west consist of Sumatra, Java, Borneo, Celebes, and their smaller adjacent islands. These largest of the East Indies islands sit on the Sunda Shelf, a submerged extension of the Malay Peninsula. To the east is the Sahul Shelf on which sits the island of New Guinea, of which the west half was part of the NEI. These two shelves are no more than 650 feet deep. Between the two shelves are three smaller groups of islands, Celebes, Molucca Islands, and the Lesser Sunda Islands. The waters in this central area are up to 14,800 feet deep. The term Lesser Sunda Islands has been used by different geographers to define a variety of islands with their categorizations differing greatly. For the purposes of this book the Lesser Sunda Islands is the

Map 47
Netherlands East Indies (and British and Portuguese East Indies possessions)

Map 47
Netherlands East Indies (and British and Portuguese East Indies possessions)

THAILAND

FRENCH INDOCHINA

SOUTH CHINA SEA

PHILIPPINES

NETHERLANDS EAST INDIES

MILES
0   100   200   400

MALAY STATES

Singapore

Malacca Strait

Medan

Fort de Kock

Padang

Mentawai Is.

SUMATRA

Palembang

Banka I.

Billiton I.

Karimata Strait

Natoena Is.

Kuching

Singkawang

SARAWAK

BRUNEI

Labuan I.

Brunei

BRITISH NO. BORNEO

Sandakan

Tarakan

DUTCH BORNEO

Balikpapan

Bandjermasin

Macassar Strait

CELEBES SEA

Mendado

CELEBES

MOLUCCA SEA

Morotai I.

Halmahera I.

Molucca Is.

Molucca Passage

Ceram I.

Buru I.

Amboina I.

BANDA SEA

JAVA SEA

Batavia

Bandoeng

JAVA

Soerabaja

Madura

Bali I.

Lombok I.

Sumbawa

Flores I.

FLORES SEA

Sumba I.

Lesser Sunda Is.

Alor I.

Wetar I.

Dili

TIMOR

Portuguese Timor

Dutch Timor

Okusi Ambeno

AUSTRALIA

Sunda Strait

INDIAN OCEAN

Christmas I.

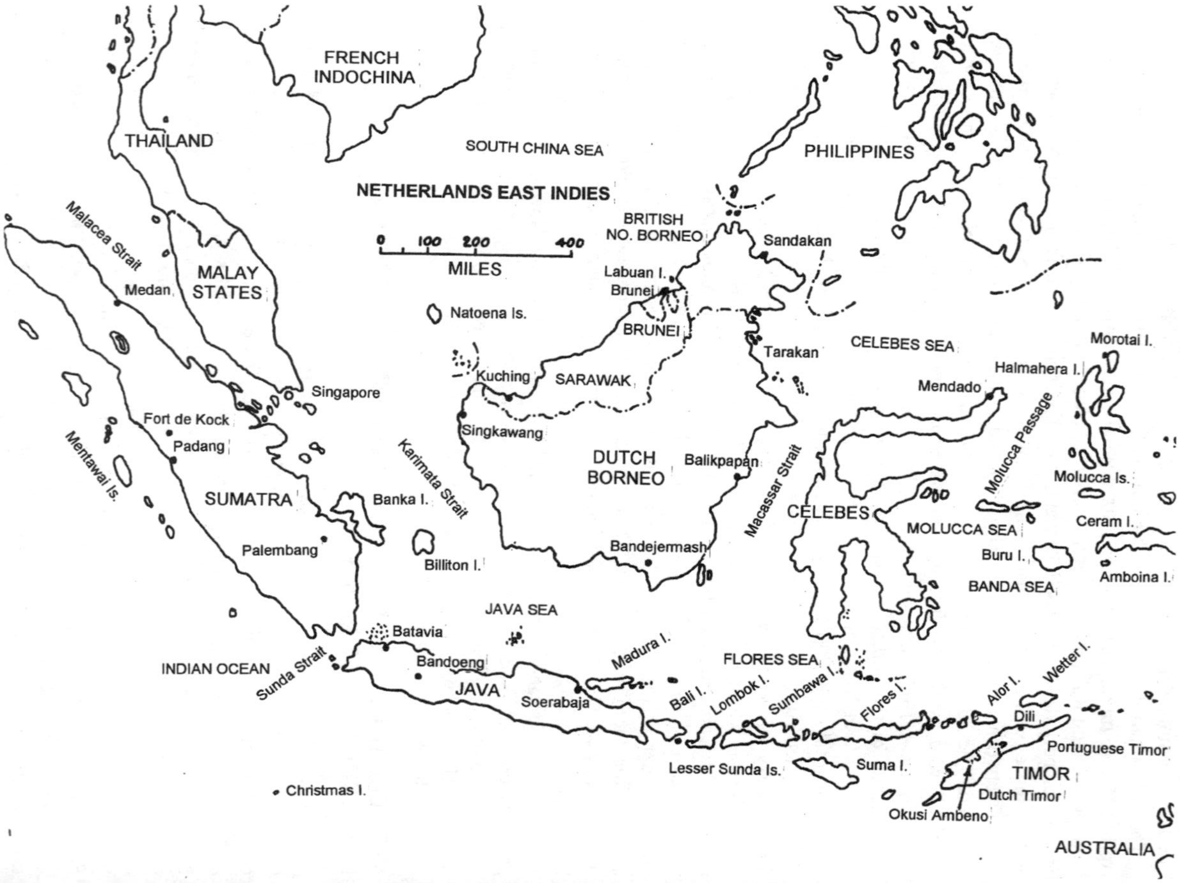

chain running east from Java toward northwest Australia. The term Greater Sunda Islands generally includes Sumatra, Java, Borneo, and Celebes, but is not used in this work. The East Indies have also been divided into two island chains by geographers:

Southwest Chain	Northeast Chain
Sumatra	Borneo
Java	Celebes
Lesser Sunda Islands	Molucca Islands
Timor	New Guinea
Tanimbar Islands	Kai Islands
	Aroe Islands

As with many other island groups the individual islands and integral smaller groups bear different names. The names used today are provided for clarity.

World War II	Current
Sumatra	Sumatera
Java	Java or Jawa
Borneo	Kalimantan
Celebes	Sulawesi
Molucca or Spice Islands	Maluku Islands
Lesser Sunda Islands	Nusa Tenggara
Dutch or West New Guinea	Papua* (was Irian Jaya 1973–2000)

*Not to be confused with Papua New Guinea on the east half of the island.

The archipelago stretches from off the west coast of the Malay Peninsula (occupied by Thailand, the Malay States, and Singapore prior to World War II) and runs east above Australia to western New Guinea, a distance of 3,200 miles with a width of 1,200 miles. If overlaid on the East Indies the Continental United States would stretch from the northwest end of Sumatra to Dutch New Guinea's eastern border with the Australian New Guinea territories. The total land and sea area is 774,000 square miles, about one-quarter the size of Australia. Most of the land area is located between the equator and latitude 10° south, although large areas of land, northwestern Sumatra, northern Borneo, Celebes' northern peninsula, and part of the Molucca Islands, lie above the equator. The northwest end of Sumatra is at longitude 96° east and the border separating Dutch New Guinea from the Australian New Guinea territories is at longitude 141° east. There are 13,667 islands and islets in the archipelago, of which less than one-third are inhabited. Besides the main islands, there are sixty smaller island groups. The South China Sea and the Pacific lap the north side of the East Indies and the Indian Ocean is on the west and south sides. Most geographers consider Sumatra, the westernmost large island, to be completely within the Indian Ocean. Militarily it was assigned to the China-Burma-India theater while the rest of the East Indies was within the Southwest Pacific Area. Some 35,900 square miles of "inland seas" are enclosed within the archipelago to include, from west to east, the Java, Flores, Sawoe, Celebes (today Sulawesi), Molucca (today Maluku), Ceram (today Seram), Banda, Timor, and Arafura Seas. On many contemporary maps these may be identified by their Dutch names, for example, *Java Zee* or *Moluksche Zee* (Molucca).

Dutch geographic terms were used on many contemporary maps and are still encountered today. *Zee*—sea, *Straat*—strait, *Eiland(en)*—island(s), *Archipel*—archipelago, *Groot*—great or large (island), *Klein*—small (island), *Baai*—bay, *Golf*—gulf, *Kaap*—cape.

The archipelago spans times zones 18–21, but there were six special time zones within the region in World War II. Northwestern Sumatra was in time zone 18:30, southeastern Sumatra was zone 19 (the adjacent Malay States was in zone 19:20), most of the island of Borneo (except British North Borneo on its northeast end) and Java were in zone 19: 40; Celebes, British North Borneo, and the islands to the south of Celebes were in zone 20, the Molucca Islands were in zone 20:30, and Dutch New Guinea was in zone 21.

The Netherlands or Dutch East Indies was considered a part of the Kingdom of the Netherlands, what the Dutch referred to simply as the Netherlands Indies (*Nederlands Indië—Ned. Indië*). (The Netherlands West Indies, or Netherlands Antillies, are in the Caribbean.) The Japanese call the East Indies the *Higashiindo* or *Ran-in*. Not all of the East Indies, however, were part of the Netherlands East Indies. The northern one-third of the island of Borneo was called British Borneo and included North Borneo (British possession), Sarawak, and Brunei (both British protectorates). Labuan Island off of Brunei was a British possession, one of the Straits Settlements, which included Singapore. East Timor was a Portuguese colony as were Okusi Ambeno, an enclave on West Timor, and Ataúro Island off Timor's north coast. These non-Dutch possessions are discussed below in the Borneo and Timor sections.

The East Indies are continental volcanic islands, essentially two roughly parallel mountain ranges. Most islands are dominated by central east-to-west mountain ranges, some reaching over 12,000 feet, bordered by narrow coastal plains. The highest peak in the East Indies is on west New Guinea at 16,532 feet. There are approximately 400 volcanoes on the islands; over 100 are active. Major eruptions have occurred to include Gunung Tanbora on Sumbawa in 1815 killing 92,000 and Krakatau killing 36,000. Earthquakes are common, but seldom severe. The volcanic origins have deposited fertile soils on the lowlands, which are most abundant on Java, Sumatra, Borneo, and New Guinea. Streams and rivers flowing from the mountains across the plains are common. The north lowland sides of the islands are dominated by rain forests of hardwoods. The southern lowland sides are covered with nipa palm and mangroves. The hills and mountains are forested with oak, chestnut, various other hardwoods, and dense underbrush.

The East Indies was once a land bridge connecting Asia and Australia. As such, a wide variety of indigenous animals are found on the islands, although some species are restricted to certain islands. Crocodiles, birds, reptiles, and amphibians of all types abound on all the islands.

The East Indies weather patterns are driven by the its location between two major land masses, Asia and Australia, with their own distinctly different weather conditions. Year-round most winds are moderate and predictable. The northwest monsoon wet season is from November to March with rainfall in the lowlands averaging 70–125 inches. The season's rains are caused by moisture picked up as the winds cross the Indian Ocean from Asia. The rain varies from island to island with the westernmost receiving more as the effects of the Australian desert diminish. Java receives about ninety inches annually and Borneo and Sumatra from 118 to 157 inches. In the mountains the annual rainfall can be as much as 240 inches, although up to 400 inches have been recorded on the north side of Java's mountains. The dry season is from June to October with the monsoon winds coming from the south and east. The temperate range is moderate with little variance throughout the year. Java experiences a daily year-round temperature range of 70°F–90°F. Humidity ranges between 70 and 90 percent. Typhoons occur, but are of little danger in the well-protected inland seas. Swift currents in some of the narrower straits pose more of a danger to mariners.

The fossilized remains of early humans have been found on Java estimated to be as old as 500,000 years. The East Indies' proximity to Southeast Asia and India resulted in waves of migrants from those regions bringing extensive Indo-Malaysian ethnic influence. Over the centuries this has been mixed with other waves of immigration from Southwest Asia, China, and some from Melanesia. Today over 300 ethnic groups are recognized, but all owe their origins to mainland Asia. Hinduism and Buddhism were introduced in the early centuries A.D. from India. Vast Indianized empires flourished during this period with the control of islands seesawing through continual warfare. Islam was introduced to the East Indies by Arab traders around A.D. 1000 and the religion gradually spread. By 1400 it was well established in the west, but it took another 200 years to take hold in the east.

The first known Europeans to visit the East Indies were the Portuguese in 1509. Roman records dating from A.D. 150 mention Borneo, however. Portuguese explorers soon descended upon the islands in search of spice and religious converts. They established a trading center in the Moluccas, but within a few years were being challenged by the Spanish from the Philippines. The rivalry ended in 1580 when Spain annexed Portugal. The Portuguese/Spanish foothold in the East Indies was tenuous due to Indonesian opposition when a small Dutch fleet arrived in 1596. The Netherlands had received its independence from Spain in 1581 and was seeking economic independence as well. The East Indies spice trade would provide that. In 1602 the United East India Company (*Vereenigde Ooslindische Compagnie—VOC*) was established by the Dutch parliament. The VOC was more than a trading firm, it had the powers of colonial government, but was motivated solely by commerce. Jakarta on Java was seized in 1619, renamed Batavia, and made the headquarters of the VOC. For the next 200 years the VOC expanded its control through the East Indies by means of war with the local sultans and changing political alliances. Brutal, corrupt, and short-sighted, the VOC exploited the islands without mercy. The VOC ruled indirectly though the subjugated sultans. In 1795 the Netherlands was occupied by France and the VOC was abolished in 1798. The Netherlands, now a French protectorate, took direct control of the islands and a French governor general was appointed. French control was short-lived. In 1811 the British occupied Java and turned the colony over to the British East India Company. The British though, after attempting to establish some reforms in what was essentially a slave colony, returned control of the East Indies to the Dutch government in exile in 1816.

A new order was established and the East Indies were made a formal colony of the Netherlands. The government, traders, and local sultans still prospered while the peasants were exploited. The government enacted what was known as the Cultivation System (*Culuurstelsel* in Dutch, *Tanam Paksa* in Indonesian), which forced farmers to cultivate crops for commercial purposes first and for local consumption second. However, slavery was abolished, some reforms introduced, and the infrastructure improved. The last local resistance on Java was suppressed during the 1825–30 Java War. Wars were to continue throughout the East Indies as the Dutch consolidated their control and expanded through the islands. Besides the Java War, the most notable and bloody of these conflicts were the Padri War from 1821 to 1838 and the Aceh War from 1873 to 1903, both on Sumatra. It was not until 1860 that a more liberal Dutch government introduced major reforms, some degree of free enterprise, and abolished government monopolies over exports. Expansion continued into the new century and beyond World War I. The Dutch had gained a huge economic empire, which they ruled through local leaders and continued to exploit for its rich resources. But, a strong sense of nationalism seethed in many of the colony's millions of inhabitants. In 1927, the Indonesian Nationalist Union (Party after 1928) was established with a policy of creating mass organizations, noncooperation with the colonial government, and eventually obtaining independence. A nationalist named Achmed Sukarno was its leader and became a dominating factor in Indonesian politics until his death in 1970.

The NEI was administered by a governor general who was also commander in chief of the Royal Netherlands Indies Armed Forces. In 1942 the governor general was A.W.L. Tjarda van Starkenborgh Stachouwer. The governor general was assisted by a cabinet, a Council of the Indies (seating two Dutch and two Indonesians), and the People's Council (*Volksraad*), a parliamentary body with sixty-one members selected by the Crown. These included twenty-five Dutch, thirty Indonesians, and five nonnatives (Chinese, Arabs, etc.). The Department of Civil Administration was comprised of Dutch and Indonesian administrators with the latter expanding in the prewar years, governing 491,000 Indonesians and 33,000 Dutch. Java, the center of Dutch power, was administered differently than the rest of colony. Java and its adjacent Madura Island were divided into three provinces (West, Middle, East Java) and two self-governing Indonesian sultanates, Djokjakarta and Soerakarta. The rest of the islands were assigned to self-governing governments with indirect Dutch control: Sumatra with its capital at Medan, Borneo with its capital at Bandjermasin, and the Great East with its capital at Makassar on Celebes. The Great East included Celebes, the Moluccas, west New Guinea, Timor, Bali, and Lombok. Each government was subdivided into residencies and provinces.

Prior to the war there were approximately 220,000 Dutch including those with native blood; about 80 percent were born in the East Indies and known as *blijers* (stayers). Dutchmen who came out to the NEI from the Netherlands to work in government service or for a commercial enterprise and then would return home were known as *trekkers* (travelers). There were almost 70,000,000 Indonesians, 1,300,000 Chinese, and 120,000 other Asians and Arabs. The total population was 70,476,000, but there were uncounted thousands of primitive natives living in remote areas. The population was unevenly distributed over the vast area with approximately 50,000,000 living on Java and Madura. The vast majority of the Indonesian and Arab populations were Islamic, but there were some Protestants, Catholics, and a small number of Buddhists.

Regardless of Dutch exploitation of the resources, most land was owned by Indonesians and only Indonesians could buy land from Indonesians. Land could only be leased by non-Indonesians under contract with strict legal stipulations. Vast quantities of sugar, rubber, spices (nutmeg, clove, cinnamon, pepper, ginger, etc.), natural pharmaceuticals, coffee, tobacco, tea, tapioca, copra, vegetable products (fibers, resins, gums), timber, rice, vegetables, petroleum, tin, bauxite, manganese, nickel, copper, sulfur, coal, diamonds, platinum, gold, and silver were exported. Over 6,000 factories, workshops, and processing plants handled these products. The NEI's value for products of military necessity was substantial. Besides food, the East Indies produced 90 percent of the world's quinine (needed to prevent and treat malaria), 70 percent of the kapok (for life vests and rafts), 38 percent of the rubber, plus militarily valuable metals and oil, all resources lacked by Japan. Unlike many areas in the Pacific, Java and Bali, off its east end, were developing a tourist trade prior to the war owing to the natural beauty and accessibility from Australia, India, and the Philippines.

Java was supported by a well-developed infrastructure with Sumatra a far second. The other islands were largely poorly developed except in the principal cities. In the entire East Indies there were 43,450 miles of roads with the most on Sumatra and fewer on smaller Java. These two islands possessed coastal and cross-island road networks, although there were many areas inaccessible by land. Coastal and interisland boat and steamer traffic were important. Only parts of southern Celebes possessed roads as did a few of the larger islands in the Lesser Sunda Islands, but these were limited and poorly developed. There were few if any improved roads on the other islands including New Guinea and Borneo, the second and third largest islands in the world. On Java there were 3,437 miles of railroad, 1,139 miles on Sumatra, and nine miles on Celebes. Telegraph lines connected most of the cities and towns on all islands with 876 stations on Java and 502 on the other islands as did telephone lines and cable systems. There were about 100 radio-telegraph and radio stations throughout the islands plus a single station in Batavia, Java capable of communications with the Netherlands. Airfields were found at the larger cities and many key towns. Most of the islands possessed good seaports, but support facilities were limited except on Java and some ports on Sumatra. There were seventeen major cities in the East Indies with a population of over 50,000. Twelve were on Java.

Defense of the East Indies, 1942

The Netherlands East Indies possessed its own armed forces, the Royal Netherlands Indies Army (*Koninklijk Nederlands Indisch Leger*) organized in 1830. Under the command of Lieutenant General Hein ter Poorten, in 1941 it contained 35,000 troops, of which 28,000 were natives (about one Dutch officer or NCO to forty native soldiers), plus a large reserve and home guard of both Dutch and Indonesians. The regulars were well trained and disciplined, but the reserves (*Reservekorps* and *Landstorm*) and home guard (*Stadswacht*) were much less so. An Indonesian militia began to be raised in June 1941. Much of the Army's equipment was obsolescent and units were often underequipped.

The Air Force, Royal Netherlands Indies Army (*Militaire Luchtvaat*) had 140 obsolescent American-made fighters and light bombers plus eighty reconnaissance aircraft, light transports, and trainers. Most of the aircraft were based on Java and under the command of General van Oyen.

There were three Sea Forces in the Netherlands Indies (*Zeemacht Nederlands-Indië*) under Vice Admiral Conrad E. L. Helfrich and mostly based at Soerabaja (today Surabaja), Java, the principal naval base: Netherlands Indies Navy (*Nederlands Indië Marine*) with ten mine warfare craft, fifteen coastal submarines, and a patrol boat; Netherlands Indies Squadron (*Nederlands Indië Eskader*) with four light cruisers and seven destroyers commanded by Rear Admiral Karl W.F.M. Doorman; and the Militarized Government Navy (*Gemilitairiseede Gouvernementsmarine*), a customs and patrol service, with 15 patrol boats. A battalion-sized Royal Netherlands Marine Corps (*Koninklijk Nederlands Korps Mariners*) detachment was attached to the Royal Netherlands Indies Army.

In 1940 Japan, after the United States, Singapore, and Britain, received more exports from the NEI than any other country including the Netherlands. In September of that year Japan began to pressure the NEI government for increased deliveries, especially of oil, and announced that its *Greater East Asia Co-Prosperity Sphere* included the NEI, much to the indignation of that government. That same month Japanese troops entered French Indochina. A conflict broke out between French Indochina and Thailand (Siam before 1939) in January 1941 and Japan negotiated a peace settlement. Amid growing concerns of Japanese expansionism, U.S., British, Australian, New Zealand, and Netherlands officials held a secret security conference in Singapore in April. The British proposed to hold Singapore at all costs, that the United States reinforce the Philippines to launch attacks on Japan in event of war, and provide military aid to the NEI. The United States agreed to none of the proposals and agreed only on continued aid to China. On 10 May Germany invaded the Low Countries and the Netherlands fell on the 15th. The NEI remained autonomous. Vichy France agreed to place Indochina under combined Japanese and French protection in July. The NEI responded by canceling all exports to Japan and freezing Japanese bank accounts as did Britain. The small British Eastern Fleet and the U.S. Asiatic Fleet were provided minor reinforcements, but little else was done. There were 65,000 British, Indian, and Australian troops in Malaya and Singapore. Australia provided two infantry battalions to reinforce the small Dutch garrisons on Amboina and Timor. There were other units on some of the larger islands to include Sumatra and Borneo, but most of their forces were concentrated on Java. An Indian battalion garrisoned British Borneo.

With the Japanese attack on Pearl Harbor, the Philippines, Malaya, and Thailand on 8 December *(X-Day)*, the NEI government declared war on Japan and interned all Japanese citizens. On 9 December the British battleship HMS *Prince of Wales* and battle cruiser *Repulse*, Force Z, were sunk in the South China Sea by Japanese aircraft from Indochina leaving the Allies without any battleship force in the Pacific. British Borneo was invaded on 16 December. The first Dutch territory seized by Japan was the tiny Tamelan Islands between Borneo and Singapore on 27 December. The American-British-Dutch-Australia Command (ABDACOM) was established on 15 January 1942 at Batavia, Java to defend Burma, the Philippines, NEI, and the approaches to northwestern Australia. The remnants of the U.S. Asiatic Fleet was ordered to Java from the Philippines at the end of December. The main goal of this combined command was to establish the 3,500-mile-long "Malay Barrier" following the Malay Peninsula's mountain chain and through the East Indies to western New Guinea inclusive. ABDACOM was under British Lieutenant General Sir Archibald Wavell with American Lieutenant General George H. Brett as his deputy. U.S. Admiral Thomas C. Hart commanded the naval forces based at Sorabaja, Java and British Air Marshall Sir Richard Peirse controlled the air forces.

ABDACOM's forces were too diverse, too widely spread, and insufficient for the task as were its logistics, but mainly, there was too little time to develop an effective defense. The disparity between the opposing forces can be demonstrated by regional naval strength. At the beginning of the war there were ninety-four Allied warships ships in the region as opposed to 230 Japanese. Besides weak forces and limited unity of command, the Malay Barrier possessed another serious flaw, it had no depth of defense. If the Japanese penetrated the weak defenses the only positions to fall back to were Australia and India. A U.S. convoy bound for the Philippines was diverted to Australia after the Japanese attack. Aboard was an artillery brigade and USAAF personnel. One of its units, 2d Battalion, 131st Field Artillery, was later dispatched to Java to be the only American ground unit to fight in the NEI.

The Japanese conquest of the NEI was to begin on 11 January 1942. While there was no fixed time schedule, it was estimated to require 150 days. The Japanese goal was to defeat the Allied forces in Thailand, Burma, the Philippines, and NEI; gain control of the economic resources of what she called the *Southern Resource Zone*, especially Singapore and the NEI, and establish a southern defense zone through the NEI. The NEI's oil was of primary importance. Japan had received 80 percent of her oil from the United

States, but this source ceased with the July 1941 American trade embargo. Japanese forces assigned to seize the NEI were subordinate to the *Southern Army* (sometimes incorrectly listed as *"Southern Area Army"*), headquartered in Saigon, Indochina under General Count TERAMOTO Kumaichi. Air support would be provided by the *3d Air Army* also headquartered in Saigon. The *Southern Army* was responsible for operations in the Philippines, Thailand, Burma, eastern New Guinea, and the NEI. The *16th Army* was the main force responsible for the NEI, but two other armies were also involved. The *25th Army*, mainly responsible for Malaya, would take Sumatra, Borneo, and Celebes while the *14th Army* would send elements from the Philippines to support *25th Army* operations on the latter two islands. The *2d Fleet* would provide naval support. The divisions and forces assigned to these armies that would serve in the East Indies are listed below:

16th Army, Lieutenant General IMAMURA Hitoshi, deployed from Japan

2d Division (2d Field Artillery; 4th, 16th, 29th Infantry), Lieutenant General MARUYAMA Masao, deployed from Japan.

48th Division (1st and *2d Formosa Infantry, 47th Infantry, 48th Mountain Artillery)*, Lieutenant General TSUCHIHASHI Yuitsu, released by *14th Army* from operations on Bataan in the Philippines.

56th Infantry Group (146th Infantry), 56th Division (aka *Sakaguchi Detachment*), Major General SAKAGUCHI Shizuo, released by *14th Army* from Mindanao, Philippines.

25th Army, Lieutenant General YAMASHITA, Tomoyuki, deployed from Hainsan Island, Indochina to attack Malaya and Thailand. Elements committed to the NEI included:

Guards Division (2d, 4th, 5th Guards Infantry; Guards Field Artillery), Lieutenant General MUTO Akira, deployed from Singapore (aka *Konoe Division*, redesignated *2d Guards Division* in June 1943).

38th Division (38th Mountain Artillery; 228th, 229th, 230th Infantry), Lieutenant General SANO Tadayoshi, deployed from Hong Kong.

35th Infantry Brigade (124th Infantry, 18th Division) (aka *Kawaguchi Detachment*), Major General KAWAGUCHI Kiyotake, deployed from Indochina.

Various *special naval landing force* units would also participate.

Only the main islands are addressed here with the focus being on those on which military operations were conducted and in the sequence in which the Japanese invaded between January and April 1942. The details of smaller islands on which Allied landings took place in 1944–45 are discussed under the Liberation of the East Indies.

Borneo, East Indies (British and Dutch Borneo). Borneo is the largest island in the East Indies and the world's third largest. It constitutes the largest Dutch land holding in the NEI even though the northern one-third of the island was under British control. Borneo measures 600 miles east to west and is over 500 miles wide. It covers an area of 284,000 square miles subdivided into Dutch Borneo (210,600 square miles), North (British) Borneo (29,500 square miles), and the British protectorates of Sarawak and Brunei (50,000 and 2,226 square miles, respectively). Borneo lies to the southwest of the Philippines, Celebes is to the east separated by the Straat Makassar, Java is to the south, and Sumatra and the Malay Peninsula are to the west. The South China Sea laps its northwest coast, the Sulu and Celebes Seas its northeast, and the Java Sea its south coast. The equator passes through the island's center. The name Borneo is derived from

Burnei or Brunei, an ancient Malay kingdom, not to be confused with the contemporary Brunei, on the northwest coast dating from the thirteenth century. There was no overall native name for the island and the term Borneo was conferred by Europeans. The Portuguese unsuccessfully attempted to establish a settlement at Bandjermasin in 1690, but were forced out by the natives. The Dutch built a fort there in 1743 and another at Pontianak in 1778. A small Arab colony was established on the west coast in 1771.

Borneo's central interior from the east to the west coast and the northern coast are extremely mountainous. Much of the interior was unexplored and the heights of the mountains were not accurately known. The highest peak is Mount Kinabalu on the northeast end of North Borneo. It is 13,455 feet and it was also the highest in the NEI exclusive of New Guinea. Most of the granite mountain chain running southwest to northeast through Sarawak and North Borneo ranges from 2,000 to over 7,000 feet as do the mountains in the interior. The highest known interior mountain was Mount Raja at 7,474 feet in the Schwaner Gebergt just west of center. The mountains, covered by both dense rain forests and large scrub brush areas, are rugged with ridges and gorges cut by rivers and streams flowing toward the coasts. The largest river is the Barito flowing through the south-central portion of the island. The capital of the government of Borneo, Bandjermasin, is located near the river's mouth. Other large river systems include the Mahakam on the east-central coast providing a fertile delta, the Kapoeas on the west-central coast, and the Mujong in western Sarawak. The larger rivers are navigable, but sandbars often block their mouths to large craft and rapids are found farther inland. Most of the south and lower west coasts are covered well inland by wide mangrove swamps. The rest of the lowlands are overgrown by thick forests. The coastlines are rocky and often dangerous to small craft.

Villages are scattered along the coast and the interior is dotted with remote villages even though the terrain is rugged. Most of these are located on rivers on which they rely for transportation and communications. Rice farmers were forced to find suitable rice-growing lands well into the interior. Except in the few areas with fertile volcanic soil there is little good farmland. Spices, vegetables, fruits, rice, cotton, sugarcane, coconuts, coffee, and tobacco were cultivated. Petroleum, tin, bauxite, manganese, nickel, copper, sulfur, coal, diamonds, platinum, gold, and silver were mined. Even though mining was only on a limited scale, few resources remain today. The main diamond mines were at Landak and Pontianak; the coal was in the Pengaron, Brunei, Kitei, and Bandjermasin areas; and large oil-producing areas were on the Mahakam Delta and around Samarinda on the east-central coast and Tarakan Island off the upper east coast. The oil was shipped from the new port at Balikpapan south of Samarinda. This was then one of the world's richest oil production centers. Borneo abounds with wildlife including monkeys, orangutans, tigers, tapirs, Malay bears, ox-like bantengs, deer, crocodiles, elephants in the north, and rhinoceros in the northwest. The lowlands and coastal areas are extremely hot and humid, but the uplands of the interior are moderate in climate and comfortable for Europeans, especially in the north. The November-to-May rainy season brings with it strong winds, which have effects well inland.

Dutch Borneo was divided into the South and East District with its capital at Bandjermasin, also the capital of Dutch Borneo, and the West District with its capital at Pontianak. The South and East District covered 149,000 square miles with a population of 1,400,000 and the West District covered 57,000 square miles supporting 830,000 people. Dutch administration was not fully established on Borneo until the 1930s. The population included about 6,000 Europeans, 2,100,000 Indonesians of at least six ethnic groups, 140,000 Chinese, and 13,000 other Asians and Arabs. Three widely separated areas were developed by the Dutch, Balikpapan on the east-central coast for petroleum production, Bandjermasin on the south-central coast for agriculture, and Pontianak on the upper west coast near the border with Sarawak for mining. Dutch Borneo's only limited road systems were found in these three areas and were not interconnected. The largest city was Bandjermasin with 65,600 inhabitants.

The northern one-third of the island of Borneo was called British Borneo and included North Borneo, a British possession, Sarawak, and Brunei, both British protectorates ruled by sultans.

North Borneo was located on the extreme northeast end of the island and covered 29,500 square miles. It was chartered to the British North Borneo Company in 1881 upon the transfer of the rights originally acquired by an American adventurer in 1865. A British governor administered the colony and answered to the British Secretary of State for the Colonies. The capital was at Sandakan on the northeast coast with a population of 13,800. The colony's population was over 252,000 Malayans and 50,000 Chinese with a small number of Europeans. The main port was at Jesselton on the northwest-central coast as was the colony's only developed road system. The interior is mountainous with a thin coastal strip. The 900 miles of coastline are rugged and indented with bays and inlets. The thirty-five-square-mile Labuan Island is off of Brunei in the mouth of Brunei Bay. It had been a British possession since 1846, first part of Singapore, but it was made a separate colony in 1912 within the Straits Settlements, which includes Singapore far to the southwest. It had a population of 8,960 Malayans, Chinese, and a few Europeans. Its capital is Victoria.

Sarawak covers 50,000 square miles of the Borneo's northwest coast. A British subject, James Brooks, obtained title to the land from the Sultan of Brunei in 1842. He effectively ruled the land as the "White Rajah." In 1888 Sarawak was recognized by the Crown as an independent state and granted British protectorate status. Brooks, who was knighted, established the Rajah as a hereditary line and his descendants continued to rule. At the beginning of the war the Rajah was Sir Charles Vyner Brooks represented by a special commissioner. Sarawak's population was almost 490,600 Europeans, Malayans, and Chinese. Most towns and villages were along the coast with few found inland. The capital was Kuching, with a population of 30,000, and is twenty-two miles inland on the Sarawak River near the country's west end. Miri, on the upper northwest coast near Brunei, was the main oil production center and there was an oil refinery at Lutong. Oil and rubber were Sarawak's main exports.

Brunei is situated on the upper northwest coast of British Borneo between Sarawak, which had been part of Brunei until 1842, and North Borneo. It covers 2,226 square miles and is divided into two separate areas by Brunei Bay; there is no land connection between the two areas. Brunei was ruled by an Islamic sultan under British protection from 1888. A British resident, responsible for administration, was established in 1906. Brunei City, located twenty miles inland west of Brunei Bay, was the capital with a population of 11,000. The population of the country was about 39,000, mostly Malayans. It has a narrow, flat coastal plain with mountains in the east and hilly lowlands in the west. The highest elevation is Bukit Pagon at 6,069 feet in the east. An oilfield was located at Seria on the coast near the Sarawak border. Rubber production was also a major economic resource.

Besides its oil, rubber, and mineral resources, Borneo was strategically important as it lies astride important shipping lanes on all sides: South China Sea, Sulu and Celebes Sea, Straat Makassar, and the Java Sea. Dutch defenses on Borneo were virtually non-existent other than some air units at Singkawang II on the upper west coast of Dutch

Borneo. The British possessed only very small garrison and police forces in British Borneo. The Indian 2d Battalion, 15th Punjab Regiment defended Kuching, the capital of Sarawak, with a company at Miri. The Sarawak Volunteer Corps (local British volunteers), Sarawak Rangers (native militia), and Borneo police were attached to the Indian battalion.

The brigade-size *Kawaguchi Detachment* and elements of the *Yokosuka 2d SNLF* deployed from Cam Ranh Bay, Indochina and landed unopposed at Miri on the upper northwest coast of Sarawak and North Borneo on 16 December 1941. The oilfields at Miri and Seria in Brunei and the refinery at Lutong were destroyed prior to the Japanese arrival. The following day Dutch aircraft began three days of strikes on Japanese shipping. Despite British and Dutch air attacks and Dutch submarine attacks on the Japanese convoy, on 24 December two battalions of the *Kawaguchi Detachment*, which had re-embarked on the 22nd, landed at Kuching at the west end of Sarawak. The Indian battalion lost two companies attempting to defend the airfield and the survivors were forced to withdraw to Sanggau, Dutch Borneo and placed under Dutch command. The Dutch aircraft at Singkawang II withdrew to Sumatra. On 3 January 1942, the Japanese landed unopposed on Labuan Island in Brunei Bay. On the 7th, Japanese troops in Sarawak crossed the border into Dutch Borneo on the west coast and the next day occupied Jesselton, North Borneo. The Royal Air Force (RAF) terminated flights over Borneo from Malaya on the 9th. On 11 January, the 5,500-man *Sakaguchi Detachment* and elements of the *Kure 2d SNLF* from Mindanao, Philippines landed on Tarakan Island off the upper east coast of Dutch Borneo. The Japanese landed on the island's east coast, opposite the Dutch defenses on the other end of the island, and seized the oilfield and airfield. The island was defended by the Dutch VII Garrison Battalion plus artillery and antiaircraft troops with a strength of 1,300 men. The garrison surrendered the next day after a brief, but stout resistance. Over 250 Dutch soldiers were murdered for their resistance, most by drowning, by order of Major General SAKAGUCHI. The next day Japan declared war on the NEI. The Japanese landed at Sandakan, North Borneo on 17 January; the capital surrendered the next day and on the 19th North Borneo surrendered. On 23 January units of the *Sakaguchi Detachment* and elements of the *Kure 2d SNLF* landed unopposed at Balikpapan on the east-central coast. The 1,100 Dutch troops of the VI Garrison Battalion plus artillery and antiaircraft units destroyed the oil installations prior to the landing. Some of the garrison was evacuated, but most were forced to surrender after only minimal resistance. Eighty soldiers and civilians were murdered by the Japanese in reprisal for burning the oil facilities. The next day the Japanese discovered the secret Samarinda II Airdrome to the north of Balikpapan near inland Longiram and commenced air attacks. The few remaining aircraft were evacuated on the 28th, but the 500-man garrison remained to await the expected arrival of U.S. aircraft. When they failed to appear most of the garrison attempted to organize as guerrillas, but the Japanese paid Dajak natives to successfully hunt them down, with many being murdered over the next months. On the 29th a Japanese force from Sarawak occupied Pontianak on the west-central coast. By 13 February Bandjermasin on the southeast end of Borneo was occupied by a battalion of the *Sakaguchi Detachment* moving overland from Balikpapan. The 500-man Dutch garrison attempted to destroy facilities of use to the enemy, but most of the native troops deserted. Borneo was secured by the Japanese, who planned to develop it as an economic base, especially for the exploitation of its oil and other natural resources. Crews of technicians and laborers had been prepared to quickly repair the oil production facilities and place them in operation.

Celebes, Netherlands East Indies. Celebes is located about 150 miles east of

Borneo across Straat Makassar. To the north is the Celebes Sea and the Philippines. Less than 200 miles to the south are the Lesser Sunda Islands across the Flores Sea. Celebes' east side is bounded by the Moluksche and Banda Seas on which lie the Molucca Islands. Celebes is an unusually shaped island with four large peninsulas thrusting from its central landmass. Jutting from the north and then curving sharply eastward is the longest, the Minahassa Peninsula with a length of some 500 miles; its average width is forty miles. It encloses the north side of Golf van Tomini with the Schildpad Eilanden. The gulf's south side is closed by the island's smallest peninsula pointing to the northeast. It in turn serves as the north side of Golf van Tolo. The Banggai Eilanden lie off the peninsula's south side. A broad peninsula runs out to the southeast. Off its end are several large islands. Between this peninsula and another jutting south from the island is Golf van Bone. The island's sprawling shape makes it difficult to provide meaningful dimensions, but from the west-central coast to the end of the smaller northeast peninsula it measures approximately 350 miles and some 500 miles south to north from the end of the south peninsula to where the north peninsula turns eastward. It covers 38,786 square miles with a 3,404-mile coastline.

Celebes is extremely mountainous with several volcanoes and peaks as high as 8–9,000 feet found on all of the peninsulas. The highest peak is Mount Rantekombola at 11,335 feet high near the base of the south peninsula and overlooking Golf van Bone. Rivers are few owing to the island's mountain-dominated narrow peninsulas. Few were able to cut channels through the steep slopes as runoff flows directly off the slopes a short distance into the sea. The whole of the island is covered with rain forests; timber was a principal industry. There are few lowlands, but coconut and coffee plantations were found on these. Gold, silver, maganese, nickel, copper, coal, and asphalt are the island's principal industries. Rice, maize, vegetables, tobacco, and coconuts are grown. Fishing is important and salt is evaporated on the coast.

The island was poorly developed and the number of towns and villages limited. Most were on the coasts with few found in the rugged mountains. The population was about 3,100,000 Indonesians (seven ethnic groups), Chinese, and small numbers of Europeans. The Chinese were to prove particularly hostile to the Japanese. The island capital was Makassar on the west side of the southern peninsula near its end. This also served as the capital for Celebes District and Dependencies, administrative divisions that covered most of the island. The Manado District encompassed the remote northern Minahassa Peninsula. The district capital was at Manado City near the peninsula's northeast end. The south peninsula with the island capital had a well-developed road system running around both sides, around the north end of Golf van Bone, and up to the west-central coast. There were also several cross-peninsula connecting roads, allowed by a central plain on which farming took place. The southeast peninsula and the islands off its end had a few developed roads. The northeast end of the Madano Peninsula was served by a road system. There were a few other remote roads connecting towns in some areas, but none of the road systems were interconnected.

Celebes was defended by the Celebes Defense Force with the Celebes Garrison Battalion, ten assorted reserve and home guard companies, and minimal artillery and anti-aircraft units. The 3,100 troops, under the command of Colonel M. Vooren, garrisoned Menado (1,500 men) on the end of the northern Minahassa Peninsula, Makassar (1,200) the island capital on the south peninsula, and Kendari (400) on the southeast peninsula. Most European women and children were evacuated to Java in January 1941, but the dependents of military personnel remained. Most of them were relocated to villages in the interior when the threat of invasion appeared.

The Japanese invasion of Celebes came at the same time as the landing at Tarakan Island off the upper east coast of Dutch Borneo, 11 January. The *Sasebo Combined SNLF*, commanded by Captain MORI Kunizo, came ashore at Kema on the southeast side of the Minahassa Peninsula near its end. At the same time the *Yokosuka 1st SNLF*, staging from Davao, Mindanao in the Philippines, parachuted on to the airfield at Menado City on the opposite side of the peninsula; Kema and Menado were connected by a cross-peninsula road. The parachute landing occurred at 0900 hours and the airfield was soon secured. The small Dutch garrisons were overrun and most were wiped out. Some prisoners were executed in reprisal of the 130 *SNLF* paratroopers killed. Elements of the *Kure 1st SNLF* next came ashore at Kendari on the lower northeast coast of the southeast peninsula on 24 January. They secured the Kendari Airdrome after only limited resistance with most of the small garrison surrendering. The airfields at Menado and Kendari were both made operational by the Japanese and preinvasion air strikes were launched from them on Java. The Battle of Makassar Strait was fought on 4 February. A Japanese force of two carriers, two seaplane tenders, and fifteen destroyers headed south through Straat Makassar to launch preinvasion air strikes on Java. An Allied force of three cruisers and six destroyers, adequate to at least turn back the Japanese force, attempted to intercept. Japanese land-based bombers attacked the Allied force damaging two cruisers and forced them to withdraw before engaging the carrier force. It was yet another example of the value of air power in naval operations. On 9 February, naval landing troops landed at Makassar, the island's capital near the end of the south peninsula, and Celebes was soon secured.

Prior to the end of the Celebes operation, the Japanese seized Amboina Island (aka Ambon) off the southwest end of Ceram (approximately forty-five by 200 miles) in the Molucca Islands 400 miles to the east of Celebes. Boeroe Island is about thirty-five miles to the west. Ambonia is only about thirty miles long east to west and two to three miles wide. The Laitimor Peninsula is located on the south-central portion of the island on which is its major town and port, Ambon City. It was the second largest naval base in the NEI. The island is mountainous with the highest point being 3,405 feet near its east end. Ambonia was defended by 2,800 Dutch troops under General Major J. R. L. Kopitz. His main unit was the Molukken Infantry Battalion backed by numerous artillery and antiaircraft batteries. Also present was the Australian 2/21st Infantry Battalion with 1,170 men. Allied air and naval elements had already withdrawn before the Japanese arrived. This included a U.S. seaplane tender and its patrol wing of ten flying boats.

The *Ito Detachment (38th Infantry Group* with *228th Infantry, 38th Division)* under Major General ITO Takeo, and the *Kure 1st SNLF* from Davao, Mindanao landed at two points on the east end of the peninsula on 31 January. The Dutch surrendered on 1 February and the Australians fought until surrendering on 3 February. The Australians lost over 300 men and the rest of the force went into captivity. On 9/10 February *SNLF* troops beheaded 230 Australian and Dutch troops and buried them in a mass grave at Laha Airdrome. An Australian War Cemetery is located near Ambon City.

The Dutch garrison at Makassar on the southern peninsula had decided that it was incapable of conducting an effective defense and prepared to fight a guerrilla war. A base was prepared at Enrekang 110 miles to the north of Makassar and 400 additional natives recruited. Almost 8,000 IJA troops landed just to the south of Makassar on 9 February without resistance. They attacked north to the town against light resistance and soon secured it. They encountered heavy resistance north of the town as the Dutch withdrew toward Enrekang. By the end of the month the native troops had deserted and about 300 Dutch soldiers surrendered.

Timor, East Indies (Dutch and Portuguese Timor). Timor is the southernmost large East Indies island and the easternmost in the Lesser Sunda Islands. It is 400 miles northeast of Darwin, Australia. Java is 670 miles west-northwest, Celebes is to the northwest, and the Molucca Islands are to the north. A string of smaller Sunda islands lie to the north of Timor, namely Flores, Adonara, Lomblen, Pantar, Alor, and Wetar, separated by the Sawoe Sea. A few smaller islands are scattered to the east of Timor to include the Tanimbar Eilanden. The Banda Sea is to the north and Timor Sea to the south. Off the southwest end is Roti Island. Timor is 280 miles long from the northeast to the southwest and varies from fifty to sixty miles in width tapering to points at both ends. It covers 11,864 square miles.

Timor is dominated by an arid, scrub-brush-covered mountain chain running its length, but there are numerous fertile valleys and lowlands. Forests of teak, eucalyptus, sandalwood, casuarina, bamboo, and coconut palms cover most of the coastal and lowland areas. Most of the mountains are 3–5,000 feet high, but higher peaks exist. On the Dutch southwest half the highest is 7,963 feet while on the Portuguese half 9,721-foot Mount Tata Mailau dominates the area. On the border between the two halves is a 5,003-foot mountain. The mountains are a tangled maze of ridges, narrow valleys, and ravines. Most of the few rivers and streams flow out of the mountains to the southeast coast. Most of the island is ringed with suitable landing beaches. The wildlife includes deer, monkeys, crocodiles, and marsupials reflecting Timor's proximity to Australia.

The southwest half of the island belonged to the NEI and the northeast half was a Portuguese colony covering 7,330 square miles. The capital of Portuguese Timor was at Dili (aka Dilli) on the north-central coast of the colony. It had been administered by Macao Colony, adjacent to Hong Kong, but was made a separate colony in 1926. The small islands of Ataúro (Kambing) and Jako, situated between Dutch Alor and Wetar Islands to the north, were also Portuguese possessions. On the north-central coast of Dutch Timor was a roughly fifteen-by-thirty-five-mile Portuguese enclave called Okusi Ambeno. Its main town was Okusi. Dutch Timor's capital was Koepang on the southwest end. The outlying islands administered from Koepang and Dutch Timor totaled an area of 24,449 square miles. The Portuguese began trading on the island in 1520 followed by the Dutch in 1613. From about 1640 the Dutch fought for control of western Timor and finally drove the Portuguese to the east half in 1655. The duel occupation of the island was informal until a series of treaties signed between 1860 and 1914 established the boundaries. The Dutch population before the war was about 150, mostly administrative officials, police, and soldiers. There were approximately 400,000 Islamic Indonesians and 4,000–5,000 Chinese and Arabs. Melanesian aboriginal Atonis of unknown numbers, driven into the mountains by the Indonesians, still practiced headhunting. Long-established inland villages, attesting to the hostility of tribal warfare, were surrounded by eight- to ten-foot-high walls of piled rock and rubble. On Portuguese Timor were some 500,000 predominately Christian Indonesians, 2,000 Chinese, 300 Portuguese, and small numbers of Arabs and Japanese. Timor had few valuable resources. The Dutch purchased sandalwood, maize, hides, and copra. The Portuguese side exported sandalwood and wax and there was a small cotton clothing industry. An improved road ran the island's length. On the Dutch side it generally ran up the center of the island and swung toward the north coast near the border. From there it followed the north coast until it turned sharply to cut across the island to terminate on the upper south coast. Some 100,000 Timorese ponies were a primary means of transport on the island. Active Japanese interest in Timor began in 1939 when they established an airmail service between Palau in the Western Carolines and Dili, for which there was no need. The airmail planes were purely reconnaissance flights transiting through the East Indies.

Dutch defenses were under the command of Colonel N.L.W. van Straten and included the Timor Garrison Battalion, a company from VIII Garrison Battalion, and an artillery battery totaling 600 troops. To stiffen the island's defense, owing to its proximity to Australia, the Australians sent 1,320 troops of the 2/40th Infantry Battalion, 2/2d Independent Company (commandos), and an antiaircraft battery. These troops, under Brigadier W.C.D. Veale, had been on Timor since 12 December. He established the Combined Defence Headquarters at Penfui Airdrome. On 17 December, 2/2d Company and 260 Dutch troops landed at Dili, Portuguese Timor under the protest of the governor, Ferreirade de Caralho. A diplomatic agreement had previously been reached by Britain, Australia, the Netherlands, and Portugal that the governor of Portuguese Timor would request Australian troops if the colony was attacked. Portugal and its colonies were declared neutral. Since the Australian/Dutch force arrived prior to his request he was opposed to the landing and threatened resistance. The Portuguese had 400 colonial troops, mostly natives. Regardless, the local populace was friendly and the Dutch occupied the city and Australians the airfield. To appease the Portuguese the Dutch troops were ordered to return to the west. The 2/2d Company, however, was decimated by malaria. An 800-man Portuguese reinforcement force was en route from Mozambique on the east coast of Africa and was due to arrive at Dili on the 20th. The subsequent Japanese landing caused the force to be recalled before it landed.

On Dutch Timor the Australian battalion defended the Baai van Koepang beaches northeast of Koepang City and the airfield while the Dutch covered the beaches to the west of the city. Penfui Airdrome, six miles inland, was employed as a staging base for aircraft en route to Java from Australia. A light Japanese air attack hit the airfield on 26 January and on the 30th a heavy air raid was delivered to cover the Japanese landing on Ambonia. On 15 February the Australians attempted to reinforce the garrison with another infantry battalion and a U.S. 75mm gun battalion, originally slated for the Philippines, but the convoy was turned back by Japanese air attacks. The RAAF squadron at Penfui was withdrawn on the 19th. That same day the Japanese launched a large carrier air raid on Darwin, Australia sinking ten U.S., Australian, and British ships. Dili was shelled that night as the Japanese invasion fleet prepared to land at Koepang and Dili. The *Ito Detachment (38th Infantry Group* with *228th Infantry, 38th Division)* under Major General ITO Takeo, having taken Ambonia, was the main landing force accompanied by 300 men of the *Yokosuka 3d SNLF.*

In the morning of 20 February the Japanese landed on the south coast of Dutch Timor to the south of Koepang and the defenders' rear. Some 350 IJA paratroopers of the *1st* and *2d Raiding Regiments* parachuted in five miles northeast of Babau at 0830 hours. About 350 more were dropped in on each of the two following days. After three days of fighting most of the Australian force surrendered losing eighty-four men and over 170 wounded. Brigadier Veale had withdrawn his headquarters to the east, and with 250 troops who had escaped the general surrender, later linked up with 2/2d Independent Company in Portuguese Timor. On 25 February ABDACOM, failing to halt the Japanese advance, was dissolved and Australian and American forces on Java and elsewhere in the NEI were placed under Dutch command.

On Portuguese Timor the Japanese landed on the night of the 20th near Dili disregarding Portugal's neutrality. After sharp engagements with the invaders, the 2/2d Company withdrew to the southwest on 3 March and began fighting as guerrillas in the Ramelau Range. Later in the month Brigadier Veale joined the company and a base was established at Mape southwest of Dili and fifteen miles inland from the south coast. The company, now known as Lancer Force, with other Australian and Dutch troops, natives, and a few Portuguese, conducted an effective guerrilla war even raiding Dili in mid-

April. More Portuguese and natives joined the Australians and before long, a well-developed guerrilla force was operational. Brigadier Veale was evacuated in late May and the company was supplied by air and sea from Australia. The Japanese attempted to eliminate the guerrillas on several occasions, but to no avail. Some native factions sided with the Japanese, however, believing that they would be given their independence. The Japanese built an airfield at Fuiloro, where in 1934 Japanese "agricultural specialists" had acquired soil samples.

Australia gave consideration to reconquering the island in June, but sufficient forces were not available. MacArthur desired that Lancer Force remain in place to support possible future operations. On 23 September 2/4th Independent Company was landed at Betano Bay on the south coast opposite of Dili to reinforce Lancer Force. The two companies and their guerrillas assumed a more passive role as the Japanese were reinforced and their puppet native troops became more aggressive. Between August and October the *48th Division (1st* and *2d Formosa Infantry, 47th Infantry, 48th Mountain Artillery)* under Lieutenant General TSUCHIHASHI Yuitsu arrived from the Philippines. It relieved the *Ito Detachment* and garrisoned Koepang, Dili, and Malaca on the east end of Timor. Japanese propaganda was also having an effect and more natives were siding with the Japanese. The 2/2d Company was finally withdrawn in December after eleven months in action. The 2/4th Company departed in January 1943 leaving behind an organized guerrilla force and intelligence collection elements. Hundreds of Dutch and Portuguese refugees departed with the Australian companies. The independent companies and their guerrillas killed 1,500 Japanese, but failed to take any prisoners. The Australians lost only forty men in this period.

The *48th Division* was especially well established on Portuguese Timor's north-central coast around Dili, but only strong patrols entered other areas for brief periods. The Japanese maintained they were there to protect the colony from Dutch and Portuguese colonialism and essentially held the Portuguese hostage. Over 40,000 Portuguese Timor natives died during the Japanese occupation through starvation, lack of medicine, reprisals, and fighting as guerrillas.

Sumatra, Netherlands East Indies. Sumatra is the second largest island in the East Indies and the fourth largest in the world covering 182,859 square miles. It stretches from approximately 5° S 105° E, off the west end of Java, 1,000 miles northwest to 5° N 95° E. The equator runs across the island's central portion. With a width of 215 miles across its southeast end, it gradually tapers to a point on its northwest end.

The southwest coast is lapped by the Indian Ocean; most geographers place the entire island within the Indian Ocean. Regardless, its east coast faces the Java Sea and the South China Sea touches its lower northeast coast as the sea emerges from between the Malay Peninsula and Borneo. Sumatra's upper northeast coast is separated from the Malay Peninsula by the forty-to-eighty-mile wide Strait of Malacca. Singapore and the British Straits Settlements lie at the southeast tip of the Malay Peninsula. Two groups of islands, Riouw and Lingga Archipels, off the end of the Malay Peninsula were governed from Sumatra. Java is separated from Sumatra by the fifteen-mile-wide Sunda Strait (aka Straat Soenda). Small, low, and swampy islands lie close along the central-northeast coast in the Strait of Malacca and further offshore around the southeast entrance of the strait. Two larger islands, Bangka and Billiton, lie off of Sumatra's east coast near Palembang. A string of islands stretch along Sumatra's southwest coast in the Indian Ocean lying roughly eighty miles offshore. The largest of these, from northwest to southeast, are: Simeuloeë, Nias, Batoe Eilanden (Pini, Masa Tanahmasa, Tanahbala), Siberoet, and Mentawai Eilanden (Sipora, Noord Pagal, Zuid Pagal).

A mountain chain, the Barisan Gebergte, runs the island's length along the southwest coast allowing only a very thin coastal lowland. These mountains range from 5,000 to 12,000 feet high, the highest being Mount Kerinji at 12,483 feet southeast of Padang on the central-southwest coast. The southeast two-thirds of the island's lower northeast coast is covered by alluvial flatlands. Numerous rivers and streams flow across the swampy flatlands toward the northeast coast, which is entirely edged by broad swamps. The largest is the Hari River, which is navigable 300 miles inland and is located on the lower northeast coast along with other large river systems. From Toba Meer (Lake Toba), located on the island's centerline about one-third of the island's length from its northwest end, the mountains stretch from coast to coast. Toba Meer, covering 500 square miles, is an oval-shaped mountain lake with a large island in its center. Numerous smaller lakes are found in this region. The island is densely forested with oak, chestnut, ebony, iron-wood, sandalwood, camphorwood, rubber trees, palms, and bamboo. Elephants, rhinoceros, orangutans, monkeys, tapirs, tigers, and wild boars inhabit the island. The coastal climate is hot and wet while the highlands are mild and wet.

Before the arrival of Europeans, Sumatra was divided into sultanates of changing alliances until dominated by the Srivijaya Empire in the eleventh century. The Javanese defeated this empire in 1377 and much of Sumatra fell under the domination of the Majapahit Kingdom. The arrival of the Portuguese, Dutch, and English in the 1500s led to the establishment of fortified settlements on the coast and warfare among the different sultanates as the Europeans vied for control. The British withdrew their claims after treaties with the Dutch in 1824 and 1871 giving the latter complete control of the islands. Dutch authority was not fully established until after a series of wars with resisting sultanates early in the twentieth century.

The Dutch Government of Sumatra was organized into districts, residencies, and provinces, which included the nearby islands. The government's capital was Palembang fifty miles inland on the Musi River near the island's southeast end. Other major cities included Medan on the upper northeast coast, Padang on the central-southwest coast, Teloekbetoeng (aka Oosthaven) on the southeast end, and Koetaradja on the northwest end. Sumatra had an extensive and well-developed road system meandering the island's entire length. A road followed most of the southwest coast; there were areas in which no road edged the coast, as well as inland roads crossing the mountains and providing access to the inland lowland areas where much of the agriculture took place. Two-thirds of the swamp-covered lower northeast coast could not be accessed by roads. The scattered villages on this coast depended largely on water transportation, although there were native tracks leading inland. The upper one-third of the swampless northeast coast was edged by a road and railroad running from Koetaradja on the northwest end through Medan to inland Ramauparapat. The Padang-Fort de Koch area on the central-southwest coast too was served by a small rail system. Another rail system ran from the ferry port at Teloekbetoeng (Oosthaven) on the southeast end to Palembang. There were a total of 1,139 miles of railroad. Ferries provided connections to Leboehan and Anjer Lor on the northeast end of Java and thus to Batavia, the capital of the NEI and Java. There were fourteen airfields on Sumatra with others under construction plus one on Bangka Island. Towns and villages were found on most of the coast, although they were sparse along the swampy lower two-thirds of the northeast coast and virtually none were found on the very swampy east coast. Villages were found on most of the larger offshore islands. Numerous villages were also found inland, especially in the valleys and foothills covered with fertile volcanic soil. Sumatra is very rich in resources, although many had yet to be developed prior to World War II. Agriculture produced rubber, coffee, tea, tobacco, palm products, and hemp. Oilfields, the most productive in Southeast Asia, and two refineries, the huge Pladjoe and Soengai Refineries, were located at Palembang at the confluence of the Musi and Komering Rivers. Coal was mined at Ombilin and Boekitasem, tin mines were found on the northeast coast islands of Banga and Billiton, and bauxite was mined in the Riouw Archipel. Palembang is fifty miles inland on the Musi River, but was a principal seaport. The principal towns were connected by a crude telephone and telegraph system.

Sumatra and its adjacent islands had a population of over 2,300,000. Most were Indonesians, divided into eleven ethnic Malayan groups, constituting over 2,000,000 of the population. They were predominantly Islamic with a few Christians. There were about 6,000 Dutch and other Europeans, 140,000 Chinese, and 13,000 other Asians and Arabs. Palembang (108,200) was the largest city followed by Medan (76,600), Padang (66,900), and the Koetaradja area.

The second largest grouping of Royal Netherlands Indies Army units defended Sumatra under the command of General Major Overakker, some 4,500 troops. This force included seven garrison battalions named after the towns they were based at: Fort de Kock, Medan, Permatansiantar, Padang, Sibolga, Djami, and Palembang. Also stationed at Palembang was a machine gun company, an antiaircraft battery, and four artillery batteries. Large numbers of British ground forces, RAF units and service personnel, and some Australians would also fight on Sumatra. The Sumatra airfields were valuable to the British for the defense of Singapore and Malaya as the Japanese *25th Army* swept down the Malayan Peninsula between December 1941 and February 1942. The Japanese would seize Sumatra in two phases, the first beginning in mid-February when southeast Sumatra was invaded and the other in mid-May when the northwest was seized. Prior to the invasion though, an air war was fought over Sumatra as fighting intensified on the Malay Peninsula.

The *25th Army* invaded Malaya by amphibious assault on 8 December 1941 and the *15th Army* pushed into Thailand from Indochina. Dutch aircraft from the NEI reinforced RAF units at Singapore as British and Indian, and later, Australian troops resisted the Japanese invasion. The Allied forces were pushed down the peninsula and withdrew to Singapore at the end of January. Most of the RAF and RAAF aircraft were withdrawn to Sumatra at that same time, from where they continued to operate to support Singapore. Some 3,250 air service personnel were withdrawn to Sumatra as well. The assault on Singapore began on 8 February and the city surrendered on the 15th with 64,000 Allied troops going into captivity.

To reinforce Sumatra, the 7th Australian Division was readied, but would not be deployable until 21 March. The Allies harbored few illusions about their ability to hold Sumatra or even Java. At Airdrome P1, eight miles north of Palembang, there were two fighter squadrons while at Airdrome P2, forty miles south-southwest of Palembang and unknown to the Japanese, were eight light bomber squadrons. These aircraft continued to attack targets in Malaya. On 14–15 February a British company-size tank squadron arrived at Oosthaven along with Australian machine gun and pioneer battalions. However, they did not land, but were ordered to Java. The advanced staff of the 7th Australian Division arrived and the 21st Australian Brigade was en route from India. It was determined that the Division's elements would not arrive in sufficient time from the Middle East and it was subsequently ordered to Ceylon.

On 14 February 260 IJA paratroopers of the *1st Raiding Regiment*, staging from Kahang and Kluang Airdromes in Malaya, were dropped on P1 Airdrome, which they quickly seized from a small Dutch detachment and armed RAF service troops. Another

100 paratroopers were dropped near the two refineries followed by 100 more the next day. More paratroopers reinforced the first echelon on the 15th and by that afternoon Palembang was occupied. Air support was provided by the *3d Air Division* operating from Malaya and IJN shore and carrier-based aircraft. The amphibious assault force staged from Cam Ranh Bay, Indochina landing elements of the *229th Infantry, 38th Division* on Bangka Island on the 14th. The main body of the *229th Infantry* reinforced by a battalion of the *230th Infantry* arrived at the mouth of the Musi River on the 15th and moved up the river toward Palembang on the 16th. They were delayed by the approach of a Dutch, Australian, British cruiser and destroyer force detected north of Sunda Strait. Japanese land and carrier-based air attacks drove off this force on the 15th. The RAF attacked Japanese shipping in the Banka Strait launching from Airdrome P2, which had not been discovered by the Japanese. The air attacks inflicted some damage on the Japanese landing barges on the Musi River, but were unable to halt the advance inland. On the 17th 1,900 British troops, 2,500 RAF service personnel, 700 Dutch soldiers, and 1,000 civilian refugees were evacuated from Oosthaven to Java, although they were forced to abandon their equipment. Surviving aircraft were also withdrawn to Java. Most of the refinery facilities were destroyed by the withdrawing troops. A party of British volunteers returned to Oosthaven and destroyed the abandoned equipment on the 18th. On the 23rd a Japanese-instigated anti-Dutch revolt broke out on northern Sumatra. By the 24th the Japanese had secured most of southern Sumatra. IJA and IJN aircraft began using the bases on southeast Sumatra to attack Java. Survivors of sunken ships attempting to escape from Singapore came ashore on Banka Island after the Japanese had seized it. The Japanese bayoneted to death forty British soldiers and then forced twenty one Australian Army nurses into the sea and machine-gunned them (one nurse and one soldier survived to later report the murders).

Most of the surviving Dutch forces had withdrawn to the northwest, but many of the native troops deserted to include those of the northwest garrisons that had not yet been engaged. On 12 March, the *Guards Division*, sailing from Singapore, landed at Medan on the upper northeast coast and a detachment landed at Koetaradja on the northwest end of Sumatra encountering little resistance. Divisional elements later linked up with a detachment of the *38th Division* moving up the island from Palembang. On 17 March troops of the *38th Division* entered Fort de Koch on the central-southwest coast where they released Achmed Sukarno, a nationalist leader, from jail. On the 28th General Major Overakker surrendered 2,000 Dutch troops at Koetarjane, a mountain village sixty-five miles northwest of Toba Meer.

The war would have little impact on Sumatra because of its relatively remote location. Some Allied air attacks were launched on the island's ports and in April and July 1944 Allied ships, including a Dutch cruiser, shelled Sabang, and in August, Padang.

Java, Netherlands East Indies. Java was the political, cultural, and economic center of the NEI and by far the most well-developed island. It also possessed the largest population, more than found in the rest of the NEI. Twelve of NEI's seventeen largest cities were found on Java. The island is small when compared to others in the East Indies, approximately 661 miles long east to west and 200 miles wide across its center portion. (see Map 48) The rest of the island's width varies from forty to 180 miles. Java covers 51,038 square miles together with adjacent Madoera Island. Running eastward from the southeast end of Sumatra, the two islands are separated by the fifteen-mile-wide Sunda Strait (aka Straat Soenda). Madoera Island (aka Madura), twenty by 110 miles, lies immediately off the eastern portion of the north coast and was governed as part of Java. Straat Madoera separating the island from Java is less than a mile wide. The Lesser

Map 48
Java, Netherlands East Indies

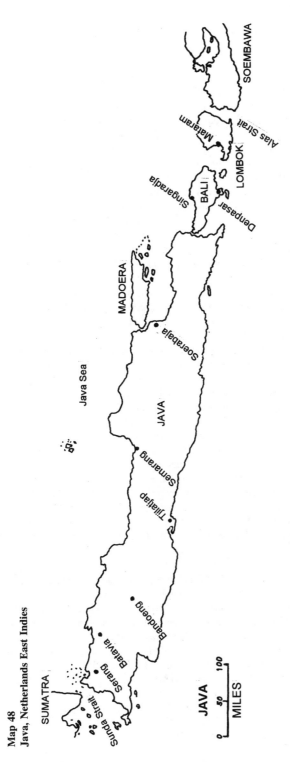

Translation of a Japanese Dutch troop strength estimate.

Sunda Islands run eastward toward Timor from Java's east end (discussed below). Borneo is approximately 250 miles to the north of Java across the Java Sea. The Indian Ocean edges Java's south coast.

A 7–11,000-foot-high spine-like mountain chain runs the island's length. Over thirty of the 112 volcanoes were active, the highest being Mount Semeru at 12,060 feet. Most volcanoes are clustered in the western portion of the island and others are widely scattered over the rest. Limestone ridges edge the mountains providing only narrow lowland coastal strips, especially on the south coast were the mountains hug the shore. Scattered 1,000-foot-high plateaus are found along the south side of the mountain range. Rivers are few and many are shallow with most running out of the sloped mountains and across the narrow plains to the north coast. On the coastal plains the climate is hot and humid, but the temperatures are moderate even at low elevations in the mountains.

Dense rain forests cover the mountains with teak, casuarina, rasamala, banyan, sago palms, and bamboo. Vast bamboo stands are found on the western portion of the island. There are virtually no coastal swamps. Even though the island is mountainous, almost two-thirds of the land was cultivated in some manner. The rich volcanic soil produces fruit trees, sugarcane, coffee, tea, rubber trees, and spices. Rice and maize are the main food crops. Rubber plantations were found across the east and west, coffee in the east, sugarcane in the east and central portions, and tea in the west.

Java and Madoera's population was over 43,000,000, mostly Indonesians with 200,000 Dutch and other Europeans, 600,000 Chinese, and 54,000 other Asians and Arabs. This huge population made it the most densely populated island in the Pacific and today it is one of the most densely populated areas in the world. The Javanese natives are divided into five ethnic groups. Most are Muslims.

The fossilized remains of the "Java Man" were found at Trinil in 1891 indicating man had inhabited the island for at least 800,000 years. Indian traders visited the island in the first century bringing Hinduism. The Mataran Kingdom flourished on the island in the eighth century and gradually converted to Buddhism by the tenth century. The Srivijaya Empire on Sumatra dominated western Java after a series of wars, but the Kediri Kingdom retained control of eastern Java. The Srivijaya Empire was in turn defeated by the Javanese Majapahit Kingdom. Javanese kingdoms rose and fell as the island was unified and splintered through the thirteenth and fourteenth centuries. Arab Muslim traders had long visited Java, but economic pressures caused many Javanese to join the Muslims and convert. Most ports in the east broke away from the Majapahit Kingdom early in the sixteenth century and the kingdom began to unravel. Other kingdoms were established in central and western Java. By the time of the arrival of Europeans there were five principal kingdoms on the island.

The Dutch first arrived in 1596 with Batavia falling under their control in 1619. From the 1670s the United East Indies Company, formed in 1602, began to assert its control over the Javanese kingdoms gaining complete control after a series of revolts and wars by 1743. In 1755 the last vestiges of the Mataran Kingdom, the most powerful when the Dutch first arrived, were splintered into the sultanates of Surakarta and Jogjakarta on the south-central coast. The rest of the island was divided into three provinces: West Java (Batavia), Central Java (Semarang), and East Java (Soersabaja), which includes Madoera Island. The British briefly controlled the island from 1811 to 1816.

A well-developed road system ran along the north coast with another largely down its center in the east and west, but edged the south coast in the central portion to avoid the higher mountains. There were no fewer than twelve cross-island roads connecting the two east to west roads. Railroad lines of 3,437 miles followed much of the route of the two east-to-west roads with numerous spurs and cross-island connections. Most towns were connected by telephone and telegraph. Coastal craft served most towns and villages. The main commercial port and naval base was Soerabaja (aka Surabaya) (341,700 population) on the eastern portion of the north coast opposite of Madoera. Batavia (533,100) is the capital of the NEI and Java located on the north coast near the island's west end. To Indonesians Batavia was originally known as Jakarta and nicknamed the "Mother City" (*Ibu Kota*). It was divided into Old Batavia (aka Lower City) and the modern Weltvrevredan where most of the city's 37,100 Dutch lived. The 409,700 natives and 78,800 Chinese lived in Old Batavia. Buitenzorg, about forty miles south of the capital in the cool mountains, was the island's social capital and the residence of the governor general. Samarang (217,800) was the third largest commercial city after Batavia and Soerabaja and located on the north-central coast. The north coast was more heavily populated than the south.

The Lesser Sunda Islands is a closely spaced archipelago running westward from the east end of Java. The larger of these islands include: Bali almost touching the east end of Java, Lombok, Soembawa, Soemba just to the south of the main chain, Flores, and then a line of much smaller islands to the north and east of Timor. Numerous small islands and islets are scattered through the chain. Bali and Lombok were the most fertile and economically important.

The defense of Java was coordinated through three military departments, I, II, and III, coinciding with the West, Central, and East Java Provinces (Surakarta and Jogjakarta fell under Military Department II). In 1941 there were 9,000 Dutch regulars, 126,000 native troops (40,000 home guard), and 17,000 Dutch volunteers under the command of Lieutenant General Hein ter Poorten, also commander of the Royal Netherlands Indies Army. Upon mobilization the three departments became divisions, although they were essentially "paper divisions" lacking the strength, firepower, tactical mobility, and service support assets of actual infantry divisions. Only the 1st Division approached the capabilities of a true division, but was still only a large brigade.

1st Division (1st and 2d Infantry; 1st Artillery, Mobile Unit), General Major W. Schilling.

2d Division (4th Infantry, Zuid Regiment), General Major P.A. Cox. This was intended to be a reserve force.

3d Division (6th Infantry, Soerabaja Garrison Regiment, 2d Artillery, Dutch Marine detachment), General Major G.A. Ilgen.

Additionally there were a small number of artillery, antiaircraft, engineer, cavalry, and military police units assigned to the divisions along with separate reserve (*Landstrum*) battalions. Fortress units with coast defense guns were located at Batavia, Tjilatjap, and Soerabaja plus an inland fortress at Bandoeng in the central western mountains. This was the location of the Dutch headquarters. On Madoera were three independent battalions of Dutch-led native auxiliaries prepared to fight as guerrillas.

Australia committed assets to defend Java as it was realized that it would become the major base if secured by the Japanese from which they would support their other occupied islands, exploit its vast resources, and threaten Australia 800 miles to the southeast. On 3 January the Australians proposed that the 7th Armoured Brigade would be deployed to Java, but it would not arrive until late February (it was subsequently diverted to Australia). Commander-in-Chief of Eastern Forces, General Wavell, commanding Commonwealth forces in Burma and Malaya, moved his headquarters from Singapore to

Batavia on 5 January. There he established ABDACOM on 15 January. Java was obviously the next Japanese target.

Commonwealth ground forces were under the command of British Major General H.D.W. Sitwell. These included five British battalion-size antiaircraft regiments (two without guns) and service units with 3,500 troops. He also commanded 3,000 Australians including the understrength 2/3d Machine Gun Battalion (without machine guns and vehicles), 2/2d Pioneer Battalion, and some service companies. The service companies were organized into an infantry battalion and the machine gun and pioneer battalions too would fight as infantry as part of Blackforce under Brigadier Arthur S. Blackburn along with a British company-size tank unit, B Squadron, 3d Hussars. Blackforce was deployed around Buitenzorg south of Batavia and west-northwest of Bandoeng (Bandung in Australian documents). The three Dutch "divisions" defended in their assigned districts. The American 2d Battalion, 131st Field Artillery had arrived from Australia on 11 January and was initially positioned at Madang in support of the Dutch 3d Division.

Allied air forces on Java were under the command of British Air Vice Marshall P.C. Maltby (equivalent to a general) with ten Dutch squadrons, three RAF light bomber, and two RAF fighter squadrons numbering 12,000 personnel. This included ground service personnel, some of whom were organized into defense units. The main airfields were Kalibanteng (Kalidjati in Australian documents) and Tjilitjam. A small number of U.S. fighters arrived from Australia on the 24th; others had been turned back by the Japanese. Some U.S. bombers were also present.

As with the future Allied campaign to neutralize Rabaul, New Britain, the Japanese had surrounded Java by seizing Borneo, Celebes, Timor, Sumatra, and others islands in the East Indies to cut off the island from outside support and from which to launch air attacks. Unlike Rabaul, however, the Japanese would take the Allied stronghold by direct assault. Japanese preinvasion air attacks were launched from Celebes beginning on 3 February and continued through the month.

Bali Island immediately off the east end of Java had not originally been a Japanese target. They had planned to employ airfields on southern Borneo to support the Java invasion, but heavy rains prevented this. Bali's Denpassar Airdrome on its south-central coast was free of rain in March. Bali, a tourist attraction even before World War II, was covered with lushly forested mountains over 4,000 feet high. The highest peak is on the east end at 10,308 feet. The island measures approximately ninety miles in length from east to west and fifty-five miles across the center, but tapers sharply to both ends. A circular road system encircled the central peaks linking the north and south coasts and the main towns. Bali was nicknamed "Island of the Gods." Bali's only defense was the Prajoda Corps of 600 Dutch-led native auxiliaries. On 19 February, 2,000 troops of the *Kanemura Detachment (3d Battalion, 1st Formosa Infantry, 48th Division)* landed unopposed, except by American air attacks launched from Java, on the southeast coast at Sanur. They advanced across the small southern peninsula and secured the airfield by late morning without encountering resistance; most of the native troops had deserted. Darwin, Australia was bombed for the first time on that date. The Dutch had failed to demolish the airfield in the confusion and the next day Japanese aircraft arrived there to support the Java invasion. On 19–20 February a Dutch and Australian cruiser and destroyer force attempted to engage the invasion force and a series of sharp engagement followed in the Battle of Badoeng Strait. A Dutch cruiser was damaged and a destroyer sunk. The Japanese suffered only three damaged destroyers and a transport damaged by air attack. Badoeng Strait (aka Bedung Strait or Straat Lombok) is a fifteen-mile-wide passage between Bali and Lombok Islands.

On 23 February certain key individuals begin to be evacuated from Java and AB-DACOM was dissolved on the 25th. On the same day two Japanese convoys were detected approaching Java from the north. Allied naval forces were dispatched to intercept the invasion convoys. On the 27th, an effort to intercept the eastern Japanese convoy resulted in the loss of two Dutch cruisers; a Dutch and two British destroyers were sunk while the rest of the force fled to Batavia and Soerabaja ending the Battle of the Java Sea and Allied sea power in the East Indies. The next day the remaining Allied ships attempted to withdraw to Australia through the Sunda Strait between Java and Sumatra after the Allied naval command was dissolved. The ships ran into the Japanese landing forces resulting in one U.S. and one Australian cruiser sunk as were one each U.S., British, and Dutch destroyers during the Battle of Sunda Strait. The Japanese lost a minesweeper and a transport plus three transports damaged, all to their own torpedoes. Only four U.S. destroyers made it to Australia. By 2 March the few Allied ships remaining in the Java area were scuttled.

Regardless of the sea battle the Japanese landed on Java on the night of 28 February. The *2d Division* landed at two points on the island's northwest corner on Sunda Strait, at the town of Merak and to the east in Baai van Bantam, where the *16th Army Headquarters* also landed. The *Shoji Detachment (230th Infantry, 38th Division* in Hong Kong) landed well east of Batavia at Eretanwetan to move inland, seized the main British airfield at Kalibanteng, and cut the coast roads to the east. Its first casualties were inflicted by air attack upon landing. It captured the airfield the next day wiping out most of the British defenders, antiaircraft, and armed ground service personnel. By the 7th it had taken Lembang just to the north of Bandoeng. The *Sakaguchi Detachment (56th Infantry Group* with *146th Infantry, 56th Division)* landed at Kragan east of Cape Apiapianom on the north-central coast and west of Soerabaja, the main Allied naval base. The 48th Division followed it ashore, advanced east, and soon captured the city and port preventing the Dutch from destroying the naval base. A destroyer damaged in the Battle of Badoeng Strait, the USS *Stewart* (DD-216), had capsized in dry dock and was salvaged and made operational by the Japanese, who designated it Patrol Vessel No. 102. The Dutch destroyer *Banckert*, also sunk in dry dock at Soerabaja, was salvaged and refitted as Patrol Vessel No. 106. The Dutch forces and Battery E of the U.S. artillery battalion were evacuated to Madoera where they surrendered on the 5th. While the *48th Division* advanced east, the *Sakaguchi Detachment* moved to the southwest against light resistance and took the inland town of Surakarta. It then continued to the west on both coastal and inland routes.

The *2d Division* in the west attacked east toward Batavia and Buitenzog. Blackforce, now supported by the U.S. 2d Battalion, 131st Field Artillery, attempted to counterattack on 1 March, but most of the supporting Dutch forces had been ordered east to defend Bandoeng. Blackforce could now only conduct a delaying action, which it did through the 5th suffering 100 casualties after holding off two-thirds of the *2d Division*. The effort allowed the Dutch to evacuate Batavia by the 5th moving their troops to Bandoeng. On 2 March the Dutch 1st Division conducted a counterattack to the east driving the *Shoji Detachment* from Soebang and lead elements of the Dutch battalion-sized Mobile Unit (light tanks, armored cars, lorried infantry) reached Kalibanteng Airdrome. The Dutch regiment sent to exploit the counterattack's success was all but destroyed by Japanese air attacks and the survivors fled. By the 5th, however, most Dutch and Allied units in the west had closed on Bandoeng.

The *Sakaguchi Detachment* now occupied Tjilatjap on the south coast and southeast of Bandoeng cutting off any hope of evacuation by sea. The native troops were badly demoralized and desertions were increasing. By 7 March all Allied aircraft had either been destroyed or evacuated. On the 8th Lieutenant General Hein ter Poorten surrendered 66,250 Netherlands Indies troops (11,300 Dutch) and on the 9th the Japanese claimed victory. The Dutch had advised the Commonwealth forces that guerrilla warfare would be impractical owing to the general hostility of many of the natives, which any guerrilla force would have to rely on for support. Some 5,600 British, 2,800 Australian, and 541 American troops plus 371 U.S. sailors, survivors of the USS *Houston* (CA-30) sunk during the Battle of Sunda Strait, were surrendered by Major General Sitwell on the 12th. The Japanese were convinced that there was an entire Australian division on the island and Sitwell was pressured for ten days to reveal the location of the rest of his forces. The Japanese had conquered the East Indies in sixty days; they had allotted 150.

Small Dutch and Indonesian elements were able to evade the Japanese and a modest guerrilla effort was begun in some areas. One such was Special Mission 43 operating southwest of Bandung, but most were captured by September 1942. Approximately 200 Dutch, Australian, and British servicemen were later captured on eastern Java. They were forced into pig baskets, taken to sea, and thrown overboard in shark-infested waters. The rest of the *38th Division* later arrived on Java, but in October it was sent to Rabaul. In May most of the larger islands in the Lesser Sunda Islands were occupied by the Japanese followed by others throughout the NEI.

Netherlands New Guinea. Netherlands or Dutch New Guinea (*Néerlandaises Nieuw-Guiena*) covered the western half of the world's second largest island (see Map 49). It was code-named ABATTOIR, CRINGLE, and WASSAIL. The general characteristics of the island of New Guinea as a whole are discussed in the previous New Guinea section. The researcher might refresh him/herself prior to continuing in this section (pp. 148, 149). Dutch New Guinea bordered the Australian territories of North-East New Guinea and Papua sharing a 500-mile border across the island's center on longitude 141° east. From the border to Dutch New Guinea's west end, Cape Fatagar, it is approximately 660 miles. Dutch New Guinea's total land area is 151,789 square miles. Attached on the north side of the island's narrow west end is a 135-by-230-mile landmass called the Vogelkop Peninsula (FIDDLESTICK, MOONSTRUCK) (today known as the Jazirak Doberai). Virtually an island in its own right, it is attached to the mainland by a ten-mile-wide, fifteen-mile-long isthmus. The Vogelkop and the mainland's tail enclose the over 100-mile-long, ten-to-twenty-mile-wide McCluer Golf opening on to the Ceram Sea to the west. The east side of the Vogelkop and the island's north coast enclose the Geelvink Baai (STIRRUPUNP) (today called the Teluk Cenderawasih). This broad bay's northward opening is protected by the Schouten Eilanden (ASTRONOMY, GASTRONOMY) to include Noemfoor, Biak, and Japen. The Schoutens cover 660 square miles of land and had a population of 25,000. The first two would become Allied objectives. Off the west end of Dutch New Guinea lie the Molucca Islands. The largest is Halmahera followed by Ceram to its south and Boeroe to Ceram's west. A comparatively small island, Morotai, off the north end of Halmahera, too would be an Allied objective. The Aroe (INSTITU-TION) and Kai Eilanden lie to the south of New Guinea's tail and southeast of Ceram. To the south-southwest of the Kai Eilander is the Tanimbar Eilander, which actually lie closer to Timor to their west-southwest. These three islands groups, covering 6,760 square miles, were administered from New Guinea and were occupied by the Japanese.

The westward extension of eastern New Guinea's Bismarck Mountains are the permanently snow-capped Sneeuw Gebergte (Snow Mountains). The range is topped by peaks reaching over 15,000 feet with the highest, Carstensz (today called Puncak Jaya), being 16,404 feet in the west-central portion. Where the island's west tail narrows the

Netherlands New Guinea

mountains drop to 3,000–4,000 feet. The mountains on the Vogelkop vary from 3,000 to 9,000 feet with Kwoka on the north coast being 9,842 feet. The Vogelkop's Tamrau Mountains form a series of roughly north-to-south-running ridges interspersed with narrow river valleys, the rivers flowing to the south into McCluer Golf. The mountains are just as rugged and covered with the same vegetation as on eastern New Guinea. The southeastern coastal and border area is a vast 100-mile-wide grass-covered plain. Westward from the plain and up the southwest coast is a huge swamp-covered plain and river delta coursed with sluggish rivers flowing to the south. The Asmat Swamp is the world's largest. The large Frederik Hendrik Eiland immediately adjacent to the south coast is flat and swamp-covered. As the south coast curves to the northwest the Sneeuw Mountains come close to the shore with rivers and streams found at close intervals flowing out of the mountains. On the extreme southeast coast and inland plains, east of Frederik Hendrik Eiland, are numerous villages. Most of the inland villages were situated on rivers, their only means of contact with the outside world. The south coast curving to the northwest of Frederik Hendrik Eiland was virtually uninhabited until reaching the west tail. Villages, while sparse, were found on the rugged coast. The Vogelkop's coast was populated as was the west side of Geelvink Baai and the Schouten Eilanden. The bay's east side was sparsely populated. Returning to New Guinea's interior, the rugged Sneeuw Mountains drop steeply, 45°, to the north into a central east-to-west river valley. There the Tarikoe River flows from the west meeting the Taritatoe flowing from the east. At the rivers' swampy confluence they combine into the Mamberamo River, which flows northwest to the coast forming the largest river system on the island. It is navigable for seventy miles. Most other rivers on the north coast are short due to their flowing out of the narrow coastal mountain chain. To the north of the narrow river valley is a comparatively low mountain range varying from 2,000 feet to the 6,742-foot Tatawasi. The larger towns and villages are found along the north coast, which is edged with mangrove swamps in many areas.

Like eastern New Guinea, the western portion was discovered piecemeal. A Portuguese explorer, Jorge de Menezes, was the first European to sight western New Guinea in 1526 and is said to have bestowed the name Papua (*Ilhas dos Papuas*; some sources claim *Oz Papuas*). The Spaniard Ynigo Ortez de Retes, exploring the northwest coast in 1545, named the land New Guinea (*Nuevo Guinea*). The Dutchman William Jansz explored the west and south coasts in 1605. Jacob Lemaire and William Schouten of the Netherlands discovered and named the Schouten Islands, explored some of New Guinea's north coast, and claimed the island for the Netherlands in 1615. Dutch settlement of western New Guinea's south coast was slow and limited even though the local sultan was friendly. In 1793, the British East India Company established a post on Manaswari Island in Geelvink Baai, but remained only briefly. The Dutch claimed the west coast New Guinea in 1828. They built a fort on Geelvink Baai in 1834, but abandoned it the next year because of the inhospitable climate. In 1848 the Dutch, British, and Germans informally divided up the island even though they had no permanent presence. The Dutch were given control of the north coast at this time. In 1885, the Germans and British formally agreed to latitude 141° east as the border between German and British New Guinea in the east and the Dutch in the west, but no treaty was made between the Netherlands and Germany. In 1895, the border between the British Territory of Papua (turned over to Australia in 1906) and Dutch New Guinea was agreed on with a slight adjustment to allow the bend of the Fly River, which crossed latitude 141° east, to be included within British territory. The Dutch did not establish a permanent administrative post on New Guinea until 1898. In 1914, Australia took over German New Guinea as the Territory of North-West New Guinea and was granted trusteeship in 1920 formally recognizing latitude 141° east as the border.

Until 1935 the Dutch were established only along the coasts, but that year expeditions searching for oil and precious metals in the interior began in earnest. Regardless, the east-central portion along the Dutch New Guinea border remained largely unexplored until 1959. The Geelvink Baai and McCluer Golf on the west end of Dutch New Guinea provide numerous good anchorages. The main port on the south coast was Merauke situated four miles up the Merauke River near the Papua border. Other important settlements were Fakfak near Cape Fatagar south of the entrance to McCluer Golf, Manokwari on the northwest shoulder of Geelvink Baai, Sorong Island off the west end of the Vogelkop, and Okaba on the south coast to the west of Merauke. Administratively Dutch New Guinea was part of the Government of the Great East with its capital at Makassar on Celebes. Mainland Dutch New Guinea was divided into the North, West, and South Divisions with their administrative centers at Manokwari, Fakfak, and Merauke, respectively. Manokwari was also the provincial capital. The Japanese *South Seas Development Company* had been granted timber concessions on Geelvink Baai and a small area at Manokwari where they had experimented with cotton growing since 1932. The known native population was about 320,000, while there were many more uncounted in the interior. There were fewer than 300 Europeans, 1,400 Chinese, and a few thousand other Asians. Other than police and a few small home guard detachments, there were no Netherlands Indies Armed Forces units on New Guinea at the beginning of the war.

There were no improved roads on Dutch New Guinea nor on any of the nearby islands, only simple native tracks. The only airstrips were found at Manokwari and Fakfak. Two seaplane bases were located at Modowi on the south coast of New Guinea's western tail.

Japanese interest in Dutch New Guinea was initially limited. Unlike eastern New Guinea it was of little strategic use and its resources were undeveloped and remote. There were no enemy forces there posing a threat to other Japanese operations in the area and no requirement for airfields or anchorages on mainland western New Guinea. Suitable anchorages and airfields in more strategically viable locations were found in the Molucca Islands to the west. In April 1942 IJN landing forces occupied various sites on the north coast. Dispatched from Amboina to the west, a small landing force first secured Babo (HANGDOG) on the south-central shore of McCluer Golf on 2 April. Sorong Island (GOLDENBOUGH, NEWCOMER) on the west end of the Vogelkop, Manokwari, the province capital on the northwest shoulder of Geelvink Baai, and Nabire on the south end of the bay were soon occupied. Hollandia on Humbolt Bay, just twenty miles west of the Australian Territory of North-East New Guinea, was secured on 20 April. Airfields were built and barge-staging bases established to support operations in North-East New Guinea. The Japanese made no effort to occupy the southwest and south coasts, but did establish garrisons, including air and naval bases, on the Aroe, Kai, and Tanimbar Eilander to the south and southwest of Dutch New Guinea. These islands were frequently attacked by Australian and U.S. aircraft from Australia. Some fifteen settlements in the swampy deltas of the mainland's south and southwest coasts remained in Dutch hands. Merauke became the Dutch military and administrative center of Dutch New Guinea. They were reinforced by small Australian detachments in 1943, but this was not publicly announced until early 1944. It perplexed some that the Japanese had not occupied the Klamono oilfields thirty miles inland from Sorong Island. The Dutch had failed to destroy these valuable fields, then considered one of the world's richest. It is thought that the Japanese obtained enough oil from more assessable fields in the East Indies. The fields' value was because the oil required no extensive refining other than "topping" to remove naphtha and then could be used to fuel ships. The fields could provide up to 25,000 barrels a day once developed. U.S. plans for this rich oil are discussed in the Sansapor–Cape Opmarai section below.

Next to China and the Philippines, the Japanese occupation of the NEI was the most brutal and repressive in the Pacific War. The territory saw over three years of hardship, poverty, famine, and forced labor. Some 4,000,000 Indonesians were employed as forced laborers (*romusha*) as well as comfort women. Another 270,000 laborers were shipped to other islands and Burma, many never to be seen again. A total of 42,233 Dutch servicemen were imprisoned, and 126,250 Dutch civilians were interned, men, women and children, including Governor General van Starkenborgh Stachouwer, under severe living conditions. They received insufficient food and scant medical supplies. The sexes were segregated in the camps with boys over ten living in the men's camps. Said to have been treated worse than American and British internees in other areas, some 26,000 Dutch civilians and servicemen died through neglect and murder. As the Allies moved closer to the islands the internees were relocated to inland camps in an effort to delay their liberation. Many British, Australian, and American prisoners of war taken in the East Indies were sent to Southeast Asia, China, and Japan as forced labor and others were kept in the East Indies for the same purpose. The approximately 60,000 native troops taken into captivity were released in early 1943 as the Japanese granted the Indonesians some degree of independence as a means of gaining their support.

Japan's victory in the East Indies gave the empire rich resources and a position from which to defend its southern periphery, but Japan now had to deal with a diverse population of over 70,000,000 covering an expansive area, 774,000 square miles, with a marginal infrastructure, and their own limited resources inadequate to support the region. The Netherlands government-in-exile in London formed a NEI consultative board on 17 June 1942. In August, an Insular Corps (*Korps Insulinde*) of Dutch and Indonesian volunteers and conscripts was raised with intelligence collection and civil affairs elements. A NEI government-in-exile was established on Ceylon off of India (today's Sri Lanka) by royal decree on 19 September. Dr. Hubertus J. van Mook, former Minister of Colonies, was appointed Governor General of the NEI.

Indonesians initially greeted the Japanese as liberators, and the Japanese recruited large numbers of Indonesians to assist in running the islands' military administration. Sumatra fell under the same military administration as Malaya being ruled by *7th Area Army* in Singapore. Sumatra was occupied by the *25th Army* headquartered at Fort de Kock under Lieutenant General SAITO Masatoshi (replaced by Lieutenant General TANABE Moritake in April 1943). Its units included the *2d Guards Division*, and the *15th* and *16th Independent Garrison Units*, which were reorganized and enlarged as the *25th* and *26th Independent Mixed Brigades* in November 1943. Java, Lesser Sunda Islands, Timor, Molucca Islands, Dutch New Guinea, and Aroe, Kai, and Tanimbar Eilander to the south and southwest of New Guinea were under *16th Army* administration from Bativia commanded by Lieutenant General IMAMURA Hitoshi. IMAMURA's rule of Java was considered too liberal by *Southern Army* and he was replaced by Lieutenant General HARADA Kumakashi on 6 November 1942. The *16th Army* initially controlled two divisions on Java, the *2d Division*, until September 1942 when it relocated to Rabaul, and the *48th Division*, until late 1942 when it moved to Timor as its garrison. The *38th Division*, after elements had conducted operations throughout the NEI, assembled on Java in late 1942 and moved to Rabaul in October. The *13th* and *14th Independent Garrison Units* were assigned to *16th Army* as well and these were enlarged and reorganized as the *27th* and *28th Independent Mixed Brigades* in November 1943. Northern Borneo was under the control of *37th Army* headquartered at Jesselton. The Lieutenant General BABA Masao had under his command the *56th* and *71st Independent Mixed Brigades* in North and South Bórneo, respectively, both organized in 1944. Dutch Borneo was initially under IJN administration as was Celebes, the Moluccas, and western New Guinea. The *5th Division (5th Field Artillery, 11th, 21st, 42d Infantry)* was deployed from Thailand in late 1942 to garrison Amboina Island off of Ceram.

On the surface the Japanese appeared to give Indonesians responsibilities they were denied under Dutch rule, although top positions were held by Japanese officers. In April 1942 various Indonesian political leaders recognized Japan as the "protector of Asia" and even adopted the Japanese calendar making 1942 the year 2602. In the meantime the Japanese plundered the East Indies of their resources resulting in rice shortages on Java. The Japanese also encouraged Indonesian nationalist organizations, which had been repressed by the Dutch. Indonesian political leaders soon found that they were able to gain concessions from the occupiers in exchange for "popular support." Achmad Sukarno, already one of the foremost leaders of the nationalist movement, emerged as the chairman of the *Empat Serangkai* (Four-leaf Clover), a committee of four who coordinated the various nationalist parties and organizations allowed by the Japanese. Muhammad Hatta was his deputy. Sukarno convinced the Japanese that popular support could only be gained by mobilization of the people though mass organizations representing their goals and aspirations. In March 1943, the *Pusat Tenaga Rakjat* (Center of the People's Power—*Putera*) was established. Youth organizations formed by the Japanese were incorporated into the program and local Indonesian councils were established. The Japanese goal was to use Indonesian nationalism and their fear of a return to Dutch control to gain popular support and aid in the resistance of an Allied attempt to reconquer the islands. An estimated 25,000 Indonesians were selected and trained for attachment to the Japanese units as auxiliary troops (*Heiho*). A paramilitary force was raised in the form of the *Pembela Tanah Air* (Defenders of the Homeland—*Peta*) and grew to 35,000. The Japanese called it the *Java Boei Giyugun* (Java Defense Volunteer Army) and it was the only one of the paramilitary forces to be lightly armed. Police forces were formed and other paramilitary units raised, but they were armed with nothing more than bamboo spears. These included the 50,000-person *Jibakutai* (Self-destruction Unit), who swore to give their lives to the defense of the homeland; 80,000-person *Shishintai* (Pioneer Corps), 50,000 in the *Hizbuallah* (Muslim Youth Corps), 50,000 in the *Gakutai* (Student Corps), and over 1,280,000 in the *Keibodan* (Civilian Defense Corps). Millions participated in Japanese and nationalist-sponsored youth groups. The Indonesian goal of such widespread collaboration was to lighten the burden of the occupation and establish a political infrastructure as a means to gain independence when Japan was defeated.

Regardless of apparent Japanese tolerance, small guerrilla organizations were established in some areas, but accomplished little. The East Indies and the islands were too large for the Japanese to fully control and they occupied only the major cities. In December 1942 the Japanese arrested the leaders of the Salvation Army in the NEI as subversives. In October 1943 the Chinese and Dyaks in North Borneo rebelled, but this effort was crushed.

By 1944 it became obvious to the Japanese that the *Putera* was a tool to achieve Indonesian nationalistic aims and did little to reinforce Japanese dominance. It was readily apparent to the Japanese that few Indonesians embraced the concept of the *Greater East Asia Co-Prosperity Sphere*. They dissolved the *Putera* in February 1944 and replaced it with the *Jawa Hokokai* (People's Loyalty Association). Sukarno remained in charge, but he was ordered to emphasize Japanese interests. The NEI government-in-exile on Ceylon appointed department heads for the new Dutch administration when the islands were liberated. That summer the Japanese premier announced that Indonesia would be granted its independence. The issue of Indonesian independence was extremely controversial within the Japanese government and armed forces. Few ministries, the IJA or IJN, or even different levels of military command agreed on the degree of indepen-dence, and how and when it was to be granted. The *25th Army* on Sumatra did not even want Indonesian political participation much less their independence. The promise of independence was more of an effort to gain additional popular support, but little was acquired. In February 1945, much of the *Peta* revolted against the Japanese. The short-lived revolt was crushed and the *Peta* disbanded. In August, with the Japanese empire crumbling, Sukarno was summoned to Saigon and promised immediate independence. Upon Sukarno's return he was kidnapped by radical nationalist youths demanding that he immediately declare independence and attack the Japanese occupation troops that very night, 16 August. They argued that in order for the Allies to recognize their independence, they would have to seize it from the Japanese, not have it granted to them by their occupiers. Sukarno proclaimed independence the next day, three days after Japan's an-nouncement that it would surrender, and the Indonesian Revolution was launched with uprisings throughout the islands. Sukarno was the new republic's president and Hatta the vice president. This convinced the British, who were responsible for the area's liberation, to take the self-proclaimed Republic of Indonesia seriously.

In the spring of 1944 the war was coming closer to the Netherlands East Indies. The Allied East Fleet shelled Sabang on north Sumatra (BELSHAZZER) on 19 April. On the 22d U.S. forces striking from eastern New Guinea landed at Hollandia on the north coast of Dutch New Guinea.

The *Southern Army*, headquartered in Saigon, was responsible for the East Indies and the Philippines. The *16th Army*, commanded by Lieutenant General HARADA Kumaka-shi and headquartered at Bativia (CASTOROIL, ROOSTER), Java (JOURNALBOY), controlled all IJA occupation forces in the East Indies until January 1943.

Japanese efforts to reinforce the East Indies to establish a new "absolute zone of national defense" began in the fall of 1943. Two major headquarters were transferred to the East Indies from Manchuria and the regional command structure was greatly reor-ganized. Japanese forces in the East Indies, other than Sumatra, were under the control of the *2d Area Army* initially headquartered at Davao, Mindanao, the Philippines arriving there on 23 November 1943. Commanded by General ANAMI Korechika, the *2d Area Army* assumed command of the *2d, 18th*[3] and *19th Armies* on 1 December 1944, some 170,000 troops, along with the *7th Air Division*, organized in January 1943. The *7th Air Division* was initially based at Amboina, but it was released to the *8th Area Army* to operate in eastern New Guinea in May/June 1943. The Japanese named the theater the *North Australia Front*.

The *2d Army*, which deployed from Manchuria, was under the command of Lieutenant General TESHIMA Fusataro. Headquartered at Manokwari on the northwest shoulder of Geelvink Baai, it was responsible for northwest Dutch New Guinea west of latitude 140° east and north of the Sneeuw Mountains. It had 50,000 troops and was assigned, in the order of their arrival:

The *36th Division (222d, 223d, 224th Infantry)*, under Lieutenant General NAGANO Yuichiro, was deployed from China in December 1943. It was positioned at Wakde Island and Sarmi on the north-central coast of Dutch New Guinea. The *222d Infantry (Biak Detachment)* defended Biak Island in the north opening of Geelvink Baai.

Both the *32d* and *35th Divisions* were deployed from China and suffered severe losses in personnel and equipment by air and submarine attack while en route to the East Indies.

The *32d Division (32d Field Artillery, 210th, 211th, 212th Infantry)* was under Lieutenant General ISHII Kaho (Yoshio in some documents). En route to Halmahera (FEARSOME) the division lost almost half of its infantry and artillery. Arriving in early May the Division was responsible for the defense of Halmahera and other islands in the Moluccas.

The *35th Division (4th Independent Mountain Artillery, 219th, 220th, 221st Infantry)*, under Lieutenant General IKEDA Shunkichi, was deployed to Dutch New Guinea via the Philippines and Halmahera and arrived in late May and early June 1944. Its units were eventually positioned at Manokwari and Sorong.

Prior to the arrival of the *32d* and *35th Divisions*, first the *3d Division*, then the *14th Division* were to be deployed from China, but these units could not be released owing to developments in that theater. Other units under the control of *2d Army* were the *1st* and *2d Field Base Units* located on Halmahera and at Monokwari, respectively. The *57th Independent Mixed Brigade* under Major General ENDO Shinichi was sent from Japan and arrived in October 1944 at Menado to garrison northern Celebes (AGGREGATE, DOTTY).

The *19th Army*, under Lieutenant General KITANO Kenzo, was organized on 7 January 1943 with 50,000 troops and made responsible for southwestern Dutch New Guinea; the Aroe, Kai, and Tanimbar Eilander to the south and southwest of New Guinea; Ceram (BAGAY, PLETHORA) and Boeroe Islands to the west; Timor, and the Lesser Sunda Islands. This left the *16th Army* responsible only for Java and Madoera. The *16th Army's 5th* and *48th Divisions* were transferred to the *19th Army*, which was headquartered on Amboina. The *48th Division*, now commanded by Lieutenant General KOKUBU Shinshichiro, continued to garrison Timor (CAVIARE, LUMPSUGAR) with its headquarters at Koepang. In early 1944 the *5th Division* under Lieutenant General YAMADA Seiichi was moved from Amboina to garrison Kai, Aroe, and Tanimbar Eilander, its headquarters on the former, plus Modowi and Mimika on the western south coast of Dutch New Guinea. The *46th Division (123d, 147th Infantry,-145th Infantry* in the Bonins) under Lieutenant General KOBUBU Shinshichiro arrived from Japan in early 1944 to garrison the Lesser Sunda Islands (*46th Division* redeployed to Malaya in August 1945).

The *2d Southern Expeditionary Fleet* was based at Soerabaja, Java. Under it were the *21st Special Base Force* at the same location, the *22d* at Balikpapan, Borneo; the *23d* at Macassar, Celebes; and the *24th* at Ende, Flores Island. The *4th Southern Expeditionary Fleet* was headquartered at Amboina with the *25th Special Base Force* at Kaimana on the south side of the Dutch New Guinea's western tail, the *26th* at Kau Bay, Halmahera; the *27th*[4] at Wewak, North-East New Guinea; and the *28th* at Manokwari on the northwest shoulder of Geelvink Baai. The *2d Guard Force* was on Tarakan Island, Dutch Borneo; the *3d* on Bali, *5th* at Hollandia, New Guinea; and *20th* on Amboina. The *23d Air Flotilla* was based at Kendari on Celebe's southeast peninsula.

Liberation of the East Indies, 1944–45

There was no overall Allied plan or intention to completely liberate all of the East Indies. The largely U.S. operations were executed by MacArthur's Southwest Pacific forces, but there was valuable RAN and RAAF participation along with small Dutch contributions. The main goal was to clear the north coast of Dutch New Guinea to eliminate any enemy threat in the area, secure airfields to support further advances to the west, and establish bases from which to support the liberation of the Philippines to the northwest. The Australian operations to regain Borneo were significant undertakings intended to further cut Japanese communications and shipping routes between the East Indies and the Home Islands as well as with Southeast Asia. They also protected the south flank of American operations thrusting into the Philippines. If necessary Borneo offered the Allies a base from which to launch operations at Sumatra, Java, the Lesser Sunda Islands, and Celebes.

The Dutch were able to participate to a limited extent in these operations being represented by a few air units, Netherlands Forces Intelligence Service teams, and Netherlands Indies Civil Administration parties. The latter would begin entering New Guinea with U.S. forces on 2 May 1944 to reestablish Dutch administration. In September 1944, Australia agreed to host 30,000 Dutch troops if the Netherlands government raised an army to assist in the liberation of the NEI. In October the Netherlands government began to recruit for this army in liberated southern Netherlands. In late 1943 the U.S. Marine Corps had begun training a Royal Netherlands Marine Corps brigade in North Carolina for eventual employment in the NEI.

Allied operations, the RENO Plan, on the northwest coast of Dutch New Guinea (ABATTOIR, CRINGLE, WASSAIL), were a continuation of the drive along the island's north coast to the west from Australian North-East New Guinea. The long north coast of Dutch New Guinea may be divided into two dissimilar areas.

From the border with North-East New Guinea to Kaap d'Urville on the northeast shoulder of Geelvink Baai, about 250 miles, the coastline is fairly consistent. There were few bays or significant terrain features. The few areas of military value were occupied by the Japanese as airfield sites and barge-staging bases and these became the Allied objectives. Beaches were narrow and closely edged by the area's vegetation, which might be dense forests, scrub brush, or mangrove swamps. Most coastal areas were backed by narrow swamps. The mountain slopes came close to the coast, but there were narrow coastal plains in many areas. Numerous small rivers and streams flowed out of the mountains and into the sea.

The Geelvink Baai area presented a much different coastal terrain. The comparatively large Schouten Islands, described later, lie at the massive bay's northward opening. On the west side of the bay is the rugged Vogelkop Peninsula, described earlier. Its coast is largely faced with cliffs and beaches are few.

Hollandia. The first U.S. operation in Dutch New Guinea took place on 22 April 1944, the same date they landed at Aitape on the north coast of North-East New Guinea approximately 100 miles east of the Dutch New Guinea border. Operation RECKLESS was a double-enveloping amphibious assault designed to secure the Hollandia area (RECKLESS) with Humboldt (LETTERPRESS) and Tanahmeran (NOISELESS) Bays, and the airfields located inland between the two bays. Hollandia is 125 miles to the northwest of Aitape.

The Hollandia area is defined by a twenty-five-mile long chain of mountains, the Cyclops, emerging five to ten miles from the coast about twenty miles west of the North-East New Guinea border (see Map 50). The forested mountains are almost 7,000 feet high dropping steeply into the sea. On their south side they drop just as steeply toward the Lake Sentani Plain on which were a number of villages. Numerous small streams flow out of the mountains on both the north and south sides, into the sea and the lake. The coast is indented by Humboldt Bay, situated at 2°30' S 141°50' E, on the east end of the Cyclops Mountains providing the best anchorage between Wewak and Geelvink Baai. The bay has a number of good landing beaches and an unimproved road on the west side of Humboldt Bay running from Hollandia Village, the local government office,

Hollandia, Netherlands New Guinea

THE HOLLANDIA OPERATION

22-26 April 1944

LANDINGS
AT HUMBOLDT BAY
22 April 1944

LANDINGS
AT TANAHMERAH BAY
22 April 1944

provided some degree of access inland to the Sentani Lake area. At the head of Humboldt
Bay is an inner bay, Jautefa Bay, delineated from Humboldt by narrow sand spit peninsulas. The beaches in Jautefa Bay are backed by mangrove swamps. Hollandia Village
sits on the west side of Humboldt at the foot of the Cyclops. At the west end of the
Cyclops is Tanahmerah Bay. Slightly smaller than Humbodlt, its opening out to the sea
to the northwest provides less protection than Humboldt and fewer landing beaches,
which are backed by mangrove swamps. The beaches are narrow, thirty yards, and the
ground behind the beaches is rugged with access inland via only a native track leading
to the lake from Dèparprè Village at the head of a smaller bay, Déparpré Bay, on the
southeast end of the larger bay. Mangrove swamps were found behind most beaches. A
line of low hills run parallel with the south coast of Tanahmerah Bay behind which is a
small river. Beyond the river is a small unnamed mountain chain dubbed by the Allies
as Mountain Range "A." The vegetation in the area is comprised of thick forests and
underbrush. There are areas of scrub brush and open, grass-covered areas around Lake
Sentani as well as swampy areas. Lake Sentani, about 15-½ miles long east to west and
from one to four miles wide, is situated on a plain at the foot of the Cyclops Mountains.
A somewhat improved road ran along the base of the mountains north of the lake, but
crossed many streams flowing out of the mountains. The route to the lake from either
bay crossed numerous low hills and defiles ideal for a delaying defense. To the south of
the lake the land is flat, but thickly forested, for thirty to forty miles inland until rising
into the mountains. Annual rainfall at Humboldt Bay is 90–100 inches, 130–140 inches
at Tanahmerah Bay, and 60–70 at the lake. In April about nine inches of rain was
expected on almost half of the month's days. The Dutch had attempted to develop the
area agriculturally, but gave up in 1938 because of disease, unhealthy climate, and problems with local labor. The Japanese occupied the area in early April 1942 and began to
build airfields north of the lake in early 1943.

With the Allies advancing up North-East New Guinea's coast, in late 1943 the north-
central New Guinea coast was essentially undefended between Wewak in the east for
some 370 miles to Sarmi in the west. The Japanese undertook to reinforce the Hollandia
and Aitape areas, which were nominally under the control of the battered *18th Army*
some 200 miles to the east. It was unable to reinforce the Hollandia area so the *2d Area
Army* undertook the task itself. The *18th Army's 51st Division* was ordered to move west
to Hollandia while the *20th Division* was to garrison Aitape. Neither could be in place
until May. To prepare defenses in advance, Major General KITAZONO Toyozo of the
3d Field Transport Command was dispatched from Hansa Bay to Hollandia in early
April. The Hollandia area had been developed as one of the largest Japanese air base
complexes outside of Rabaul. There were three airfields, Hollandia, Sentani, and Cyclops,
on the north side of Lake Sentani, inland and roughly midway between Humboldt and
Tanahmerah Bays. The *9th Fleet Headquarters* and *4th Air Army Headquarters* were in
the area, but they evacuated prior to the American landing.

At the time of the U.S. landing the Hollandia area was defended by 15,000 IJA and
IJN troops, but only about 20 percent could be considered combat troops: a garrison and
two antiaircraft battalions, a few automatic weapons companies, plus the *90th Naval
Base Force*. The *3d Field Transport Command* was the senior headquarters overseeing
a hodgepodge of transport, engineer, airfield, air service, medical, signal, and supply
units plus stranded aircrews. Alerted to the possibility of an Allied landing on the New
Guinea coast on 17 April, defenses were frantically rushed. An invasion force was sighted
on 19 April and massive American air strikes hit Aitape, Hollandia, and Wakde-Sarmi
on the 21st destroying the few aircraft that had not been evacuated.

The purpose of Operation RECKLESS was to secure airfields on the north-central coast of New Guinea to support future operations in the Geelvink Baai area to the west. The area would also be developed as a base to support the reconquest of the Philippines. The 6th Army (ALAMO Force) under Lieutenant General Walter Krueger was responsible for both Operations PERSECUTION (Aitape) and RECKLESS (Hollandia). The dual operation was a strategic bypass of Japanese-held Wewak intended to isolate the forces there. They would later be dealt with by the Australians. It would be a long leap. Hollandia is 275 miles northwest of Hansa Bay, then the most advanced Allied enclave on New Guinea. The bypass concept was an extension of the island-hopping strategy.

The RECKLESS Task Force was built around I Corps commanded by Lieutenant General Robert L. Eichelberger. His two divisions formed two landing forces plus the RECKLESS Task Force Reserve with the 34th Infantry detached from the 24th Infantry Division. Amphibious support would be provided by the 2d Engineer Special Brigade. The 24th Infantry Division (19th, 21st Infantry) under Major General Frederick A. Irving comprised the NOISELESS Landing Force for Tanahmeran Bay. The Division had conducted an incomplete rehearsal at Taupota Bay on the New Guinea coast south of Goodenough Island, its base. The 24th Infantry Division would make the main effort to drive toward the operation's objective, the Lake Sentani airfields. The 41st Infantry Division (162d, 186th Infantry) under Major General Horace H. Fuller formed the LETTERPRESS Landing Force for Humboldt Bay. The Division's 163d Infantry was detached to the PERSECUTION Task Force for the Aitape landing to be conducted the following month. The 41st Infantry Division, based at Finschhafen, conducted its rehearsals near Lae. It would conduct a supporting attack from the east as the 24th Infantry Division drove for the airfields from the west. They would contain any Japanese fleeing east from the 24th Infantry Division's assault. The ships of the Western Attack Group (Task Group 77.1) left the Goodenough Island and Cape Cretin staging areas between 16 and 18 April. The convoys sailed around the east and north sides of the Admiralties and assembled northwest of Manus on the 20th, along with the convoy bound for Aitape, before approaching their target areas.

Dawn on 21 April (D-Day) was overcast with light rain and rough seas as U.S. Navy and RAN cruisers and destroyers opened fire on the landing beaches. The 24th Infantry Division's 19th Infantry and part of the 21st Infantry came ashore in landing craft on Beach RED 2, an 800-yard-long beach on the northeast side of Tanahmeran Bay at 0800 hours (H-Hour). Only very light small-arms fire was received and there were casualties. The ground behind the beaches proved to be extremely swampy and hilly making movement inland difficult. Even more critical was the scarcity of suitable ground for supply dumps, vehicle parks, assembly areas, and bivouac sites. The beachhead soon became choked with men, supplies, and vehicles. An accompanying Marine tank company had to be reembarked as the terrain was so rough they could not find parking spaces much less maneuver. Unloaded artillery sank into the mud.

A company of 1st Battalion, 21st Infantry landed unopposed aboard amphibian tractors on the narrow Beach RED 1 inside Déparpré Bay, which was fronted by a previously unknown coral reef. The rest of the battalion came ashore in landing craft. Scheduled for H+25 (0725 hours), the landing was delayed twenty minutes as the amphibian tractors negotiated the reef. The move inland was further delayed by swamps and the maze of wandering trails made it difficult to find the trail heading toward Lake Sentani. This battalion was to advance toward Lake Sentani and the airfields as soon as possible with the rest of the Division following from RED 2 via RED 1. Patrols from RED 2 expected to find a road or trail linking the beachhead with RED 1 about two miles to the south, but it did not exist. The absence of a simple jungle trail and the ruggedness of the terrain, delaying the construction of a road, virtually immobilized a division and caused drastic changes in plans. Masses of troops, men, and supplies were piling up in the beachhead and there was no way to move them over the intervening swampy and hilly terrain to RED 1 and the trail to Lake Sentani, the Division's main objective. Landing craft were used to shuttle men and supplies to RED 1, but it too suffered from lack of space for dumps and assembly areas. Follow-on supply convoys bound for Tanahmeran Bay had to be diverted to Humboldt Bay; there was no room in the 24th Infantry Division's cramped beachheads.

To make matters worse, it was found that the fourteen-mile-long "road" to the airfields, previously thought capable of supporting vehicular traffic, was a crude native track with hairpin turns on the hillsides climbing 60° slopes and beset with mud slides. Vehicle movement was out of the question, but the 1st Battalion, 21st Infantry advanced up the trail nonetheless with the 3d Battalion following. They initially met no enemy opposition, but lack of supplies coming forward would severely slow their advance. Two infantry battalions, two antitank companies, two cannon companies, and elements of various service and support units, 3,500 men, were detailed to manpack supplies for the two forward battalions, but as rains increased and the distance to the forward elements grew, it proved to be almost impossible. The weather cleared enough to allow limited supply drops on the 26th and the units made it to Hollandia Airdrome after a monumental effort. Fortunately resistance had been light, but sufficient to delay the advance further.

The 41st Infantry Division landed at the southwest end of Humboldt Bay at 0700 hours. The 162d Infantry landed on Beach WHITE 1 on the right flank securing Hollandia Village to the north. It was followed ashore by the 186th Infantry. The 3d Battalion, 186th Infantry landed on WHITE 2 on the north peninsula enclosing Jautefa Bay. It was to have crossed the peninsula barging through the mangrove swamps on its far side aboard amphibian tractors plunging into the inner bay and then land again on WHITE 4 on the northwest side of that bay. The amphibian tractors could not make it through the swamps, so the tractors swam through the bay's entrance between the two peninsulas. They landed on WHITE 4 and secured the road from Hollandia heading inland toward the airfields. A single company of the 186th Infantry landed on WHITE 3 on the south peninsula to secure the southern flank. Most units experienced very light opposition.

The 41st Infantry Division had its own logistics problems, but not as serious as the 24th's. WHITE 1 and 2 became very congested with supplies and equipment, a matter made worse by stacks of Japanese stores piled in the area; the Japanese had used Humboldt Bay as their own supply transfer point. WHITE 3 was very steep, as were the other beaches, and on the wrong side of the bay to be of use. On the morning of the 23d the 186th Infantry began advancing south to swing west toward Lake Sentani eight miles from the bay. The road was much better than any found in the area, but heavy rains stifled vehicle traffic and enemy resistance stiffened as the unit moved west. On the night of 23/24 April a Japanese air attack succeeded in destroying ammunition and ration dumps on WHITE 1 magnifying the Division's supply problems. Regardless, the main effort was shifted from the 24th Infantry Division to the 41st. A jetty was reached on the east end of the lake on the 24th to be used as a base for future operations. The 34th Infantry, 24th Infantry Division, the RECKLESS Task Force Reserve, was landed in Humboldt Bay on the 24th after diverting from Tanahmerah Bay. As units pushed along the lake's north shore, two companies of the 1st Battalion, 186th Infantry boarded amphibian tractors at the jetty at 1000 hours, 25 April and conducted a landlocked amphibious operation up the lake to Nafaar Village on the north-central shore, between Cyclops and Sentani Airdromes, landing at 1150 hours without opposition. A second such operation occurred at 0800 hours on the 26th when two companies of 2d Battalion, 186th Infantry departed Nefaar aboard amphibian tractors and landed at Ifaar one mile to the west and near the Cyclops Airdrome at 1000 hours against light fire. The rest of the battalion landed there in the early afternoon. Only scattered resistance was encountered as units closed in on the airfields, which were all secured on the 26th. At 1645 hours patrols from the 186th Infantry west of Hollandia Airdrome made contact with the 21st Infantry moving slowly from the west. Mopping up took place in the area and base development began. On 25 May the 41st Infantry Division departed Humboldt Bay for the Biak landing.

The bulk of the Japanese had withdrawn to the west bypassing the 24th Infantry Division to its south as it struggled eastward on its native track. They completed their assembly at Genjem Village about fifteen miles west of Lake Sentani and then made for Sarmi 120 miles to the west. Regardless of the general Japanese withdrawal, almost 1,000 Japanese stragglers in the area were killed during mop-up operations through 6 June. Between 22 April and 6 June U.S. losses in the Hollandia area were 124 KIA, 28 MIA, and 1,057 WIA. Over 3,300 Japanese were killed and 611 prisoners taken. Japanese elements retreating from Aitape to the east had assembled at Arso Village about twenty miles inland and south of Humboldt Bay about 1 June. They then proceeded westward, but most were never again seen.

Base development began quickly at Hollandia when the area was turned over to the Services of Supply on 6 June. The airfields were expanded by the USAAF and Base "G" was built around Lake Sentani, the largest on northwest New Guinea. In the original plan six airfields were to be built at Hollandia, but because of swamplands and rain, only the three existing fields were rebuilt. This massive complex housed the headquarters for U.S. Army Forces in the Far East, Allied Land Forces, Allied Air Forces, 7th Fleet, and 6th and 8th Armies as well as troop-staging camps. Naval Advance Base, Hollandia was built on Humboldt Bay. Ship-unloading facilities, supply and ammunition depots, ship repair facilities, and support installations were built there. A fuel depot was built on Tanahmerah Bay. These bases were invaluable for staging and supporting operations in the southern Philippines. The Allied headquarters were moved forward into the Philippines as the offensive continued. The Army base was closed down before the war's end. The Navy base was closed on 1 November 1945 and turned over to Dutch authorities. After the war Hollandia was renamed Sukarnapura, then Jayapura in 1962 (its original native name was Numbai).

Wakde-Sarmi. Following the Hollandia operation, the tempo of the Allied advance along the coast of Dutch New Guinea increased. The decision to secure the Wakde-Sarmi area was made while the Hollandia landing was still underway (see Map 51). The Wakde-Sarmi area is about 140 miles northwest of Hollandia and had been developed as a defensive position with three airfields. The Allies wanted to establish their own airfields there as well as a base for light naval forces and a troop-staging base.

Most of the coast in the objective area was backed by vast mangrove swamps extending well inland. In the middle of the objective area was Maffin Bay, nothing more than a shallow, curving indentation on the coast offering no protected anchorage. A number of villages were scattered along the bay shore. The objective area extended approximately ten miles along the coast in either direction. Immediately inland from the bay are the Irier Mountains, a roughly five-mile-wide range of 1,000-foot-plus high hills extending about ten miles inland. The highest hill is Mount Basbassi at 1,400 feet toward the south end. Unfinished Maffin Airdrome was at the foot of the mountains near the coast and the mouth of the Woske River, which runs along the northwest side of the mountains.

Map 51
Wakde-Sarmi, Netherlands New Guinea

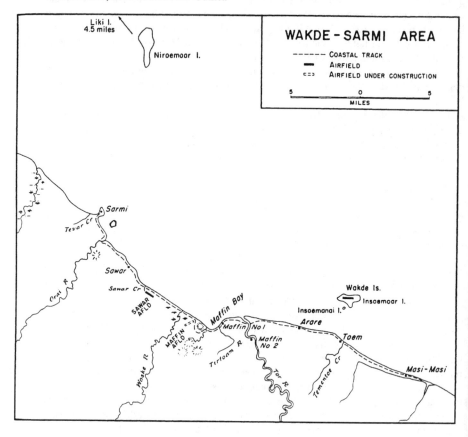

Three miles to the northwest of Maffin Airdrome (HEADWAY) was Sawar Airdrome (VAR-
NISH). The northwest end of the objective area was the village of Sarmi (NOSERING), the
local government office, perched on the mile-long Sarmi Peninsula. A tiny island, Van-
doemoear, to the southeast of the peninsula defined Sarmi Harbor. This had no port
facilities other than a small jetty and offered little protection. Several villages were clustered along the coast and inland between Sarmi and Sawar Airdrome. Inland, from the
Woske River and up the coast, the land was swamp-covered. To the east of Maffin Bay
the inland ground was only mildly swampy, but thickly covered with patches of rain
forest and underbrush. The largest river in the area, the Tor (aka Oedoeahit), flows
through to the east of the Irier Mountains. Much of the land between the river and the
mountains is swampy. Some ten miles east of Maffin Bay the coastal swamps are again
found in the vicinity of Tememtoe Creek and the Araren River. A track ran along the
coast connecting the villages.

The village of Arare was located about four miles east of the Tor River on the dry
coastal area. This would be the main landing site. Approximately four miles to the
northeast of Arare and two miles off the coast were the Wakde Islands, one of the

operation's primary objectives. Isoemoar Island, the larger of the two, was generally known as Wakde Island (STICKATNOUGHT) to the Allies. A large and well-developed airfield complex occupied much of the island. Off Wakde's south shore is a small islet, Insoemanai, measuring about 800 yards east to west and 250 yards in width. Wakde Island is 3,000 yards long east to west and 1,200 yards wide. A small peninsula juts out of the south-central coast like a shark's fin. At the end of the peninsula is a twenty-five-foot-high knoll. The rest of the island is about fifteen feet above sea level and flat. A small jetty was located at the base of the peninsula's west side and nearby were a cluster of plantation houses. A simple packed coral road network allowed access to all parts of the island. Much of the island was densely covered by coconut palms and underbrush, except where it had been cleared for the almost 5,000-foot-long airfield, taxi ways, and support facilities. The beaches are narrow, twenty to thirty feet wide, and gradually sloping packed sand and coral fragments. On the east coast are low limestone cliffs with small caves. Both islands are surrounded by 20–200-yard-wide fringe coral reefs. Wakde's terrain did not lend itself to the defense, but the Japanese built about 100 pillboxes, bunkers, and fighting positions.

About twenty miles to the northwest of Maffin Bay and twelve miles offshore are the Koemamba Eilanden. The two main islands are Niroemoar (one by three miles) and Liki (two by three miles) to its northwest. Both are hilly, 469 and 970 feet, respectively.

To the Japanese the *Maffin Bay Sector*, as they called it, was the forward defensive position of Geelvink Baai some 100 miles to the northwest. While effort had been expended to develop the sector's airfields, little had been done to prepare ground defenses. Preparations began immediately on defenses to face an amphibious assault after the Allies landed at Hollandia. The *36th Division (223d, 224th Infantry,-222d Infantry* on Biak Island), now under Lieutenant General TANOUE Hachiro, was based in the sector with 14,000 troops. This included attached antiaircraft, airfield, and service units under the *4th Engineer Group* plus the *91st Naval Garrison Force*. Much of the *224th Infantry (Matsuyama Force)* was ordered by *2d Area Army* to move toward Hollandia to establish a blocking position at Armopa, about halfway between Sarmi and Hollandia. The remaining 11,000 troops concentrated their defenses at Maffin Bay and westward along the coast as well as on Wakde Island. The coast east of the Tor River to the Tementoe River, opposite of Wakde Island, was left undefended. Constant Allied air and PT boat raids hampered the defenders' preparations. A Dutch bomber squadron participated in the raids along with U.S. and Australian aircraft. The Allies estimated that there were only 6,500 troops in the area, but while their overall estimate was far too low, their assessed combat troops strength of 4,000 was higher than actually present.

The reinforced 163d Infantry, 41st Infantry Division was selected for Operation STRAIGHTLINE and designated TORNADO Task Force under Brigadier General Jens A. Doe, who had commanded the Aitape operation. The 128th Infantry, 32d Infantry Division and the separate 158th Infantry were designated the ALAMO Force Reserve, for both Wakde-Sarmi and Biak. The 3d Engineer Special Brigade would support the operation. After changes in plans, it was decided to land at Arare well east of the Japanese defenses on firm ground devoid of swamps. Wakde Island was too small for the main landing. It would become too congested with men, supplies, and equipment and the buildup would be conducted under fire. A landing at Arare allowed dumps to be established and then Wakde could be assaulted in a shore-to-shore operation.

The landing force, after various delays caused by surf and the late arrival of supporting units, staged from Airape on 15 May 1944. En route the Eastern Attack Group laid over at Humboldt and Tanahmerah Bays to pick up additional service troops. The force departed the Hollandia area on the 16th arriving off of Arare at dawn on the 17th (D-Day) in a chilly drizzle and calm seas.

At 0730 hours, 3d Battalion, 163d Infantry landed without opposition at Arare. The rest of the battalions followed it ashore with the 2d moving east toward Tementoe Creek and the 1st moving to the east and establishing a bivouac to prepare for the D+1 assault on Wakde. The 3d Battalion sent elements west to cross what the Americans dubbed as the "Unnamed Creek" and the Japanese called Tenbin River to set up a defensive position at the mouth of the Tor River. A platoon of Company E, 2d Battalion was then reloaded on landing craft and occupied tiny Insoemanai Island off of Wakde in the late morning. The rest of the company soon followed along with the Provisional Groupment, two artillery battalions, and a cannon company under the 191st Field Artillery Group. The artillery would support the next day's Wakde assault and began preparatory fire in the early afternoon. The mainland beachhead was well consolidated by nightfall and little was seen of the enemy.

There were over 800 Japanese on Wakde. The core of the defense was the *9th Company, 3d Battalion, 224th Infantry* and 150 IJN guard troops. The rest were engineers, air service, and other service troops. Naval gun fire, air strikes, and artillery from Insoemanai prepped the island on the morning of the 18th. The reinforced 1st Battalion, 163d Infantry landed at the jetty at the base of the peninsula at 0910 hours under heavy small-arms fire. Despite the in-depth defenses of mutually supporting pillboxes, the north shore of the island was reached at 1330 hours and over three-quarters of the island was cleared by nightfall. On the 19th the assault troops pushed toward the northeast bottling up the survivors in a pocket on that end of the island by nightfall. The pocket was cleared the next day, but mop-up continued for days. Work on the airfield began on the 19th and it was operational on the 21st. Only four prisoners were taken. American losses were forty dead and 139 wounded.

Two smaller operations were conducted on the 19th when Companies E and I, 163d Infantry were sent to clear Niroemoar and Liki Islands to the northwest. Neither was occupied by the Japanese and USAAF radar warning sites were established. The units in the mainland beachhead, while awaiting the outcome of the Wakde assault, conducted local patrols.

Ashore the Japanese to the west of the beachhead were being pounded by naval gunfire, artillery, and air strikes resulting in considerable casualties and the loss of many of their ammunition and ration dumps. The *Matsuyama Force* that had been sent to the east was ordered to return and prepare to attack the beachhead from that direction while the *223d Infantry (Yoshino Force)* attacked from the south and southwest on the night of 25 May. The separate 158th Infantry Regiment, the ALAMO Force Reserve, arrived on the morning of 21 May and landed without incident. It would spearhead an attack sixteen miles to Sarmi to the west commencing on 23 May. The attack was launched by crossing the Tor River on a foot bridge that had been captured intact and moved up the coast reaching Lone Tree Hill on the 26th. On 25 May Brigadier General Doe departed to accompany the 41st Infantry Division for the Biak operation and Brigadier General Edwin D. Patrick took over as the TORNADO Task Force commander.

The Japanese had established an extremely effective defensive position on Lone Tree Hill just to the east of Maffin Airdrome. The attack stalled and was called off on the 29th and defenses were improved on the Snaky River just east of the hill. The 163d Infantry was scheduled to redeploy to Biak and the 6th Infantry Division was to begin arriving on 5 June. The 158th Infantry was pulled back about 1–½ miles from the hill to await relief by the 6th Infantry Division. On the night of 30/31 May, the planned

Japanese counterattack, after numerous delays, was launched by the *Yoshio Force*. The *Yoshio* and *Matsuyama Forces* were never able to effectively coordinate the planned pincer attack. The TORNADO Task Force was positioned along some twelve miles of coast in twenty-one separate perimeters. The *Yoshio Force* attacked positions in the center to the east of the Tor River finding only antiaircraft gun sites. While causing some damage and much confusion, the attack achieved little and the Japanese withdrew. Most of the 163d Infantry departed for Biak on the 30th.

The 6th Infantry Division (1st, 20th, 63d Infantry) under Major General Franklin C. Silbert landed at Toem (TOPHEAVY) between 5 and 14 June. The untried division assembled, unloaded supplies and equipment, and acquainted itself with the combat area while patrolling and mopping up. The attack on Lone Tree Hill was renewed on 20 June as ALAMO Force pressured the new division to secure the Maffin Bay area for a staging base to support future operations. The Arare-Toem area's terrain, beach, and surf conditions were ill suited for the purpose. The hill was occupied on the 22nd, but a difficult fight followed to hold it as the Japanese still controlled part of the hill. Two American battalions were cut off atop the hill. In order to secure the hill, a shore-to-shore amphibious assault was executed by two companies of the 3d Battalion, 1st Infantry on the 24th. They landed west of the hill in Maffin Bay aboard amphibian tractors at 0900 hours. Other units followed as the lead companies attacked east and west, but swamps and dense forest prevented much headway. The battalions trapped on the hill began clearing the enemy positions and caves on the slopes. When the battalions came off the hill they numbered only about 200 men each. The Japanese began withdrawing, but the hill was not fully secured until 25 June. Mop-up to the west and south continued into July and the Maffin Bay area was not fully secured until 9 July. The remaining Japanese withdrew to the west of the Woske River. The 6th Infantry Division was scheduled for an operation on the Vogelkop Peninsula and had to depart on 15 July. The 31st Infantry Division arrived at Maffin Bay on the 14th to relieve the 6th and it continued the mop-up and defense of the area. The Division commander assumed the role of TORNADO Task Force commander. It gave the Division, which had not seen combat, valuable experience. The 25th and 33d Infantry Divisions arrived later to stage for operations. On 2 September the Wakde-Sarmi operation was declared completed. From 17 May to 1 September U.S. losses in the area were approximately 400 dead, fifteen missing, 1,500 wounded and injured. An estimated 3,870 Japanese were killed and fifty-one taken prisoner. More are believed to have died on Lone Tree Hill buried in caves and fighting positions. Of the many who withdrew to the west, it is not known how many died of disease and starvation. Some 2,000 disorganized Japanese were believed to be still holding out in the area, but they made no effort to hamper American operations as Maffin Bay turned into a major staging area for the Philippines. Wakde Airfield developed into a large installation used by both the USAAF and Navy (FPO SF 3415).

In the north opening of the Geelvink Baai is a group of islands known as the Schouten Eilanden comprised of Biak, Noemfoor, and Japen (FLONCED). The first two would be secured by U.S. forces in May and June 1944 to provide airfields to support operations in the southern Philippines 900 miles to the northwest.

Biak Island. Biak code-named HORLICKS, is the largest and northernmost of the Schouten Eilanden and is situated at 10°00' S 131°00' E. Biak is technically two islands, the main and larger island of Biak and Soepiori Island on its northwest side (see Map 52). The two are separated by a very narrow stream-like strait called the Sorendidori River. For this reason Biak is usually considered a single island. Noemfoor Island is approximately sixty miles to the west of Biak and Japen is about the same distance to

Map 52
Biak and Soepiori Islands, Schouten Islands, Netherlands New Guinea

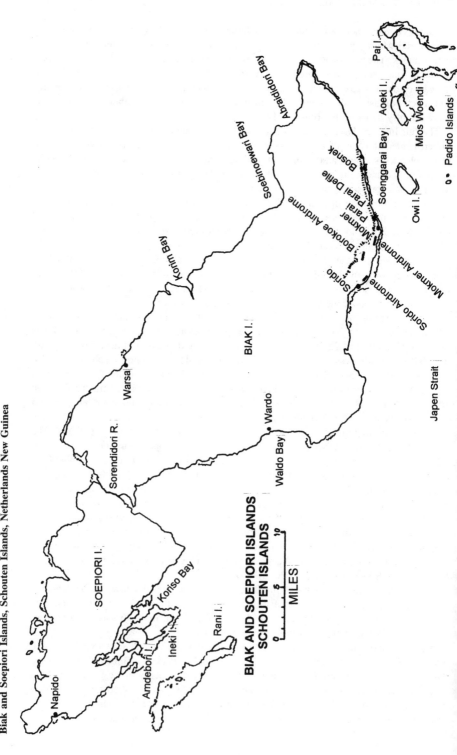

BIAK AND SOEPIORI ISLANDS
SCHOUTEN ISLANDS

MILES
0   5   10

the south. Off the southeast coast of Biak are the Padaido Eilanden, over a dozen forested islets covering a twenty-one-by-thirty-five-mile area. The Wakde-Sarmi area is 130 miles to the southeast.

Biak measures approximately forty-five miles northwest to southeast and is about twenty miles across its center, its widest point, and covers 950 square miles. Both ends taper out to less than ten miles in width. Soepiori is less than twenty-five miles in length and about ten wide at its east end. Biak's surface is covered by a series of very rough terraced coral ridges with spur ridges reaching 2,428 feet on its northwest end. River valleys are found on the northeast end (the largest), west-central coast, and northeast-central coast. The highest elevation on Soepiori is 3,392 feet. Its mountains lie in clusters and large ridges along the upper southwest coast, down the island's center and along the east end in an L shape, and on the northeast coast. The step-like construction of Biak's ridges provides some flat areas at different elevations, but they were also described as levee-like, that is, high coral limestone embankments. A cave-pocketed, rugged, narrow, 180- to 250-foot-high coral ridgeline parallels part of the south coast. The top of the ridge is wooded, but behind it the broken plateau is covered with scrub brush. Further inland the rising ground is interspersed with patches and bands of forest until about two to three miles inland when the scrub gives way to dense forest. A trail ran behind the ridge parallel with the coast less than a mile inland. The southeast interior one-third of the island has large broken-surfaced flat areas 150–200 feet above sea level. The entire island is grown over with dense rain forests and underbrush. Rainfall is heavy, about 100 inches per year, but there are few streams, other than in the three small river valleys. The rain permeates into the coral, especially on the eastern half of Biak, and is carried off by underground streams into the sea. Rains were to hamper the operation.

Most of the few villages were along the south coast with Bosnek, the government center, located on the central-southeast coast. About twelve miles to the west of Bosnek is Sorido, from which a track crosses the island to Korim Bay on the central-northeast coast. There are no port facilities or protected anchorages although there were two short jetties at Bosnek (SLUMBERLAND) and three at Soenggarai Bay at Parai just to the east of Mokmer (GRIND-STONE, MARSHMELLOW), itself roughly midway between Bosnek and Sorido. An area of vertical cliffs was found backing Parai and called the Parai Defile by U.S. troops. The entire coast is fringed by a 200- to 600-foot-wide reef. At low tide the reef was dry, but planners had no information on how deep the water was at high tide. In many areas there were coral cliffs edging the coast and, often, where there were no cliffs, mangrove swamps were found. From east of Bosnek the steep coral ridge closely hugs the coast allowing a 400 to 800-yard-wide strip. A road follows this strip atop a ten-to-fifteen-foot-high coral shelf. Small villages, with many of their houses built on stilts over the water, were found there. From Mokmer the ridge turns inland and a gradual, but rugged, slope rises one to two miles from the coast. On this narrow, scrub-brush-covered coastal plain the Japanese built three airfields, from east to west, Mokmer (the largest) (SWEETACRES), uncompleted Borokoe (the Japanese called it Sorido No. 2), and Sorido No. 1 (the smallest). Their heaviest defenses were constructed along this section of the coast where a barrier reef swings out from the fringing reef. At Sorido, the coastal road turns north and degenerates into a track heading north. A native trail continues along the coast. At Bosnek, the coral ridge backing the town is actually a vertical cliff. Atop the cliff the Japanese had cleared an airfield site, but no other work was accomplished. Two additional fields were also planned for the area. Intended to be used mainly by the *23d Air Flotilla*, their usefulness ceased when Allied aircraft began operating from Hollandia.

The Japanese forces on Biak were designated the *Biak Detachment* and were built around the *222d Infantry, 36th Division* under Colonel KUZUME Naoyuki. Attached were antiaircraft, airfield construction, transport, and service units plus the *19th Naval Garrison Force* and IJN antiaircraft units. The *Biak Detachment* totaled 12,000 troops and was slated to be reinforced by the *221st Infantry, 35th Division* on Halmahera to the west. The Allied estimate was 4,400 men with about half being combat troops. The service units were converted to combat units as the invasion fleet approached. The defenses were concentrated on the south coast atop the ridge running from Soriari west to Soenggarai Bay inclusive. Where the coast bends at Mokmer and the ridge turns inland there was a gap in the defense. Heavy defenses were found on the inland ridge overlooking Mokmer Airdrome. Artillery was hidden in cave positions. Owi Island (SPIRIT-SAIL), one of the largest and closest to Biak of the Padido Eilanden, is 2-½ miles southeast of Mokmer and defined Soenggarai Bay. It measures about three miles from northeast to southwest and is 1-½ miles wide. It is mostly flat, but there are two narrow parallel ridges over 100 feet high running much of its length. Most of the island is covered with scrub brush, but a wooded band follows the northwest coast and bends around the southwest end.

The landing site selected for Operation HORLICKS was at Bosnek with its two jetties and near the east end of the defenses. The 41st Infantry Division (162d, 186th Infantry, −163d Infantry at Wakde-Sarmi), with significant support units attached, under Major General Horace H. Fuller comprised the HURRICANE Task Force. The 2d Engineer Special Brigade supported the operation. The 128th Infantry, 32d Infantry Division, and the separate 158th Infantry were designated the ALAMO Force Reserve, for both Biak and Wakde-Sarmi. Z-Day was set for 27 May, ten days after the beginning of the Wakde-Sarmi landing. The HURRICANE Task Force conducted a limited rehearsal at Humboldt Bay and departed for Biak on 25 May aboard the Western Attack Group. U.S., Australian, and Dutch aircraft had been heavily preping the area.

The Western Attack Group arrived off the south coast of Biak in the early morning of 27 May. The landing beaches were GREEN 1–4 located near the eastern end of the Japanese defensive positions in the vicinity of Bosnek. The *Biak Detachment Head-quarters* was initially in this area just over one mile inland. The stronger-than-anticipated westward-flowing current caused some units to land as much as 3,000 yards west of their assigned beaches. One unit came ashore in a 2,000-yard-wide mangrove swamp, but being aboard amphibian tractors, it was able to gain the coastal road. Most of the lead 186th Infantry landed on their designated beaches at or very shortly after the designated H-Hour, 0730 hours. The 162d Infantry soon followed it ashore. Some confusion resulted in units being in the wrong areas and beachhead congestion was soon experienced on the narrow coastal strip. More confusion arose because of the inaccuracy of maps. Enemy air attacks did not begin until after 1100 hours. As the 186th Infantry established defenses facing the ridge above them, the 162d Infantry moved west down the coastal road before halting for the night.

On the morning of the 28th the 162d resumed its westward attack down the coast and soon began to experience stiffing resistance. The *Biak Detachment Headquarters* relocated west to the inland ridge north of Mokmer Airdrome and a strongpoint known as West Caves. The next day it was realized that to continue the attack on such a narrow frontage with the enemy controlling the heights above the entire length of the column was impractical. In the early afternoon the attacking column's rear elements began to withdraw and the lead battalion was extracted by amphibian tractors and landing craft. To date U.S. casualties were light, but enemy resistance was stronger and more aggressive than expected. This, coupled with the terrain restrictions and severe water shortages, resulted in a call for reinforcements. The 503d Parachute Infantry Regiment was moved to Hollandia and placed on standby. The 163d Infantry (-2d Battalion) arrived on 31 May. On 1 June the attack was resumed with the 186th Infantry mounting the ridge and moved west in the vicinity of the surveyed airstrip while the 162d attacked along the coast. The advance was slow and Mokmer Airdrome was finally reached on 7 June. Most of the remaining Japanese troops were concentrated around the West Caves strongpoint northeast of Mokmer Airdrome, but many had moved to a low ridge north of the airfield. Another strongpoint known as the East Caves was situated in the south side of the ridge above Mokmer Village. The cave strongpoints were comprised of huge caves systems of unknown depth, large sinkholes, smaller caves, and field fortifications organized into dense integrated defensive positions. Between 11 and 15 June a concerted attack was made to the north and west.

In the meantime work began on Mokmer Airdrome. There were grave concerns over the operation's progress and the lack of an operational airfield to support the coming Marianas campaign. On 1 June Owi, Aoeki, and Mios Woendi Islands were reconnoitered. Owi was selected for an airfield site and work began on the 3d. A PT boat base was established on tiny Mios Woendi, five miles to the southeast of Owi. Lieutenant General Eichelberger, commanding I Corps, was sent to Biak on 15 June to take over the RECKLESS Task Force relieving Major General Fuller of the responsibility, but he would retain command of the 41st Infantry Division. However, he requested relief from that command as well, which was reluctantly granted, and Brigadier General Doe took command of the Division. Additional reinforcements were still required and on 18 June the 34th Infantry, 24th Infantry Division arrived from Hollandia and was immediately committed.

In the meantime the Japanese planned to reinforce Biak with 5,000 troops in a series of operations known as *KON*. These were to be conducted in conjunction with the larger *A-GO Operation*, an effort in which the remaining main battle units of the Japanese fleet were to be assembled to confront the U.S. Pacific Fleet. It was deemed critical that Biak be held as its airfields were needed to support *A-GO*. Japanese air attacks on Biak had continued since the landing and they increased in support of the reinforcement effort. The 35th Division on Sorong and Halmahera began to move by water to Moanokwari from where elements would stage to Biak. The first *KON Operation* was an effort to move part of the IJA's *2d Amphibious Brigade* from the Philippines to Biak. The convoy was detected by Navy patrol bombers at a far greater distance from Biak than the Japanese had anticipated. They were unaware that the Americans had already established a base at Wakde Island. Fearing interception by American ships, the first *KON Operation* was recalled on 3 June and the unit was landed at Sorong on the west side of the Vogelkop Peninsula. A second attempt was made on the 7th, but the convoy only carried a small number of *219th Infantry* troops. Again fearing compromise, these troops too were diverted to Sorong. A final attempt was made to move the *2d Amphibious Brigade* from Sorong to Biak on the 12th, but it too was canceled as the *A-GO Operation* was put into effect when it became apparent that the United States would invade the Marianas. While large-scale reinforcement had not been possible during the *KON Operations*, an estimated 1,200 troops of assorted companies from the *35th Division's 219th* and *221st Infantry* and previously uncommitted elements of the *36th Division's 222d Infantry* were infiltrated to Biak by landing barge during the month of June. The *Biak Detachment* committed these elements piecemeal as they arrived rather than concentrating the fresh troops in a counterattack.

A major effort was made between 18 and 27 June to reduce the remaining Japanese strongpoints to the northwest of the airfields. Work on Mokmer Airdrome resumed on the 20th and on the 23rd part of the field was in use by fighters. The West Caves was destroyed on the 27th. Operations to clear the remaining enemy to the north and west of the airfields had begun on the 20th and continued through the 30th. No major effort was made to clear the East Caves, although probed and barraged with mortars and artillery, until the end of June. The Japanese had largely abandoned the position by that time. On 28 June Lieutenant General Eichelberger departed Biak leaving Major General Fuller in command of the HURRICANE Task Force. A final strongpoint known as the Ibdi Pocket still held out above the coastal mangrove swamp west of the GREEN Beaches. It was finally reduced after an incredibly tenuous defense on 25 July signaling an end to organized resistance.

Numbers of Japanese had retreated to the north in an effort to organize a guerrilla war, but they were short of supplies and ammunition and lacked heavy weapons. An estimated 4,000 Japanese still held out in the north. In early July American patrols into the north began, but significant efforts did not begin until August. On 2 August the 2d Battalion, 163d Infantry landed at Korim Bay on Biak's north-central coast and pushed south to link up with a battalion of the 162d Infantry moving overland from the airfields on the 15th. Remaining Japanese units were ordered to assemble at Wardo on the west-central coast to stage for a final counterattack. Some of the units moving there were interdicted by American patrols. On the 17th the 1st Battalion, 186th Infantry landed at Wardo to dash any hope of such an effort. The battalion went on to land on the southeast and northwest ends of Soepiori Island to clear enemy elements there. A small number of Japanese are known to have evacuated the islands by small boat.

Because of the different units involved it was difficult to determine the exact number of U.S. casualties on Biak. It is estimated that between 27 May and 20 August 400 were killed, 2,000 wounded, 150 injured, and five missing plus over 7,200 nonbattle casualties, many with scrub typhus and unidentified fevers. At least 4,700 Japanese were killed and 220 captured by 20 August. Unknown numbers were killed in later mop-up actions to include those on Soepiori Island or who died of starvation and disease. It was later estimated that the total Japanese dead was at least 8,000 and another 240 prisoners were taken. Almost 600 Javanese and Indian laborers were freed along with 300 Formosans.

The airfield on Owi Island was operational by 21 June. In July it was extended to 7,000 feet and a second 7,000-foot runway was completed in August. The 5,000-foot Mokmer Airdrome was extended to 7,000 feet by the end of July and the 4,000-foot Borokoe Airdrome was operation at the same time. It was soon extended to 5,500 feet. Sorido Airdrome was operational in August with 4,000 feet of runway. None of the fields, though, were ready for use to support the Marianas campaign, which had been the original intent of the operation. Landing ship unloading areas, docks, and jetties were built at Bosnek, Parai, and Mokmer. Depots and storage areas were built at Base "H" around Sorido west of the airfields. The Navy built a seaplane base at Mios Woendi Island along with a landing craft repair facility and in September a temporary advance submarine base. Other Navy support facilities were built on nearby Noesi and Oreiv Islands. The 41st Infantry Division remained on Biak until the end of January 1945. Naval Advance Base, Biak (FPO SF 3505) was closed on 19 January 1946. Since 1968 northwest Biak has been maintained as a nature reserve.

Noemfoor Island. Noemfoor, code-named TABLETENNIS, is located approximately seventy miles to the southwest of Biak across the Japen Strait and is the westernmost of the Schouten Eilanden in the north opening of Geelvink Baai. Manokwari, a key Japanese base and headquarters of the *2d Army* on the northwest shoulder of Geelvink Baai, is fifty miles to the west.

Noemfoor is fourteen miles long from north to south and eleven miles wide across the center (see Map 53). The island's oval shape is broken by Broe Bay dipping deeply into the northeast coast. The six-mile-long bay is oriented south-southeast creating a 5-½-mile-long peninsula varying from one to 4-½ miles in width. Several mangrove swamp-covered islands block much of the bay's entrance. Mangrove swamps penetrate deeply into the bay's western shore with smaller, scattered swamps on the east side. The entire east or seaward side of the peninsula is lined by broad mangrove swamps. Small mangrove swamps are found scattered around northwest, north, and south coasts. A 1-to-1-½-mile-wide coastal strip rising to over 100 feet above sea level runs around the south coast to the northwest where is widens to three miles. Near Broe Bay it narrows back to a mile in width. The Broe Peninsula too is only 100 or so feet above sea level. The northern one-third of the island is fairly level gradually sloping upward to the south where it is becomes rugged and hilly. Just south of the island's center the highest ground climbs to 670 feet. Southeast of this is Hill 380. Most of the island is covered with dense rain forests and underbrush. Rain was heavy and frequent during the operation. The entire island is surrounded by a fringing coral reef of varying width. It is narrow on the west side, but is over a mile wide on the north and south sides. It narrows again on the east side. The entrance to Broe Bay is covered by a broad reef. Offshore waters are deep allowing ships to approach from any direction.

The island's 5,000 inhabitants lived in villages on the south and north coasts as well as around Broe Bay. Tracks or trails followed most of the coastline from the southeast around to the north. From the southeast coast an inland trail runs up the Broe Peninsula where it connects to trails running along the bay's east shore and around its south end. From there a trail crosses the southern portion of the island between Hills 670 and 380 to the lower west coast in the vicinity of the 4,000-foot-long Namber Airdrome at Roemboi Bay. The 5,000-foot Kamiri Airdrome was on the beach on the northwest side. On the island's north end was the unfinished 5,000-foot Kornasoren Airdrome. Japanese airfield construction had begun in late 1943.

The *Noemfoor Defense Detachment* consisted of the headquarters of the *219th Infantry, 35th Division*, the Regiment's *3d Battalion*, two companies from the *222d Infantry, 36th Division*, and a provisional battalion comprised of construction, transport, and airfield units. The 2,000 troops were under the command of Colonel SHIMIZU Suesada. U.S. estimates were up to 3,250 troops. Some 600 Formosan laborers and 2,000 Javanese slave laborers had been brought to the island. The Japanese defense focused on the main Kamiri Airdrome on the northwest coast, but small elements were also positioned at the other two airfields.

Noemfoor was to be secured for two reasons, to provide additional airfields to support future operations and to deny its use by the Japanese as a staging site for sending reinforcements to Biak from Manokwari; it was roughly midway between the two. The CYCLONE Task Force was formed by ALAMO Force under the command of Brigadier General Edwin D. Patrick, who had commanded the TORNADO Task Force at Sarmi. The Task Force consisted of the separate 158th Infantry, which would conduct the amphibious assault, and the 503d Parachute Infantry, which would parachute onto Kamiri Airdrome if needed for reinforcement. Also assigned were the No. 62 Works Wing (airdrome construction) of the RAAF and significant antiaircraft and support units. Elements of the 2d and 3d Engineer Special Brigades would provide landing craft. The Task Force would

Map 53
Noemfoor Island, Netherlands New Guinea

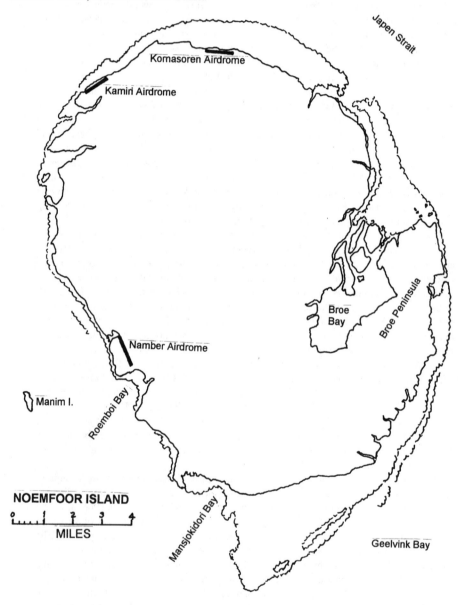

Japen Strait

Kornasoren Airdrome

Kamiri Airdrome

Broe Bay

Broe Peninsula

Number Airdrome

Manim I.

Roemboi Bay

NOEMFOOR ISLAND

0   1   2   3   4

MILES

Mansjokidori Bay

Geelvink Bay

field 8,000 troops, of which 7,000 would land on D-Day, 2 July 1944. The 34th Infantry, 25th Infantry Division at Biak was the Task Force Reserve. USAAF and RAAF units would fly support missions.

The Noemfoor Attack Force (Task Force 77) departed Toem (Wakde-Sarmi) on 29–30 June. After passing to the north of Noemfoor and then turning south the Attack Force arrived off of the northwest coast in the early morning of 2 July. Beach YELLOW was 800 yards wide and extended along the west end of the Kamiri Airdrome, which was on the edge of the high-water line. The beach was comprised of loose sand with a very gradual slope and forty to sixty feet across to the tree line. Since the assault troops were landing directly into the island's strongest defenses the naval bombardment was the heaviest delivered in the Southwest Pacific to date. This was reinforced by bomber attacks. The bombardment's smoke and dust, combined with a thick haze, made visibility poor.

The 158th Infantry's landing at 0800 hours was without opposition. The amphibian tractors carrying the first waves overran the airfield and the troops dismounted behind the coral ledge on the far side. The troops moved inland with little resistance. By late afternoon a 3,000-yard-long, 800-yard-deep beachhead had been established. There were only two dozen U.S. casualties and 115 enemy dead were counted. The next day units moved out of the beachhead in an effort to find the enemy. The 503d Parachute Infantry was ordered to parachute on to the secured Kamiri Airdrome to reinforce the ground troops because of the unknown situation as to enemy strength and to speed up the island's occupation. Because of a shortage of transport aircraft, one battalion a day would be dropped between 3 and 5 July. Staging from Cyclops Airdrome at Hollandia, the Regiment's 1st Battalion jumped in at 1000 hours. The low drop altitude, parked vehicles, equipment and supply dumps, wrecked Japanese aircraft, and trees along side the runway resulted in seventy-two casualties among the 739 paratroopers. The 3d Battalion jumped in the next day, and even though additional precautions had been taken, the 685 men suffered fifty-six injuries. The 2d Battalion's jump was canceled and it was flown to Mokmer Airdrome on Biak the next day. It embarked aboard landing craft and arrived at Noemfoor on 11 July.

On 4 July Kornasoren Airdrome was secured. Units had moved around the island's north and west coasts as well as inland in an effort to locate the elusive enemy. Only light resistance was encountered. On the same day the enemy was discovered on low hills north of the island's center and the Japanese attempted to attack. Most were destroyed by the 5th. On 6 July, the 2d Battalion, 158th Infantry was landed at Roemboi Bay on the southeast end of Namber Airdrome meeting no resistance. It was now apparent that the Japanese had scattered inland in small groups. The 158th Infantry was assigned the northern half of the island, the 503d Parachute the southern. The only large group of 400–500 Japanese that offered organized resistance was found on Hill 670 near the island's center on 16 July. Prisoners reported Colonel SHIMIZU to be with this group. This force managed to exfiltrate to Hill 380 to the south from which it again withdrew on 15/16 August. Another contact was made on the 17th, but the group continued to evade. With only limited contacts being made with small disorganized groups, the island was declared secure on 31 August. The 503d Parachute and 158th Infantry remained on the island until November 1944 and January 1945, respectively, still mopping up.

The United States lost seventy KIA and 345 WIA on Noemfoor. A total of 1,960 Japanese were known dead and 247 were captured along with 623 Formosan laborers. Almost 300 of the Formosans had died earlier because of Japanese mistreatment. The

Netherlands Indies Civil Administration party found that 400 of the island's 5,000 natives had been impressed for labor. Natives, most of whom had moved into the interior to avoid the Japanese, captured approximately fifty and killed a similar number. Over 3,000 Javanese laborers of all ages and sexes had been brought to Noemfoor in November 1943. They were severely mistreated and no provision was made for clothing, quarters, medication, and little food provided. Some 400 survived with only ten to fifteen accidentally killed by U.S. forces.

Work on the Kamiri Airdrome (FUNNYBONE, SPOILSPORT) had begun on D-Day and it was ready for limited use on 6 July. It was later extended to 5,400 feet. Nambur Airdrome was to be the next one improved, but it was on a poor site and the effort was switched to Kornaroren (LONGLEG). A 7,000-foot bomber runway was completed on 27 July in time to support operations on the Vogelkop Peninsula. A second 7,000-foot runway was completed in early August. The Noemfoor airfields later supported operations on Morotai Island and Borneo.

Sansapor-Cape Opmarai. The mountainous Vogelkop Peninsula branches to the northwest off the west end of Dutch New Guinea's tail. Its east side is bounded by Geelvink Baai and the south side by McCluer Golf. Halmahera Island in the Molucca Islands lies to the west. The Japanese occupied positions on the Vogelkop at Manokwart on the northeast corner: Sorong, a small island off the west end, Babo on the south shore of McCluer Golf, and Nabire on the south end of Geelvink Baai.

MacArthur's staff proposed several objectives on the Vogelkop where airfields could be established to support operations toward the Philippines; Mindanao is 600 miles to the northwest. It was desirable to have airfields between Noemfoor to the east and the future objective of Morotai to the northwest. As the tactical and strategic situations changed these early plans were canceled. One of the main plans was to capture Sorong and Waigeo Islands, the latter being a much larger island sixty miles northwest of the former. Another operation, for which a massive effort had begun in the States, was to capture and develop the Klamono oilfields thirty miles inland from Sorong Island. The formation of the 5,000-man Engineer Petroleum Production Depot had begun in California. This organization was to move to and operate the Klamono oilfields to supply ships with fuel in-theater. Its oil required little refining before it could be burned by ships. The effort's manning, shipping, and support requirements were found to be more demanding than simply shipping the fuel from the States and the project was canceled.

A new plan was developed to secure an enclave on the north-central coast of the Vogelkop in an area unoccupied by the Japanese. The Sansapor-Mar area was selected, later to be known as the Sansapor-Cape Opmarai Operation (see Map 54). The Sansapor-Cape Opmarai area (GLOBETROTTER) is on the northwest coast of the Vogelkop about eighteen miles southwest of Kaap de Goede Hoop (aka Cape Jamersba), the peninsula's northernmost point. Sorong is sixty-five miles to the southwest and Manokwari is 140 miles to the east. Reconnaissance determined that good landing beaches and suitable sites for airfields were available.

The objective area between Cape Sansapor on the west flank and Cape Opmarai on the east was approximately twelve miles broad. Less than two miles to the southwest of Cape Sansapor was the Sansapor coconut plantation and a village by the same name. Sansapor Bay, a shallow curve in the coast, is on the west side of the cape into which flows the Sekowa River. Approximately fourteen miles further to the southwest of Cape Sansapor is Mega Bay where a later landing would take place. Roughly in the center of this area was Mar Village (aka Warsai) on the east side of the swampy mouth of the Wewe River. Inland more swampland was found stretching from either bank of the river.

Overlooking Cape Sansapor are steep hills that climb toward 4,300-foot high Mount Tonkier about twelve miles inland. A roughly 350-foot-high hill, Mount Sowewe, lies on the coast between Cape Sansapor and Mar. Immediately to the east of Mar is Mount Tafel, 1,400 feet high. Numerous streams flow out of the hills and the lowlands between the hills. Much of the lowlands, especially along rivers, is swampy. The hills and dry ground are covered with rain forests and underbrush, though less dense than ordinary. Opposite of Mar and 3 and 5 miles offshore, respectively, are Middleburg and Amsterdam Islands comprising the Mios Soe Eilanden. Neither island is much over a mile in length.

The Japanese operated a small barge-staging base at Cape Sansapor on the Sorong-to-Manokwari route and it was thought to be manned by no more than 100 sea transport troops. Aerial reconnaissance detected cleared strips near the mouth of the Wewe River that might indicate initial clearing of an airstrip. If this proved to be the case an up to 700-man airfield construction unit might be in the area. Further ground reconnaissance in mid-June 1944 determined that airfields could be constructed near Mar and on Middleburg Island. No Japanese were found in the immediate area. The previously detected cleared strips proved to be overgrown, abandoned native gardens. D-Day was set for 30 July.

The 6th Infantry Division (1st, 63d Infantry, -20th Infantry remaining at Wakde-Sarmi) under Major General Franklin C. Silbert was designated the TYPHOON Task Force. The Task Force was heavily augmented by engineer units to construct airfields. The Division first had to be relieved from its mopping-up operations at Sarmi and assembled giving it only a week and a half to plan, train, rehearse, draw supplies and equipment, and load-out on already overcrowded beaches at Maffin Bay. The Attack Force (Task Force 77) sailed from Maffin Bay on 28 July. To obtain complete surprise and because no enemy were expected in the area, no prelanding bombardment, aerial or naval, was conducted. Instead, U.S., Australian, and Dutch aircraft raided Manokwari, Sorong, Halmahera, Ceram, and Amboina as a diversion. Even the convoy's route was a deception effort in that it sailed along the north coast of New Guinea, then between Biak and Japen, then Biak and Noemfoor, and then westward along the equator as though making for Sorong or Halmahara before turning sharply south to the objective.

The 1st Infantry landed without opposition at 0701 hours, 30 July on Beach RED located between two small, unnamed coral-edged capes to the east of Mar. Small detachments aboard amphibian tractors landed on Middleburg Island right after 0730 hours and on Amsterdam at 1130 hours. Neither island was occupied by the enemy. Three unarmed Japanese were killed on the mainland the first day. Beach RED provided good landing sites for LSTs, but the beach sand was very soft inhibiting wheeled vehicle movement and the jungle behind the beach allowed for only limited dump and assembly areas. Units moved inland and established a beachhead line 800 yards deep before nightfall.

On 31 July, the 3d Battalion, 1st Infantry boarded landing craft at the mouth of the Wewe River and landed at 0844 hours on Beach GREEN at Cape Sansapor to the west. There was no opposition and it was apparent that the Japanese had hastily abandoned their badge staging base. The beachhead was expanded inland as much as eight miles and along the coast to the Koor River to the east of Cape Opmarai and the Sekowa River southwest of Cape Sansapor, some thirty miles. Work had begun immediately on airfields between Beach RED and the Wewe River and on Middleburg Island. Patrols were sent out and on 3 August 110 sick and wounded Japanese were captured at a crude hospital near Cape Opmarai, probably barge passengers who had been dropped off for treatment after suffering air attacks.

Map 54
Sansapor-Cape Opmarai, Netherlands New Guinea

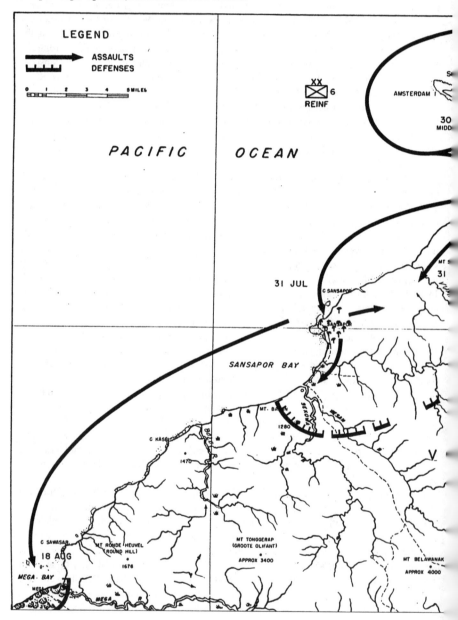

LEGEND

ASSAULTS
DEFENSES

0 1 2 3 4 5 MILES

XX
6
REINF

AMSTERDAM I

30
MIDD

PACIFIC   OCEAN

MT S
31

31 JUL

C SANSAPOR

SANSAPOR

SANSAPOR BAY

MT BA

1280

C KASG

1470

MT RONDE HEUVEL
(ROUND HILL)

1676

MT TONGGERAP
(GROOTE OLIFANT)
APPROX 3400

MT BELAWANAK
APPROX 4000

C SAWASAR

18 AUG

MEGA BAY

MEGA

MEGA R

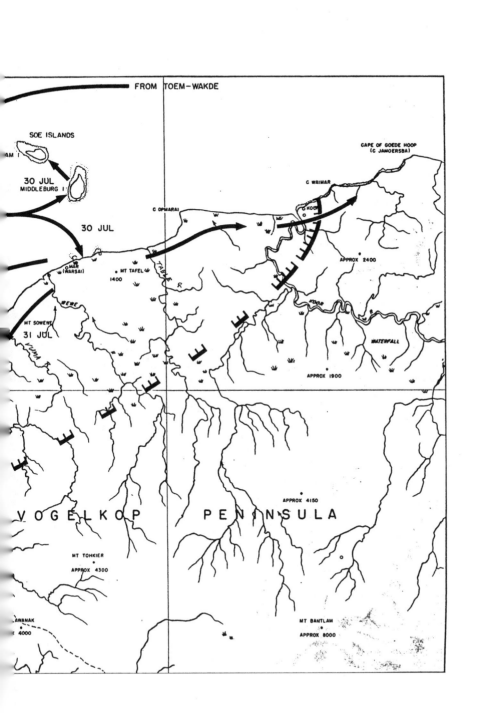

FROM TOEM-WAKDE

SOE ISLANDS

CAPE OF GOEDE HOOP
(C JAMOERSBA)

30 JUL
MIDDLEBURG I

C WAIMAR

C OPMARAI

30 JUL

O KOOR

APPROX 2400

OMAR
(WARSAI)

MT TAFEL
1400

MT SOWEWE

WATERFALL

31 JUL

APPROX 1900

VOGELKOP   PENINSULA

APPROX 4150

MT TOHKIER
APPROX 4300

AWANAK
4000

MT BANTLAM
APPROX 8000

During the May and June fighting on Biak the *35th Division* at Sorong and Halmahera began moving to Manokwari by water from where it would stage to reinforce Biak during the unsuccessful *KON Operations*. Much of the *35th Division* was now at Manokwari on which Allied air attacks from Wakde, Biak, and Noemfoor increased. Many of the ration dumps were destroyed and the 12–15,000 troops there could no longer be supported. Even with Sorong only sixty-five miles from Sansapor, the *35th Division* and *2d Amphibious Brigade* was powerless to undertake any offensive action because of a lack of watercraft. Overland movement was impractical as insufficient supplies and ammunition could not be carried to sustain an offensive, especially since barges could not deliver it as they advanced east. The *2d Army* at Manokwari ordered the *35th Division* there to return to Sorong by foot beginning in early July. The *2d Army Headquarters* began an overland move 150 miles south to Windehsi where the Vogelkop Peninsula's isthmus joins the mainland. The *1st Independent Brigade* under Major General FUKA-BORI Yuki, assembled largely from the *2d Field Base Unit*, and the *28th Special Base Force* remained at Manokwari.

On 15 August the TYPHOON Task Force was alerted that *35th Division* elements were moving west past the beachhead. The 6th Infantry Division increased its patrols inland and established ambushes to interdict the Japanese who were attempting to avoid the area by moving further inland. Elements of the 1st Infantry were landed briefly at Mega Bay thirty miles to the southwest of Mar on 18 August to search for the evading enemy. The 20th Infantry arrived at Mar on 23 and 25 August to rejoin its parent division. At that time Major General Silbert turned over command of the Division and the Task Force to Brigadier General Charles E. Hurdis as he departed to assume command of X Corps. Light Japanese air raids were received on 25, 27, and 31 August. By the end of the month the Division had killed 385 Japanese and took 215 prisoners, many being Formosans. Most of the *35th Division* made it to Sorong, but the mere presence of the 6th Infantry Division forced the hunger-weakened and ill troops to divert to the south through more rugged country and large numbers died along the way. TYPHOON Task Force losses between 30 July and 31 August were fourteen dead, thirty-five wounded, and nine injured. Over 800 men were diagnosed with scrub typhus or fever of unknown origin; nine died.

The 5,400-foot-long Middleburg Airdrome (HAIRLESS) was operational on 17 August for fighters. The 6,000-foot Mar Airdrome, intended for medium bombers, was operational on 3 September and was soon extended to 7,500 feet. They supported operations on Morotai and interdiction operations were flown from them throughout the Molucca Islands. A small PT boat base was built of Amsterdam Island in early August. The 6th Infantry Division remained at Sansapor-Cape Opmarai until departing for the Philippines in December 1944.

The Japanese forces remaining on the Vogelkop: *2d Army, 35th Division, 1st Independent* and *2d Amphibious Brigades* were cut off from *2d Area Army* forces on Halmahera, Ceram, and Celebes and incapable of mounting any offensive action due to short supplies and lack of air and naval support. The *2d Army Headquarters* was later able to move to Celebes.

Morotai Island. The final major U.S. operation in the NEI was executed on Morotai Island, code-named INTERLUDE. Morotai is located approximately twenty miles off of Halmahera Island's northern peninsula separated by the Morotai Strait (see Map 55). The west end of New Guinea is 230 miles to the southeast, Celebe's Minahassa Peninsula is 220 miles west-southwest, and Mindanao is 300 miles northwest. It is the northernmost

Map 55
Morotai Island, Netherlands East Indies

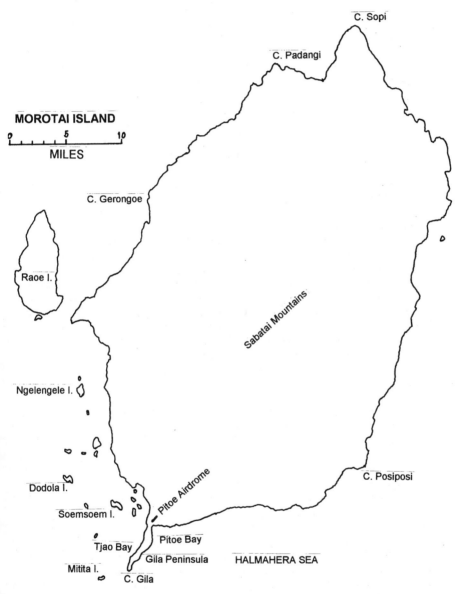

of the Molucca Islands and one of the most remote within the NEI being far out of the
way of shipping lanes.

Halmahera Island (aka Jailolo), code-named FEARSOME, is the largest of the Molucca
Islands measuring about 220 miles from north to south and some ninety miles at its
widest to cover 7,000 square miles. It somewhat appears to be a miniature version of

Celebes 170 miles to its west in that it is comprised of four peninsulas. The island is mountainous with the highest elevation being 4,947 feet in the center. Clustered off its southwest coast is Batjan Island with three smaller islands. Just to their south are the Obi Eilanden. These small islands are essentially mountaintops reaching from the Ceram Sea to 6,926 and 5,285 feet, respectively. The *32d Division*, only at half strength because of losses suffered while en route to the island, garrisoned Halmahera and Batjan along with the 1st *Field Base Unit* and *10th Expeditionary Unit*. The Division fell under the *2d Area Army* headquartered on Celebes and was responsible for the defense of Morotai. Also on the island was the *26th Special Base Force*. Regardless of the *32d Division's* low strength, there were almost 30,000 troops on Halmahera, but less than one-third were combat troops. The Japanese had begun construction on nine airfields on the island, mostly in the north where the troops were concentrated, and most were completed. Once the Americans landed on Morotai, reinforcements would be sent from Halmahera.

Morotai measures forty-eight miles northeast to southwest and twenty-eight miles across the center covering an area of 695 square miles. The island's shape appears similar to Noemfoor, only six times larger and with much higher elevations and more rugged. The island is mountain-covered with four parallel ranges running north to southwest. From east to west these are: Sangowo, Sabatai, the largest and central chain, Tjio, and Waja Boela Mountains. The highest areas are found in the southern Sabatai Mountains' southwest end with Mount Sabatai at 3,575 feet and the north end of the Tjio Mountains topping 3,435 feet. The entire island is covered with dense rain forest and underbrush. The mountains drop close toward the coast on all sides of the island except the southwest. There a broad river plain, known as the Doroeba Plain, covers an area about nine miles east to west and stretches over four miles inland gradually sloping up to the foothills of the Sabatai Mountains. Over this plain flows the Tjao and Pilowo Rivers to the west into Tjao Bay. Scores of rivers and streams flow out of the mountains with so many inland tributaries that in many areas they are encountered at less than one-mile intervals one after another. Between these are smaller streams, ravines, and gullies.

Jutting five miles to the west-southwest off the island's southwest end is a less than one-mile-wide Gila Peninsula (1°55' N 128°07' E) separating Tjao Bay on its west side and Pitoe Bay on the east. A foot trail ran most of the peninsula's length along its west side toward the end, Cape Gila (aka Cape Dehegila). The peninsula is flat and covered with palms and underbrush. The east side of the peninsula is free of obstacles, but is exposed to rough seas. The west side has coral reefs, but Tjao Bay offers protected waters because of the barrier reefs to the west. Aerial photographs showed the beaches to be very gently sloping and covered with white sand. Two landing beaches were selected on the peninsula's west side. A Japanese airstrip, Pitoe, was located just north of the peninsula's base on the Tjao Bay (west) side. Its construction was abandoned because of drainage problems. The Americans would build two airfields on the Doroeba Plain near the peninsula's base and to the east of the Japanese field.

The rest of Morotai's coastline is varied with numerous shallow indentations and mixed types of beaches. A narrow coral reef fringes the entire island. On the west coast were three areas of mangrove swamps, the southernmost being between the Tjao and Pilowo Rivers. Off the west coast are sixteen or so islets mostly surrounded by barrier reefs. Across from Tofoe Bay on Morotai's west-central side is Raoe Island. Its south end is only 1-½ miles from Morotai while its north end is nine miles away as Morotai's coast turns northeast. The four-by-nine-mile island is hilly with its highest elevation being 1,640 feet.

Small villages were scattered around the coast with most found along the south. There were no inland villages. Morotai was inhabited by 9,000 natives and a single Dutch missionary. There were no developed industries or plantations nor was there a government administrative center. The island fell under the jurisdiction of the Sultanate of Ternate on Halmahera, which was indirectly governed by the Dutch. Nor were there any roads. A native track followed the south coast from Tjao Bay around to Cape Posiposi on the southeast side. A trail looped inland from the south-central coast into the southwest end of the Sabatai Mountains and then back to the Tjao Bay following the Pilowo River. A similar trail ran inland from the northwest coast to the northeast end of the Tjio Mountains and turned back to the northeast coast. There was more or less a coastal trail around Raoe Island connecting the five villages.

Morotai was seized by U.S. forces in conjunction with the Palaus operation and for one of the same reasons, to protect MacArthur's east flank as he attacked into the Philippines. Its possession would also provide a site for fighter and bomber airfields to support operations in the southern Philippines. These would be the nearest Allied airfields to Mindanao. The Australians hoped to use the airfields to support their upcoming Borneo operations.

The ALAMO Force designated XI Corps Headquarters under Major General Charles P. Hill as the TRADEWINDS Task Force to execute Operation DAREDEVIL. Its main operating force was the 31st Infantry Division (124th, 155th, 167th Infantry) under Major General John C. Persons, located at Wakde-Sarmi with the 124th Infantry at Aitape. The 126th Infantry, 32d Infantry Division was the Task Force Reserve. Included in the Task Force were significant antiaircraft units, much of the 4th Engineer Special Brigade, and other combat support elements to total 28,000 troops. A huge engineer and service force, with RAAF airdrome construction units, added another 40,200 troops. As a further backup the ALAMO Force Reserve was the 6th Infantry Division garrisoning Sansapor-Cape Opmarai. D-Day would be 15 September.

The 2d Area Army at Menado on northern Celebes assessed that the next Allied thrust westward after the seizure of Sansapor in July 1944 would be Halmahera. Allied air attacks had been increasing on the island through August and early September. Two battalions of the 211th Infantry, 32d Division were sent from Halmahera to garrison Morotai, but in mid-July they were returned to the main island to bolster its defense. To provide some degree of defense for Morotai, the Division formed the 2d Provisional Raiding Unit, a commando-type organization comprised mainly of Formosan enlisted men under Major KAWASHIMA Takenobu and other Japanese officers. Its advance elements arrived on the south end of Morotai on 12 July, but the last elements did not arrive until 19 August. The unit consisted of only four raiding companies plus a few minor support elements to total about 500 troops. The raiding companies remained in the southwest while a small joint force, a rifle platoon, engineer platoon (both from the 32d Division), and a detachment of the 26th Special Base Force garrisoned the island's northeast end at Cape Sopi, perhaps 100 men or so. The unit made efforts to make it appear that a larger force defended the island to include constructing dummy gun positions and camps, and lighting numerous campfires at night.

Because of the dispersal of the TRADEWIND Task Force's elements and limited facilities, the load-out took place at different locations. The 31st Infantry Division (-124th Infantry) loaded at Maffin Bay, the 124th and 126th Infantry at Aitape, air units at Hollandia, and the many engineer and support units at Finschhafen, Hollandia, Aitape, Maffin Bay, and Sansapor. Limited rehearsals were conducted at Aitape and west of Wakde. The convoys departed at different dates to rendezvous at Maffin Bay on the 11th and departed the next day. The Morotai Attack Force (Task Force 77) moved well out to sea to the north of New Guinea to ensure that Japanese lookouts along the coast did not report the movement. Ships were reported leaving Hollandia to the *2d Area Army* and that headquarters believed Halmahera would soon face a landing. To reinforce the deception, Allied aircraft attacked Japanese airfields on Batjan Island while the U.S. Navy shelled installations on northwest Halmahera. Preinvasion reconnaissance flights over Morotai had been limited as were air attacks. The naval shore bombardment of southwest Morotai did not begin until two hours before the 15 September landing.

The morning provided excellent visibility, a calm sea, and light winds. Aboard amphibian tractors, the 155th and 167th Infantry landed on Beach RED on the west side of the base of the Gila Peninsula and just to the south of the abandoned Japanese airstrip. There was no opposition to the 0830 hour (H-Hour) landing. The 155th immediately moved to the north of the airstrip and the 167th to the south. The 124th Infantry came ashore in landing craft on Beach WHITE a mile to the south at 0831 hours. It was extremely fortunate the landing was unopposed. Beach and offshore conditions proved atrocious.

Beach RED, rather than being composed of firm white sand forty to fifty feet deep with a 100–135-yard-wide fringing reef, proved to be one of the worst beaches encountered in the Southwest Pacific. The apparent white sand beach turned out to be three feet of gray clay and mud covered with a thin crust of sand. The reef varied from one to five feet in depth and was covered with coral heads, loose coral boulders, and potholes. Landing craft could not approach closer than forty yards to the beach even at high water. LSTs could not approach closer than eighty yards and their vehicles and equipment had to be transloaded into smaller landing craft and ferried closer to shore. Scores of vehicles were swamped in the unevenly deep reef waters or became bogged down in the beach mud. Ashore the beach was narrower than expected and there were insufficient areas to assemble supplies and equipment.

Beach WHITE to the south, on which the 124th Infantry landed, was almost as bad. The fringing reef was expected to be eighty yards wide, but turned out to be 150 yards. Its surface varied from inches to over five feet deep and was just as studded with coral heads, boulders, and potholes as RED. Larger landing craft could only close to within 100 yards of shore and their discharged vehicles drowned out or sunk in the beach mud. Regardless, the 124th made it ashore to move up the peninsula and took up position to the right of the 167th Infantry with its own right flank resting on Pitoe Bay. The beach area to the north of WHITE was no better and much narrower, fifteen to twenty feet. Unloading had all but ceased by 1500 hours and only 40 percent of the vehicles and supplies had been unloaded. A more suitable beach was found ¾-mile to the south of WHITE and was designated NEW WHITE Beach and most landing craft were diverted there. Because of the impossible conditions on RED and with NEW WHITE being far from ideal, a survey party selected an alternate beach on the east side of the peninsula. This much wider beach offered very good reef and beach conditions. Located just to the south of the peninsula's base and opposite of Beach RED, it was designated Beach BLUE. Some unloading continued on RED and NEW WHITE after channels were blasted through the reef and coral landing ramps constructed from the reef edge to shore and across the mud beach to firm ground. Inland the peninsula was mostly dry and roads to the main island were cleared.

A dozen Japanese were killed the first day and one captured as the assault troops worked their way inland to establish the beachhead line. The next day the three regiments resumed their advance with negligible resistance. The 126th Infantry landed and took up reserve positions on the Gila Peninsula. By the 20th a perimeter was established averaging 1–¼ miles deep and extending twelve miles across the island's southwest end. The *7th Air Division* based on Celebe launched light air raids beginning on D+1, but these were generally ineffective. The Japanese had withdrawn inland avoiding decisive engagement. The raiders attempted some small night infiltration attacks, which were ineffective despite claims of success. On the 17th U.S. patrols were landed on the islets off the west coast and at points along the west and southeast coast to forestall the enemy's movement along coastal trails. Other patrols were landed on the northwest coast and the northeast end on the 18th and 19th. Raoe Island was secured on the 21st. Some Japanese attempted to flee from Morotai, but most were intercepted by PT boats. Allied aircraft continued to attack Japanese bases in the Moluccas in an effort to prevent effective reinforcement of Morotai. ALAMO Force was dissolved and it reverted to its formal title, 6th Army, on 15 September. There were no changes in unit assignments or missions. In the beachhead work on two new airfields was begun. The new Pitoe fighter field, inland from Pitoe Bay and east of the old Japanese strip, was partly operational on 4 October; however, it was abandoned and designated the Pitoe Crash Strip for disabled aircraft. Escort carriers were able to provide fighter support for the beachhead's defense and the fighter field's approach interfered with that of the more important Wama bomber field. Pitoe also had serious drainage problems. Wama Airdrome was operational on 4 October with a 4,000-foot length and later extended to 5,000. In late September construction of a parallel runway was begun at Wama. The 7,000-foot Pitoe Airdrome was partly operational by 17 October. Japanese air raids increased somewhat and continued into the early months of 1945, but they had little effect.

The *32d Division* on Halmahera made some effort to land reinforcements on the west and southeast coasts on 29 September in the form of three provisional raiding detachments drawn from the Division's regiments. These detachments ran into frequent U.S. patrols and ambushes on the coastal tracks and were unable to link up with the *2d Provisional Raiding Unit* in the southern Sabatai Mountains until 20 October.

In early October the *2d Area Army* deducted that the United States had no intention of landing on Halmahera or elsewhere in the Moluccas and ordered the *32d Division* to renew its efforts to reinforce Morotai. The *3d Battalion, 210th Infantry* landed on the southeast coast on 9 October. It too was unable to link up with the *2d Provisional Raiding Unit* until 20 November, but by that time it numbered only 100 men because of ambushes, starvation, and disease. Some 1,900 troops of the *211th Infantry* are claimed to have landed on the west coast across from Raoe Island on 16 November and Colonel MORTIS assumed command of Japanese forces on the Morotai. Many of the reinforcements may have gone down with their barges when interdicted by the U.S. Navy. The Navy intensified the blockade and the *Morotai Detachment* was unable to be resupplied. The U.S. forces were largely unaware of these landings and believed that the naval patrols were successfully interdicting most reinforcement attempts. The terrain, weather, lack of supplies, and aggressive American patrols negated Japanese offensive efforts and the remaining Japanese pulled deeper into the mountains and dwindled away. In the meantime the Japanese claimed to have inflicted over 4,000 U.S. casualties and heavy damage on equipment though early December. Total U.S. Army and Navy casualties on Morotai were forty-five KIA and 103 WIA. The United States killed 305 Japanese and took fifteen POWs, but hundreds perished in the mountains and en route aboard sunken barges.

The 31st Infantry Division remained on Morotai providing base security until it departed for the Philippines in April 1945 being relieved by the 368th Infantry, 93d Infantry Division (Colored). A PT boat base was set up on Soemsoem Island in Tjao Bay to interdict barge reinforcement attempts from Halmahera. Later the small Naval Advance

Base, Morotai (FPO SF 936) was built on Gila Bay and the peninsula. It operated a troop and supply ship unloading facility and a small craft repair facility until it was disestablished on 21 January 1946 and turned over to the RAN. From January 1945 Morotai was developed as a staging base for Australian units destined to invade Borneo far to the west.

In the spring of 1945 the considerable Japanese forces in the East Indies constituted no major threat, being cut off from the Home Islands by Allied offensive operations on New Guinea and the Philippines. These forces included:

Western New Guinea—10,000 troops in two very weak divisions and two brigades essentially cut off from the rest of the East Indies.

Lesser Sunda Islands, Timor, and Ceram and other Banda Sea islands—60,000 troops in two strong divisions.

Celebes and Molucca Islands—45,000 troops in a division and a brigade.

Java—35,000 troops in two strong brigades.

Borneo—31,000 troops in two brigades and a regiment.

The South Pacific Area command felt it was obligated to commence operations in the East Indies because of international agreements when the command was established in 1942, to enhance the U.S. government's position and prestige in the Far East with the reestablishment of the Netherlands government in Batavia, Java, and to actively employ the I Australian Corps forces originally planned for use on Luzon.

In the summer of 1944 Australia proposed that a Commonwealth force be organized to secure the East Indies after the Allies were reestablished in the Philippines. This force would be made a distinct British command separating the East Indies and Australia from the Southwest Pacific Area command. MacArthur rejected the proposal based on existing command agreements and the necessity of retaining Australian forces under a combined command to more effectively implement Allied strategy in the region. NEI government in exile and the Southwest Pacific Area command agreed on a civil affairs accord to transfer military government control to the Dutch as NEI areas were liberated. It was decided that operations to retake Borneo, both British and Dutch, would commence in May 1945.

Borneo, East Indies (British and Dutch Borneo). As a refresher, the island of Borneo is the second largest in the East Indies (after New Guinea). Borneo was code-named BRIGANTINE. It is located west of Celebes, north of Java, east of Sumatra and Malaya, and southwest of the Philippines (see Map 56). On the north coast were the British protectorates of Sarawak and Brunei plus the British possession of North Borneo (SCARECROW), collectively known as British Borneo. The southern two-thirds of the island was Dutch Borneo. The various oilfields on Borneo were estimated to have provided 40 percent of Japan's fuel oil and 25–30 percent of her crude and heavy oils in 1943–44. Borneo sits astride two key north-to-south sea lanes. On the island's west side is the Straat Karimata with Sumatra on the other side allowing access into the South China Sea from the Java Sea, and on the east side is the Straat Makassar with Celebes on the far side providing a route from the Java Sea to the Philippines. The Java Sea itself to the south is the main east to west sea lane through the Netherlands East Indies.

The operating force tasked with liberating Borneo was the I Australian Corps under Lieutenant General Sir Leslie Morshead. Its 7th Australian Division (18th, 21st, 25th Brigades) was commanded by Major General E.J. Milford. The 9th Australian Division

Borneo, East Indies (including British and Dutch Borneo)

Borneo, East Indies (including British and Dutch Borneo)

(20th, 24th, 26th Brigades) was under Major General Sir George F. Wootten. This force had been slated to land on northern Luzon on 31 January 1945, but Operation LOVE II was canceled by MacArthur. This was to have been the principal operation on Luzon and executed in advance of 6th Army's main effort landing on Lingayen Bay in February. The Australian 1st Tactical Air Force (No. 10 Group prior to October 1944) provided much of the air support for the operations and was backed by USAAF and USN air units. Obtaining sufficient shipping proved to be a major problem for I Corps as most of the 7th Fleet's assets were committed to operations in the Philippines. In many cases units were forced to be transported long distances to Borneo by cramped landing ships and craft rather than troops transports. U.S. Navy Seabee battalions participated in all three operations on Borneo.

Japanese forces on Borneo were under the command of the *37th Army* now head-quartered at Weston, North Borneo. Lieutenant General BABA Masao had 31,000 troops in only two brigades and a regiment under his command. The *56th Independent Mixed Brigade* was under Major General AKASHI (personal name unknown) at Tawau, North Borneo on the coast near the Dutch Borneo border. The *71st Independent Mixed Brigade* was in Balikpapan, Dutch Borneo under Major General YAMAMURA H. (personal name unknown) with elements garrisoning the Bandjermasin (OVERSCENTED) area on the island's south end. The *25th Independent Mixed Regiment* was at Jesselton, North Borneo. Two garrison battalions were at Kuching (JANET) in western Sarawak. IJN units on the island included the *22d Special Base Force* under Rear Admiral KAMADA Michiaki at Balikpapan on the east-central Dutch Borneo coast and the *2d Guard Force* on Tarakan Island off the northeast coast of Dutch Borneo, both reinforced by IJA elements. There were over 3,300 Japanese civilian employees. Airfields in North Borneo were located at Jessleton and Sandakan in North Borneo, two on Labuan Island, Brunei City, and Kuching in Sarawak. In Dutch Borneo there were airfields at Bengkajang, Pangkauanboeoen, Bandjermasin, two at Balikpapan, Longiram, and Tarakan Island.

The Japanese occupation of Borneo was harsh and the treatment of prisoners of war captured in 1942 was among the most savage atrocities inflicted in the region. In October 1943 many of North Borneo's 50,000 Chinese, aided by Djaks, rebelled seizing Jesselton on the northwest central coast. The revolt was crushed and many of the participants were executed. That same month Special Operations Australia elements, "Z" Special Unit, began to be inserted in North Borneo and Sarawak to collect intelligence and raise guerrilla forces.

In 1942, over 2,400 Australian prisoners of war had been brought from Singapore to Sandakan on the northeast coast of North Borneo to construct an airfield. When the airfield was completed they were allowed to waste away in a camp until January 1945 when just over 1,000 were still alive. The Sandakan Death March was conducted in three phases as the surviving prisoners were marched to Ranau some 120 miles inland to the northwest. The first group of 455 prisoners departed on 29 January and arrived on 6 February with 230 alive. The second group departed with 566 on 29 May and a week later 203 arrived at Ranau. The last group of seventy-five fit men left at the end of July and all died or were killed en route. The 291 sick and injured left at Sandakan were murdered. On 1 August the thirty-two prisoners remaining alive at Ranau were murdered. Only two of the original 2,400-plus prisoners survived captivity by escaping. A group of 144 Dutch soldiers captured in 1942 had been allowed to live with their families at Samarinda on the east-central coast of Dutch Borneo north of Balikpapan. On 30 July 1945 they and their families were taken inland to Loakoeloe where the wives were hacked and bayoneted to death before their husbands and children, the children thrown alive down a 600-foot mine shaft, the men beheaded, and the men and women's bodies were dropped into the mine. The site was discovered by 7th Australian Division soldiers searching for the missing Dutch.

I Australian Corps would conduct three major operations to liberate Borneo: Tarakan Island, Brunei Bay and Labuan Island, and Balikpapan between May and July 1945.

Tarakan Island, Dutch Borneo. Tarakan (aka Pamoesian) (FLATCATCHER) is a small island in the Sesajap River delta 2-½ miles off the northeast coast of Dutch Borneo separated from the mainland by the Batagau Strait (see Map 57). The Celebes Sea laps its east coast. The roughly triangular-shaped island is fifteen miles long from the northwest side to the south end and eleven miles across the north end. The island's central portion is covered with low, but rugged hills reaching a little over 100 feet. Most of the island is thickly wooded with palms, hardwoods, and underbrush. From the west-central coast around the north end to the east-central coast is a one-to-two-mile-wide mangrove swamp through which streams flow out of the hills. The lower east coast and south end are edged with a narrower belt of mangroves. A small island less than ¾ mile across, Sadau, is situated ½ mile off the west-central coast.

Tarakan Town lies on the lower southwest coast with the main portion of the town 2,000 yards inland. Small scattered, brush-covered hillocks are found between the beaches and the town. The well-developed town sits on the west side of the Pamusian River with low, marshy ground on that flank. On the coast to the southwest of the main town were four piers for loading oil. Three good roads led from the dock area into the town. This would be the location of the landing beaches, know as the Lingkas Beaches. The Japanese had driven in rows of pipes, rails, and posts reaching 125 yards offshore as a landing craft obstacle the length of the Lingkas Beaches. The town was backed by low hills and about one mile to its northwest was the Tarakan Airfield. Three miles to the north of the airfield and just northwest of the island's center was the Djoeata (aka Juata) Oilfield while the smaller Sesanip Oilfield was just to the northeast of the airfield. The oilfields had been destroyed by the Dutch, but the Japanese had rebuilt them. They were one of the key reasons the island was designated an objective. From the Djoeata Oilfield a track led to Djoeata Village on the northwest coast. There were no coastal roads or tracks because of the swamps.

The seizure of Tarakan, Operation OBOE I, would allow Allied airfields to be constructed to support further Australian operations on Borneo as well as provide a base for the reintroduction of Dutch administration in the NEI. The British and Australians were committed to this last factor as they too were colonial powers desiring to reestablish themselves in their lost territories. The landing was set for 1 May 1945 (P-Day).

RAAF units began attacks on Japanese airfields elsewhere on Borneo, Celebes, and Java twenty days prior to the landing. Attacks on Tarakan itself and other nearby targets on Borneo began on 12 April. The oil storage tanks at the oilfield and Lingkas were destroyed so the Japanese would not ignite them to interfere with the landing. The 26th Brigade, 9th Division under Brigadier D.A. Whitehead was heavily reinforced with engineers and support troops to 12,000 men, almost a division in its own right. It was accompanied by a Dutch Insular Corps company plus adminstrators to total 400. The Brigade staged from Morotai on 30 April aboard the 7th Fleet's Tarakan Attack Group (Task Group 78.1), sailing north of Celebes. The Japanese had recently relocated an infantry battalion from Tarakan to Balikpapan to the south, but there were still 2,100 troops there, both IJA troops of the *455th Independent Infantry Battalion* under Captain

Map 57
Tarakan Island, Dutch Borneo

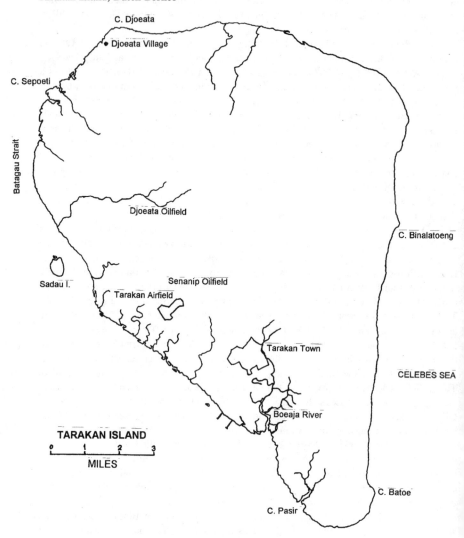

MATSUMOTO Saichiro and the *2d Guard Force* under Captain MIZOGUCHI Kunio. Virtually all of the defenders were concentrated around Tarakan Town.

On P-1 a commando squadron and an artillery battery landed on Sadau Island six miles northwest of the Lingkas Beaches to cover the engineers breaching the beach front obstacles. The next morning saw two infantry battalions landing on Beaches RED on the left and GREEN on the right at 0918 hours without opposition. (The two main landing beaches were separated by Beach YELLOW.) The assault battalions encountered light opposition as they moved inland to Tarakan Town. Unloading difficulties were experienced at the beaches when the falling tide exposed 500 yards of deep black mud coursed with tidal drainage channels. At high tide the beaches were ten to fifteen yards wide and comprised of soft mud. On shore the soft clay soil was pitted with water-filled bomb and shell craters because of the high water table. Regardless, the Australians were firmly established ashore by nightfall. The next morning the airfield was reached and Tarakan Town was cleared by the 5th. (On 8 May the surrender of German forces in Europe was announced.)

The bulk of the Japanese defenders had dug in on a ridge to the north and northeast of the town and a costly effort was undertaken to clear this area. Once this was accompanied the Australians worked inland to the north where the Japanese had fallen back to Hills 105 and 102, the Fukukaku area, and dug in deeply. The Dutch company cleared the southern lob of the island. The Australians continued the attack into the hills and the Japanese held out until 14 June under repeated assaults. At that time the Japanese commander, demoralized as no effort had been made to reinforce the defenders, released the survivors in small groups to fend for themselves. They withdraw to the north and east with the Australians in pursuit. The island was declared secure on 21 June, but some 1,000 Japanese were still roaming the hills in small bands. Mop-up operations continued well into August and the smaller Boenjoe Island, about fifteen miles to the northeast, was cleared. The reconstruction of the Tanakan Airfield was plagued with drainage problems and it was not operational in time to support the Brunei Bay or Balikpapan operations. The oilfields could not be made operational until after the war owing to Japanese holdouts and serious damage to the facilities.

Many consider the Tarakan operation not to have been worth the cost. Australian 1st Tactical Air Force units remained on Morotai too far to the west to provide effective support. U.S. carrier aircraft and USAAF fighters from Sanga Sanga on Tawitawi Island in the southwest end of the Philippine's Sulu Archipelago initially supported the operation. Australian air units were moved there to support ground operations on northeast Borneo when it became apparent that the Tarakan Airfield was unusable.

Australian losses on Tarakan were 225 killed and 670 wounded. Several hundred Indonesian and Chinese laborers were liberated along with 7,000 island inhabitants. The Japanese lost over 1,600 and 252 captured. Some Japanese elements managed to withdraw to the northwest to join up with the garrisons around Brunei Bay. About 300 surrendered after VJ-Day.

Brunei Bay, Brunei and Labuan Island, Straits Settlements. The Brunei Bay (MAINSHEET) area on the upper northwest coast of Borneo abuts four different political divisions: The Sultanate of Brunei was divided into two areas separated by a few-miles-wide strip of Sarawak territory, which edged the bay's south side at two points. The two Brunei areas were on the west and south sides of the bay. The bay's east side was edged by North Borneo. Labuan Island (OATMEAL) is on the east side of the bay's northward entrance and was administratively part of the Straits Settlements along the west coast of Malaya. All four of these political divisions were under British control or protection prior to the war.

Brunei Bay is about 160 miles to the southwest of Borneo's northeast end, Cape Sempang Mangayan. The bay covers some 500 square miles and offers an excellent protected anchorage. The entire coast of British Borneo fronts the South China Sea. Overland, Tarakan Island is about 180 miles to the southeast of Brunei Bay across the Maitland Range. Except for narrow flat coastal strips, the entire area is covered with rugged hills up to 2,000 feet high, although most are lower. The hills and coastal strips are heavily forested.

The Japanese units defending the area included the *56th Independent Mixed Brigade,*

25th Independent Mixed Regiment, and detachments of the *22d Special Base Force* and the *2d Guard Force*. Elements were detached from the brigades to garrison other areas. All were under the *37th Army* now headquartered at Melalap, inland due east from Brunei Bay's north end. At the time of the 10 June 1945 Australian landing elements of the *56th Independent Mixed Brigade* were deployed around Brunei Bay and inland just to the northeast, this latter concentration acting as a mobile reserve to react to landings either in Brunei Bay or along the upper northwest between Jesselton and Cape Sempang Mangayan. Other Brigade elements and the *25th Independent Mixed Regiment* were deployed in that sector. These units totaled almost 5,000 troops plus some 650 on Labuan Island and 1,550 around Seria and Miri fifty to seventy miles to the southwest of Brunei Bay. Still other Brigade elements, about 1,500 troops in the St. Lucia Bay area at Tawau, were positioned on the lower southeast coast of North Borneo in the vicinity of the border with Dutch Borneo and north of Tarakan Island. Much of the forces at Tawau had been ordered to move overland in March to "reinforce" the units around Brunei Bay. The arduous trek cost many their lives and they arrived so exhausted and sick with only light weapons and limited supplies that they were of little value to the defense.

The 9th Australian Division (-26th Brigade on Tarakan Island) on Morotai was assigned the mission of securing this large area. The Division was much reinforced with I Corps and base troops to almost 31,000 men. After conducting extensive rehearsals at Morotai, the Division was transported to the northwest through the Philippine's Sulu Islands, past the southwest end of Palawawan to arrive outside of Brunei Bay on the morning of 10 June (Z-Day). The troops completed the 1,100-mile journey aboard landing ships of Task Group 78.1 rather than troop transports under crowded and otherwise uncomfortable conditions. RAAF and USAAF units neutralized airfields and other targets in the area as U.S. Navy and RAN ships provided fire support.

The 20th Brigade landed at two points on the west side of Brunei Bay without opposition. One battalion landed on Beach GREEN at Brunei Bluff defining the west side of the bay's entrance while another battalion landed on Beach WHITE on Muara Island just to the south of Brunei Bluff. The island was unoccupied by the enemy and the bay's entrance was secured. A company from that battalion was sent up the Brunei River at the west side of the bay followed by the rest of the battalion overland after it departed Muara Island.

Labuan Island in the bay's entrance and to the east of Brunei Bluff measures about twelve miles northeast to southwest along its northwest shore and some six miles across the center where a portion of the island protrudes to the southeast. At the end of the protrusion is Victoria Harbour and the main town of Labuan. The north end of the harbor and the west side of the peninsula on the harbor's west side are covered with mangrove swamps. The island is mostly low and flat with a few hillocks and largely forested. Less than 1-½ miles north of the town is Labuan Airfield. Roads run north and west out of the town to allow access to those sides of the island. On the northwest-central coast was Timbalai Airfield. Only a few trails served the southern portion of the island, which was largely undeveloped.

The 24th Brigade landed two battalions on Labuan Island's southeast protrudance and the north side of Victoria Harbour on Beach BROWN at 0915 hours. Initially experiencing no opposition, the battalions moved inland and became engaged north of the town. On the 12th the Japanese were found concentrated in a 600-by-1,000-yard stronghold dubbed "The Pocket" on the north edge of the mangroves at the harbor's head and west of Labuan Airfield. The Pocket fell on the 21st and the battalions moved north and west to clear the rest of the island. At least 400 Japanese were killed on Labuan, half of those died in The Pocket. The prelanding bombardment and subsequent fighting had destroyed most buildings on the island and the island's 3,000 inhabitants were mostly homeless. A third 24th Brigade battalion was landed on the east side of the bay on the 17th and it took Weston and soon Lingkungan as it pressed inland. On the 19th another battalion landed near the bay's northeast shoulder and with the battalion to the south advanced east toward Beaufort, which they took on the 27th. The 24th Brigade continued to advance up the coast into mid-July, but North Borneo's capital, Jesselton (DUCHESS), was not secured until 28 September.

In the meantime on the southwest side of Brunei Bay the 20th Brigade conducted other small-scale landings at 0915 hours to clear the south shore and moved southwest along the coast toward Seria, which was secured on the 22nd. One battalion was landed farther to the southwest in the Miri-Lutong area, seventy miles from the bay, on the 20th. The area had been abandoned by the Japanese, but there were some small pockets of resistance along the coast. The Japanese had ignited the thirty-seven oilwells at Seria as they withdrew, but the well-head fires were soon extinguished by engineers. The oilfields at Miri and other oil production facilities were captured intact. The two Australian elements soon linked up. During this period a number of Indian prisoners of war captured in 1942 were found. Many had been murdered by the retreating Japanese. On the 27th the Japanese positions inland were found and attacked with the aid of Dyak guerrillas. All along the North Borneo coast the Japanese were withdrawing inland to the northeast or along the northwest coast toward Kuching near Borneo's west corner where a Japanese garrison was located. The Australians conducted aggressive patrols to hurry them, but there was no intent to pursue. The Japanese moving to the northeast concentrated along the northeast coast around Sandakan (ADELPHI, JEWESS, STRANGLEHOLD) to make a final stand, but they were never attacked. The 9th Division's main objective, to secure the coast and key facilities, was accomplished. They controlled a 5,000-square-mile area requiring only limited mopping up and security patrols.

The Australians now had to care for thousands of civilians in the area. This effort was coordinated by the British Borneo Civil Affairs Unit staffed by both British and Australians. Australian losses in the operation were 114 dead and perhaps three times that number wounded. Five American landing craft crewmen were also killed. Over 1,200 Japanese dead were counted, but large numbers perished in the hills attacked by headhunters. About 130 Japanese were taken prisoner.

Balikpapan, Dutch Borneo. The final large-scale Australian operation of the war and the last large amphibious assault in the Southwest Pacific Area, since the Lingayen Gulf landing on Luzon in January, took place on 1 July 1945. Balikpapan (TWILFIT, VIOLET) is located on the southeast-central coast of Dutch Borneo. Celebes is 200 miles to the east across the Straat Makassar. The town of Balikpapan, the largest in Dutch Borneo, is situated on the lower east side of Balikpapan Bay, which opens southeast onto Straat Makassar. Klandasan, almost as large as Balikpapan, is situated on a blunt point on the bay's east shoulder facing the coast. To the north of Balikpapan and its adjacent villages is Sumbir River. North of the river are mangrove swamps. Most of the sparsely populated west shore of Balikpapan Bay is lined with mangrove swamps and wide river inlets. The bay's entrance is about 2-½ miles across and it runs inland to the north about nineteen miles with a width of one to 2-½ miles. A well-developed road following a pipeline ran from Klandasan past Balikpapan and inland north to Samarinda. A coast road, also following a pipeline, ran from Klandasan to Samarinda and then turned inland. Balikpapan was mainly an oil-loading port with numerous oil storage tanks outside of the town and behind Klandasan. The oilfields and most of the refineries were well inland

and to the north at Sambodja and Samarinda, although there was a refinery outside of Balikpapan. The 5,000-foot Sepinggang Airfield was located on the coast four miles east of Klandasan and Manggar Airfield was situated on the coast thirteen miles east of Balikpapan. Inland from the coast and beyond the towns the country was hilly and forested.

The Japanese defending the Balikpapan area included part of the *71st Independent Mixed Brigade* and most of the *22d Special Base Force*. There were an estimated 3,100 troops Balikpapan along with 1,100 Japanese and Formosan laborers, but many were oil production staff and service troops. The naval base force manned a considerable number of coast defense guns and antiaircraft weapons well hidden in the hills. Another 1,500 troops were at Samarinda sixty miles to the north where the main oilfields were located. Defenses had been constructed on the east shoulder of Balikpapan Bay at Klandasan and the entire coastline from Klandasan to Manggar was festooned with timber obstacles covered from light defensive positions. The strongest defensive positions were located on the inland hills to the northeast of Klandasan and to the east of Balikpapan. Japanese battalion strongpoints were located in the Klandasan area, at Manggar up the coast, and on the northbound road north-northeast of Balikpapan.

The 7th Australian Division on Morotai with 21,000 troops was reinforced by 12,000 I Australian Corps, base, and engineer troops. Two Dutch Insular Force companies participated. After rehearsals the reinforced Division embarked aboard the Balikpapan Attack Group (Task Group 78.2) and sailed north of Celebes and then south through the Straat Makassar arriving off of Klandasan on the morning of 1 July (F-Day). The prelanding naval bombardment, fired by U.S., Australian, and Dutch ships, was the most intense ever conducted in the Southwest Pacific Area. This had been preceded by twenty days of massive air attacks by USAAF, U.S. Navy, U.S. Marine Corps, RAAF, and Dutch aircraft. Since Tanakan was not yet operational the fighter support had to fly from Sanga Sanga far to the north and bombers came from Palawan, Morotai, and Samar. A massive mine-sweeping effort was made prior to the landing as the offshore waters of Balikpapan had been liberally seeded in an effort to curtail Japanese oil shipments. From 26 June U.S. Underwater Demolition Teams blew gaps through the landing obstacles. The prelanding bombardment ignited many of the oil storage tanks behind Klandasan and columns of black smoke rose to 1,000 feet.

The 18th Brigade landed on the left directly into Klandasan while the 21st Brigade landed on the right just to the east of the town at 0855 hours. The U.S. Army's 672d Amphibian Tractor Battalion landed the lead assault troops. Opposition was very light upon landing, but gradually increased as the troops moved inland. The 18th Brigade secured its beachhead and advanced north and northwest. The 21st Brigade moved northeast and east securing Mount Malang, a hill just over a mile inland and northeast of Klandasan, as well as Stalkudo on the coast to the east. The next day Sepinggang Airfield was secured as were objectives to the north. The 25th Brigade landed on the 2nd and prepared to advance north. On the 3rd Balikpapan was seized and light aircraft were able to use the Seppinggang Airfield. The Manggar Airfield was occupied on the 5th. Japanese resistance continued to stiffen as the Australians advanced inland. Knowing the war was coming to a conclusion, commanders had been cautioned to reduce casualties. Extensive use of artillery, naval gunfire, and air strikes was employed to support the advance. Part of the 18th Brigade leapfroged up the upper reaches of Balikpapan Bay beginning on the 5th aboard amphibian tractors and landing craft engaging Japanese elements on the west side as they sent patrols inland. Some Indian prisoners were liberated in this area. The other brigades continued to advance north and northeast.

The Japanese finally abandoned their positions on the north road on the 21st and withdrew to the northeast. Sambodja, some fifteen miles inland from Manggar and twenty-eight miles northeast of Balikpapan, was occupied on the 18th. The Japanese in this area too began to withdraw to the northeast. Most of the remnants later moved west with some continuing in that direction all the way across the island to the Japanese garrison at Kuching on the northwest corner, a journey of 500 miles that few completed. Others turned south after moving west and headed for Bandjermasin on the south coast where another Japanese garrison was located. Elements of the *22d Special Base Force* were still on the west side of Balikpapan Bay and attempted to infiltrate the port area where a number of small engagements were fought into early August. The Balikpapan area was essentially considered secure by the end of July.

At least 1,800 Japanese died in the Balikpapan area and sixty-three prisoners were taken. Australian losses were 229 KIA and 634 WIA. For the entire Borneo operation Allied losses were 436 KIA, three MIA, and 1,460 WIA. The Allies counted 5,693 Japanese dead, but many more were killed or died of disease, starvation, and wounds, plus 536 prisoners were captured.

World War II may have ended, but August and September 1945 was only a new beginning of warfare and political turmoil in the former Netherlands East Indies. At the cessation of hostilities Australia was assigned responsibility for Borneo, the NEI east of Lombok Island, Ocean and Nauru Islands, all of Australia's prewar territories (Papua and North-West New Guinea, the Bismarcks). Some 192,000 Japanese military, auxiliaries, laborers, and civilians were in the Borneo and NEI areas. This included four armies, seven divisions, and six brigades plus IJN forces. The surrender of Japanese forces in these areas commenced after the formal 2 September surrender in Tokyo Bay and were accepted by Australian officers. On Borneo no less than eight groups of forces or garrisons surrendered at Balikpapan, Bandjermasin, Jesselton, Kuching, Labuan, Penadjam, Temadeong, and Tenom to bring an end to the *37th Army*. Japanese forces on Celebes surrendered at Mendado and Macassar. Forces in the Moluccas Islands surrendered at Morotai and Ceram to include the *2d Army (2d Area Army* had been deactivated 13 June 1945 on Celebes and *2d Army* assumed control of units formerly assigned to it). At Batavia, Java the *16th Army* surrendered in October. A final small group surrendered at Bandoeng in January 1946. Timor surrendered on 11 September. The *25th Army* surrendered on Sumatra at Padang and Koeta Radja.

Besides repatriating the Japanese, the Australians were responsible for operating a military government in selected areas, assisting the Dutch to reestablish authority, provide aid to Indonesians, return slave laborers to their home islands, recover and evacuate Allied prisoners of war, and maintain order in the resulting political vacuum caused by the war's sudden end. Only limited Australian forces were available to occupy selected areas. Japanese commanders in areas not initially occupied by Allied forces were directed to maintain law and order under Australian authority, a mission the Japanese performed well according to Allied rules. The Dutch had originally planned to reoccupy Java with two brigades and Sumatra with one. In the face of Japanese-trained Indonesian armed forces and the inability to deploy sufficient Dutch forces to the NEI, the British filled the vacuum. On Java and Sumatra the 23d, 26th, and 5th Indian Divisions under XV Indian Corps, along with HQ, RAF, NEI, were deployed in October and November 1945 as occupation forces under British command. By early 1946 the Netherlands government was reestablished in most areas and Australian forces were relieved.

Indonesian nationalism was rampant since Sukarno declared the Republic of Indonesia

(*Republik Indonesia*) on 17 August 1945. A long and involved period of negotiation ensued between the Dutch and self-proclaimed Indonesian government and was brokered by the British. Violence escalated in many areas with clashes between Indian units, which included British troops, and the Indonesians, who declared war. In December Dutch forces began arriving and before long a full-scale civil war broke out. The Indian/British forces departed in December 1946 after losing 975 KIA/MIA and 1,670 WIA. Fighting resumed as the Dutch attempted to retain or, rather, regain control. The Netherlands government finally relented and granted the NEI its independence on 27 December 1949. The Royal Netherlands Indies Army was disbanded on 29 July 1950. The Dutch lost over 2,500 dead.

The Dutch, however, retained control of Dutch New Guinea, separated from the rest of the East Indies in 1946, as a place of residence for Indonesian-born Dutchmen and resident Dutch citizens wishing to remain under Netherlands administration. After fighting between Dutch and Indonesian forces, Dutch New Guinea was integrated into Indonesia in August 1962 as Irian Barat (West Irian), but was soon renamed Irian Jaya (Victorious Irian); Irian was the native name for the island. Many of the Dutch had previously departed New Guinea. Pro-Dutch Amboina and Ceram fought their own war of independence against Indonesia, which soon failed. Sarawak became a state of the new Malayan Union in 1957 when the Malay States were granted independence from Britain. North Borneo became Sabah, a self-governing state in 1963, and Labuan Island, now Pulau Labuan, became a federal territory of Malaysia. Beginning in December 1962 Indonesia challenged the Commonwealth over these territories, which were still under protection of the Crown. Known as the Confrontation, first Indonesian-sponsored insurgents and then Indonesian Regular Army units fought a protracted border war with British, Australian, New Zealand, and Malaysian forces. A peace treaty was finally signed between Malaysia and Indonesia in August 1966. Brunei remained a British protectorate, until given complete independence in 1984. There have since been numerous revolts and troubles throughout culturally, religiously, ethnically, politically mixed Indonesia. In 1975, after Portuguese Timor was granted independence, Indonesia invaded East Timor, supposedly to control the resulting instability, and soon annexed it. Troubles have recently ignited when East Timor voted for its independence in a 1999 referendum resulting in United Nations intervention with mainly Australian troops. Today Indonesia has the largest Islamic population outside of the Middle East with a population of over 214,000,000.

The Netherlands supports very proactive programs involved with veteran and survivor organizations assisting former prisoners and internees of the Japanese. The Museum of the Royal Netherlands Indies Army is located in Arnhem, the Netherlands.

THE PHILIPPINES

Next to the Greater Sunda Islands of the Netherlands East Indies the Philippine Islands constitute the largest archipelago in the world spanning an area of over 1,150 miles from north to south and about 700 miles across (see Map 58). If they were overlaid on the United States the islands would stretch from the Great Lakes into Florida and from West Virginia into Arkansas. The islands stretch from latitude 5 to 22° north and lie between longitudes 117 and 127° east. The center is located at 250°04' S 130°06' W. Their west side is bounded by the South China Sea and the east by the Philippine Sea, unbroken by islands for 600 miles until reaching the Palaus. On the Philippines' southwest side are the Sula and Celebes Seas separating them from the East Indies' Borneo and Celebes

Map 58
Philippine Islands

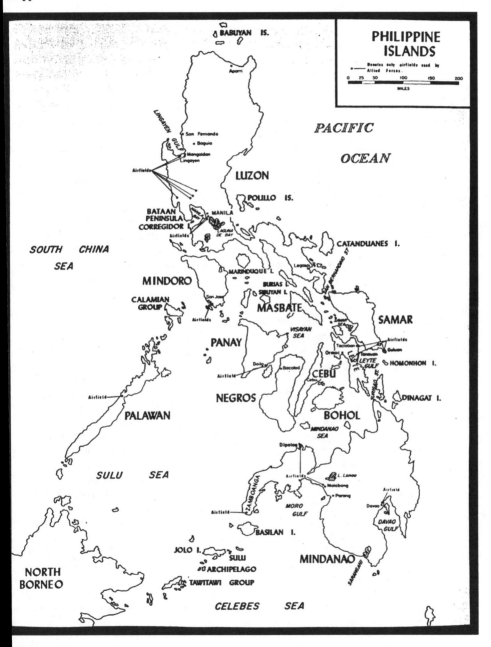

Islands. To the north of Luzon, the northernmost of the main islands, it is only 220 miles across the Luzon Strait to Formosa, Japanese territory, while mainland Indochina is 750 miles to the west. From Manila, Pearl Harbor is 5,300 miles to the east-northeast while Tokyo is only 1,800 miles to the north-northeast. The Philippines were in time zone 20.

The Philippine Islands (PI) were code-named EXCELSIOR and the Japanese knew them simply as *Hito*, although the term *Firippin* was sometimes used. In the native Tagalog it is the *Philipinas*. While commonly referred to simply as the Philippine Islands, officially the country was known as the Commonwealth of the Philippines, a title established in 1934.

The Philippines consist of 7,083 islands and islets comprising 114,400 square miles of land, slightly more area than Arizona. There are so many islands that only 2,773 were named; some 4,600 bear names today. Only 466 of these islands are larger than one square mile, but there are a number of very large islands. The two largest, Luzon and Mindanao, account for over two-thirds of the land area, more than 77,700 square miles. The combined coastline of these islands is 12,000 miles, the same as the continental United States. About 600–700 of the islands were populated; some 1,000 are today. The sheer number of islands and vastness of the Philippines prevent all but a cursory study of the main islands focusing on those on which actions were fought.

The continental-type islands are of volcanic origin being formed some fifty million years ago; there are still about twenty active volcanoes. Earthquakes and landslides constitute hazards. They are rugged and mountainous with the highest elevation being Mount Apo at 9,691 feet on southern Mindanao. Valleys are interspersed with rocky, terraced mountains, hills, and ridges running the length of the islands, of which most are oriented roughly north to south. Spurs and fingers run off many of the ridges. Only Luzon and Mindanao have extensive lowlands. Vegetation varies greatly ranging from dense hardwood forests covering 70 percent of the land to scrub tree and brush-covered areas to open grasslands. The trees include teak, ebony, ironwood, and cypress plus native hardwoods such as apitong, yakal, lauan, camagong, ipil, narra, and mayapis. About 19 percent of the Philippines land area is considered arable with the river valleys and plains possessing extremely fertile volcanic soil. In the southern islands coral limestone composes much of the soil. The coastlines are often rocky and lined with cliffs, although suitable landing beaches are found in many areas, especially within the numerous bays and gulfs. In the Philippines the term "gulf" is commonly used to identify large bays. Coastal swamps with mangroves and nipa palm are found in some areas. The beaches are frequently wide with few, if any, natural obstacles. Access inland varies though to include level coastal plains to gradually rising terraced slopes to hills and ridges. Water is abundant on most islands with significant rivers found on the larger ones.

The eleven largest islands make up 95 percent of the landmass: Luzon, Mindanao, Samar, Negros, Palawan, Panay, Mindoro, Leyte, Cebu, Bohol, and Masbate in descending size. The Philippines are divided into three main areas: Luzon in the north, the largest island; Mindanao in the south, the second largest island; and the Visayas (sometimes spelled Visayans) in the central portion. The Visayas surround the Visayan and Sibuyan Seas and consist of the last nine islands listed above and 6,000 smaller islands covering 33,000 square miles.

Although the Philippines are located in the tropics, the climate is considered mild and not oppressively hot as found on most other Pacific islands. Hot and humid periods occur though in April and May; however, there is more variation between day and night high and low temperatures than there is with seasonal differences. There is only a 10°F difference between the coolest and hottest months. Most of the islands receive over seventy inches of rainfall annually, but some areas receive in excess of over 200 inches. The eastern portions of the islands receive most of their rainfall between October and April, the northeast monsoon. The southwest monsoon blows from June through September delivering its rains in the western portion. The islands' central mountains affect the monsoons with the windward areas receiving the heaviest rains and leeward sides considerably less. Southern Luzon, part of the Vises, and most of Mindanao experience no pronounced dry season while other islands endure a March-to-May dry season. The Philippines sit astride the typhoon belt and up to six a year can strike the islands. Malaria and other tropical diseases are a problem, but plague and smallpox, prevalent before the arrival of the Americans, were under control.

The Philippines have long been inhabited by humans; the earliest bones found, on Palawan, date to 22,000 B.C. Stone tools have been found dating back to 30,000 B.C., but human presence is believed to date back to about 40,000 B.C., humans having arrived in the islands about the same time as on Australia and New Guinea. Settlers from China, themselves migrating from Southeast Asia, arrived in the Philippines in about 1500 B.C. Over the next 2,000 years cultures evolved in the Philippines as it became a crossroads between China, India, Southwest Asia, the South Seas, and East Indies as countless kingdoms rose and fell. Hinduism and Buddhism were introduced and much influence and control were gained over the Philippines by the Javanese and Sumatran kingdoms to the south such as Sri Vijaya (650 B.C. to A.D. 1377) and Majapahit (1292–1478). Islam began flowing into the Philippines in the early 1400s and flourished for a short time. Trade with China grew and was largely controlled by that empire.

Ferdinand Magellan discovered the Philippines in 1521 first sighting Samar on the archipelago's east-central edge. He named the islands Archipelago of Santa Lazaro claiming them for Spain even though flourishing kingdoms were well established there. Magellan was killed on Mactan island, adjacent to today's Cebu City, as the Spanish helped one of the ruling rajas put down a rebellion. Four more Spanish expeditions arrived between 1525 and 1542, with the leader of the last renaming the islands in honor of the heir to the Spanish throne, Philip II (1556–1598). Philip decreed the Philippines a colony of Spain in 1565 with the first capital on Cebu. Manila was selected as the capital in 1571. The distant colony, being ruled from New Spain (Mexico), saw little initial development. The Spanish influence saw the widespread introduction of Catholicism and the halt of the spread of Islam. Spain ruled the Philippines as a closed colony for over 250 years, at a financial loss, but it served as an important port of call for the galleon trade routes between the New and Old Worlds. The British seized Manila in 1762 during the Seven Years' War. It was returned to Spain after the war, but the mistreated Chinese merchants rebelled against Spanish rule and China began increased trade with England in the area. Foreign trade increased and the Philippines became more open. With Mexico's independence from Spain in 1821, the Philippines was ruled directly from Madrid. With exposure to foreign trade, especially from 1834 when the colony was opened to free international trade and external influence, a Philippine nationalist movement developed. A series of revolts occurred over such issues as the exclusion of Filipinos from religious orders, education reform, and personal freedoms. By the mid-1800s the Philippines was no longer a backwater, but possessed growing agricultural and business enterprises, educational institutions, banking, and well-established elite classes. The revolts were brutally crushed, but other idealists filled the void left by those killed and exiled. By 1896 the Katipunan Rebellion was well established with the goal of gaining independence from Spain.

Relations between Spain and the United States had seriously deteriorated by 1897 as a similar revolt boiled in another Spanish colony, Cuba. As war between the two countries became imminent, agreements were made between the United States and the exiled Filipino government in Singapore and Hong Kong. The United States declared war on Spain on 25 April 1898 and the U.S. Asiatic Squadron entered Manila Bay on 1 May destroying the small Spanish fleet. The Filipino rebellion grew and on 12 June the Philippines were declared independent from Spain. The United States had no desire to gain control of Spain's disassembled colonies, but German, Japanese, French, and British warships were arriving at Manila and it was apparent that there were designs to take over and divide up the struggling nation as had been done in China. The United States felt it had no choice but to take over the Philippines in order to prevent her exclusion from trade by imperial powers. The Treaty of Paris saw the acquisition of the Philippines, Guam, and Puerto Rico by the United States from Spain for $20 million. The treaty was not well received in the Philippines, which had just declared its independence. Faced with the prospect of being taken over by another foreign power, the government proclaimed the First Philippine Republic on 23 January 1899. Hostilities with the United States began on 4 February and continued for two years. It took 126,000 U.S. troops to subdue the Philippines at a cost of over 4,200 American and 16,000 Filipino dead plus another 200,000 civilians who died of starvation and disease. The rebellion's leader was captured in March 1901 and he was persuaded to call an end to organized resistance. The United States declared an end of military rule on 4 July 1901, but limited resistance continued until 1903. Other groups such as the Moros continued to resist for a number of years. It was America's only success in defeating a large-scale guerrilla movement. An American governor-general and council of state governed the Philippines until 1935.

Between 1900 and 1902, the United States swept away Spanish laws, outlawed slavery, installed modern civil laws, and extended the American Bill of Rights to Filipinos. In 1907 the Philippine Assembly was freely elected and the first Filipino president was installed, Manual L. Quezon, who continued to dominate Philippine politics until his death in 1944. An increasingly large measure of self-rule was granted. The U.S. Tydings-McDuffle Act of 24 March 1934 established the Philippine Commonwealth. As such it was an autonomous commonwealth under the protection of the United States. It was to be granted its independence on 4 July 1946 as the Republic of the Philippines. In anticipation of independence a constitution was approved in 1935. The United States maintained some degree of control over the Philippines' national debt, foreign loans, currency, imports, exports, foreign relations, immigration, and national defense through the U.S. High Commissioner to the Commonwealth of the Philippines, Francis B. Sayr. There were 160 Americans and over 22,700 Filipinos in government service. The Commonwealth was divided into forty-eight provinces headed by appointed Filipino governors.

Economically the country was well developed. Manila had become a regional commercial center for the distribution of American goods and the main port of entry. Smaller ports of entry were Cebu, Hoilo, Zamboanga, Jolo, Legaspi, and Davao, all with good port facilities. There were another 200 ports of call throughout the islands for interisland steamers and ferries making roads and railroads of secondary importance on many islands. On Luzon there was a telephone system and most cities and principal towns on other islands were linked by telephone, telegraph, and radio. Most provincial governments operated telephone systems so that many *barrios* (villages) had at least one phone linking them to the outside. Submarine cables linked Manila to Guam, Shanghai, and Hong Kong and there were four transoceanic radio stations. There were 13,750 miles of roads throughout the islands and over 700 miles of railroads on Luzon and almost 133 miles on Panay and Cebu. All of the larger islands possessed well-developed road systems with coastal roads and one to four connecting cross-island roads depending on its size. The entire length of the Philippines could be driven from the north end of Luzon through Samar and Leyte and to southern Mindanao and required only three ferry crossings.

A brief discussion of the naming of communities in the Philippines will aid researchers. Villages and small towns were referred to as *barrios* (today they are called *barangays*) while cities are called municipalities. Sometimes the principal town on an island carries the island's name. To differentiate between the two, the community will be called, for example, Cebu City, which is on the island of Cebu. Multiple barrios bearing the same saints' names (San, Santa, Santo) will be found throughout the islands with sometimes more than one of the same name on the same island. Barrios named San Josè are found on most of the larger islands. Province capitals often bear the name of the province. Frequently the barrio located at the mouth of a river will bear the river's name.

The Philippines is an agrarian culture with the principal crops being rice (a main staple of the Filipinos), coconuts, sugarcane, coffee, tobacco, maize, and tropical fruits. The chief exports were hemp, coconut products (coconuts, copra, coconut oil), tobacco, and lumber. Hemp, from the abaca tree, was an important export and the loss of the Philippines to the Japanese made hemp and Manila rope a scarce product forcing world navies to search for alternatives. It is for this reason that nylon rope was developed. Interestingly, much of the hemp production was handled by the large Japanese community on Mindanao. Embroidered materials were also an important export. Mining was not fully developed, but there are significant deposits of gold, silver, iron, chrome, manganese, copper, and lead, some of which had been tapped. Animal life includes a domesticated water buffalo known as the carabao (practically a national symbol), deer, wild pigs, and mongoose. Cattle and pigs constitute the main livestock population.

In 1941, the Philippines had a population of 16,771,900. Some 6,400,000 lived in the Visayas, 920,000 on Leyte, and most of the rest on Luzon. The vast majority were Filipinos of Malayan stock with a mixture of Spanish and Chinese blood speaking over sixty-five different, but related dialects. There is a small population of an aboriginal pygmy race known as the Awtas. The Moros, a name given by the Spanish, are a Filipino Islamic warrior society who live on western Mindanao, southern Palawan, and the Sulu Archipelago. They have long remained outside of mainstream Filipino society and still do. In 1937 the Tagalog dialect, the most common among the wealthy and influential of central Luzon, was adopted as the basis of the national language, Pilipino. Twice as many people spoke the Visayan dialect. English was also adopted as an official language. Within the Philippine Army most of the officers spoke Tagalog while many of the rank and file spoke other dialects. While there are similarities between dialects, few can understand each other. In 1941 about 27 percent, mainly on Luzon, spoke English and only 3 percent Spanish. The majority of Filipinos were Catholic. There were approximately 9,000 Americans residing on Luzon and small numbers on other islands. There were also 117,000 Chinese and 30,000 Japanese, most of whom (about 15,000) lived in the vicinity of Davao on Mindanao and most others in the Manila area. Most were interned at the commencement of hostilities.

The Philippine Army, advised and supplied by the United States, included a small Philippine Army Air Corps, 500 men with forty aircraft. The existing Insular Constabulary, a 5,000-man professional national militarized police organized in 1901, was included in the Army as the Philippine Constabulary Division under Major General Guillermo Franciscom, who retained control of the Constabulary under the Japanese. There was no navy, just a small Army Off Shore Patrol, which was to have received motor torpedo boats. There was also a U.S. Army and Navy presence plus the Philippine

Scouts (PS), a component of the U.S. Army. The Philippine Scouts was considered a well-trained and disciplined force comprised of Filipino rank and file and led by U.S. Army officers, but included Filipino officers as well.

The Philippines had no conventional military tradition when the Commonwealth was authorized to organize an army in 1935. The president-elect, Manuel Quezon, asked his friend, General Douglas MacArthur, former Chief of Staff of the U.S. Army, to serve as the Military Advisor of the Commonwealth Government to establish and develop a system of national defense by 1946. A regular force of 10,000 troops was planned and was to be backed by a reserve of 400,000, a goal to be achieved by 1946. The regular force included the 1st Regular Division and the Philippine Constabulary Division, which continued its police duties with detachments stationed throughout the islands. Conscription was introduced, but required only a 5-½-month training period before transfer to the reserves. A military academy to train officers was established at Baguio on Luzon, also the summer capital. The Commonwealth was divided into ten military districts, each with one reserve division projected to grow to three. Divisions, regiments, and many battalions were commanded by U.S. Army officers. Defense plans for the larger islands were developed, and since these were intended for use by the Commonwealth once full independence was granted, they did not include U.S. military or naval participation. Officers and NCOs were trained for cadre leadership positions and as instructors in 1936 and conscription began in 1937. Training was conducted at camps scattered throughout the Philippines with the U.S. Army providing training and technical assistance.

Overall U.S. military command was maintained by the Philippine Department, established in 1913, with headquarters in Manila. It was under the command of a major general until 1941. General MacArthur had retired from the U.S. Army in 1940 to become the Commander-in-Chief of the Philippine Army and a field marshal, but when war with Japan appeared likely he was recalled to active duty as a lieutenant general and assumed command of the newly formed U.S. Army Forces in the Far East on 27 July 1941. As such he was also Commanding General, Philippine Department. The day prior the Philippine Army was placed under his command. The principal formations within the new command were the Philippine Division, the Harbor Defense of Manila and Subic Bays, the Far East Air Force under Major General Lewis R. Brereton at Clark and Nichols Fields, various separate units, and the Philippine Department, which became a supply and administrative organization for the U.S. and Philippine Armies. The Philippine Division (31st, 45th, 57th Infantry), organized in 1921, was comprised mainly of Philippine Scout units, with the 31st Infantry solely American-manned, totaling 10,500 troops. It was commanded by Major General Jonathan M. Wainwright and stationed at Fort William McKinley south of Manila. Harbor Defense of Manila and Subic Bays, headquartered at Fort Mills on Corregidor under Major General George F. Moore, included four U.S. Army and Philippine Scout coast artillery and antiaircraft regiments with 5,300 troops. The Far East Air Force consisted of fewer than 280 aircraft, of which only half were considered modern, and 5,600 personnel. These forces totaled 10,500 U.S. Army and 12,000 Philippine Scouts.

U.S. Navy elements in the Philippines were under the Asiatic Fleet under Admiral Thomas C. Hart and the shore establishment was commanded by Rear Admiral Francis Rockwell of the 16th Naval District. The Asiatic Fleet (Task Force 5) possessed only three cruisers, thirteen World War I destroyers, twenty-nine mostly old submarines, six gunboats, a patrol wing with twenty-four aircraft, and some service vessels. Under the Naval District were 1,700 Marines of the 4th Marines, recently evacuated from China, and the 1st Separate Marine Battalion. In all there were about 20,000 American service personnel in the Philippines.

The Philippine Army had been fully mobilized by progressively calling up the reservists giving it a strength of 120,000 troops, but they were underarmed, ill-equipped, and only partly trained. Large unit-level training and maneuvers had never been conducted because of the lack of funds. Most units were much under strength with few of the divisions approaching their modest 8,600-man authorization. Many divisional subunits were never formed and all units lacked even basic equipment and materiel. There was virtually no artillery. One hundred cargo ships of equipment and materiel were scheduled in the first months of 1942 along with 22,500 American troops in two infantry regiments, artillery units, support units, and advisors, but time had run out.

Philippine Army units on Luzon included: 1st Regular, 11th, 21st, 31st, 41st, 51st, 71st (-), and 91st (-) Divisions (the two-digit divisions being reserve) with 76,750 troops. In the Visayas were the 61st Division (-) and the 74th and 75th Infantry Regiments (Provisional). On Mindanao were the 81st (-), 101st, and 102d Divisions plus single regiments detached from the 61st, 71st, and 91st. On 4 November 1941, North and South Luzon Forces, commanded by Major General Jonathan Wainwright and Brigadier General (later Major General) George M. Parker, respectively, were organized to oversee the training and tactical control of Philippine Army units on Luzon. The Visayan-Mindanao Force was formed for the same purpose in the central/southern Philippines under Colonel (later Major General) William F. Sharp headquartered on Cebu. The headquarters moved to Mindanao at the end of December. The Philippine Army was placed directly under MacArthur's command when hostilities erupted.

Defense of the Philippines, 1941–42

Anticipating a Japanese attack, U.S. air patrols sighted Japanese aircraft as early as 4 December 1941 within twenty miles of Luzon. The Japanese successfully launched air attacks on the main U.S. airfields around Manila on the morning of 8 December destroying almost 100 aircraft on the ground. The Japanese landed a naval landing force on small Batan Island, the northernmost in the Philippines on the same day. The small garrison was defeated and work began on an airfield. Most Japanese air and ground forces committed to the Philippines were launched from Formosa to the north under the command of Lieutenant General HOMMA Masaharu's (correctly spelled HONMA) *14th Army* backed by the *5th Air Group* with 307 aircraft under Lieutenant General OBATA Hideyoshi. The *14th Army* at the time consisted of the *16th Division (9th, 20th, 33d Infantry, 22d Field Artillery)* under Lieutenant General MORIOKA Susumu and *48th Division (1st* and *2d Formosa Infantry, 47th Infantry, 48th Mountain Artillery)* commanded by Lieutenant General TSUCHIHASHI Yuitsu. IJN forces included the *3d Fleet,* reinforced by elements of the *1st* and *2d Fleets,* under Vice Admiral TAKAHASHI Ibo and the *11th Air Fleet* under Vice Admiral TSUKAHARA Nishizo with 444 aircraft.

Luzon. The largest and northernmost of the main Philippine islands is approximately 340 miles long north to south and 130 miles across at its widest (see Map 59). It covers 40,814 square miles and is about the size of Virginia. The Picol Peninsula juts 200 miles to the southeast from the main body of the island toward Samar. The irregular-shaped peninsula varies from ten to forty miles in width. Luzon's topography varies greatly with several mountain ranges running north to south with the Sierra Madre along the upper east coast with a maximum elevation of 6,188 feet, the broad Cordillera Moun-

Map 59
Luzon, Philippine Islands

tains running up the center with Mount Pulog at 9,613 feet, and the Caraballo Mountains on the west-central coast with the highest elevation being 6,686 feet. On northern Luzon is found the islands' largest river, the Cagayan, which flows north between the Cordillera and Caraballo Mountains in a fifty-mile-wide valley, the second largest food-producing area on Luzon. Numerous tributaries feed the river from the mountains. Another river valley, the Agno/Pampanga described below, is found on central Luzon reaching from Lingayen Gulf to Manila Bay. Lingayen Gulf is twenty miles wide and thirty miles deep and served both the Japanese and Americans with their main landing site. The adjoining river valley provides a natural corridor to Manila. Manila Bay, slightly larger than Lingayen Gulf, but protected by Bataan Peninsula, provides an excellent anchorage. The city of Manila, the commonwealth capital, sits on the southeast shore with a population of 623,400. A large lake, Laguna de Bay, lies to the southeast of Manila and a smaller one, Lake Taal, to the south. Numerous bays and gulfs with good landing beaches are found on both the east-central and west-central coasts. The two main Far East Air Force bases were Clark Field almost fifty miles northwest of Manila and Nichols Field on the city's south edge (today called Villamor Air Base); small airstrips were scattered throughout the islands. U.S. Navy bases included Olongapo Navy Base on the north end of Subic Bay at the upper northwest base of Bataan, Mariveles Navy Section Base at the south end of Bataan, and Cavite Navy Yard on the southeast side on Manila Bay. Satellite facilities included a radio station and seaplane base at nearby Sangley Point

At dawn of the 10th two landing forces, the *Tanaka* and *Kanno Detachments*, comprised of reinforced elements of the *2d Formosa Infantry* and over 4,000 troops, landed at Aparri on the north end of Luzon and Vigan on the upper west coast, respectively. These units linked up on the island's northwest corner on the 12th, but elements also moved south. They were intended to secure local airfields and as diversionary landings to attract U.S.-Fil forces, but MacArthur withheld the North Luzon Force to attack the main Japanese force when it appeared. Also on the 10th the Japanese Batan landing force secured Camiguim Island off the coast north of Aparri for its airstrip. Cavite Navy Yard was heavily bombed.

On the 12th the 2,500-man *Kimura Detachment* with the *33d Infantry* and *Kure 1st SNLF* from the Palaus landed at Albay Gulf on the southeast end of Luzon's long tail, the Picol Peninsula. This force seized Legaspi and its airstrip and then moved slowly up the peninsula after defeating elements of the South Luzon Force's 41st and 51st Divisions. Heavy air attacks continued against the few remaining U.S. aircraft and bases. U.S.-Fil ground forces harassed the advancing Japanese, but most concentrated to meet the expected main landing in Lingayen Gulf 130 miles north of Manila. By the 14th three IJA air regiments had arrived at the captured airfields as well as some IJN air elements in the south. The IJA and IJN had designated an operational boundary across Luzon on latitude 16° north, from the south end of Lingayen Gulf on the west coast to Casiguran Sound on the east; the IJN was initially responsible for southern Luzon operations.

On 16 December Japanese forces from the Palaus landed on Mindanao (discussed below). The main Luzon landing on the east shore of Lingayen Gulf came on 22 December with the *47th Infantry* and *1st Formosa Infantry* landing at Agoo and Caba, respectively. They experienced heavy surf, rain, and poor visibility. U.S.-Fil opposition was initially moderate, but increased. By the next day the remainder of the *48th Division* was ashore along with the *16th Division's 9th Infantry*. Some 43,000 Japanese troops would land in Lingayen Gulf. Also on the 23rd the landing force linked up with the *Tanaka Detachment* pushing down from the north. On the 24th the *16th Division*, staging from Amami O Shima in the Ryukyus, landed only with its *22d Infantry* at multiple points in Lamon Bay on the east side of the Picol Peninsula where it joins Luzon's main land mass. Linking up with the *Kimura Detachment* pushing up the peninsula, the *16th Division* battled the South Luzon Force as it withdrew northward toward Manila.

On the 25th the *Matsumoto Detachment* from Davao landed on Jolo Island in the Sulu Archipelago stretching to the southwest of Mindanao. By the 27th the *48th Division* had routed the 11th, 71st, and 91st Philippine Divisions. This positioned the *48th Division* at the north head of the vast Agno/Pampanga River Valley. The Agno flows north on the valley's west side and the larger Pampanga flows south on the east side to empty into Manila Bay. This level valley provides a natural corridor for military operations running from the south end of Lingayen Gulf 130 miles to Manila. The 5,000-square-mile valley, flanked on both sides by mountains, is an average of forty miles in width with several roads and a railroad running its length. Its numerous rivers and streams, however, proved only minor obstacles to movement south. The valley and the area around Manila is the largest food-producing area in the Philippines.

On the 26th MacArthur realized there was little hope of external reinforcement and that his meager force, stripped of air support, would be unable to contain the Japanese invaders. He ordered all U.S.-Fil forces on Luzon to withdraw to the Bataan Peninsula and the fortified Manila Bay islands under War Plan ORANGE 3. The Bataan Force under Major General George Parker was formed on 24 December to organize the defense of the peninsula. The South Luzon Force was taken over by Brigadier General Albert M. Jones. The Philippine Department directed the evacuation of supplies to Bataan and Corregidor. Some stockpiles of supplies and ammunition had previously been accumulated on the peninsula. That night, Headquarters, U.S. Army Forces in the Far East and the Philippine government moved to Corregidor. On the 27th Manila was declared an open city, meaning there would be no resistance to its occupation and that it could not be bombed or shelled. Japanese internees were released. Military installations were set afire by withdrawing U.S.-Fil troops and looting broke out. On the 28th the Japanese drive to Manila from the north began and by the end of the month they had pushed well over halfway down the valley. The North Luzon Force was conducting a fighting withdrawal on successive defense lines to Bataan to the southwest and the South Luzon Force was withdrawing through Manila with the intent of reaching Bataan as well. Because of the coastal swamps, many tributaries, and vast river deltas on the north side of Manila Bay and northwest of Manila, the South Luzon Force had to skirt these to the north moving through the town of San Fernando before turning southwest to enter Bataan. In effect they were withdrawing toward the Japanese advancing from the north. The Japanese moved to trap half of the U.S.-Fil forces, but the North Luzon Force held the route open in a series of holding and rear guard actions to allow their comrades from the south to pass through San Fernando by 2 January 1942. The advance guards of the *48th* and *16th Divisions* occupied Manila on the same date and restored order. All U.S.-Fil forces had closed on Bataan by the 6th. The remnants of the Asiatic Fleet were ordered to Java at the end of December.

On 6 January, North Luzon Force became I Philippine Corps under Major General Wainwright and Bataan Force became II Philippine Corps under Major General Parker. The South Luzon Force Headquarters was dissolved and the Philippine Department provided supply and administrative functions. The Philippine Division served as the reserve. Sailors and airplaneless airmen were organized into provisional infantry units: Air Corps Regiment, Philippine Air Corps Battalion, Naval Rifle Battalion. The Japanese underwent a reorganization as well. The *14th Army* was preparing an immediate assault on Bataan before U.S.-Fil forces could dig in, but on the eve of the attack orders were received to release the *48th Division* and *5th Air Group* for redeployment to Java and Thailand, respectively. The *48th Division* was relieved by the *65th Brigade* on 7–8 January and the *9th Infantry* was attached to it. The *65th Brigade (122d, 141st, 142d Infantry)*, under Major General NAKA Akira, had landed at Lingayen Gulf on the 1st. The few remaining IJA air elements were formed into the *10th Independent Air Unit* and the minimal IJN ships, *Land Force* units, and air units were organized into the *3d Southern Expeditionary Fleet* under Vice Admiral SUGIYAMA Rokuzo.

Bataan Peninsula. Bataan, a province, thrusts south from the Luzon mainland bounded on the east side by Manila Bay and the west by the much smaller Subic Bay (see Map 60). The peninsula is approximately forty miles long north to south, twenty-five miles across at its widest (near the north end), but eighteen miles wide near its south end and twenty miles across at its landward base. Over 75 percent of its 420 square miles is covered with extremely dense jungle, bamboo, and undergrowth. The peninsula is dominated by two mountains, 4,222-foot Mount Natib in the north and the 4,700-foot Mount Bataan on the south end. Both are actually clusters of rocky volcanic peaks varying from 3,000 to over 4,000 feet. More accurately the cluster of peaks on the south end is known as the Miriveles Mountains. The mountain sides are creased with ridge fingers, ravines, and stream-filled gorges. Scores of rivers and streams radiate outward from the mountains crossing narrow coastal plains averaging fifteen miles wide on the east coast and ten miles on the west. The rivers and streams cross-compartment the swampy coastal plains and serve as obstacles to advance. The peninsula is densely over-grown with forests and undergrowth. Between Mounts Natib and Bataan is an east-to-west low, swampy valley ten to fifteen miles wide. Improved Route 111, Pilar-Bagac Road, crosses this from the east coast to the west. Route 110 follows the entire coastline, but it was improved only on the east side, East Road, as far as Tobang near the southeast corner. The rest of the road was unimproved around the south end, Miriveles Road, and up the west coast, West Road. Route 74 crossed the peninsula's landward base between Mount Natib's foothills and the Zambales Mountains to the north. The west shore was cliff-lined with rock outcroppings. The swampy coastal terrain made malaria and other tropical diseases a problem for both belligerents. Miriveles Navy Section Base was on the south end at Sisiman Bay with a small airstrip, seaplane base, and ammunition depot. Bataan and Cabcaben Fields, dried rice patty strips, were on the southeast end of the peninsula.

I Philippine Corps dug in to the west of Mount Natib with the 1st Regular, 31st, and 91st (-) Divisions and the now-dismounted 26th Cavalry (PS) while II Philippine Corps established a defensive line east of Mount Natib with the 11th, 21st, 41st, and 51st Divisions and the 57th Infantry (PS). The 2d Regular Division was formed from Con-stabulary troops. Mount Natib created a ten-mile-wide gap between the two corps, but the terrain was virtually impassable by a large force. The first line of defense was known as the Mauban-Abucay Line, named after the coastal barrios on which its ends were anchored. The Philippine Department, in addition to its supply and administrative activ-ities, was assigned a defense sector until 26 January with the 71st Division (-). There were 15,000 U.S. troops, 65,000 Filipino troops (Philippine Army and Philippine Scouts), and 26,000 American and Filipino refugees on Bataan.

The *14th Army* launched its offensive on 9 January with the *65th Brigade* attacking south along Bataan's east coast. On the 10th a battalion secured the Olongapo Navy Base on Bataan's base on the west side. Fort Wint on Grande Island, protecting the entrance to Subic Bay, had been evacuated on 24 December. The *65th Brigade* soon ran

Map 60
Bataan Peninsula, Luzon Island

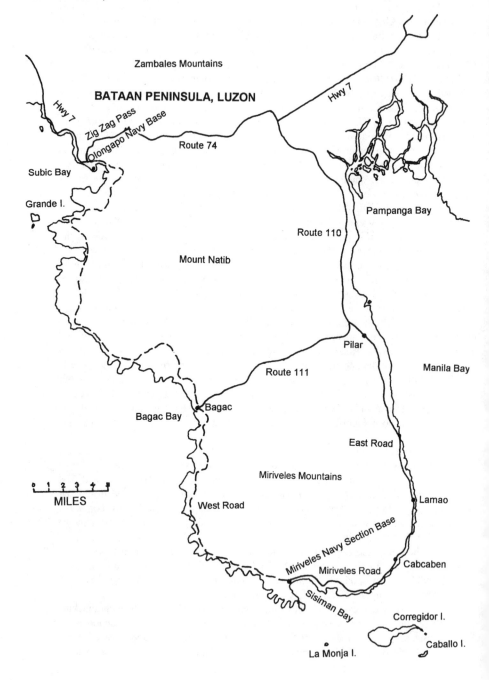

into stiff resistance taking two weeks to advance fifteen miles against II Philippine Corps. The Corps was pushed back when Japanese units outflanked the U.S.-Fil forces by moving through the foothills of Mount Natib on the 22nd. On the 13th the *20th Infantry* had been dispatched to Olongapo and began to advance down the west coast. This was the *Kimura Detachment* under Major General KIMURA Naoki, commander of the *16th Infantry Group*. This force made good initial advances destroying significant I Philippine Corps elements, but it too became stalled. In an effort to regain momentum, a battalion of the *20th Infantry* was landed on the southeast coast on 23 January behind U.S.-Fil lines and a separated element landed further down the coast. The units were soon pinned down and wiped out by 1 February. The rest of the *16th Division* arrived on Bataan's west coast on 28 January. A second battalion landed just to the north of the first on the night of 2 February and it too was cut off as the *16th Division* pressed south. To this point the Japanese had suffered almost 3,000 dead, over 4,000 wounded, and some 10,000 were seriously ill. To date the U.S.-Fil forces had suffered 50 percent casualties. The Japanese suspended offensive operations on 8 February, even though the *16th Division* still attempted to extract a battalion trapped behind U.S.-Fil lines until the 15th. The Japanese were exhausted and on the 22nd withdrew a few miles to the north to await reinforcement, a luxury the U.S.-Fil forces could not look forward to. Regardless, the defenders, after having long fought on half-rations, occupied the abandoned Japanese positions.

On 8 February the U.S. government was astounded to receive a message from President Quezon proposing that the United States grant the Philippines immediate independence, that the country be declared neutral, the Philippine Army be disbanded, and U.S. and Japanese forces would withdraw. Disheartened by a sense of abandonment, America's "Germany first" policy, and Lend-Lease program for Britain, Quezon was desperate to save his country. MacArthur attached his comments essentially endorsing Quezon's proposal. President Roosevelt rejected the proposal.

The Japanese high command was not initially concerned with the prolonged and costly effort to eliminate the U.S.-Fil forces bottled up on Bataan since they were jubilant over their many successes in the Netherlands East Indies, the Asia mainland, the Solomons, and elsewhere. Realizing the gravity of the situation in early February, the *4th Division* (*4th Field Artillery; 8th, 37th, 61st Infantry*) under Lieutenant General KITANO Kenzo, was ordered from Shanghai along with three regiments detached from other divisions (*41st Infantry, 5th Division; 62d Infantry, 21st Division; 124th Infantry, 18th Division*) tasked with securing other islands, and significant artillery to include large-caliber howitzers to reduce Corregidor as well as bomber units. These units arrived on Luzon between mid-February and early April. The battered *65th Brigade* had to be rebuilt with it and the *16th Division* receiving 7,000 replacements. In the process the *14th Army's* chief of staff was relieved for failure to achieve scheduled goals. On 11 March, the Luzon Force was formed under General Wainwright to control all U.S.-Fil units on Bataan. Its headquarters was located in the foothills of the Mariveles Mountains northeast of the Mariveles Navy Base. General MacArthur was ordered to evacuate his staff to Australia the next day and with him went President Quezon and numerous government officials. A Philippine government in exile was established in Wellington, Australia. Quezon later went to Washington, DC, where Roosevelt signed a bill extending his term of office until liberation, but he died in New York State on 1 August 1944. Vice President Sergio Osmeña succeeded him.

Preliminaries for the renewed Japanese offensive were launched on 12 March with the *16th Division* and *65th Brigade* driving in the U.S.-Fil outposts. The U.S.-Fil second defense line wrapped around the north edge on Mount Bataan from Bagac on the west coast, just to the south of Route 111, to Orion on the east coast, the Bagac-Orion Line. In the meantime Major General Edward P. King assumed command of the Luzon Force while General Wainwright moved to Corregidor to prepare for its defense. After extensive training in assault of the intricate and in-depth U.S.-Fil defenses, the main offensive was launched on 3 April. The *16th Division* in the west conducted a diversion and fought a holding action while the *4th Division* and *65th Brigade* in the east executed the main assault. They soon broke through the defenses and the disease-ridden, malnourished U.S.-Fil forces (the troops were now on quarter rations and the cavalrymen had eaten their last horses) were unable to effectively establish the planned third defense line on the flanks of Mount Bataan. II Philippine Corps was essentially destroyed in the east leaving I Corps' east flank exposed and it retreated. General King surrendered the Luzon Force to Major General NAGANO Kameichiro, commanding *21st Infantry Group (62d Infantry)*, on 9 April at the Experimental Farm Station near Lamao on the southeast side of the peninsula. Over 12,000 U.S. and 63,000 Filipino personnel surrendered; some 3,000 made it to Corregidor. The subsequent sixty-five-mile Bataan Death March to Camp O'Donnell, a former Philippine Army camp, resulted in the death of 600 Americans and between 5,000 and 10,000 Filipinos. Now only 10,260 U.S.-Fil troops held out on Corregidor and the other Manila Bay fortified islands.

   Manila Bay Fortified Islands. Four heavily fortified islands guarded the sixteen-mile-wide entrance to Manila Bay. The most important, largest, and best known of these is Corregidor Island, "The Rock," two miles off the south end of Bataan (see Map 61). Tadpole-shaped Corregidor is 3-½ miles long and 1-½ miles across its roughly circular head at its west end. A narrow two-mile-long tail undulates to the east. The tail is connected to the head by a 600-yard-wide necking rising only a few feet above sea level. This low area is known as Bottomside on which was located a barrio, San Josè, for Philippine Scout dependents and civilian employees, support facilities, and boat docks on both sides. The rest of the tail is a rugged ridge spine with hills and ravines. Kindley Landing Strip is located near the east end of the tail. Overlooking Bottomside on the tail's highest ground is rocky Malinta Hill with the 1,400-foot Malinta Tunnel, begun in 1922 and completed in 1932. The tunnel complex included headquarters, hospital, mess, power generation, living quarters, etc. housed in twenty-four thirty-foot-wide, 400-foot-long lateral tunnels, plus connected hospital (twelve laterals) and quartermaster (eleven laterals) tunnel complexes. On a level plateau on the base of the island's head above Bottomside is Middleside. Here were officer and NCO family quarters, the hospital, dependents' schools, and a service club. The island's head rises 400–500 feet to Topside containing headquarters, barracks, parade ground, and a golf course. The garrison's flagpole had been removed from a Spanish ship sunken in Manila Bay in 1898. Topside is faced with rocky cliffs overlooking scattered, narrow beaches. Several ravines give access to the beaches. Most of the island was covered with trees and brush. The entire island was provided a good road network to include the tail. A narrow-gauge railroad system on Topside served most of the twenty-three coast defense gun batteries. These were armed with fifty-six 12-, 10-, 8-, 6-, and 3-inch guns, 12-inch mortars, and 155mm guns collectively known as Fort Mills. There were also a number of 3-inch antiaircraft guns and searchlights. Known as the Gibraltar of the East for obvious reasons, Corregidor split the entrance of Manila Bay into the North and South Channels. While unquestionably formidable, it was provided little protection from a direct amphibious assault.

   Caballo Island is 1-¾ miles south of Corregidor and covers only 1/4 square mile. Its west half is comprised of three brush-covered hills with an elevation of 380 feet and

Map 61
Corregidor Island

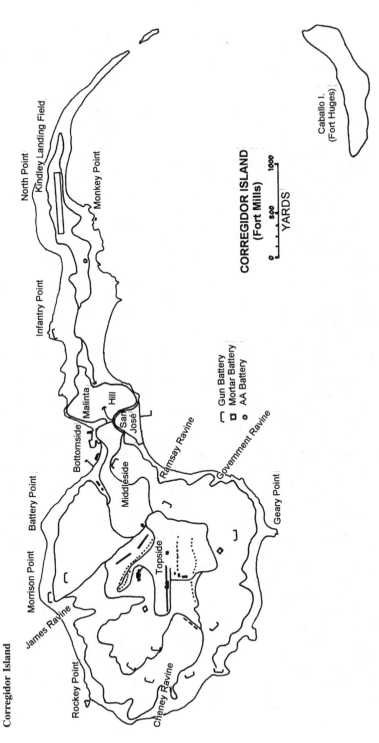

North Point

Kindley Landing Field

Monkey Point

Infantry Point

Malinta
Hill

San
José

Ramsay Ravine

Government Ravine

Geary Point

Bottomside

Middleside

Battery Point

Morrison Point

James Ravine

Rockey Point

Cheney Ravine

Topside

Gun Battery
Mortar Battery
AA Battery

CORREGIDOR ISLAND
(Fort Mills)

0   500   1000
YARDS

Caballo I.
(Fort Huges)

near vertical cliffs lining the shore. Its east half is a low, level sand spite surrounded with beaches. Fort Huges was armed with seventeen 14-, 6-, and 3-inch guns and 12-inch mortars in eleven batteries to add to the coverage of South Channel. El Fraile Island is 4-¼ miles south-southeast of Corregidor in the South Channel. Its Fort Drum was unique as the tiny rock had been leveled to water level and a 350-foot-long, 144-foot-wide battleship-shaped fortress, Fort Drum, was built atop it. The "Concrete Battleship" or "USS Drum" was forty feet high with walls up to thirty-six feet thick. It mounted two twin 14-inch gun turrets with two 6-inch guns on either side of the "hull" and included a battleship-like "bird cage" fire control tower. Carabao Island is 7-½ miles south of Corregidor and 500 yards off the south shore of Manila Bay. The long, narrow, barren, rocky island is surrounded by 100-foot high cliffs atop which is Fort Frank. Here were mounted nineteen 14- and 3-inch guns, 12-inch mortars, and 155mm guns. Fort Wint on Grande Island, centered in the entrance of Subic Bay, had been evacuated on 24 December. The south shore of the 2,200-by-3,300-foot island was lined with a ridge with a 150-foot elevation on the southwest end. It mounted twelve 10-, 6-, 3-inch and 155mm guns. These islands too had tunnel systems.

Over 5,700 U.S. and Philippine Scout troops manned the four coast artillery regiments (59th, 60th, 91st, 92d) and other units comprising the Harbor Defenses. U.S. Army, U.S. Navy, U.S. Marine Corps, Philippine Scouts, and Philippine Army units on the Manila Bay fortified islands totaled 10,260 men directly under Headquarters, U.S. Army Forces, Far East commander Major General Wainwright. The reinforced 4th Marines was responsible for Corregidor's beach defenses.

Concentrated air attacks on Corregidor and the other islands began on 29 December 1941 and continued until 6 January 1942, although there were still occasional raids. Artillery from the mainland joined in on 5 February. Air attacks began anew on 24 March and heavy artillery joined in after the fall of Bataan. The *4th Division* was tasked to seize Corregidor on 5 May *(X-Day)*. The landing force departed southeast Bataan and missed its intended north shore beaches between Infantry and Cavalry Points after a severe pounding by coast defense guns. The *1st Battalion, 61st Infantry Regiment* landed near the east end of the island's tail between Cavalry Point and North Point near Kindley Field. The *2d Battalion, 61st Infantry* landed nearby. The *4th Infantry Group* with the *37th Infantry* and a battalion of the *8th Infantry* were to have landed on the west portion of the island, but limited landing craft allowed only two battalions to be lifted. The Japanese fought up the island's tail to Malinta Hill by 1000 hours the next morning. The *3d Battalion, 61st Infantry* landed at dawn. At that point General Wainwright, realizing defeat was inevitable, surrendered to protect the over 1,000 wounded and many noncombatants. He also ordered other U.S.-Fil forces elsewhere in the Philippines to surrender within four days.

Besides well over 1,000 wounded, up to 800 defenders died. Among the surviving U.S.-Fil prisoners of war were seventy-two Army and eleven Navy female nurses. References are in conflict over Japanese casualties. One reports 900 dead and 3,000 wounded, which appears excessive. The *33d Infantry, 16th Division* occupied Carabao, Caballo, and El Fraile Islands on 7 May after they surrendered.

Visayas. The existing Visayan-Mindanao Force was split on 4 March. The Mindanao Force under Brigadier General William F. Sharp consisted of the 81st (-), 101st, and 102d Divisions, two regiments detached from the 61st Division, and one regiment from the 71st and 91st Divisions, plus Army Air Forces units serving as ground troops, a total of 25,000 troops. The command was headquartered at the Del Monte Airfields and was also responsible for Panay. The Visayan Force was comprised of the 61st (-) and 71st (-) Divisions,

Map 62
The Visayas, Philippine Islands

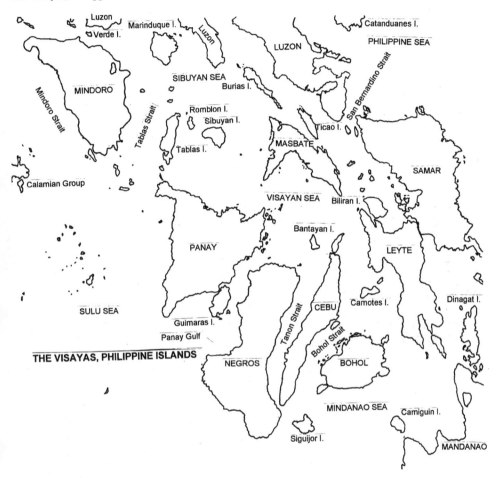

From an Allied report depicting guerrilla dispositions.

two provisional infantry regiments, and two regiments detached from the 81st Division, some 20,000 troops. This command was under Brigadier General Bradford H. Chynoweth and was responsible for Cebu (on which it was located), Panay, Negros, Leyte, Samar, and Bohol (see Map 62). None of the other Visayas were garrisoned. On 16 April the two forces were reconsolidated as the Visayan-Mindanao Force under Major General Sharp after Cebu had fallen.

Cebu. Cebu lies between Negros to its west and Bohol to the east (see Map 63). The ten-to-fourteen-mile-wide Tanon Strait separates Cebu from Negros; the strait is only two miles wide at its south end. Cebu is approximately 135 miles long north to south and twenty miles wide across the center covering 1,695 square miles making it the ninth largest island. A road follows most of the coast with a cross-island road connecting Cebu

Map 63
Panay, Negros, and Cebu

Masbate

Carabao I.

Visayan Sea

Pandan

Capiz

Ciyo East Passage

Jalauo River Valley

PANAY

Bantayan I.

Bogo

Pototan

Caoiz

San José de
Buenavista

Tigbauan Iloilo

Guimaras Strait

Bacolod

Guimaras I.

CEBU

Pulupandan

San Carlos

Panay Gulf

Toledo

Cebu City Opon
Talisay

PANAY, NEGROS, AND CEBU

Binalbagan

Mactan I.

NEGROS

Tanon Strait

Carcar

Bohol Strait

Orong

Argao

Tanjay

Dumaguete   Siguijor I.

City on the east-central coast with Toledo on the west. A railroad runs along the east coast from Argao through Cebu City to Danao. A mountainous spine runs the island's length with its highest point being 3,599 feet. Cebu was defended by the Philippine Army's 82d and 83d Infantry, Cebu Military Police Regiment, and miscellaneous units totaling 6,500 troops under Colonel Ivan C. Scudder. On the morning of 10 April 1942 the *Kawaguchi Detachment (124th Infantry)* landed at Cebu City, the principal town, and Toledo on opposite sides of the island. They landed at up to five other sites as well, but neither Japanese nor U.S. records identify the locations. The MP Regiment was driven from Cebu City on the first day. The Japanese then moved from both coasts to cut the island in two on the central cross-island road. The defense collapsed on the 12th and on the 19th the Japanese declared the island secured. Numerous small units had withdrawn to the mountains and were preparing for guerrilla operations with supplies they had hidden.

   Panay. Panay lies to the northwest of slightly larger Negros separated by the ten- to twelve-mile-wide Guimaras Strait. The Sibuyan Sea is on its north side, the Sulu Sea to its west and southwest, and the Visayan Sea to the east. Mindoro is to the northwest and Masbate to the northeast. Guimaras Island lies close off the southeast coast opposite of Iloilo, the principal city. Panay, the sixth largest, is roughly triangular in shape measuring about seventy-five miles wide and ninety-five miles long and covers 4,448 square miles. The island's central portion is occupied by a north-to-south Jalauo River Valley flanked by mountains, the highest elevation being in the larger western chain at 6,726 feet. A road follows the coastline and a cross-island road runs up the central valley from Iloilo to Capiz on the north side. A railroad parallels this approximate route. Panay was defended by 7,000 men of the 61st Division (63d, 64th, 65th Infantry) plus some Constabulary under Colonel Albert F. Christie. The *Kawamura Detachment (41st Infantry)* landed unopposed at Iloilo and Capiz, at both ends of the cross-island road, on 16 April. On the 18th another small force landed at San Josè de Buenavista on the lower west coast. After several engagements the Philippine forces fell back largely intact to the mountains and were well prepared to conduct a guerrilla war, but the Japanese controlled the roads and key towns. They declared the island secure on the 20th.

   Leyte and Samar were still held by a 2,500-man U.S.-Fil force, Negros was held by 3,000 troops, and there were 1,000 men on Bohol, but the Japanese were unconcerned with these small forces; if necessary they would be reduced later. All were preparing for guerrilla operations.

   Mindanao. The second largest and southernmost of the Philippine's large islands was not as well developed as Luzon. Mindanao is irregularly shaped, about 300 miles across, with its coasts indented by numerous inlets, bays, and gulfs. It covers 36,906 square miles, slightly larger than Indiana. It had a poor road system, although there were two highways. Route 1 ran from Digos on Davao Gulf on the southeast-central coast northeast across the island to Parang on the west coast, cut across the base of the Zamboanga Peninsula, and followed the north coast to the extreme northeast end. Route 3 ran from Cagayan on the north-central coast winding south to link back up with Route 1 midway between Parang and Digos. While barrios and towns lined the north and east coasts there were few on the other coasts other than around Davao Gulf, where Davao City is located, the island's principal town. The three important Del Monte airfields were located at Tankulan ten miles inland from the north-central coast. The Far East Air Force's heavy bombers had been moved there to protect them from air attack and were then to be employed to attack enemy shipping approaching the Philippines from the north. The island is mountainous with the Diuata Mountains running along the east coast, but the highest peak is Mount Apo, a 9,691-foot volcano on the west side of Davao Gulf. The Agusan River flows north almost the entire length of the east coast along the inland side of the Diuata Mountains through a marshy valley to empty into the Mindanao Sea. The shorter Mindanao River, also in a swampy valley, is located on the west-central portion of the island emptying into Bongo Bay. Both are navigable. The Zamboanga Peninsula juts almost 150 miles westward from the upper west coast and then turns southwest.

On 16 December 1941, the *Sakaguchi Detachment* from the Palaus with the *56th Mixed Infantry Group Headquarters*, under Major General SAKAGUCHI Shisuo, *146th Infantry*, and *SNLF* elements, landed at Davao. This force was detached from *16th Army* involved in the occupation of Borneo and Java. Landing with it was the *Miura Detachment* with the *1st Battalion, 33d Infantry* from the *16th Division*. Davao was defended by 2,000 Filipino troops, who were soon forced to withdraw. The *Matsumoto Detachment* departed on the 23rd to occupy Jolo Island to the west. The *Miura Detachment* remained to establish a seaplane base and the airfield outside of Davao was placed into operation. Jolo was occupied on the 24th after defeating 300 Constabulary. Both Davao and Jolo were then used as launch sites for operations in Borneo to the southwest. The Japanese made no effort to secure the entire island through the first months of 1942. The *Miura Detachment* was contained at Davao and Digos and the Philippine Army units, assigned defense sectors about the island, continued to train. MacArthur hoped that Mindanao would be able to hold out until he was able to mount an offensive from Australia and use the island as a forward base of operations to reconquer the Philippines.

On 29 April the *Kawaguchi Detachment (124th Infantry)*, after securing Cebu, landed in the Moro Gulf on the west-central side of Mindanao and advanced north up Route 1 as well as to the east while the Miura Detachment moved west on Route 1 from Digos to meet them. About 220 *32d Naval Base Force* troops landed at Zamboanga on the north coast of the Zamboanga Peninsula on 2 March and established a seaplane base. The *Kawamura Detachment (41st Infantry)*, after seizing Panay, landed at Cagayan in Macajalar Bay near where Route 1 and 3 joined on the north-central coast. While the Filipino troops resisted to the extent of their capabilities, on 10 May the Mindanao Force surrendered.

Major General Wainwright released Major General Sharp commanding the Visayan-Mindanao Force to the command of MacArthur when he surrendered Corregidor, but on the night of the 7th he attempted to reassume command to order the force to surrender. Wainwright feared that the 11,000 surrendered troops on the fortified islands might be massacred if the southern forces did not meet Japanese demands. MacArthur ordered Sharp to ignore Wainwright. A truce was arranged and meetings held between Sharp and the Japanese. Once appraised of the situation in the north by a staff officer sent by Wainwright, Sharp surrendered his forces on 10 May. Many of the far-flung units were without communications and some were already executing raids and harassing attacks on the Japanese. Panay surrendered on 20 May and Leyte and Sumay on the 26th, but only about 10 percent of the officers and men surrendered in both cases; most went into the hills. *The Nagano Detachment (62d Infantry)* occupied Negros, Bohol, Leyte, and Samar between 20 and 25 May. Negros did not surrender until 3 June and then only about 40 percent of the troops turned themselves in. By 9 June, the units that had decided to surrender had done so. Approximately 7,000 American civilians were interned at one time or the other. Their internment was erratic with some not confined until 1943 and others released later. Many of the elderly and infirm were never interned. Most were detained in camps on Luzon where they were not generally overly mistreated. American prisoners of war were confined in camps under harsh conditions throughout the Philippines, although most were on Luzon. Many prisoners were shipped to Burma, Japan, and China under extremely brutal conditions as forced labor.

A total of 129,400 IJA troops, 12,800 IJA *Air Service*, and 49,800 IJN personnel, including the *3d Fleet*, had been committed to the conquest of the Philippines. The *14th Army* was detached from the *Southern Army* on 29 June and placed under the direct control of the *Imperial General Headquarters*. It was directed to stabilize and secure the Philippines and establish a military government. Lieutenant General HOMMA was recalled to Japan being replaced by Lieutenant General TANAKA Shizuichi. HOMMA was given a conquering general's welcome, but was not permitted to deliver his report to the Emperor. He was considered disgraced for his refusal to continue the attack on Bataan without reinforcements and failing to meet the time schedule. For this he was placed on the reserve list in August 1943. Tried for violating the rules of war and held responsible for the Bataan Death March, he was shot at Los Baños, Luzon, while his subordinates were hanged, on 3 April 1946.

The Japanese occupation was repressive, but many areas on larger islands and hundreds of remote inhabited islands remained unoccupied. The Japanese actually controlled only twelve of the forty-eight provinces. A combination of rugged terrain, the occupation force's self-confinement to the cities and larger towns, the resentment of the Filipino people, and their faith in the return of American forces led to the organization of a massive resistance movement. Guerrilla units were raised independently in mid-1942 and were gradually unified throughout the Visayas and on Mindanao by MacArthur's General Headquarters in Australia. Owing to the extent of Japanese occupation on Luzon, guerrillas kept a low profile until late 1944 when they arose in large numbers in support of the American invasion. In central Luzon the 30,000-person People's Anti-Japanese Army, the *Hukbo ng Bayan Laban sa Hapon* or *Hukbalahap*, arose independent of American support. The Huk resistance was a strongly nationalist movement and would continue its own guerrilla war after liberation. Guerrilla leadership was provided by hundreds of American and Filipino servicemen from all branches and organizations who had refused to surrender. In October 1943, most Filipino prisoners of war were released by the Japanese under the General Amnesty Order when the puppet Philippine government was formed and some joined the guerrillas. Supplies and arms were delivered by submarine and flying boat. Until the American invasion guerrilla activities throughout the islands were generally low-keyed and avoided large-scale operations. Some units suffered when they attempted too ambitious of operations. While they harassed the enemy, they mainly built up and developed their strength to support the coming invasion. The guerrillas were credited with killing 8–10,000 Japanese during the occupation. They were extremely valuable in providing intelligence information to the General Headquarters, aiding reconnaissance teams, and recovering downed airmen and escaped prisoners of war. The guerrilla movement was not without its internal problems, however. There were conflicts between the different groups with many having their own political agendas, or vied for power, recognition, or simply exploited local civilians. Animosities between groups were common, even after the U.S. invasion, with some units openly fighting each other. Once the invasion came the guerrillas' real value was realized as they continued to provide up-to-date intelligence, served as scouts and guides, secured roads and barrios in advance of the Americans, and harassed the Japanese in the rear. The guerrilla units were of varied organization, but in the Visayan-Mindanao area were subdivided into the old 4th–10th Military Districts with many units picking up the designations of former Philippine

Army units. Some units were sufficiently well supplied, organized, and trained to conduct low-level conventional operations alongside U.S. units. An estimated 260,000 Filipinos served in guerrilla organizations to include combatants and support. Even more were in the underground and auxiliary organizations.

After the surrender the Japanese ordered remaining Philippine government officials to return to work. In an effort to lighten the occupation's harshness, most did. Philippine government officials soon proposed a provisional executive under the authority of the commonwealth. Japan turned down the proposal as some Philippine officials sought trade agreements with Japan. Fearing accusations of sedition with the enemy should the United States return, many were reluctant to follow this path. Jorge Vargas, former mayor of Manila, formed a provisional council of state unrelated to the commonwealth. In late 1942 all political parties were abolished and the *Kapisanan Sa Paglilingkod Sa Bagong Philipinas* or *Kalibapi* (Association for Service in the New Philipines) was formed under Vargas. Youth and women's auxiliaries were formed and the Supra party boasted some 1,500,000 members in 1944. In the meantime Japan attempted to convert Philippine production to military ends. Much of the harvest went to feed the occupation troops. The average citizen did what was necessary to survive the occupation confused by the choices of resistance and collaboration. It was soon realized that Japan's promise of "Asia for the Asians" did not translate to equality, as often demonstrated by the heavy-handed military government and frequent outright brutality. Food, medicine, and consumer products were in drastically short supply and inflation soared. Refusal to deliver food quotas, sabotage, and passive resistance increased. Because of initial Japanese export of food and materials from the Philippines and the massive influx of troops, rice and other foodstuffs actually had to be imported from Thailand and Indochina.

In early 1943, Japan offered the Philippines the opportunity for self-government under a new constitution supporting their *Greater East Asia Co-Prosperity Sphere*, if the new country would declare war on the United States. Believing America would forgive collaboration under the circumstances and that Japan would retaliate if the offer was rejected, the offer was reluctantly accepted. The puppet Republic of the Philippines, given token independence in October 1943 under President José P. Laurel, former Secretary of the Interior, declared war on the United States in September 1944. Of course no active effort was undertaken by the new republic and the following month U.S. forces landed on Leyte.

Some effort was made by the Japanese military administration to raise pro-Japanese armed forces, mainly to combat guerrillas. Little success was achieved in this area because of the widespread hatred of the Japanese, the faith that America would return, and general sympathy for the guerrillas. The Constabulary was retained for police duties and former Philippine Army officers were given Constabulary commissions. The Japanese pressured the government to increase the Constabulary's size and level of training to combat the growing guerrilla threat, but they were at the same time reluctant to arm it, fearing the weapons would end up in guerrilla hands. For the most part the Constabulary performed only as a police force, although some counterguerrilla actions were undertaken by a few units.

In December 1944 the Japanese combined several local efforts to raise armed units to form the *Kalipunang Makabayan, ng mga Pilipino* or *Makapili* (Patriotic League of Filipinos), a resurrection of a Spanish-era guard originally comprised of Indians imported from Mexico. With a recruiting goal of 20,000, fewer than 5,000 volunteered mainly from central and southern Luzon. Under the command of General Artermio Ricarte, the *Makapili* dug fortifications, served as guides, and gathered intelligence for the Japanese.

Elements also conducted counterguerrilla operations with the *8th Division*. In October 1944 Ricarte also formed the *Hoan Giyugun* or *Giyugun* (Security Force), but little came of it because of the siphoning of funds. Many of the *Makapili* and *Giyugan* were tried for treason after the war, but few of the Constabulary were.

Lieutenant General KURODA Shigenori took command of the *14th Army* and the military government in May 1943. In August 1944, the army was upgraded to the *14th Area Army* to provide a single headquarters responsible for the defense of the Philippines. KURODA considered the Philippines to be indefensible because of its size and the limited forces available to him. He took no action to improve the situation and roads and railways fell into disrepair. Regardless, the Philippines became the key supply distribution center for the occupied Netherlands East Indies, Malaya, Burma, and New Guinea as well as a link to those far-flung forces with the Home Islands. KURODA's protector, Premier TOJO, was dismissed after the fall of Saipan, and KURODA was replaced by General YAMASHITA Tomoyuki in September 1944. At this time the *14th Area Army* consisted of the *16th* and *30th Divisions* and the *30th, 31st, 32d*, and *33d Independent Mixed Brigades*. The fall of the Marshalls and Marianas in early and mid-1944 coupled with the loss of eastern New Guinea led the Japanese high command to realize that the Philippines would soon become an Allied objective. To the Japanese the Philippines, the "east wing of the Southern Sphere," would be the decisive battle of the war and their last line of defense in the south. Their loss would cut Japan off from its extensive forces and resources in the East Indies. The Japanese high command felt that fifteen divisions, eight brigades, and significant air units would be required to defend the Philippines, but only half that number were available. The Japanese had developed sixty-eight airfields scattered throughout the Philippines.

Preparations for the coming American invasion began in mid-May 1944 after the Allied April success at Hollandia on eastern New Guinea. Reinforcements and aircraft flowed into the Philippines, new units arrived, and existing units were upgraded; for example, the four brigades were enlarged to divisions. This effort lasted through the summer into September, the month prior to the U.S. invasion of Leyte. The *Southern Army* headquarters, controlling forces in Southeast Asia and the South Pacific under Field Marshall Count TERAUCHI Hisaichi, moved from Saigon, Indochina to Manila in mid-May. In September 1944, the *14th Area Army* was directly responsible for Luzon with four divisions, three brigades, and the *2d Tank Division* en route. Its subordinate *35th Army*, under Lieutenant General SUSUKI Sosaku, defended the Visayas and Mindanao with four divisions and a brigade. The *14th Area Army* mustered 224,000 troops in addition to air service personnel, laborers, and civilians employees.

Liberation of the Philippines, 1944–45

In May 1944, Admiral Nimitz suggested establishing U.S. positions on the coast of China and opening supply lines to the interior. Supplying the massive, but ill-equipped, Chinese Army would force Japan to reinforce the mainland and stretch its forces thinner. Consideration was given to invading Formosa, 670 miles southwest of Japan, before it could be reinforced, and bypass the Philippines.

MacArthur opposed the plan to bypass the Philippines contending, with additional naval support, he had the forces to liberate them. Nimitz agreed to an alternate plan that included recapturing much of the Philippines between October and December 1944. Depending on the situation, either Luzon would be invaded in February 1945 or Formosa-Amoy Area (on mainland China) in March. This would be followed by the Bonin Islands in April and the Ryukyus (with Okinawa) in May. MacArthur insisted on liberating Manila on Luzon for obvious personal and political reasons. More important than these reasons is the fact that the liberation of Manila and Luzon would be a severe psychological victory over Japan. Because of the complexities and difficulties of securing Formosa (discussed in the Okinawa Gunto section), simultaneous invasions of Okinawa and Luzon were proposed meeting the approval of both the Pacific Ocean Area and Southwest Pacific commands.

MacArthur's General Headquarters developed the MUSKETEER II plan in August 1944 consisting of a series of sequential operations. Operation KING I envisioned a landing on the south end of Mindanao on 15 November 1944 followed by KING III, a 7 December landing on Mindanao's Zamboanga Peninsula. KING II, the Leyte landing, would take place on 20 December. In September it was recommended to Admiral Nimitz and General MacArthur that the Palaus and Yap be bypassed; only Ulithi should be seized to provide an advance naval base to support operations in the Philippines. It was also recommended that the Leyte assault be advanced two months as the air defenses in the Philippines were found to be weak. Nimitz approved canceling Yap, but ordered the Palaus and Ulithi operations to continue and that Leyte be seized as soon as possible. The date of 20 October 1944 was set. Morotai Island in the Molucca Islands, part of the East Indies off the west end of New Guinea and southeast of Mindanao, was to be secured as well. Once supporting bases were secured in the central Philippines, LOVE and MIKE series of operations would be executed in the northern Philippines with the goal of liberating Luzon.

Leyte. In some respects Leyte (CYCLONE, later ACCOUTERMENT) was an unusual choice for America's first objective in the Philippines, largely because of its location within the archipelago. (see Map 64). Much larger Mindanao, defended by substantial forces, is to its south, Samar is to the northeast, and other Japanese defended islands of the Visayas, Panay, Negros, Cebu, Bohol, are to its west. Leyte was deep within the Japanese defenses with no clear approach from the open sea; small islands would have to be first secured. The nearest Allied airfields were 500 miles away on Peleliu and Morotai, beyond fighter range. The selection of Leyte was unusual too in that MacArthur's original 1942 plan for the liberation of the Philippines was to employ Mindanao as the base of operations. That plan, however, hinged on the ability of the U.S.-Fil defenders being able to retain the island. Even as late as August 1944, MacArthur planned for the initial primary landing in the Philippines to be on Mindanao. Heavily defended Mindanao, perhaps so because the Japanese had learned of his earlier plan, was ruled out as the first major objective.

Leyte is situated in the eastern portion of the Visayas 340 miles south of Manila. Samar is separated from Leyte by the 13-½-mile-long, ¼- to-½-mile-wide San Juanico Strait (LACUNA) on the northeast side (Samar is discussed below). While navigable by small craft, it experiences strong tides and rip currents. Leyte is 115 miles long from the northwest to the southeast, fifteen miles wide at its narrow center, forty-five miles wide across the upper end, and thirty-five miles at the lower. It covers 2,799 square miles making it the eighth largest. A densely forested mountain range runs the length of the island with sharp ridges and ravines. The southern third of the island is extremely rugged with a very narrow coastal strip. The central portion is dominated by the mountains, the highest being 4,426 feet, but a five-to-ten-mile-wide coastal plain edges the east side facing Leyte Gulf. This coastal plane runs northward toward the island's northeast end widening out into the Leyte Valley. The fertile valley opens out on to the Samar Sea with a width of twenty-five miles on the north coast. It was here that the United States planned to build airfields to support operations in the rest of the Philippines; the Japanese

Map 64
Leyte, Philippine Islands

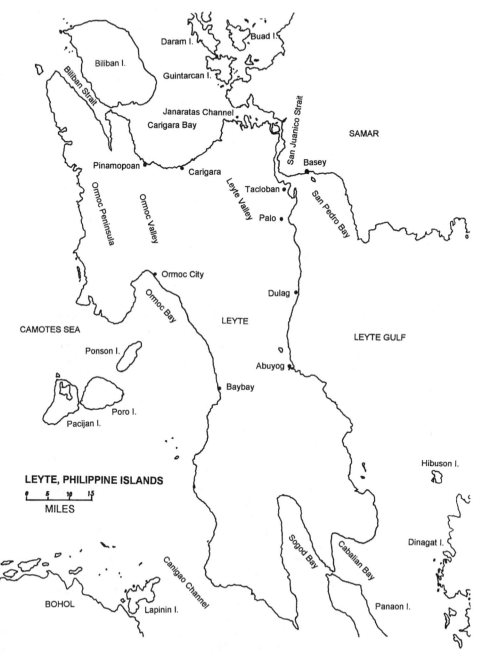

Daram I.

Buad I.

Biliban I.

Guintarcan I.

Biliban Strait

Janaratas Channel

Carigara Bay

San Juanico Strait

SAMAR

Pinamopoan

Carigara

Basey

Leyte Valley

Tacloban

Ormoc Peninsula

Ormoc Valley

Palo

San Pedro Bay

Ormoc City

Dulag

Ormoc Bay

LEYTE

CAMOTES SEA

LEYTE GULF

Ponson I.

Abuyog

Baybay

Poro I.

Pacijan I.

Hibuson I.

LEYTE, PHILIPPINE ISLANDS

0   5   10   15
MILES

Sogod Bay

Cabalian Bay

Dinagat I.

BOHOL

Canigao Channel

Lapinin I.

Panaon I.

From a Japanese topography assessment.

already had six airfields in the area. Difficulties would be encountered as the valley floor was covered with inundated rice paddies disrupting its natural drainage. As a result there was a very high water table, often only inches below the surface. The majority of Leyte's population of almost 1,000,000 lived on the upper northeast coast and the island's north end. Tacloban, the principal city with a population of 31,000, is on the northeast coast at the south entrance of the San Juanico Strait. A road skirts most of the island's coast, except for double-ended Ormoc Peninsula on the northwest end. A cross-island road runs across the narrow isthmus connecting Abuyog on the east coast and Baybay on the west. The roads, however, were only suited for fair weather, are unpaved, and incapable of supporting heavy, two-way military traffic. Off the northwest end of Leyte, separated by the narrow Biliban Strait, is Biliban Island. Panaon Island is immediately off the south end of Leyte near Sogod Bay, which deeply indents that end of the island. Off the west-central side of Leyte are the Camotes Sea, Pacijan, Poro, and Ponson.

The east coast facing Leyte Gulf (LUBRICATE) provided the best landing beaches. An eighteen-mile-wide sector was selected on Leyte's upper east coast, part of it protected by San Pedro Bay. The bay was enclosed by Leyte on the west and Samar Island on its north and east sides; San Juanico Strait opened into the bay's northwest corner. This would allow American forces rapid access to the Leyte Valley to begin airfield construction. The firm, sand beaches are very narrow, but the plain beyond is flat and the coastal road would allow mobility once gained. There were coastal mangrove swamps and flooded rice paddies in some areas and very few tracks provided exit from the beaches to the coastal road. Ormoc Bay on the east coast provided good beaches, but the roads were poor and it would require the 3–4,000-foot mountains to be crossed before reaching Leyte Valley. Ormoc Valley on the north side of the bay and at the southern base of the Ormoc Peninsula was also considered key terrain for the control of the island. Ormoc City offered port facilities and a good anchorage. The five-mile-wide, thirteen-mile-long valley was accessible by road connected to the north coast at Pinamopoan on Carigara Bay. The low, marshy valley need not be occupied though; it could be controlled from the surrounding hills. A landing on Carigara Bay on the north coast would provide rapid access to Leyte Valley, but the bay is shallow and more exposed to air attack from the north. The coast is also swampy and faced or flanked by hills. The rugged south end of the island was considered militarily unimportant.

Samar. Samar (PORCUPINE, ROSEBUD, WITCHCRAFT), the third largest island, lies to the northeast of smaller Leyte. Only small Japanese elements secured the south end of the island and it would play a minor role in the Leyte campaign. Samar is approximately 200 miles long northwest to southeast and 110 miles across at its north end. It covers 5,124 square miles. Its northwest corner is only about ten miles from the end of Luzon's Bicol Peninsula separated by the San Bernardino Strait. The Samar Sea is on the island's southwest coast separating it from Masbate. Samar is dominated by two low mountain clusters with the highest elevation being 2,654 feet in the north. Samar's southeast end is covered with foothills. The highest elevation in this area is a 1,529-foot peak overlooking San Pedro Bay. Roads on the southeast end of the island were poorly developed. An improved road ran from Basey on the north end of San Pedro Bay along the island's southwest coast and around the north end. A spur road crossed the island's center to the northeast coast between the two mountain clusters.

There was an active guerrilla force on Leyte, but it would play a minor role in the battle. American guerrilla commanders on Mindanao and Panay both understood they were authorized to raise guerrilla units in the 9th Military District, Leyte and Samar. This resulted in two Filipino-led guerrilla groups in opposition with each other. The two groups joined battle in August 1943 together suffering up to 300 casualties, but the smaller group's power was broken and most joined what was known as the 92d Division. In late 1943, the Japanese offered amnesty to the guerrillas if they were to surrender and many did. The Japanese soon began conducting operations to hunt down those who remained in the hills and turned their frustration on civilians. Seeking revenge, the guerrillas fought back killing 430 Japanese and wounding 200. On the eve of the Leyte landing the 92d Division numbered active 3,200 guerrillas.

The main Japanese force on Leyte was the *16th Division (9th, 20th, 33d Infantry, 22d Field Artillery)*, which had fought through the Philippine campaign. It was responsible for the defense of Leyte and Samar. Now under the command of Lieutenant General MAKINO Shiro it was considered the strongest division in the *35th Army*, to which it was subordinate. It was concentrated on Leyte with only four companies detached to secure larger Samar. Under the 10,600-man division were service units, several air base units, and elements of the *36th Naval Garrison Unit* at Ormoc and Tacloban. Elements of the *30th Division* on Mindanao were to reinforce Leyte if attacked. Most of the *16th Division's* forces were deployed in depth in the southern and central portions of the Leyte Valley.

Allied air strikes on Leyte began on 1 September 1944 and carrier strikes commenced in October to neutralize the approaches. This included attacks in the Ryukyus. The Leyte assault would be the largest amphibious assault to date in the Pacific. The Leyte Ground Assault Force (CYCLONE Landing Force) was the 6th Army with 202,500 troops under Lieutenant General Walter Kruger. Two recently organized corps were under 6th Army, X and XXIV Corps. There was also a two-division 6th Army Reserve and a 6th Army Service Command. While the two corps were new, all six assigned divisions, except the 96th Infantry Division, were combat experienced.

X Corps, 51,500 troops, Major General Franklin C. Silbert:

1st Cavalry Division, Special (1st Brigade—5th, 12th Cavalry, 2d Brigade—7th, 8th Cavalry), Major General Verne D. Mudge.

24th Infantry Division (19th, 34th Infantry; -21st Infantry detached for separate missions), Major General Frederick A. Irving.

XXIV Corps, 53,000 troops, Major General John R. Hodge:

7th Infantry Division (17th, 32d 184th Infantry), Major General Archibald V. Arnold.

96th Infantry Division (382d, 383d Infantry; -381st Infantry as 6th Army Afloat Reserve), Major General James L. Bradley.

6th Army Reserve, 28,500 troops:

32d Infantry Division (126th, 127th, 128th Infantry), Major General William H. Gill. It remained at Hollandia, New Guinea until 14 November.

77th Infantry Division (305th, 306th, 307th Infantry), Major General Andrew D. Bruce. It was located at Guam until moved to Manus in mid-November and then landed on Leyte on 23 November.

Other major 6th Army units included the 2d Engineer Special Brigade, 32d Antiaircraft Artillery Brigade, and 20th Armor Group. The 40th Antiaircraft Artillery Brigade would arrive in mid-December.

The Fifth Air Force, augmented by the Thirteenth Air Force, would support the operation along with aircraft from 3d Fleet carriers. RAAF elements would conduct supporting attacks on Japanese installations in the East Indies. The 7th Fleet under Vice Admiral Thomas C. Kinkaid was organized as the Central Philippine Attack Force (Task Force 77). The 7th Amphibious Force (Northern Attack Force, TF 78) delivered X Corps while the 3d Amphibious Force (Southern Attack Force, TF 79) transported XXIV Corps. Numerous task groups provided various gunfire (six battleships, six cruisers), air support (eighteen escort carriers), escort, and other supporting missions, a total of 738 ships.

The 1st Cavalry Division shipped out of Manus Island in the Admiralties while 24th Infantry Division and 6th Army Service Command departed from Hollandia, New Guinea on 13 October after conducting limited rehearsals. After conducting rehearsals on Maui for the Yap landing, XXIV Corps, its divisions, and the Marine V Amphibious Corps Artillery departed Hawaii in mid-September (XXIV Corps Artillery was supporting VAC in the Marianas). The Yap operation was canceled and the Corps staged at Manus Island. It departed for Leyte between 11 and 14 October rendezvousing with the X Corps convoy north of New Guinea on 17 October. A severe storm struck Leyte Gulf between 14 and 17 October, but it had abated by the time the invasion force arrived on 20 October (A-Day) with clear skies.

On A-3, prior to the invasion fleet entering Leyte Gulf, the 6th Ranger Battalion secured Homonhon and Sluan, small islands on the north side of the bay's entrance, and the north end of Dinagat Island south of the entrance. Their beaches were designated BLACK 1–3, respectively, and they landed in the morning of 18 October under poor weather conditions. After eliminating minimal opposition, beacon lights were set up to guide the fleet during its passage on the night of the 19th. Shore bombardment began on A-1. At 0930 hours, A-Day the 21st Infantry secured the Panaon Straits without opposition. This was a narrow gap between Mangatao Point on the south end of a peninsula on the east side of Sogod Bay on Leyte's south end and the north end (Liloan Point) of Panaon Island. A PT boat base was established there. H-Hour on 20 October was 1000 hours for all assault regiments.

X Corps landed on to the southeast of Tacloban between San José on the Corps' north flank and Palo on the south. The 1st Cavalry Division came ashore on Beach WHITE receiving little fire as the Japanese defense line was set up inland beyond the coastal swamps. After crossing the swamps the troopers pushed inland and secured Cataisan Peninsula jutting northward, on which the Tacloban Airfield is located. The 24th Infantry Division landed on Beach RED south of the cavalry division. Opposition here was stiff resulting in the loss of several landing craft and others being driven off. The landing was made on schedule, but was somewhat disorganized. The infantry had to negotiate marshy ground along the Palo River and its tributaries running parallel with the shore. It was in this sector that General MacArthur made his historic "I shall return" landing in the Philippines. XXIV Corps landed eleven miles to the south between San José[5] and Dulag. The 96th Infantry Division landed between San José and the Calabasag River on Beaches ORANGE and BLUE and made good progress inland even though an unexpected swamp was encountered. Light opposition was experienced, although artillery and mortar fire was heavy in some areas. The 7th Infantry Division landed straight into the town of Dulag with its Beaches VIOLET and YELLOW located between the Calabasag (north) and Daquitan (aka Marabang) (south) Rivers. A swamp on the south edge of Dulag forced one of the assault battalions to land ¼ mile from the rest of the division. Opposition was limited, but stiffened as the units moved inland. Inland swamps slowed all landing units' progress as well, but Dulag Airfield, one mile inland from the town, was soon secured.

The *4th Air Army* and IJN aircraft executed major air attacks beginning on 24 October targeting ships and supply dumps ashore. They also provided aerial cover for the Japanese convoys rushing reinforcements to Leyte. The IJN launched the first of the *SHO (Victory) Operations* with *Combined Fleet* units converging on Leyte with the aim of striking the American 3d and 7th Fleets on 25 October. The *2d Air Fleet* began arriving on Luzon prior to this. A series of four naval battles were fought between 24 and 25 October in the central Philippine waters and known as the Battles of Sibuyan Sea, Surigao Strait, Samar, and Cape Engaño. Collectively they are commonly known as the Battle for Leyte Gulf although none occurred in the gulf. Contemporary newspapers dubbed it the "Second Battle of the Philippine Sea," but only one of the actions, off Samar Island, took place there. When the engagements were over the Japanese had lost four battleships, four aircraft carriers, seven cruisers, nine destroyers, and five transports. The IJN also suffered damaged ships to include two battleships, seven cruisers, and five destroyers. U.S. Navy losses were one escort carrier sunk and three damaged and three destroyers sunk and four damaged. The third decisive naval battle had been fought by the IJN resulting in its most severe losses. The *Combined Fleet* would no longer be able to mount a significant threat against Allied naval forces. A new Japanese tactic was experienced during the Battle of Samar, which was to plague the Navy through the rest of the war. At 0740 hours, 25 October an IJN fighter intentionally crashed into the USS *Santee* (CVE-29). This was the war's first planned *kamikaze* ("divine wind") suicide attack, what the Japanese called *Tokubetsu Kogeki* ("special attack"), *Tokko* for short. These initial attacks were limited, sinking nine ships and damaging twenty-one, but would increase in the future.

Because of the distance of U.S. airfields from Leyte, limited numbers of aircraft, and the need that most carrier aircraft be committed to counter the *SHO Operation*, American air forces were unable to check the flow of Japanese reinforcements to Leyte, the *TA Operation*. Units were at first shipped piecemeal to Leyte between 23 and 30 October. The *41st Infantry, 30th Division* and four independent infantry battalions from different islands were shipped to Leyte and disembarked at Ormoc. These units moved north up the Ormoc Valley and then east toward Carigara intending to enter the Leyte Valley from the north. In the meantime XXIV Corps in the south, despite counterattacks, had pushed almost halfway across the island and into the mountains seizing the San Pablo, Burauen North and South (aka San Diego) Airfields. They would not be usable until November, however. XXIV Corps also attacked north linking up with X Corps on the 25th at the Bibahaan River. X Corps had mainly extended its beachhead north, driving north to take Tacloban, the first city to be liberated in the Philippines, on the 21st and toward the San Juanico Strait on the 24th. It soon secured both sides of the strait. The beachhead continued to grow and by 2 November most of the Leyte Valley was cleared. Japanese forces were pushed into the mountains in the south and center. The main American drive was now west along Carigara Bay toward Carigara Town.

The *1st Division (1st, 49th, 57th Infantry, 1st Field Artillery)* under Lieutenant General KATAOKA Tadasu was shipped down from Luzon with 12,000 men and landed at Ormoc on 1–2 November. On 9 November 10,000 troops of the *26th Division (12th, 13th Independent Infantry, 11th Field Artillery)* under Lieutenant General YAMAGATA Kurihanao were landed. The *35th Army Headquarters* arrived from Cebu on 2 November. These initial reinforcement successes came to an end on 10 November when five transports and their escorts were sunk at the mouth of Ormoc Bay while attempting to deliver 2,000 *26th Division* troops from Luzon. Another convoy with unknown numbers of troops was destroyed late in November. Other convoys arrived with supplies with some ships being sunk during unloading. The main body of the *68th Independent Mixed Bri-*

gade under Major General KURUSU Takeo arrived at San Isidro on the Ormoc Peninsula's upper west coast on 7 December, but its four transports were sunk after only part of the 4,000 troops disembarked. On 9–11 December, 3,000 troops of the *77th Infantry Brigade, 102d Division* under Major General KONO Takeishi unloaded at Palompon on the lower Ormoc Peninsula (many U.S. Army documents refer to this unit as the *"77th Infantry Regiment"*). The division headquarters, under Lieutenant General FUKUE Shinpei (numerous variations in the spelling of both names are encountered in references),[6] had arrived on 17 November. Regardless of the general success of deploying some 45,000 troops to reinforce the defense of Leyte, the commander of the *14th Area Army* attempted to convince the commander of the *Southern Army* the folly of the effort urging that the troops be retained for the defense of Luzon.

Between 1 November and 3 December the *1st* and *102d Divisions* counterattacked 24th Infantry Division, which had advanced to Carigara at the northwest end of the Leyte Valley. Regardless, the 24th Infantry Division seized Carigara on 2 November and began fighting into the Ormoc Valley; its 21st Infantry rejoined it on the 7th. The 32d Infantry Division landed on 14 November and relieved the exhausted 24th. In the south the 7th Infantry Division had pushed across the island and controlled the approaches to Baybay. It then began to drive north up the west coast. The 32d Infantry Division, joined by the 1st Cavalry Division (reinforced by 112th Cavalry Regiment, Special on 14 November), fought their way down the Ormoc Valley reaching Kananga about halfway down its length to link up with the 77th Infantry Division from the south on 21 December. The 77th Infantry Division had landed unopposed at Ipil on 7 December, 1-½ miles north of the 7th Infantry Division's lead elements. The 77th took over the drive north to Ormoc City, which it seized on 10 December. The 77th then pressed north up the valley to link up with X Corps as the 7th pushed across the southern end of the valley. XXIV Corps Artillery arrived from Saipan and relieved VAC Artillery on the 11th. On 25 December, elements of the 24th Infantry Division landed at Calubian near the north end of the Ormoc Peninsula and drove across to the west coast. Units of the 77th Infantry, 1st Cavalry, and 32d Infantry Divisions next pushed westward across the Ormoc Peninsula reaching the west coast on 29, 28, and 31 December, respectively.

In the XXIV Corps sector in the southern Leyte Valley the 11th Airborne Division (187th Glider, 188th and 511th Parachute Infantry)[7] under Major General Joseph M. Swing, came ashore on 18 November at Bito on Leyte's west coast on the narrow isthmus. It secured that sector with the 96th Infantry Division to its north. On 5 December the *16th* and *26th Divisions*, and *68th Independent Mixed Brigade* in the central mountains attempted a counterattack in the 96th Infantry and 11th Airborne Division sectors supported by elements of the *3d* and *4th Raiding Regiments* (battalion-size parachute units of the *2d Raiding Brigade, 1st Raiding Group*), the *WA Operation*. Some 400 Japanese paratroopers jumped onto the Buri, San Pedro, and Bayug Airfields at dusk on 6 December, but were wiped out by the 11th Airborne Division. The counterattack was defeated eliminating any serious opposition in the Leyte Valley and central mountains. The 38th Infantry Division (149th, 151st, 152d Infantry) under Major General Henry L.C. Jones arrived on 16 December to stage for a future operation, but elements were pressed into action for the mop-up. The guerrillas assisted U.S. forces through the campaign by harassing Japanese units in the rear, providing intelligence on their troop movements, and serving as scouts and guides.

On 26 December, the island was declared secure and control of mop-up operations on Leyte and Samar was transferred to 8th Army under Lieutenant General Robert L. Eichelberger. X and XXIV Corps continued their mop-up operations under 8th Army securing the west coast on 1 January 1945. Japanese remnants held out in the central mountains and the hills of the Ormoc Peninsula and mop-up continued until 8 May 1945. In January and February X Corps units cleared Samar assisted by the Americal Division, which began arriving on 24 January. Other units involved in the mop-up included the 108th Infantry (arrived 15 March) and 1st Filipino Infantry Regiments (arrived 8 February), a U.S. Army unit. Some 5,000 Japanese troops remained on Leyte and Samar. Less than 2,000 were evacuated to Cebu and other islands along with the *102d Division Headquarters* departing on 5 January. Those left behind remained under the nominal command of the *16th Division*. The *35th Army* staff was to be moved to Mindanao. Evacuated on 18 March by two vessels, they arrived at Cebu City on 24 March, two days before the Americans landed on Cebu.

Leyte was a tough campaign requiring the commitment of seven U.S. divisions for the main battle alone, more than any other campaign to date. It had a benefit that the planners had not considered. The American landing had attracted many more Japanese forces to the island than had been expected, the equivalent of more than three divisions. This resulted in a battle of attrition and the destruction of better than four divisions through direct combat, lost on reinforcement attempts, and their remnants stranded and hunted down. The *Combined Fleet* was essentially neutralized and Japanese aircraft losses were tremendous. The end result was reduced opposition during later island campaigns.

Between 20 October and 25 December 1944 the 6th Army lost over 1,600 dead and almost 4,500 wounded on Leyte. Another 1,360 were killed and 4,400 wounded during the 26 December 1944 to 8 May 1945 mop-up. Japanese sources have variously estimated that between 59,400 and 70,000 personnel, including air service and IJN, served on Leyte. The 6th and 8th Armies claimed to have killed over 80,500, one-third during the mop-up phase, and captured 830. Japanese sources estimate some 49,000 were killed to include those lost during the mop-up phase.

Naval base development soon began on Leyte (FPO SF 3201) and Samar (FPO SF 3149). The headquarters of the 7th Fleet and Philippine Sea Frontier Headquarters was located at Tolosa eleven miles south of Tacloban. Weather and terrain conditions made base construction on Leyte largely impractical. The Army established Base "K" just to the northwest of Tacloban at Anibong Point, a site rejected by the Navy. A small administrative naval station was established at Tacloban. A seaplane base was built on Jinamoc Island in San Pedro Bay five miles east of Tacloban. Most of the area Navy bases were established on Samar, which provided better terrain for construction. The main naval base was built at Guiuan on the end of a peninsula jutting eleven miles from the southeast corner of Samar into Leyte Gulf. It included an administrative center, quarters, support facilities, and two 7,000-foot runways., which were mainly used by the USAAF. Tubabao Island, lying immediately offshore to the west of the peninsula, housed a receiving station connected to Guiuan by a 515-foot bridge. A ship repair facility was built on Manicani Island eight miles west of Guiuan. A PT boat base was built near Saledo at the base of the peninsula. The long, narrow island of Calicoan runs southeast off the end of the peninsula. A large supply depot and support facilities were built there.

Prior to operations thrusting into the northern Philippines the MUSKETEER plan was refined as MUSKETEER III on 26 September 1944. Approved on 13 October, the plan envisioned seizing a foothold on southern Mindoro off the southwest coast of Luzon on 15 December. This was necessary as poor weather conditions continued to hamper airfield development and air operations on Leyte and would hinder air support of the Luzon landing scheduled for 20 December. Mindoro would also provide airfields closer to the main objective. The lightly defended main islands in the Visayas, Panay, Negroes, Masbate, Cebu, and Bohol would be secured concurrently. A total of two armies, four corps, including one Australian, and fourteen divisions (two Australian) were envisioned for this operation, although it was not necessary to commit all.

Mindoro. This seventh largest of the Philippine islands is about half the size of New Jersey covering 3,794 square miles (see Map 65). It measures approximately 110 miles from its northwest corner to its south end and is fifty-eight miles across its north end. Mindoro was code-named UNIQUE. It is separated from the south end of the main Luzon landmass by the 7-½-mile-wide Veroe (Verde) Island Passage. About twenty-four miles to the northeast of Mindoro is Marinduque Island. Panay is to the southeast, the small Calamian Group and Palawan are to the southwest across the Mindoro Strait (DENTIST, RHUMB), and Tablas and Sibuyan Islands are to the east. A broad, forested mountain range reaching elevations of over 8,000 feet runs the length of Mindoro. The highest peaks from north to south are Mounts Halcon (8,484 feet), Baco (8,160 feet), and Wood (6,230 feet). A narrow scrub-brush-covered coastal plain runs from the northeast coast around the south end and up to the northwest corner. On the east coast the plain averages fifteen miles in width, it narrows considerably on the south end, and averages ten miles in width up the southwest coast. Numerous streams and rivers flow out of the mountains across the plains. Mindoro was underdeveloped and possessed a poor road system. An unimproved track followed most of the coastline. The only improved road, Route 1, ran inland parallel with the northeast coast to avoid Lake Naujan and the swampy streams. It connected Bongabong on the lower east coast and Calapan on the northeast. A short narrow gauge railroad connected San Josè (UMERRING) and San Augustin on the lower west coast. Tracks crossed the mountains from east to west in the south, center, and northwest. San José Airfield was located inland from the lower west coast near the south end. A large number of barrios lined the coasts, but with the most populated areas being on the south end and the northeast. Mindoro's population was 117,000.

About twenty-four miles to the northeast of Mindoro across the Tablas Strait is Marinduque Island. The roughly circular island is some twenty-plus miles across covering 354 square miles. It is mountainous with its highest elevation being 3,878 feet on the south coast. A road encircles the island and tracks cross the mountains. Barrios are scattered along the coast, but most are found on the south and northwest sides. It would be an American objective as well.

Mindoro was defended by only 1,000 IJA and IJN personnel, mostly airfield service, and 200 marooned sailors. They were under the operational control of the *8th Division* on Luzon. The main combat units were two provisional rifle companies provided by the *105th Division* on Luzon and a company-size diversionary (commando) unit. They were concentrated in the vicinity of the San José Airfield near the south end.

The 6th Army formed the Western Visayan Task Force under Brigadier General William C. Dunckel, assistant commander, 24th Infantry Division to execute Operation LOVE III. The combat units were the 19th Infantry, 503d Parachute Infantry, and a battalion of the 21st Infantry. An antiaircraft group, four engineer battalions for airfield construction, a RAAF airdrome construction squadron, and service troops backed up the infantry, a total of over 16,500 men. The task force departed the east coast of Leyte aboard 7th Fleet ships on 12 December, skirted to the north of Mindanao, and approached Mindoro from the south as air strikes were conducted on Luzon. A beachhead was to be established on the lower west coast near the south end and three airfields were to be built. The western Visayas experienced less rain than Leyte and Samar where weather severely hampered construction and air operations.

Map 65
Mindoro, Philippine Islands

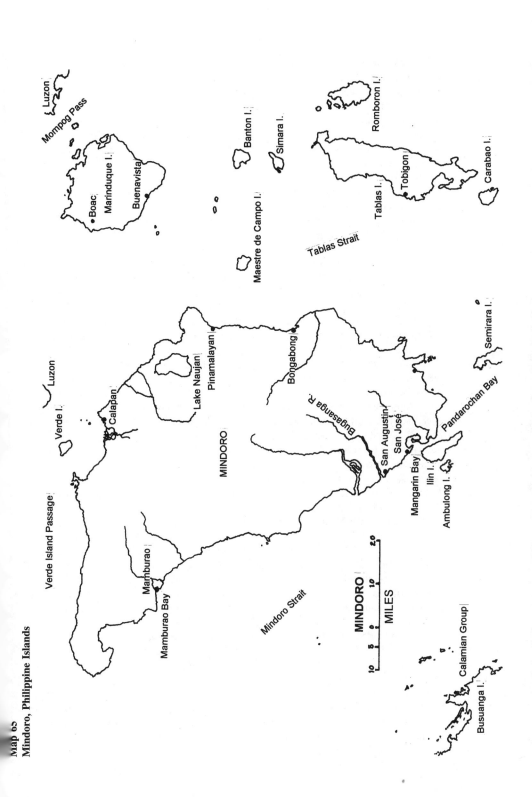

At 0730 hours, 15 December (U-Day), the 503d Parachute landed unopposed on Beaches GREEN and BLUE flanking the mouth of the Bugasanga River. The 19th Infantry came ashore on Beach WHITE to the southeast. All beaches were wide, flat, and sandy. Rain hampered the operation, but Japanese air attacks from Luzon were light, although some damage was inflicted on ships. The units moved rapidly inland with virtually no opposition to establish an outpost line up to seven miles deep and seventeen miles across. Most of the Japanese withdrew northeast and then up the east coast. Work began immediately on the three airfields: Ellmore Field on the Bugasanga River and west of the old San José Airfield, which was unusable, Hill and Atkinson Fields to the south of Ellmore and nearer to the coast. Ellmore was operational on 22 December. Murtha Field was later built to the southeast of Ellmore.

Japanese air raids continued including *kamikaze* attacks, which sank six and damaged seven ships. A Japanese cruiser-destroyer raid sortied from Baie de Camranh (Cam Ranh Bay), Indochina and attempted to attack American shipping off Mindoro and shell the beachhead on 26 December. They managed to deliver a bombardment before being driven off by Allied aircraft with the loss of a destroyer and damage to two cruisers. The rest of the 21st Infantry arrived before the end of the month. Japanese air attacks intensified until 5 January 1945 when they redirected their attention to invasion convoys bound for Luzon. The Mindoro landing attracted sufficient Japanese aircraft and about fifty were lost to reduce the air threat to the Luzon invasion. Ashore the infantry units, aided by guerrillas, patrolled and pursued Japanese stragglers. Battalion and company-size landings were conducted on the east coast on 1, 11, and 21 January and on the upper southwest coast on 2 January. The final Japanese pocket was wiped out on 24 January on the northeast coast. Some Japanese may have been evacuated, but others fled to the mountains. Ambulong, a small island off the south end of Mindoro, was secured on 6 January. A company of the 19th Infantry landed on Marinduque Island to the northeast and cleared a small pocket of resistance on the 11th; most of the Japanese had previously been destroyed by guerrillas. The remaining Japanese evacuated on the 21st.

Besides providing much-needed airfields to support the Luzon campaign, Mindoro served as a base from which to conduct diversionary operations oriented at drawing Japanese troops to southern Luzon and from which to secure other islands in the area by elements of the 19th and 21st. These included Nasugbu Point, Luzon on 29 January, Verde Island in the Verde Island Passage between Mindoro and Luzon, Lubang Island off the northwest coast of Mindoro on 28 February, and Romblon and Simara Islands to the northeast of Tablas Island on 11 and 12 February, respectively. The Navy built a PT boat base and small port facility at San José. Casuality records are aberrant because of the different units involved and included operations on other area islands, but U.S. ground forces lost approximately 100 KIA and 200 WIA on Mindoro. Japanese losses are unknown, but numbered into the hundreds with small numbers of prisoners taken.

Luzon. At this point the reader might refresh him/herself with Luzon's physical description provided earlier in this section. Japanese forces on Luzon were extensive in December 1944. Subordinate to the *Southern Army*, which returned to Saigon on 17 November, was the *14th Area Army* headquartered in Manila with 275,000 troops under the command of General YAMASHITA Tomoyuki. MacArthur's staff estimated only 152,500 troops. Forces under *14th Area Army* were a tank and six infantry divisions, most of which lacked at least a regiment lost on ships sunk en route to Luzon or units that had been sent to Leyte, two independent mixed brigades, a hodgepodge of provisional and independent units, extensive service troops, and the *4th Air Army* under Lieutenant General INANA Masazimi. Over 30,000 replacements, stranded on Luzon because of lack of shipping recovered wounded, and troops rescued from sunken transports during the reinforcement of Leyte, were formed into new units or assigned as fillers for existing units. IJN forces included the headquarters of the *Southwest Area Fleet* and the *3d Southern Expeditionary Fleet* headquartered in Manila, both under Vice Admiral OKOCHI Denshichi, along with the *31st Special Base Force* under Rear Admiral IWABUCHI Sanji. There were 31,000 IJN personnel on Luzon.

General YAMASHITA felt that Luzon could not be held with the forces available and lacked the capability to conduct a mobile defense over such a large and rugged area. He choose a static defense abandoning the Manila area and its plains, left essentially undefended Lingayen Gulf where the Japanese had landed in 1941 and was an obvious American landing site, and rejected MacArthur's concept of withdrawing to Bataan as a trap. He felt Lingayen Gulf and the Agno/Pampanga River Valley corridor to Manila were indefensible as his troops would be exposed to air attacks and the maneuver and firepower of American ground units. He decided to concentrate his forces in three mountain strongholds that the Americans could only overrun at great cost in lives, materiel, and time. Light defenses and delaying actions would be fought on Lingayen Gulf and the Agno/Pampanga Valley. Thousands of tons of supplies were moved into the mountain strongholds.

The main stronghold was in the central Cordillera Mountains of northern Luzon to the east and northeast of Lingayen Gulf and included the food-producing Cagayan Valley in the northeast. The *14th Area Army* established its headquarters at Baguio, a summer mountain resort at 5,000 feet about twenty-five miles northeast of Lingayen Gulf. The *Shobu Group* with 152,000 troops was assembled in the mountains with the *2d Tank (-), 10th (-), 19th, 23d*, and *103d Divisions, 58th Independent Mixed Brigade*, and other elements directly under YAMASHITA's command. An isosceles triangular-shaped redoubt was established and anchored on Bontoc at it north end and Baguio and Bambang fifty miles to the south, the two towns being separated by thirty-five miles. The *23d Division* with the *58th Independent Mixed Brigade* attached established light defenses on the east shore of Lingayen Gulf and would conduct a fighting withdrawal into the redoubt. The *10th Division (-)* defended the southern approaches to the redoubt. The *2d Tank (-)* and *19th (-) Divisions* would defend the Agno/Pampanga Valley as they withdrew, but were prepared to conduct counterattacks into the valley or toward Manila. The *103d Division* established scattered defenses along the upper west coast and would withdraw east into the Cagayan Valley. They and elements of the *2d Tank* and *19th Divisions* would hold the valley until supplies could be withdrawn into the redoubt. The *Tsuda Detachment* set up defenses on the east coast on Dingalan Bay and Cape Encanto. The *61st Independent Mixed Brigade* was stationed on Batan and Babuyan islands off the north coast of Luzon.

The *Shimbu Group* with 80,000 troops was under Lieutenant General YOKOYAMA Shizuo, commander of the *8th Division*. His forces included the *8th (-)* and *105th Divisions* and *31st Special Base Force*, with 16,000 IJN personnel. This group defended the south end of Luzon including Manila, the east side of Manila Bay, and the Bicol Peninsula. He was to defend the mountains east and northeast of Manila and conduct delaying actions on the Bicol Peninsula. While forces, mainly IJN, initially garrisoned Manila, the city was not to be defended after the Americans arrived.

The 30,000-man *Kembu Group* was assigned the southern portion of the Caraballo Mountains on the west side of the Agno/Pampanga Valley and the part of the valley on which Clark Field and Fort Stotsenburg were located. During the Group's preparations it was under different commanders, but by the time of the invasion the Group was placed

302   PACIFIC ISLAND GUIDE

under Major General TSUKADA Rikichi, commander of the *1st Raiding Group*, a division-level parachute and glider unit. The *Kembu Group* included the *2d Glider Infantry Regiment* of the *1st Raiding Group* (its only remaining unit), *2d Mobile Infantry (-)* of the *2d Tank Division*, and the *39th Infantry (-)* of the *10th Division* plus a larger part of the *4th Air Army* (elements were attached to the *Shobu* and *Shimbu Groups*), and 15,000 IJN antiaircraft, air service, construction troops under the commander of the airplaneless *26th Air Flotilla*, Rear Admiral SUGIMOTO Ushie.

Regiments and brigades assigned to these divisions and forces were as follows:

Shobu Group/14th Area Army

2d tank Division (3d Tank Brigade 2d Mobile Infantry), Lieutenant General IWANAKA Yoshiharu.

10th Division (10th, 63d Infantry, 10th Field Artillery, 39th Infantry), Lieutenant General OKAMOTO Yasuyuki.

19th Division (73d, 75th, 76th Infantry, 25th Mountain Artillery), Lieutenant General YOSHIHARU Kane.

23d Division (64th, 71st, 72d Infantry, 17th Field Artillery), Lieutenant General NISHIYAMA Fukutaro.

58th Independent Mixed Brigade, Major General SATO Bunzo.

103d Division (79th, 80th Infantry Brigades), Lieutenant General MURAOKA Yoshitake.

Tsuda Detachment (11th Independent Infantry, 26th Division), Colonel TSUDA Tsukada.

Shimbu Group

8th Division (8th Field Artillery, 17th, 31st Infantry, -5th Infantry on Leyte), Lieutenant General YOKOYAMA Shizuo.

105th Division (81st, 82d Infantry Brigades), Lieutenant General TSUDA Yoshitake.

The Japanese estimated that the main American landings would occur at either Lingayen Gulf or Batangas on the south end of the main Luzon landmass. The Batangas area provided a good road network and was a shorter distance from Manila to the north than the city was from Lingayen. The capture of Mindoro immediately across the narrow Verde Island Passage from Batangas and the recent diversionary operations in the area convinced many Japanese staff officers of the Batangas option by mid-December. They further estimated the landing would occur in mid-January. On 19 December the *14th Area Army* began deploying units in accordance with the defense plan and additional units were deployed in the south in the event of a landing at Batangas. It was not until the invasion convoy was off of Bataan that a landing at Lingayen Gulf was confirmed.

Operation MIKE I, the main 6th Army landing in Lingayen Gulf (SARTORIAL), Luzon (SATANIC, later WHITEWASH), was scheduled for 20 December 1944 as was LOVE II, a supporting landing at the mouth of the Cagayan River on Luzon's north coast. LOVE II, with the I Australian Corps and its 7th and 9th Divisions, was canceled. The 8th Army's planned 10–20 January supporting landing in Dingalan Bay on the east-central coast with the 33d Infantry Division and 158th Infantry and 503d Parachute Infantry Regiments was also canceled. Eight divisions were assigned to 6th Army under General Walter Krueger for the Luzon assault. The staging areas for the assigned units were widely scattered and are included in the following order of battle.

I Corps, Major General Innis P. Swift:

6th Infantry Division (1st, 20th, 63d Infantry), assault, Sansapor, Major General Edwin D. Patrick.

43d Infantry Division (103, 169th, 172d Infantry), assault, Aitape, Major General Leonard F. Wing.

32d Infantry Division (126th, 127th, 128th Infantry), follow-on, Leyte, Major General William H. Gill.

33d Infantry Division (123d, 130th, 136th Infantry), follow-on, Finschhafen-Toem, Major General Percy W. Clarkson.

XIV Corps, Major General Oscar W. Griswold:

40th Infantry Division (108th, 160th, 185th Infantry), assault, New Britain, Major General Rapp Brush.

37th Infantry Division (129th, 145th, 158th Infantry), assault, Bougainville, Major General Robert S. Beightler.

1st Cavalry Division, Special (1st Brigade—5th, 12th Cavalry, 2d Brigade—7th, 8th Cavalry), follow-on, Leyte, Major General Verne D. Mudge.

112th Cavalry Regiment, Special, follow-on, Leyte, Brigadier General Julian W. Cunningham.

6th Army Reserve:

25th Infantry Division (25th, 35th, 161st Infantry), Nouméa, Major General Charles L. Mullins, Jr.

158th Infantry Regiment, Noemfoor, Brigadier General Hanford MacNider, Jr.

Other major 6th Army units included the 4th Engineer Special Brigade, 68th Antiaircraft Artillery Brigade, and 13th Armored Group. Task Force 77, the Luzon Attack Force, was provided by the 7th Fleet with 7th Amphibious Force (TF 78) transporting I Corps and 3d Amphibious Force (TF 79) carrying XIV Corps. The many units assembled in Leyte Gulf arriving from their far-flung staging areas between 1 and 5 January. There were no fewer than twelve task groups supporting the operations. Among these were a bombardment force of six battleships and six cruisers and twenty-one escort carriers for close air support. The 3d Fleet would provide additional carrier support attacking targets, especially airfields, throughout the Philippines and elsewhere.

The postponement of the Mindoro landing had a corresponding impact on the Lingayen Gulf landing, originally set for 20 December. The landing, MIKE I, was moved to 9 January 1945 (S-Day) taking advantage of favorable tide and moon conditions. Lead elements of the invasion force departed Leyte Gulf on 2 January with the rest of the task groups sailing by the 6th. The forty-mile-long convoy sailed west north of Mindoro, then northwest skirting the west side of the Visayas. Japanese air attacks on the convoy, to include *kamikazes*, began on the 4th resulting in one ship sunk and twenty-four damaged before the fleet entered Lingayen Gulf. By 13 January a total of twenty-four ships were sunk and sixty-seven damaged by *kamikazes*. The preliminary bombardment of the landing areas on the south end of the gulf began on 6 January and continued even though there was no response from the enemy, no Japanese were seen, and Filipinos were seen attempting to organize a welcoming parade. The landing forces entered the gulf at 0400 hours, 9 January. H-Hour was set at 0930 hours; the landings would be completely unopposed except for the mounting air attacks on the fleet.

S-Day was clear, but lightly overcast, with light surf and winds, and hot—much different than experienced by the Japanese in December 1941. The landing beaches were level and free of natural or manmade obstacles, but narrow. Inland the coastal plain too was level, but there were numerous swamps and rivers and streams edged with swamps and these edged with rice paddies. There were also large areas of salt evaporators bordering some streams, shallow, dyked containment ponds in which seawater was evaporated by sunlight and the salt recovered. There was a well-developed road network, however, linked to the roads heading south through the Agno/Pampanga River Valley corridor to Manila 120 miles to the south. The valley though was flanked by foothills, then forested mountains. There was only one small airstrip in the area located on the west side of Dagupan. Several towns and barrios were scattered along the coast and inland.

I Corps came ashore on the eastern portion of the gulf's south end centered on San Fabian, a small town beside the mouth of the Patalan River. The 43d Infantry Division landed on Beaches WHITE 1 and 2 to the east of San Fabian, and WHITE 3 directly in front of the town. To the west of San Fabian the 6th Infantry Division landed on Beaches BLUE 1 and 2. The 43d Infantry Division's mission included securing the grass-covered terraced ridge lines progressively rising in steps from 100 to 600 feet on the east flank. Six Japanese battalions were dug-in in in-depth defensive positions there.

The boundary between I and XIV Corps was the wide mouth of the Dugupan River; then from the Dugupan Town (APPREHEND) it followed a road inland. XIV Corps' 37th Infantry Division landed on Beaches CRIMSON and YELLOW to the east of the Lingayen Airfield while the 40th Infantry Division landed on Beaches GREEN and ORANGE directly in front of the airfield and just to the east of Lingayen Town. Inland swamps made for slow going, but there were no enemy units in the XIV Corps' sector.

I Corps's movement south was slowed by the resistance on its north flank, but XIV Corps made good headway until reaching the Clark Field complex (eleven airfields) on 23 January. The *Kembu Group* delayed the advance for a week and Clark was not in American hands until the end of the month. The 1st Cavalry Division arrived on the 26th to reinforce XIV Corps. Its 1st Brigade was mounted aboard trucks and with armor support drove toward Manila while the rest of the division mopped up in its wake. The brigade reached the northern outskirts of Manila on 3 February.

Operation MIKE VI was commenced on 29 January (X-Day) when XI Corps, under Major General Charles P. Hall, landed at San Antonio above Subic Bay twenty-five miles to the northwest of Bataan Peninsula. This landing is commonly referred to as the Zambales Landing after the province it occurred in. XI Corps and its 38th Infantry Division (149th, 151st, 152d Infantry) under Major General Henry L.C. Jones, and reinforced by the 34th Infantry from the 24th Infantry Division, staged from Leyte. Guerrillas reported the landing area free of enemy, the bombardment was canceled, and the landing made unopposed. The 38th Infantry Division was held up by a Japanese force at Zigzag Pass northeast of Olongapo. It required almost two weeks for the defenses to be reduced resulting in the replacement of the 38th Infantry Division commander by Brigadier General William C. Chase. XI Corps fell in on the west flank of XIV Corps and cut off Japanese forces on Bataan. Some of these evacuated to the mainland across Manila Bay and to Corregidor.

To reinforce the drive to Manila yet another amphibious assault was executed on 31 January as part of Operation MIKE VI. The 11th Airborne Division (187th, 188th Glider Infantry) under Major General Joseph M. Swing, staging from Leyte, landed at Nasugary Bay just to the south of the entrance to Manila Bay at 0815 hours without opposition. The Division pushed inland against light resistance with the aim of approaching Manila fifty-five miles to the north. The Division's 511th Parachute Infantry, 1,455 men, flying from Mindoro, parachuted on to Tagaytay Ridge at 0815 hours, 3 February, but some troops were misdropped five miles east-northeast of the intended drop zone. The 11th Airborne fought its way to the southern outskirts of Manila by 5 February.

Considering Manila (GRANNY, NIRVANA, STEAMROLLER) to be indefensible, General

YAMASHITA ordered the *Shimbu Group* to destroy bridges and key installations and evacuate the city. Admiral IWABUCHI Sanji ordered his 16,000 troops to remain and fought a tenuous battle lasting from 4 February to 4 March. Manila was one of the largest cities in the Pacific region and much of the city center was comprised of heavily constructed modern concrete buildings intended to resist earthquakes. A large, massively constructed Spanish fortress area near the port, the Intramuros, was defended by the *Manila Naval Defense Force*, the last stronghold in the city to fall. The "Walled City," as the Intramuros was known, had modern government buildings built throughout it. Massive artillery was required to blast the defenders out of their strongpoints, but air strikes were restricted. Much of the city was devastated to include many landmarks and its infrastructure shattered. Shortly before the city's fall MacArthur declared the Commonwealth of the Philippines to be reestablished. XIV Corps lost over 1,000 dead and 5,500 wounded. As many as 100,000 Filipinos may have died in Manila, with thousands wounded, many being murdered by retreating Japanese. About 16,000 Japanese troops, mostly IJN, were killed inside and on the outskirts of Manila. Some forty miles south of Manila was the Los Baños Internment Camp with 2,150 U.S. civilians. Fearing the Japanese might murder the civilians, 130 men of Company A, 1st Battalion, 511th Parachute Infantry jumped onto a drop zone immediately outside the camp on 23 February. The rest of the battalion landed by amphibian tractor from Laguna de Bay. In less than twenty minutes all of the 250 Japanese guards were dead with no loss to the American civilians and one paratrooper died and one was wounded.

On 14 February the 151st Infantry (South Force) boarded landing craft at Olongapo on Subic Bay and landed at Mariveles on the south end of Bataan. The 1st and 149th Infantry (North Force) swept down Bataan's east coast beginning on the 12th. At Pilar the North Force split with part of it moving south to link up with the South Force at Limay on the 18th. Another element moved across the peninsula's central east-to-west Pilar-Bagac Road and linked up with another element of the South Force at Bagac on the 21st. On 16 February the 1st Battalion, 503d Parachute Infantry parachuted on to Corregidor with its drop zone on Topside while 3d Battalion, 34th Infantry assaulted the Rock's south coast landing at Bottomside. Over 2,000 U.S. troops initially assaulted Corregidor, which was defended by 5,670 Japanese, mainly IJN troops. The first lift of paratroopers began landing at 0833 hours, 16 February having staged out of Mindoro. The amphibious assault hit the Beach BLACK at 1028 hours followed by the second lift of paratroopers at 1240 hours. Two additional battalions landed from the sea the next day. Corregidor was cleared and back in American hands at 1600 hours, 26 February. MacArthur returned to Corregidor on 2 March, nine days short of three years from when he was ordered to leave, and the American flag was again raised on the former Spanish flagpole. American losses were 445 KIA, 560 WIA, and 340 injured by the hazards of the small rubbled drop zone and other accidents. There were thirty-five Japanese prisoners taken; the rest of the defense force was destroyed. The other Manila Bay fortified islands were cleared between 27 March and 16 April by elements of the 38th Infantry Division.

While the Battle for Manila continued, XIV Corps began an offensive to clear southern Luzon on 20 February by first attacking eastward from Manila. On 14 March XIV Corps was relieved by XI Corps and the *Shimbu Group* was driven south down the Bicol Peninsula. Although XI Corps took over operations, the in-place divisions continued to operate in the south. Divisions fighting in the south were the 1st Cavalry, 11th Airborne, 6th, 38th, and 43d Infantry Divisions. To this was added a significant guerrilla force known as U.S. Army Forces in the Philippines, Northern Luzon (USAFIP[NL]) under the command of Colonel Russell W. Volckmann. Well organized, it contained 20,000 men organized into the 11th, 14th, 15th, 66th, and 121st Infantry Regiments along with service elements. Supported by U.S. artillery battalions, they fought as conventional units alongside U.S. units. Separated from the *14th Area Army*, the *Shimbu Group* was re-designated the *41st Army* in March 1944 under Lieutenant General YOKOYAMA Shizuo (former commander of the *8th Division*). Two small amphibious landings were made on the peninsula to cut off retreating Japanese. On 1 April, the 158th Infantry landed at Legaspi in Albay Gulf on the lower east end of the Bicol. On 27 April the 5th Cavalry landed at Pasacao on the west-central coast. Southern Luzon was declared secure on 31 May.

I Corps was assigned the responsibility of clearing northern Luzon and began opera-tions against the bulk of the *Shobu Group* on 21 February. Engagements were fought in the valleys, hills, and ridges until the end of the war as the Japanese withdrew deeper into the mountains more intent on survival than on defending the island. The 6th Army was relieved by the 8th Army for the mop-up of northern Luzon on 30 June with the in-place divisions generally remaining. Divisions fighting on northern Luzon included the 25th, 32d, and 33d Infantry Divisions.[8] The guerrillas played a valuable role in clearing northern Luzon with many units undertaking direct combat action in addition to their normal intelligence-collecting and guide duties. Approximately 61,100 troops were surrendered by General YAMASHITA to Major General William Gill commanding the 32d Infantry Division on 3 September at Baguio, the former southwest corner anchor of the *Shobu Group's* mountain stronghold.

Casualties on Luzon were heavy on both sides. U.S. Army losses were 8,310 KIA and 29,560 WIA. Over 93,400 U.S. troops suffered nonbattle injuries, disease, and illness, the highest nonbattle casualty rate experienced by the United States in any World War II campaign. An estimated 205,535 Japanese died on Luzon including those who suc-cumbed to disease and starvation while 9,050 were taken prisoner prior to the surrender. Japan's materiel losses were significant as well. In October 1944 the *4th Air Army* had 300 aircraft on-hand in the Philippines. Between October 1944 and January 1945 it received 2,300 additional aircraft. In mid-January thirty aircraft remained to be evacuated. This does not include the hundreds of IJN aircraft lost.

U.S. naval base construction began soon after Manila fell. The existing base at Cavite was refurbished (FPO SF 954). At nearby Sangley Point (FPO SF 961) a 5,000-foot airfield was built and the seaplane base expanded. A headquarters complex for the 7th Fleet was built on the Manila waterfront along with a communications center. Construc-tion on a large advance base began at Olongapo on Subic Bay (FPO SF 3002). A sub-marine base, ship repair facilities, amphibious training base, supply depot, and support facilities were built. The base remained in operation as the U.S. Navy's largest Pacific base after Pearl Harbor until 1991 when the Philippine Senate rejected the renewal of the American lease on Subic Bay Navy Base and the United States left the following year. The former base has since developed into a successful free-trade zone. The Army established three major logistics bases: Base "M" at Lingayen Gulf, Base "X" in Manila, and Base "R" at Batangas. The Clark Field complex was developed into a large air base by the USAAF. Other USAAF fields were constructed at Del Carmen, San Franando, and San Marcelino to the south of Clark; Nielson and Nichols on the edge of Manila; and Lipa and Batangas on the south end of the main Luzon landmass. Clark continued as a major Air Force base until 1991 when Mount Pinatubo erupted forcing the base to be abandoned by the United States.

Visayas. The Visayan Islands (INTEGER) comprise the central portion of the Phil-ippines and consist of the main islands of Palawan, Samar, Negros, Panay, Cebu, Masbate, Bohol, and Jolo. Operations to clear the central Philippines began before Luzon was secured. These operations were intended to secure airfields to support future operations into the East Indies and free Filipinos in the area from the Japanese. The VICTOR operations were part of the larger plan MONTCLAIR III, which included operations to secure the East Indies scheduled for May. The VICTOR operations began at the end of February 1945 and were completed in April. The 8th Army under Lieutenant General Robert L. Eichelberger with X Corps, Americal, 24th, 31st, 40th, and 41st Infantry Divisions, 2d and 3d Engineer Special Brigades, and 503d Parachute Infantry Regiment was responsible for the Visayas and Mindanao. Also at 8th Army's disposal were large and well-developed guerrilla forces on the larger islands.

Japanese forces were under the control of the *35th Army* commanded by Lieutenant General SUSUKI Sosaku. He was succeeded by Lieutenant General MOROZUMI Gyosaku, commanding the *30th Division* on Mindanao, after his death on 14 June. The *35th Army's* control of units in this area was tenuous at best after the staff evacuated Leyte in late December 1944. Japanese units defending these islands included the *30th, 100th,* and half of the *102d Divisions, 2d Air Division,* the *54th, 55th,* and *77th Independent Mixed Brigades,* and smaller units plus the *33d Base Force* and other IJN elements. There were over 102,000 Japanese including 53,000 IJA combat and service troops, 19,400 IJA *Air Service,* 15,000 IJN, and 14,800 noncombatants and civilians.

Palawan. Lying outside of the main grouping of the Visayas, Palawan (UNCEASING) stretches to the southwest toward Borneo with Mindoro lying 120 miles to its northeast. Situated between Palawan and Mindoro is the Calamian Group with Busuanga and Gulion Islands being the largest in the group. Palawan defines the north side of the Sulu Sea. The South China Sea flanks its northwest side. The elongated island is 270 miles long northeast to southwest with a width of fifteen to thirty miles to cover an area of 4,500 square miles, making it the fifth largest. About one-third of the island's length from its northeast end is Honda Bay on the southeast side creating a seven-mile-wide isthmus. A mountain chain runs the length of the island with its highest elevation being 5,850 feet near the southwest end. Most of the population is found on the northeastern one-third of the island. The island was underdeveloped and lacked improved roads. An unimproved track followed the coastline and a few tracks crossed the island. Palawan essentially runs perpendicular to the rest of the islands in the Philippines resulting in its southwest side catching the full brunt of the June-through-September southwest monsoon.

The Japanese had two airstrips and a seaplane base at Puerto Princesa on the south side of Honda Bay on the east-central coast. They served as a way station for air and small-craft traffic between Borneo and the Philippines. The island's long coastline provided hidden anchorages for a sheltered passage between Borneo and the Philippines. The Puerto Princesa area was defended only by two detached companies of the *174th Independent Infantry Battalion* on southern Negros plus the *131st Airfield Battalion.* The *174th's* parent unit was the *78th Infantry Brigade* on Cebu. The battalion commander, Captain KOJIMA Chokichi, was the senior officer on Palawan. Detachments of these companies garrisoned Dumaran Island off the northeast end of Palawan and Conon and Pandanan Islands off the southwest end. About 1,200 of the 1,750 IJA and IJN personnel on Palawan were concentrated at Puerto Princesa. Of these 900 were IJA *Air Service* and 250 IJN personnel. In February most of the personnel moved to the 4,220-foot Thumb Peak ten miles northwest of Puerto Princesa and prepared defenses.

The 8th Army was assigned the task of securing the occupied islands bordering the Sula Sea in early February. Operation VICTOR III was executed by the much-reinforced 186th Infantry, 41st Infantry Division numbering 8,150 men under Brigadier General

Harold Haney, assistant division commander. Staging from Mindoro on 26 February and transported by the Palawan Attack Group (Task Group 78.2), the regiment landed at Puerto Pincesa at 0850 hours on the 28th (H-Day). The town is located on a peninsula enclosing the east side of a bay bearing the same name as the town. The landing beaches were on the south end of the peninsula adjacent to the two airfields. No Japanese were found in the area. Between 3 and 8 March three Japanese strongpoints were reduced in the mountains. Dumaran Island was seized on 9 March. Through the month of March U.S. patrols pursued the Japanese though the mountains of central Palawan as they attempted to avoid contact. Buguanga and Conon islands off the northeast end were secured between 9 and 17 April while Balabac and Pandanan Islands off the southwest end were seized between 12 and 21 April. Airfield construction at Puerto Princesa was slow because of poor soil conditions, even when the 4,500-foot Japanese concrete runway was extended. A field was not operational until 20 March. The last element of the 186th Infantry was relieved by the 368th Infantry, 93d Infantry Division (Colored) in early July. American losses were ten KIA and forty-five WIA. The Japanese lost at least 890 dead and twenty prisoners.

The seizure of Mindanao and the Sulu Archipelago, discussed below, occurred through March and May. The Southern Visayas, Panay, Cebu, Negros, and Bohol, were the next phase of the VICTOR operations. VICTOR was split into two related operations because of geographic compartmentalization created by the north-to-south mountain chain on Negros. The area was divided into Panay and northwest quarter of Negros to the west, VICTOR I, and the remainder of Negros, Cebu, and Bohol to the east, VICTOR II. VICTOR I and II's goals were to secure these islands, and coupled with the previous occupation of Leyte and Samar, cut off Japanese forces remaining in the southern Philippines.

Panay. Panay (DEVOTION) lies immediately to the northwest of Negros and is described earlier in this section. There were 2,500 troops assigned to the reinforced *170th Independent Infantry Battalion* of the *77th Infantry Brigade* under Lieutenant Colonel TITSUKA Ryoichi based at Iloilo on the lower southeast coast, the principal city. Among these were over 1,000 airfield service troops and 400 civilians. Half of the garrison had been sent to Leyte in October 1944. The Japanese operated three airfields on the island's southern portion, San Fernando, Santa Barbara (TIRING), and Mandurriao with Loctugan on the north coast. In December, it was considered to withdraw the Panay garrison to Negros, but U.S. air interdiction and lack of shipping made this impractical. Instead, the Japanese defense plan realistically called for a limited defense of Iloilo followed by a withdrawal into the western mountains to fight a guerrilla war, a plan similar to that accomplished by the U.S.-Fil defenders almost three years earlier. A series of strongpoints were established in the Bolo area (where the machete-like tool evolved) in the foothills and delaying positions set up on their approaches in the Jalauo River Valley. A detached company defended San José de Buenavista on the lower west coast.

The 40th Infantry Division (185th Infantry, -108th and 160th Infantry for the Panay operation) under Major General Rapp Brush, staged from Lingayen Gulf, Luzon on 15 March aboard the Panay Attack Group (Task Group 78.3), without benefit of a rehearsal. The 185th Infantry landed unopposed at 0900 hours, 18 March (G-Day) at Tigbauan twelve miles west of Iloilo. The assault waves were greeted by a formal parade of guerrilla units in starched khakis. The 22,500 guerrillas, half of whom were armed, would be of great aid to the 40th Infantry Division as they already controlled three-quarters of the island. Iloilo was secured on 20 March, but the Japanese had destroyed 70 percent of the third largest commercial center in the Philippines. The Japanese rear guard broke through guerrilla roadblocks to rejoin the main force in the interior. Elements of the

185th Infantry cleared Gumimaras Island between 20 and 23 March; the few defenders fled into the hills. A small Japanese detachment on tiny adjacent Inampulugan Island was wiped out on the 22nd. There were minor skirmishes between the Japanese and U.S. guerrilla forces in April and May, but no major effort was made to decisively engage the Japanese. The Jalauo River Valley was cleared to the north coast and the north and south coasts patrolled while the guerrillas secured most of the island's interior and other coastal areas. Security of the Panay was turned over to the guerrillas in late June. To that date the United States had lost twenty KIA and fifty WIA. Japanese losses were almost 1,000 dead, lost mainly to the guerrillas. Approximately 1,560 Japanese troops surrendered at the war's end.

Negros. Negros (BAMBI), lying between Panay and Cebu, is approximately 140 miles long north to south, thirty-five miles across its north end, twenty-two miles across its center at the narrowest point, and fifty miles across its widest in the south. It covers 4,903 square miles making it the fourth largest island in the Philippines and just slightly smaller than the state of Connecticut. The island's large southern lob is almost entirely occupied by mountains over 4,000 feet high with a very narrow coastal strip. A chain of over 4,000-foot-high mountains runs up the east coast allowing for a three-to-ten-mile-wide coastal plain on the west coast and only a mile of less wide strip on the east. The rugged mountains rise on the northern portion to 8,087 feet at Canlaon Peak (contemporary references report the highest elevation as 6,243 feet). The western coastal plain is planted with sugarcane fields and rise paddies. Small rivers and streams flow out of the mountains across the coastal plains and strips with most being on the west-central and upper west coat. The largest river is the Ilog on the central-west coast. It and its tributaries cleft deeply into the southern mountains and create a large swamp area at its mouth. While barrios were scattered along the coasts, the majority of the population lived west-central and upper west coast and the north end. An improved road ran around most of the island, but its southwest end was served with an unimproved track. There were several short, narrow-gauge railroad lines serving the island's sugarcane industry, mainly on the upper west coast.

Northern Negros was defended by the *77th Infantry Brigade, 102d Division* under Major General KONO Takehi. Three of the Brigade's five infantry battalions were detached to defend other islands, however. There were numerous service and support units, which had been reorganized into combat units. Northern Negros had been a major airfield complex for the *2d Air Division.* There were seven airfields operated by the *6th Air Sector Unit* on the upper west and north end, Silay, Manalpa, Bacolod, Tanzaa, Talisay, Fabrica, and Salavia plus Binalbagan (IJN) with Dumaguete near the south end. In all there were almost 12,000 troops on Negros, but only some two-thirds of the troops were armed and stocks of supplies and ammunition were low, contrary to the situation found on most defended islands, which were initially well stocked. The Japanese left rear-guard detachments on the north and upper west coast to blow up the bridges and delay the Americans. As much equipment and supplies as possible were moved into a northern mountain stronghold. Prior to the American landing the guerrillas controlled most of the southern and central portions of the island.

American operations on northern Negroes were part of the VICTOR I operation in conjunction with the seizure of Panay. It was also referred to as Negros Occidental after the province that occupied the western and northern portions of the island. The 40th Infantry Division (-108th Infantry) on Panay departed Iloilo on 28 March aboard Task Group 78.3. The 185th Infantry landed unopposed at Pulupandan at 0900 hours on the 29th (G-Day) on Negros' upper west coast across from Guimaras Island. The 160th

Infantry soon followed and units spread to the north and east. The American attack had been so swift that none of the bridges had been blown by the Japanese. By 8 April the Japanese rear guards had withdrawn to the mountain stronghold and guerrillas hurried Japanese detachments to the southwest of the stronghold. The 503d Parachute Infantry, which had been prepared to conduct a parachute reinforcement, came ashore after garrisoning Corregidor on the 7th and was attached to the 40th Infantry Division. The three regiments launched an attack on the stronghold on the 9th. The Japanese defenders had excellent observation of the grass-and-brush-covered hills around their stronghold and were able to resist until overrun on 2 June. A considerable number of Japanese were able to flee into the mountains and they had been successful in tying down a division for almost two months. While the fighting was taking place in the northern mountains, the Division's reconnaissance troop followed the east coastal road almost to Dumaguete near the southeast end. There it linked up with the 164th Infantry after it landed on 26 April (see below). The 40th Infantry Division returned to Panay in late June while 503d Parachute remained to garrison Negros and mop up until the end of the war.

Approximately 4,000 Japanese were killed by 9 June. Another 3,350 died in mopping-up actions and of disease and starvation. About 250 had been taken prisoner. At the end of the war 6,150 remaining Japanese surrendered. U.S. losses had been 370 KIA and 1,025 WIA with most lost during the April and May reduction of the mountain redoubt.

Southeastern Negros, what was known as Negros Oriental after the province, was assigned to VICTOR II forces, which were in the process of securing Cebu to the east. The Americal Division's 164th Infantry (-) staged from Talisay on Cebu and landed unopposed at Looc five miles north of Dumaguete on the southeast coast on 26 April. Contact was made with the 40th Infantry Division patrol from the north immediately after landing. Dumaguete was mostly burned by the withdrawing Japanese, but it was quickly secured.

The Japanese garrison on southern Negros was under a separate chain of command from those forces in the north. The understrength *174th Independent Infantry Battalion (-)*, air service personnel, and 150 marooned sailors in the area totaled 1,300 troops. They were under the command of Lieutenant Colonel OIE Satoshi and subordinate to the *78th Infantry Brigade, 102d Division* headquartered on Cebu. The Japanese dug in inland among the foothills west of Dumaguete. The Japanese repulsed the first American and guerrilla attacks on their main stronghold. On 6 May attacks were resumed and the stronghold was overrun on the 28th. A final strongpoint was reduced between 7 and 12 June and the south end of the island was declared secure on the 14th. The area's security was turned over to the guerrillas on 20 June when the 164th Infantry departed. U.S. losses were thirty-five KIA and 180 WIA. The Japanese lost 530 dead and fifteen prisoners. At the end of the war 880 Japanese surrendered.

Cebu. Cebu (BANZAI, OXYGEN), immediately off the east coast of Negros, was previously described in this section. Cebu was to be secured under Operation VICTOR II by the Americal Division (132d, 182d Infantry, -164th Infantry) under Major General William H. Arnold. The 14,900-man division staged from Leyte aboard Cebu Attack Group (Task Group 78.2) on 24 March after conducting rehearsals there.

Cebu was the most strongly defended island in the Visayas with 14,500 troops, most of whom were concentrated in and around Cebu City on the east-central coast. Many of the personnel, however, were service and support troops as Cebu had been the *35th Army's* main supply base supporting the defense of Leyte and then its attempted evacuation. Included were 1,700 civilians. The main IJA headquarters on Cebu was the *102d Division* under Lieutenant General FUKUE Shinpei.[9] The division's combat units though

consisted only of the *78th Infantry Brigade Headquarters* under Major General MA-
JOME Takeo and the *173d Independent Infantry Battalion*. The rest of the division was
either detached to garrison other islands or had been lost on Leyte. The various service
elements and large numbers of transport and shipping units were reorganized as combat
units. The *33d Special Base Force*, under Rear Admiral HARADA Kaku, and its *36th
Guard Unit* were also included in the strength. Some 1,700 troops held a position in
northern Cebu under Lieutenant General KATAOKA Tadasu, commander of the *1st
Division*, whose headquarters had arrived for Leyte. These *1st Division* elements were
obstinately called the *1st, 49th,* and *57th Infantry Regiments*, but were each less than
battalion-sized. The *102d Division* stronghold was prepared near Guadeloupe in the foothills to the northwest of Cebu City. The Japanese operated only one airfield on Cebu,
Lahug, two miles north of Cebu City.

The American Division came ashore at 0828 hours, 26 March (E-Day) at Talisay four
miles southwest of Cebu City. The 182d Infantry landed in the southwest part of the
town and the 132d Infantry on the northeast edge over wide sand and gravel beaches
faced with palms. Mines created a great deal of confusion before the units moved inland
to the north and northeast. Cebu City was secured the next day and the day after that
Mactan Island two miles across Cebu Harbor was cleared as was Lahug Airfield. The
outer defenses of the Japanese stronghold were cleared by 2 April. The stronghold was
immediately attacked and was not cleared until the 18th. On 10 April the 164th Infantry
arrived at Cebu, but only briefly participated in the fight between 12 and 20 April. It
then prepared for its southeastern Negros operation and departed on the 25th (see above).
The stronghold fell sooner than expected as the Japanese decided to withdraw to the
north extricating about 7,500 troops. U.S. forces pursued as the *102d Division* and IJN
remnants attempted to link up with the *1st Division* element in the north. Flanking landings were made along the coast to cut off the Japanese withdrawal. The first week of
May saw engagements with the *1st Division* in the north. In early June the two U.S.
regiments were joined by two newly equipped guerrilla regiments and soon shattered the
Japanese resistance. The survivors withdrew deeper into the mountains and were still
harassed by the guerrillas. The American Division disengaged on 20 June to assemble at
Cebu City and prepare for the invasion of Japan. The guerrillas continued the mop-up
and patrol. The U.S. Army built the large logistics Base "S" on the island.

An estimated 5,550 Japanese died through combat, disease, and starvation on Cebu
between the landing and the war's end and 405 prisoners were taken. In August 1945
8,550 Japanese surrendered. American losses were 420 dead, 1,730 wounded, and over
8,000 nonbattle casualties, a large percentage of whom were disabled by hepatitis and
malaria.

Bohol. Bohol (MERRYMAID) is situated fifteen miles off the lower east coast of Cebu
separated by the Bohol Strait. On its north is the Camotes Sea, the Mindanao Sea is to
the south. Leyte is twenty miles to the northeast across the Canigao Channel. The oval-
shaped island is the tenth largest of the Philippines, covering 1,534 square miles. It is
seventy-two miles wide from northeast to southwest and thirty-seven miles across the
center from north to south. Most of the island is covered by low mountains, the highest
being 2,838 feet, allowing only a thin coastal strip around most of the south, southeast,
and northwest coasts. The north and northeast coats are edged by wider plains. Rivers
and streams run out of the mountains at roughly even intervals around the island. The
largest river, the Inabanga, flows into the sea on the upper northwest coast, but provides
only a small valley. The smaller Sampelangon and Loay Rivers on the southwest end
provide larger valleys. An improved road circled the entire island and a number of tracks

crossed the mountains. Panglao Island lies less than one mile off the southwest end and Lapinin Island the same distance off the northeast side.

Bohol was defended by 330 troops of two companies detached from the *174th Independent Infantry Battalion, 78th Infantry Brigade*. The parent battalion was on southeast Negros. There were no Japanese airfields on Bohol. Guerrillas reported that the Japanese had withdrawn into the hills inland from the south-central coast near Cambuyo on the Manaba River.

The 3d Battalion, 164th Infantry, Americal Division staged from Leyte to secure Bohol. The battalion landed unopposed at Tagbiliran on 11 April, secured by guerrillas, on the island's southwest end. One company followed the coast around to the northwest side of the island and met no resistance. The rest of the battalion moved east along the south coast and made contact with enemy elements seven to eight miles inland from the south-central coast on the 15th. An enveloping attack was made on the 17th with action lasting through the 20th. The last effective resistance was eliminated on the 23rd as the Japanese withdrew north across the island. The 3d Battalion, 164th Infantry departed on 7 May leaving a detachment of the 21st Reconnaissance Troop and the guerrillas to mop up.

Through the first week of May the Japanese had lost 105 dead and fifteen prisoners. Only fifty surrendered at the end of the war, the rest having been killed by the guerrillas or died of disease. Americans losses were seven KIA and fourteen WIA.

The conquest of Mindanao was to be conducted in two operations, VICTOR IV on the western Zamboanga Peninsula and the adjacent Sulu Archipelago beginning in mid-March 1945 and VICTOR V on the southwest coast of the island's main landmass commencing in mid-April. Besides these two major landings a number of supporting and flanking landings would be executed in what proved to be a very complex series of operations. The goal of VICTOR IV was to secure the Basilan Strait off the end of the Zamboanga Peninsula as well as the numerous passages through the Sulu Archipelago into the Sulu Sea. This was considered to be one of the main approaches to the Philippines and mainland Asia from the Southwest Pacific. VICTOR V's goal was to defeat the significant Japanese forces on Mindanao and free the island.

Zamboanga Peninsula, Mindanao, and the Sulu Archipelago. The physical characteristics of Mindanao, the second largest and southernmost of the Philippines, is described earlier in this section.

The Zamboanga Peninsula juts almost 150 miles in a ragged arch from western Mindanao (SILVERSAND, SILVERWARE, SPRIGHTLY, VOTER). On its north and west sides is the Sulu Sea and on the other is the Moro Gulf. (See Map 66). A small number of coastal islands are found along the Moro Gulf side. A chain of mountains runs the length of the peninsula with the highest peak being Mount Matindang at 7,956 feet on its broad central portion. The southern end of the peninsula where most of the action took place was covered with mountains over 2,000 feet high and averages fifteen miles in width. The south end was dominated by a 4,380-foot peak. A very thin strip of level plain edges the south end's west coast. This plain widens out on the south end to over five miles, but narrows again to an average of three miles on the east coast. The peninsula widens out to almost eighty miles in width at its central portion, but narrows considerably before it joins the island's main landmass.

The Sulu Archipelago stretches approximately 250 miles from the south end of the Zamboanga Peninsula (FURNACE) to the northeast-central coast of Borneo. The chain consists of over 100 islands and scores of islets and reefs forming a barrier on the south

Sulu Archipelago and Zamboanga Peninsula, Mindanao

Sulu Archipelago and Zamboanga Peninsula, Mindanao

MINDANAO

Illana Bay

Dumanguilas Bay

Olutanga I.

Sibuguey Bay

MORO GULF

Zamboanga Peninsula

Sirawai

Zamboanga City

Basilan Strait

Lamitan

Basilan I.

Loksap

Tapiantana Group

CELEBES SEA

Samales Group

SULU SEA

Jolo I.

Jolo City

Jolo Group

SULU ARCHIPELAGO

Tupal Group

Pangutaran I.

Pangutaran Group

Tawitawi I.

Tawitawi Group

Sanga Sanga I.

SULU ARCHIPELAGO AND
ZAMBOANGA PENINSULA,
MINDANAO

MILES

0 10 20 30 40 50

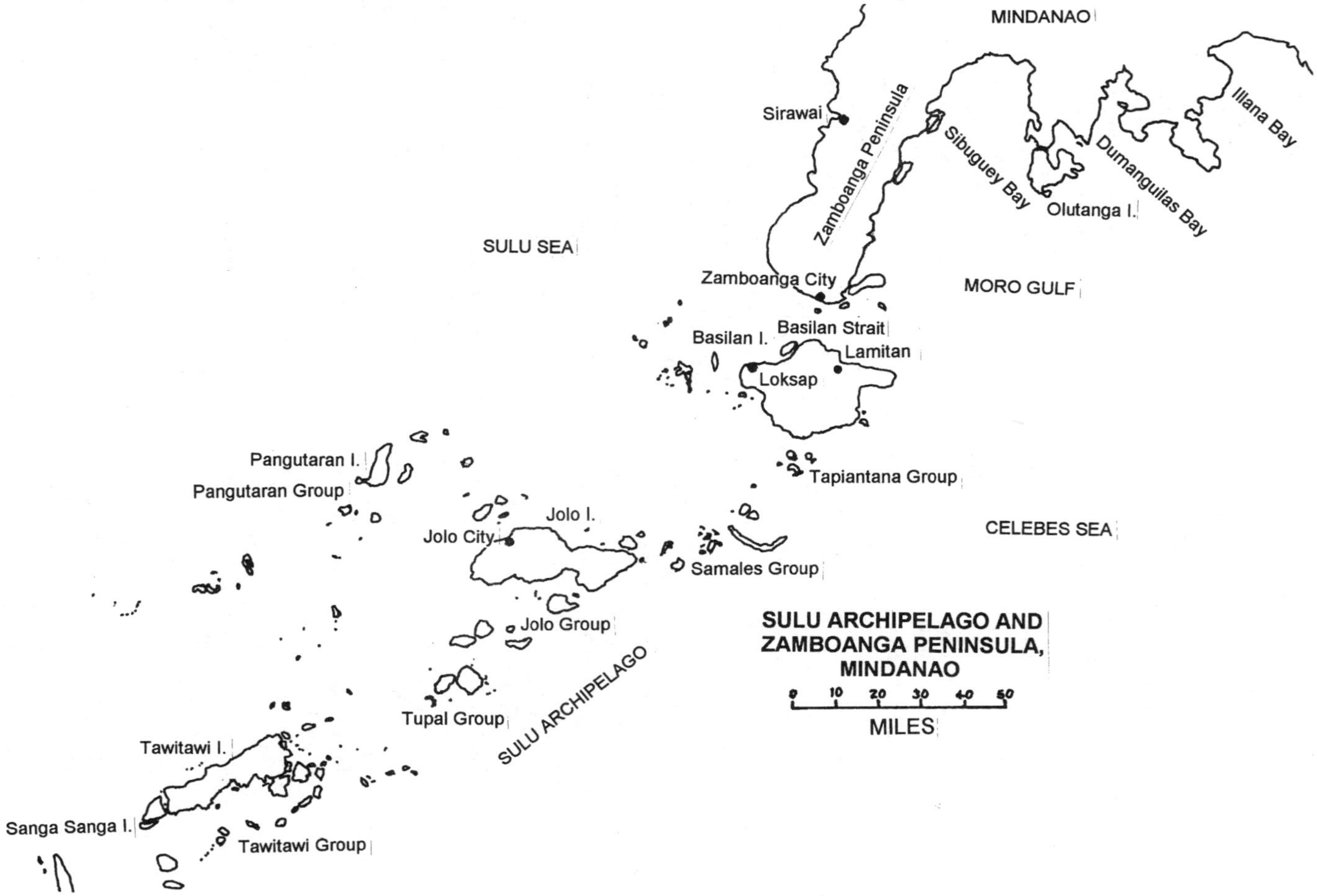

side of the Sulu Sea (ACCOUTERMENT, RULER) and the north edge of the Celebes Sea (TRIBESMAN). Three of the islands are of significant size. Basilan (twenty by thirty-six miles, 3,317 feet elevation) is immediately off the tip of the Zamboanga Peninsula. Jolo in the middle of the archipelago is the second largest (fourteen by forty miles, 2,664 feet). Tawitawi is the smallest of the three (ten by thirty miles, 1,800 feet) near the chain's southwest end forty miles from Borneo. The islands were populated by 300,000 Islamic Moros (*tao Sutig*) under the spiritual leadership of Sultan Mohammed Janail Abirir II. The sultan had the distinction of fighting the Spanish and then the Americans, but surrendered to Brigadier General John J. Pershing in 1911. He became resolutely loyal to the United States and the old sultan fought the Japanese from his mountain retreat on Jolo.

Japanese forces on Mindanao and the Sulu Archipelago were under the control of the *35th Army* headquartered on Cebu. These forces were split into two separate commands because of the island's size. The boundary between the two sectors was just east of Lake Lanao at the base of the Zamboanga Peninsula. The Zamboanga Peninsula in the west was the responsibility of the *54th Independent Mixed Brigade* (-detachments to other islands) under Lieutenant General HOJO Tokichi. The *33d Guard Force* plus IJA and IJN *Air Service* units were in the area. These units totaled almost 9,000 personnel. The main position in the Sulu Archipelago was on Jolo Island. It was defended by the smaller *55th Independent Mixed Brigade* under Major General SUZUKI Tersuzo. He controlled 3,000 IJA troops and 500 attached IJN personnel. Japanese forces on the main landmass of Mindanao were under the overall command of Lieutenant General MOROZUMI Gyo-saku with 58,000 IJA and IJN personnel. He would later assume nominal command of the *35th Army* when its commander was killed on 14 June. There were 17,000 Japanese civilians in the Davao area, the island's principal city on the south-central coast, of whom 5,000 had been conscripted as laborers. MOROZUMI directly commanded the largely Korean-manned *30th Division (40th Field Artillery, 74th Infantry*, battalions from *41st* and *77th Infantry)*. Service and airfield units plus the headquarters of the *2d Air Division*, commanded by Lieutenant General TERADA Seiichi, were also attached to the *30th Division*. These units were responsible for the defense of western and northern Mindanao. Southern and eastern Mindanao were the responsibility of the *100th Division (75th, 76th Infantry Brigades)* under Lieutenant General HARADA Jiro, who was largely left to his own devices by General MOROZUMI. Also under his command were air service and airfield units as well as the *32d Special Base Force* under Rear Admiral DOI Naoji. Most of the service units attached to both divisions were reorganized into combat units. Japanese airfields in the area included six in the northwest at Patag, Lumbia, Del Monte, Malaybalay, Valencia, and Dansalan; three around Davao at Licanan, Sasa, and Matina; two on the tip of the Zamboanga Peninsula, and Bongao on the southwest end of Tawi-tawi Island near the southwest end of the Sulu Archipelago.

Guerrillas on Mindanao were well organized under the 10th Military District head-quartered at La Paz in the northeast and under the command of Colonel Wendell W. Fertig. The 38,000 guerrillas were well armed and organized into the 105th (6,600), 106th (3,900), 107th (2,500), 108th (15,000), 109th (4,300), and 110th (5,400) Divisions plus the Maranao Militia Force (9,500 Moros). Moro guerrillas on the Sulu Archipelago were under the Sulu Area Command with 1,500 men.

The 41st Infantry Division (162d, 163d Infantry, -186th Infantry), under Brigadier General Jens A. Doe, was assigned to VICTOR IV with the mission of securing the Zamboanga Peninsula. The Division staged from Mindanao aboard the Zamboanga Attack Group (Task Group 78.1) on 8 March 1945. Rehearsals had been conducted with amphibian tractors as the beaches were fronted with fringing reefs and coral heads. Bombardment of the landing beaches began on the 8th. The fighter strip under construction on Palawan, intended to support the Zamboanga landing, was not operational by the time of the landing. To alleviate this problem two companies of the 21st Infantry, 24th Infantry Division were flown into Dipolog Airfield on the north shore of the peninsula 135 miles to the northeast of the landing site on 8 March, two days before the landing. The field was secured by guerrillas of the 105th Division, which had been using it for resupply flights since late 1944. A Marine fighter squadron arrived the next day and provided close air support to the landing force from behind Japanese lines until 15 March when they relocated to the newly completed strip at Zamboanga City. Mindanao's distance from other island airfields and the fact that most carriers were committed to Okinawa and other operations made the possession of airfields in the immediate area critical.

The 162d Infantry landed at the barrio of San Mateo three miles west of Zamboanga City at 0915 hours, 10 March (J-Day) under very light small arms fire. The 163d Infantry came ashore immediately behind the lead regiment. The abandoned Wolfe Airfield behind the landing beach was immediately secured. The next day San Roque Airfield on the northwest side of Zamboanga City and the town itself were secured. The American troops, assisted by guerrillas, advanced north into the low hills meeting their first strong opposition on the 12th. The strongpoints were overrun by 24 March and the surviving Japanese withdrew up the west coast hoping to be rescued. Battalion-size flanking landings were made on the west coast on 26 April and 17 and 21 May as the Japanese fled. Harassed by guerrillas, they were forced to withdraw back into the mountains. Most remnants concentrated in the broad north-central portion of the peninsula where they were contained by 105th Division guerrillas. The 41st Infantry Division was relieved by units of the 368th Infantry, 93d Infantry Division (Colored) in early July. Near Zamboanga City two airfields, Calarian and Moret Fields, were built that proved invaluable to the fighting on eastern Mindanao.

An estimated 6,400 Japanese were killed or died of starvation and disease on the peninsula, while 1,100 were taken prisoner, many surrendering to the guerrillas. At the end of the war 1,385 surrendered. U.S. losses on the peninsula were 220 KIA and 665 WIA.

Operations in the Sulu Archipelago commenced on 16 March. A rifle company landed near Lamitan on the northeast coast of Basilan Island ten miles off the end of Zamboanga Peninsula on that date, but made no contact with the small Japanese detachment. Two guerrilla companies relieved them and pursued the Japanese, who had withdrawn to the interior. A PT boat base was established on the island. The 2d Battalion, 163d Infantry landed on Sanga Sanga and Bongo Islands off the southeast end of guerrilla-controlled Tawitawi Island (also spelled Tawi Tawi) (SOYABEAN) 200 miles from the end of the peninsula on 2 April. A 6,500-foot fighter strip was built on Sanga Sanga and was operational on 2 May. This field soon allowed RAAF units to support operations on northeast Borneo. Two Americans were killed and four wounded before the small Japanese detachment was destroyed. The 163d Infantry (-) landed on the north coast of Jolo (GABBLE, PENSIONER) at 0845 hours, 9 April, five miles east of Jolo City. The beach was very lightly defended with the bulk of the *55th Independent Mixed Brigade* having withdrawn to two strongholds, one on Mount Daho six miles southeast of Jolo City and the other six miles southwest of the town on Mount Tumatangus. The Daho stronghold was overrun between 15 and 22 April and the Tumatangus reduced between 25 April and 2 May, although small pockets held out. The Moro guerrillas participated in both operations and continued the mop-up. The 163d Infantry was relieved by units of the 368th Infantry,

93d Infantry Division (Colored) on 19 June. American losses on Jolo were thirty-five KIA and 130 WIA. Approximately 3,780 Japanese died and thirty were taken prisoner. Only ninety survived the Moros to surrender after the war.

Eastern Mindanao. Operation VICTOR V was conducted by X Corps under Major General Franklin C. Sibert with two infantry divisions and the 3d Engineer Special Brigade. The 24th Infantry Division (19th, 21st, 34th Infantry), under Major General Roscoe B. Woodruff, would lead the assault while the 31st Infantry Division (124th, 155th, 167th Infantry), commanded by Major General Clarence A. Martin, would arrive a few days later. The 24th Infantry Division staged from Mindoro aboard Task Force 78.2 on 11 April heading for Illana Bay. The bay is an extension of Moro Gulf on the south side of the Zamboanga Peninsula near where it joins the island's main landmass. Located on the west-central side of Mindanao, the Mindanao River Valley opens out on to it. The Japanese expected the main landing on Davao Gulf (OBERON) ninety miles to the east. This is where they had landed in 1942 and it was there that most of the *100th Division* and *32d Special Base Force* were concentrated around Davao City (DELTA). The Japanese considered the second most likely landing area to be Majcajalar Bay on the north-central coast. Thus Illana Bay was lightly defended and subsequently selected for the main landing. The Mindanao Valley possessed a road system allowing access to the north and east, Davao Gulf area, and also provided airfield sites to support later operations in the island's east and north.

While the invasion force was en route word was received from the guerrillas of the 108th Division, who essentially controlled 95 percent of the island, that they had occupied the Malabang-Parang area, the landing site at the head of Illana Bay, and that the Japanese had withdrawn inland. The landing commenced on 17 April (R-Day) when Ibus Island off of Malabang was secured by engineers at 0730 hours (See Map 67). At the same time 3d Battalion, 21st Infantry landed at Malabang (REBELLIOUS) to be greeted by guerrillas. The main landing took place at Parang twenty-two miles to the south of Malabang. Bongo Island, fourteen miles due west of Malabang, was secured 0745 hours. The 19th Infantry landed at Parang at 0900 hours soon followed by the 21st Infantry. Following two routes, the units immediately moved inland heading for Fort Pikit 35 miles inland. The routes skirted Lake Labas and the Libungan Marsh, roughly halfway to the fort, which was reached on the 21st. Engineers aboard landing craft moved up the Mindanao River and secured the fort in advance of the infantry. Japanese resistance was light, but the poor roads slowed movement.

The 31st Infantry Division came ashore at Parang on 22 April staging from Morotai Island to the southeast of Mindanao. The American units converged on Fort Pikit, but soon split again on two routes at Kabacan (ALLECTION). The 24th Infantry Division moved southeast on Route 1 toward Davao Gulf to attack the bulk of the *100th Division* and the 31st Infantry Division moved north up Route 3 (Sayre Highway) to engage the *30th Division*. The intent was to decisively engage both enemy divisions and keep them separated. The Japanese had planned to withdraw into the virtually unexplored mountains of east-central Mindanao after the Americans had established their beachheads.

Rushing to the head of Davao Gulf, the 24th Infantry Division reached the area on 24 April and pushed north and south along the shore against heavy resistance. Davao City was secured on the 31st. Much difficulty was encountered in the area west of Davao because of the abaca (hemp) plantations. The twenty-foot-high banana-tree-like plants were planted at ten-foot intervals with ten feet between rows. Shoots had grown densely between the untended plants reducing visibility to a few feet. Fire fights occurred in the plantations' oppressive heat at ranges of two to four yards. By 1 May, the 24th Infantry

Map 67
Mindanao, Philippine Islands

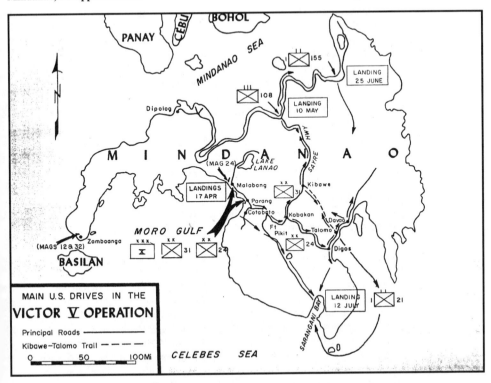

Division held a three-to-five-mile-wide coastal strip along the gulf's shore with the *100th Division* in the foothills. It was not until the end of May that the Japanese were pushed back and they established a second defense line. This line was not broken until 10 June and the Japanese began to retreat north. Part of the 24th Infantry Division were relieved by units of the 162d Infantry, 41th Infantry Division on 9 June. The remnants of the *100th Division* and other units in the southeast pulled into the central mountains near Maglusa to establish a stronghold.

Meanwhile the 31st Infantry Division advancing in the north against the *30th Division* fought a tough battle up a north extension of the Mindano Valley through April and into May. The terrain was extremely difficult in this area with countless gouges to be crossed and mud slides caused by heavy rains. The 41st Infantry Division's 162d Infantry came ashore in early May to take over rear area security and this allowed the 31st Infantry Division to commit more combat power to its advance. To place more pressure on the Japanese the 108th Infantry, 40th Infantry Division landed without opposition at Agusan in Macajalar Bay (LUMINOSITY) on 10 May. It pushed the Japanese out of the Del Monte area and linked up with the 31st Infantry on the 23rd. Most of the remnants of the *30th Division* fled to the northeast in an effort to establish strongholds in the mountains. On 23 June, 1st Battalion, 155th Infantry landed unopposed near the mouth of the Agusan River in Butuan Bay on the island's north coast and moved south to attack the rear of the *30th Division*.

On 30 June eastern Mindanao was declared secure as organized resistance had ceased. Mop-up continued in the extremely rugged rain-forest-covered mountains drenched by heavy rains into August. The guerrillas took over much of the mop-up as the exhausted units of the 24th, 31st, 40th, and 41st Infantry Divisions gradually disengaged. A final operation was conducted in July. Some *100th* and *30th Division* elements had withdrawn south to the Sarangani Bay area about seventy-five miles southwest of Davao City. This had been one of the landing sites for the originally planned early capture of Mindanao, but became the final assault landing site in the Philippines. Guerrillas had kept pressure on Japanese units in this area when the 1st Battalion, 21st Infantry landed near Buayan at the head of the bay on 12 July. A provisional infantry battalion of antiaircraft troops had moved south from the Mindanao Valley and linked up with the landing force on 13 July. The Japanese were pushed inland and organized resistance collapsed on 25 July.

By 30 June, when the island had been declared secure, 10,540 Japanese had been killed in combat and 600 prisoners were taken including 250 combatant civilians. Another 2,325 were killed between that date and the end of the war by U.S. and guerrilla units. A total of 21,100 Japanese died in combat or by disease and starvation on eastern Mindanao and 2,696 prisoners were eventually captured. At the end of the war 52,910 surrendered. Total U.S. losses were 820 dead and 2,880 wounded.

MacArthur declared the Philippines liberated on 5 July and hostilities formally ceased in the Philippines on 15 August 1945. The elements of four U.S. divisions on Luzon were still engaged in mop-up actions along with 118,000 guerrillas throughout the islands. The numerous other U.S. 6th and 8th Army divisions in the Philippines were preparing for the invasion of Japan. Selected guerrilla units were being reorganized and equipped as regular Philippine Army units and the Constabulary. The Philippine Constabulary and the Integrated National Police Force were combined in 1991 to form Philippine National Police. The U.S. Army reestablished the Philippine Scouts as well when on 6 April 1946 the Philippine Division, which was carried as captured and not disbanded, was redesignated the 12th Infantry Division (Philippine Scouts). The Division was inactivated on 30 April 1947, but component units remained in existence until the Philippine Scouts were disbanded in December 1948. Some Philippine Scouts units performed occupation duty on Okinawa and Guam.

Total U.S. ground casualties in the Philippines was 10,380 dead and 36,550 wounded. An estimated one million Filipinos died from all causes during the Japanese invasion, the occupation, and the U.S. invasion either fighting in the Philippine Army and the other armed organizations, as guerrillas, through Japanese reprisals, Allied bombing, and from fire by both the Japanese and Americans. War crimes trial affidavits list 131,028 Filipino civilians murdered in seventy-two large-scale massacres and remote incidents. Thousands of U.S. military prisoners and civilian internees were liberated, but many had died in captivity, often being murdered. Of the 381,550 IJA and IJN personnel in the Philippines 255,795 were killed in combat or by disease and starvation. There were 11,745 prisoners taken and 114,010 surrendered after 15 August.

With the reestablishment of the Commonwealth government under President Sergio Osmeña trade and security issues were quickly resolved with the United States. A major issue in Philippine politics was that of collaboration with the Japanese by government officials, businessmen, landlords, and other individuals. This was actually the issue of old grievances between the elite and the farmers and workers. José Laurel, president of the Japanese puppet government, maintained that he was first loyal to the Philippines and second to the Japanese. His collaboration was an effort to ease the burden of occupation through the Japanese-dominated Council of State and he faced down the Japanese on many issues. Osmeña and Laurel reconciled after the American invasion, but neither won the April 1946 presidential election. Manuel Roxas won to become the first president of the new Republic of the Philippines established on 4 July 1946 as scheduled in 1935. In 1948, he declared amnesty for all arrested collaborators, except those who had committed violent crimes.

There are few monuments or preserved battle sites in the Philippines, but there is a military cemetery outside of Manila and a monument and some artillery pieces are displayed at Lingayen Gulf. Corregidor and the other Manila Bay fortified islands were stripped of scrap metal and anything else salvageable immediately after the war and allowed to deteriorate. Many of the heavy coast defense guns and mortars still remain, however, as do their crumbling concrete fortifications. Headquarters, barracks, and other buildings are largely deteriorated. The Philippine government was established a Corregidor Memorial Office on the island and some restoration of selected sites, facilities, and tunnels is underway. Day tours of Corregidor are available and arrangements may be made to visit other fortified islands. A small naval station is located on fortified Caballo Island. Philippine military museums, all located near Manila, include: Army at Fort Bonifacio, Makati; Air Force at Villamor Air Base, Pasay City; Navy at San Felipe Naval Base, Cavite; National Police (Constabulary) at Camp Crame, Quezon City; and Armed Forces of the Philippines at Camp Aguinaldo, Quezon City.

NOTES

1. Australian Imperial Force units (volunteer units permitted to serve overseas, conscripts were not) prefixed by "2/" identify them as the second reiteration; they had previously been raised to serve in World War I.

2. The 1st Cavalry Division, serving as dismounted infantry, was organized differently than standard infantry divisions. It had two cavalry brigades, each with two cavalry regiments organized into two battalion-size cavalry squadrons. This gave the cavalry division only eight maneuver squadrons, rather than nine battalions, which were smaller than infantry battalions.

3. The *18th Army* operated on eastern New Guinea and is discussed in the preceding New Guinea section.

4. The *27th Special Base Force* was formed by consolidating the *2d* and *7th Base Forces*, the former having retreated from Lae-Salamaua.

5. By coincidence two barrios named San José were located on the north flank beaches of both X and XXIV Corps.

6. General FUKUE was relieved of command on 1 January for attempting to evacuate the remnants of his units to Cebu without authority. He was reinstated on 24 March as *IGHQ* failed to respond to *35th Army* charges. He was shot after the war for the execution of Allied POWs in Singapore.

7. On 4 December 1944 the 11th Airborne Division's Battery A, 457th Field Artillery Battalion parachuted in at Manarawat, Leyte. Staging from San Pablo, 120 men were dropped to establish firing positions near the west-central coast.

8. On 23 June 1944 the 11th Airborne Division's reinforced 1st Battalion, 511th Parachute Infantry—1,030 men—parachuted on to Camalaniugan Airfield staging from Lipa Airfield southeast of Manila. The operation saw the first limited use of gliders in the Pacific. The objective was Aparri on the north coast of Luzon, the last port held by the Japanese, but it was secured by 6th Army troops as the unit dropped.

9. General FUKUE had been relieved of command, but was reinstated on 24 March when General SUZUKI Sosaku, commanding *35th Army*, arrived.

READING SUGGESTIONS

Bergerud, Eric M. *Touched by Fire: The Land War in the South Pacific.* New York: Penguin Books USA, 1996.

Breuer, William B. *MacArthur's Undercover War: Spies, Saboteurs, Guerrillas, and Secret Missions.* New York: John Wiley and Sons, 1995.

Bureau of Yards and Docks. *Building the Navy's Bases in World War II, Vol. II.* Washington, DC: US Government Printing Office, 1947.

Cannon, M. Hamlin. *United States Army in World War II: Leyta: The Return to the Philippines.* Washington, DC: US Government Printing Office, 1987.

Chapin, Capt John C. . . . *And a Few Marines: Marines in the Liberation of the Philippines.* Washington Navy Yard: History and Museums Division, Marine Corps Historical Center, 1997.

Cogan, Frances B. *Captured: The Japanese Internment of American Civilians in the Philippines, 1941–1945,* Athens, GA: University of Georgia Press, 2000.

Coletta, Paolo E. and Bauer, K. Jack (Editors). *United States Navy and Marine Bases, Overseas.* Westport, CT: Greenwood Publishing Co., 1985.

Craven, Wesley F. and Cate, James L. *The Army Air Forces in World War II: Plans and Early Operations, January 1939 to July 1942, Vol. 1.* Chicago: University of Chicago Press, 1948.

Craven, Wesley F. and Cate, James L. *The Army Air Forces in World War II: The Pacific: Guadalcanal to Saipan, August 1942 to July 1944, Vol. 4.* Chicago: University of Chicago Press, 1950.

Craven, Wesley F. and Cate, James L. *The Army Air Forces in World War II: The Pacific: Matterhorn to Nagasaki, June 1944 to August 1945, Vol. 5.* Chicago: University of Chicago Press, 1953.

Doland, Ronald E. (Editor). *Area Handbook Series: Philippines: A Country Study.* Washington, DC: Government Printing Office, 1993.

Drea, Edward J. *Defending the Driniumor: Covering Force Operations in New Guinea, 1944.* Ft. Leavenworth, KS: Combat Studies Institute, 1984.

Frederick, William H. and Worden, Robert L. *Area Handbook Series: Indonesia: A Country Study.* Washington, DC: US Government Printing Office, 1993.

Garand, George W. and Stonebridge, Turman R. *History of US Marine Corps Operations in World War II: Western Pacific Operations, Vol. IV.* Washington, DC: US Government Printing Office, 1966.

General Staff, GHQ, Southwest Pacific Area. *Reports of General MacArthur, The Campaigns of MacArthur in the Pacific, Vol. I.* Washington, DC: US Government Printing Office, 1966.

General Staff, GHQ, Southwest Pacific Area. *Reports of General MacArthur, Japanese Operations in the Southwest Pacific Area, Vol. II.* Washington, DC: US Government Printing Office, 1966.

Gillespie, Oliver A. *The Pacific: Official History of New Zealand in the Second World War 1939–45.* Wellington, NZ: Department of Internal Affairs, 1952.

Greenfield, Kent R.; Palmer, Robert R.; and Wiley, Bell I. *United States Army in World War II: The Fall of the Philippines.* Washington, DC: US Government Printing Office, 1947.

Hough, Lt. Col. Frank O. and Crown, John A. *The Campaign on New Britain.* Washington, DC: US Government Printing Office, 1952.

Hough, Lt. Col. Frank O.; Ludwig, Maj. Verle E.; and Shaw, Henry I., Jr. *Pearl Harbor to Guadalcanal, Vol. I.* Washington, DC: Government Printing Office, 1958.

Krancher, Jan A. (Editor). *The Defining Years of the Dutch East Indies, 1942–1949: Survivors' Accounts of Japanese Invasion and Enslavement of Europeans and the Revolution that Created Free Indonesia.* New York: MacFarland and Co., 1996.

Lebra, Joyce C. *Japanese-Trained Armies in Southeast Asia.* New York: Columbia University Press, 1977.

Livingston, Willaim S. and Louis, William R. (Editors). *Australia, New Zealand, and the Pacific Islands since the First World War*. Austin: University of Texas Press, 1979.

Long, Gavin M. *The Six Years War: A Concise History of Australia in the 1939–1945 War*. Canberra: The Australian War Memorial and the Australian Government Publishing Service, 1973.

Miller, John, Jr. *United States Army in World War II: Cartwheel: The Reduction of Rabaul*. Washington, DC: US Government Printing Office, 1959.

Milner, Samuel. *United States Army in World War II: Victory in Papua*. Washington, DC: US Government Printing Office, 1957.

Morison, Samuel E. *History of US Navy Operations in World War II: The Rising Sun in the Pacific, 1931–April 1942, Vol. III*. Boston: Little, Brown and Company: 1948.

Morison, Samuel E. *History of US Navy Operations in World War II: Breaking the Bismarcks Barrier, 22 July 1942–1 May 1944, Vol. VI*. Boston: Little, Brown and Company, 1950.

Morrison, Samuel E. *History of US Navy Operations in World War II: New Guinea and the Marianas, March 1944–August 1944, Vol. VIII*. Boston: Little, Brown and Company, 1952.

Morison, Samuel E. *History of US Navy Operations in World War II: Leyte, June 1944–January 1944, Vol. XII*. Boston: Little, Brown and Company, 1966.

Morison, Samuel E. *History of US Navy Operations in World War II: The Liberation of the Philippines, Luzon, Mindanao, the Visayas 1944–1945, Vol. XIII*. Boston: Little, Brown and Company, 1959.

Nalty, Bernard C. *Cape Gloucester: The Green Inferno*. Washington Navy Yard: History and Museums Division, Marine Corps Historical Center, 1994.

Philippine Army (no author), *Philippine Army: 100 Years*, www.army.mil.ph/pa100yrs.htm.

Rasor, Eugene L. *The Solomon Islands Campaign, Guadalcanal to Rabaul: Historiography and Anointed Bibliography*. Westport, CT: Greenwood Publishing Co., 1997.

Rasor, Eugene L. *The Southwest Pacific Campaign: Historiography and Anointed Bibliography*. Westport, CT: Greenewood Publishing Co., 1996.

Shaw, Henry I., Jr. and Kane, Maj. Douglas T. *History of US Marine Corps Operations in World War II: Isolation of Rabual, Vol. II*. Washington, DC: US Government Printing Office, 1963.

Smith, Robert R. *United States Army in World War II: The Approach to the Philippines*. Washington, DC: US Government Printing Office, 1984.

Smith, Robert R. *United States Army in World War II: Triumph in the Philippines*, Washington, DC: US Government Printing Office, 1963.

Taaffe, Stephen R. *MacArthur's Jungle Victory: The 1944 New Guinea Campaign*. Saint Lawrence, KS: University of Kansas Press, 1997.

Tanaka Kengoro. *Operations of the Imperial Japanese Armed Forces in Papua New Guinea Theater during World War II*. Tokyo: Japan Papua New Guinea Goodwill Society, 1980.

Whitman, John W. *Bataan: Our Last Ditch*. New York: Hippocrene Books, 1990.

Young, Donald J. *The Battle of Bataan: A History of the 90 Day Seige and Eventual Surrender of 75,000 Filipino and United States Troops to the Japanese in World War II*. Jefferson, NC: McFarland & Company, 1992.

4

Central Pacific Area

The Central Pacific Area, as a strategic military zone, was a broad band of ocean stretching from the west coast of the United States to China (see Map 68). Its southern boundary was the equator, with a small notch cutting down into the South Pacific Area to take in Canton Island. Its southern boundary began at 110° west longitude, ran north to 11° north latitude and then angled to the northeast to the Mexico/Guatemala border. Just off the northwest end of Dutch New Guinea the boundary made a 90° turn north at longitude 130° east to 20° north latitude where it turned back to the west, south of Formosa. This allowed the Philippines and most of the Netherlands East Indies to fall within the Southwest Pacific Area. The area's northern boundary was latitude 42° north running from the California/Oregon state line across the Pacific, clipping the south end of Hokkaido Island, the northernmost of the main Japanese Home Islands, and striking shore just to the south of the Korea/China border. The rest of Japan fell within the Central Pacific Area. Mainland Asia abutted the area's western boundary and was encompassed by the China-Burma-India Theater.

In the eastern-central portion of this vast body of water are the Hawaii Islands and most of the other U.S. island possessions discussed in the U.S. South and Central Pacific Possessions section. In the southwest quadrant of the area are the Marshall, Caroline, and Mariana Islands, comprising the Japanese Mandated Territory for the most part. In the central-western portion are the Volcano Islands with Iwo Jima, and the Nansei Shoto with the Ryukyus and Okinawa. The Ellice and Gilbert Islands, which actually lie in the South Pacific Area, are discussed in this section to retain operational continuity.

GILBERT AND ELLICE CROWN COLONY

This Crown Colony evolved in the 1890s up through just a few years before the war. Prior to that the two island groups and associated islands were under no formal jurisdiction other than local native rule, missionary groups attempting to instill some form of order, and white traders who reigned control through might. The commander of the HMS *Royalist*, H.M. Davis, first proclaimed protectorate status over the Gilbert Islands in 1892 in an effort to curtail wholesale exploitation. A resident commissioner was installed on Ocean Island in 1900. The local native rulers requested that the Gilbert and Ellice Islands be annexed by Britain in 1915 and Ocean, Fanning, Washington, and Union Islands were added in 1916. The Crown colony was formerly established that same year, the latter island being ceded to New Zealand in 1925. Christmas Island was added in 1925 and the Phoenix Islands followed in 1937. The Gilberts and Ellices were discovered piece-meal between 1764 and 1824, largely by British explorers. The Gilberts were named after one of these, a Royal Navy officer visiting the islands in 1788. The native I-Tungaru refer to the group as the Land of Beru.

The Gilbert and Ellice Islands form a long chain of small, scattered atolls and islands. They stretch from 03° N 173° E southeast to 03° S 177° E. The Ellices run from 05° N 176° E southeast to 05° N 179° W. The Phoenix Islands lie to the east. Some 300 miles northwest of the Gilberts is the Marshall Islands while 600 miles to the southwest of the Ellices are the Samoa Islands and to the south is Fiji. To the southwest of the Gilberts is Ocean Island. East of the Gilberts and north of the Phoenix Islands are the U.S. possessions of Howland and Baker Islands, which are discussed in this section.

There are sixteen coral atolls and islands of significance in the Gilberts with 166 square miles of land and nine atolls in the Ellices with fourteen square miles. While all of the atolls of the Gilberts and Ellices had European names bestowed upon them, under British administration the native names were used. Most rise no more than twelve feet above sea level, hard sand overlying a coral rock base and minimal soil. The vegetation is normally coconut palms and underbrush. The Gilberts and Ellices were affected by fewer natural and imported diseases than many other Pacific islands. The most serious diseases suffered by the natives were tuberculosis, yaws, and leprosy, but these were kept under control. Malaria, filariasis, smallpox, and plague were unknown in the Gilberts. Dysentery was present and its prevalence on Tarawa increased after the assault due to the thousands of unburied bodies. Dengue fever also appeared after the battle. There are no natural sources of freshwater; catchment basins were required to collect rainwater. The period from October to March experiences westerly winds and rains. The northeasterly trade-winds from March to October provide milder temperatures. While the annual rainfall is between 150 and 180 inches, there is a five-to-seven-year drought cycle and at the time of the November battle the Gilberts was experiencing one. Afternoon high temperature was in the mid- to high 90s with high humidity and a night low of 72°. All of the Gilberts and Ellices are located in time zone 24. (The Phoenix Islands were in time zone 1.) Ocean and Nauru Islands are discussed at the end of this section.

The natives of the Gilberts were warlike Micronesians while those in the Ellices were Polynesians; the Phoenix Islands were unpopulated. Both races, however, were far from being "pure" as there had been intermingling during migrations of both groups through the island chains and from Samoa. When the British took over they halted an ongoing war and this led to much confusion over land titles, which was a complex issue with the Gilbertese. Eventually a Native Lands Commission was established in an effort to sort it out, but by the time of the war many claims and counterclaims had not yet been resolved. Under British rule nonnatives cannot buy land and the Crown took numerous measures to allow the natives a high degree of self-rule. A few British and French missionaries were scattered though the islands with most of the natives adopting Chris-tianity. Prior to the war there were approximately 28,000 natives and less than 100 Europeans in the Gilberts along with a few Chinese. While the population was compar-tively small, the Gilberts, because of their 166 square miles of land, were the most heavily populated islands in the Pacific. In the Ellices there were only 4,200 natives and barely

Map 68
Central Pacific Area

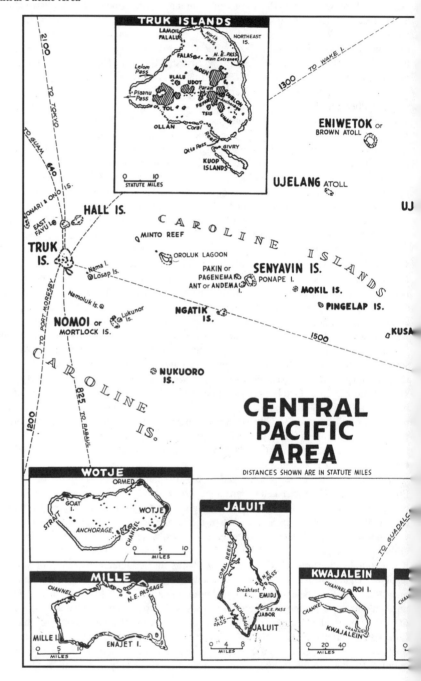

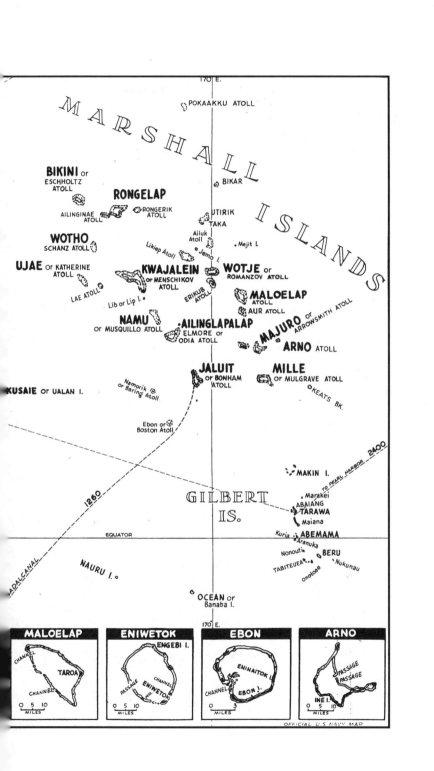

170 E.

⌀ POKAAKKU ATOLL

MARSHALL ISLANDS

BIKINI or
ESCHHOLTZ
ATOLL

⌀ BIKAR

RONGELAP

⌀RONGERIK
ATOLL

AILINGINAE
ATOLL

UTIRIK
TAKA

WOTHO
SCHANZ ATOLL

Ailuk
Atoll

Likiep Atoll

• Mejit I.

Jemo I.

UJAE or KATHERINE
ATOLL

LAE ATOLL

KWAJALEIN
or MENSCHIKOV
ATOLL

WOTJE or
ROMANZOV ATOLL

Lib or Lip I.

ERIKUB
ATOLL

MALOELAP
ATOLL

AUR ATOLL

NAMU
or MUSQUILLO ATOLL

AILINGLAPALAP
ELMORE or
ODIA ATOLL

MAJURO or
ARROWSMITH ATOLL

ARNO ATOLL

JALUIT
or BONHAM
ATOLL

MILLE
or MULGRAVE ATOLL

KUSAIE or UALAN I.

Namorik
or Baring Atoll

⌀KEATS BK.

Ebon or
Boston Atoll

MAKIN I.

TO PEARL HARBOR 2400

GILBERT

IS.

• Marakei

ABAIANG
TARAWA

1260

• Maiana

EQUATOR

Kuria **ABEMAMA**

• Aranuka

Nonouti

BERU

NAURU I. ⌀

TABITEUEA

• Nukunau

GUADALCANAL

Onotoa

⌀ **OCEAN** or
Banaba I.

170 E.

MALOELAP	**ENIWETOK**	**EBON**	**ARNO**
CHANNEL **TAROA** CHANNEL 0 5 10 MILES	ENGEBI I. PASSAGE CHANNEL **ENIWETOK** I. 0 5 10 MILES	CHANNEL **ENINAITOK** I. **EBON** I. 0 3 MILES	PASSAGE PASSAGE **INE** I. 0 5 10 MILES

OFFICIAL U.S NAVY MAP

any Europeans. About 2,000 natives had been voluntarily resettled in the Phoenix Islands by the British just prior to the war in an effort to relieve overcrowding. The atolls offer a meager existence, but some are more densely populated than more fertile and larger islands found elsewhere. Most Europeans had evacuated the islands before the Japanese arrived.

On the war's eve Mr. V. Fox-Strangeways was the colony's resident commissioner on Ocean Island answering to the high commissioner for the Western Pacific in Fiji. A small European staff administered the fiscal, health, education, and law enforcement needs of the colony through six district officers with native administrative staffs. Each island also had a native magistrate who held court with village headmen. Australian trading firms dealt with exports (copra and phosphate) and imports. Subsistence farming included bananas, breadfruit, taro, and papaw. A lagoon-side road, surfaced with coral mud, ran the length of every island in the colony, but the primary means of land transportation was bicycle. At low tide the coral reefs could usually be traveled by foot from island to island. Canoes and launches provided local transportation between atoll islands and small steamers provided service between the atolls. There were no airfields in the colony prior to the arrival of the Japanese.

The Gilberts' importance to the Japanese was to serve as an outer guard for their bases in the Marshalls some 300 miles to the northeast. Bases in the Gilberts would allow the Japanese to attack the southern flank of American task forces moving toward the Marshalls. They also provided advance air bases to scout the approaches in the southern arc, and once the Americans occupied the Ellice Islands 700 miles to the southeast of the Gilberts, they were used to keep those developing bases under surveillance and harass them by air attack. The Japanese occupied some of the Gilbert Islands in December 1941. After the Marine raid on Butaritari in August 1942, the Japanese seized Nauru and Ocean Islands and began reinforcing Butaritari and Tarawa, a process that lasted into 1943.

Ellice Islands

The Ellice Islands (aka Fagoon Islands, though seldom used) were code-named MOLE-HILL and later RECUPERATE. The Japanese called them *Erisu Shoto.* They consist of nine atolls stretching about 300 miles from the northwest to the southwest: Nanomea, Niutao (aka Speiden or Lynx), Nanumanga (aka Nanomama), Nui (aka Netherland), Vaitupu (aka Tracey), Nukufetau, Funafuti, Nukulaelae (aka Mitchell), and Niulakita (aka Nura-kita or Sophia). Three of these atolls, Funafuti, Nanomea, and Nukufetau, were occupied by U.S. forces in October 1942 and August 1943 to secure the northern approaches to the Samoas and Fiji, place the Japanese-held Gilberts under surveillance, and support future operations in the Gilberts by the 4th Marine Base Air Defense Wing and Seventh Air Force elements. This preliminary phase to Operation GALVANIC was launched by the Marine Corps' Defense Force, Samoan Group. In conjunction with the occupation of these islands an Army task force secured Baker Island (which see below). New Zealand coastwatchers were established in the Ellices prior to the war and were still in place when the Americans arrived. While the Japanese did not occupy any of the Ellice Islands, they did bomb the administrative center on Funafuti on several occasions after occupying the Gilberts.

Funafuti Atoll. Funafuti (pronounced Fun-na-fut-ti) was code-named FETLOCK until February 1943 when it was renamed HAEMETITE and later HURL. The atoll is located at 08°31′ N 179°08′ E. It is in the southern portion of the Ellices with the other two later

Map 69
Funafuti Atoll, Ellice Islands

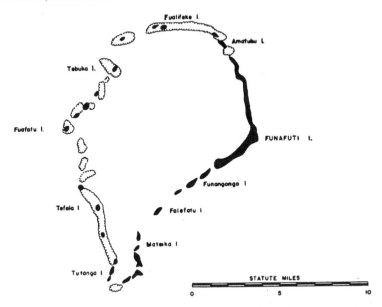

U.S. occupied atolls to the northwest, Nukufetau at 43 miles and Nanomea at 235. Naura Island is 870 miles to the northwest of Funafuti.

The atoll is irregularly shaped measuring about 13-½ miles from north to south and ten miles across making it the largest in the Ellices (see Map 69). It is comprised of thirty islands with Fongafale Island, which the Americans generally called Funafuti Island, on the northeast side. This reversed L-shaped island is eight miles long and 50–150 yards wide, but its elbow provides a 700-yard-wide area. The sheltered lagoon has several entry passages for shallow draft ships, but the main entrances are Te Buabua (north) and Te Ava Mateika (south) and on the southeast side to the southwest of Fongafale. The former was dredged by the Navy. Two others on the northwest side are Te Ave i de Lape and Te Afualilku. A ragged string of islets stretch away from the southwest end of Fongafale about nine miles and then a scattered line of islets and broken barrier reefs run north to curve around to Fongafale's northwest end. The islands are covered by palms and salt brush. Mangrove swamps line parts of the oceanside shores. There were 680 natives on the island at the time of the U.S. occupation, who remained.

Funafuti was discovered by a Captain De Peyster in 1819. It was the administrative center for the Ellice Islands, a district of the Gilbert and Ellice Islands Crown Colony, and the only authorized port of entry in the district. A hospital and gaol were located there. It is historically noteworthy to geologists in that in 1897 Professor Sir Edgewood David drilled a borehole to 1,100 feet and proved Darwin's theory of the origin of coral reefs.

Operation FETLOCK, the Funafuti Atoll Occupation, was executed on 2 October 1942 by the Marine 5th Defense Battalion. The occupation was not publicly announced, or even commonly known within the Navy, until after the Japanese discovered it on 27 March 1943. Ten Japanese air attacks were launched from Nauru Island staging through

Map 70
Nanomea Atoll, Ellice Islands

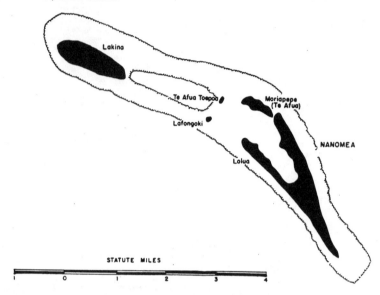

Tarawa between March and November 1943. Seabees constructed a 5,000-foot airfield on Fongafale's elbow, which was operational at the end of the month. By April 1943 it was extended to 6,600 feet allowing B-24 bombers to attack Nauru on the 20th and Tarawa on the 22nd. Small seaplane and PT boat bases were built. A floating naval base, since space ashore was limited, in the form of Service Squadron 4 was activated at Funafuti on 1 November 1943 to support operations into the Gilberts. The naval base ashore was commissioned on 15 November (FPO SF 225). Funafuti later supported operations in the Marshalls. It was here that chartered tankers transferred their fuel to fleet oilers, which transported it into the combat zone to fuel warships. As the war moved north the base lost much of its value other than as an aircraft way station. Roll-up began in May 1944 and the base was closed on 12 June 1946. The airfield is still operational being the lone airport in the nation of Tuvalu.

Nanomea Atoll. Nanomea, sometimes spelled Nanumea, was earlier know as St. Augustine. It was code-named PHILISTINE. The northwestern most of the Ellice Islands is 460 miles southeast of Tarawa Atoll. It is located at 05°39' N 176°08' E.

Nanomea is an elongated atoll just under seven miles long northwest to southeast (see Map 70). The largest island is Y-shaped Lolua about three miles long and a mile wide across the top of its "Y" on the northwest end. An islet, Moriapepa (aka Te Afua), lies off the north arm of the "Y." Oval-shaped Lakina Island is situated on the atoll's northeast end and is about 1-⅓ miles long and ⅓ mile wide. Two little islets, Te Afua Toepoa and Lafongoki, lie between the two main islands. The islands are surrounded by a slug-shaped coral reef with a ⅓-by-1-½-miles-long, oval-shaped lagoon lying between the two main islands. It offered no protected anchorage. The islands are densely covered with salt brush and palms.

Nanomea Atoll was occupied by the Marine 7th Defense Battalion on 18 August 1943. The Japanese conducted an air attack on 7 September and another attack on 7 November.

Map 71
Nukufetau Atoll, Ellice Islands

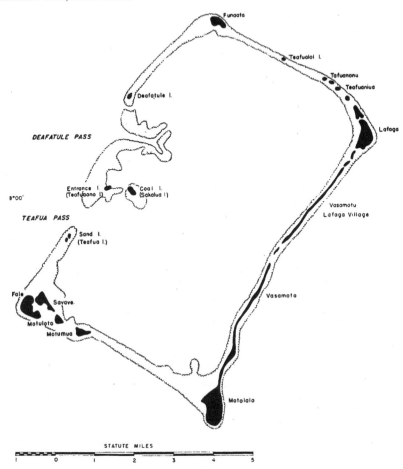

The 6,000-foot bomber field built on Lolua Island was operational in late September (FPO SF 337). It ran up the lower arm of the "Y" and on to the northeast arm. A 3,000-foot fighter strip crossed the bomber strip. The first bomber raids on the Gilberts and Marshalls were staged from Nanomea in November. A sixty-foot-wide, 1,500-foot-long channel was cut into the small lagoon on the northwest side to allow small craft to enter. The USAAF took over the Navy-built airfield in December. Roll-up of the base began in May 1944 and it was closed in December 1944.

Nukufetau Atoll. Nukufetau, sometimes spelled Nuku Fetau, was code-named PIC-AROON. It was also known as De Peyster after its discoverer, though this was a seldom-used name. The atoll is situated at 08°0' N 178°30' E and is 650 miles southeast of Tarawa.

The atoll is rectangular-shaped with a length of about 9-¼ miles northeast to southwest, a width of 5-½ miles, and a twenty-four mile perimeter (see Map 71). There are

Map 72a
Baker Island, Phoenix Group

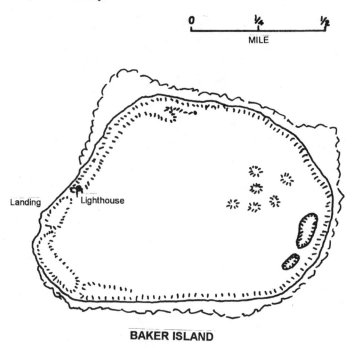

BAKER ISLAND

twenty-two islands and islets scattered around this perimeter, which is a narrow coral
barrier reef with only two breaks on the northwest side. Motolalo Island is the atoll's
largest and is located on the south corner. Running about 3-½ miles from its less-than-
a-mile-across oval lobe is a narrow sandbar terminating about halfway up the atoll's
length. Another long, narrow sandbar continues toward the east corner on which Lafaga
Island is located, the atoll's second largest. Six islets dot the northeast end of the atoll's
barrier reef and another is at the north corner. Four larger islets are clustered at the west
corner and the southwest end is open other than the unbroken barrier reef. Only five
islets are scattered across the atoll's northwest side. Two gaps in the barrier reef allow
access to the lagoon, the main Teafua Pass in the south portion and the narrow, twisting
Deafatule Pass in the north. The lagoon itself was shallow allowing access to only small
craft. For this reason supplies and equipment had to be unloaded from larger ships at
Funafuti sixty miles to the south and transferred to Nukufetau aboard landing craft.
Motolalo Island was swampy, but densely covered by palm trees and salt brush.

The Marine 2d Airdrome Battalion, an antiaircraft and air base defense unit, occupied
Motolalo Island on 27 August 1943. A 3,500-foot fighter strip was operational on 9
October. It crossed the island from east to west. A 6,100-foot bomber strip, which crosses
the fighter strip north to south, was opened at the end of that same month (FPO SF 333).
A 1,000-foot causeway was built to link sections of the atoll. Nukufetau served as an air
base to attack the Gilberts. In early 1944 the air units had moved north and roll-up began
in May. It remained in use as an alternate staging and emergency airfield until closed in
December 1944. The main inhabited island today is Savave on the atoll's west corner.

Map 72b
Howland Island, Phoenix Group

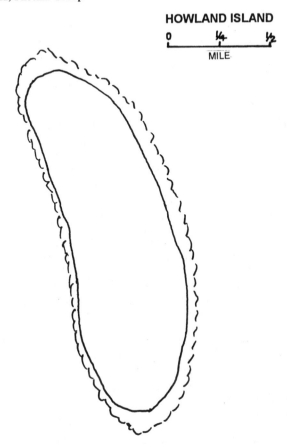

HOWLAND ISLAND

0   ¼   ½

MILE

The three original Marine units occupying the Ellice Islands were relieved by the 51st Defense Battalion, split between the islands, on 23–27 February 1944.

Baker and Howland Islands, Phoenix Group

Baker Island was code-named TURNOVER and Howland Island was UMPTEEN. These two islands are included in the Phoenix Group, but are approximately 400 miles to the northeast of the main group (see Maps 72a and 72b). Baker is situated at 0°13' N 176°31' W and Howland at 0°48' N 176°38' W. They are approximately 1,650 miles southeast of Pearl Harbor and are both some 480 miles due east of the Gilberts and northeast of the Ellices. Tarawa is 500 miles to the east. Baker, while smaller than Howland, was more militarily important and lies thirty miles southeast of the former.

The two islands are similar in formation being of low coral sand with a closely fringing coral reef. The highest elevation on Baker is twenty-six feet and on Howland is ten feet with both islands' elevated areas being on the west coasts. Saucer-shaped Baker has an elevated rim and a lower center, and is roughly a mile across. Howland is an oval oriented north to south and is just over 1-½ miles long and slightly less than a mile wide. There are no ship anchorages, but boat landings can be made on both islands' west shores. The vegetation found on both is low scrub brush, grasses, and prostrate vines. Baker is sparsely vegetated in scattered clumps while Howland is almost completely covered by brush and had a stand of fifteen-foot-high trees just northeast of the center in a mounded area known as "King-Doyle Park." Howland, like Baker, is lower in the center than its shoreline. The central area is very flat making it ideal for an airfield. Both islands are hot, humid, windy, and receive little rainfall. Sea and shore birds abound and Howland is infested with gray rats.

While claimed by Britain, the islands were annexed by the United States in late 1935 without dispute on the basis that they were named in the American Guano Act of 1856. Both islands were worked for guano until depleted in about 1890. Colonists from Hawaii landed on both islands in 1935 and built lighthouses on the west shores. Operational beacons remain to this day. The islands were placed under the Department of the Interior in May 1936.

In 1937, a 2,400-foot airstrip was constructed on Howland to provide Amelia Earhart and Frederick Noonan a refueling stop between New Guinea and Hawaii for their round-the-world flight attempt. On 2 July, en route to Howland, they disappeared and were never again seen. The search, conducted by substantial U.S. Navy forces, was halted on 18 July. The Japanese thought there was an operational airfield on the island and planned to strike it during the Pearl Harbor attack. It was later bombed by the United States to prevent its possible use by the Japanese and later the Japanese did the same to deny it to the United States. It was repaired by U.S. forces in late 1943 for use as an emergency landing strip.

On 11 August 1943, an Army defense force landed on Baker (APO SF 457) with antiaircraft and engineer battalions, and a fighter squadron in conjunction with the Marine Corps' Ellice Islands occupation. In September an airfield was constructed to support future operations in the Gilberts. Nothing militarily significant occurred on the islands and by 1945 neither was in use.

The islands have been unoccupied since the war and the airfields are overgrown. In 1974, both islands were placed under the control of the Fish and Wildlife Service of the Department of Interior and are part of the National Wildlife Refuge System as unincorporated territories. Both islands are restricted and can be entered only by special permit, usually granted to scientists and researchers.

Gilbert Islands

The Gilbert Islands were code-named OVERFED. The Japanese called them *Girubato Shoto*. Located roughly halfway between Hawaii and Australia, they are approximately 2,400 miles southwest of the former and 2,800 miles northeast of the latter. The southernmost of the Marshall Islands is less than 300 miles to the northwest of the northernmost of the Gilberts, Butaritari (Makin) Atoll. Straddling both the International Date Line and the equator they are situated between 03°30' N 173°00' E and 03°00' S 177°00' W. The Gilberts are divided administratively into three districts with sixteen atolls and islands, listed from northwest to southeast. The Northern District included: Little Makin (aka Pitt), Butaritari (administrative center), Marakei (aka Matthew), and Abaiang (aka Charlotte). The Central or Tarawa District held: Tarawa (administrative center), Maiana (aka Gilbert or Hall), Kuria (aka Woodle), Apamama, Aranuka (aka Henderville), and

Nonouti (aka Sydenham). The Southern or Beru District consisted of: Tabiteuea (aka Drummond), Beru (aka Francis, administrative center), Nukunau (or Nikunau, aka Byron), Onotoa (aka Clerk), Tamana (aka Rotcher), and Arorae (Hope).[1]

Most of the Europeans had evacuated the colony before the Japanese arrived, but a few remained. Three of these atolls were temporally occupied by the Japanese on 9 December 1941: Butaritari, Marakei, and Abaiang, who interned the Europeans they found on the former. The next day they conducted an air raid on Tarawa, the administrative center. A second raid followed on the 24th and Japanese forces landed the same day. By that summer the Japanese felt the islands faced little danger from the Americans and reduced the already small garrisons. On 17–18 August 1942 Marines raided Makin Island, Butaritari Atoll destroying a seaplane base before withdrawing. This resulted in a build-up of forces in the Gilberts and the fortification of selected islands in the Butariyari and Tawawa Atolls. Japanese coastwatchers were placed on other area atolls. Five Europeans and seventeen unarmed New Zealand coastwatchers on other atolls (Beru, Tamana, Maiana, Nonouti, Kuria) were captured and used for forced labor. On 15 October, all twenty-two captives held by the Japanese were murdered (the missionaries and nuns were not molested for propaganda purposes). In May 1943 the *Combined Fleet* enacted plans for the *Z Operation*. It envisioned a new defensive line running from the Aleutians, through the Marshalls and Gilberts, and then the Bismarcks. It would contain a series of strongly defended islands that would sufficiently delay any American effort to take them enabling IJN forces to attack the American invasion fleet.

In November 1943, with the Ellices secured as forward air bases, the Americans were prepared to strike north to seize Tarawa, Butaritari (Makin), and Apamama Atolls in the Gilberts and Nauru Island (Operation GALVANIC). The seizure of the Gilberts would place American forces in a position to thrust into the Japanese Mandated Territories, the Marshalls to the north, and the Carolines to the northeast. Possession of the Gilberts would allow the Americans reconnaissance of the Marshalls, which were out of range from existing American bases. The Marine Corps was assigned Tarawa and Apamama, and the Army Butaritari.

The islands were returned to British control before the war was over and they remained in colonial status. Racial tensions between the Polynesian Ellice Islanders and the Micronesian Gilbertese coupled with economic competition led to the establishment of separate colonies in 1976. In 1978 the Ellice Islands were given their independence from Britain and the nation of Tuvalu was established. Its capital is Funanfuti (aka Vaiaku) on Funafuti Island. It is a constitutional monarchy, but consideration is being given to establishing a republic. The Gilbert, Line, and Phoenix Islands were granted independence by the United Kingdom in 1979 as the Republic of Kiribati (pronounced "Keeribas"). Betio is the main shipping port and nearby Bairiki is the nation's capital and business center. Japan built a satellite ground station on Tarawa Atoll in 1985 as did China in 1997.

Tarawa Atoll. Tarawa (pronounced Ta-ra-wa), aka Cook or Knox Atoll, both little used, was code-named INCREDIBLE. The main assault took place on Betio Island (pronounced Bay-shio), aka Bititu on old charts, code-named HELEN and later, LONGSUIT. Tarawa is the northern most of the of the Gilbert Islands in the Central District and is at 1°30' N 173°00' E. It is located 2,390 miles southwest of Pearl Harbor. The nearest atoll in the group is Abaiang about ten miles to the north and Maiana is some twenty miles south. Makin Atoll, the other main objective of Operation GALVANIC, is 105 miles to the north.

Tarawa is a triangular-shaped coral atoll (see Map 73). The eighteen-mile-long north-

Map 73
Tarawa Atoll, Gilbert Islands

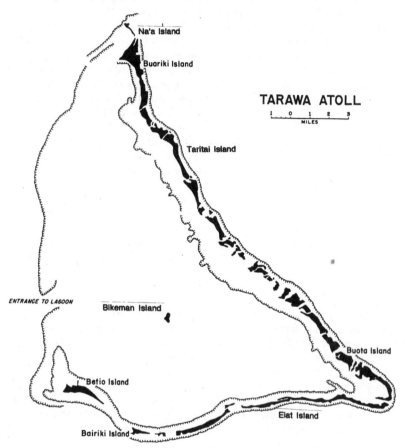

east side, with some forty-two islands and islets, is oriented northwest to southeast while the southern twelve-mile-long base, with five islands, runs roughly west to east. Most maps in official histories depict considerably fewer islands for simplicity and because at low tide many small islets "merged" into one. Seldom too do they depict little Bikeman Island in the middle of the lagoon, the remnants of the ancient volcanic caldera. The 12-½-mile-wide northwest side of the lagoon is devoid of islands, but is barred by a submerged barrier reef with a one-mile-wide lagoon passage 3-½ miles north of Betio. The atoll's largest island, Betio, is both the southern- and westernmost in the atoll and the assault's main objective.

Betio is 800 yards wide at its west end tapering to Takaronro Point on the east end of its 3,800-yard length (see Map 74). The 291-acre coral sand island (about the size of the Pentagon and its parking lots or one-third the size of New York's Central Park) has a maximum elevation of only ten feet with most of it below six feet. There are no streams or ponds; brackish water is obtained from wells and freshwater from rain catchments. Most of the island is covered with palm trees. The Japanese cut very few of these bringing

Betio Island, Tarawa Atoll

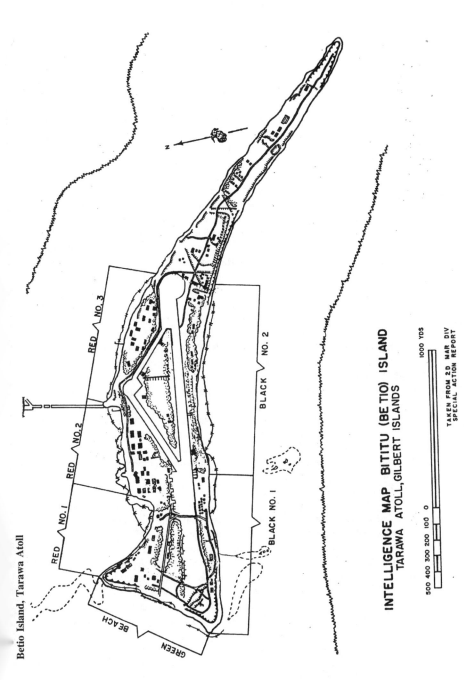

INTELLIGENCE MAP BITITU (BETIO) ISLAND
TARAWA ATOLL, GILBERT ISLANDS

500 400 300 200 100 0   1000 YDS

TAKEN FROM 2 D MAR DIV
SPECIAL ACTION REPORT

Marine Corps intelligence map of Japanese defenses.

thousands of palms from other islands to build defenses. Most palms on the island were destroyed during the battle and were replanted some years later. The beaches are thirty to fifty yards wide at low tide; water lapped the sea wall at high tide. A 500–1,200-yard-wide fringing reef surrounds the island.

Tides played a crucial role in the battle almost leading to an American defeat. A dodging tide was expected during the assault, that is, a neap tide that ebbed and flowed several times a day in an unpredictable manner. The Marines hoped for a high dodging tide, which would have maintained a water depth over the reef sufficient to allow landing craft to cross. The period of dodging tides would have ended on 22 November. This later period's spring tides would have been high, but were either too early in the morning for a daylight landing or too late to allow a beachhead to be secured before dark. A low dodging tide occurred and landing craft were unable to cross the reef even at "high tide." This proved near disastrous.

Tarawa was in the Central, or Tarawa, District of the Gilbert and Ellice Crown Colony and was the district capital and the port of entry for the Gilberts. There were seven villages: Betio, Baririki, Abaokoro, Noto, Buariki, Nabeina, and Buota. The district capital was located on Betio along with the government hospital, King George V School for Native Boys, and the colony gaol. It was also headquarters for the Burns Philp Trading Company Ltd. and two smaller trading firms. The leper station was on Naa Island (aka Lone Tree Island) at the atoll's extreme north end. London Missionary Society and (French) Roman Catholic missions were on the atoll. The main export and source of native employment was copra. Fishing and government service were additional sources of employment. A 1,600-foot-long Government Pier (referred to as the Long or Central Pier in Marine documents) jutted into the lagoon from Betio's north-central portion and became an important landmark during the battle. The 150-foot-long Burns Philp Pier was 400 yards east of the Long Pier. Both piers were built of coconut logs. A simple packed-coral, lagoon-side road ran the entire length of the atoll; most gaps between islands could be crossed at low tide. Some 2,700 native Micronesians lived on the atoll when the Japanese seized it. Most of the thirty Commonwealth citizens were evacuated to Fiji, but a few remained to be interned along with twenty-four coastwatchers on nine of the Gilberts' sixteen atolls. Most of the missionaries and nuns, widely scattered on different islands, had not yet been evacuated. The Japanese forced the natives on Betio to move to other islands in the atoll to fish for themselves and the occupiers. Natives and internees were also used as forced labor to prepare defenses.

On 10 December 1941 a detachment of the *51st Guard Force*, after landing on Makin, came ashore on Betio where the missionaries and nuns had assembled to await evacuation to Ocean Island. They were only mildly harassed and none were interned. The Japanese rounded up a few Europeans and soon left. They returned on 24 December searching for coastwatchers, collecting seven. The Japanese returned again on 3 September 1942 to search all of the atolls and rounded up all seventeen remaining coastwatchers and five Europeans. *SNLF* troops arrived on 15 September with construction troops arriving in December. The original troops were reorganized as a special base force (defense troops) on 15 February 1943 and a new naval special landing force arrived on 17 March to be reinforced by more construction troops in May. At the time of the American landing the *3d Special Base Force (-)* formerly *Yokosuka 6th SNLF)*, *Sasebo 7th SNLF (-)*, *111th Construction Unit (-)*, and a detachment of the *4th Fleet Construction Department* were on Tarawa. Collectively, this 4,866-man force was known as the *Gilberts Area Defense Force* under Rear Admiral SHIBASAKI Keichi, with detachments detailed to Butaritari and Apamama Atolls as well as Ocean and Nauru Islands to the west. Intelligence estimated 2,500–3,100 troops.

Betio was to be the core of the Gilberts defense and was converted to what was arguably the most strongly defended locale of its size in the world. Over 500 pillboxes, bunkers, and shelters were built of coconut logs, concrete, and steel with dozens of coast defense and antiaircraft gun positions and all-around inshore obstacles. A 4,400-foot coral runway occupied much of the island's western portion. The airfield's existence, which had begun to be built in October 1942, was not discovered until a U.S. bomber raid on 26 January 1943. The Japanese concrete command post bunker was located on the north side of the airfield near its east end and south of the Burns Philp Pier. A three-to-five-foot-high coconut and coral rock sea wall was built around virtually the entire island. The Japanese expected the Americans to land on the island's ocean, or south, side with a second choice being the west end. The Americans landed on the lagoon, or north, side. Admiral SHIBASAKI claimed the Americans could not take Tarawa with a million men in a hundred years.

Nauru Island (see below), 390 miles west of the Gilberts and the only other Japanese-held island in the area with a completed airfield, was determined to be too well defended. Tarawa was the main Japanese bastion, possessed the area's largest airfield, and was headquarters of the *Gilberts Area Defense Force*. Carrier strikes on Tarawa began in September and Army Air Forces bomber raids began in mid-November. The U.S. Fifth Fleet marshaled at Efaté in the New Hebrides and at Pearl Harbor. All forces had sailed for the Gilberts by early November arriving predawn on the 20th. The landing craft were launched by 0430 hours.

The Marine Corps' 17,447-man Southern Landing Force, formed around the 2d Marine Division (2d, 6th, 8th, 10th [artillery] Marines) under Major General Julian C. Smith, was subordinate to V Amphibious Corps commanded by Major General Holland M. Smith. The division departed Wellington, New Zealand, and conducted rehearsals at Efaté, New Hebrides. The Fifth Fleet's Southern Attack Force (Task Force 53) set sail for the Gilberts on 13 November and arrived inside Tarawa's lagoon before dawn on the 20th.

Beaches RED were on the western north shore of Betio: Beach RED 1 near the west end, RED 2 west of the Long Pier, and RED 3 east of the Long Pier and centered on either side of the short Burns Philp Pier. Reinforcements landed on Beach GREEN on the island's west end on D+1. BLACK 1 and 2 on the western south shore were not used. Bairiki Island (CORA), 3,000 yards to the southeast of Betio, was cleared and artillery established there and on Eita Island (ELLA) 5,500 yards to the southeast.

Landing at 0845 hours, the 2d Marines secured tenuous beachheads around the Long Pier and on the island's northwest corner while the 8th Marines carved out a beachhead east on the Central Pier. On D+1 they cut the island in two across the center and seized the west end after additional troops landed there. On D+1 and D+2 battalions of the 6th Marines were landed on Beach GREEN on the island's west end. The Marines held two-thirds of the island by D+2 as they pushed westward, but pockets of Japanese still held out in the rear. The island's east end was reached on D+3 and Betio was declared secure at 1321 hours, 23 November 1943. Between 21 and 26 November small Marine units cleared the remainder of the atoll pushing a Japanese company north that had escaped from Bairiki Island. It established a defense on Buariki Island (SARAH) at the north end of the atoll and was wiped out on 26 November. The division scout company reconnoitered the unoccupied Abaiang, Marakei, and Maiana Atolls between 29 November and 1 December.

The Marines suffered their highest casualty rate in the briefest time during the seventy-six-hour Betio assault: 904 KIA, 93 POW, 2,233 WIA, and 88 MIA. Japanese troop and Korean laborer loses were 4,690 KIA with 17 Japanese and 139 Korean POWs. Approximately 175 Japanese were KIA with two POWs taken during their final stand on Buariki Island on 26 November.

Within a few days after the assault reconditioning of the airfield began and it was operational on 18 December. By early January 1944 it had been expanded and upgraded to a 6,600-foot strip named Hawkins Field (FPO SF 907) and employed to support the Marshalls operation. A 6,000-foot strip, Mulinix Field (FPO SF 908, APO SF 240), was established by the Army Air Forces on Buota Island (DIANA) at the atoll's southeast corner. Collectively, U.S. Air Bases, Tarawa Atoll was assigned FPO SF 808. A Marine cemetery was established behind Beach RED 2 and is known today as Memorial Garden.

The Tarawa assault was extremely controversial because of the extensive casualties, 18 percent of the landing force, which shocked the American public. The lessons learned were invaluable and reduced casualties in later operations. This resulted in improvements in naval gunfire techniques, new pillbox assault tactics, routine and expanded employ-ment of amphibian tractors to land the assault waves, introduction of specially designed amphibious command ships, improved radio procedures, replacement of light tanks with mediums, increased numbers of flamethrowers, bazookas, and demolitions, the necessity for Underwater Demolition Teams (frogmen) to clear obstacles, and a myriad of other tactical details.

Mullinix Field was closed on 9 December 1944 and Hawkins was transferred to the USAAF on 1 June 1945. It was closed soon after the war. Hawkins Field is now covered by houses, shops, and water storage tanks. The modern Bonriki Airport is on Buota Island, the former Mulinix Field. Concrete bunkers and gun positions are still scattered over Betio. Four British-made 8-inch guns, long rumored to have been captured at Sin-gapore (no 8-inch guns were there), are on the island's opposite ends. They are actually from an order of eight guns purchased from Britain in 1905 and positioned on the Jap-anese Home Islands. Much of the wartime Marine cemetery was subsequently bulldozed over when the airfield was expanded. All that remains today is a Memorial Garden near the shore end of the now demolished central pier. Two jetties sheltering a small boat port have been built to the east of the central pier. In 1968, the Marine Corps erected a monument to the battle on Betio. By 1986 the monument was in danger of being removed to make room for a Japanese-built fish-cold-storage plant. Two years later the 2d Marine Division Association dedicated a nine-ton Georgia granite monument. There is also a memorial in memory of the twenty-two British subjects murdered by the Japanese.

Butaritari (Makin) Atoll. Butaritari Atoll, commonly called Makin (pronounced "Muckin," but commonly called "Maken" by the Americans) after its principal island, was earlier known as Touching. In official documents Butaritari and Makin were used interchangeably for both the atoll and the island. Its code name was KOURBASH and later PLAYFUL. Butaritari is 105 miles north of Tarawa and is the northernmost of the Gilbert Islands. The nearest atoll in the group, other than Little Makin Atoll about four miles north of the Butaritari's east end, is Abaiang some seventy miles due south. Makin is in a key position to support future operations into the Marshalls and Carolines. Kwajalein Atoll in the central Marshalls is 450 miles to the northwest and Truk in the eastern Carolines is 1,265 miles west-northwest. Butaritari is situated at 3°10' N 172°50' E.

The triangular-shaped atoll's southeast side is about eighteen miles long and comprised of two long narrow islands averaging 500 yards in width (see Map 75). Both have a maximum elevation of twelve feet. Westernmost Makin Island (aka Butaritari Island), the atoll's largest, is ten miles long with a three-mile-long cross-T on its southwest end. Kuma Island is 6-½ miles long and slightly narrower than Makin. Both are joined by a

Map 75
Butaritari (Makin) Atoll, Gilbert Islands

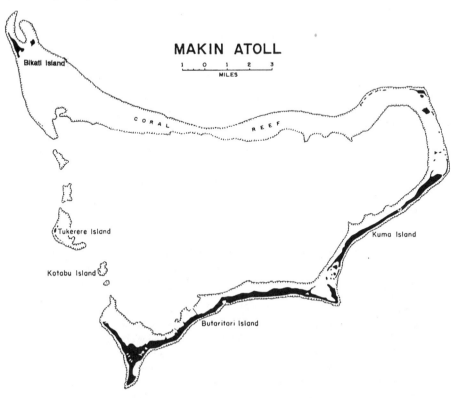

MAKIN ATOLL

Bikati Island

1 0 1 2 3
MILES

CORAL REEF

Tukerere Island

Kuma Island

Kotobu Island

Butaritari Island

continuous reef that turns north off the northeast end of Kuma for about four miles and then, after broadening out, runs west for some twenty miles. A few scattered islets dot the reef's east end, but the north arm is virtually islandless except for two small islets on the flared-out east end. The west side of the atolls has several coral heads and shoals lying across the entrance to the lagoon. One islet of any significance sits in the center of the open west side. Other coral reefs are scattered across the central and eastern portions of the lagoon (not shown on the map).

Little Makin Atoll (aka Makin Meang) is about four miles north of the Butartari's east end and is a six-mile-long elongated coral reef. The main island on the north end is 2-¾ miles long and a ½-mile wide with a few islets scattered in a line off its south end.

Makin Island's western portion was covered by coconut palms, thicker on the south side, and salt brush. The lagoon side of the north arm of the "T," Flink Point, and its junction with the long arm is lined with mangrove swamps. Much of the central portion was covered with salt brush and swamp, except near the shores. The whole of the junction with the T's crossarm is swamp-covered with interspersed lakes. The eastern portion was again covered with palms thickening toward the east end. A packed-coral motor road ran along the lagoon side the island's entire length and almost to the end of the T's south arm, Ukiangong Point, but only halfway up the T's north arm. Just west of the island's center portion was the old British administrative center, which included the government house and native hospital. There were four roads crossing the government area connecting to a simple road running along the oceanside in the central area only. The island's native numbered about 1,700 prior to the war. When the Japanese occupied the island they were ordered to relocate to other islands. The natives worked the coconut plantations, harvested taro, and fished. There were several villages, but the main one was Butaritari east of the government area. The second largest was Ukiangong near the T's south end. Four concrete or stone piers jutted out into the lagoon from this area (from east to west): Government Wharf (250 yards long), Stone Pier (150 yards), King's Wharf (300 yards with an unloading "island" at its end), and On Chong's Wharf (200 yards). The entire island was bordered by reefs on both sides, 100–200 yards across on the southern oceanside and 500–1,500 yards wide on the northern lagoon side. The sand beach on the oceanside was about twenty yards wide while there was virtually no beach on the lagoon side. The lagoon side was selected for the landing in the area of the wharves, which the landing craft could guide on and would later be used for unloading landing ships. That side's wider reefs were assessed to pose no major obstacle as they were flat and sufficiently deep at high tide for landing craft. At low tide they were completely exposed. The Army, however, experienced similar tidal problems on the lagoon side as the Marines did at Tarawa.

On 8 December 1941 a company of the *51st Guard Force* from Juluit Atoll, Marshall Islands, landed on Makin. A seaplane base and radio station were established in the former government area. There were only 73 IJN personnel, under the command of Sargeant Major KANEMITSU, based there in August when the Marines struck. Transported by two submarines, at 0530 hours, 17 August, two companies of the 2d Raider Battalion landed by rubber boat on Beach Z on the south shore and northeast of the Japanese base. The 221 raiders attacked the base claiming eighty-three Japanese dead. They shot down two seaplanes and the submarines sank a small transport and a patrol craft with deck gunfire. The Japanese launched two air attacks from the Marshalls. They were scheduled to withdraw that same night, but surf conditions delayed the withdrawal until the next night at 2030 hours. The Marines lost eighteen KIA, sixteen WIA, and twelve MIA. Actual Japanese losses were forty-six KIA; twenty-seven survived by hiding. It was later discovered that nine of the Marine missing had become separated and were left behind. They surrendered when Japanese reinforcements were flown in. The prisoners were taken to Kwajalein Island in the Marshalls and were executed on 16 October 1942. The raid, originally intended as a diversion for operations in the Solomons, achieved little and resulted in the Japanese heavily reinforcing and fortifying the Gilberts. None of the reinforcements were diverted from the Solomons.

On 20 August the Japanese flew in an advance party by seaplane; they had not and would not build an airfield on the island, and the relief force soon arrived by ship. Nauru and Ocean Islands were soon occupied and on 15 September the 1,500-man *Yokosuka 6th SNLF* arrived at Tarawa from Japan. Detachments were deployed to Butaritari and Apamama. On 15 February 1943, the *Yokosuka 6th SNLF* was redesignated the *3d Special Base Force* and placed in command of all forces in the Gilberts *(Gilberts Area Defense Force)*. An improved float-plane base was operational by July.

At the time of the American landing Butaritari was defended by the *Makin Detachment* of the *3d Special Base Force*, detachments of the *11st Construction Unit* and *4th Fleet Construction Department*, and IJN *Air Service* personnel with 798 troops under Lieutenant ISHIKAWA Seizo (U.S. Army estimated 500–800 troops). The defenders fortified the central portion of Makin Island around the old government area and the seaplane base on the lagoon side. Unlike Tarawa, Makin was only lightly defended. The 3,000-yard-wide main defense area was flanked by cross-island antitank ditches. The east tank barrier (five feet deep, thirteen feet wide) was about 300 yards west of Stone Pier and the more heavily fortified west tank barrier (six feet deep, 14-½ feet wide) was about 350 yards east of On Chong's Wharf. A 100–200-yard-wide band had been cleared through the palms to provide a clear field of fire over the ditches. This clearly identified the locations of the Japanese positions to naval gunfire observers and aircraft. King's Wharf was located in the center of the defense area; Government Wharf was 1,000 yards east of the east antitank ditch with Butaritari Village filling the lagoon-side area between the ditch and wharf. The predominance of shore defenses were oriented toward the ocean-side as the defenders expected a landing force to follow the raider's example. The largest coast defense guns were six 80mm (3.2-inch) pieces with half oriented to the ocean and the others on the lagoon.

The original plan for Operation GALVANIC called for the occupation of Tarawa and Nauru, but the latter was considered too strongly defended and Butaritari was substituted. The selection of Butaritari also made it easier to support the operation as the two main objectives were only 105 miles apart; Nauru was 390 miles to the east. The naval force was the 5th Fleet's Northern Attack Force (Task Force 52). The Army's 6,470-man Northern Landing Force was built around the 27th Infantry Division's 165th Infantry Regiment, elements of the 105th Infantry, and other reinforcing units. The landing force was under the direct command of Major General Ralph C. Smith, the 27th Division's commander, and was subordinate to V Amphibious Corps. The division loaded out of Pearl Harbor and undertook rehearsals at Maui. It then sailed for the Gilberts arriving off the west end of Makin Island before dawn on 20 November.

The main landing was preceded by a platoon of Army infantrymen and a platoon of reconnaissance Marines securing unoccupied Kotabu Island 1-½ miles north of Flink Point at 0643 hours. The first waves of amphibian tractors, the Army's first use of the reef-crossing vehicles, came ashore on Beaches RED (left; no number) and RED 2 (right) on the west end of the island's "T" crossarm at 0832 hours. Some of these had been fitted with 4.5-inch rockets, their first use in such a manner. The beaches were undefended and free of manmade obstacles, but the coral was unexpectedly studded with rocks, which prevented the following landing craft from approaching the beaches forcing the troops to wade ashore. It was later assessed that if the beaches had been well defended the landing forces would have been devastated. The accompanying tanks had a difficult time negotiating the swampy terrain between the beaches and the west tank barrier 2,500 yards to the east. Large-caliber shell holes contributed to the problem. The south and north ends of the "T" were secured within hours. The second attack landed at 1041 hours on Beach YELLOW on the lagoon side between the King's Wharf and On Chong's Wharf. With amphibian tractors in the lead the landing force experienced only very light fire on the approach. Once ashore the troops attacked in both directions trapping the defenders of the west tank barrier between two forces. The beachheads were well established by nightfall. The attack resumed the next day with remaining pockets of resistance overrun and the east tank barrier cleared on the 22nd. At noon the same day a company was landed by amphibian tractor on the lagoon side at a narrow isthmus of the island 4,000 yards beyond the east tank barrier to block fleeing Japanese as the main force swept east. Kuma Island to the east of Butaritari had been reconnoitered on the 21st. A small force was landed at 1400 hours, 22 November on the lagoon side 2,000 yards from Kuma's southwest end and advanced to that end of the island to block any Japanese who may have escaped from Makin. Makin Island was declared secure at 1030 hours, 23 November.

Most of the assault troops departed on the 24th leaving an element to secure the construction troops. U.S. Army losses were sixty-six dead and 158 wounded. All of the Japanese defenders were killed except for just over 100 captured personnel, mostly Korean laborers. While Army casualties were light, the Navy suffered heavily when the USS *Liscome Bay* (CVE-56) was sunk by a submarine while operating southwest of Butaritari with the loss of over 600 hands. The Army built the 7,000-foot Starmann Airfield on Butaritari Island to the east of the main defense area. It was completed in early January 1944 and supported operations in the Marshalls and Carolines. The airfield was built on sand and could only support fighters, but it is still operational as a commercial airport.

Apamama Atoll. Officially named Abemama Atoll, Apamama was used in virtually all U.S. documents during the war and this name will be used in this study. Abemama was earlier known as Hopper or Roger. The atoll was code-named BOXCLOTH and later BUMPKIN. Abemama is located in the center of the Gilbert Islands' Central District about seventy-five miles southeast of Tarawa. It is situated at 0°33' N 173°83' E. Since many of the islands/islets did not have names their code names are used here.

Oval-shaped Apamama Atoll is fifteen miles long northwest to southeast and six miles across (see Map 76). Its lagoon provided a deep, well-protected anchorage. The ends of the atoll and the northeast side was bordered by six islands and islets. The largest is the main island of Apamama (STEVE), hook-shaped, and about seven miles long and 1,000–2,000 yards wide. It is only twelve feet above sea level. It occupies most of the northeast side to the lagoon and hooks around its northwest end. Off its southeast end is the next largest island, OTTO, and in between the two is the islet OSCAR. On the southeast end of the lagoon is the third largest island, crescent-shaped JOHN. The islet ORSON lies between it and OTTO, while JOE, another islet, is off its west end. From the west end of JOE a submerged coral reef runs northwest to Entrance Island, actually an islet. The main entry to the lagoon, South Passage, runs to the northwest of it. Another submerged coral reef continues to the northwest to Abatiku Island, then hooks northeast connecting with STEVE (Apamama Island). A secondary entrance, Western Passage, lies between Abatiku and STEVE. The gaps between the islands and islets between STEVE and JOE could be easily forded at low tide. The islands are covered with coconut palms and salt brush. Almost 1,000 natives lived on the atoll in several villages with Tabontebike being the government station.

The Japanese first occupied Apamama on 31 August 1942 with a small *SNLF* detachment from Jaluit. This force departed on 4 September. A small detachment of the *6th SNLF* soon reoccupied the island. In February 1943 the *6th SNLF* was redesignated as the *3d Special Base Force* and the detachment on Apamama fell under the *Gilberts Area Defense Force*. In mid-October 1943 the atoll appeared to be unoccupied by the Japanese. The V Amphibious Corps Reconnaissance Company was given the mission of reconnoitering Apamama to determine if it was occupied. If occupied in strength, elements of the 6th Marines would assault the atoll on 26 November 1943. Loaded aboard a submarine the company traveled first to Tarawa and then to Apamama. It was attacked and damaged by a U.S. destroyer while en route, but was able to proceed arriving in the afternoon of 20 November. The company landed by rubber boat on JOE's west end at 0445 hours the next morning; they intended to land on JOHN to the east, but the current swept them west. The company moved across JOHN engaging a Japanese patrol. The

Map 76
Apamama Atoll, Gilbert Islands

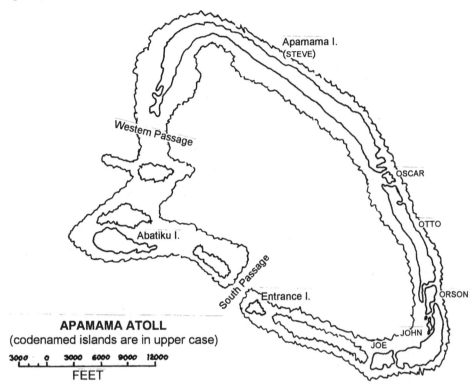

Apamama I.
(STEVE)

Western Passage

OSCAR

OTTO

Abatiku I.

South Passage

Entrance I.

ORSON

JOHN
JOE

APAMAMA ATOLL
(codenamed islands are in upper case)

3000 0 3000 6000 9000 12000
FEET

Marines found twenty-three defenders dug in on the south end of OTTO after approaching it from ORSON on the 23rd. The company attempted to withdraw and outflank the strongpoint by rubber boat, but was pinned down. The submarine shelled the strongpoint and the next morning the marines found that all of the defenders who were not killed by the shelling had committed suicide. Marine losses were two KIA and two WIA. On the 25th the 3d Battalion, 6th Marines occupied the atoll and was reinforced by the 8th Defense Battalion. Construction soon began on a 7,000-foot bomber strip, O'Hare Field, on the northwest hooked end of Apamama Island and was operational on 15 January 1944. It still serves as a commercial airport.

NAURU ISLAND

Nauru Island has been known as Pleasant, Shank, and Nawodo, and was code-named APHORISM. It is 390 miles west of the Gilberts, 155 miles northwest of Ocean Island, its nearest neighbor, 425 miles southwest of Jaluit Atoll, and 1,010 miles southeast of Truk. It is situated at 0°31' S 166°56' E; that is, twenty-six miles south of the equator. Being located roughly halfway between the Gilberts (time zone 24) and the Solomons (time zone 23), it is the only island in time zone 23:30.

Nauru is oval-shaped, 3-¾ miles long northeast to southwest, 2-¾ miles across the

Map 77
Nauru Island

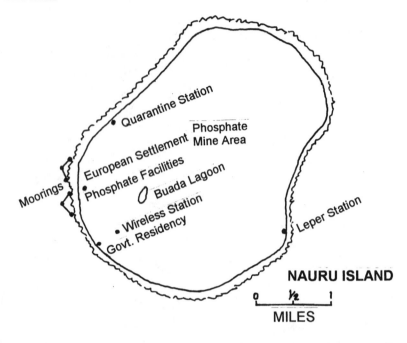

southern portion, and covers 8.2 square miles (see Map 77). The island is comprised largely of tribase phosphate of lime rock, extremely valuable as fertilizer. Nauru is edged with a narrow beach, a fertile coastal stripe 150–300 yards wide, then rises as a 100-foot coral rock cliff to a plateau. The island's interior is rocky and barren with low hills and shallow valleys. The highest elevation is 213 feet. The mining has left jagged coral pinnacles up to fifty feet high. Because of the strip mining there is little actual soil, except around Buada Lagoon, a small lake near the island's southwest side. The island is fringed with a narrow coral reef, which drops off steeply. Both Nauru and Ocean Islands are massive submarine mountains with just the peak emerging from the sea. The reef, dotted with coral heads, is exposed at low tide. On the east side the shore is very slightly indented by Enniberri Bay, but there are no protected anchorages there or elsewhere. Manmade ship moorings are positioned off the west shore for the phosphate freighters. The high temperatures run into the 90°F range and humidity is high. Average annual rainfall is 120 inches and storms are frequent often causing ships to lie off the island awaiting clam weather to allow loading. Most of the rain falls during the November to February westerly monsoon season. The easterly tradewinds prevail the rest of the year. Tropical diseases were almost nonexistent, but there was a leper station on the island's southeast side on the south end of Enniberri Bay. Vegetation is largely confined to the coastal strip and included palms, pandanus trees, some hardwoods, and brush. Tropical plants, fruits, and vegetables flourish around Buada Lagoon. Most indigenous birds and animals disappeared because of the destruction of their habitats though mining.

Native Nauruans are a mix of Polynesian, Micronesian, and Melanesian. They lived peacefully until the 1870s when the introduction of firearms and alcohol resulted in a vicious war leading to the death of almost half the population by the time Germany annexed the island. Nauru was discovered by an English Captain Fearn in 1798, which the British called Pleasant Island. Nauru was annexed by Germany in 1888, which used the native name, but it ignored Ocean Island, it being less hospitable. It was not until 1900 that it was discovered, quite by accident, that the island was comprised largely of the highest-quality phosphate. It was estimated that there was phosphate sufficient to supply Australia and New Zealand for a century. The German government granted a concession to the British Phosphate Company, in which Germany held shares, plus received a royalty on every ton of exported phosphate. Mining began in 1906. In November 1914 Nauru was seized without opposition by an Australian detachment. In 1919 the League of Nations granted Britain, Australia, and New Zealand combined authority over the island, effective in 1920. The phosphate mine was now under the British Phosphate Commission.

At the beginning of the war there were about 1,800 native Nauruans. The island was also populated by some 1,500 indentured Chinese laborers, 50 islanders from other islands, and 170 Europeans. The natives retained ownership of the land and were paid royalties on the phosphate. Their others needs were also provided by the administration. They did not work the mine. Only the coastal strip was inhabited. A 12-mile-long road circumscribes the island's shore and a number of roads run across the island to facilitate mining. There was also a narrow-gauge railroad that hauled phosphate to the west shore where large cantilevers conveyed the rock directly into ships' holds moored offshore. The government station and wireless station were on the south end of the island along with most service facilities. A number of small villages dot the coastal strip.

The war came to Nauru on 6 December 1940 when the German commerce raiders *Komet* and *Orion*, disguised as the Norwegian *Narvik* and the Japanese *Nanyo Maru*, sank five Commonwealth freighters awaiting loading in three days. The captured survivors were released by the Germans on Emirau Island near the end of the month. An Australian artillery troop was placed on the island as a nominal defense force. Mining and transport operations continued until 9 December 1941 when Japanese aircraft from the Marshalls bombed Nauru. The Chinese and Europeans, other than seven including the administrator, Lieutenant Colonel F.R. Chalmers and some Australian coastwatchers, were evacuated in February 1942 by a French destroyer and steamer. On 25 August 1942 the Japanese occupied undefended Nauru and it was garrisoned by two companies of the *43d Guard Force* from the Carolines. Construction soon began on an airfield on the southwest coast's fringe and it was completed in March 1942. In August 1942 the island was reinforced, as a result of the Marine raid on Makin Island, and in February 1943 the occupying unit was designated the *43d Guard Force Dispatched Landing Force* and made subordinate to the *Gilberts Area Defense Force*. The Japanese deported 1,200 Nauruans to Truk as forced labor with about one-third dying.

B-24 bombers from Funafuti first bombed Nauru on 20 April 1942. Especially heavy attacks were executed on the eve of the November 1943 Gilberts operation to completely neutralize it. The United States initially desired to seize Nauru and to establish a base there to support operations into the Marshalls and Carolines. It was to be secured in November 1943 at the same time as Tarawa and Apamama Atolls in the Gilberts. A division was assessed as necessary to take the small island and was to land on the northwest coast. The U.S. Army's 27th Infantry Division actually began training for the mission. Nauru though was considered too strongly defended and too difficult to support while operations were being conducted in the Gilberts far to the east. Butaritari in the

Gilberts was substituted. Air attacks by the USAAF and Navy continued to the end of the war. On 14 September 1945, IJN Captain SOEDA Hisayuki surrendered 3,700 troops to Brigadier J.R. Stevenson of the Australian Army.

The surviving Nauruans returned from Truk in January 1946. The U.N. placed Nauru under Australian trusteeship after the war. In anticipation of the eventual exhaustion of the phosphate, it was proposed to relocate the islanders to Curtis Island off the north coast of Queensland, Australia when that time came. The proposal was rejected. In 1968, it was granted independence as the Republic of Nauru and became a member of the Commonwealth. In 1970 the control of the mine was transferred from the British Phosphate Commission to the Nauru Phosphate Corporation. Various investment and commercial development efforts are being undertaken to replace the phosphate income when that runs out in a few years. Nauru is the third smallest country in the world; Monaco and Vatican City are smaller.

OCEAN ISLAND

Ocean Island was also known as Banaba, its native name, and Baanopa. The name Banaba is becoming more commonly used today. It was code-named CAPILLARY. The island is located 240 miles southwest of Tarawa Atoll, 155 miles southeast of Ocean Island, its nearest neighbor, and 420 miles south-southwest of Jaluit Atoll. It is situated at 0°52' S 169°35' E in time zone 24, the same as the Gilberts.

Ocean Island is oval-shaped appearing similar to Nauru in shape, but oriented differently and smaller. (see Map 78). It is 1-¾ miles long east to west and about the same across its east end, 1-¼ miles across the center portion, six miles in circumference, and covers 1,500 acres. The island is a volcanic cone with the lip of the rocky-sloped cone 276 feet above sea level. The cone's caldera is a shallow bowl. Ocean Island is edged with a narrow beach behind which is a 100-yard-to-¼-mile-wide gently slopping coastal fringe. Much of the island was covered with brush and woodlands, except where strip mining was underway. The mining has resulted in limestone pinnacles up to eighty feet high. The island is honeycombed with an extensive cave system, known as *bangabangas* to the Banabans and considered sacred. It was from these that water was obtained (rainwater seepage) until strip mining allowed rainwater to collect on the surface. The climate was similar to Nauru Island's. The south coast was slightly indented by Home Bay, flanked by Solomon's Point (Sydney Point on some maps) on the island's southeast corner and Lillian Point on the south side. Near the point is Ooma (pronounced "Uma"), the European community. The bay offers little protection, but it was here that phosphate freighters were loaded. A road ran around the coastal fringe from the west end to near Solomon's Point. Other roads ran into the cone to serve the mine.

When phosphate was discovered on Nauru in 1900 it was realized that Ocean Island was similar. No nation had bothered claiming Ocean Island. Britain immediately annexed the island on 28 November 1900. The British Phosphate Company soon began mining operations. The island was included in the Gilbert and Ellice Islands Crown Colony in 1916. The native Micronesian Banabans retained ownership of the land and received royalties from phosphate export; they did not work the mines. The headquarters of the British Phosphate Commission (Company prior to 1920) was based on the island as was the government administrative center for the Gilbert and Ellice Islands Crown Colony when the resident commissioner was installed there in 1900. At the beginning of the war there were approximately 140 Europeans, 640 native Banabans, 900 indentured Chinese, and 1,200 Gilbertese. The latter two groups worked the mines.

Map 78
Ocean Island

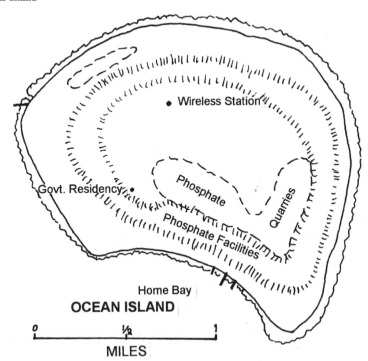

On 9 December 1941 Japanese aircraft from the Marshalls bombed Ocean Island putting a halt to mining operations. An Australian artillery troop was placed on the island as a defense force. It and most of the Europeans and Chinese were evacuated in February 1942 by a French destroyer and steamer. Six Europeans remained behind, the administrator, Mr. C.G.F. Cartwright, three New Zealand coastwatchers, and two missionaries. In March 1941 Rabi Island (pronounced "Rambi") near Vanu Levu in Fiji, had been purchased by the Australian government, using Banaban natives' phosphate royalty funds, to relocate the islanders to. This did not occur in time. On 26 August 1942 the Japanese occupied undefended Ocean Island and it was garrisoned by two companies of the *62d Guard Force* from Jaluit. The six Europeans are believed to have been murdered, but their remains were never found. The loss of Nauru and Ocean Islands caused a severe shortage of fertilizer in Australia and New Zealand. The United States was able to provide only one-third of those countries' needs. In August 1942 the island was reinforced and in February 1943 the defending unit was designated the *62d Guard Force Dispatched Landing Force* and made subordinate to the *Gilberts Area Defense Force*. No airfield was built there. Most of the Banabans and Gilbertese were taken to Kusaie, Nauru, and Tarawa where they were employed as forced labor. Some 160 Gilbertese were kept on Ocean Island to fish and build fortifications for the Japanese and would have been incorporated into the defense force if the island was attacked. The Allies never made any plans to assault Ocean Island, but did conduct frequent air raids. Two days after the

Japanese surrender the Gilbertese were murdered. One survived to testify in the subsequent war crimes trial. On 2 October 1945 IJN Lieutenant Commander SUZUKI Nahoomi surrendered his force of 400 men to Brigadier J.R. Stevenson, Australian Army.

The phosphate deposits were depleted in 1980 with all but 150 acres of the island's 1,500 acres strip-mined and the island was virtually abandoned. Some 4,000 Banabans now live on Rabi Island, Fiji where they moved to immediately after the war once collected from the various islands the Japanese had deported them to and 300 remain on Ocean Island. The Gilbert, Line, and Phoenix Islands were granted independence by the United Kingdom in 1979 as the Republic of Kiribati and Ocean Island was included.

JAPANESE MANDATED TERRITORY

A Japanese expeditionary force took control of the German possessions of the Marshall, Caroline, and Mariana Islands in October 1914 soon after World War I erupted. In December 1920 Japan was granted a Class C mandate by the League of Nations to govern the former German possessions, effective 1 April 1922. (These islands had been purchased by Germany from Spain in 1899.) These became known as the Japanese Mandated Territories or simply the Japanese Mandate. In December 1914 the Japanese established the *South Seas Defense Force*, from the *2d South Seas Squadron*, to garrison and administer the former German possessions. The civilian-run *South Seas Bureau (Nan'yo-Cho)* was organized in 1920 when the League of Nations adopted the terms of the Mandate. The *South Seas Bureau* was directly under the *Ministry of Overseas Affairs*, and divided into six administrative districts: Palaus, Marianas, Marshalls, and West, Central, and East Carolines. The *Bureau* was headquartered on Koror Island in the Palau Islands, West Carolines, itself organized into five sections: General, Financial, Police, Economic Development, and Communications. Virtually all commercial activities were under the control of the *South Sea Development Company (Nanyo Kohatsu Kabushiki Kaisha)* and the *Nankai Trading Company*.

Japan undertook a vigorous settlement policy and a major economic development effort in the islands. By the late 1930s Japanese settlers outnumbered the natives. The Japanese and native population in 1940 was 131,200. After serving the required two-year notice, Japan withdrew from the League of Nations in 1935 and the Mandate became a "closed territory" with Westerners restricted from entry. The popular press of the time called it "Japan's islands of mystery." Japan is often accused of "illegally" fortifying the Mandates, but she was under no obligation to the United States not to. The Five Power Naval Treaty, signed in 1922, was merely an agreement between Japan and the United States to maintain the status quo in regard to fortifications and navy bases in certain possessions. The Mandate was not included in the agreement. As late as 1938 the Japanese still claimed the islands were not being fortified. The *4th Fleet* was activated on 15 November 1939 to defend the Mandated Territory. It was organized as an amphibious force rather than a conventional combat fleet. Admiral SUETSUGU Nobumasa, prewar Commander-in-Chief of the *Combined Fleet*, described the Marshalls, Carolines, and Marianas as "made to order for Japan." Each of the three groups was provided with an independent defense system, centered around Jaluit, Truk, and Saipan, respectively, within which air and naval forces could be marshaled, serviced, and supplied as well as raids and operations mounted out of the range of Allied bases and reconnaissance aircraft.

An American bastion, Guam, was situated at the south end of the Marianas, long a thorn in Japan's side. Yap Island, West Carolines was another problem for Japan. A treaty, recognizing Japan's right of control, gave the United States equal rights to matters relating to the island's internationally important German-built telephone cable center and the later radiotelegraphic station.

The Mandated Territory with the Marshall, Caroline, and Mariana Islands totaled some 1,458 islands, islets, and reefs providing 860 square miles of land. They span an area of 2,500 miles from east to west (130° to 175° E) and 1,200 miles north to south (0° to 22° N). These islands extend across two time zones, 22 and 21.

The larger islands are of volcanic origin, most of which are heavily populated. The smaller islands, especially in the Marshalls and Carolines, are coral atolls, most of which were uninhabited or bear little population. The Marshall Islands lie in the eastern portion of the Mandates and are northwest of the Ellice Islands. The Caroline Islands extend in a long band to the west of the Carolines, its east end aligned with the east end of the Solomons far to the south and its west end with the west end of Netherlands New Guniea to the south. The Mariana Islands run north in a crescent from the Western Carolines toward the Kazan Retto with Iwo Jima.

The area encompassed by the Japanese Mandate includes most of the region known as Micronesia. The natives are predominantly Micronesians with an admixture of Polynesian, especially in the eastern and central islands where they are often referred to as "Kanakas," the native word for "man." Those in the west and north have more Malay blood and are called "Chamorros." They also possess a great deal of Spanish and Filipino blood. Most of Micronesia was Christianized by the late 1800s and Japan allowed the natives to continue their religious practices. Militarily the Mandated Territory provided Japan with a barrier to the Australian, British, American, and French possessions to the south, an outer defense belt. They also viewed these islands as forward bases for the conquest of those same territories. They were also economically valuable to Japan with the main exports being sugar, maize, coffee, phosphate, bauxite, fruits, vegetables, fish, and wood products. The climate of these islands was similar with a northeast tradewind from December to May. This is the dry season with very little rain, April being the driest month. From June to November the southwest monsoon brings five to fifteen inches a month, an annual mean of eighty-one inches. Temperatures range from the high 60°Fs at night to the high 90°Fs in the day. Humidity can be high. Freshwater is scarce with rain catchment being the main source, especially on the atolls.

The former Japanese Mandate was turned over to U.S. control by the United Nations on 2 January 1947 as the Trust Territory of the Pacific Islands. The postwar status of each group of islands in the former Japanese Mandate is discussed in the appropriate section.

MARSHALL ISLANDS

The Marshall Islands, code-named BULLY, *Maasyaru Shoto* to the Japanese, spanning from 162° to 173° E and 5° to 15° N, is centered on 09°00' N 168°00' E, roughly 2,500 miles southwest of Hawaii, 2,500 miles southwest of Japan, and 1,000 miles northeast of New Guinea. The East Caroline Islands are roughly 500 miles to the west and Guam is 1,500 miles in the same direction. The Marshalls contain twenty-nine atolls, five separate islands, and 867 reefs providing seventy square miles of land and covering some 750,000 square miles of ocean area. The Marshalls span an area of 800 square miles of ocean. Counting the atoll's islets there are 1,152 islands/islets. The islands are arranged in two parallel chains running northwest to southeast, separated by roughly 100 miles, the eastern Radak (Sunrise) Group with sixteen atolls and islands and the western Ralik

(Sunset) Group with eighteen atolls and islands. The Marshalls are about 160 miles northwest of the Gilberts and are basically an extension of that group. Those militarily important atolls with separate entries are identified in the following table by an asterisk (*). The number of islands/islets is provided, when known, along with other names from north to south. The native names were generally used by both the Allies and the Japanese.

Ralik Group (western)		*Radak Group* (eastern)	
Ebon (Boston, Covell)	21	Taongi (Gasper, Rico, Smyth)	—
Namorik (Baring)	3	Bikar (Dawson)	3
Kili (Hunter)	1	Utirik (Button, Kutusov)	—
Jaluit* (Bonham)	50	Taka (Suvarov)	—
Ailinglapala (Elmore, Helut, Odia)	21	Mejit (Miadi, New Year)	1
Jabwat	1	Ailuk (Tindal, Watts)	10
Namu (Musquillo)	—	Jemo (Steeo-to, Temo)	1
Lib (Princessa, Tebut)	1	Likiep (Count Heiden, Legieb)	44
Ujae (Katherine)	—	Wotje* (Romanzoff, Romanzow)	64
Lae (Rae, Brown†)	14	Erikub (Bishop, Egerup, Junction)	52
Kwadjalin* (Menschikoff, Mentshikow)	38	Maloelap* (Araktcheeff, Calvert, Kaven)	64
Wotto (Shanz)	—	Aurh (Aur, Auru, Ibetson, Traversey)	32
Ailinginae (Ailinglablab)	—	Majuro* (Arrowsmith, Madjuro)	33
Rongelap (Pescadore)	—	Arno (Aruno, Daniel, Pedder)	14
Rongerik (Radokala)	48	Mille* (Miri, Mulgrave, Mili)	30
Bikini (Eschscholtz)	10	Knox (Narik)	10
Eniwetok* (Brown)	40		
Ujelang (Arecifos, Casobos, Providence)	13		

Both large and small coral atolls (Kwajalein is the world's largest) comprise most of the Marshall's land area varying three to twenty feet above sea level. The highest point in the islands is on Likiep at thirty-four feet; the average elevation is seven feet. The larger islands are covered with coconut palms, pandanus trees, breadfruit trees, and salt brush of varying densities. The smaller ones are bare or covered with salt brush. Virtually all atolls and islands are surrounded by coral reefs, which generally lie closer to shore on the lagoon side. The beaches are narrow and either flat or very gently sloping for the most part. The native Marshallese are Micronesians with much Polynesian influence.

The first of the Marshall Islands was discovered by a Spaniard, Alonso de Salazar in 1525 and Alvaro de Saavedra in 1529. Spain though did little to establish ownership of the islands until annexing them in 1686, but not much effort was made to develop or even retain them. In the late 1700s and early 1800s more islands were discovered or "rediscovered" by various Russian (who made the first detailed maps explaining the Russian names of some islands), English, and American explorers. They were named after a British Captain John Marshall who discovered some of the islands in the southern

---

†Not to be confused with Eniwetok Atoll, which was also commonly known as Brown Atoll.
*Entries for these atolls can be found in the text.

Radak Group. There was no government within the islands and freebooters, adventurers, and traders did as they pleased. In 1880 an economic competition evolved over the islands between Australia and Germany. This lasted until Germany annexed the islands in 1902; they had been purchased from Spain in 1899. Australia maintained some trading connections in the islands until October 1914, when Japan, acting as an ally of Britain, seized the Marshalls. Japanese trading firms took over control of the islands and the Australian interests dwindled. Besides interning German citizens, Japan drove half-German, half-Marshallese out of the islands, who fled south to the British-controlled Gilberts. The first simple airstrip to be built in the Marshalls was laid out on Roi in the mid-1930s. The only available prewar population figures date from 1935, 10,000 natives and 490 Japanese. Except for Eniwetok and Ujelang Atolls (administered by the *Ponape* or *East Carolines District* from Ponape Atoll), the Marshalls' administrative center was the *South Sea Bureau's Jaluit* or *Marshalls District* on Jaluit Atoll, which was a major naval base prior to late 1943.

Preinvasion air attacks forced the Japanese to withdraw their ships to Truk in the East Carolines. The *4th Fleet*, headquartered at Truk, was responsible for the defense of the Marshalls and its main operating unit in the Marshalls was the *6th Base Force*. This unit had arrived in March 1941 and was first based on Wotje. It relocated to Kwajalein in August. Later in the year guard forces arrived to garrison the islands. IJN air bases in the Marshalls included land-plane fields on Roi at the north end of Kwajalein, Mille, Maloelap, Wotje, and Eniwetok (an uncompleted field was on Kwajalein Island) and seaplane bases at Jaluit, Wotje, Majuro, Taongi, and Utirik. Regardless of all these airfields, by the time of the American invasion there were only a few aircraft remaining on Eniwetok; all others had been destroyed by relentless carrier and bomber air attacks. A submarine base had been established on Kwajalein Island. On 1 February 1942 a U.S. carrier task force ventured into the Marshalls and launched air attacks on Jaluit, Kwajalein, Milli, Maloelap, and Wotje as well as Makin in the Gilberts. While they were unsettling to the Japanese, little damage was inflicted. In September 1943 the *Imperial General Headquarters* designated a new *National Defense Zone* anchored in the Marianas, Carolines, and running through the eastern portion of Dutch New Guinea. The Solomons, Bismarcks, and eastern New Guinea had been lost or were about to be. The Marshalls, while outside of this zone, were not abandoned. A delaying action was to be fought there while defenses in the new zone were established. The IJA was tasked with sending units from Japan, North China, and the Philippines to support the delaying action. Reorganized units designated *South Sea Detachments* and the new *1st Amphibious Brigade* were sent to Kwajalein, Jaluit, Maloelap, Wotje, Mille, and Eniwetok in late 1943 and January 1944.

With the Gilberts securely in American hands in November 1943, the next step toward Japan was to be Operation FLINTLOCK, the conquest of the Marshalls. Planning began in September 1943, but it was not until mid-December that the plans were finalized after many changes. It was apparent that the hard lessons learned at Tarawa were integrated into the planning. New innovations were introduced as well, such as dedicated amphibious command ships, Underwater Demolition Teams whose frogmen would clear offshore mines and obstacles, amphibious trucks (DUKW or "Ducks"), and the routine use of armored amphibian tractors to land the assault troops under enemy fire and cross the reefs. The operation was to commence on 30 January 1944. The 5th Fleet was responsible for the operation and its joint Marine and Army assault forces were under V Amphibious Corps commanded by Major General Holland M. Smith. Of the four Marine and four Army infantry regiments assigned to the Marshalls invasion, only two of the Army regiments had seen combat in the Aleutian Islands, and that was under near-Arctic conditions. The main effort was the seizure of the centrally located Kwajalein Atoll to provide a major fleet base to support operations into the Marianas and Carolines, the securing of other selected islands, and the neutralization of bypassed islands by air attacks. The first preinvasion air attacks inflicted on the Marshalls began in mid-November 1943 with carrier strikes and then bombers from the Ellice Islands and Canton Island. On 23 December bomber raids were launched from the Gilberts, as were most subsequent attacks. The attacks were aimed at Japanese airfields and installations on Mille, Maloelap, Jaluit, Wotje, and Kwajalein Atolls and continued up to the invasion. (It is interesting to note that the first theoretical plan for an invasion of the Marshalls was developed by a Marine officer, Major Earl H. Ellis, in 1921. It called for the seizure of Eniwetok, Ujelang, Wotje, and Jaluit Atolls.)

Most of the naval forces for the invasion assembled at Hawaii, but others steamed from Fiji, the Solomons, Ellice Islands, and San Diego, California. The main task forces assembled in the Hawaii Islands where the Army units had conducted rehearsals while the Marines had rehearsed on the California coast. American planners studying aerial photographs of the Marshalls saw that the initial Japanese defensive positions were built on the ocean side, but because of the lagoon-side landings on Makin and Tarawa, they had began construction of defenses on the lagoon side. Most of the defenses had no depth and were poorly integrated. The plan called for lightly defended Majuro Atoll in the lower portion of the eastern chain to be seized first. On 31 January the Marines would seize small islands in the vicinity of Roi-Namur in the north end of Kwajalein Atoll in the center of the Marshalls' western chain and the Army would do likewise near Kwajalein Island at the south end of the atoll. The Marines would assault Roi-Namur the next day as the Army attacked Kwajalein Island. On 17 February, Eniwetok Atoll on the northwest corner of the Marshalls would be seized by a joint Marine and Army force. The other islands in Japanese hands, Mille, Maloelap, Jaluit, and Wotje, were bypassed and relentlessly pounded by air attacks until the war's end.

Task Force 51 departed the Hawaii Islands 22–23 January 1944 heading southeast for a distance of 2,200 miles. Carrier air attacks commenced on the Japanese-held islands on the 29th along with gun attacks. On the 30th the Northern and Southern Attack Groups separated and headed for the north and south ends of the huge Kwajalein Atoll.

The seven militarily important atolls are discussed below. Those assaulted by U.S. forces, Majuro, Kwajalein, and Eniwetok, are discussed first followed by the atolls that were bypassed and remained in Japanese hands.

Majuro Atoll, Marshall Islands

Majuro, also known as Arrowsmith, was code-named SUNDANCE and later, POSTSCRIPT. It was sometimes earlier spelled as Madjuro. Robert Louis Stevenson dubbed it the "Pearl of the Pacific" during his 1889 visit. Majuro is in the lower portion of the eastern Radak Group about 280 miles southeast of Kwajalein, sixty-five miles northwest of Mille, ninety-eight miles south of Maloelap, and 117 miles northeast of Jaluit. It is situated at 7°10' N 171°10' E.

The elongated soil atoll is twenty-six miles east to west and six miles wide. (see Map 79). Most of its circumference is edged with a continuous reef with the only openings on the north-central side. The lagoon is entered though the two-mile-wide Catlin Pass. The lagoon is 150–210 feet deep offering an excellent protected anchorage, but there are some coral heads in the western portion. Majuro Island (LAURA) is the largest of the

Majuro Atoll, Marshall Islands

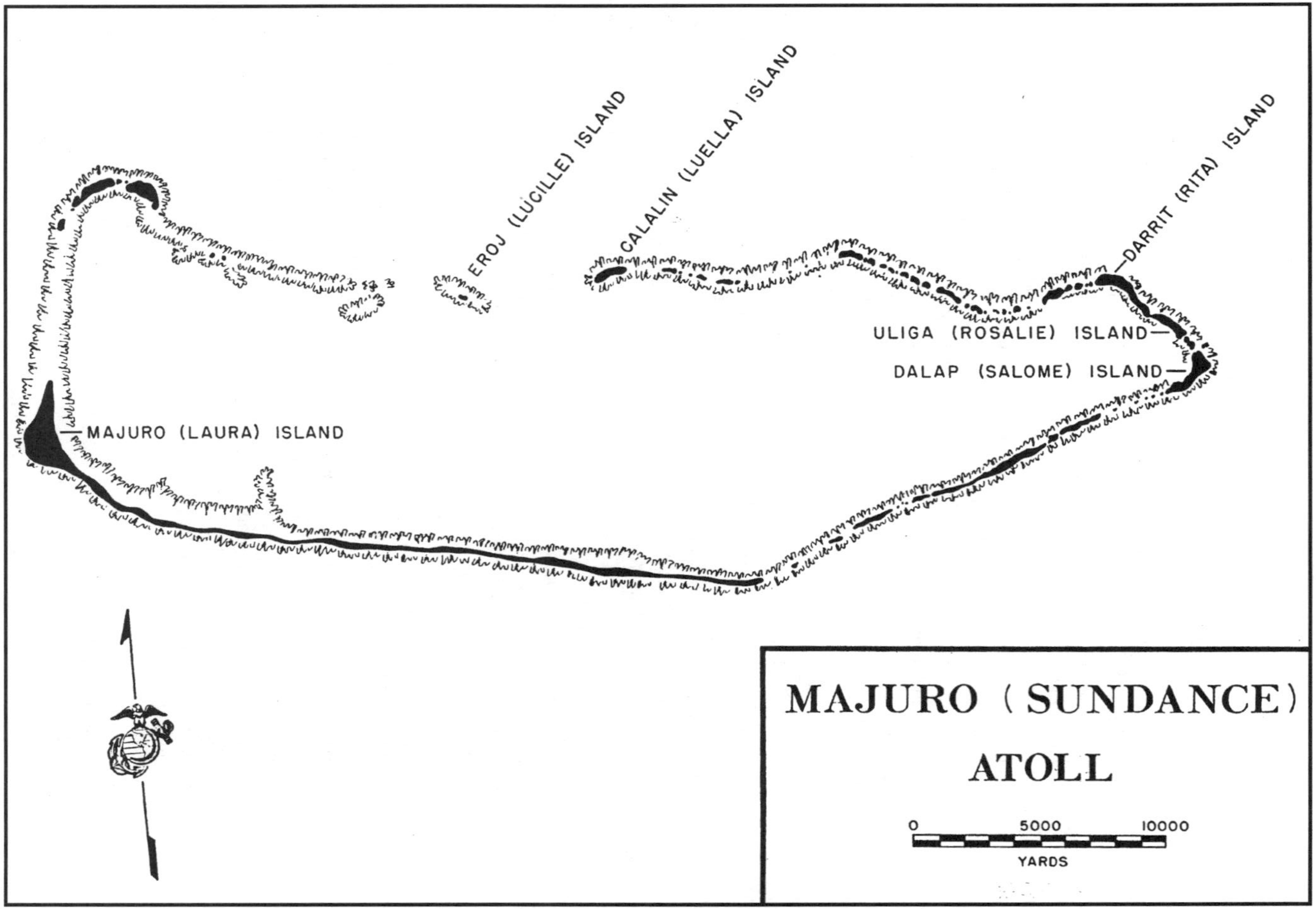

MAJURO (SUNDANCE)
ATOLL

0   5000   10000
YARDS

DARRIT (RITA) ISLAND

ULIGA (ROSALIE) ISLAND

DALAP (SALOME) ISLAND

CALALIN (LUELLA) ISLAND

EROJ (LUCILLE) ISLAND

MAJURO (LAURA) ISLAND

atoll's fifty-seven islets. It is a thin, not over 300 yards wide, ribbon twenty-one miles long running from the atoll's southeast corner, where a 1 by 1-¾-mile wide oval sits, southeast to where the reef makes a northeastward turn. Sandbar islets are scattered along that side of the reef for about twelve miles. On the narrow east end of the atoll are three larger islets, from south to north, Dalap (SALOME), Uliga (ROSALIE), and Darrit (RITA). More small islets dot the reef along its north side to Calalin Pass, which is flanked on its east side by Calalin Island (LUELLA) and west by Eroj Islet (LUCILLE). The submarine reef, with some gaps, continues northwestward, to a few islets situated on the atoll's northwest corner. The reef on the west end is free of islets. The thirty-three islands and islets are covered with low salt brush. The atoll experiences heavy rains.

The Japanese had built a small seaplane base on Darrit Island on the atoll's northeast corner. It included a 400-foot-long timber pier, a narrow-gauge railroad leading from the pier to a group of warehouses, and various support facilities. Majuro was added to Operation FLINTLOCK's list of objectives on 26 December. Being lightly defended it was to be secured and used as a base on which to build airfields that would aid in keeping the line of communications open to Kwajalein and protect that route from the bypassed Japanese-held islands to the north and south. It was also to be used as a temporary fleet anchorage if necessary.

The SUNDANCE Landing Force, 2d Battalion, 106th Infantry Regiment, detached from the 27th Infantry Division, and the VAC Reconnaissance Company, was assigned to lightly defend Majuro Atoll. The landing force was delivered by Task Group 51.2, the Majuro Attack Group. At about 2300 hours, 30 January, a platoon of the reconnaissance company landed by rubber boat on Calalin Island making them the first American troops to land on an island possessed by Japan since before the war. The rest of the company landed on other islands and found that the Japanese had abandoned the atoll, even the seaplane base on Darrit Island, a year earlier. Only an IJN warrant officer, who was captured, and three civilians, who fled, were found on Majuro Island overseeing Japanese property.

The SUNDANCE Landing Force occupied Darrit and Dalap Islands and the Marine 1st Defense Battalion soon arrived. The U.S. Navy quickly developed the previous Japanese seaplane base on Darrit Island into their own. On Dalap Island a 5,800-foot airfield was built and was usable as an emergency landing strip in less than two weeks. Existing Japanese facilities and supplies were utilized. Minimal fleet support facilities were built and the air facilities were expanded as Fleet Anchorage, Naval Base, and Naval Air Facility, Majuro. A 4,000-foot fighter strip was built on Uliga Island and a coral causeway was built connecting Dalap and Uliga Islands as well as others to provide a 35-mile-long road, which has been paved and is still in use. The 4th Marine Base Defense Aircraft Wing Headquarters was based at Majuro Atoll. U.S. submarines soon began evacuating natives from Japanese-controlled islands that would continue to be bombarded, to both protect them and deny the Japanese their labor, and they were housed on Majuro to total 4,000. The Navy provided for the natives' needs and after the war returned them to their home islands. The base remained fully operational through the war and was closed on 23 June 1947.

Kwajalein Atoll, Marshall Islands

Kwajalein Atoll, pronounced "Kwa-dja-lin," almost no accent, was earlier known as Menschikoff or Mentshikow. It was initially code-named CARILLON and later EYRIE, PORCELAIN, and ROWLOCK, and eventually nicknamed "Kwaj." Kwajalein is near the geographic center of the Marshalls and in the central portion of the western Ralik Group. Namu Atoll, the nearest to it, is about forty miles to the southeast. Kwajalein is 337 miles southeast of Eniwetok and 245 miles northeast of Jaluit. Truk in the Carolines is 925 miles to the west and Guam in the Marianas is 1,320 miles to the west-northwest. Kwajalein Atoll is located at 09°10' N 167°25' E.

Kwajalein is the largest atoll in the world measuring sixty-six miles in length and twenty miles wide, so wide that islands on the other side cannot be seen (see Map 80). The lagoon covers 655 square miles making it large enough to shelter the entire U.S. Pacific Fleet. There are ninety-three islands and islets, of which thirty-eight islands are of significant size, but there are only just over six square miles of land. The atoll forms a misshapen triangle with numerous breaks in the reef allowing entry into the lagoon. The atoll forms two arms, the south and the west, with a small portion projecting to the north, areas generally referred to as western, southern, and northern or northeastern Kwajalein. While islands and islets are scattered on most of the reef's length, there is the fifteen-mile wide Tabik Channel (only the western part is passable at low tide because of a submarine reef) on the south side of the west arm; the larger islands are concentrated in four areas. Two of these were bypassed by the war, the west end of the western arm with Ebadon Island (GODFREY) and smaller ones, the second largest in the atoll, and the eastern portion of the west arm's south side, an area east of the Tabik Channel and where the southern arm turns south, with Ennugenliggelap, Yebbenohr, and Nell Islands being the most notable. On the end of the southern arm is the atoll's largest island, Kwajalein Island, while on the northern lode are the twin islands of Roi and Namur. North of Kwajalein Island is the much smaller, but defended, Ebeye Island. These were Operation FLINTLOCK's main objectives. Both of these areas possessed numbers of smaller islands, some of which were used for artillery firing positions to support the assault on the main islands. Even though these island objectives were in the same atoll and part of the same operation, they were very much fought as independent battles. Kwajalein and Roi-Namur Islands are forty-two miles apart.

The numerous small adjacent islands in the vicinity of Kwajalein and Roi-Namur were all code-named and these will be used in the following discussion since many of the native names are very similar, difficult to pronounce, and some had no known native names. The code name will follow the native name in parentheses with its first use. Note that for the most part the island code names adjacent to Roi-Namur began with "A" and those near Kwajalein had code names beginning with "B" or "C"; there were exceptions. See also the accompanying maps.

Roi-Namur Islands. The twin islands of Roi (BURLESQUE) and Namur (CAMOUFLAGE) are at the corner of the northward projecting barrier reef at 09°25' N 167°30' E making them the northernmost islands in Kwajalein Atoll. Their code names are a rare instance of signifying some meaning; Roi had been stripped of vegetation to make room for the airfield while Namur was heavily covered with palms and brush. Both islands are irregularly shaped and separated by 500 yards, but connected by a sandbar along the lagoon side and a concrete causeway halfway between the lagoon and oceansides (see Map 81). A low, brush-covered, triangular-shaped piece of land projected north from the sandbar, its end (Pauline Point) crossed by the causeway. Roi measures 1,170 by 1,250 yards while Namur is 800 by 890 yards. Both islands had well-developed road systems. A figure "4"–shaped airfield (one 4,300 and two 2,700-foot runways), taxiways, and dispersal areas occupied most of Roi and there were few buildings other than hangars and shops. The airfield's shape was noted by the assaulting 4th Marine Division. All airfield support facilities, shops, and barracks were concentrated on Namur's south and

Map 80
Kwajalein Atoll

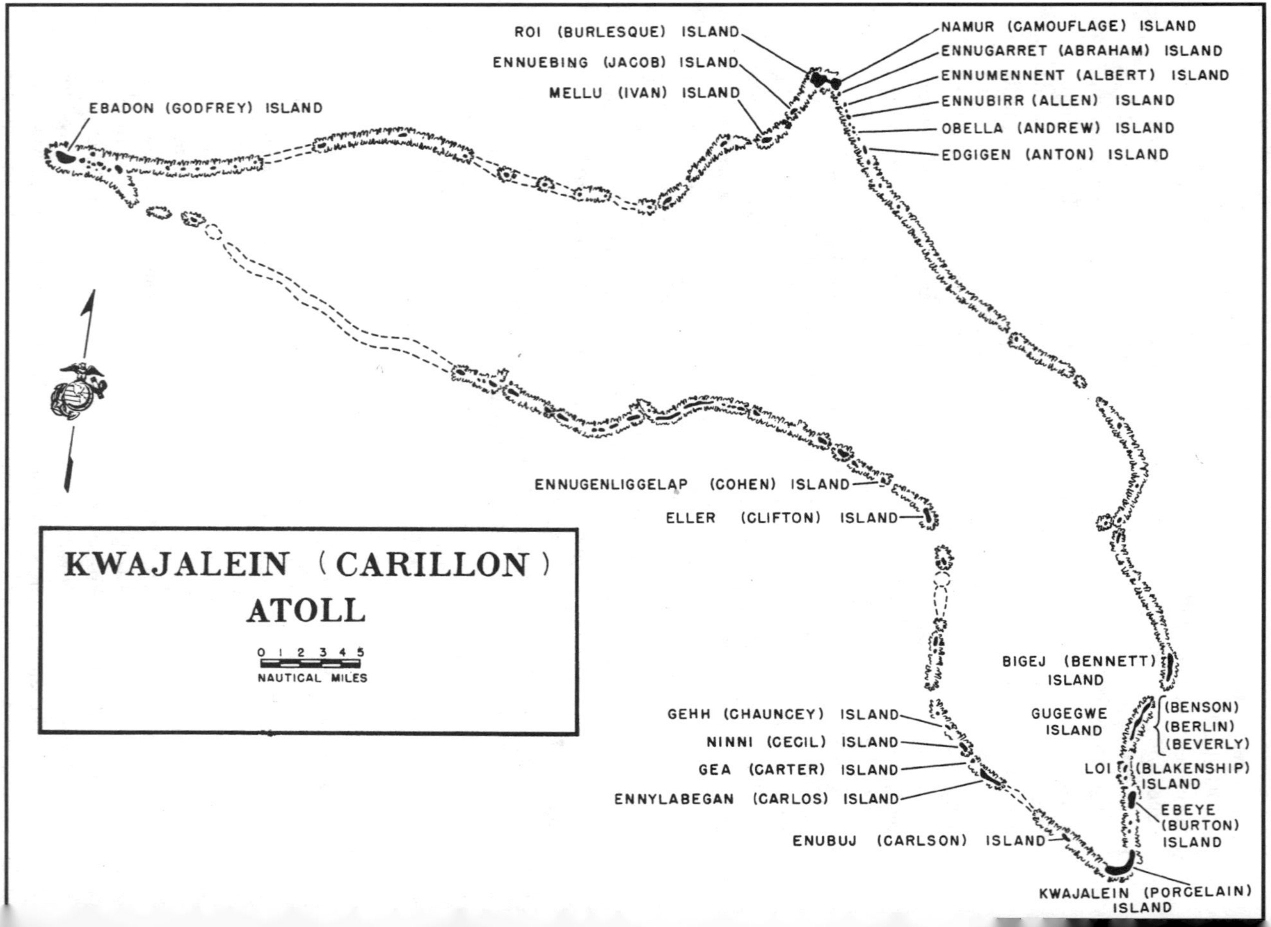

KWAJALEIN (CARILLON)
ATOLL

0 1 2 3 4 5
NAUTICAL MILES

ROI (BURLESQUE) ISLAND

ENNUEBING (JACOB) ISLAND

MELLU (IVAN) ISLAND

EBADON (GODFREY) ISLAND

NAMUR (CAMOUFLAGE) ISLAND

ENNUGARRET (ABRAHAM) ISLAND

ENNUMENNENT (ALBERT) ISLAND

ENNUBIRR (ALLEN) ISLAND

OBELLA (ANDREW) ISLAND

EDGIGEN (ANTON) ISLAND

ENNUGENLIGGELAP (COHEN) ISLAND

ELLER (CLIFTON) ISLAND

BIGEJ (BENNETT) ISLAND

GUGEGWE ISLAND

LOI

(BENSON)
(BERLIN)
(BEVERLY)

(BLAKENSHIP) ISLAND

EBEYE (BURTON) ISLAND

KWAJALEIN (PORCELAIN) ISLAND

GEHH (CHAUNCEY) ISLAND

NINNI (CECIL) ISLAND

GEA (CARTER) ISLAND

ENNYLABEGAN (CARLOS) ISLAND

ENUBUJ (CARLSON) ISLAND

Map 81
Roi-Namur Islands

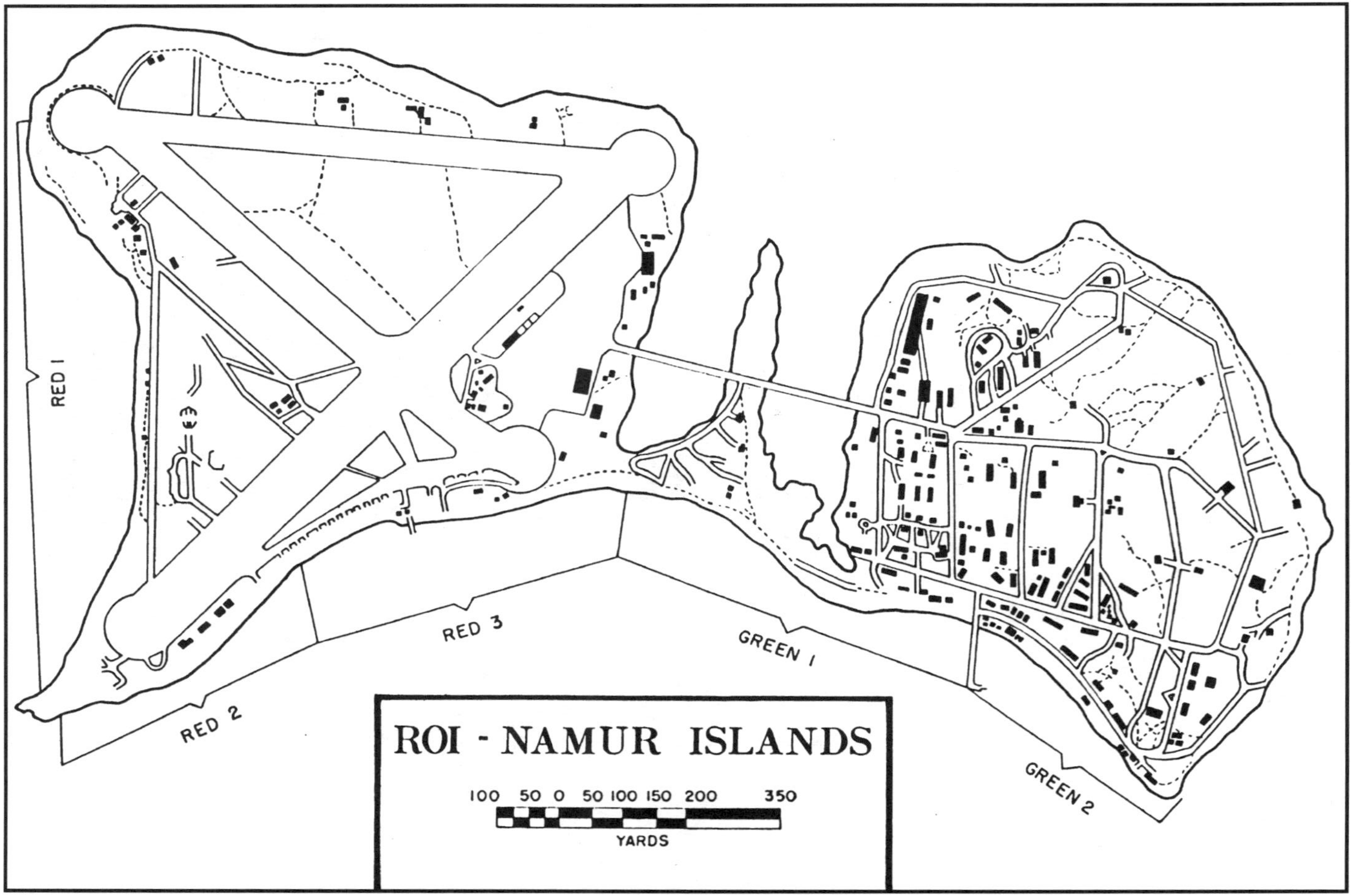

ROI - NAMUR ISLANDS

GREEN 2

GREEN 1

RED 3

RED 2

RED 1

100 50 0 50 100 150 200   350
YARDS

west portions. The L-shaped, 450-foot-long Yokohama Pier jutted into the lagoon from the center portion of Namur while a much shorter pier was located on the lagoon side on Roi near its southeast corner. Both islands are low and flat. On the oceanside the reef is 125–450 yards broad and falls steeply into the sea resulting in a very heavy surf. On the lagoon side the reef is more gradually sloped and brushed by light surf. Three sandbars lie close off the southeast corner of Namur. A line of small islands and islets run southeast from Namur along the atoll's barrier reef. The largest of these, and the closest, are Ennugarret (ABRAHAM) (460 yards away), Ennumennent (ALBERT), Ennubirr (ALLEN), and Obella (ANDREW). About two miles to the southwest of Roi is tiny Ennuebing Island (JACOB) on the edge of the narrow JACOB PASS and two miles farther is the larger Mellu Island (IVAN) beside the main entrance into the lagoon, Mellu Channel (IVAN PASS). Most of the defenses were on Roi's north and west shores and Namur's north and east shores. Light defenses were being built on the south shores by the *61st Guard Force Dispatched Force, 24th Air Flotilla Headquarters*, under Rear Admiral YAMADA Michiyuki, the service personnel of airplaneless air units, and a detachment of the *4th Fleet Construction Department*. Of the 3,000 personnel, over 2,000 were air service staff, but they were organized to fight.

Kwajalein Island. Kwajalein Island (PORCELAIN) is a crescent-shaped island with its concave side on the lagoon or north side (see Map 82). It is 2-½ miles long and averages 800 yards wide for most of its length, but narrows to 300 yards at the northern end. Kwajalein Island is situated at 09°42' N 167°44' E on the extreme south end of the atoll. Kwajalein and its adjacent islands were covered with palms, pandanus trees, and salt brush, with the woods being the densest on Kwajalein's north end. The west end was wooded as well, but there was a large clearing in which a radio direction finder complex was built, known as the Wart Area. A low antitank sea wall was constructed along the shore and this proved to be a minor obstacle to the landing force. A motor road encircled the entire island with several connecting roads crossing the island. Two 100-yard-long wharves, Center Pier, were located on the north-central shore and the L-shaped, 500-yard-long Nob Pier jutted into the lagoon 800 yards from the north end. Numerous support buildings, shops, barracks, and warehouses were built along the north shore beginning in the Center Pier area and toward the north end, which possessed numerous large structures. A large building complex was located inland where the island turned distinctly north and was known as the Admiralty Area, the island headquarters. Most of the Japanese defenses were built along the oceanside and the north and west ends. The 5,000-foot-long airfield was located on the island's central portion near the Center Pier. On the oceanside the 100–130-yard-wide reef is smooth and level, completely exposed at low tide. A heavy surf pounds the east shore, turns into a rolling surf on the south shore, and is moderate at the southwest corner. On the lagoon side the water is calm, but the reef is 500–800 yards wide and studded with boulders and coral outcroppings. On all sides of the island the beaches are ten to twenty yards wide rising to higher ground. On the north and west ends the beaches rise even more gradually and extend inland 250 and 450 yards, respectively. Prior to the assault on Kwajalein Island four smaller nearby islands would be occupied. Enubui Island (CARLSON) is three miles northwest of Kwajalein. It is 2/3-mile long and less than 300 yards wide and was the site of a radio station. A 100-foot-long pier was located on the island's lagoon side. Some 4,300 yards northwest of CARLSON is Ennylabegan Island (CARLOS),[2] one mile long and 300 yards wide. Between the two lies the so-called CARLOS PASS, but not even small craft could pass over its submarine reef. Two islets are located nine miles northwest of Kwajalein and 1/2 mile beyond CARLOS, Gea (CARTER) and Ninni (CECIL) Islands. The

Map 82
Kwajalein Island

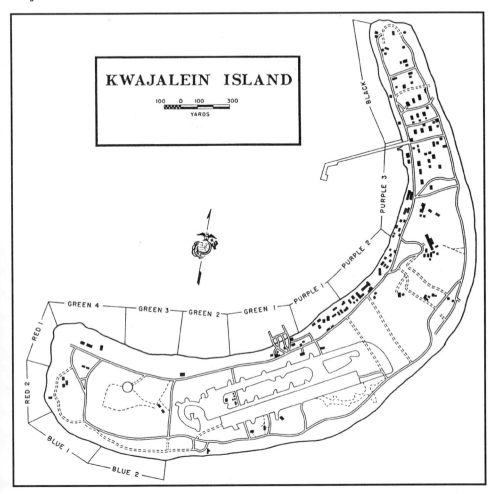

KWAJALEIN ISLAND

100   0   100   300

YARDS

two sit on either side of the 1/2 mile-wide Gew Channel (CECIL PASS), a narrow, but usable entrance into the lagoon, through which the attack force would enter single file. Gehh Island (CHAUNCEY) to the northwest of CECIL was secured after the main landing. Kwajalein Island was the headquarters for the *61st Base Force*, under Rear Admiral AKIYAMA Monzo, *6th Submarine Base Force, 6th Communications Unit*, a detachment of the *4th Fleet Construction Department*, air service personnel, and the main body of the *61st Guard Force* along with a company of the *Yokosuka 4th SNLF* to total 4,000 IJN personnel. Also present were over 800 IJA troops of the *1st Amphibious Brigade*, either assigned to aid with the island's defense or en route to Wotje Atoll.

   Ebeye Island. North of Kwajalein Island is a string of small islands and islets that were to be cleared after the main landing. The most important of these, and the third most strongly defended in the atoll, was Ebeye (BURTON). Located 2-½ miles north of

360

PACIFIC ISLAND GUIDE

Map 83
Ebeye Island, Kwajalein Atoll

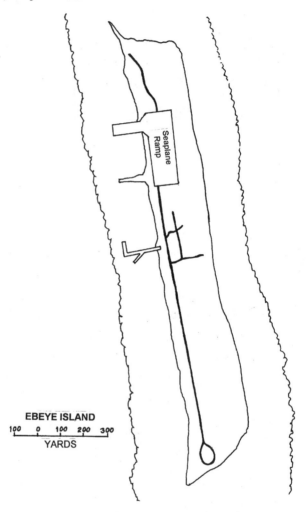

EBEYE ISLAND

100   0   100   200   300

YARDS

Kwajalein Island, the rectangular-shaped island is 1,770 yards long north to south and 250 yards wide (see Map 83). It is situated at 09°45' N 167°45' E. The offshore reefs and beaches were similar to Kwajalein's. BURTON was dotted with palms and brush with the densest brush and small mangroves along the oceanside. An improved road ran along the island's lagoon side. The L-shaped concrete Bailey Pier, with a secondary pier angling off the south side, jutted 1,600 feet into the lagoon from the island's center. Two 100-yards-long seaplane ramps occupied the northern portion of the lagoon side. Numerous support buildings, hangars, shops, and barracks were scattered over the island with the densest concentration in the center. Near Bailey Pier was a radio direction finding station. As with other islands in the atoll the main defenses were built on the oceanside, but on BURTON additional positions had been built in the vicinity of the seaplane ramps. The

Map 84
Northern Kwajalein Atoll

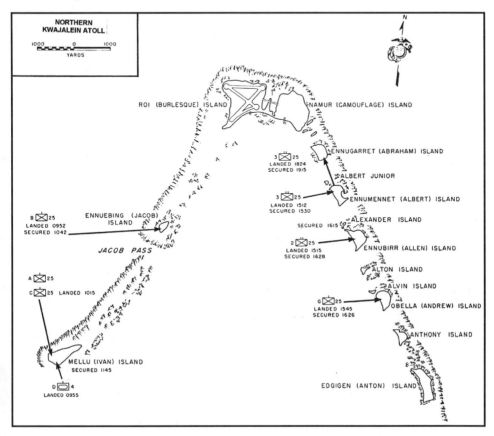

island was defended by detachments of IJN guard force, communications, and air service personnel, some 500 personnel.

Northern Kwajalein Atoll (Roi-Namur). The Northern Attack Force (Task Force 53) took up station west of Roi-Namur with the 4th Marine Division (14th [artillery], 20th [engineer], 23d, 24th, 25th Marines) aboard in the early hours of 31 January 1944 (D-Day; see Map 84). Under the command of Major General Harry Schmidt, the division had departed San Diego, California in mid-January 1944 to be the first Marine division committed directly to combat from the States conducting the longest shore-to-shore amphibious assault in history (4,300 miles), until the 8,000-mile 1982 British expedition to the Falkland Islands.

Phase I of the operation called for the 25th Marines to secure JACOB and IVAN guarding IVAN PASS into the lagoon southwest of Roi. Elements landed on the islets at 0955 hours (H-Hour) and both were secured at 1015 hours allowing the Navy task force to enter the lagoon. A-Hour saw elements of the regiment landing on ALLEN, ALBERT, and ANDREW southeast of Namur between 1510 and 1545 hours. All were secured within an hour followed by a landing on ABRAHAM at 1830 (B-Hour) and it was secured in forty-five minutes. Supporting regimental and battalion weapons were emplaced on ABRAHAM, the nearest to Namur, and four battalions of artillery were emplaced on JACOB, IVAN, ALBERT, and ALLEN with one battalion on each. An estimated thirty-five Japanese were killed and five prisoners taken on the offshore islands while the Marines lost eighteen KIA, eight MIA, and forty WIA.

Phase II was to have begun at 1000 hours (W-Hour) on 1 February when the 23d Marines were to have assaulted Roi and the 24th Marines Namur, but assembly of the amphibian tractors delayed the assault for two hours. With two battalions abreast in amphibian tractors, the 23d Marines came ashore on Beaches RED 2 and 3 on the Roi's south shore at 1157 hours. The Marines swept across the airfield and it was declared secure at 1802 hours. The 24th Marines landed on the south shore of Namur at 1155 hours on Beaches GREEN 1 (west of Yokohama Pier) and 2 (east of the pier). This regiment also secured the causeway and sandbar connecting the two islands. At 1305 hours a massive explosion shook Namur creating a 1,000-foot mushroom cloud, which almost covered the island, and showering palm trees and huge chunks of concrete for hundreds of yards. Marines attacking a large concrete bunker on the southeast had thrown in satchel charges and this detonated scores of torpedoes and two adjacent ammunition magazines. Twenty Marines were killed and about 100 injured, over half of the casualties suffered by 2d Battalion, 24th Marines on Namur. The 24th Marines pushed about three-quarters of the way across more heavily defended Namur by nightfall. Natalie Point on the north end was reached at 1215 hours the next day and the island was declared secure at 1418 hours. The Marines counted 3,472 enemy dead on both islands, but hundreds were buried in bunkers. A total of ninety-one prisoners were taken. The Marines lost 206 KIA, 181 MIA, and 531 WIA.

By 6 February forty-seven other islands in the atoll had been searched by the 25th Marines. The only Japanese air attack that managed to reach the islands (carrier strikes had neutralized all airfields in the Marshalls) was executed on 12 February. The attack struck Roi destroying much of the Marines' ammunition stockpiles, killing thirty personnel and wounding 400.

Southern Kwajalein Atoll (Kwajalein and Ebeye). The Southern Attack Force (Task Force 52) arrived off of the west end of Kwajalein with the 7th Infantry Division (Reinforced) (17th, 32d, 53d Infantry), under Major General Charles H. Corlett for the 1 February main landing.

Like the Marines to the north the Army too secured small islands northwest of Kwajalein, CECIL, CARTER, CARLSON, and others on order on 31 January. Japanese lookout posts were on these islands, but an estimated 250–300 defenders secured CARLSON. The 17th Infantry was assigned this mission. In the early dawn darkness CHAUNCEY was mistaken for CECIL and it was landed on. This resulted in a skirmish before the mistake was realized. Most of the force was withdrawn and landed on CECIL before noon. CHAUNCEY, however, was defended by a larger force than realized and the small American element had to be withdrawn. One-mile-long CARLOS was secured quickly. CARLSON, the largest of the offshore islands, was assaulted at 0912 hours. Expecting resistance, all the landing force found were twenty-four Korean laborers, who were taken prisoner. Four battalions of the division artillery were soon landed to support the next day's main landing on Kwajalein Island. CHAUNCEY, previously mistakenly landed on, was cleared by the 7th Reconnaissance Troop on 2 February resulting in 125 enemy dead.

At 0930 hours (H-Hour), the 7th Infantry Division assaulted the west end of Kwajalein Island. The 184th Infantry hit Beach RED 1 on the north portion and the 32d Infantry landed on RED 2 to the south with the two regiments landing by amphibian tractor on about a 500-yard-wide front. They immediately advanced up the length of the island halting for the night just short of Center Pier after having overrun about half of the airfield. The next day the advance pushed almost to the Admiralty Area where the island turns north. Resistance increased as the soldiers fought their way up the island's length. The numerous buildings, debris from bombing and shelling, and large numbers of craters served as obstacles to the advance as well as provided the defenders cover. By nightfall on 3 February the assault troops had advanced almost to the long Nob Pier. Nero Point of the north end was cleared at 1920 hours, 4 February, but the island had been declared secure at 1610 hours. American losses were fifty-eight dead, two missing, and 170 wounded. Approximately 4,450 Japanese died on Kwajalein Island and 176 prisoners, mostly Koreans, were captured.

The remainder of the small islands in southern Kwajalein Atoll were to be secured by the 17th Infantry. The most important of these, the nearest to Kwajalein, and the most heavily defended was Ebeye Island (BURTON). The regiment assembled on CARLOS for the 3 February assault. A 500-yard-wide beach designated ORANGE 4 was selected as it was faced with the lightest defenses. It was on the island's lagoon, or west side near the south end. The regiment came ashore at 0935 hours, cut across the island's south end, and turned north. By night half of the island had been cleared as far as Bailey Pier. The attack continued on the 4th with the north end being reached at 1210 hours and the island declared secure at 1337 hours. The 17th Infantry had lost seven KIA and eighty-two WIA while an estimated 450 Japanese were killed and seven prisoners taken. Other elements of the 17th Infantry secured the small islands to the north of BURTON between 1 and 5 February. Almost 450 Japanese were killed on these islands and a few prisoners taken at a cost of six American dead and eleven wounded.

The Kwajalein Atoll operation, lasting from 31 January to 8 February, was completed. Roi's 4,300-foot-long main runway was quickly made operational to be soon followed by the two secondary runways. Besides missions into the Carolines and Marianas, aircraft from Roi operated against the bypassed Japanese-held islands in the Marshalls. The air base was commissioned in May 1944 (FPO SF 825). An aviation supply base was built on Namur and the sandbar connecting the two islands was widened and thickened with coral dredged from the lagoon allowing another road to be constructed as the Japanese causeway was insufficient for heavier traffic. On Kwajalein Island the 5,000-foot Japanese runway was extended to 6,300 feet and support facilities built. The Army first used the airfield, but turned it over to the Navy on 1 July 1945 as Naval Air Base, Kwajalein (FPO SF 824). The Navy established a seaplane base on Ebeye Island (BURTON) and the headquarters of Naval Operating Base and Commander, Marshalls-Gilberts was established there as well (FPO SF 807). A joint communications center was built on Enubuj Island (CARLSON). A complete ship repair station was built on North Gugegwe Island (BERLIN). After the U.S. occupation the islands were commonly known only by their code names. The base remained operational, at a reduced capacity, and gradually closed out with Roi-Numar being closed early.

In 1951 the remaining facilities were turned over to the Bureau of Aeronautics. Kwajalein played a support role for the atomic bomb tests as Bikini Atoll. U.S. missile-testing programs increased in the late 1950s and the Pacific Missile Range was established originating at Camp Cooke (later renamed Vandenberg Air Force Base), California and extending to Kwajalein Atoll. In 1958 the Navy took control of Kwajalein and the Kwajalein Pacific Missile Range Facility was developed. Control of Kwajalein was transferred to the Army on 1 July 1964, with the Navy retaining overall control of the Pacific Missile Range. Over the years an extensive missile-testing and launch complex was developed, which is still operated by U.S. Army, Kwajalein Atoll. The airfield on Kwajalein is known as Bucholz Army Airfield.

Eniwetok Atoll, Marshall Islands

Code-named DOWNSIDE during the landing, Eniwetok was later code-named BABA-COOTE and BEGRUDGE. Eniwetok (pronounced "En-ni-we-tok," all vowels short, no accent), was commonly known as Brown Atoll. Today it is spelled Enewetok. It is 540 miles northwest of Jaluit, 337 miles northwest of Kwajalein, and is the northwestern most atoll in the western Ralik Group. Ujelang is its nearest neighbor about 130 miles to the southeast, itself the westernmost of the Marshalls. Eniwetok is located at 11°30' N 162°15' E.

The roughly circular atoll with some thirty islands and islets is twenty-one miles across from northwest to southeast and seventeen miles across the center (see Map 85). The five-mile-wide Wide Passage on the south side is the main entrance to the 388-square-mile lagoon, capable of providing a good anchorage for up to 2,000 ships. The namesake island, Eniwetok Island (PRIVILEGE) is the largest in the atoll and is on the east side of Wide Passage. It was commonly known as Brown Island and this name was used by the Japanese (*Chairo Jima*). From Eniwetok the atoll forms an almost unbroken circular reef line all the way around its sixty-four-mile circumference to an islet on the west side of Wide Passage. Parry Island (HEARTSTRINGS, later OVERBUILD), the third largest in the atoll, is 2-¼ miles to the northeast of Eniwetok island. On its north end is the one-mile-wide Deep Passage into the lagoon. On the north side of Deep Passage is Japtan Island (LADYSLIPPER). About 1-½ miles inside the lagoon and centered on Deep Passage is Jeroru Islet (LILAC). Following the curve of the reef around to the north side of the atoll is a string of scattered islets terminating at Engebi Island (FRAGILE, later OUTGENERAL), the second largest. Another line of islets runs to the southeast of Engebi. The westernmost portion (West Spit) of the atoll's reef has no islands. There are two islets about one-third of the way between West Spit and the west side of Wide Entrance that were code-named POSY. Roughly five miles to the southeast of POSY is a narrow unnamed passage. A short string of islets stretches southeast of this to the west side of Wide Entrance. The fringing coral reef is further offshore on the oceanside of the islands. On the lagoon side the reefs lie closer ashore with gaps or are almost nonexistent. The Japanese established light defenses on the three largest islands and these were assaulted by a joint Marine and Army force. These islands each had one or two short piers and boat landings.

Prior to the war the Japanese had established no military facilities in Eniwetok Atoll. It was not until December 1942 that work began on an airfield on Engebi Island. It was not completed until mid-1943. A small detachment of the *61st Guard Force* arrived in January 1943 from Kwajalein to establish lookout posts on Engebi and Eniwetok. They were relieved by a sixty-man detachment in October 1943, which emplaced two 120mm guns of Engebi. The airfield was not used until November when it became a ferrying way station for aircraft withdrawing westward into the Carolines. When it became apparent to the Japanese command that the Americans might soon move on the Marshalls, a combat unit was deployed to Eniwetok.

A new IJA unit, the *1st Amphibious Brigade*, had been organized in Manchuria from a railroad security unit under Major General NISHIDA Yoshima. It was sent to Truk in the Carolines where some of its 4,000 troops were detached for duty at Maloelap, Kwajalein, and Wotje. The remaining 2,600 troops of the self-contained unit arrived at Eniwetok on 4 January 1944, a month and a half before the Americans would attack. Defenses were nonexistent and work began employing construction troops, laborers, air-

Map 85
Eniwetok Atoll, Marshall Islands

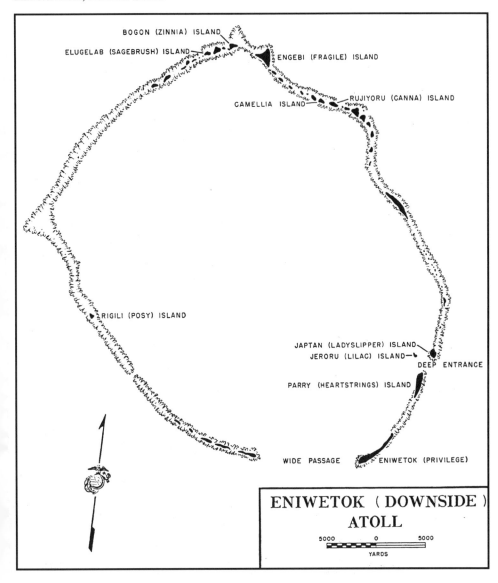

field service personnel, and marooned sailors and airmen. A total of 3,500 Japanese were at Eniwetok with more combat effectives than at Kwajalein, but the latter's defenses were much more superior. The headquarters of the *1st Amphibious Brigade* and most of the combat troops were emplaced on Perry, 1,350 troops and laborers. On Engebi were almost 1,300 troops and laborers, but with a higher percentage of support personnel to combat troops than found on Parry. Just over 800 troops were on Eniwetok. Only hasty

Map 86
Engebi Island, Eniwetok Atoll

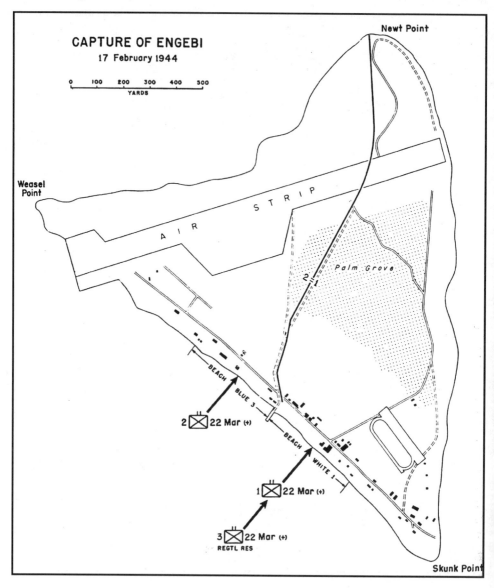

CAPTURE OF ENGEBI
17 February 1944

0   100   200   300   400   500
            YARDS

Newt Point

Weasel
Point

AIR STRIP

Palm Grove

BEACH BLUE 3

2 ⊠ 22 Mar (+)

BEACH WHITE 1

1 ⊠ 22 Mar (+)

3 ⊠ 22 Mar (+)
REGTL RES

Skunk Point

defenses were prepared on all islands, but some of the most effective were those on Eniwetok. Since the defensive positions were of simple construction few were detected by U.S. aerial photography.

Engebi Island. Engebi is positioned on the north end of the atoll. The low and flat triangular-shaped island measures 1,500 yards on its concave northwest side, 2,000 yards on its east, and 2,100 yards on the southwest (see Map 86). A 3,950-foot airfield paralleled the northwest shore, the only airfield in the atoll. To obtain this length the air-field's southeast end, near the island's east corner, Weasel Point, had been extended slightly into the lagoon by coral fill, an engineering effort the Japanese seldom undertook. Most of the support facilities were built along the southwest shore, along which ran an improved road from the airfield to Skunk Point on the south corner. Roads ran from there along the east shore to Newt Point on the north corner. A short pier was positioned on the center of the southwest shore. Most of the island was lightly vegetated with brush and scattered palms, but the east-central position was more thickly covered by palms and underbrush and the north corner was covered by very dense brush. The surrounding coral reef was broad and flat with no natural obstacles on the southwest, lagoon, side.

Eniwetok (Brown) Island. Eniwetok is located on the east side of Wide Passage on the atoll's southeast rim. It is two miles long from the northeast to the southwest and ¼-mile wide near the southwest end (see Map 87). It was unique among the atoll's islands in that the lagoon side was faced with a steep eight-to-fifteen-foot bluff imme-diately behind the narrow beach, the maximum elevation found in the atoll. This proved to be a difficult obstacle to overcome. An unimproved road ran almost three-quarters of the island's length from the southwest end. Only limited support facilities had been built on Eniwetok. On the southeast, oceanside, shore the coral reef extended 100–200 yards offshore and about 70–150 yards off the southwest end. Along the southern portion of the northwest, lagoon, shore the coral reef extended 200–500 yards offshore, but pre-sented no major obstacle. Another reef edged the nearshore area. Along about three-quarters of the rest of the island's northwest shore there were broken fringing reefs and coral outcroppings.

Parry Island. Parry is a teardrop-shaped island located on the south edge of Deep Entrance on the atoll's southeast side and is 2-¼ miles to the northeast of Eniwetok. It is two miles long and just under 600 yards wide near its north end, Neck Point (see Map 87). The south end, tapering to a point, was named Slumber Point. An unimproved road followed the circumference of the shoreline. A small seaplane base complex was located on the upper central portion of the west, lagoon, side as was a radio direction finding station. There were two piers; the longer southern one was known as Valentine Pier. The island is low and flat with most of it densely covered with palms and brush. The upper portion of the west side was relatively clear though. On the east, ocean, side and north end the coral reef is 200–300 yards wide. On the lagoon side the reef fringes the shoreline most of the island's length, but along the upper central portion it is free of reefs, although there are a few coral outcroppings 300–500 yards offshore from this area as well as off the lower west shore.

Operation CATCHPOLE, the occupation of Eniwetok Atoll, was originally scheduled for 1 May 1944 by employing units that were to have executed the planned Kavieng, New Britain occupation, but that operation was canceled and CATCHPOLE was moved up to mid-February 1944. The Eniwetok Expeditionary Group (Task Group 51.11) was formed to execute the operation, but it was first sent from Hawaii to Kwajalein arriving there on 3 February. Its landing force, Tactical Group 1, was tasked as the floating reserve for Operation FLINTLOCK. The 8,000-man Tactical Group, Brigadier General Thomas E. Wat-son 1 was a joint provisional force formed by V Amphibious Corps and built around the separate 22d Marines and the 106th Infantry (-2d Battalion) detached from the 27th Infantry Division. Not needed at Kwajalein, the Expeditionary Group departed the atoll on 15 February. Carrier air strikes on Eniwetok had begun on 30 January, when all of the Japanese aircraft on Engebi were destroyed, and continued up to the landing.

Map 87
Eniwetok (Brown) and Parry Islands, Eniwetok Atoll

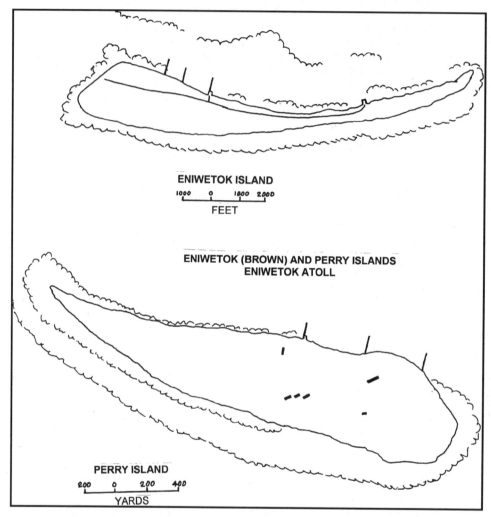

ENIWETOK ISLAND

ENIWETOK (BROWN) AND PERRY ISLANDS
ENIWETOK ATOLL

PERRY ISLAND

    The Expeditionary Group arrived outside of the southeast entrances to Eniwetok's
lagoon on the early morning of 17 February (D-Day). Bombardment of Japtan, Engebi,
Eniwetok, and Parry began immediately. The transports bearing the landing force entered
through Wide Passage and the bombardment force entered through Deep Passage. By
1400 hours, VAC Reconnaissance Company had secured unoccupied Aitsu (CAMELLIA)
and Rujioru (CANNA) Islands southeast of Engebi to block any enemy attempting to
escape from Engebi. At 0327 hours, 18 February Marine scouts secured Bogon Island
(ZINNIA) to the northwest. Artillery battalions were emplaced on the first two completing
Phase I. The two artillery battalions were to support the Engebi assault, which was
thought to be the most strongly defended island.

Phase II began the next day as the 22d Marines assaulted Engebi landing on the lagoon side on Beaches BLUE 3 and WHITE 1, the two beaches separated by the central pier. Landing at 0845 hours (W-Hour), the lead battalions rolled up the beach positions and pushed across the island meeting the heaviest resistance in the central palm grove and the south corner near Skunk Point. The island was prematurely declared secure at 1450 hours. Organized resistance was finally overcome at 0800 hours on the 19th. Over 1,200 Japanese, Okinawans, and Koreans died on Engebi and sixteen prisoners were taken. American losses were eighty-five dead and missing and 521 wounded.

Phase III began on the 19th when both Eniwetok and Perry Islands were to be seized. The 106th Infantry, backed by a Marine battalion, assaulted the lagoon shore of Eniwetok Island landing on Beaches YELLOW 1 and 2 at 0917 hours (Y-Hour). The island was soon cut in two. An Army and a Marine battalion attacked toward the southwest end where the strongest resistance was encountered, but it was reduced by 1900 hours. A Japanese counterattack had caused some confusion at noon, but this was defeated. One Army battalion pushed up Eniwetok's long, narrow tail to its northeast end. Progress was slow on this end of the island and it was not cleared until 1630 hours, 21 February. Although it had taken longer to secure the island than planned, American losses were only thirty-seven KIA and ninety-four WIA. The Japanese lost about 800 men and twenty-three were captured.

The longer-than-expected effort to secure Eniwetok delayed the assault on Parry. In the meantime the Army artillery battalion previously emplaced on CANNA was relocated to Eniwetok to support the Perry landing. Weapons and ammunition problems had become acute. Grenades, demolitions materials, artillery ammunition, and even individual weapons were donated by other units to resupply and replace losses in the 22d Marines. At 0900 hours (Z-Hour), 22 February the 22d Marines landed on the upper portion of the lagoon side on Beaches GREEN 2 and 3. By 1330 hours the north end had been reached while the seaplane base area and the rest of the island had been cleared to about midway down its length. An attack by three Japanese tanks was launched too late to be effective. American tanks had already been landed and easily defeated the lighter Japanese machines. The American advance halted for the night 450 yards from the south end. That sector was cleared by 0900 hours on the 23rd and the island was declared secure thirty minutes later. The Japanese lost about 1,300 men and twenty-five were captured. American losses were approximately 170 dead and 230 wounded.

The 106th Infantry reverted to its parent division's control and remained as a garrison force until returned to Hawaii in April. The 22d Marines moved to Kwajalein Atoll for area island security. It then conducted twenty-nine, mostly unopposed, landings to clear the many islands during the Lesser Marshalls Operation, Operation FLINTLOCK, JR., securing the mostly unoccupied Wotho, Ujae, Lae, Namu, Ailinglapalap, Namorik, Ebon, Bikini, Rongelap, Utirik, Airluk, and Likiep Atolls, and Kili and Mejit Islands between 7 March and 5 April 1944.

Base development soon began on Eniwetok when the Japanese airfield on Engebi Island was restored. A new 3,950-foot fighter field was begun on Eniwetok Island and was commissioned as Wrigley Airfield. On the southern portion of the island a new 6,800-foot bomber field was built, Stickell Field. A seaplane base was built on Parry Island using the Japanese facilities. Limited naval base facilities were built on Eniwetok Island. Eniwetok, being the nearest U.S. air base to the Marianas, became a major staging base for attacks on those islands. It was there that the task forces assembled for the Marianas campaign in the summer of 1944. The advanced fleet base also supported the British Fleet Train (service elements) operating in the Pacific in 1945. Wrigley Field was closed on 18 September 1944. The naval air base and naval station on Eniwetok were closed on 23 May 1947.

Jaluit, Wotje, Maloelap, and Mille Atolls, Marshall Islands

Jaluit Atoll is located near the south end of the western Ralik Group. Its nearest neighbor is Kili Island about thirty miles to the southwest. Kwajalein Atoll is 245 miles to the northwest and Majuro Atoll is about 110 miles to the northeast.

Wotje and Maloelap (also spelled Maloelab or Maoloclap) Atolls are in the central portion of the eastern Radak Group while Mille Atoll is at the south end of the group. Majuro Atoll is situated between Maloelap, ninety-eight miles north, and Mille, sixty-five miles southeast. Wotje is 164 miles east of Kwajalein, Maloelap is seventy miles southwest of Wotje, and Mille is 165 miles south-southeast of Wotje. Due east of Mille is Jaluit at 145 miles. Wotje is considered a part of the Romanzow Group along with the small Erikub Atoll to the south and a few scattered islands between the two atolls. These four atolls' code names and latitude and longitude are (see Map 68, pp. 324–25):

Jaluit (DEADWOOD, FILLET)	06°00' N 169°35' E
Wotje (CREOSOTE, ADIPOSE, IRONMONGER)	09°30' N 170°00' E
Maloelap (CORDIAL)	08°75' N 171°00' E
Mille (CADDIE, LOCKMAN)	06°13' N 171°58' E

The atolls are similar to others in the Marshalls being roughly oval reefs with numerous low islands and islets surrounding a lagoon. The islands are covered with palms, pandanus trees, and salt brush.

Jaluit is about twelve miles across its broader southern end from East to West Points, but only four miles wide at its north end, and almost thirty miles long from west-northwest to east-southeast. Of its fifty islands the largest is the long, narrow, L-shaped (with an extremely long vertical arm) Jaluit Island. Jabur Island was the administrative center of the Marshalls and the Japanese developed a major naval base on Jaluit Island because of its deep, well-protected lagoon. It possessed only a seaplane base and no land airfield. Other Japanese installations were on Emidj and Enybor Islands to the north of Jaluit Island. By the time of the American invasion of the Marshalls the base's fleet and air activities had been withdrawn.

Wotje Atoll is thirty miles long from east to west and eight to twelve miles across. Most of its sixty-five islands are found along its east rim, where the largest islands are located, the central south side, and a few scattered along the western north side. The largest island is Wotje Island on the extreme east central end. Both a T-shaped land airfield and a seaplane base were found there.

Maloelap is about thirty miles long from northwest to southwest and eight to fifteen miles wide. The largest of its sixty-four islands are on the southeast end. Located there is the main island, Taroa, on which an X-shaped airfield was built. It was considered by the United States to be the most important Japanese airfield between Tarawa and Truk.

Mille Atoll is about twenty miles long from the west-northwest to the southeast and about ten miles across. Its thirty islands are distributed around most of the atoll's rim with the east side being open. A large X-shaped airfield, with third runway connecting the arms of the "X" on one side, was built on the main Mille Island. This was the only airfield in the Marshalls that was within Japanese fighter range of the Gilberts to the southeast. It was from there that some of the strikes were flown on Tarawa and Makin during the Gilberts campaign.

These islands were subordinate to the *6th Base Force* on Kwajalein, formed in December 1941, itself under the command of the *4th Fleet* at Truk, and their defense was the responsibility of the *6th Defense Force*. In October and November 1941 the *51st, 52d,* and *53d Guard Forces* were sent to defend Jaluit, Maloelap, and Wotje, respectively. In the summer of 1943 these guard forces were redesignated the *62d, 63d,* and *64th,* respectively, and the new *66th Guard Force* was assigned to Mille in June. Mille was intended to be used as an aircraft staging base for offensive operations into the Ellice, Fiji, and Samoan Islands. IJA units began arriving in the Marshalls in late 1943 as the new *National Defense Zone* was established. Among these was the *3d Battalion, 107th Infantry* of the *52d Division* assigned to Mille. The senior IJN commander in the bypassed Marshalls was Rear Admiral MASUDA Nisuke headquartered on Jaluit.

Prior to the execution of Operation FLINTLOCK at the end of January 1944 it was essential that the airfields on these atolls be completely neutralized to ensure the security of the invasion fleet. These bases had previously been subjected to air attacks during the course of the Gilberts campaign, but beginning in November 1943 they were struck by repeated heavy carrier air strikes and Army Air Force bomber raids, launched from the Ellice Islands and Canton Island. The first post-Gilberts strikes were delivered on Mille, Jaluit, and Maloelap on 18, 23, and 26 November, respectively. Jaluit, from which the Japanese had withdrawn most aircraft, was effectively neutralized on the same day as the first strike, but raids continued. Mille was quickly neutralized by 2 December, but stubborn Maloelap did not succumb until 2 January 1944. Attacks on Wotje were not launched until 13 December and by the 26th it was neutralized. Raids continued on all of these atolls through the Marshalls campaign to further soften the defense forces. There were 13,700 IJN personnel, IJA troops, and civilian employees on the four atolls: Jaluit—2,200, Maloelap—3,100, Wotje—3,300, and Mille—5,100.

After the capture of the Marshalls these four islands were bypassed by U.S. forces and effectively placed under a state of siege by the 4th Marine Base Defense Air Wing on Kwajalein with its aircraft groups operating from Engebi Island in Eniwetok Atoll, Roi in Kwajalein, and Majuro Atoll. Navy and Army aircraft participated in the reduction of the bypassed Marshalls as well. The post-Marshalls campaign attacks began in March 1944 and lasted until the war's end. Including the pre-Marshalls campaign attacks, the attacks during the campaign, the three armed services' air arms dropped almost 13,000 tons of bombs on Japanese installations in these four atolls. While the Japanese arguably became some of the most practiced antiaircraft gunners in the Pacific, for the flyers it was a monotonous campaign of daily "milk runs" in an unending effort to destroy the garrisons, although they admittedly received valuable bombing practice before moving on to more offensive operations. Japanese attempts to grow crops were countered by fire bombings and aerial spraying with diesel fuel. Of the 13,700 Japanese on the atolls, by the war's end 2,564 had been killed in action and 4,876 died of disease and starvation. On all but Jaluit, where Rear Admiral MASUDA managed to maintain morale and prevent starvation, the defenders of the other islands were thoroughly demoralized by the war's end. On 2 September 1945, Vice Admiral HARA Chuichi, commanding the *4th Fleet*, and Lieutenant General MUGIKURA Shunsaburo, commanding the *31st Army*, surrendered on Truk. This surrender applied to the forces on the bypassed Marshall Islands. Rear Admiral MASUDA commanding those forces from Jaluit committed suicide rather than answer questions regarding missing airmen that had been shot down over the islands.

In 1949 the Marshall Islands became the Marshall Islands District of the Trust Territory of the Pacific Islands administered by the United States, along with the Marianas and Carolines, the former Japanese Mandated Territory. Nuclear testing was conducted at Bikini and Eniwetok Atolls in the early 1950s. The inhabitants of Bikini were relocated to Rongerik Atoll to allow the twenty-three nuclear detonations to be conducted. Kwajalein Atoll was developed as a missile testing facility. The Trust Territory adopted a constitution in 1979. It entered a Compact of Free Association with the United States on 21 October 1986, in effect granting its independence from U.S.-administered U.N. trusteeship as the Republic of the Marshall Islands (its Independence Day is 1 May 1979 when the proclamation of the Republic was made.) The nation's capital is Delap, Uliga, and Darrit Islands in Majuro Atoll (collectively called the D-U-D Municipality), the site of the massive World War II naval base. The Marshallese have sought and received compensation for the dislocations and inconveniences caused by nuclear weapons testing over the years. The Republic joined the U.N. in 1991. The U.S. Army still operates the Kwajalein Pacific Missile Range Facility. Kwajalein Island is off-limits to nongovernment and nonmilitary personnel. The facility's 1,500 Marshallese employees live on Ebeye Island and are shuttled by boat. Ebeye is a transit point for unofficial visitors. The Republic claims Wake Island and is in mild dispute with the United States over this issue. The Marshalls rely heavily on U.S. grants and revenues from the missile facility. Coconut products, fruits and vegetables, fishing, tourism, and embryonic offshore banking provide limited income. Tourism has increased because of the fantastic wreck diving available at Kwajalein, Bikini, and Jaluit, with the first two atolls being designated historic sites by the U.S. government under Project SeaMark. War relics can still be seen ashore on Maloelap, Mille, and Jaluit. Besides the native languages, English is an official language and Japanese is still spoken.

MARIANA ISLANDS

The Mariana Islands, code-named GATEWAY, is the smallest group of the three comprising the Japanese Mandated Territory, but has by far the most land area. The Japanese called them *Mariana Shota*. It is some 300 miles due north of the West Caroline Islands separated by the Challenger Deep of the Marianas Trench, the world's deepest known ocean depth at 36,198 feet. The Philippines are 1,500 miles to the west. Eniwetok, the northwestern most of the Marshalls, is 1,300 miles to the east. Pearl Harbor is 3,400 miles to the east and Tokyo is 1,260 miles to the north-northwest. Approximately 500 miles to the northwest is the Kazan Retto with Iwo Jima. The chain of islands stretches from 20°32' N 144°54' E south to 13°15' N 144°43' E. The Marianas were in time zone 21 while most of the rest of the Mandated Territory was in time zone 22. Guam though was in time zone 22.

The Marianas is a 425-mile-long chain of hilly volcanic islands running north to south in shallow curve, its concave side to the west. Those in the north are essentially volcanic peaks rising 6,000–12,000 feet from the ocean's bottom. The southern islands are larger land masses and the most important militarily and economically (see Map 88). These islands rise from even deeper depths, Saipan for example from 36,000 feet. The island with the highest elevation is Anatahan at 2,585 feet. Farallon de Medinilla, north of Saipan, is the lowest island in the chain with an elevation of 266 feet. The total land area, exclusive of Guam, is 177 square miles; Guam alone adds another 225 square miles. There are no atolls in the Marianas. Many of the islands are fertile. The predominant vegetation is scrub trees, ironwood trees, brush, and sword, cogon, and bunch grass with

Map 88
Southern Mariana Islands

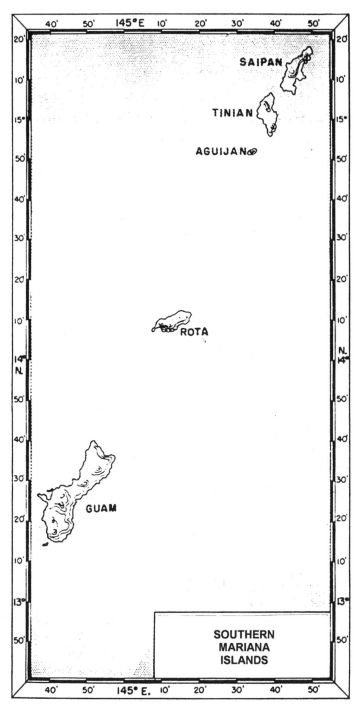

SOUTHERN
MARIANA
ISLANDS

some palms. Mangrove swamps are found on some islands. There are many open grass-covered areas. Streams are nonexistent on the islands with the notable exception of Guam, the only one with a reliable water supply. Beaches are usually small and most of the coastlines are edged with coral limestone cliffs. Coral reefs lie close to shore on most of the islands presenting a major obstacle to landings in many areas. From north to south the fifteen Mariana Islands are:

Island	Dimensions (miles)	Elevation (feet)
Fallon de Pajaros (Uracas)	2 diameter	1,047
Maug	1 diameter	748
Asunción	1 diameter	2,923
Agrigan (Agrihan)	2½ × 6	3,166
Pagan	2½ × 8	1,883
Alamagan	1½ × 2¼	2,440
Guguan	1 × 2½	988
Sariguan (Sarigan)	1½ diameter	1,800
Anatahan	1½ × 5	2,585
Farallon de Medinilla	2 long	266
Saipan	5½ × 12½	1,554
Tinian (Bona Vista)	5 × 10½	564
Agùijan (Agiguan, Goat)	2 × 3	584
Rota (Barpana, Luta)	5½ × 12	1,612
Guam	10 × 32	1,334

The Zelandia Banks is located between Guguan and Sariguan Islands and the Esmeralda Banks is twenty-four miles west of Tinian. Early in the twentieth century these volcanic cones projected above sea level, but are now submerged.

The Marianas were discovered by the Portuguese explorer Ferdinand Magellan in 1521 while leading a Spanish fleet in the first circumnavigation of the earth. After crossing the entire Pacific and missing all other island groups, he sighted what he named *Islas de los Velas Latinas* (Islands of the Lateen Sails) after the rigging style of the native boats. They were also dubbed *Islas de los Ladrones* (Islands of the Thieves) owing to certain practices the natives inflicted on visitors. That name was commonly used well into the twentieth century. Spain claimed the islands in 1565 and officially named them *Las Marianas* after Queen Maria Anna in 1668. The Chamorro natives rebelled against Spanish rule on several occasions with the last revolt being in 1695 against Spain's imposition of Christianity. Spain brutally put down the revolt driving many of the Chamorros from Guam, the center of the troubles. Many fled to the northern Marianas, where they were pursued and almost wiped out, and others moved south to the Carolines. Where there had been some 75,000 Chamorros, there were 3,500 counted in the 1710 census. The Chamorros built large stone monuments in remembrance of these events on Guam and Tinian, which can still be seen. Christianity was eventually accepted by the survivors in the late 1700s. Spain's hold on the islands at the end of the 1800s was tenuous at best and little had been done to develop them. In the mid-1800s a small group of Americans attempted to colonize Saipan, but was frustrated by the Spanish governor. In 1899 the islands, except Guam, were purchased from Spain by Germany and annexed in 1902.

On 21 June 1898 the cruiser USS *Charleston* landed a Marine detachment on Guam and accepted the surrender of the Spanish governor. The island was soon a U.S. possession. In October 1914 the Japanese seized the other islands from Germany and gained their control as a mandated territory in 1920. The *South Seas Bureau Marianas District* administrative center was at Garapan on Saipan. This had also been the German seat of government. The Japanese developed the fishing industry in the islands and on Saipan and Tinian a sugarcane industry flourished.

A legend persists that Amelia Earhart and Fred Noonan were imprisoned on Saipan after their aircraft's 2 July 1937 disappearance while en route to Howland Island from New Guinea for their round-the-world flight attempt. It has been claimed that they were actually conducting a spy flight over the Japanese Mandates on behalf of the U.S. government when they disappeared. The Marianas are some 800 miles north of New Guinea and about 2,300 miles northwest of Howland Island. No real evidence exists to support this theory.

The defense of the Marianas was the responsibility of the *4th Fleet* headquartered at Truk. The *5th Base Force* was established on Saipan prior to the war along with the *5th Communications Unit* and *5th Defense Force* and these units were directly responsible for the Marianas. The *5th Base Force* was tasked with planning the seizure of Guam just prior to the war. In April 1942 the *5th Base Force* was redesignated the *5th Special Base Force*. At that time there were only 1,500 personnel assigned to the command. Only the three largest islands, Saipan, Tinian, and Guam, all at the southern end of the chain, played major roles in the war. Minor Japanese installations were located on Rota and Pagan Islands. Prior to the invasion the *31st Army*, under Lieutenant General OBATA Hideyoshi on Truk was made responsible for IJA units in the Marianas; it later moved to the Palau Islands. While the *4th Fleet* had overall responsibility for the area, once an island was attacked the senior IJA commander on the island would assume command of all Japanese forces. The Marianas began to be heavily reinforced between February and May 1944. These larger islands allowed the Japanese to adopt new defensive tactics. Unlike the central Pacific atolls they were large enough to allow a defense in depth, although this was not always fully taken advantage of, and some degree of maneuver. They were also small enough for all or most of the main landing sites to be defended unlike the larger South and Southwest Pacific islands. Those islands too had limited the defender's ability to maneuver because of their size, the dense vegetation, and rugged terrain.

The U.S. command had long planned to seize the southern Marianas as part of its drive toward Japan. The importance of the Marianas was due to a technological advance. The long-range B-29 bomber had been fielded, but was forced to operate from China placing the nearest target in Japan at 1,600 miles. Supplying fuel, bombs, and materials for the bombers from India was a major logistical effort. The Marianas would provide ideal B-29 bases allowing the "Superfortresses" to range most of the Home Islands. The United States formed the largest joint expeditionary force to date to seize the Marianas. Two Army and three Marine divisions and a large Marine brigade were assembled for the operation under two Marine amphibious corps. The landing force, the Expeditionary Troops (Task Force 58), was under the command of Marine Lieutenant General Holland M. Smith. The overall Joint Expeditionary Force (Task Force 51) was commanded by Vice Admiral Richmond K. Turner.

Operation FORAGER was to commence in mid-June 1944 with the assault of Saipan followed by Tinian and then Guam. Preparations were begun in March. All of the assigned divisions were in the Hawaiian islands, except for one Marine division and the

Marine brigade destined for Guam, which were on Guadalcanal. Carrier air strikes on the islands had begun in February 1944 and were followed by almost daily bomber raids from Bougainville and later the Admiralties right up to the invasion. Heavy air attacks were also inflicted on Truk to the southeast to neutralize that main base.

Saipan Island, Mariana Islands

Saipan was code-named TATTERSALLS. The second largest island in the Marianas is 100 miles northeast of Guam. Tinian is three miles off the south end of Saipan. Farallon de Medinilla, the southernmost of the Northern Marianas, is about thirty miles to the northeast. Saipan is situated at 15°15' N 145°45' E.

Saipan measures 12-½ miles from northeast to southwest and 5-½ miles across the center and covers eighty-five square miles (see Map 89). The fifty-four miles of coastline are mostly faced with cliffs of varying height providing only fourteen miles of beaches, most of which are on the west side. The west side and the south end, while possessing most of the usable beaches, also provide barrier reefs. Fringing the south end the reef's edge extends further offshore as it runs up the east coast, up to 1,500 yards off the center portion of the island at Mutcho Point. North of the point is Tanapag Harbor formed by a long, submerged coral reef arm curving out from the upper east coast, after which the reef runs back close ashore along the upper east coast. The south end of the reef arm is off of Mutcho Point and a channel had been dredged into Tanapag Harbor. The harbor does not indent the coast, but the offshore reef arm provides some protection for what is called Saipan Lagoon. The harbor is defined by Mutcho Point on its south side and the town of Garapan, the island's largest, and Flores Point on the north side. It is from twenty to fifty feet deep. The port possessed four large piers, the largest being 700 yards long with spur piers. Approximately 3,000 yards northwest of Tanapag Harbor is Maniagassa Island, about 300 yards in diameter covering ten acres. Projecting from the southeast corner of the island is Nafutan Peninsula and 4,000 yards north across Magicienne Bay (aka Lau Lau Bay) is Kagman Peninsula. The bay's shore is faced by broken cave-riddled cliffs and fringed by a narrow beach with coral outcroppings and a coral reef, the only one on the east side.

The southern third of the island is a rolling plateau 200–300 feet above sea level. The island's main 4,500-foot Aslito Airfield (aka Isloto) is located on the plain at the base of the Nafutan Peninsula. On the lower west coast is a roughly 2,000-yard-wide plain on which is located the marsh-surrounded freshwater Lake Susupe near Afetna Point. South of the point is the island's second largest town, Charan Kanoa, and to its north is an emergency landing strip. Another airfield was located on the island's north end at Marpi Point at the base of 833-foot-high Mount Marpi, but was uncompleted. A seaplane base was located at Flores Point on the north edge of Tanapag Harbor. The island's center is dominated by the 1,554-foot Mount Tapotchau rising from the north edge of the southern plateau. A rugged 400–934-foot ridge line runs seven miles north to Mount Marpi. Caves and ravines were common in the hills. Some 70 percent of Saipan was planted with sugarcane, a serious impediment to ground troops. The rest of the island, the hilly areas, was covered by low scrub trees, brush, and high, dense grasses. Aslito Airfield had been built in 1934, the first in the Marianas, and the seaplane base in Tanapag Harbor in 1935. The emergency strip and the uncompleted airfield on the north end had been begun in 1944.

An improved road follows the west coast from the south end's Cape Obiam to Marpi

Map 89
Saipan Island

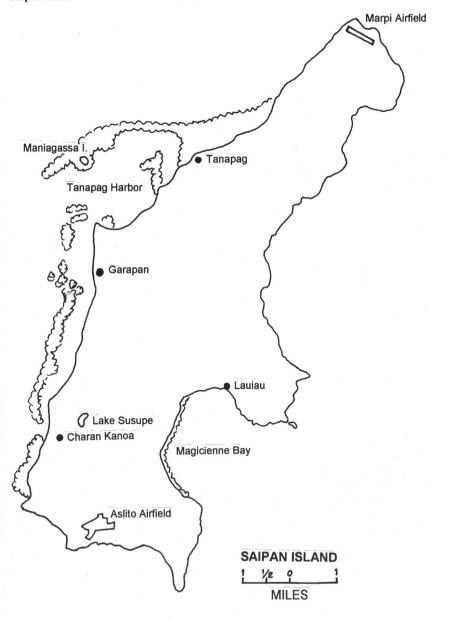

Marpi Airfield

Maniagassa I.

● Tanapag

Tanapag Harbor

● Garapan

● Lauiau

𝒞 Lake Susupe

● Charan Kanoa

Magicienne Bay

Aslito Airfield

SAIPAN ISLAND

1 ½ 0 1

MILES

Point on the north end. The road loops around the north end and reconnects with itself on the west coast. Three other roads cross the northern ridge connecting to a road running down the east coast to Kagman Peninsula, along Magicienne Bay to Aslito Airfield and around the south end where it connects with the west coast road. The island also possessed an extensive narrow-gauge railroad system to transport sugarcane. It ran around most of the coast. The island's population was over 20,000 Japanese, about 4,000 Chamorros, and 1,000 Kanakas. Some Japanese civilians, mainly women and children, had been evacuated prior to the invasion, but many women and children remained to suffer the coming battle.

Minimal defensive installations were not built on Saipan until 1940–41 regardless of American fears that the islands were being fortified. The *43d Division (118th, 135th, 136th Infantry)*, commanded by Lieutenant General SAITO Yoshitsugu, was sent to Saipan from Japan in late May 1944. The *1st Expeditionary Unit* also arrived from Japan in May and was reorganized as the *47th Independent Mixed Brigade* under Colonel OKA Yoshiro. Two additional infantry battalions, detached from other islands, plus artillery, antiaircraft, tank, engineer, and service units were present. IJN units included the regimental-size *41st* and *55th Base Forces*, the parachute-trained, battalion-size *Yokosuka 1st SNLF*, and service units under the *5th Special Base Force*. There were 25,500 IJA troops present along with 6,200 IJN personnel on Saipan. The *43d Division* doubled as the *Northern Marianas Army Group* responsible for Saipan and Tinian.

The 66,800 men of the Northern Troops and Landing Force (Task Group 56.1), the joint Marine and Army force under V Amphibious Corps, commanded by Lieutenant General Smith, conducted final rehearsals in May and prepared for the operation. The expeditionary force departed Hawaii between 25 and 30 May. Under VAC were the 2d Marine Division (2d, 6th, 8th, 10th [artillery], 18th [engineer] Marines) commanded by Major General Thomas E. Watson, 4th Marine Division (14th [artillery], 20th [engineer], 23d, 24th, 25th Marines) commanded by Major General Harry Schmidt, the 27th Infantry Division (105th, 106th, 165th Infantry) under Major General Ralph C. Smith, and XXIV Corps Artillery. While VAC, a Marine command, controlled the landing force for Saipan and later Tinian, its combined artillery assets were under the Army's XXIV Corps Artillery. XXIV Corps itself was engaged in the Philippines with VAC's Artillery attached.

The force arrived off of southwest side of Saipan on the morning of 15 June 1944 (D-Day). The reserve regiments of the 2d and 4th Marine Division conducted a demonstration off of the northern west coast while the assault regiments loaded into amphibian tractors. This was the first Marine Corps two-division assault. The 2d Marine Division landed south of Garapan and north of Afetna Point with the 2d Marines on Beaches RED 1–3 while the 8th Marines came ashore on their right on Beaches GREEN 1–3. The first troops landed at 0843 hours (H-Hour). The 4th Marine Division landed to the south of the 2d with the 23d Marines on Beaches BLUE 1 and 2 and the 25th Marines on YELLOW 1–3 north of Agingan Point on the island's southwest corner. The regiments fought inland against stiff resistance to capture Aslito Airfield on the 18th and the southern third of the island to the central Mount Tapotchau was cleared by the 22nd, although a Japanese pocket on the southeast corner at Nafutan Point was not cleared by the Army until 27 June. The 27th Infantry Division, initially the landing force reserve, came ashore between 17 and 20 June and its regiments were fed into the advancing line or employed for rear-area mop-up. For the first time flamethrower-armed tanks were used in combat by the Marines as were napalm fire bombs dropped by the Army Air Force.

The Battle of the Philippine Sea occurred on 19–20 June when the Japanese launched *A-GO Operation*, the naval counterattack of the American Marianas invasion force. This was to be the largest carrier air battle of the war. While the Japanese committed significant assets to include nine carriers and 470 aircraft, the Americans had fifteen carriers and almost 1,000 aircraft. When it was over virtually all of the Japanese aircraft had been downed in what was dubbed "The Great Marianas Turkey Shoot" along with land-based aircraft destroyed as well as three carriers and two tankers sunk and seventeen of twenty-five submarines lost. The U.S. Fleet lost no ships, but did lose about 130 aircraft. The battered Japanese fleet withdrew and made no more efforts to attack the invasion force.

The push into central Saipan began on the 22nd June with the 2d Marine Division on the left, the 27th Infantry Division on the right, while the 4th Marine Division cleared the Kagman Peninsula on the island's east side. As the Americans advanced north the 27th Infantry Division assumed the left of the line as the 2d Marine Division cleared Garapan area, and the 4th Marine Division fell in on the right. Problems arose when the Army division in the center lagged behind the aggressively advancing 2d and 4th Marine Divisions exposing their interior flanks. This resulted in the relief of the Army division commander by Marine General Holland Smith on 24 June. Major General Sanderford Jarman took over temporary command of the 27th Infantry Division. The argument of whether or not the relief was justified continues to this day, but regardless, the action led to a serious souring of Marine Corps and Army cooperation and affected command relationships to the end of the war.

The drive north resumed on the 27th, but was a slow, grinding process for all units with the Japanese launching several vicious counterattacks through the remainder of the campaign. Aslito Airfield was made operational for U.S. fighters on 29 June. As the enemy was pushed north onto the narrower end of the island the 2d Marine Division was pinched out of the line on 30 June, but would mop up Garapan. The division would also rest and prepare for the assault on Tinian. The 4th Marine Division would continue to advance on the right and the 27th Infantry Division on the left. The final push north began on 5 July and as the island narrowed further the 27th Infantry Division too was pinched out of the line on the 6th leaving the 4th Marine Division to clear the north end. Saipan was declared secure at 1615 hours on 9 July. Tiny Maniagassa Island off of Tanapag Harbor, where a coast defense gun battery had been emplaced, was seized on 13 July by Marines who killed or captured the thirty-one-man garrison while suffering one man wounded.

Of the 31,600 Japanese troops, 23,811 were buried (many more were uncounted in bunkers and caves), 1,780 were captured (including 838 Koreans), 14,560 civilians were interned (including 1,173 Koreans, 3,129 native islanders), and an estimated 22,000 Japanese, Okinawans, and Korean civilians (two out of three) committed suicide, were murdered by Japanese troops (to prevent their surrender), or were killed by Japanese or American fire. Japanese civilian suicides were often accomplished by throwing themselves off of cliffs into the sea, an act the U.S. armed forces attempted to halt. American losses were 3,225 dead, 326 missing, and 13,600 wounded.

The Battle for Saipan was both militarily and politically a decisive engagement. Japan's *National Defense Zone* had been breached, the Japanese Navy had suffered an aerial defeat that it could not rebuild, an American base was secured from which B-29 bombers could attack the Home Islands. Even though Saipan was one of the mandated islands, it was considered to be more of a Japanese territory because of its extensive colonization. The impact of the landing on Japan was serious. On 26 June, well before Saipan had fallen, Emperor HIROHITO requested of the Foreign Minister to find a diplomatic way to end the war. The Japanese government delayed announcing the island's fall and when it did the Prime Minister, War Minister, and Chief of Army General Staff TOJO Hideki and his cabinet were forced to resign on 18 July. The Navy Minister and the Chief of Navy General Staff also stepped down.

The Army Air Forces soon began building two massive airfields for B-29 bombers, Kobler and Isely[3] (former Aslito) Fields, and the extensive support facilities required for the bombers. Fully operational by mid-December 1944, Isely was the main operating field and Kobler (FPO SF 957) was used for spare bombers and transport flights. The former Japanese railroad had been made operational and put to use even before the fighting was over. By 25 July Tanapag Harbor had been cleared and refurbished allowing its use by ships. On 1 September Naval Operating Base, Saipan (FPO SF 3245) was commissioned and work soon began on developing Tanapag Harbor. The seaplane base at Flores Point was rebuilt. Naval depots, repair bases, and support facilities were constructed. The Navy completed the former 4,500-foot Japanese airfield at Marpi Point (FPO SF 959) in July 1945 extending it to 7,000 feet and building a second 3,500-foot runway. They also built a new 5,000-foot airfield on Kagman Peninsula (FPO SF 958). After the war naval base funding and resources were channeled to Guam and in 1948 it was decided to close the base on Saipan and it was decommissioned on 30 June 1949. The port, though, has become the main seaport for the Commonwealth of the Northern Mariana Islands. The town of Chalan Kanoa is now the administrative center for the Commonwealth of the Northern Mariana Islands. A Japanese memorial exists at Marpi Point on the north end known as "Banzi or Suicide Cliff" where Japanese soldiers and civilians threw themselves off.

Tinian Island, Mariana Islands

Tinian Island, earlier known as Bona Vista, was code-named TEARAWAY. Tinian is three miles due south of Saipan separated by a channel with a swift northeastward current (see Map 90). Guam is about eighty-five miles to the southwest. Tinian is located at 14°58′ N 145°37′ E.

Tinian is a low island compared to others in the Marianas. A volcanic island, it is covered by rich red soil on a limestone base. The island covers about fifty square miles and measures 10-¼ miles from the northern Ushi Point to the southern Lalo Point and five miles at it widest across the center. While it is mostly flat, there are two hills near the northwest end, the 390-foot-above-sea-level Mount Maga and just to its southeast, the 564-foot Mount Lasso, the location of the Japanese command post. On the south end was a 580-foot rugged, limestone unnamed hill mass with cliffs and ravines. Most of the island is comprised of a roughly 200-foot-high central plateau. All level land was cultivated with sugarcane, about 90 percent of the land, so much that Tinian produced half again as much sugar as larger, but hilly and wooded, Saipan. Cultivated square or rectangular farm plots bordered by small irrigation ditches or windbreaks of trees and hedgerows covered the plateau. The cane fields were crisscrossed with a grid of one-lane dirt roads. A narrow-gauge railroad system running out of Tinian Town with spurs to the southeast side, the west coast, and the north end hauled cane to the refineries. Other level ground was occupied by four airfields, 4,700-foot No. 1 and 3 near the north end at Ushi Point, 5,000-foot No. 2 on the east shore at Gurguan Point, and the uncompleted No. 4 northwest of Tinian Town. Hilly ground, unsuited for cultivation, was covered with low scrub trees and dense brush. Other than two small villages adjacent to Airfield No. 1, the only town on the island was Tinian Town on the southwest coast. It sat on Suharon Bay and possessed minimal port facilities. Indenting the upper east coast is Asiga Bay.

Map 90
Tinian Island

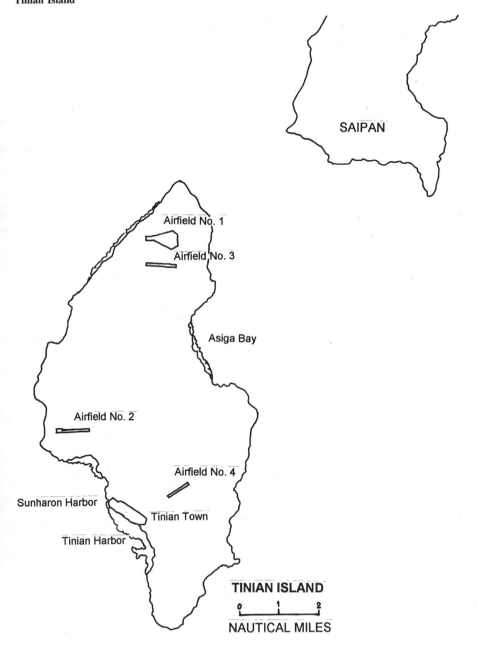

SAIPAN

Airfield No. 1

Airfield No. 3

Asiga Bay

Airfield No. 2

Airfield No. 4

Sunharon Harbor

Tinian Town

Tinian Harbor

TINIAN ISLAND

0   1   2

NAUTICAL MILES

About 18,000 Japanese civilians inhabited the island. Most were employed by a commercial sugar firm. The native Chamorros were long before forcibly relocated to smaller islands and continued fishing.

Located approximately five miles south of Tinian is uninhabited Aguijan Island, aka Agiguan or Goat Island. It measures about two by three miles and covers 2.7 square miles. Its elevation is 584 feet and it is surrounded by steep cliffs making access difficult. It is situated at 14°53' N 145°35' E.

The defenders of Tinian were subordinate to the *Northern Marianas Army Group* headquartered on Saipan. Like the American invasion plan, the Japanese defense plans for Saipan and Tinian were linked. On 7 July, prior to Saipan's fall, the command of Tinian forces was shifted to the *Southern Marianas Army Group* on Guam. The main unit on Tinian was the *50th Infantry Regiment*, detached from the *29th Division* on Guam. The regiment, reinforced by a fourth battalion from Saipan, was under the command of Colonel OGANTA.Kiyoshi. IJA forces fielded 5,050 troops. Also defending the island were 4,100 IJN troops under Captain OYA Oichi. These included the *56th Guard Force*, construction and air service troops, most of whom were reorganized into rifle units. Vice Admiral KAKUTA Kakuji, commanding the *1st Air Fleet*, was present, but did not assume any degree of command over the battle.

Most of the island is edged with jagged 6–100-foot limestone cliffs presenting a difficulty for invasion planners. While ringed with coral reefs, these did not pose the problems the cliffs did. Gaps in the cliffs were few and narrow allowing the defenders to concentrate on the most likely landing sites. The most suitable beaches were on Sunharon Bay in front of and flanking Tinian Town, but they were heavily defended. Another possible site was Beach YELLOW on the northern east shore at Asiga Bay. While considered the second most likely beach by the Japanese commander, it was only a 125-yard-wide gap in the twenty-to-twenty-five-foot cliffs.

Two other beaches existed, WHITE 1 and 2, on the northwest shore. The Japanese commander considered WHITE 2 to be a possible secondary landing site and directed that light defenses be established there. Regardless, the Japanese did not consider the WHITE beaches to be viable options for the Americans still fighting on Saipan. They were simply too small for the Americans, who preferred to assault beaches suitable for a full regimental landing team.

Owing to the extent of defenses on the other beaches, the fact that the assault troops would be weary after a prolonged and difficult fight on Saipan, and that Tinian could be secured at a comparatively leisurely pace, American planners were led to seriously consider the WHITE beaches, regardless of their drawbacks. Preparatory strikes on Tinian began before the Saipan assault. Beginning on 11 June, the Southern Marianas endured 3-½ days of air strikes, which destroyed all Japanese aircraft and sunk much of the area's shipping. Shellings of Tinian occurred frequently while Saipan was still fought over and increased after 26 June. Just over a week after the 15 June Saipan landing, U.S. artillery began shelling Tinian from the south end of Saipan. Soon, thirteen Army and Marine XXIV Corps Artillery battalions were concentrated on the south tip of Saipan to interdict targets on Tinian and support the assault.

Out of necessity this book cannot provide detailed analysis and study of the many factors affecting each of the amphibious operations. An example of some of the factors and planning requirements for selecting beaches is beneficial to students of geo-military studies, however. A discussion of the selection of Tinian's beaches provides an extraordinary example. Beaches suitable for amphibious operations were scarce on Tinian. The best were located on the southwest shore at Tinian Town. This is also where the Japanese command expected the Americans to land and contained the highest concentration of troops. The four Tinian Town beaches (designated ORANGE, RED, GREEN, and BLUE) totaled 2,100 yards in width, but were separated by 200–2,000-yard sections of low cliffs.

The selection of the actual landing beaches was a subject of much debate in the highest levels of 5th Fleet. The Navy preferred the wider beaches at Tinian Town and its Sunharon Bay to protect small craft unloading operations during the expected foul weather. These were extensively defended and YELLOW beach on the northeast shore was only slightly less well defended. The WHITE beaches were under serious consideration by the Marines owing to the apparent limited Japanese effort to develop defenses there. The Navy was also reluctant to begin a fight that would force the Marines to drive down the full length of the island, only to prolong the battle.

The main concern over the WHITE beaches was their size. Both were flanked by low cliffs and coral outcroppings, and overlooked by Mount Maga only 2,000 yards to the south. They were under easy observation from the Japanese command post on Mount Lasso 4,000 yards to the south. Airfields No. 1 and 3, both east of the beaches, were ringed with antiaircraft guns, although most had been knocked out. Three 140mm guns were dug in at Faibus San Hilo Point less than 3,000 yards southwest of WHITE 2. A wooded strongpoint with trenches, dugouts, light machine gun, and rifle pits was 500 yards northeast of WHITE 1. Coincidentally, the local Japanese found the two beaches with their white sands and clear waters ideal for swimming—they called them the "White Beaches."

WHITE 1 was located 1,000 yards west of the end of Airfield No. 1. It was only sixty yards wide, hardly the usual 1,200 yards desired for a regiment landing with two battalions abreast. It offered a 200-yard-wide approach across the fifty-or-so-yard-wide coral reef. The beach was as shallow as it was narrow, only a few yards at low tide. Coral outcroppings and ledges littered the beach, which was backed by a twenty-to-thirty-yard-wide belt of brush. An equally wide belt of low trees, free of underbrush, backed the brush line. Beyond these were sugarcane fields crisscrossed by dirt roads.

WHITE 2 was 1,000 yards to the south-west of WHITE 1. It was 160 yards wide, but only the center sixty-five yards were free of coral outcroppings and ledges. Those on the rest of the beach averaged 3-½ feet in height. The beach offered a 400-yard-wide approach. A sloping 1-½-to-2-foot-high manmade coral rock seawall was located behind the beach, but vehicles could mount it with ease. A narrow belt of brush and scattered trees backed the beach and then the usual cane fields and grid of roads.

Both beaches were flanked by six-to-ten-foot-high coral cliffs. While low, they were sharp and jagged and undercut by wave action making them difficult for Marines to scale.

While senior commanders argued the pros and cons of the WHITE beaches, the Marines and Navy conducted a reconnaissance of the WHITE beaches and Beach YELLOW to cancel their reservations. They were far smaller than any previously attempted on which to land a regiment, much less a reinforced division to be followed by a second. If one of the WHITE beaches was unsuited, one might be used along with YELLOW. This plan offered a two-prong attack, but the two beaches were on opposite sides of the island and separated by 6,000 yards of enemy-infested terrain. Reconnaissance of the WHITE beaches was encouraging and the Navy finally agreed to the plan.

Habitually, supplies were landed directly onto beaches from amphibian tractors and trucks ("Ducks"), and ramped landing craft. Supplies were stockpiled in dedicated dumps, then moved inland and distributed to frontline units. The tiny WHITE beaches precluded this practice. Supplies would have to be hauled inland by tractors and Ducks and dumps established well clear of the beaches. They would be congested enough with landing and departing amphibious vehicles. This meant that the two lead assault regiments, one on each beach, had two essential missions besides closing with and destroying the enemy: (1) they had to make contact with each other over the 1,000-yard interval between the beaches to establish a single beachhead; (2) they would have to plunge inland as far and as fast as resistance permitted to provide the depth necessary for supply dumps, artillery positions, command posts, aid stations, and reserve units.

The assault-loaded transports and landing craft bearing the 4th and 2d Marine Divisions departed Saipan on the night of 23 July and within hours were positioned off of the WHITE beaches. The 27th Infantry Division would remain on Saipan as the area reserve and continue mopping up; it would not land on Tinian. (The Guam assault had begun on 21 July.) The morning of the landing, 24 July 1944 (J-Day), the 2d Marine Division conducted a feint off of Tinian Town to reinforce the enemy's belief that that was where the main assault would be aimed. Air attacks swept the island between gunfire lulls of the bombardment force and XXIV Corps Artillery on southern Saipan. Underwater Demolition Team frogmen attempting to destroy coral boulders and any antiboat mines on WHITE 2 were foiled by a rainstorm. A battleship, two cruisers, and four destroyers supporting the assault fired round after round directly into the beaches in hopes of destroying any mines. Thirty gunboats fired guns and 4.5-inch rockets into the beach areas. This was followed by on-call aircraft strikes. Air observers reported possible mines remaining on the beaches. Artillery on Saipan laid smoke on Mount Lasso to deny the Japanese observation of the beaches. The Marine amphibian tractors churned shoreward regardless of possible mines.

On WHITE 1 Company E, 2d Battalion, 24th Marines churned ashore at 0747 hours and the rest of the battalion followed in a column of companies as did the 1st Battalion. Eliminating resistance from caves and crevasses, the 24th Marines had secured a line 1,400 yards inland by 1600 hours. The 25th Marines assaulting WHITE 2 took advantage of the "wider" beach and landed two battalions abreast, that is with both battalions in company column. Resistance stiffened as the 25th Marines pushed inland preventing them from reaching Mount Maga. However, the two regiments quickly established contact between the two beaches. Despite the small beaches, mines, resistance, and rain, 15,600 Marines were ashore the first day. Lieutenant General Holland Smith, in a rare favorable statement, called the Tinian assault "the perfect amphibious operation." This is often attributed to the operation's many departures from accepted amphibious doctrine and flexibility in planning, factors critical for any successful military operation.

The 2d Marine Division came ashore the following day and the drive south resumed. It slowed as the Japanese were pushed onto the island's narrow and rugged southern end. Organized resistance dwindled by 1 August and the island was declared secure at 1855 hours. The Marines lost 330 dead and over 1,570 wounded. Over 5,000 Japanese dead were counted and thousands more buried in caves and bunkers. Prisoners numbered 250 by one count and 500 by another, possibly owing to confusion with civilian internees. Regretfully, some 4,000 civilians were killed in the preinvasion bombardment and during the fighting ashore.

Naval Base, Tinian was established at Tinian Town on Sunharon Bay (FPO SF 3247) as a cargo ship port to supply the bomber units. The island was literally leveled when new airfields were constructed; over 8,000,000 cubic yards of coral fill were used to construct the six main runways, taxi ways, and handstands. Immense support facilities were built. The first was the 6,000-foot West Field built for the Navy in November 1944, using the old No. 2 Airfield. Two 8,500-foot runways were added to West Field and it was taken over by the Army Air Forces as a B-29 base. It was ready in March 1945, though still used by the Navy as Naval Air Base, Tinian. North Field was built over the old No. 1 and 3 Airfields. It was operational in February 1945 and by May had four 8,500-foot runways for B-29s. Mine Assembly Plant No. 4 served as an aerial mine depot for the B-29s mining Japanese ports and assembled more mines than all other U.S. mine depots together. It was from Tinian that B-29s launched to drop atomic bombs on Hiroshima and Nagasaki on 6 and 9 August 1945. The air bases were closed after the war and much of the debris was bulldozed to the island's edges. The center of the island has overgrown with brush and high grasses. The naval base and naval air base were closed on 1 June 1947. Today the former Tinian Town is known as San Jose and much of the island is leased by the U.S. military for training.

In 1949 the U.N. granted the United States trusteeship over the Mariana Islands, the former Japanese Mandated Territory, as part of the Territory of the Pacific Islands, which included the Marshalls and Carolines. On 8 January 1978 the covenant agreement and the constitution were adopted and the islands became the Commonwealth of the Northern Mariana Islands on 4 November 1986. A local governor was elected at that time. The commonwealth is in political union with the United States and administered through the Office of Insular Affairs of the U.S. Department of the Interior. The town of Chalan Kanoa is now the commonwealth capital. The islands have no significant exports, other than a growing garment industry with most of the workers being Chinese. Huge numbers of other foreign workers, mainly Chinese, are unemployed. Most coconut, vegetable, fruit, and cattle production is consumed locally. The commonwealth's main source of income is tourism, of which about 75 percent are Japanese seeking a tropical climate.

Guam (Mariana Islands)

Prior to World War II the U.S. government officially designated the island simply as "Guam" deleting the appendages "Island" and "Mariana Islands," the latter to sever any identity with the Japanese Mandated Territory. After its capture by the Japanese it was renamed Great Shrine Island (*Omiya Jima*). Guam was code-named STEVEDORE. It is situated at 13°26' N 144°43' E. Guam is located at the southern end of the Mariana Islands. Saipan is 100 miles to the northeast and Rota Island is forty-seven miles in the same direction. Kwajalein Atoll in the Marshalls is 1,000 miles to the east and Ulithi Atoll in the Carolines is 400 miles to the southwest.

Guam is by far the largest island in the Marianas with 225 square miles (see Map 91); the total land area of the other fourteen islands in the chain is 177 square miles. It is thirty-two miles long from north to south and ten miles wide across its north and south lobes. Across the narrow central isthmus the island is four miles wide. This lowland isthmus, with Agana Bay on the west coast and Pago Bay on the east, separates the island's much different ends. Temperatures are moderate to hot with a night low of 69° and a high of 91°. Humidity is high and daily rains are experienced July to December.

The south end is dominated by a rugged hill chain running close to the west coast to Agana, the island's main town. The elevations are not as high as those found on Saipan, but nonetheless rugged and possess caves and ravines. Mount Lamlam near the lower west coast is 1,334 feet high. Notable peaks running north from Mount Lamlam are Mounts Alifam (869 feet), Tenjo (1,022 feet), Chachao (1,046 feet), and Alutom (1,082). The vegetation on Guam is more lush, dense, and tropical than found on the other islands of the chain. The south is covered with sword, cogon, and bunch grass and scrub forest,

Map 91
Guam

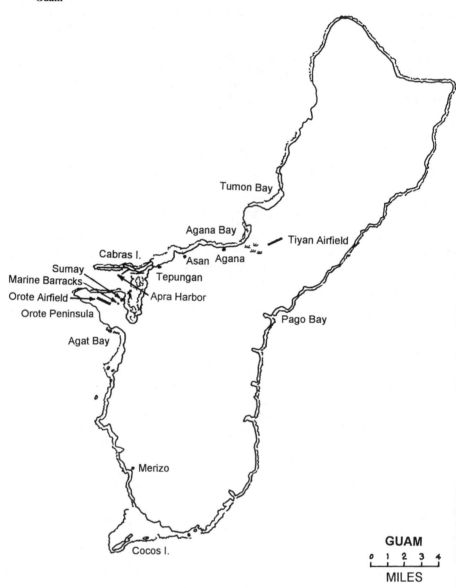

although Mounts Lamlam, Taene, and Alifan were forested with large stands of hard-woods. The southern valleys are fertile and under cultivation with rice and vegetables. The soil on the island's southern half is red volcanic clay, which turns into a thick mud after heavy rains. Numerous rivers and streams flow out of the hills to the sea; Guam is the only island in the Marianas with rivers and streams and is self-sufficient for water.

The largest rivers, Talofofo, Ylig, and Pago, flow toward the east coast. A large swamp is located inland from the southeast coast and another swampy area is found on the west side of the isthmus along the Agana River on the east side of the town of Agana. Much of the isthmus is covered with coconut palms.

The northern portion of the island consists of a 400–500-foot high limestone plateau. It has rolling terrain and is broken by three hills, Mounts Barrigada (674 feet), Santa Rosa (870 feet) on the central upper east coast, and Machanao (610 feet) at the north end at Ritidan Point. The vegetation is extremely dense making off-trail movement almost impossible in many areas. It consists of tropical forest, underbrush, and undergrowth. The higher hilltops are barren being covered only by sword grass and scrub brush. Some cattle ranching was undertaken in the north.

The northern coastline, from Tumon Bay on the west coast, just north of the isthmus, around the north end, and down the east coast to Pago Bay, is edged with limestone cliffs from 100 to 600 feet high. Narrow coral reefs fringe this coast. The southern coastline, like the inland area, is much different. The southern east coast too is fringed with a narrow coral reef, but the cliffs are lower and there are breaks. The south and southeast coasts are beat by a heavy surf and the former has rugged offshore reefs reaching out over two miles. Reef-surrounded 1-½-mile-long Cocos Island lies about 1-½ miles off the southwest end of Guam. The southwest coast to is faced with low cliffs rising directly into the hills and possessing a very poor road system.

Only a fifteen-mile stretch of the central portion of the lower west coast had suitable beaches with narrow, low reefs, and beaches of sufficient width and depth. The reefs are 25–700 yards wide, but there are numerous breaks. Jutting from the center of this portion of the coast is Orote Peninsula. Apra Harbor (aka San Luis d'Apra) lies on the peninsula's north side and Agate Bay on the south. The four-mile-long peninsula is about ½-mile wide near its base, where rice paddies lie, widens to 1-¾ miles wide, then tapers gradually to a point. It is faced with 100–200-foot-high cliffs on all sides. Most of the peninsula was covered with scattered palms and scrub brush, except around the Orote Airfield on the seaward end. A mangrove swamp is located near the coast on the peninsula's north shoulder. Off the peninsula's west end is Orote Island and off its south-central side is Neye Islands, both small rocky islets less than 100 yards offshore. The prewar Marine barracks was located on the high ground above the southeast side of Sumay, itself located on the north-central side of the peninsula along with the cable station and Pan American seaplane station. A dredged boat and seaplane channel protected by breakwaters allows access to Sumay. It was the second largest town with 2,000 inhabitants.

Apra Harbor on the peninsula's north side does not extend to the shore as the shore is barred by a broad reef, but nonetheless offers the best protected harbor in the Marianas. Located in the center of the harbor 1,200 yards northeast of Sumay were the crumbled ruins of a small Spanish-era fort, *Fuerte de Santa Cruz*, perched on a low reef and often awash by the sea; it had no military value. Piti Navy Yard was located at the north end of Apra Harbor with Tepungan Village 400 yards to its northeast. There a 500-yard-long causeway connects the mainland with two-mile-long, boomerang-shaped Cabras Island, which protects the harbor's north side. A submarine reef, Luminao Reef, extends west from the island's seaward end on which a one-mile-long breakwater, five feet above high-tide level and thirty-six feet wide, had been built in 1941 using limestone blocks quarried on Cabras Island. An 800-yard-long pier ran southwest into the harbor from Cabras' seaward end and protective jetties and fueling docks ran along the island's south shore. The over 1,000 contract workers employed on these projects had been evacuated prior to December 1941. The planned 4,500-foot Orote Airfield had been staked out, to be finished by the Japanese.

The main landing beaches were selected on either side of the Orote Peninsula. To the south of the peninsula in Agat Bay were the Agat Beaches near Agat Village on their north edge and Bangi Point on their south. Two islets, Yona and Alutom, lay off Bangi Point. About seven miles to the north of the Agat Beaches were the Asan Beaches centered on Asan Village. The beaches were bounded by Adelup Point on their east side (the coast bends here) and Asan point on the west. The narrow coastal plains behind both of the beaches were covered with dry rice paddies.

Guam was discovered by Fernando Magellan on 6 March 1521. Spanish occupation was effected when priests and soldiers established a mission in 1668. The United States gained control of Guam from Spain in 1998 when Marines landed and the Navy was given responsibility for the island's government after being granted control of the island by the Treaty of Pairs. A Navy captain served as the governor and commandant of the naval base, but a degree of civilian control was permitted. The Guam Congress consisted of a House of Council and a House of Assembly. There were several court systems. The governor had final say on most issues, however. Spanish colonial law, modified as necessary by the governor, was still in effect. Guam was first and foremost a naval station, albeit a small one capabilities wise, but it essentially encompassed the entire island and its three-mile territorial limits. A navy yard was established at Piti, the port of entry, in 1899 and a Marine barracks at Sumay in 1901. The Navy proposed to build defenses on Guam and in 1905 established a coaling station at Piti. In 1908 it was decided to concentrate on developing Pearl Harbor, but six 6-inch guns were emplaced in 1909. Other proposals for Guam's defense were made before and after World War I to protect the route to the Philippines, but little was done. In March 1921 a Marine seaplane unit was stationed there, the first Marine aviation unit to serve in the Pacific, until withdrawn in February 1931. The 1922 Washington Navy Conference, where both the United States and Japan agreed not to fortify their western Pacific possessions, was enacted and was to have an impact on the island's future military development. In the intervening years little was done to develop the naval station or improve the island's defenses. The coast defense guns emplaced there were removed by 1930. There were no airfields on Guam, although at least two were planned. The Navy renewed its efforts after Japan withdrew from the League of Nations to gain approval for defense on Guam, but was told in 1938 that it would be inappropriate to make further requests of Congress. The 1939 Hepburn Board urged that Guam be developed as an advanced fleet base and the 1940 Greensdale Board recommended a more modest base development, but neither gained much for the island. In 1941 Guam was given a Category "F" defense rating meaning that no new defenses would be established and existing naval forces, being what they were, would only destroy facilities and materials to prevent them from falling into enemy hands. Congress also feared that any effort to develop defenses on Guam would only intimidate and provoke Japan into rash action. Guam's fate was sealed. Some limited base improvement construction was approved and contract work began in May 1941, fuel tanks on Cabras Island, road improvements and extension around the island, and building the breakwater on the north side of Apra Harbor.

Guam's exports, mainly copra and coconut oil, were a sixth of what its imports were. In 1936, Pan American Airways established a seaplane station at Sumay on the San Francisco-Manila-Hong Kong route. Communications were maintained via the Navy radio stations and a commercial cable station was established in 1903 by the Pacific Cable Company.

Agana, the administrative center, sits on Agana Bay on the west side of the isthmus with a 1941 population of 12,550. Numerous villages were scattered about the island, mainly along the coast. Approximately eighty-five miles of improved road allowed access to most areas on the island. These are connected by unimproved roads and jungle tracks in other areas. Most of the coast is fringed by roads and a cross-island road crosses at the isthmus.

In 1941 the island's population was 23,400, which included 21,500 Chamorros, 800 nonnatives (Americans, Chinese, Japanese, etc.), and over 400 Navy and Marine personnel. The official language was English, but Chamorro was retained and spoken at home and some Spanish was still spoken. The Chamorros were not American citizens, but U.S. nationals. It was reported at the time that the Chamorros preferred to be called Guamanians (that does not hold true today).

By executive order in January 1941, foreign warships and ships of commerce were not permitted to enter the Naval Defense Sea Area and Naval Air Space Reservation three miles around the island; exceptions were granted. Prior to this Japanese trading schooners were permitted to visit the island. In March Japanese aircraft were detected overflying the island (learned later to be photoreconnaissance flights); Japan apologized. In April plans were announced to expand the naval station and improve the harbor. That same month saw a slight expansion of the Guam Insular Force Guard, a Guamanian-manned, militia-type naval station guard originally formed in 1901. No further efforts were made to fortify the island in fear of complicating ongoing negotiations with Japan. With growing fears of war 104 American dependents and almost 1,000 construction workers were evacuated to Hawaii and the States in October. Further war warnings were issued; Japan had already made the decision to attack.

In December 1941, Naval Forces, Guam, under the command of Captain George J. McMillin, consisted of the Administrative Group, Navy Hospital, a Navy Radio Station at Agana, a Navy Radio Station at Libugon, and the Navy Yard at Piti plus the Marine Barracks at Sumay. There were 271 Navy personnel, including Guamanian messmen and bandsmen, and 122 Marines. At 0445 hours, 8 December (7 December in Hawaii) the naval governor was notified of the Pearl Harbor attack. IJN aircraft from Saipan attacked the Marine barracks and Pan American Hotel at 0827 hours and the USS *Penguin* (AM-33) was damaged off of Orote Point and scuttled. Civilians were evacuated from Agana and Sumay while some fifty Japanese nationals were arrested and detained in the Agana jail. A second attack followed at 1700 hours. That night nine Saipan native infiltrators landed by dugout at Ritidian Point on the north end and three were apprehended. At 0830 hours, 9 December air attacks resumed. The Marines dug in near their barracks on Orote Peninsula along with naval station personnel and the crew of the USS *Penguin*. Other naval craft included the USS *Robert L. Branes* (AG-27) (damaged, but captured), YP-16 (burned), and YP-17 (damaged, but captured). The USS *Gold Star* (AG-12), the Guam station ship, was in the Philippines at the time of the attack. The 246-islander Guam Insular Force Guard, led by a few Marines, secured government buildings in Agana. The eighty-islander Guam Insular Patrol, the island's police force with twenty-nine Marines assigned, was stationed in villages across the island.

The 370-man *5th Company, Maizuri 2d SNLF* from Saipan landed on Dungcas Beach north of Agana at 0215 hours, 10 December and attacked and captured the Insular Force Guard in Agana. The IJA's 4,886-man *South Seas Detachment*, from Haha Jima, under Major General HORII Tomitaro and built around the *144th Infantry Regiment*, had been organized specifically for capturing Guam and later Rabaul. It landed at the same time. One battalion landed at Tumon Bay north of Dungcas Beach and moved south toward

Agana. Another landed at Talofofo Bay on the east coast and moved northwest and another landed on the southwest coast near Merizo and moved north to attack the Marines at Sumay. After token resistance the governor surrendered at 0700 hours, 10 December making Guam the first piece of American territory to fall into Japanese hands. Marine losses were five KIA and thirteen WIA. Navy losses were eight KIA and four Guam Insular Force Guards were killed with a total of twenty-two Navy and Guam Insular Force wounded. About thirty civilians were killed by strafing and bombing. Japanese losses were one dead and six wounded. The few remaining American civilians were interned and later exchanged with diplomatic personnel along with four U.S. Navy nurses.

The Chamorros suffered heavily under Japanese rule. Besides changing the Guam's name to Omiya Jima, the island's capital of Agana was renamed Akashi (Bright Red Stone). Japanese only was taught in the schools and rationing was instituted. A Japanese firm, *South Seas Development Company*, took over all Guamanian business enterprises. Many people died or otherwise suffered from poor food and limited medicines. Group punishment was inflicted when individuals were accused on infractions of the occupation regulations. The Japanese built two small airfields, a 4,500-foot strip on Orote Peninsula and a 5,000-foot strip at Tiyan (aka Agana) 2-½ miles east of Agana, which was not quite completed by the 1944 invasion. An airfield was cleared, but no other work accompanied, at Dededo three miles northeast of Tiyan and near Tumon Bay on the west coast. Chamorros, including women and children, were forced to help with their construction along with building fortifications. The Japanese performed little other military construction on the island only exploiting its resources. When the island began to be reinforced in 1944 the schools and churches were closed, more restrictive rationing imposed, and punishments were harsher.

With the fall of the Marshalls the Japanese began to reinforce the Marianas, including Guam, to a total of 11,500 troops. The *29th Division (18th, 38th, 50th Infantry)*, under Lieutenant General TAKESI Takahina, arrived on Saipan via Japan from Manchuria in February 1944 and then moved to Guam the following month; its *50th Infantry* was moved on to Tinian. (The *13th Division* was to have been sent in its place.) Almost half of its *18th Infantry* was lost when its transport was torpedoed en route from Japan, but it was rebuilt and its *1st Battalion* remained on Saipan. The division doubled as the *Southern Marianas Army Group* responsible for the defense of Guam and Rota. Tinian was transferred to its command on 7 July, before Saipan's fall. A reinforcement unit, the *6th Expeditionary Unit*, arrived in April and was reorganized into the *48th Independent Mixed Brigade* (four battalions) under Major General KIYOSHI Shigematsu and the *10th Independent Mixed Regiment (-1st Battalion* on Rota). There were also antiaircraft units and three tank companies with thirty-three to thirty-eight tanks. IJN personnel totaled some 7,600 troops of the *54th Guard Force, 60th Antiaircraft Defense Unit*, and marooned sailors and air service troops organized for ground combat. The Japanese concentrated most of the *38th Infantry* on Agat Bay, *54th Guard Force* on Orote Peninsula, part of the *18th Infantry* near Apra Harbor, and most of the *48th Independent Mixed Brigade* at Agana Bay. Elements of the *10th Independent Mixed Regiment* were positioned around the south and east coasts. Interestingly, Lieutenant General HIDEYOSHI Obata, commanding *31st Army* headquartered in the Palau Islands and to which the forces in the Marianas were responsible, was stranded on Guam when the Americans landed. He continued to direct the overall defense of the Marianas, but left the defense of Guam to Lieutenant General TAKESI.

The recapture of Guam was essential to the American advance across the Pacific, not only as a point of honor, but because of its need as an advance navy operating base and on which to build airfields to base B-29-bombers. Guam was scheduled to be assaulted on 18 June 1944. This was delayed until 21 July for several reasons. It was discovered that a Japanese fleet was approaching the Marianas from the Philippines and the landing was postponed so as not to endanger the Southern Attack Force (Task Force 53) heading for Guam. With the Battle of the Philippine Sea over and the naval threat passed, another delay was imposed because of the stronger-than-expected resistance on Saipan. This required the Expeditionary Troops Reserve, the 27th Infantry Division, to be committed. It was originally envisioned to employ this division on Guam alongside the Marines. Fearing that additional reinforcement might be required on Saipan, the 1st Provisional Marine Brigade, slated for Guam, was retained in the area as the Expeditionary Troops Reserve while the 3d Marine Division withdrew to Eniwetok to await the invasion of Guam. In the meantime it was decided to release the General Reserve at Hawaii, the 77th Infantry Division, to the Southern Troops and Landing Force for use on Guam. The entire division could not deploy immediately and it was decided to delay the invasion longer until it arrived in its entirety at Eniwetok. With Saipan secured it was finally decided to assault Guam on 21 July.

The 54,690 men of the Southern Troops and Landing Force (Task Group 56.2) and III Amphibious Corps, under Major General Roy S. Geiger included the 3d Marine Division (3d, 9th, 12th [artillery], 19th [engineer], 21st Marines) commanded by Major General Allen H. Turnage; the 1st Provisional Marine Brigade (4th, 22d Marines) under Brigadier General Lemuel C. Shepherd, Jr.; the 77th Infantry Division (305th, 306th, 307th Infantry) commanded by Major General Andrew D. Bruce; and IIIAC Artillery. The latter division's 305th Infantry was initially attached to the 1st Provisional Marine Brigade as its reserve. The 26th Marines was detached from 5th Marine Division in the States and deployed as the Expeditionary Troops floating reserve, but it did not land and was redeployed to Hawaii at the end of July.

Both the 3d Marine Division and 1st Provisional Marine Brigade undertook rehearsals on Guadalcanal while the 77th Infantry Division did the same in Hawaii. The Marine formations staged through the Marshalls at Kwajalein, cruised offshore of Saipan in the event they were required ashore, then assembled at Eniwetok in early July to await the arrival of the 77th Infantry Division later in the month. Between 11 and 18 July the Southern Attack Group departed Eniwetok and arrived off the island's west coast between 20 and 21 July. Besides earlier air and naval strikes, Guam was subjected to a thirteen-day air and naval bombardment prior to the landing. W-Day was 21 July and the Marines came ashore at 0830 hours.

The 3d Marine Division landed on the Northern, or Asan, Beaches that were located between Adelup and Asan Points and centered on the town of Asan on Guam's west-central coast. The 3d Marines landed on Beaches RED 1 and 2. The 21st Marines landed on GREEN in a column of battalions and the 9th Marines hit BLUE just to the northeast of Asan Point.

The 1st Provisional Marine Brigade came ashore on the Southern, or Agat, Beaches. These beaches were seven miles southwest of the Northern Beaches and separated by Agana Harbor and Orote Peninsula. The 22d Marines landed on Beach YELLOW 1 and 2 adjacent to Agat town. The 4th Marines landed on WHITE 1 and 2 north of Bangi Point. The 305th Infantry came ashore on W-Day and W+1.

The 306th Infantry landed on W+2 on the WHITE beaches followed by 307th on W+3 on the same beaches as the rest of the 27th Infantry Division. The 305th Infantry was returned to its parent division's control on 24 July.

Japanese resistance was stiff on both beaches, which were dominated by high ground, and the Marines were only able to establish shallow beachheads by nightfall. The Japanese counterattacked both beachheads, the first of many, and while small elements managed to infiltrate the frontlines, the attacks failed to make significant penetrations. Progress was slow for the first few days as the Marines fought to link-up the two beachheads and push inland up the high ground. Cabras Island was secured on the 24th and Orote Peninsula was closed off from the mainland the next day. The peninsula was cleared by the 1st Provisional Marine Brigade on 29 July, where 2,500 Japanese died, while the 77th Infantry Division took over the right flank and the 3d Marine continued to advance on the left. Marines from the north beaches linked-up with soldiers from the south beaches at 1745 hours, 28 July.

The Americans concentrated pushing north after the link-up. The 77th Infantry Division reconnoitered the southern portion of Guam in force, but found no organized enemy resistance. Most of the defenders had withdrawn to the north. On 31 July the drive north began with the 3d Marine Division on the left and the 77th Infantry Division on the right while the Marine brigade secured the beachhead and patrolled southern Guam. Progress was slow, but on 6 August the Americans approached the wider northern lobe of the island. The 1st Provisional Marine Brigade went into the frontline that night on the 3d Marine Division's left, which was now in the center. The Americans closed in on the last enemy centers of resistance with the Army overrunning the strongpoint on Mount Santa Rosa on the upper east coast on 8 August. The Marines reached Ritidian Point on the northwest corner and the Army Pati Point on the northeast on 10 August and the island was declared secure at 1131 hours.

Almost 11,000 Japanese bodies had been counted with more buried and undiscovered. Thousands of Japanese were still hiding in the island's northern forested hills. Mop-up continued long after the island was secured. By the end of August 1945, a total of 18,400 dead had been counted, 1,250 prisoners were taken, and some 500 Japanese civilians interned. The last organized group of Japanese, forty-six men, surrendered on 11 September 1945. Marine and Army patrols hunted down scores of Japanese holdouts along with the Marine-advised Guam Combat Patrol and Guam Police long after V-J Day. Dozens were still surrendering years after the war, with the last surrendering in 1960, until one more surrendered in 1972. American casualties were over 1,700 KIA and almost 6,000 WIA.

Orote Airfield (FPO SF 939) was rebuilt and extended to 5,000 feet and was operational on 29 July allowing its use by Navy and Marine fighters supporting the ground troops. North and Northwest Airfields, each with two 8,500-foot B-29 bomber runways, were built near Ritidian and Pati Points, respectively. These were operational in February and June 1945, respectively. It was from North Field that the first B-29 raid on Japan was launched from the Marianas on 24 February 1945. The 7,000-foot Agana Field was built over the old Japanese Tiyan strip east of Agana and used by transports. A second 6,000-foot runway was later constructed. The 7,000-foot Harmon Field (first called Depot Field) was built to the north of Agana on the site of the cleared Japanese strip. It headquartered the XXI Bomber Command from early December and then the Twentieth Air Force from July 1945 where it remained until May 1949.

The development of port facilities at Apra Harbor was given the highest priority. Most existing facilities had been destroyed and the towns of Agana, Sumay, and Piti leveled. Piers were built on Cabras Island and the bottom dredged. In early October a typhoon struck Guam and much of the port construction completed to date was destroyed, but was soon rebuilt. The breakwater was extended to more completely protect the harbor to total 17,000 feet. Naval Operating Base, Guam (FPO SF 926) became a major cargo port, repair facility, and submarine base. An extensive island-wide permanent road construction project was also undertaken. Among the road projects was a twelve-mile-long packed-coral-surfaced road connecting Agana and Sumay to become the first four-lane highway in the Pacific. Numerous supply depots, hospitals, and troop camps were built. Guam, along with Okinawa, became a major staging base for the planned invasion of Japan. Housing was built for 15,000 Guamanians.

Guam remained an important naval base after the war. One postwar role was the trials of forty-four Japanese war criminals. Since Guam remained American soil there were no disputes over its continued use as a base as was experienced in the Philippines and Japan. Permanent facilities and improvements continued through the postwar years. Headquarters for U.S. Naval Forces, Marianas (FPO SF 943) sits atop Nimitz Hill on the west side of Agana and was the administrative center for the U.S. Commonwealth of the Northern Marianas and the U.S. Trust Territories of the Pacific Islands. U.S. Army, Mariana and Bonin Islands was headquartered on Guam as well. The 1st Provisional Marine Brigade was activated at Camp Witek, Guam in June 1947 as a Pacific area contingency force. It departed for the States in April 1949 and Fleet Marine Force, Guam was formed for administrative control of Marine units on Guam and remained until April 1950. Naval Operating Base, Guam was redesignated Naval Base, Guam in 1952, then as Naval Station, Guam in 1956. It became a ballistic missile submarine home port and Naval Air Station, Guam remained operational, the old Orote Airfield. Naval Supply Depot, Guam is located around Apra Harbor. The naval magazine, communications station, calibration lab, and regional medical center remain operational to support Pacific and Asia contingency operations. From 1965 to 1972 B-52 bombers flew missions to Vietnam from Andersen Air Force Base, renamed from North Field in 1947. Guam housed over 100,000 Vietnamese refugees in 1975 and 6,600 Kurd refugees from Iraq in 1996.

Guamanians were granted American citizenship on 1 August 1950 and it became the Territory of Guam. Naval administration ceased in 1949 and was transferred to the Department of the Interior. A local governor was elected at that time. The island is an organized, unincorporated territory of the United States with its own local government. It is under the jurisdiction of the Office of Insular Affairs, U.S. Department of the Interior. In 1962 Guam's ports were opened to foreign visitors. Today the former town of Agana is known as Hagatna. Prior to the war there were no snakes on Guam. Today the island is infested by brown tree snakes, which have devastated the bird and small-animal populations. They are thought to have been introduced to the island via wartime cargo ships from Australia. A Marine Corps war dog cemetery for the twenty-five scout and messenger dogs killed on Guam is located on Oronte Point.

Rota and Pagan Islands, Mariana Islands

These two comparatively small islands were occupied by Japanese forces, but were not assaulted by the United States. Both were part of the Japanese Mandated Territory.

Rota Island. Rota (STIMULATE) is forty-seven miles northeast of Guam and sixty-nine miles southwest of Saipan. Situated at 14°08' N 145°12' E, it is the southernmost and nearest of the Japanese-mandated islands to the American possession. Rota is 10-½ miles long from northeast to southwest, three miles wide, and covers thirty-eight square miles. It is ruggedly mountainous with Mount Manria on the southwest end being 1,625 feet above sea level. It has a rugged coastline faced with cliffs and no harbor, but the open Sosanyaya Bay indents the island's southwest end. The island's population was small with the main village being Songsong, involved in fishing and sugarcane growing, and located on the south coast. It was at Rota that the Japanese Guam invasion forces from Haha Jima and Saipan rendezvoused on 9 December 1941.

The Japanese built an airfield on Rota near the northeast end before the U.S. Marianas invasion. The *50th Infantry* was scheduled to move to Rota on 15 June 1944 to garrison the island, but the appearance of the U.S. Saipan invasion force caused it to remain on Tinian. The *1st Battalion, 10th Independent Mixed Regiment* was sent to garrison Rota on 23 June from Tinian. The *3d Battalion, 18th Infantry* soon followed as a counter-landing force for Saipan or Guam, but was returned to Guam on 19 June as sea conditions and American patrols made the plan impractical. Rota was subordinate to the *Southern Marianas Army Group (29th Division)* on Guam until it fell on 10 August 1944. It then fell under the control of Pagan Island. The Japanese garrison of 1,000 IJA troops, 500 IJN air service personnel, and 500 laborers were destined to sit out the war.

Pagan Island. Pagan is approximately 180 miles north of Saipan. To its south is tiny Alamagan Island and to the north is Agrihan Island (aka Agrigan). Located at 18°07' N 145°46' E, it is the fifth island from the northernmost in the chain. Pagan is 2-½ miles wide across the larger north lobe and eight miles long. The smaller south lobe is connected to the north by a one-mile-wide neck. The island possesses three active volcanoes reaching a height of 1,870 feet (Mount Pagan) on the north end and two more on the south lobe (1,883 and 1,798 feet), but regardless, was populated. A narrow plain is situated on the island's center neck, but the island is divided by a series of cross-island cliffs. Its coastline is rugged, rocky, and lined with cliffs. The only landing sites are at Apaan Bay on the west coast on which the main settlement is located, Shomushon, and an area on the east side.

The Japanese had built an airfield on the north end of the narrow neck prior to the U.S. invasion of the Marianas. The *9th Independent Mixed Regiment* arrived on Pagan from Japan with 3,500 troops to garrison the island in May 1944 along with 800 IJN personnel, mainly air service, and 1,000 laborers. The regiment was commanded by Colonel AMAU Umehachi, who became the senior military commander remaining in the Marianas after Guam's fall.

Air attacks began on Rota and Pagan on 11 June 1944 and continued intermittently until the war's end as both islands were bypassed by U.S. forces. The Rota garrison surrendered on 2 September 1945 to Marine Colonel Howard N. Stent from Guam. The Pagan garrison surrendered to U.S. Army representatives from Saipan on the same date.

Small U.S. Navy installations were established on the islands after the war, Rota (FPO SF 3261) and Pagan (FPO SF 3083).

CAROLINE ISLANDS

The Caroline Islands, code-named HIGHWAY, and called *Karorin Shoto* by the Japanese, span a vast stretch of ocean from 130° east longitude at the Palau Islands on the west end to 163° east longitude and Kusaie Atoll on the east, a distance of some 1,700 miles. From north to south the band of islands stretches from 10° N to the equator, although most of the islands lie north of 05° north latitude. The northernmost atoll is Ulithi and the southernmost is Nukuor. The Marshalls are to the east, the Solomons, Bismarcks, and New Guinea are to the south, the Philippines are to the west, and the Marianas lie to the north. Most of the Eastern Carolines lie in time zone 22 along with the Marshalls, but the Western Carolines, Western Group (Yap), Palau Islands, and a few of the westernmost islands in the central Namonuito Islands, are in time zone 21 along with the Marianas (see Map 68, pp. 324–25).

The Carolines contain 549 islands of every description from small sand islets, to coral atolls, to large mountainous volcanic islands with a total land area of approximately 830 square miles. Most of these islands comprise forty-five atolls or small island groups. The area is so vast and there are so many islands that geographers grouped the islands into seven loosely related groups, which is open to interpretation.

The study of these islands is made difficult because they bear so many alternative names, which seldom agree from map to map making it impractical to identify the "common" name of many islands. The common names listed here are those used by the armed forces in World War II, and for militarily unimportant islands, the names provided on the National *Geographic Society's Pacific Ocean Map of 1943*, which appears to be the native names used by the U.S. armed forces to identify these islands. The alternative names include Japanese, native, and earlier English or German names. The Japanese names are italicized and in some cases were used by the U.S. armed forces. Atolls and islands on which Japanese garrisons were established are marked with an asterisk (*). From east to west these groups include:

Eastern Group or Senyavin Islands

*Kusaie** (Strong, Ualan)

Pingelap (*Pigerappu*, McCaskil, Musgrave)

Mokil (*Mikiru*, Wellington)

*Ponape** (Ascension, Puynipet)

Ant (*Anto*, Andema)

Pakin (Peguenema)

Ngatik (*Natikku*, Raven)

*Oroluk** (Bordelaise)

Nomoi Islands or Mortlock Group (southeast of Truk)

Nukuoro (Dunkin, Montverde)

Lukunor *(Rukunori)*

*Satawan**

Etal (Etaru)

Namoluk *(Namorukki)*

Kapingamarangl (Greenwich) (south of Nukuoro Island)

Truk Islands

Losap (Rosoppu, Duperrey)

Nama (D'Urville)

Truk* (*Torakku Toh*, Hogoleu, Ruk)

Kuop

Namonuito Islands (*Namonuito Shoto*) or **Central Group**

Hall (*Murilo*, Muriro)

Nomwin (Namolipiafane)

East Fayu (*Rukute*)

Namonuito (Anonima, Bunker, *Ororu*)

Pulap (Pourappu, Tamatam)

Puluwat* (*Endabi Shoto*, Enderby, Kata)

Pulusuk (*Shukku*, Suk)

Pikelot (*Pigerotto*, Lydia)

Satawal (*Sasaon*, Tucker)

West Faiu (*Fuiyao*)

Lamotrek* (*Namochikku*, Swede)

Elato (*Erato*, Haweis)

Gaferut (*Gurimesu*, Grimes, High)

Olimarao *(Onomarai)*

Ifalik (*Furnkku*, Wilson)

Faraulep (*Furaarappu*, Gardner)

Woleai* (*Mereyon*, Thirteen, Ulie)

Eauripik (*Yorupikku*, Euripik, Kama)

Western Group

Sorol (*Sororu*, Philip)

Fais.(*Fuhaesu*, Tromelin)

Ulithi* (*Uraushi*, Uluthi, Nackenzie)

Yap* (Yappu)

Ngulu (*Kurru*, Lamoliork, Matelotas)

Palau Islands

Babelthuap* (Palau, Arrecifos, Baberudaobu)

Arakabesan*

Koror* (*Kororu*, Koror)

Urukthapel (*Urukethaburu*, Uruktapi)

Aurapushenuru

Eil Malk (*Makarakaru*, Eimalk, Irakong)

Peleliu* *(Periryu)*

Angaur* (*Angauru*, N'Year)

Other islands to the west-southwest of the Palaus include:

Sonsorol

Pulo Anna

Merir

Tobi (*Tokobe*)

Helen Reef

To confuse matters more than the Japanese Mandated Territory was divided administratively into the *Palau*; and *West, Central*, and *East Caroline Districts*, which do not necessarily coincide with the above geographic groups. The Allies tended to simplify matters by loosely separating the Carolines into two groups: the Eastern Carolines comprised of the Eastern Group, Nomoi Islands, Truk Islands, and Namonuito Islands; and the Western Carolines, code-named ARTERIAL, with the Western Group and the Palau Islands.

The larger islands are fertile with coconut palms, pandanus trees, hardwoods, breadfruit trees, and salt brush, usually very dense. The smaller ones are bare or covered with salt brush and palms. Virtually all atolls and islands are surrounded by coral reefs. The beaches are narrow and either flat or very gently sloping. The larger islands are heavily populated while most of the atolls were uninhabited. The natives are Micronesians with Polynesian influence, but vary racially from island to island. Most are Kanakans as found in the Marshalls, but those in the Carolines have more Malay blood. The climate was hot and humid. From September to November westerly winds predominate, bringing an average of ten inches of rain a month. The rest of the year the islands experience up to four inches a month. While malaria was not present, dengue fever and dysentery were.

The Palau Islands were first visited by the Portuguese explorer Ruy Lopez de Villa-lobos in 1543. Spain later explored the islands and annexed the Carolines as the New Philippines along with the Marshalls and Marianas in 1686. Spain concentrated its minimal colonization efforts in the Marianas and did little with the Carolines. In the late 1700s and for much of the 1800s adventurers and traders considered the islands a no-man's-land and did as they pleased. In 1885 Germany claimed Yap in the Western Carolines, but Spain protested and Germany withdrew. German traders still worked the islands and in 1899 they were sold to Germany, which took possession on 1 October 1899. A Japanese expeditionary force seized Yap in 1914 and in 1922 the Carolines became part of the Japanese Mandated Territory. The international cable and radio stations on Yap were under Japanese control, but after U.S. protests in 1921, Japan granted the United States complete right of access to Yap and a say in the stations' operation.

The *South Seas Bureau* administrative center for the entire Japanese Mandated Territory was on Koror Island in the Palau Islands. Four of the six districts that the Mandated Territory was divided into were in the Carolines: *Palau District* headquarters on Koror, *West Carolines District* on Yap, *Central Carolines* on Truk, and *East Carolines* on Ponape. The principal harbors in the Carolines are Babelthuap, Angaur, Yap, Truk, Ponape, and Kusaie, the latter two being fair-weather ports. Fruits and vegetables are grown for local consumption. Coconut products were a main export as were fish and marine products. Effort was made to establish a cattle, goat, and pig industry, but it met with little success. Adequate fish, vegetables, and fruits were produced to support the population, but large quantities of rice were required to be imported for the Japanese colonists.

When Japan withdrew from the League of Nations in 1935, the Carolines, like the rest of the Japanese Mandate, was closed to the West. The Japanese developed Truk as a major naval base. Like Rabaul on New Britain, one of the main goals of the Carolines campaign was to neutralize the base, and like Rabaul, that would be accomplished without direct assault. Truk would be surrounded, cut off, and neutralized by air and sea attack.

When Japan established a new *National Defense Zone* in September 1943 part of its line ran through the Carolines. They fought a delaying action in the Marshalls to the east, which American forces overran in early 1944. On the southern portion of the *National Defense Zone* in New Guinea the Allies hammered away at the Japanese forces struggling to maintain their foothold there. The Americans next assaulted deep into the Mandates and seized the Marianas in the summer of 1944. The Americans now had strong bases to the south (Solomons, Bismarcks, eastern New Guinea), the east (Marshalls), and the north (Marianas) of the Carolines. Rather than attempt to seize the numerous Japanese bases in the Carolines, or even bypass selected bases, in a drive

westward to Truk, the Americans attacked the extreme Western Carolines, the Palau
Islands. In effect, all of the Caroline Islands were bypassed and Truk basically surrounded, although not completely cut off. Yap was to have been seized, but the operation
was canceled in mid-September. At the same time it was recommended to cancel the
Palaus operation as well, but Nimitz ordered it to continue along with the Ulithi occupation, which was necessary as an advanced naval base to support operations in the
Philippines. The attack on the Palau Islands, though, had another purpose. It was to
protect MacArthur's eastern flank for his northward dive into the Philippines. The necessity to do so has been long debated, because it was a costly battle providing only
marginal strategic benefits.

To defend the Carolines portion of the *National Defense Zone* the Japanese retained
only limited forces. Two IJA divisions and a brigade had been lost in the Marianas.
Significant IJN base, guard, and special naval landing forces had been lost there as well
as in the Gilberts and Marshalls. The *Central Pacific Area Fleet* was headquartered at
Truk under Vice Admiral NAGUMO Chuichi. All remaining naval forces, mainly shore
organizations, were under its direct command. Most warships had been withdrawn. What
naval aircraft remained were under the *14th Air Fleet* also at Truk. Its operating arm,
the *4th Fleet*, had been rendered ineffective with the fall of the Marianas. IJN Land
Forces included the *4th Base Force* at Truk and *30th Base Force* in the Palaus plus six
guard forces on various islands.

The *31st Army* was headquartered on Saipan to control all IJA units in the Japanese
Mandate. It was under the direct command of the *Central Pacific Area Fleet*. In the
spring of 1944 when the *National Defense Zone* was established through the Carolines
all IJA forces in the area fell under the *2d Area Army* headquartered in the Philippines.
The *14th Division* was in the Palau Islands along with the *49th* and *53d Brigades* and
the *52d Division* and *51st Brigade* were at Truk. The *52d Brigade* defended Ponape Atoll
and the *50th Brigade* Woleat Atoll. There were an estimated 55,300 IJA troops in the
Carolines.

Palau Islands, Caroline Islands

The Palau Islands are the westernmost of the Carolines and known as *Parao Shoto* by
the Japanese. Pronounced "Pelew," they were code-named DRAGONMAN and later FULL-
CRY and SCHOOLGIRL. Truk is 1,035 miles to the east, Yap is 350 miles to the northeast,
and Guam is 730 miles to northeast. The west end of New Guinea is about 600 miles
due south and Mindanao Island in the Philippines is 600 miles due west across the
Philippine Sea. Pearl Harbor is 4,600 miles to the northeast and Tokyo is 2,400 miles to
the north. The Palaus are located at 07°30' N 134°30' E.

There are approximately 100 islands and islets in the Palaus covering 185 square miles
of land (see Map 92). There are another 100 smaller islets and exposed reefs. All of the
islands are very irregularly shaped and mountainous belying their volcanic origins. The
string of islands runs from the small Kayangel Atoll in the northeast ninety miles to
Angaur Island in the southwest. A broken barrier reef lies between Kayangel Atoll and
the main island of Babelthuap, an area that the Kossol Passage (aka Kossol Roads),
seventy miles north of Peleliu, allows ships to transit from west to east and provides an
excellent anchorage. Southwest of Babelthuap lie much smaller scattered islands including Arakabesan, Koror, Aurapushenuru, Urukthapel, Eil Malk, Peleliu, and Angaur. A
seventy-seven-mile-long barrier reef runs along the west side of the islands from the
Kossol Passage, close along Babelthuap, bends westward several miles from the central

Map 92
Palau Islands, Caroline Islands

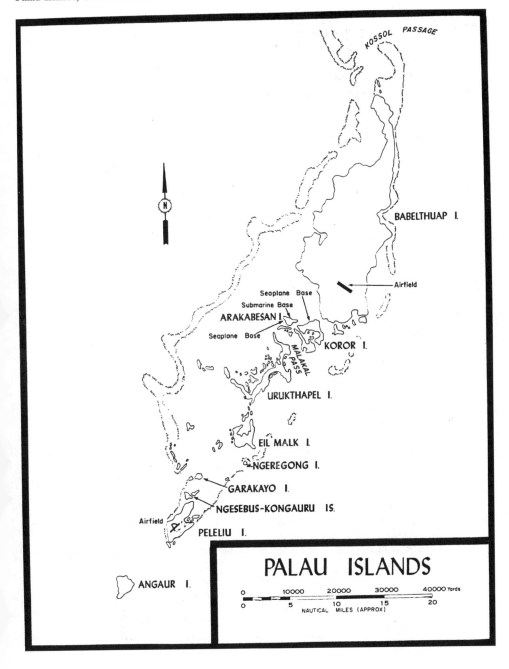

KOSSOL PASSAGE

BABELTHUAP I.

Airfield

Seaplane Base

Submarine Base

ARAKABESAN I.

Seaplane Base

KOROR I.

MALAKAL PASS

URUKTHAPEL I.

EIL MALK I.

NGEREGONG I.

GARAKAYO I.

NGESEBUS-KONGAURU IS.

Airfield

PELELIU I.

ANGAUR I.

PALAU ISLANDS

| 0 | 10000 | 20000 | 30000 | 40000 Yards |

| 0 | 5 | 10 | 15 | 20 |
NAUTICAL MILES (APPROX)

islands, and then swings back to Peleliu. This provides a large protected lagoon. The east side of the islands has fringing reefs and small scattered barrier reefs lie offshore. Most of the islands are fertile and very densely vegetated with palms, ironwood, bayan, and pandanus as well as grass-covered areas. Mangrove swamps are found in many coastal areas. The islands are very rugged uplifted coral and limestone, a maze of ridges, hills, steep-sided pinnacles, ravines, and gorges honeycombed with caves. The roughness of the terrain on Peleliu came as a complete surprise to the invaders. The rugged terrain was not realized until naval and air bombardment had stripped the island's thick concealing canopy.

The islands were discovered by the Spandaird Ruy Lopez de Villalobos in 1543 and were claimed by Spain in 1686. Spain made no effort to colonize the islands, however. Germany gained control in 1899 followed by Japan in 1914. In 1941, there were 16,000 Japanese colonists and only 6,250 natives on the islands. Over half of the natives lived on Babelthuap and most of the Japanese lived on Koror, Peleliu, and other southern islands. Well-developed Koror Town was the capital of the Mandated Territory, the headquarters of the *South Seas Bureau* as well as the military headquarters for the *4th Fleet* established there in 1939. While an administrative center, the Palaus had few military installations other than a small naval base comprised of submarine and seaplane bases on Arakabesan, a seaplane base on Koror, and airfields on Babelthuap, Peleliu, and Ngesebus. The airfield on Peleliu was built before the war and used for reconnaissance missions into the Philippines and the Netherlands East Indies. A carrier group used the islands as a base for its air strikes into the Philippines in 1941. Palau also served as a staging base for troops en route to the Philippines and Netherlands East Indies and in 1943 for the same purpose for units reinforcing the Marshalls. In February 1942 the *4th Fleet Headquarters* relocated to Truk Atoll.

Babelthuap Island. U.S. forces did not land on Babelthuap. It was too large and too well defended making it not worth the cost. Commonly known as Palau Island, it will be referred to here as Babelthuap, its Japanese name, to prevent confusion with the Palau Islands. It was also known as Arrecifos and Baberudaobu. Today it is called Babeldaob. It is by far the largest island in the Palaus and for that matter the largest in the Carolines being about sixteen miles long north to south and ten miles across. Hilly and rugged, its highest elevation is 794 feet, Mount Ngerchelchauus. The hills are covered with dense rain forests, but a good road system allowed access to most coastal areas. The island essentially comprises the northern half of the group and is situated at 07°30' N 134°30' E. Babelthuap Airfield was located inland near the southeast corner. Babelthuap is noted for its ancient ruins of comparatively advanced construction and rows of basalt monoliths of unknown origin and age. A cluster of over 200 small jungle-topped limestone knobs dot a twenty-mile stretch of water south of Koror known as the Rock Islands. Koror Island with the administrative center and a seaplane base, Arakabesan Island with its submarine and seaplane bases, and Aurapushenuru Island are located off the southwest end of Babalthuap.

Peleliu Island. The main objective of the Palaus assault sits on the southwest end of the Palaus barrier reef at 07°00' N 134°15' E. Angaur, the other objective, is seven miles to the southwest while Eil Malk, the nearest large island, is eight miles to the northeast. Babelthuap is twenty-five miles in the same direction. Peleliu (its Japanese name was Periryu) was code-named EARTHENWARE. Its ancient native name was Odesangel.

Often described as a lobster claw in shape, Peleliu is about six miles long from the northeast to the southwest and just over two miles across (see Map 93). The main part

Map 93
Peleliu Island, Palau Islands

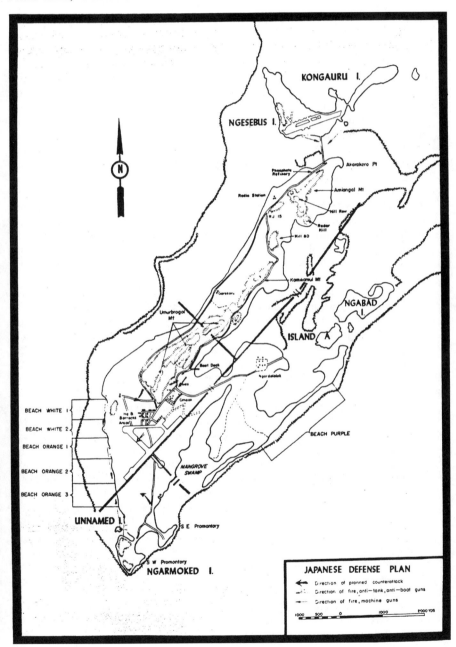

KONGAURU I.

NGESEBUS I.

Phosphate
Refinery

Akarakoro Pt

Radio Station

Amiangal Mt

Hill Row

RJ 15

Radar
Hill

Hill 80

Kamilianui Mt

NGABAD

Umurbrogol
Mt

Garekoru

ISLAND A

Boat Basin

Ngarekelok

Bkoss

Camp

Ngardololok

BEACH WHITE 1

Hq &
Barracks
Areas

BEACH WHITE 2

BEACH ORANGE 1

BEACH PURPLE

BEACH ORANGE 2

MANGROVE
SWAMP

BEACH ORANGE 3

UNNAMED I.

S E Promontory

S W Promontory
NGARMOKED I.

JAPANESE DEFENSE PLAN

Direction of planned counterattack
Direction of fire, anti-tank, anti-boat guns
Direction of fire, machine guns

1000   500   0   1000   2000 YDS

of the island is elongated, but a sprawling peninsula, almost an island in itself, is attached to the southeast side by a narrow 300-yard-wide isthmus. Most of its shores are lined with mangrove swamps. Much of the southern third of the island, its widest portion, is generally flat, but covered by dense scrub woods and scattered palms, as is the southeastern peninsula. On this area lies the well-developed X-shaped airfield and a road system. The northeastern two-thirds of the Peleliu Island is a 3,500-yard-long arm, averaging 1,000 yards wide. It is covered by an extremely rugged spine of rocky ridges, coral outcroppings, rubbled valleys, gorges, crags, and sinkholes pockmarked with caves and all heavily wooded with dense underbrush. The east side of the arm's coast is lined with mangrove swamps. Many of the features in this jumbled terrain would receive nicknames from the Marines and soldiers who fought on them (discussed below). Roads, West and East, ran along both sides of the coast on the arm to its northeast end, Akaraoro Point. Here there was a phosphate refinery to process the mineral mined on the island. The southern half of the arm is dominated by the 550-foot Umurbrogol Mountain and the center portion is covered by the slightly lower Kamilianlul Mountain. Umurbrogol was faced with thirty-to-sixty-foot cliffs on its north side and lined by a mangrove swamp on the south. On the northeast end of the arm is the T-shaped Amiangal Mountain. These "mountains" were actually rocky ridges. They provided a formidable obstacle to attackers and were ideal for the defenders. Well-dug-in pillboxes and fortified cave positions were developed in depth with interlocking fields of fire providing mutual support. The natural defenses were reinforced by elaborate tunnel systems, with the most intricate being the IJN-constructed tunnels on the northern arm. It was a sign of things to come on Iwo Jima and Okinawa.

On the south tip of the island is Ngarmoked Island, which was actually connected to the main island by a narrow isthmus and also known as the Southwest Premonitory. A similar, but smaller feature, the Southeast Premonitory, was attached to the island just to the north of this. It defined the southwest end of a shallow bay choked with a mangrove swamp and was bounded on the north by a large flat peninsula.

Two islets lie on the northeast end of the peninsula, one dubbed Island "A" and the larger Ngabad Island. Off the northeast end of Peleiu's upper long arm are two more islands. The larger, roughly L-shaped Negesebus Island was connected to the main island by a 600-yard-long causeway. The second, nonoperational, airfield covered the base of the "L." Attached by a 100-yard causeway was the elongated Kongauru Island on Negesebus' east end. Both are flat, sandy, and scrub tree-covered.

The most suitable landing beaches are on the southern portion of the west coast of the southeastern portion of Peleliu, although landings could be made at almost any point providing the reef and mangroves allowed access. On the east side the reef fringes the southern coast, but is as much as 1,600 yards wide along the northern. The northwest side has reefs up to a mile wide, but it narrows to 600–700 yards along the southern portion's west coast. There it is shallow, but littered with boulders and outcroppings. The outer lip of the reef is raised and the surf is moderate. This lip prevented landing craft from reaching shore and great reliance was placed on amphibian tractors and "Ducks" as well as using barge-mounted cranes to transfer supplies and munitions from landing craft to amtracs and Ducks. In-depth defenses were dug in facing these beaches and natural obstacles on the reefs were reinforced by manmade obstacles and mines. A rocky islet dubbed "Unnamed Island" sits on the south end of these beaches on the north side of Ngarmoked Island on Peleliu's tip. From it automatic weapons and antiboat guns infiltrated the approaches to the beaches.

The incredibly jumbled and rugged terrain encountered in the Umurbrogol Pocket produced a bevy of nicknames for the many distinct terrain features, essential in order to direct fire and air strikes, to orient troops, to navigate by, and as reference points (see Map 94). Accounts and histories of the reduction of the Umurbrogol Pocket abound with these nicknames. This subject is confused as the Marines and the Army used different nicknames for these feature. Marine aviators sometimes used still other nicknames and even regiments within the 81st Infantry Division used different ones. The "Army's Terrain of Umurbrogol Pocket Map" serves as the basic reference by which to identify the features' other nicknames.

ARMY	MARINES	JAPANESE
Old Baldy	Hill 300 (considered part of Five Sisters)	Kansokuyama
Five Sisters Hill	Bloody Nose Ridge (specifically south slope)	Tenzan
Death Valley	Death Valley	
China Wall	China Wall	Nakayama (central and south portion of China Wall)
		Oyama (northern portion of China Wall—Japanese CP)
Wildcat Bowl (321st Inf)	Little Slot (Marine Air)	
Main Valley (323d Inf)		
Five Brothers Ridge	Five Brothers Ridge	
Mortimer Valley (321st Inf)	Horseshoe Valley or The Horseshoe	
Easy Valley (323d Inf)	Big Slot (Marine Air)	
Fresh Water Pond (Pond is located in depression to left of words *Mortimer Valley* on map.)	Grinlinton Pond	
Hill 100	Hill 100	
Walt Ridge	Walt's or Pope's Ridge	Higashiyama
Hill 140	Hill 140	
Baldy	Baldy Ridge	
Ridge 120	Hill 120	
Boyd Ridge	Boyd Ridge	Suifuyama or Suifuzan

Note that there were numerous other hills in the Umurbrogol Pocket designated in the 100-and 200-foot elevation range.

Angaur Island. Angaur (its Japanese name was Angauru) was code-named DOMESTIC, later TAXPAYER, and was earlier known as N'Year Island. It is located outside of the Palaus' barrier reef seven miles to the southwest of Peleliu making it the southernmost of the islands at 06°55' N 134°10' E.

Angaur is about 2-¼ miles from north to south, 1-½ miles across the center, and covers about 2,000 acres (see Map 95). The island is mostly rolling terrain, but in the northwest corner are extremely rugged coral and limestone ridges up to 200 feet high with closely packed coral pinnacles on scrub-tree-choked Ramauldo Hill. This area is rugged owing to strip mining for phosphate. In that area are three small lakes, the prod-

Map 94
Terrain of Umurbrogol Pocket, Peleliu Island

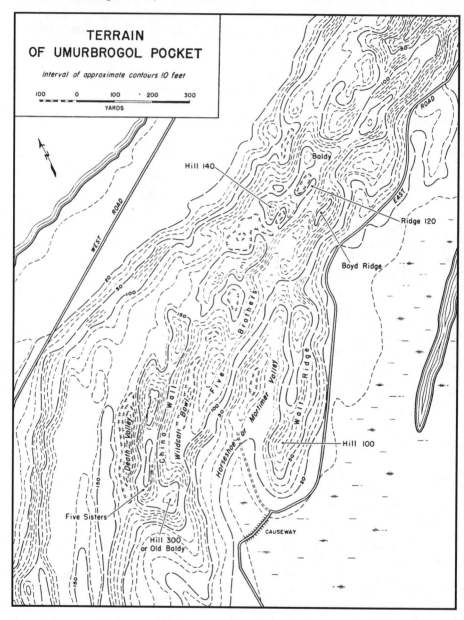

Map 95
Angaur Island, Palau Islands

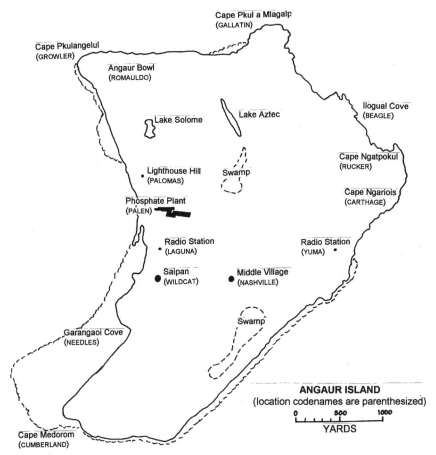

Cape Pkul a Mlagalp
(GALLATIN)

Cape Pkulangelul
(GROWLER)

Angaur Bowl
(ROMAULDO)

Lake Solome

Lake Aztec

Ilogual Cove
(BEAGLE)

Lighthouse Hill
(PALOMAS)

Swamp

Cape Ngatpokul
(RUCKER)

Cape Ngariois
(CARTHAGE)

Phosphate Plant
(PALEN)

Radio Station
(LAGUNA)

Radio Station
(YUMA)

Saipan
(WILDCAT)

Middle Village
(NASHVILLE)

Swamp

Garangaoi Cove
(NEEDLES)

ANGAUR ISLAND
(location codenames are parenthesized)

0   500   1000

YARDS

Cape Medorom
(CUMBERLAND)

ucts of mining. The two largest were called Solome and Aztec Lakes and located in bowl-like depressions. The rugged phosphate mine area was bounded on its inland side by a swamp, but the mine area could be entered along both coasts. Another larger inland swamp is found on the lower southeast side of the island. Most of the island was covered with light to dense areas of scrub brush, but much of its center is densely wooded. The town of Saipan is on the concave west coast. Just to its north was a large phosphate plant and a lighthouse perched upon a small hill. The lighthouse was toppled during the battle. From the plant a narrow-gauge railroad track ran from the west coast to the east coast at Rocky Point dividing the island in two. Five spur lines ran on to the northwest and north-central parts of the island to serve the mine. Angaur Bay on the west side had no harbor or protected anchorage. On the north end of Saipan Town is a small protected cove suitable for boats. About 400 yards north of this was a floating conveyor belt system, running from the phosphate plant, that jutted about 200 feet over the water from which freighters were loaded with phosphate. There was no airfield.

Most of the shoreline is faced by twenty-to-forty-foot cliffs. Except for the coast's center position near the phosphate refinery the west coast was fringed by coral reefs, edging the shore along the northern portion and 200–800 yards wide along the southern. The reefs drop steeply into deep water. The north and northeast coasts were coral free, but the north was faced with ridges and had no beaches. Most of the southeast coast had a 100–200-foot wide fringing reef, but its upper end was open. Its beaches had steep gradients though, and this made the unloading of supplies and equipment difficult. The landings would take place there, Beach BLUE, between Rocky Point on the south side of the beach and Cape Ngariois on the north side, plus on the northeast coast, Beach RED.

The controversy of the decision to seize the Palau Islands is beyond the scope of this book. The decision was affected by many factors to include the strategic goals and concepts of the Central Pacific and Southwest Pacific commands. It was in this region that the two commands, Nimitz' and MacArthur's, began to converge in their drive toward Japan. Numerous courses of actions and alternative objectives were considered. Regardless, the decision to execute Operation STALEMATE II, the invasion of the Palaus in mid-September 1944, fulfilled both commands' goals. Nimitz' purpose was to cut off and neutralize Truk and other Japanese bases in the area: Yap, Woleai, and Ponape, and MacArthur's desire was to protect his east flank as he thrust north into the Philippines. The question though, was either goal accomplished or best served by attacking the Palaus?

A major issue was whether Truk would have to fall to a direct assault or whether it could be neutralized from the air. The command center of all Japanese armed forces in the Mandated Territory and harboring a massive fleet base and air bases, Truk was a formidable target. A major carrier strike was executed on Truk on 17–18 February 1944. It was discovered that most of the fleet and aircraft had withdrawn to the Philippines. What few ships and aircraft that remained were largely destroyed and significant damage was inflicted on the once-mighty base. The Japanese had effectively neutralized Truk on behalf of the Allies. Nonetheless air attacks continued to hit the atoll to reduce it further.

Preinvasion air strikes in the Palaus began in March 1944 with a carrier raid and was followed by periodic carrier and bomber strikes. These strikes hit not only targets on the objective islands, but struck installations elsewhere in the Palaus and at other Caroline Island bases. Beginning in August up to the invasion the raids intensified. By the time of the September invasion, there were virtually no operational enemy aircraft in the Carolines.

Operation STALEMATE II was to be another joint affair under III Amphibious Corps commanded by Major General Roy S. Geiger. It would double as the Western Troops and Landing Force and consist of two divisions: the 1st Marine Division (1st, 5th, 7th, 11th [artillery] Marines) under Major General William H. Rupertus aimed at Peleliu and the 81st Infantry Division (321st, 322d, 323d Infantry) commanded by Major General Paul J. Mueller. It would take Angaur and other area islands. The Western Attack Group (Task Group 32) would deliver the 29,700 troops to their objectives. Two divisions were in reserve, the 5th Marine as the area reserve in Hawaii and 77th Infantry as the floating reserve at Guam, but neither was committed. Peleliu would be assaulted on 15 September (D-Day) followed by Angaur on the 17th (F-Day). Babelthuap Island to the north, along with Koror and its adjacent islands, would not be attacked owing to the former's size and defenses. The Palaus operation was conducted in conjunction with the occupation of Morotai Island on 15 September, a small island off the north end of Halmahera Island in the Netherlands East Indies, itself off the west end of New Guinea (discussed previously on page 250). Another part of the larger operation was the Eastern Troops and Landing Force under XXIV Corps with the 77th and 96th Infantry Divisions and VAC Artillery on standby at Guam. This force would seize Yap and Ulithi, northwest of the Palaus, scheduled for 5 October.

The 1st Marine Division on Pavuvu in the Russells and the 81st Infantry Division at Hawaii rendezvoused at Guadalcanal at the end of August where final rehearsals were conducted. Beginning on 4 September the ships of the Western Attack Group set sail for the Palaus 2,100 miles to the northwest arriving off the southeast coast of Peleliu under ideal weather conditions on the morning of 14 September.

The Peleliu assault has since been often described as the "forgotten campaign." This has been attributed to its being executed soon after the more publicized Marianas campaign and the questionable benefits of the operation. It appears that many correspondents accompanying the invasion lost interest in the operation when told that the island would be secured in four days. Few bothered to go ashore and the others departed the area. Until in recent years only a limited number of books have been published addressing the operation.

The Palau Islands were subordinate to *Southern Army* headquartered in the Philippines and directly commanded by the reinforced, 35,000-man *14th Division (2d, 15th, 59th Infantry)* headquartered on Koror. Lieutenant General INOUE Sadao doubled as commander of the *Palau District Group*. The main unit on Peleliu was the reinforced *2d Infantry Regiment*, which doubled as the *Peleliu Sector Unit*, commanded by Colonel NAKAGAWA Kunio. To it were attached the *346th Independent Infantry Battalion* of the *53d Independent Mixed Brigade; 3d Battalion, 15th Infantry Regiment*; plus field artillery, antiaircraft, machine cannon, and tank units—approximately 6,500 troops. About 500 infantry and artillery men of this force defended the connected Ngesebus and Kongauru Islands off the north end of Peleliu. Major General MURAI Kenjiro, commander of the *14th Division's Infantry Group*, was present on Peleliu, but it appears that Colonel NAKAGAWA was in tactical command. IJN units included detachments of the *43d* and *45th Guard Forces*: two antiaircraft units, three construction battalions, and 1,400 air base service personnel for a total of approximately 3,000 personnel. There were an estimated 10,700 IJA and IJN troops on Peleliu, not including those in later landing units and failed raids.

Angaur was defended by the reinforced *1st Battalion, 59th Infantry* under Major GOTO Ushio as the *Angaur Sector Unit* with 1,400 men. Babelthuap was defended by the *15th Infantry (-3d Battalion)* and *59th Infantry (-1st Battalion)*, plus four battalions of the *53d Independent Mixed Brigade (-346th Battalion)* under Major General YAMABUCHI Takao. The IJN *30th Base Force, 43d* and *45th Guard Forces*, and air service personnel were also located on Babelthuap, Koror, and its adjacent islands. A total of 21,000 IJA, 4,000 IJN, and up to 10,000 laborers were in the Palaus.

Peleliu. As naval gunfire and aircraft continued to pound Peleliu the 81st Infantry Division conducted a demonstration off of Babelthuap as the 1st Marine Division prepared to land. All beaches were on the west coast just north of the island's south end. Landing at 0832 hours, the 1st Marines hit Beaches WHITE 1 and 2, the 5th Marines ORANGE 1 and 2, and the 7th Marines in a column of battalions on ORANGE 3 near the island's southern tip. With all three regiments committed at once the 321st Infantry served as the division reserve. Resistance was extremely heavy, especially on the flanks, and only part of the airfield was overrun on the first day. On the second day most of the southern portion of the island was cleared to include the airfield and the south end of the Umurbrogol Mountain was reached, but little progress was made there. The 1st

Marines on the left pushed into the mountain's flank by the 20th. The 321st Infantry was detached from the 81st Infantry Division to relieve the 1st Marines on the 22nd; the 1st Marines were combat ineffective having taken 45 percent casualties. Stalled at the base of Peleliu's northeast arm, the 5th Marines cleared the southeast peninsula and nearby islets by the 23rd. The *2d Battalion, 15th Infantry Regiment* landed on Peleliu from Babelthuap on the night of 23/24, but much of it was soon destroyed. A push by the 321st Infantry and 7th Marines managed to flank the Umurbrogol along the west shore and the pocket was isolated by the 27th. The rest of the northeast arm was cleared by the 5th Marines between the 27th and 28th; the security of the eastern Peleliu was assumed by the remnants of the 1st Marines. Ngesesbus and Kongauru Islands were assaulted by 3d Battalion, 5th Marines by an amphibious landing at 0911 hours, 28 September. Ngesesbus (ACEPIECE) was declared secure at 1500 hours the next day.

The Umurbrogol Pocket on the northeast arm now became the island's focal point. The pocket was about 1,900 yards long and some 550 yards wide containing 3,000 Japanese dug in on what was arguably considered the most rugged and inhospitable terrain fought on anywhere in the Pacific. Stripped of vegetation by artillery and bombs, the barren ridges offered no cover and concealment. Marines had to carry in filled sandbags—there was no loose soil—to build positions on the bare rock in order to hold the ground they had gained. From 29 September the 7th Marines attempted to reduce the pocket until relieved by the 5th Marines on 5–6 October. They had no better luck and had spent themselves by the 14th. In the meantime the 81st Infantry Division was ordered to Peleliu from Angaur to relieve the exhausted Marines, a move that was resisted by the Marine command until ordered to do so by higher authority between the 15th and 17th. It took the 81st until 27 November to subdue the pocket in brutal fighting when the 323d Infantry completed the operation. The island was finally declared secure at 1100 hours on that date, but base development had begun long before; fighters had begun to operate from the main airfield on D+7. Peleliu was the first opposed landing supported solely by Marine aviation. The operation that had been expected to be over in four days lasted almost 2-½ months. The Marines had lost over 1,100 killed on Peleliu, 117 missing, and over 5,000 wounded. The Army lost 540 dead and over 2,700 wounded. Almost 4,000 more soldiers and Marines were out of action owing to battle fatigue, illness, or disease. Heat (115°F in the shade), high humidity, and serious water shortages were responsible for much of this. Diseases were a problems as the infestation of flies was far greater than American troops had ever encountered. An estimated 10,900 Japanese had died on Peleliu and nineteen Japanese and 200 Korean and Okinawan prisoners were taken.

Angaur. Two days after the Peleliu assault began, the 81st Infantry Division landed on Angaur. The island was thought to have been defended by two battalions rather than one. For this reason two regiments were landed on 17 September (F-Day). At 0830 hours the 321st Infantry landed on Beach BLUE on the upper southeast coast while the 322d Infantry hit Beach RED on the northeast coast about 1,600 yards to the south. The 322d managed to carve out a large beachhead on D-Day, but progress was slower for the 321st. The next day the 322d drove most of the way across the island and took the phosphate plant and the 321st cleared the area between the two beachheads. On the 19th the 322d cleared much of the west coast as the 21st pushed the Japanese in the south into two pockets. These were overcome on the 20th. This left a well-dug-in pocket of about half of the defenders on the northwest corner of the island in the rugged phosphate mine and its high ground. Regardless, the island was declared secure at 1034 hours, 20 September. On the 21st the 322d Infantry overran the last pocket. On the same date the

321st was withdrawn and sent to Peleliu to reinforce the hard-pressed Marines. The Japanese garrison was wiped out except for fifty-nine prisoners. U.S. losses were 260 KIA and 1,350 WIA.

On 24 September, Kossol Passage off the north end of Babelthuap had been cleared of mines and three days later was in use as a major fleet resupply and servicing anchorage. Kossol Roads, together with Ulithi, supported fleet operations in the Philippines.

A total of almost 10,500 U.S. casualties in all categories and services were suffered in the Palaus Islands. Babelthuap, Koror, and the other islands of the Palaus remained in Japanese hands until Lieutenant General INOUE Sadao surrendered to Marine Brigadier General Ford O. Rogers on 2 September 1945. Some 18,500 IJA and 6,400 IJN, 9,750 civilians, and 5,350 natives fell under U.S. control. Owing to Peleliu's rugged terrain Japanese soldiers managed to hide out for years, some into the 1960s. The 1st Marine Division erected a memorial on Bloody Nose Ridge or Five Sisters on the south edge of the Umubrogol Pocket.

Development of U.S. Naval Base, Peleliu (FPO SF 3252) began soon after the landing. The main Japanese airfield was rebuilt with 6,000- and 4,000-foot runways. Support facilities and hospitals were built and a small boat basin and repair facility, still called ORANGE Beach, was constructed near the south end, the south flank of the landing beaches, and incorporated "Unnamed Island." No attempt was made to use the Japanese airfield on Ngesebus Island as it was built on soft sand and was not worth the effort. On Angaur a 7,000-foot Army airfield was built and the Navy established a small boat repair facility (FPO SF 3257). The Army closed the airfield in June 1945 and Navy activities ceased there in 1946. After the war small U.S. Navy installations were operated briefly on other islands in the Palaus: Babelthuap, Koror, Ngeregong, Urukthapel, Eil Malk, and Makakal; and the Carolines: Juluit, Sorol, Yap, Namonuite, Minto Reef, Moloelap, Truk, Pakin, Ant, Kusaie, Oroluk, Ngulu, Namolus, Tonelik, Wotje, Woleai, and Ponape. Most of these were temporary sites for the repatriation of Japanese personnel, demilitarization of facilities, and clean-up.

The final surrender of World War II, Operation CAPITULATION, occurred in April 1947. In early March 1947, intelligence indicated that a small band of Japanese holdouts on northern Peleliu was planning to attack U.S. Naval Base, Peleliu installations, which included dependent housing. Marine Garrison Forces, Pacific ordered Marine Barracks, Peleliu to be reinforced on 17 March by Marine Barracks, Guam and Pearl Harbor. A force of 120 Marines located the stragglers and convinced twenty-seven soldiers of the *2d Infantry Regiment* and eight *45th Guard Force* sailors to surrender on 21–22 April. The naval base was closed later that year.

Ulithi Atoll, Caroline Islands

With the decision to cancel XXIV Corps' planned 5 October assault on strongly held Yap, the related assault on Ulithi was delayed as the forces tasked with that mission were reassigned. On 16 September it was decided to go ahead with the plan to seize Ulithi and the only unit available to the Western Landing Force and Troops was the 81st Infantry Division's 323d Infantry. J-Day was set for 22 September.

Ulithi Atoll, code-named HORROR, was also known as Urushi, its Japanese name, Uluthi, and Mackenzie. Ulithi is situated at 10°06' N 139°05' E. It is 370 miles to the northeast of the Palaus, 370 miles southwest of Guam, and ninety-three miles east-northeast of Yap. Less than forty miles to the east of Ulithi is small Fais Atoll.

Map 96
Ulithi Atoll, Caroline Islands

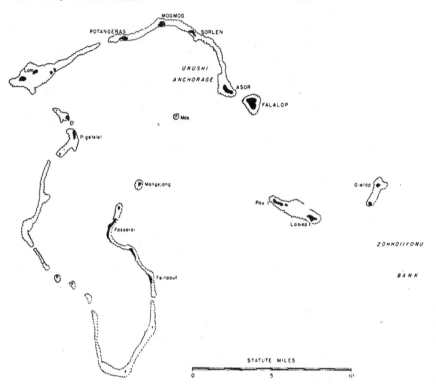

The small irregularly shaped atoll is about twenty-two miles long from north to south and fourteen miles across its wider northern portion (see Map 96). The rim reef is broken in many places, but the main entry into the lagoon are Mugai and Dowarugui Channels on the upper east side. Small islands and islets are scattered around the rim with most of the larger ones on the north side. Others are concentrated on the upper west and the lower east sides. The largest is Falalop Island (AMELIORATE) in the northeast. Running around the north side of the rim enclosing Urushi Anchorage capable of sheltering 300 ships, from Falalop are nearby Asor (IDENTICAL), Sorlen (KEENSET), Mogmog (LITH-ARGE), Potangeras (ACETYLENE), and Lam (no code name) among a cluster of islets and reefs. Sitting on the south side of the Mugai Channel is Mangejang (AMAZEMENT) and spread out to its south are Fassarai (AGGRAVATE), Lossau, Feitabul, and Pugeluc Islands. A few islets were located to the east of Ulithi on the Zohhiiyonu Bank. The islets are low and level with scattered palms and brush. The climate is hot and humid, and the area experiences heavy rain. The Japanese had a seaplane base in the atoll and an airfield on Falalop, but had abandoned the atoll several months before the U.S. landing.

The main Ulithi Attack Force (Task Group 33.1) departed the Palaus on 21 September arriving on the 22nd. In the meantime a reconnaissance party landing on the 21st had found no Japanese. After the main landing force occupied Falalop, Asor, Mogmog, and Potangeras the islands were declared secure. Elements of the 323d Infantry went on to search Ngulu Atoll between the Palus and Yap on 16–17 October, Pulo Anna Island to the south of the Palaus on 20 November, Kayangel Atoll off the north end of the Palaus on 28 November–1 December, and Fais Island to the southeast of Ulithi on 1–4 January 1945. On this island were found 17 IJN personnel and civilian employees. Eight were killed, six taken prisoner, and three are believed to have fled by boat. U.S. losses were two KIA and five WIA.

Advanced Fleet Anchorage, Ulithi Atoll (FPO SF 3011) was soon established and a new 3,500-foot airfield (Marine Air Base, Ulithi) and seaplane base were built on Falalop while other support facilities, including a fleet recreation area, were built on Asor, Sorlen, Mogmog, and Potangeras, the last three having small landing strips for local light aircraft. The facility was closed in December 1945, but an aerological station remained in operation there until 1948.

Yap Island, Caroline Islands

Yap, pronounced "Uap" and also known as Yappu, its native name, was code-named BEQUEST and later VOCALIST. It is ninety-three miles west-southwest of Ulithi and 350 miles northeast of the Paluas. Yap is situated at 09°37' N 138°08' E.

Yap is a rugged hilly island of irregular shape actually consisting of four nearly joined islands separated by very narrow and shallow channels: the largest, Yap; Tomil-Gagil off Yap's northeast; Map, north of Tomil Gagil; and Rumug, northwest of Map (see Map 97). The island is twenty-one miles long northeast to southwest and eleven miles wide across the center. The highest elevation on the southwest portion is 585 feet and on the northeast is 261 feet. The island is covered with dense forests of coconut and areca palms and bamboo. Fruits and vegetables are grown on the fertile island. Considered one of the most attractive of the Carolines, ruins of an ancient unidentified civilization are found on the island to include terraces, embankments, roads, stone wharves, and stone building platforms. There were numerous villages around the coast, which is edged by a wide barrier reef. Yap was the administrative center for the Mandated Territory's *West Carolines District* located at Yap Town on the southeast central coast on Tomil Harbor. Much of the coastline was edged by an improved road system.

Yap was defended by the eight-battalion *49th Independent Mixed Brigade*, under Colonel ETO Daihachi with 4,000 troops, the *46th Base Force* with 3,000 IJN personnel, and 1,000 laborers. Yap Airfield was located near the south end of the southwest portion and Gagiltomil Airfield was on a plateau on the south end of the northwest portion. Yap had been a prime target for STALEMATE II and assigned to XXIV Corps to take on 5 October 1944 (J-Day), but it was bypassed. Its defenders sat out the war and surrendered to the U.S. Navy in September 1945.

Note: Morotai Island, a small island in the Netherlands East Indies roughly halfway between Dutch New Guinea and the Philippines and over 500 miles to the southwest of the Palaus, was seized in conjunction with the Palau operation. Morotai is discussed in the Netherlands East Indies section.

Truk Atoll, Caroline Islands

Truk, pronounced "Chuck," was also known as Torakku Tho, the Japanese name, *Ruk*, or *Hogoleu*. It was code-named ANACONDA and PANHANDLE. Truk is located east of the center of the Carolines with the Palaus 1,035 miles to the west, Guam 555 miles to the northwest, Kwajalein 925 miles to the east, and Rabaul 690 miles to the south. Pearl

Map 97
Yap Island, Caroline Islands

Harbor is 3,260 miles to the northeast. Truk is situated at 07°43' N 151°46' E. Truk was in time zone 22, with most of the Carolines; the Palaus were in zone 21.

Truk is a large atoll about forty miles across north to south and east to west vaguely triangular in shape (see Map 98). It is also a complex atoll with about seventy islands and islets. Most of these are on the reef's 150-mile circumference rim as with most atolls, but eleven islands and about twenty islets are scattered within the 800-square-mile lagoon. Most of the rim islands on the east side are long and narrow while smaller islets are scattered densely along the northwest side. The southwest side's islets are more widely spaced. There are five main entrance passages into the lagoon: North (WAYWARD), Northeast (ALPHONSE), Otta (MONSOON) in the southeast, South or Aulap (FORCEPS), Piaanu (GLOWWORM) in the west, Passages. Just a few miles off the southeast corner of the atoll at Otta Passage is the small (five by eighteen miles) elongated oval Kuop or Kunyuna Atoll (aka Royalist Islands) while even smaller circular Losap Atoll is about sixty miles to the southeast.

The main islands inside the lagoon are, from west to east: Tol (Wednesday) (PORT-FOLIO), Udot (Monday) (PALEFACE), Param (CODLING), Fefan (CALEFACTION), Moen (Haru-Spring, today called Weno) (ANATHEMA), Dublon (Natsu-Summer) (ADHERENT), and Uman (CENTIMETER). Tol is the largest; islets located around it bear the names of

Map 98
Truk Atoll, Caroline Islands

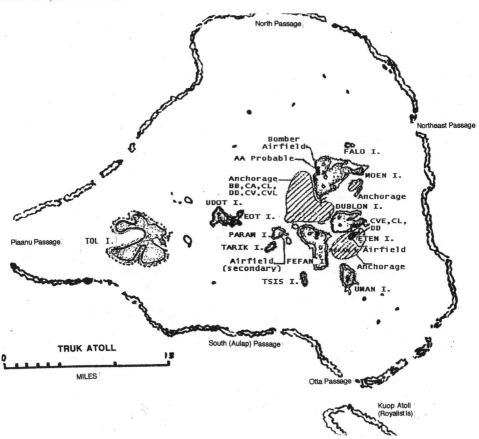

Adapted from a Navy target chart for Operation HAILSTONE.

the other days of the week. The islands inside the lagoon are covered with quite high hills,[4] overgrown with palms and brush, and edged with narrow fringing reefs.

   The two most important islands are in the western portion of the lagoon. The largest of the two and the second largest in the lagoon is Moen with two airfields (Moen 1 and 2 at the north and south corners, respectively) and a seaplane base. To the south of it is Dublon, the fourth largest in the lagoon (after Fefan), which hosted the principal town and the *Central Caroline District* administrative office. It was also the port of entry and had a seaplane base. Immediately off the south-central shore of Dublon is the eighty-six-acre islet of Eten (Bamboo) (BANNISTER). Its shoreline was bulkheaded into a rectangular shape and an airfield built on it giving the appearance of an aircraft carrier. Param, near the lagoon's center, also had an airfield. A small island on the east side of Otta Passage at the atoll's southeast corner is Mesegon Island with a small airfield. Natives were not permitted on these islands and those living on them had been moved to other islands.

Prior to the war there were almost 3,000 Japanese civilians and 18,000 natives living on the atoll.

Japanese traders were established on Truk in 1891. In 1939 the Japanese began developing Truk as the major naval base in the the Mandated Territory. It was fortified with coast defense guns covering the five entrances, which were also blocked by command-detonated mines, while other guns were positioned to prevent landings on the outer islands. The popular press of the period called it "the Japanese Pearl Harbor" or "the Gibraltar of the Pacific." It was through Truk that most of the aircraft, troops, supplies, and material were staged into the Solomons, Bismarcks, New Guinea, and elsewhere to support the Japanese conquest, and later, to defend the Empire's shrinking perimeter. In February 1942 the *4th Fleet Headquarters* arrived from the Palaus and was headquartered on Dublon Island. In July the *Combined Fleet* (elements of the *1st, 2d,* and *3d Fleets, 6th Submarine Fleet*) arrived at Truk. At its height of operation up to 1,000 ships were sometimes found in the lagoon. While it was a superior anchorage and well defended, its repair facilities were limited.

Truk was defended not only by major fleet forces and aircraft, but ground forces as well. This included the *52d Division (69th, 150th Infantry; -107th Infantry* detached to Ponape), the *51st Independent Mixed Brigade(-)*, IJA service and support troops plus the IJN's *4th Base Force, 41st Guard Force, Sasebo 101st SNLF*, and significant air base service units as well as labor units with 5,200 laborers. Lieutenant General MUGIKURA Shunsaburo commanded both the *52nd Division* and *31st Army* as well as doubling as the *Truk District Group*. Vice Admiral HARA Chuichi commanded the naval forces, *4th Fleet*, remaining in the islands. In May 1945 there were an estimated 13,600 IJA troops and 10,600 IJN personnel. Several of the atolls around Truk were defended and included:

Woleai	*50th IMB, 44th Guard Force*	5,500
Puluwat	*11th IMR, IJN detachment*	3,500
Nomoi	*Element 51st IMB, IJN detachment*	2,400
Ponape	*52d IMB, 107th Infantry, 42d Guard Force*	8,000
Kapingamarang	IJA and IJN detachments	400

The U.S. command had no desire to directly assault Truk; it would be neutralized by air and sea in a manner accomplished so effectively on Rabaul. The 5th Fleet executed Operation HAILSTONE on 17–18 February 1944. Eight aircraft carriers, six battleships, ten cruisers, and twenty-eight destroyers of Task Force 58 approached Truk from the northeast and sailed around the atoll and back to the northeast while launching thirty air strikes of significantly more power than the two Japanese strikes on Pearl Harbor. The *Combined Fleet*, which the Navy had hoped to catch in the lagoon, had taken heed of indicators of the coming attack and had withdrawn west to the Palaus on 10 February. The American strikes did sink two cruisers, two destroyers, an aircraft ferry, two submarine tenders, an auxiliary merchant cruiser, six tankers, and seventeen merchant ships, destroyed approximately 100 aircraft on the ground and in the air, and inflicted serious damage to shore installations. Task Force 58 conducted a follow-on raid on 29–30 April destroying small craft, almost 100 aircraft, and shore facilities. B-24 and B-29 bombers continued to frequently raid Truk until the end of the war with the atoll providing a good training target for newly arriving bomber units.

On 2 September 1945, Lieutenant General MUGIKURA Shunzaburo, *31st Army*, and

Vice Admiral HARA Chuichi, *4th Fleet*, surrendered the Truk garrison and the outlying garrisons, a total of 130,000 military personnel and civilians, to Vice Admiral George D. Murray aboard the USS *Portland* (CA-33). This was the largest surrender in the Pacific Ocean Area. Marine occupation forces did not arrive until 24 November and were based on Moen Island (FPO SF 3400).

In 1949 the Caroline Islands became part of the Trust Territory of the Pacific Islands administered by the United States, along with the Marianas and Marshalls. The Carolines were divided into six island districts: Ponape, Kosrae, Truk, Yap, and Palau. Like the rest of the Trust Territory the economy stagnated and the entire territory became a welfare state, what became to be known as the "Rust Territory." Unlike the Marshalls and Marianas where postwar military activities continued, the Carolines slumbered. In May 1979 the proclamation for the Federated States of Micronesia was announced and on 3 November 1986 the Compact of Free Association with the United States took effect. Truk was officially renamed Chuuk at the same time. The compact excluded the Palau District, which remained under U.S. trusteeship. Its Compact of Free Association was announced in July 1979 and took effect on 1 October 1994 and it became the Republic of Palau *(Beluu er a Belau).*

The Federated States on Micronesia is divided into four states: Kosrae, Pohnpei, Chuuk (Truk), and Yap. Its capital is Palikir on Pohnpei (Ponape) Atoll. Other than phosphate, some fish, bananas, and garments, the country has little in the way of exports. Its remote location has not promoted tourism to any degree. The approximately sixty shipwrecks of the "Ghost Fleet of Truk" in the shallow lagoon are an attraction to divers.

The Republic of Palau includes the Palaus plus the remote islands to the southwest, Sonsorol Islands, Pulo Anna, Meirr, Tobi, and Helen Reef. The country is divided into sixteen "states," essentially individual islands, with the capital being Koror. A new capital is being built on eastern Babeldaob (Babelthuap) about fifteen miles to the northeast. Exports include fish, vegetables, and local craft items. Tourism is growing because of the excellent diving. Seventy of the Rock Islands south of Koror have been designated a marine reserve and entry is prohibited, but diving is permitted in other parts of the Rock Islands. The U.S. government has designated certain areas with sunken ships as historic landmarks under Project SeaMark.

NOTES

1. Three atolls—Butaritari, Tarawa, and Apamama—were the main American objectives in 1943. In order to prevent confusion, a clarification of these atolls' names are required. Butaritari was commonly called Makin after its dominant island and the island on which the action was fought. Conversely, Makin Island was sometimes called Butaritari Island. This was an error on the part of the American intelligence. In this study the atoll is called Butaritari and the island Makin. The action in Tarawa Atoll was mainly on Betio Island, although this island is commonly referred to as "Tarawa." The approved spelling of Apamama Atoll was Abemama, but the former was used by U.S. forces and that practice will be continued in this study in order to prevent conflict with most other references.

2. Today Ennylabegan Island is commonly known as Carlos, its native name all but forgotten.

3. Aslito Airfield was first renamed Conroy Field on 18 June. XXI Bomber Command renamed it "Isley Field," its common name, but it was actually named after Commander Robert H. Isely, a Navy pilot killed during the battle for Saipan. Today it is known as Iseley International Airport.

4. The highest elevations are: Tol—1,422 feet, Udot—796 feet, Fefan—1,026 feet, Moen—1,283 feet, Dublon—1,163 feet, and Uman—945 feet.

READING SUGGESTIONS

Alexander, Col. Joseph H. *Across the Reef: The Marine Assault of Tarawa*. Washington Navy Yard: History and Museums Division, Marine Corps Historical Center, 1993.

Alexander, Col. Joseph H. *Utmost Savagery: The Three Days of Tarawa*. Annapolis: Naval Institute Press, 1995.

Bureau of Yards and Docks. *Building the Navy's Bases in World War II, Vol. II*. Washington, DC: US Government Printing Office, 1947.

Chapin, Capt. John C. *Breaking the Outer Ring: Marine Landings in the Marshall Islands*. Washington Navy Yard: History and Museums Division, Marine Corps Historical Center, 1994.

Coletta, Paolo E. and Bauer, K. Jack (Editors). *United States Navy and Marine Bases, Overseas*. Westport, CT: Greenwood Publishing Co., 1985.

Controvich, James T. *The Central Pacific Campaign 1943–1944: A Bibliography*. Westport, CT: Greenwood Publishing Co., 1990.

Craven, Wesley F. and Cate, James L. *The Army Air Forces in World War II: The Pacific: Guadalcanal to Saipan, August 1942 to July 1944, Vol. 4*. Chicago: University of Chicago Press, 1950.

Crowl, Philip A. *United States Army in World War II: Campaign in the Marianas*. Washington, DC: US Government Printing Office, 1960.

Crowl, Philip A. and Love, Edmund G. *United States Army in World War II: Seizure of the Gilberts and Marshalls*. Washington, DC: US Government Printing Office, 1985.

Garand, George W. and Strobridge, Truman R. *History of US Marine Corps Operations in World War II: Western Pacific Operations, Vol. IV*. Washington, DC: US Government Printing Office, 1966.

Gayle, Brig. Gen. Gordon D. *Bloody Beaches: The Marines at Peleliu*. Washington Navy Yard: History and Museums Division, Marine Corps Historical Center, 1996.

Graham, Michael B. *Mantle of Heroism: Tarawa and the Struggle for the Gilberts, November 1943*. Novato, CA: Presidio Press, 1997.

Harwood, Richard. *A Close Encounter: The Marine Landing on Tinian*. Washington Navy Yard: History and Museums Division, Marine Corps Historical Center, 1994.

Heinl, Lt. Col. Robert D., Jr. and Crown, Lt. Col. John A. *The Marshalls: Increasing the Tempo*. Washington, DC: HQ Marine Corps, 1954.

Hoyt, Edwin P. *Storm over the Gilberts*. New York: Mason/Charter, 1978. Livingston, William S. and Louis, William R. (Editors). *Australia, New Zealand, and the Pacific Islands since the First World War*. Austin: University of Texas Press, 1979.

Lodge, Maj. O.R. *The Recapture of Guam*. Washington, DC: HQ Marine Corps, 1954.

Morison, Samuel E. *History of US Navy Operations in World War II: Aleutians, Gilberts and Marshalls, March 1943–April 1944, Vol. VII*. Boston: Little, Brown & Company, 1951.

Morison, Samuel E. *History of US Navy Operations in World War II: New Guinea and the Marianas, March 1944–August 1944, Vol. VIII*. Boston: Little, Brown & Company, 1952.

Morison, Samuel E. *History of US Navy Operations in World War II: Leyte, June 1944–January 1944, Vol. XII*. Boston: Little, Brown & Company, 1966.

O'Brien, Cyril J. *Liberation: Marines in the Recapture of Guam*. Washington Navy Yard: History and Museums Division, Marine Corps Historical Center, 1994.

Price, Willard. *Japan's Islands of Mystery*. New York: John Day Company, 1944.

Rogers, Robert F. *Destiny's Landfall: A History of Guam*. Honolulu: University of Hawaii Press, 1995.

Shaw, Henry I. Jr.; Nalty, Bernard C.; and Turnbladh, Edwin T. *History of US Marine Corps Operations in World War II: Central Pacific Drive, Vol. III*. Washington, DC: US Government Printing Office, 1966.

Sherrod, Robert. *Tarawa*. New York: Duell, Sloan, & Pearce, 1944. Reprinted by The Admiral Nimitz Foundation.

Smith, Robert R. *United States Army in World War II: The Approach to the Philippines*. Washington, DC: US Government Printing Office, 1984.
Stockman, James R. *The Battle for Tarawa*. Washington: Historical Branch, G-3 Division, Headquarters, Marine Corps, 1954. Reprinted by The Battery Press.
Wright, Derrick. *A Hell of a Way to Die: Tarawa Atoll, 20–23 November 1943*. London: Windrow & Greene, 1996.

5

Western Pacific

The Western Pacific was not a military command, but merely a term of convenience used to define the west-central Pacific region adjacent to Japan. The islands within this region are territories of Japan. Operationally the region fell under the Central Pacific Ocean Area. Two large island groups are located in this region, the Nanpo Shoto (with Iwo Jima) and Nansei Shoto (with the Ryukyus and Okinawa). Some historians consider the Mariana Islands to be in the region as well, again for utility. Both of these groups contain smaller island groups. To clarity the topic, made more complex by the Japanese terms commonly used to identify these groups and their islands, a brief explanation is required. Translations of Japanese island-related terms are: *Shoto*—groups of islands, *Retto*—archipelago, *Gunto*—group, *Shima* and *Jima*—island.

NANPO SHOTO, JAPAN

Nanpo Shoto (Three Groups of Islands) is a chain of island groups extending 750 miles south of Tokyo Bay terminating some 300 miles north of the Mariana Islands (see Map 99). The Marianas might be considered a distant continuation of the chain. The Nanpo Shoto is comprised of three island groups, from which its name is derived. The northernmost group is the Izut Shichito (aka Izut Shoto) with six main islands (Hachijo Shima, Aoga Shima, Bayonnaise, Smith, Mitsugo Jima, Sofu Gan). The middle group is Ogasawara Shoto (aka Ogasawara Gunto or Peel Group), more commonly known to U.S. forces as the Bonin Islands. It consists of four islands: Muko Jima (Parry), Nishino Shima (Rosario), Chichi Jima (Peel, Beechy), Haha Jima (Baily, Coffin, Hillsborough) (the parenthesized names were common British names). A short distance to the south is the Kazan Retto, commonly known as the Volcano Islands. In the center of this small archipelago is Iwo Jima. To its north is Kita (North) Iwo Jima and to the south is Minami (South) Iwo Jima. Many official documents locate Iwo Jima in the Bonin Islands (Ogasawara Shoto), but it is in the Volcano Islands (Kazan Retto). This confusion occurs because both groups are located in the larger Nanpo Shoto group. It is also a common practice to refer to the two groups together as the Bonin Islands (SECLUSION).

Map 99
Nanpo Shoto, Nansei Shoto, Mariana Islands, and Western Caroline Islands

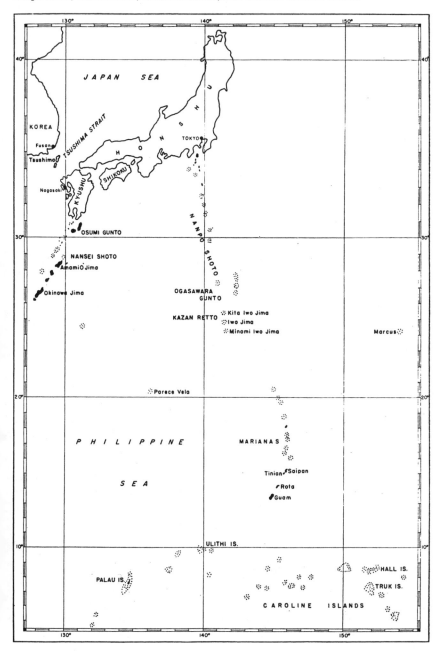

The Japanese claim they were discovered by the Prince of Ogasawara in 1593, but they were more probably long known to fishermen. Americans and Englishmen visited the islands through the 1800s. Britain claimed the islands in 1827, but little was done to maintain a hold on the islands, although a small colony of mixed European nationals and Americans was established at Port Lloyd on Chichi Jima. Commodore Matthew Perry, en route to Japan, recommended that a coaling station be established there. The Japanese began colonizing the islands in 1853 and in 1861 took over their control. All of the islands were annexed as part of Japan in 1891 when they were placed under the juris-diction of the *Tokyo Prefecture* as the *Ogasawana Branch Administration*. The Western settlement on Chichi Jima was allowed to remain, but it dwindled away by the early 1900s. Like the Mandated Territories, from the mid-1930s the islands were off limits to Westerners. A sign posted on the beach at Iwo Jima provided the warning in Japanese and English:

Notice

Trespassing, surveying, photographing, sketch-
ing, modelling, etc; upon or of these premises
without previous official permission are prohibited
by the Military Secrets Protection Law.
  Any offender in this regard will be punished
within this law.

Ministry of the Navy

Oct. 1937

Early military activities in the islands was limited, although the *Chichi Jima Branch, Army Fortifications Department* was formed in 1920 to develop defenses on that island. The Naval Arms Limitations Agreement of 1922 forestalled any further fortification. In the late 1930s, a small naval base was established on Chichi Jima and fortifications were built. The naval base on Futami Ko Harbor on the island's south side included a seaplane base, weather and radio stations, and small coastal patrol craft units. At the beginning of the war the island was garrisoned by almost 4,000 IJA troops and 1,200 IJN personnel. An IJN airfield was built on Iwo Jima in 1943 and 1,500 airfield service personnel stationed there with an air unit. The garrisons of both islands were increased in 1944 and reorganized into the *109th Division*; the parent division was on Iwo Jima while the Division's *1st Mixed Brigade* and *17th Independent Infantry Regiment (-)* were on Chichi Jima.

The only island in the Nanpo Shoto that would be assaulted was Iwo Jima. Chichi Jima (VISIONARY) and Haha Jima (MAHATMA) were considered for seizure, but were rejected because the former was more heavily fortified than Iwo Jima, surrounded by cliffs, and the ruggedly mountainous islands were ill-suited for the necessary extensive airfields.

Iwo Jima, Kazan Retto, Nanpo Shoto

Iwo Jima means Sulphur Island and Kazan Retto means Volcano Archipelago or Is-lands. Iwo Jima was code-named ROCKCRUSHER and later STARLIT and WORKMAN. To Marines during rehearsals it was known only as Island "X" or "XRAY," and later simply as "Iwo." Iwo Jima is 670 miles south of Tokyo, 700 miles north of Guam, and 625 miles north of Saipan, just under halfway between Saipan and Tokyo. It is situated at

Map 100
Iwo Jima, Kazan Retto, Nanpo Shoto

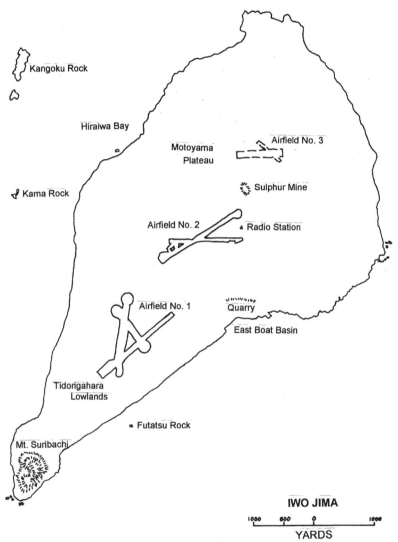

Kangoku Rock

Hiraiwa Bay

Motoyama
Plateau

Airfield No. 3

Kama Rock

Sulphur Mine

Airfield No. 2

Radio Station

Airfield No. 1

Quarry

East Boat Basin

Tidorigahara
Lowlands

Futatsu Rock

Mt. Suribachi

IWO JIMA

1000   500   0   1000

YARDS

24°44' N 141°22' E. Iwo Jima and all of the Nanpo Shoto islands were in time zone 21, the same as the Japanese Home Islands.

Geologically, Iwo Jima is a comparatively young volcanic island. The porkchop-shaped island is 4-⅔ miles long from northeast (Kitano Point) to southwest (Tobiishi Point), 2-½ miles across the wide northeast portion, and 700 yards wide at the landward base of Mount Suribachi on the southwest end (see Map 100). It covers 7-½ square miles making it the largest island in the Kazan Retto. In profile the island has the appearance of a mostly submerged whale with the gently humped northeast plateau representing its head and Mount Suribachi its tail. Mount Suribachi (aka Suribati-yama) is a dome-shaped, rocky-sided extinct volcano rising to 546 feet with a comparatively shallow caldera atop its eroded cone. Most of its north slope was covered with scrub brush, but this was burned off before the landings. There were narrow, rocky beaches around its base, but they faced only steep cliffs, boulders, and tallis. Suribachi, or rather the highest point on its rim, was code-named HOTROCKS and used as a reference point for all radar contacts (24°44'11" N 141°17'28" E), but it generally came to mean the entire mountain. The men who took it called it "Mount Sonofabitchi."

Northeastward from the base of Suribachi the southwestern part of the island forms a triangular piece of land, which the Japanese call Tidorigahara, before rising toward the plateau. In this area the ground rises from the beaches on both sides in steep terraces of coarse, black volcanic sand. The terraces are formed and shifted by wave action and high winds. The number of steps, height, and steepness of the terraces varied from area to area. Generally the terraces were eight to fifteen feet high angled from forty to forty-five degrees and then the ground rose higher from there. The volcanic sand was deep, soft, and had no adhesive qualities. It was impossible for wheeled vehicles to climb the terraces and few tracked vehicles could manage either. Most would bog down into the sand and their treads could find no purchase. Those that did make it to the top usually sank up to their bottom, frames becoming stuck. As they spun their treads in an effort to move forward they only sank deeper and piled up banks of sand behind them, creating another obstacle for following vehicles. Men sank to their ankles and found it impossible to dig foxholes on the exposed high ground; the sand would ceaselessly slide into the holes as they dug. Only large shellholes and bomb craters provided any cover, if they were large enough to have displaced sufficient sand and not simply refilled after the shell or bomb had burst. To add to the difficulties, the sand was infested with fleas. Massive effort was expended to first wench vehicles up the terraces, constantly tow them out of areas they had sunk into, and then bulldoze ramps that were covered with metal airfield matting.

The offshore waters are free of reefs and rock outcroppings. The ocean bottom rises steeply to the island; just a few feet from the beach the water is ten to twelve feet deep. The beaches are pounded by an unobstructed surf, which broached landing craft and made it extremely difficult to unload cargo. This did have the advantage, along with the soft sand, of preventing the Japanese from emplacing underwater and beach obstacles and mines. There are no protected anchorages or lagoons. The beaches are five to ninety feet wide before rising into the terraces. The beach along the southeast coast is about 3,500 yards long, a straight, clear stretch running from the base of Suribachi to the East Boat Basin where the island's northeast portion bulges out. These would be the landing beaches. Above the East Boast Basin was a rock quarry. The west beach was similar to the southeast, but 2,000 yards long and beat by heavier surf. It was later used to land supplies, with extreme difficulties, to units fighting on that side of the island. Along the island's northwest side from Hiraiwa Bay, which barely indents the coast, to Kitano Point on the northeast end, the beaches are very narrow and rocky. From Kitano Point around the east bulge to Tachiiwa Point beaches are nonexistent. The coast there is faced with shoals, submerged rocks, and rocky cliffs with little access inland. Three rocky islets are situated to the northwest of Iwo Jima, Kama Rock about 1,000 yards offshore and the larger Kangoku Rock (aka Kangoku-iwa) with a small unnamed attendant rock off its south end, some 2,250 yards off. Kangoku measures about 200 by 600 yards. It is flat, brush-covered, and about twenty feet above sea level. About 250 yards offshore and centered on the southeastern landing beaches, between Beaches RED 1 and 2, is tiny Futatsu Rock.

Atop the terraces on the Tidorighara the land levels out fifty to sixty feet above sea level and the ground is virtually devoid of cover and concealment, including vegetation. The western half was divided into scores of small local subsistence vegetable and grain garden plots in a checkerboard pattern separated by low dikes. Rice was imported from the Home Islands. Here, too, all the vegetation had been burned off. The west half of the area, that on the side nearest the landing beaches, was even more barren. Other than shallow depressions, low mounds, and shell and bomb craters there was no cover for the advancing Marines. The area was heavily mined and covered by fire from the higher ground to the north and Suribachi to the south, from which observers directed artillery, mortar, and rocket fire.

On the northern end of the Tidorighara and partly on the plateau was Motoyama Airfield No. 1 (also called Chidori Airfield by the Japanese) built up on a raised foundation with 5,025- and 3,965-foot-long runways. About 1,000 yards to the northeast on the still higher ground of the plateau was Motoyama Airfield No. 2 with 5,225- and 4,425-foot runways. On the north side of this second field are two key pieces of terrain, Hill PETER and Hill 199-0. To the northeast of the field was the sulfur mine and Motoyama Village, the largest on the island. North of the village was Airfield No. 3, only 3,800 feet in length and uncompleted. Airfield No. 1 had been built in 1943 and No. 2 was completed in 1944. The Motoyama plateau varies in general elevation from 200 to 300 feet with low sandstone hills and ridges up to 340–387 feet high. The gray-brown rock-covered ground is broken and laced with ravines and gorges. On the east side of the Motoyama are found sulfur steam vents and sulfur mud hot springs. The ground is hot in many areas and made tunneling by the Japanese extremely difficult. The sulfur permeated the island with the smell of rotten eggs. Vehicle movement on the plateau is difficult and many areas are inaccessible. The island's road system was limited and rudimentary. There is virtually no animal or bird life.

There was little vegetation on the Motoyama plateau, what there was being low grasses and scrub brush. Modest sugarcane and pineapple fields had been planted in the northeast where some thin fertile soil was found and there was a small sugar refinery. In 1943 there were only 1,100 Japanese civilians on Iwo Jima, most of whom worked the sulfur mine or the struggling sugarcane fields. Besides the main village of Motoyama in the center of the plateau, other villages of simple wooden houses existed there, two on the southwest side, Minami and Higashi, and two on the northwest, Nishi and Kita, all positioned well inland. With the exception of 400 civilians impressed into the IJN construction unit, most were evacuated before the American invasion.

The island is subtropical with a cool season lasting from December through April. Temperatures range from the high 50°Fs to the high 70°Fs. During the May-to-November warm season the temperatures are in the high 60°Fs to the mid-80°Fs. Annual rainfall is sixty inches with May being the wettest month and February the driest, but it rained frequently with accompanying high winds during the battle. There are no natural sources of water, no streams, no ponds. The Japanese sank fourteen wells, but rain catchments and storage cisterns were essential. The ground is highly permeable and no surface water is retained. The Japanese also built containment ponds to catch rainwater runoff from the two completed airfields.

Early in the war, while military strength was modestly increased on Chichi Jima, only small elements were placed on Iwo Jima to support the IJN airfield. In April and May 1944, after the fall of the Marshalls, the neutralization of Truk, and the expected battles in the Carolines and Marianas, efforts began to be made to fortify Iwo Jima. There were 5,200 IJA troops and a 1,000-man IJN *Iwo Jima Guard Force* in addition to the 1,500-

PACIFIC ISLAND GUIDE

man IJN *Air Service* unit. Efforts were further increased as the Marianas fell and additional reinforcements were sent, but many fell victim to U.S. submarines prowling the area. The defense forces dug extremely elaborate tunnel systems and incorporated the many caves and ravines into the defenses. No one knows the true extent of the tunnel and caves systems, which are believed to have totaled up to five miles, but the entire defense force and their supplies were sheltered in them. Pillboxes, gun positions, fighting positions, antitank ditches, and extensive minefields were constructed in depth in three cross-island defense lines with the first following the contour of the plateau's southwest edge and running between Airfields No. 1 and 2. The second was 1,000 or so yards behind the first cutting across the northeast end of Airfield No. 2. The third line ran across the island northeast of Airfield No. 3 only 1,000–1,500 yards from the island's northeast end. The ground before Suribachi and the peak itself was another strongpoint. The 2,000–3,000 yards of open ground between the Suribachi strongpoint and the first defense line was undefended except by direct and indirect fires from the south and north. Airfield No. 1 laid in that area. A massive quantity of coast defense guns, antiaircraft weapons, antiboat guns, heavy automatic weapons, mortars, and rocket launchers were provided the defenders. Iwo Jima has been called the most strongly defended piece of terrain ever.

Japanese forces on Iwo Jima were under the control of the *31st Army* headquartered on Truk. The major unit on Iwo Jima was the *109th Division (-)*, which doubled as the *Bonin District Group* (aka *Ogasawara Army Group*) under Lieutenant General KURIBAYASHI Tadamichi. It consisted of the *2d Mixed Brigade* and the *145th Infantry Regiment* with a total of nine infantry battalions. These were backed by numerous artillery, mortar, antitank, automatic weapons, and engineer battalions plus a few tanks. Additionally there were IJA air service personnel who were incorporated into the combat units. IJN Land Force units included numerous antiaircraft and coast defense gun units plus air service personnel organized into combat battalions under Rear Admiral ICHIMARU Toshinosuke. Total troop strength was approximately 21,000. Postwar Japanese records are in conflict as to the mix of IJA and IJN troops. One report lists 17,500 IJA and 5,500 IJN while another gives 13,586 IJA and 7,347 IJN (the latter is thought to be more accurate).

Consideration to seizing Iwo Jima was given as far back as September 1943. The island became more important after the Marianas were seized and B-29 bombers prepared to launch raids on the Home Islands. The cost of taking Iwo Jima has been argued by some as too high for the benefit of providing a midway emergency landing field. Iwo Jima served another purpose though. Being close to Japan it allowed passing bombers to rendezvous with fighters based on the island, which escorted the bombers to their targets to greatly aid in their survivability. It would also be the first landing on territory that was part of Japan and not a Mandated Territory like the Saipan. In October 1944 the decision was made to go ahead with Operation DETACHMENT. First scheduled for January 1945, it was moved to 19 February (D-Day).

The first carrier raid was made on Iwo Jima in June 1944 and regularly scheduled bomber strikes began in August and continued with increasing frequency up to the invasion. These strikes, from the Marianas, were also aimed at Chichi Jima. Iwo's aircraft were destroyed and shipping in the area was sunk. Regardless of the repeated and prolonged battering, the defense force remained intact and continued to dig in.

V Amphibious Corps, under Lieutenant General Harry Schmidt, was assigned the daunting task of seizing the island. It was known before the landing that the assault and subsequent seizure of the island would be extremely difficult and costly. Air attacks from the Home Islands were another major concern. The two assault divisions were the 4th Marine Division (14th [artillery], 23d, 24th, 25th Marines) commanded by Major General Clifton B. Cates and the 5th Marine Division (5th Shore Party, 13th [artillery], 26th, 27th, 28th Marines) under Major General Keller E. Rockey. This would be the 5th Marine Division's first action, but its regiments were fleshed out with the men of the former Marine parachute battalions and other veterans. The 3d Marine Division (3d, 9th, 12th [artillery], 21st Marines), under Major General Graves E. Erskine, would be the Expeditionary Troops Reserve. While Iwo Jima is perceived as a Marine operation, the Army's 138th Antiaircraft Artillery Group was attached along with small support elements. In all VAC totaled 71,300 troops.

The 4th and 5th Marine Divisions were training in Hawaii and the 3d was on Guam. The divisions conducted their final rehearsals at those locations and those in Hawaii departed for the Marianas in early February. On 16 February the 4th and 5th Marine Divisions departed Saipan with the 21st Marines of the 3d Marine Division following as the 5th Amphibious Force sailed north. The 3d Marine Division departed the next day. Attached to the divisions for the first time were two 1,400-man replacement drafts. They would first unload ships and then be fed to line units as replacements, but even this was insufficient to replace casualties. Before it was over artillerymen and service troops were being sent in as infantry replacements.

On the morning of 19 February the assault divisions were offshore as the massive preassault bombardment continued. Long lines of amphibian tractors advanced toward the beaches on the southeast shore receiving negligible fire with the first vehicles hitting the beach at 0859 hours. The 5th Marine Division's beaches were northeast of Mount Suribachi. The 28th Marines landed on Beach GREEN 1 while the 27th Marines landed on RED 1 and 2. The 26th Marines, as the initial VAC Reserve, landed later on different beaches. The 4th Marine Division's beaches were adjacent to the East Boat Basin. The 23d Marines landed on Beaches YELLOW 1 and 2. The 25th Marines landed on BLUE 1 and 2. The 24th Marines, the Division Reserve, landed later on different beaches. The 21st Marines from the 3d Marine Division landed later on 21 February and became the new VAC Reserve after the 26th Marines was committed to the line.

On the first day the four assault regiments pushed across the southeastern portion of the island and were on the edge of Airfield No. 1 with the 28th Marines on the left flank also attacking Mount Suribachi and reached the east shore. At 1020 Hours, 26 February, after a week of fighting, the first small American flag was raised atop Suribachi. A second larger flag was soon obtained and the photograph of its raising by five Marines and a Navy hospital corpsman taken by Associated Press photographer Joe Rosenthal made history. While the 28th Marines subdued Suribachi, the 5th and 4th Marine Divisions swung right and began pressing northeastward overrunning Airfield No. 1 on D+1. By D+5 they had fought through the first defense line and were in the process of penetrating the second. Progress was increasingly slow as the Marines advanced suffering horrendous casualties. The difficult terrain and the strength of the Japanese defenses slowed the advance to a snail's pace. On 24 February the 3d Marine Division's headquarters and 9th Marines came ashore and the division was fed into the frontline between the 5th and 4th Marine Divisions as the island's northeast end widened out. The 3d Marine Division's 3d Marines remained afloat as the Fleet Reserve until departing the area for Guam on 5 March. By 7 March most of the island had been cleared except for a rough crescent from the Tachiiwa Point on the northeast side around the north coast to just southwest of Kitano Point on the north end. The Japanese still held an area 700–1,000 yards wide around the island's end. It took more than another week to reduce most of this narrow band, although the 4th Marine Division broke through to the northeast cost on the 10th. The final pocket of resistance in the Tachiiwa Point area was overrun on 16 March and the island was declared secure at 1045 hours. A small ravine near the island's north end, Cushman's Pocket, was wiped out on 24 March, but mop-up long continued.

Much of the garrison was annihilated, but the estimated 300 remaining Japanese hiding in caves and tunnels was a gross underestimation. By the end of March, only 216 prisoners had been taken, mainly Korean laborers. As mopping up continued, by the end of May 1,600 more Japanese were killed and 870 captured. It was later discovered that 3,000 were still alive. Iwo Jima had been the costliest single campaign of the war in the Pacific. The Marines lost 6,000 dead and 17,300 wounded.

It has frequently been asked if the benefit was deserving of the cost in lives spent to secure 7-½ square miles of barren rock? Besides the very real value of providing a base for fighters escorting bombers to Japan (which began on 7 April), it was intended as an emergency landing field for those bombers. The first B-29 made an emergency landing on refurbished Airfield No. 1 on 4 March. Fifty more were to make emergency landings by 16 March, the date the island was declared secure. By the end of the war 2,251 B-29s made emergency landings on Iwo—24,761 airmen.

Airfield No. 1 had been sufficiently reconditioned to allow its use by observation planes on 26 February and transports were able to use it from 3 March. By 16 March Airfield No. 2 was usable. Development and expansion of all three airfields were undertaken and Airfields No. 1, 2, and 3 were renamed South, Central, and North, respectively. South Field became a 6,000-foot fighter strip. Central Field was expanded with a 6,000-foot fighter and two 8,500-foot bomber runways. The two bomber strips were later extended to 9,800 and 9,400 feet to better accommodate crippled B-29s. North Field was completed with a 6,000-foot fighter runway. Massive support facilities were built to support the three airfields. An attempt was made to construct a protected harbor on the southeast beaches to include breakwaters and sunken block ships (FPO SF 3150). A storm defeated this effort. Water was a continuing problem and eight of the fourteen wells drilled by the Japanese were placed in use along with stills and other efforts. IJA forces on Chichi Jima and the Bonin Islands were surrendered to Commodore J.H. Magruder on 3 September 1945. IJN forces were surrendered by Vice Admiral MORI Kunizo (who had commanded the *Sasebo Combined SNLF* to seize Celebes, NEI in January 1942) to Marine Colonel Presley M. Rixley on 13 December.

The Volcano and Bonin Islands remained under U.S. Navy control after the war. In 1951, after the formal peace treaty with Japan, the islands were placed under provisional Navy administration. The air base facilities on Iwo Jima were closed on 14 August 1946. U.S. Navy Facility, Chichi Jima (FPO SF 3148) was established on that island after the war on Futami Ko Harbor. The small communications facility, called "Yankeetown," was closed in 1968 when the Bonin Islands were returned to Japanese control. Iwo Jima is still evolving; it is now densely vegetated and there was a mild volcanic eruption on the Motoyama plateau in 1982. Atop of Mount Suribachi is a small concrete disc set flush in the rock marking the spot of the flag raising. Central Airfield is the only remaining operational field on the island.

NANSEI SHOTO, JAPAN

The Nansei Shoto (Southwestern Islands) is a curving string of widely spaced islands stretching almost 650 miles southwest of Kyushu, the southern most of the Japanese Home Islands, from approximately 30° north latitude and 130° east longitude across the

Map 101
Nansei Shoto

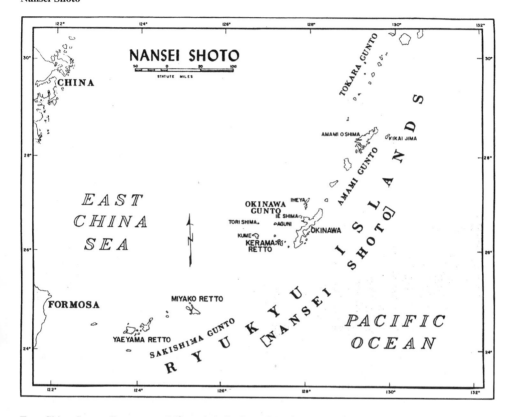

East China Sea to Formosa to 24° north latitude and 123° east longitude (see Map 101).
They are part of Japan proper and were in time zone 21 as were the Home Islands.

Ryukyu Retto (Ryukyu Archipelago or Ryukyu Islands) comprises most islands in the
Nansei Shoto string being virtually one and the same. Ryukyu is derived from the Chinese
Liuchiu ("lew-chew" or "loo-choo"), meaning "floating horned dragon." The Japanese
inability to pronounce "L" resulted in RYUKYU. The Ryukyus were code-named BUNK-
HOUSE.

The Ryukyus consists of 161 islands in five major groups (Gunto). From the northwest
end of the Nansei Shoto the five groups are:

Osumi Gunto, just off the south end of Kyushu.

Torkara Gunto, a small group of little islands.

Amami Gunto, a group of islands almost as large as Okinawa Gunto.

Okinawa Gunto, discussed below, is separated from the next group by almost 188 miles.

Sakishima Gunto, another large group less than 100 miles east of Formosa.

In addition to Okinawa Gunto the larger islands in these groups were defended by
Japanese forces. In the Amami Gunto the *21st Independent Mixed Regiment* defended

Amami O Shima and the *64th Independent Mixed Brigade* was on Tokuno Shima. The Sakishima Gunto was defended by the *28th Division* and *60th Independent Mixed Brigade* on Miyako Jima, *59th Independent Mixed Brigade* on Irabu Jima, and *45th Independent Mixed Brigade* on Ishigaki Jima.

Okinawa Gunto, Ryukyu Retto, Nansei Shoto

The Okinawa Group or Okinawa Islands are centered around Okinawa Shito or Okinawa Island. The meaning of Okinawa is open to debate as almost every source gives a different meaning ranging from "precious floating stones on the horizon" to "a rope of offering." Okinawa Gunto was code-named LEGUMINOUS and the main island was SCATTERING. It was nicknamed "Okie" by American servicemen.

Okinawa Gunto, the largest island group in the Ryukyu Retto, is approximately 320 miles southwest of Kyushu. (see Map 102). It lies 350 miles northeast of Formosa and 460 miles east of the China mainland. Manila, Philippines is 790 miles to the southwest, Guam is 1,230 miles to the southeast, and Pearl Harbor is 4,040 miles east. While not necessarily important in World War II, the fact that Okinawa is located 450 miles to the southeast of Shanghai, China and 540 miles south-southeast of Pusan, Korea was to later increase its strategic importance. The main island is situated at 26°26' N 127°41' E. Satellited around Okinawa Shima are several other islands and small groups of islands comprising Okinawa Gunto: Kerama Retto (eight islands fifteen miles west of Okinawa), Kume Shima (fifty-five miles west), Agunia Shima (forty miles west), Ie Shima (four miles west), Iheya Retto (four islands fifteen miles north), Yoron Shima (fifteen miles northeast), and an unnamed group of eight scattered islands in Kin Wan (Bay) called the Eastern Islands by the Americans (five to ten miles east). Most of these islands would play important roles in the Okinawa campaign.

The Chinese intermittently raided the Ryukyus for hundreds of years beginning in the sixth or seventh century. The Dragon Empire never attempted to attain complete sovereignty over the islands, but in 1368 demanded tribute and the Ryukyuan king declared himself a subject of China. Okinawa also had relations with Japan and managed to remain at least partly independent of both overshadowing empires. Japan gained partial control of the islands in the 1500s. In 1609, after Okinawa refused to provide troops for Japan's war against Korea, Japan invaded and devastated the island kingdom. Okinawa still maintained a semi-independent status paying tribute to both Japan and China. Commodore Matthew Perry used Okinawa as a supply base during his 1853 effort to establish trade with Japan. He raised an American flag on a hill near Shuri Castle that Americans would die for almost a hundred years later. The opening of Japan quickly established the country as a regional power and it took control of Okinawa in 1867. The Ryukyuan king was given a permanent residence in Tokyo and in 1874 the Japanese Home Ministry took total control of the islands. A Japanese governor was installed in 1879 and the islands given prefecture (*ken*) status. China still claimed the islands and Okinawans preferred their fence-sitting status between the two powers, but they were now solidly part of the Empire of the Rising Sun. Okinawa was granted a prefecture assembly and a seat in the Diet in 1920. In 1943, the *Prefecture of Okinawa* was consolidated with seven others into the Home Islands *District of Kyushu*.

Okinawa Shima is oriented northeast to southwest with a length of sixty-four miles. Its width varies from eighteen miles at the Motobu Peninsula (*Hanto*) extending east from the island's northern portion to two miles at the Ishikawa Isthmus just south of the island's midpoint. Several smaller peninsulas jute from the island's southern portion

Map 102
Okinawa Gunto

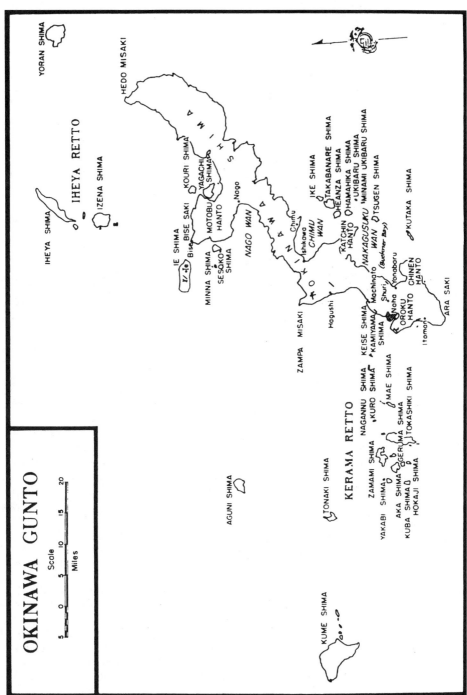

OKINAWA GUNTO

Scale

Miles

5   0   5   10   15   20

KUME SHIMA

AGUNI SHIMA

TONAKI SHIMA

KERAMA RETTO

YAKABI SHIMA
ZAMAMI SHIMA
KURO SHIMA
AKA SHIMA
GERUMA SHIMA
KUBA SHIMA
HOKAJI SHIMA
TOKASHIKI SHIMA
MAE SHIMA
NAGANNU SHIMA
KEISE SHIMA
KAMIYAMA SHIMA

YORAN SHIMA

HEDO MISAKI

IHEYA RETTO

IHEYA SHIMA

IZENA SHIMA

O K I N A W A

KOURI SHIMA
YAGACHI SHIMA
BISE SAKI
MOTOBU HANTO
Nago
NAGO WAN

IE SHIMA
Bise
MINNA SHIMA
SESOKO SHIMA

ZAMPA MISAKI

Hagushi

Machinato
Shuri
Naha
OROKU HANTO
Itoman

Ishikawa
Chimu
CHIMU WAN

IKE SHIMA
TAKABANARE SHIMA
HEANZA SHIMA
KATCHIN HANTO
OHAMAHIKA SHIMA
UKIBARU SHIMA
MINAMI UKIBARU SHIMA
OTSUGEN SHIMA
NAKAGUSUKU WAN
(Buckner Bay)
Yonabaru
KUTAKA SHIMA
CHINEN HANTO

ARA SAKI

protecting excellent anchorages. The island covers 640 square miles. The Ishikawa Isthmus divides Okinawa into two contrasting regions.

The sparsely populated north is covered with rugged, ridge-like 1,000–1,500-foot-high hills branching off a central ridge. The areas around the hills are bisected by deep ravines and gullies terminating at the coast in steep cliffs. The northwest coast's Motobu Peninsula is a dominant feature and was the center of Japanese resistance in the north. The entire area is covered by dense forests of pine, live oak, and thick underbrush. The road system was extremely limited with a only a single one-lane road following the northwest shore to the north end. Cross-country vehicle movement is impossible. The soil is red clay and sandy loam and well drained by the many small streams. This region stretches south past the Ishikawa Isthmus to the island's southern third.

The heavily populated south is characterized by rolling hills, sometimes terraced, gradually reaching over 500 feet high at the island's southern end. The hills are cut by ravines and shallow, narrow streams providing poor drainage. The further south one goes, the more hilly and broken the terrain becomes. Caves, cut by underground streams, honeycomb the hills and ridges. The central plains south of the Ishikawa Isthmus are open and gently rolling. Further south small scattered, irregular knolls dot the area and were incorporated into the defense. The hills can be steep in some areas and several escarpments and twisting limestone ridges cut across the island providing successive cross-compartment defensive lines as one advances south. Few long fields of fire exist proving ideal for Japanese short-range weapons. While some areas were lightly wooded, four-fifths of the south was cultivated with sweet potato, sugarcane, rice, and soybean fields in the valleys and on hills and plateaus. Fishing was secondary to farming as the island's principal industries. Villages and towns were scattered across the southern region and connected by a network of one-lane roads and trails. Some of these were surfaced with crushed coral, but most were dirt cart tracks. A single two-lane limestone road connected the island's only two cities of Naha and Shuri. Because of the clay soil conditions, the largely unimproved roads were totally incapable of supporting military traffic during the rainy season. Off-road traffic was impossible in most areas when the rains came. A narrow-gauge railroad connected Naha, Kobakura, Kobuba, and Yonabaru with branches linking Kobakura to Kadena and Kokuba with Itoman. The thirty miles of track mainly hauled produce and some would be returned to operation by American engineers.

Much of the coastline was fronted by limestone cliffs and scattered coral heads. The most desirable landing beaches were on the west coast south of the two-mile-wide Ishikawa Isthmus, the Hagushi Beaches edging the central plains. The beaches were named after centrally located Hagushi Village at the mouth of the Bishi Gawa (stream). Hagushi, however, was actually a mistranslation. The village's real name was Togushi. The Japanese called them the Kadena Beaches. The usual coral reef shelf paralleled the shore with a higher seaward crest 200–700 yards offshore and then deepened closer to shore. At low tide trucks could easily drive across it. The area's mean tides are four feet, but at the time of the landing a spring tide would raise the water level to six feet. The eight miles of landing beaches were gently sloping with few natural obstacles, although there were extensive seawalls up to ten feet high. The beaches were not continuous, but separated in 100–900-yard lengths by low-cliff headlands. At low tide the beaches were ten to forty-five yards wide, but at high water were completely awash. Behind the beaches sparsely vegetated and cultivated ground rose gradually to fifty feet. The beaches were selected because of their proximity to Yontan and Kadena airfields 2,000 yards inland. Their early seizure would allow land-based fighters to fly close air support and aid in the defense of the fleet.

The population of Okinawa was 435,000 and included thousands of Japanese immigrants serving as government officials, administrators, managers, and merchants. Even with representation in the government, Okinawans had little real say in their affairs. Naha is Okinawa's prefectural capital and commercial center with a preinvasion population of over 60,000. It was the island's main seaport. Shuri was slightly smaller and was the Ryukyu's traditional capital. Shuri Castle is perched on the massive ridge cutting across the island and was the ancient throne of the Ryukyuan kings. It would become a vicious battleground. On the east side of the island's southern portion is the broad Nakagusuku Wan (Bay) (ABSENCE), which was considered as a landing site.

Most population centers were villages ranging from fewer than 100 inhabitants up to over 1,000. The towns of Itoman, Nago, and Yonabaru were simply large villages with few modern buildings. Concrete and stone government and commercial buildings were numerous in Naha and Shuri, but most urban buildings and dwellings were one-story wood surrounded by low stone walls. Dwellings in villages had clay walls, thatch roofs, and were surrounded by bamboo windbreaks or low stone or mud walls overgrown with tropical vegetation. Unique to Okinawa were the stone, lyre-shaped family tombs, an important part of the indigenous animistic cult emphasizing the veneration of ancestors. Dug into hillsides, they did not provide all-around defense, but offered protection from artillery and their vulnerable sides could be covered from other fighting positions.

The two main airfields, Yontan and Kadena, were on the central plains while Machchiano Airfield was just north of Naha. Across from it on the east coast was the abandoned Yonabaru Airfield. An IJN airfield was located on Oroku Peninsula. Two airfields were located on Ie Shima.

Before the invasion 80,000 Okinawans were shipped to Kyushu aboard returning supply ships to work in factories (some were sunk en route by U.S. submarines). Another 60,000 were forced to relocate to the sparse north reducing the burden on Japanese forces in the heavily populated south.

Temperatures are moderate with a winter night low of 40°F. At the time of the battle day temperatures ranged from the 70°Fs to the 80°Fs. Humidity is high year-round. Rain is frequent, but irregular, with the heaviest occurring from May to September during the summer monsoon, ninety-three inches per year. Rain was to have a major impact on the coming battle. Moderate winds varied from south to east at the time of the battle.

Japanese and Okinawans lay claim to the same basic racial origins, the Ainu aborigines, but Okinawans have more Mongoloid and Malayan blood. Okinawans appear physically similar to the Japanese, but there the resemblance disappears. Their languages have the same roots, but are mutually unintelligible (Japanese was taught in schools, but few Okinawans were proficient). The native language is Luchuan. Bearing extensive Chinese influence, Okinawa's culture and religion were distinctly different from Japan's. Too, the Japanese viewed the Okinawans as inferior and there was broad disparity between the two races socially, economically, and politically resulting in much resentment. Japanese on the island enjoyed many privileges not conferred on Okinawans. This secondary station did not, however, exempt Okinawans from military conscription to serve the Emperor. The coming battle for Okinawa can be described as a clash between three cultures, the effects of which still reverberate today.

In the Central Pacific Area the 3d and 5th Fleets had seized the Marianas in the summer of 1944, which proved to be an extremely serious blow to Japan. MacArthur invaded the Philippines in October 1944. By the end of the year they had secured several solid footholds. In the meantime the 3d Fleet took Iwo Jima between February and March 1945.

The Japanese knew what was coming next. What they did not know was exactly where the Americans would strike. The *Imperial General Headquarters* narrowed the possible targets to Formosa off the Chinese mainland or Okinawa southwest of the Home Islands. They began to reinforce both as the American 5th Fleet and 10th Army marshaled at island bases across the Pacific.

A major concern of the U.S. high command was the possibility that Japan might conclude a separate peace with a hard-pressed China. The establishment of U.S. positions on the coast of China to open supply lines to the interior was considered. Supplying the massive, but ill-equipped, Chinese Army would force Japan to reinforce the mainland and stretch its forces thinner. This would involve invading Formosa, 670 miles southwest of Japan, before it could be reinforced, and bypassing the Philippines.

Formosa, basically a Japanese colony, had its advantages. Bypassing the Philippines would prevent a potentially protracted campaign requiring a massive commitment of U.S. forces. Formosa would provide a base from which to invade the mainland, protect sea routes to China, and launch long-range bombers at Japan.

Formosa could be a problem as well. It was well within range of Japanese air bases on mainland China, was garrisoned by five divisions, an air division, five independent mixed brigades, and an air fleet manned by 480,000 troops. It could be easily reinforced from the mainland only 100 miles away and was a large mountainous land mass 240 miles long and ninety miles wide, with elevations to 13,000 feet. It promised to be a tough campaign; Formosa was about the size of Kyushu.

In July 1944, with the Marianas campaign winding up, President Roosevelt met with Admiral Nimitz and General MacArthur. MacArthur opposed the plan to bypass the Philippines contending, with additional naval support, he had the forces to liberate them. Nimitz agreed to an alternate plan that included recapturing much of the Philippines between October and December 1944. Depending on the situation, either Luzon would be invaded in February 1945 or Formosa-Amoy Area (on mainland China) in March. This would be followed by the Bonins (Chichi Jima) in April and the Ryukyus (with Okinawa) in May.

Soon after this proposed plan was developed, Lieutenant General Millard F. Harmon, Army Air Forces, Pacific Ocean Area, proposed that Operation CAUSEWAY—Formosa, be abandoned with compelling arguments that air operations could more effectively be conducted against Japan from the Marianas. He addressed the threat of hostile forces remaining on Formosa (it was not to be completely occupied because of its size), intercept from the China mainland along the entire route to Japan, and less favorable weather. Harmon proposed that Iwo Jima be seized in January 1945 and Okinawa in June simultaneous with the invasion of Luzon. General Robert C. Richardson, U.S. Army Forces, Pacific Ocean Area, agreed with Harmon. Other key commanders tagged for CAUSEWAY favored the proposal. General Simon B. Buckner, 10th Army, stated sufficient combat and service troops were not available to secure a significant lodgment on Formosa. Admiral Raymond A. Spruance too preferred avoiding Formosa and supported his ground commanders.

In October 1944, Nimitz advised Admiral Earnest J. King of his subordinate commanders' views. The Joint Chiefs of Staff evaluated the proposals and directed MacArthur to land on Luzon on 20 December 1944 and Nimitz to assault Iwo Jima on 20 January 1945 and Okinawa on 1 March. This last operation before the planned November invasion of Japan was code-named ICEBERG.

With the United States fully securing the Philippines, Japanese forces in the Netherlands East Indies would be cut off from the Home Islands. B-29s could ceaselessly bomb

Japan from their bases in the Marianas with the Japanese denied bases in the Ryukyus from which to intercept them. American bases in the Ryukyus would further protect the flank by intercepting enemy aircraft from Formosa and China and could attack Japan as well. The forces and command structure devised for Formosa would be retained for the invasion of Okinawa Gunto. Iwo Jima was not secured until 16 March. Within days the initial operations for ICEBERG began, delayed because of Iwo Jima's delay.

Task Force 51, under Vice Admiral Richmond K. Turner, contained elements of the U.S. Army, Navy, Marine Corps, and the three services' air arms. Besides the supporting naval carrier, gunfire, and transport forces, Task Force 51 controlled Task Force 56, the Expeditionary Troops with all ground forces involved in the assault. Under the command of Lieutenant General Simon B. Buckner, Jr., it was built around the 10th Army with 182,800 initial assault troops. Two corps were subordinate to 10th Army.

XXIV Corps, Southern Landing Force, Lieutenant General John R. Hodge.

  7th Infantry Division (17th, 32d 184th Infantry), initial Okinawa assault division, Major General Archibald V. Arnold.

  27th Infantry Division (105th, 106th, 165th Infantry), initial Expeditionary Troops Floating Reserve, Major General George W. Griner, Jr.

  77th Infantry Division (305th, 306th, 307th Infantry), initial Kerama Retto assault force, then Ie Shima, Major General Andrew B. Bruce.

  96th Infantry Division (381st, 382d, 383d Infantry), initial Okinawa assault division, Major General James L. Bradley.

  81st Infantry Division (321st, 322d, 323d Infantry), Major General Paul J. Mueller. It was the Area Reserve on New Caledonia and was not committed.

The Army began the operation with 102,250 troops and rose to 190,300 by the end of June. The Marine Corps began with 88,500 troops.

III Amphibious Corps under the command of Major General Roy S. Geiger.

  1st Marine Division (1st, 5th, 7th, 11th [artillery] Marines), initial Okinawa assault division, Major General Pedro A. del Valle.

  6th Marine Division (2d, 6th, 8th, 10th [artillery] Marines), initial Okinawa assault division, Major General Lemuel C. Shepherd, Jr.

  2d Marine Division (4th, 15th [artillery], 22d, 29th Marines), Major General Thomas E. Watson. It served as the demonstration force off of Okinawa and then as a floating reserve. It soon departed for Saipan to serve as an area reserve.

Both XXIV and IIIAC possessed substantial corps artillery and combat support assets. Additional 10th Army units included the 53d Antiaircraft Artillery Brigade and 20th Armored Group.

Okinawa Gunto first felt the war on 29 September 1944 when B-29s bombed the airfields. The first raid by carrier aircraft followed on 10 October, an operation mainly intended to neutralize the air threat to the approaching Leyte invasion force. The Japanese referred to this action as the Air Battle of Formosa. The Japanese lost 500 aircraft and three dozen ships in three days. Okinawa was granted a respite until the new year brought a massive carrier raid on 3 January. The Fast Carrier Force returned on the 10th for an even more punishing raid. The January operations were in conjunction with raids on Formosa and the China coast. The Fast Carrier Force struck targets in the Tokyo area through late February. While retiring to Ulithi, the Force struck Okinawa on 1 March with an extremely vicious raid.

American submarines and patrol bombers effectively isolated the Ryukyus from Japan and Formosa sinking scores of cargo ships. Between attacks on Japan, B-29s conducted numerous raids on Okinawa. By the end of March there were almost no operational Japanese aircraft in the Ryukyus. Naha City and its port were completely destroyed as was Shuri. Between 18 and 31 March, the carriers conducted further strikes on Kyushu airfields and Japanese warships in preparation for ICEBERG. On 24 March, the Force sank an entire eight-ship convoy northwest of Okinawa. On the same date battleships shelled targets on Okinawa. Between 26 and 31 March, the British Carrier Force struck Saki-shima Gunto to the southwest of Okinawa neutralizing its airfields.

The Japanese, expecting a landing on Okinawa or Formosa at any time, alerted its air forces for *Operation TEN-GO* on 25 March. On the 27th and 31st massive B-29 strikes on the airfields effectively shut them down. The Japanese managed to launch only fifty two-aircraft attacks prior to L-Day damaging eight U.S. ships. *TEN-GO* was not able to launch until 6 April, five days after the main landing.

On 25 March, the Gunfire and Covering Force moved in with nine battleships, ten cruisers, thirty-two destroyers, and 177 gunboats to begin a massive preinvasion bombardment along with the Carrier Force. They had little effect, although the few remaining Japanese aircraft on the island were destroyed. The Japanese had pulled back from the beaches and largely refused to respond to attacks from their underground shelters.

The Army's 7th, 77th, and 96th Infantry Divisions conducted their train-up and rehearsals for Okinawa on Leyte in the Philippines while the 27th Infantry Division staged out of Espíritu Santo. The 1st, 2d, and 6th Marines Divisions were located on Pavuvu, Saipan, and Guadalcanal, respectively. The 1st and 6th Marine Divisions of IIIAC rendezvoused at Ulithi Atoll and departed for Okinawa in late March while the 2d Marine Division departed from Guadalcanal. XXIV Corps and most of its Army divisions departed from Leyte just prior to that as the 27th Infantry departed Espíritu Santo. The 10th Army and Island Command units on Oahu departed even earlier. The amphibious forces encountered rough weather en route with many groups barely making their target date.

Prior to the neutralization of Truk in February 1944 Okinawa Gunto was very lightly defended. To bolster the island's defenses, the *32d Army* was organized in April 1944 and made subordinate to the *10th Area Army* on Formosa. The *32d Army* was under the command of Lieutenant General USHIJIMA Mitsuru. The first combat unit to arrive was the *9th Division* from Manchuria in June 1944. In late June, a mere 600 survivors of the *44th Independent Mixed Brigade* arrived. U.S. submarines had attacked its convoy sending 5,000 troops to the bottom. The *15th Independent Mixed Regiment* was flown in July, Japan's first attempt to airlift so large a force. The Brigade was rebuilt under Major General SHIGEKI Suzuki with the regimental-sized *2d Infantry Unit* and *15th Independent Mixed Regiment*. The *24th Division (22d, 32d, and 89th Infantry, 42d Artillery)* followed from Manchuria, under Lieutenant General AMAMIYA Tatsumi. The *62d Division (63d and 64th Brigades)*, under the command of Lieutenant General FUJIOKA Takeo, arrived in August from China. Nondivisional artillery units were under the *5th Artillery Group* to include IJN coast defense guns. The *21st Antiaircraft Artillery Group* controlled IJA air defenses.

In June 1944 the *Labor Unit (Boeitai)* was established with about 16,600 Okinawans augmenting regular units and up to 39,000 *Boeitai* were conscripted. A further manpower pool was tapped in January 1945 when *32d Army* directed that all fit male islanders between the ages of 17 and 45 could be mobilized as labor. This included thousands more on other Nansai Shoto islands. Unknown thousands were conscripted. IJA troops numbered 67,000. About 5,000 were Okinawan conscripts assigned to regular Japanese units. Over 12,000 Korean laborers and comfort women were present. In March, 18,500 service troops were reorganized into *ad hoc*, poorly trained, ill-armed "specially established" rifle regiments and attached to the combat formations.

Some 3,825 IJN personnel and over 6,000 civilian combatant employees were assigned to the *Okinawa Naval Base Force's* coast defense gun, antiaircraft, air service, and construction units. The *Base Force* was under the command of Rear Admiral NIPPA Teiso and assigned to defend the Oroku Peninsula.

The *32d Army* had been promised another division from the Home Islands, but it never arrived. The Japanese possessed the resources to defend only approximately one-third of the island. The defense of the central plains and the Yontan and Kadena Airfields was rejected. The airfields could not be used once the Americans arrived and the *32d Army* would be quickly destroyed on the exposed plains. Moving the *32d Army* to the rugged north might prolong its survival, but this option would deprive it of its resources in the south and prevent it from forcing the Americans into close combat and inflict unacceptable losses on them.

The *32d Army's* deployment found the *62d Division* covering an area in the south from Naha and Shuri north to a line anchored on the east and west coasts on the second narrowest neck of the island, the 3-½-mile-wide Chatan Isthmus. This north-facing front was dug in on some of the first high ground encountered south of the central plains where the Americans would land. A more formidable defense line behind this was centered on the rugged 4,500-yard-long Urasoe-Mura Escarpment, Tanabaru Escarpment, and several ridges running from northwest to southeast across the island. The main defense line, however, was still farther south and centered on the Shuri Castle and a vast, rugged cross-island ridge-and-hill complex. Forces on this line were withheld from the first weeks' fighting. The weary advancing Americans would run headlong into well-prepared and formidable defenses. The *24th Division* secured the southern end of the island to prevent landings and act as the *32d Army* reserve. The *44th Independent Mixed Brigade* was southeast of the *62d* defending the Chinen Peninsula where it was thought the Americans might land on the island's southeast Minatoga Beaches. The *Okinawa Naval Base Force* secured the Oroku Peninsula southwest of the *62d Division* and was prepared to fight the Americans at the water's edge as was IJN doctrine. The island's north was not completely abandoned. The *1st Specially Established Regiment* (formed from airfield service personnel) screened the Yontan and Kadena Airfields on the central plains. The regimental-size *2d Infantry Unit*, detached from the *44th Independent Mixed Brigade*, was established on the Motobu Peninsula on the island's northwest coast to distract the Americans and tie up forces. One of its battalions was on Ie Shima just west of the Motobu along with other small elements.

Thousands of pillboxes, bunkers, weapons emplacements, and fighting positions were dug. Terrain features were incorporated into the defense and weapons were well sited with excellent overlapping fields of fire. Multiple defense lines were established across the island anchored on dominating terrain. The construction and improvement of these repeating lines would continue through the battle as the Japanese were painfully pushed south. Supplies and munitions were protected in dugouts and caves. Extensive tunnel systems were dug, over sixty miles, enough to protect the Army's 100,000 troops.

Six days prior to the scheduled landing date on Okinawa, 1 April 1945 (L-Day), as the largest assemblage of ships in history, 1,300 major ships, converged on Okinawa

Gunto as bombers and battleships continued to batter the island, the final assault would begin.

Kerama Retto. Kerama Retto (today called Shimajiri-Gun) is a group of eight rugged islands: Yakabi, Kuba, Zamami, Aka ("Happy Corner"), Keruma (called Geruma by the United States), Hokaji, Amuro, and Tokashiki (the largest, one by six miles), plus smaller islets, fifteen miles west of Okinawa (see Map 103). The islands are hilly and rocky with elevations up to 650 feet. The islands are largely covered with scrub brush and some small trees. Most of the shorelines are edged with cliffs or steep slopes, but there are small landing beaches. The islands are edged with coral reefs.

Unsuited for airfields, they were an ideal anchorage capable of accommodating over seventy ships. Kerama Kaikyo and Aka Kaikyo anchorages were in the center of the group separated by Keruma Shima. The Keramas would become the fleet's refueling, rearming, and repair base. The proposal for its early capture was initially resisted because of the fear of air attack. The need for such a base was realized during the Iwo Jima assault. The Western Island Attack Group, 77th Infantry Division embarked and swept through the Keramas from the west on 26 March (L-6) with the first landing on Aka Shima at 0804 hours (M-Hour). Five of the Division's infantry battalions secured the islands with little resistance by 29 May. Only four of the islands were defended by 975 IJN troops. Japanese losses were 530 dead and 120 prisoners. Some 1,200 civilians were interned, after almost 150 had suicided. Over 350 suicide boats were captured. American losses were thirty-one dead and eighty-one wounded. About 300 IJN troops remained unmolested on Tokashiki under a gentlemen's agreement (surrendered after V-J Day). The 77th Infantry Division reembarked on 30 March. The floating fleet base and a seaplane base were in operation before the islands were fully secured. On 31 March, patrol bombers, operating from seaplane tenders, began antishipping patrols over the East China Sea, local antisubmarine patrols, and air-sea rescue support for carrier operations.

Underwater demolition teams reconnoitered the Hagushi Beaches on 29 March. Spotter aircraft over Okinawa reported no human beings were visible. The entire island appeared deserted. Keise Shima (actually four sand islets), eleven miles southwest of the Hagushi Beaches, was secured unopposed by a 77th Infantry Division battalion early on 31 March. Marine scouts had previously confirmed the islets were unoccupied. The 420th Field Artillery Group came ashore with two battalions to support the main landing and cover southern Okinawa with their 155mm guns. The Japanese made several unsuccessful attempts to destroy the guns.

The amphibious force assembled just west of Okinawa. The Carrier Force took up station some fifty miles to the east. On 31 March, the Demonstration Group, 2d Marine Division embarked and arrived off the southeast Minatoga Beaches, which the Japanese considered the most likely site for the main landing.

At 0820 hours 1 April an eight-mile line of amphibian tractors bearing four American divisions began their run to the beaches landing at 0830 hours. Only sporadic Japanese mortar and artillery fire fell. Resistance ashore was virtually nil as the untrained airfield service troops of the *1st Specially Established Regiment* dissolved. From north to south the assault troops landed as follows:

6th Marine Division—22d Marines on Beaches GREEN 1 and 2, 4th Marines on RED 1–3. Yontan Airfield was immediately opposite of the division's beaches.

1st Marine Division—7th Marines on BLUE 1 and 2, 5th Marines on YELLOW 1–3. The Bishi Gawa (stream) on the 5th Marines' right flank was the boundary between IIIAC and XXIV Corps.

Map 16.5
Kerama Retto, Okinawa Gunto

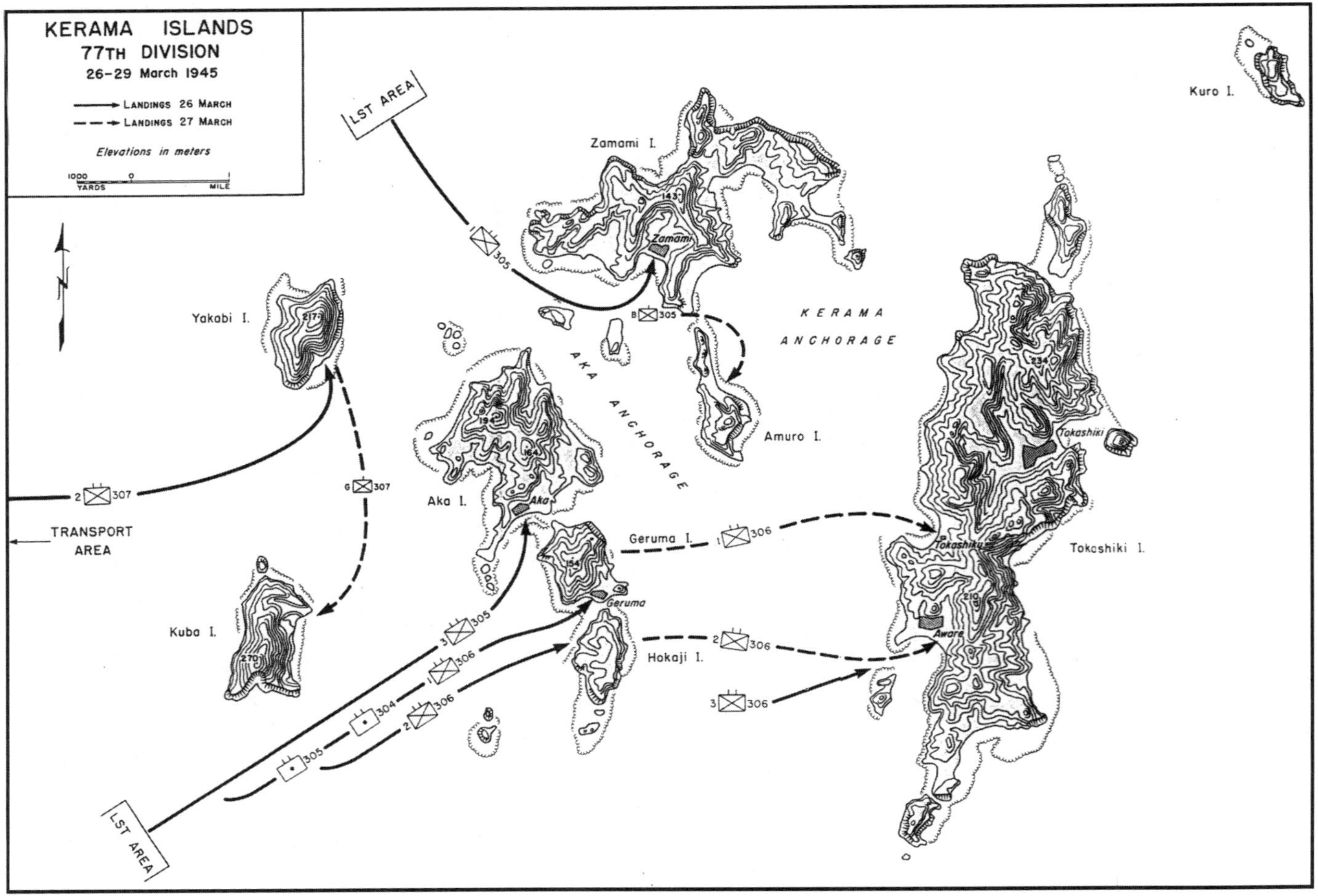

KERAMA ISLANDS
77TH DIVISION
26–29 March 1945

→ LANDINGS 26 MARCH
--→ LANDINGS 27 MARCH

Elevations in meters

1000   0   MILE
YARDS

Kuro I.

Tokashiki I.

KERAMA ANCHORAGE

Amuro I.

Zamami I.

AKA ANCHORAGE

Geruma I.

Hokaji I.

Aka I.

Geruma

Kuba I.

Yakabi I.

LST AREA

TRANSPORT AREA

1 306
2 306
3 306
B 305
305
305
305
306
306
306
G 307
2 307

7th Infantry Division—17th Infantry on PURPLE 1 and 2, 32d Infantry on ORANGE 1 and 2. Kadena Airfield was opposite the division's beaches.

96th Infantry Division—381st Infantry on WHITE 1 and 2, 383d Infantry on BROWN 3 and 4.

Massive casualties were expected among the landing force, with 50,000 troops landed in the first hour and another 10,000 by nightfall, but among the four divisions there were only 150 casualties. Late morning found the 4th Marines on the edge of Yontan Airfield and the 17th Infantry at Kadena. The two airfields were not expected to be captured until L+3. By nightfall a 15,000-yard beachhead, 5,000 yards deep in places, was firmly established.

On L+1 the two airfields were securely in American hands as were the surrounding hills. That afternoon Kadena was usable for emergency landings and Yontan was usable on L+2. The main bridge over the Bishi Gawa was captured intact and the defenders had destroyed few bridges over smaller streams. The question in everyone's mind was "Where is the enemy?"

The 6th Marine Division moved north and by 4 April had secured the narrow Ishikawa Isthmus. The 1st Marine and 7th Infantry Divisions reached the east coast on the afternoon of the 3rd and the Marines secured the Katchin Peninsula on the 5th. The 96th Infantry Division wheeled to its right and began moving south as did elements of the 7th on the east coast. By L+3 they were established on a line across the Chatan Isthmus facing south. All units were in positions they had expected to reach after two weeks of hard fighting.

The weather turned for the worse on 4 April. The sea state was such that unloading was sometimes suspended. Rains turned roads into quagmires. Entire new roads were built between rain periods and the weak native bridges replaced by steel Bailey bridges. The west coast highway was redesignated "U.S. Highway 1." Marine fighter squadrons arrived at Yontan on 7 April and at Kadena two days later to provide close air support.

In a desperate effort, *Operation TEN-ICHI* ("Heaven Number One"), the Japanese sortied the battleship *Yamato* on 6 April on a suicide mission to beach itself on Okinawa just to the south of the landing beaches and turn its massive guns on the American forces ashore and the transports. American carrier planes found the *Yamato* on 7 April sinking it, a cruiser, and four destroyers in two hours at a cost of ten U.S. aircraft. The battleship did not even make it halfway to Okinawa.

To protect 10th Army's eastern flank, the Eastern Islands lying northeast of the Katchin Peninsula in the Chimu Wan (Bay) had to be secured. This was accomplished between 6 and 11 April by elements of the 27th Infantry Division. Most of the islands were unoccupied, except for Tsugen Shima. The Japanese lost 243 men, but thirty escaped. U.S. losses were fourteen dead.

The American command could only guess at Japanese intentions. Air reconnaissance revealed nothing in the south (the Japanese were underground). Some thought the enemy may have evacuated to other islands, or had been drawn to the southeast by the demonstrations, or were waiting to counterattack; that opportunity came and passed. Still, there was little response from the enemy.

The impact of the invasion was initially more devastating in the Home Islands than to Japanese forces on Okinawa. On 3 April, news of the landing was released. This was Emperor Jimmu Day, who 2,500 years earlier, had launched the conquest of Yamato (after which the battleship was named) to "make the universe our home." Premier KOISO Kuniaki claimed the Americans would be driven from Okinawa and Saipan recaptured.

He was forced to resign the next day. Admiral (Baron) SUZUKI Kantaro was appointed by the Emperor on 7 April to find an honorable way for Japan to end the war.

On 4 April the 7th and 96th Infantry Divisions attacked south. The Japanese plan was to use the *62d Division* to hold the main northern defense line while the *24th Division* and *44th Independent Mixed Brigade* were held in reserve to destroy any new American landings on the southern coasts. The *62d* was in excellent positions on commanding terrain and had complete observation of XXIV Corps on the sparsely vegetated plain below. The artillery could fire on the Hagushi Beaches and Nakagusuku Wan.

In February the Japanese had concentrated the assets of the *6th Air Army* and *5th Air Fleet*, some 1,800 aircraft, under IJN control of Kyushu. Their mission was to execute suicide missions, what the Japanese called Special Attack, but more commonly known as *kamikaze* ("Divine Wind"). The first attacks began upon the fleet's arrival at Okinawa and were piecemeal for the first five days. On 6 April massive coordinated attacks were mounted and continued through most of the campaign. The Navy suffered its highest losses of ships and men in the Pacific because of the *kamikazes*.

Punching through the outposts, the two American divisions cautiously pushed south meeting strong resistance. The covering force held the Americans off for eight days inflicting over 1,500 casualties on the Corps, but at a cost of almost 4,500 dead. The outer Shuri defenses were now uncovered and the Corps would continue its advance against even tougher resistance.

The 96th Infantry Division attacked the low Kakazu Ridge on 9 April and was repulsed. After repeated attacks it was not until 12th that the ridge was taken. The *63d Brigade* lost 5,750 men, the 96th lost 451. During the Kakazu battles the 7th Infantry Division to the east had made slow progress in rugged terrain against stiff resistance.

Chafing at their defensive strategy, the more aggressive Japanese officers clamored for a counterattack. The counterattack was launched on 12 April. It proved to be far too weak and uncoordinated as many commanders, realizing its folly, held back their troops. The battle lasted all night and into the next. By dawn on the 14th it was all over. It delayed the American push a couple of days, but the Japanese lost hundreds and the Americans less than 100. The Americans continued to inch south and then prepared to assault the main Shuri defenses on even more rugged terrain.

While XXIV Corps fought slowly toward Shuri, IIIAC was engaged in a different kind of war. The 1st Marine Division defended Yontan Airfield, the landing beaches, and secured the zone behind XXIV Corps across the island. The 6th Marine Division had secured the Ishikawa Isthmus as far north as to where the isthmus began to widen. On 6 April the Marines launched a push up the west and east coasts. Roads in the north were very limited and the terrain rugged and densely vegetated.

The Japanese had blown bridges and laid mines, but resistance was very light. Finally, on 8 April, after combing the hills, it was determined the enemy had concentrated on the Motobu Peninsula on the island's upper west coast. The enemy was fixed in a six-by-eight-mile redoubt around the 1,200-foot-high Yae Take (Mount). The broken and steep terrain precluded the use of armor. Defending this ideal piece of terrain was the heavily armed 1,500-man *Udo Force*. The Yae Take was not cleared until the 18th. Some 700 Japanese dead were counted. Enough managed to escape in the broken terrain that they would conduct a lengthy guerrilla war in the wild north.

On 4 May, the 27th Infantry Division relieved the 6th Marine Division in the north. On 4 August, the north was finally declared secure, although there were still holdouts.

Ie Shima. Ie Shima (infrequenty called Ie Jima) was code-named INDESPENSABLE. It lies 3-½ miles off the west end of the Motobu Peninsula and twenty miles north of the Hagushi Beaches (see Map 104). It is located at 26°43' N 127°47' E. The oval-shaped island is 5-½ miles long from east to west and 2-¾ miles wide. The north and northwest coasts are faced with cliffs up to 100 feet high pockmarked with hundreds of caves. The south coast is lined with nine-to-thirty-five-yard-wide beaches broken into 125–900-yard-long sections separated by low cliffs and outcroppings. The ground slopes gently inland from the beaches. The southwest coast and parts of the south are backed by bluffs. The entire island is surrounded by a coral reef several hundred yards wide, but it was not a major obstacle. Inland the ground rises to a level plateau averaging 165 feet above sea level. Most of the island is served by a well-developed, but unsurfaced road network. Cultivated vegetable and sugarcane fields covered much of this land interspersed with clear areas of low grasses and clumps of scrub trees. Thrusting abruptly upward from the east portion of the island is Iegusugu Mountain. This is a conical limestone 600-foot-high peak, nicknamed "the Pinnacle" and covered with scrub brush and trees, and honeycombed with caves and ravines. On the Pinnacle's south side is the sprawling Ie Town of stone buildings. On the island's center were three 6–7,000-foot-long airfields in the pattern of an "XI." The island had a population of 8,000, but about 3,000 had been evacuated to Okinawa. Ie Shima was defended by 2,000 troops of the *Igawa Unit* with substantial defenses built around the Pinnacle and the town.

Minna Shima, an islet four miles south of Ie, was secured by Fleet Marine Force, Pacific Reconnaissance Battalion troops on 12/13 April and occupied by two artillery battalions on the 15th. The 77th Infantry Division was moved from its station 300 miles southeast of Okinawa and assaulted Ie Shima on the morning of 16 April (W-Day) with full naval gunfire support as well as artillery firing from Motobu Peninsula. The 306th Infantry landed on Beach GREEN at 0758 hours (S-Hour) on the southwest end while the 305 Infantry hit RED 1 and 2 on the south-central coast. Initially, as on Okinawa, there was virtually no resistance with the airfields soon overrun as the regiments swept east across the island toward the Pinnacle and Ie Town. Resistance increased the next day as the town was approached. The 307th Infantry was landed on the morning of the 17th. By the 18th the troops had closed in on the north, west, and south sides of the town and Pinnacle. The attack bogged down against fierce resistance, especially in the town's center around the administrative building, called the Government House, and the surrounding high ground known as Bloody Ridge. Most of the town was cleared on the 20th and the Pinnacle was not taken until the 21st. Ie Shima was declared secure at 1730 hours that date. The Japanese lost 4,700, but of these an estimated 1,500 were armed civilians, and 409 prisoners were taken. American losses were 128 dead and missing and 900 wounded. Tragically, the popular war correspondent Ernie Pyle was killed by machine-gun fire on 18 April. On 25–28 April the 77th Infantry Division was moved to Okinawa and was soon again in combat. The entire civilian population was removed from the island within two weeks of its being secured to prevent interference with airfield construction. They were returned after the war. Ie Shima served a final role in the war when on 19 August two white-painted Japanese bombers arrived from Tokyo bearing the Japanese surrender delegation. They were then flown to Manila on U.S. aircraft. They returned the next day and flew back to Japan. Because of misunderstandings, the American ground crew failed to provide sufficient fuel for the aircraft to return to Japan. It crashed offshore of Japan, but the envoys were rescued and delivered the terms of unconditional surrender to the Emperor on schedule.

Map 104
Ie Shima, Okinawa Gunto

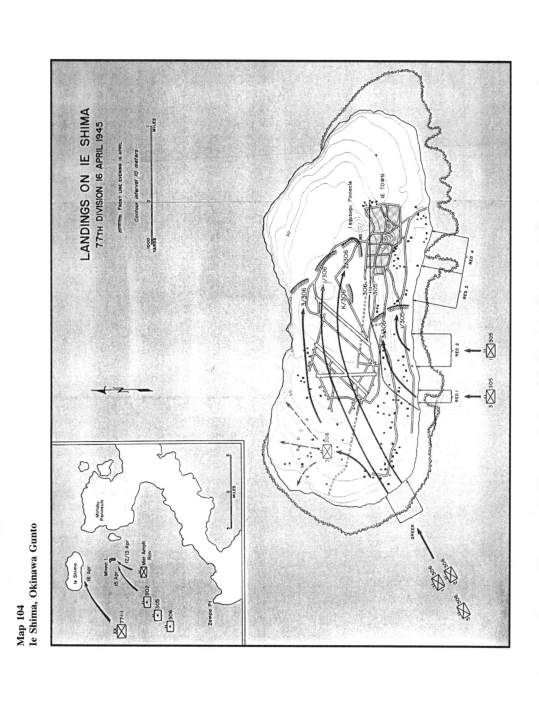

LANDINGS ON IE SHIMA
77TH DIVISION 16 APRIL 1945

Front line evening 16 April

Contour interval 10 meters

On Okinawa Shima the advancing XXIV Corps' Army divisions were now facing the Japanese main cross-island defense line, the Shuri defenses built on a series of steep ridges and escarpments. The 7th Infantry Division was on the east, the 96th in the center, and the 27th on the west. The attack was launched on 19 April, but it was the 24th before the outer Shuri defenses were penetrated. The 1st Marine Division was attached to XXIV Corps on 30 May relieving the 96th Infantry Division on the east flank. The assault continued southward through the main Shuri defenses, an effort continued until 3 May when the Japanese attempted a counteroffensive. The Japanese attacked that night with their main effort in the center and the east by the *24th Division*. The attack was supported by counterlanding raids in the American rear on both coasts. Shallow penetrations were accomplished in some areas, but the attack was repulsed. Japanese losses only served to weaken their front and the American forces continued to push south. On 7 May IIIAC resumed control of the 1st Marine Division on the west flank in anticipation of the island's widening and the necessity to place a fourth division into the line. The 6th Marine Division was soon assigned a sector on the 1st Marine Division's right and placed a single regiment into the line. (On 8 May the surrender of German forces in Europe was announced.) By 21 May 10th Army had progressed south to Shuri and Naha with the divisions on line from east to west: 96th Infantry, 77th Infantry, 1st Marine, and 6th Marine. The primary 10th Army objective was Shuri. No complete Japanese unit remained in the lines, only remnants. On the 29th the 22d Marines took Naha while an element of the 5th Marines, seizing the opportunity, crossed into the 77th Infantry Division's sector and secured Shuri Castle, much to the Army's exasperation. On the same date Army units broke through on the east coast as Japanese units were routed creating a melee of intermixed U.S. and Japanese units with both sometimes being attacked on both sides. The apparent confusion was due to a complex Japanese scheme of withdrawal. On 25 May the *62d Division* went through a defensive line of the *44th Independent Mixed Brigade* southeast of Naha and then attacked XXIV Corps elements to the east. The *24th Division* then withdrew from that sector on the 29th as the *62d Division* established a new line to the rear. The *24th Division* established a new line south of Itoman on the west coast as the *44th Independent Mixed Brigade* withdrew on the 31st to establish a line linked to the *24th Division*'s and running to the east coast. The *62d Division* then conducted a fighting withdrawal through the new lines between 30 May and 4 June. The *32d Army* successfully withdrew to the south, but of the 50,000 troops at the beginning of the operation, only 30,000 remained.

On 24 May paratroopers of the *1st Raiding Brigade* attempted an air-landed raid on Yontan Airfield staged from Japan. Only one of the five transports managed to land. A number of U.S. aircraft were destroyed and damaged on the ground, but the raiders were quickly killed.

IJN forces still held the Oroku Peninsula on the southwest coast and south of Naha (BROTHER), where the 6th Marine Division was blocked by Naha Harbor. Not to be halted by a mere body of water, the Division did what was natural and executed a shore-to-shore amphibious assault launched from the west coast north of Naha and into Naha Harbor to flank enemy forces on the Peninsula on 4 June (K-Day). The 4th Marines landed on Beach RED 1 and RED 2, south of Naha, at 0600 hours to be followed by the 29th Marines. While not given much attention, the two-regiment subsidiary operation was larger than some earlier amphibious assaults. It was the last opposed amphibious assault in World War II.

The 2d Marine Division's 8th Marines returned to the Okinawa area from Saipan on

30 May. Its 2d and 3d Battalions landed on Iheya Jima 3 June and the 1st Battalion landed on Aguni Shima on 9 June. These islands, north and west of Okinawa, were unoccupied. Radar and fighter direction centers were established on both islands.

The situation was stabilized by 31 May with most Japanese remnants positioned in the central portion of the crumbling lines. By 3 June the 7th Infantry Division pushed south on to the Chinen Peninsula on the southeast coast while the 96th Infantry and 1st Marine Divisions steadily drove south in the center. After hard fighting the Japanese remnants were driven onto the south end of the island by 11 June, although there were still substantial pockets in the American rear areas. The 8th Marines landed at Naha on 15 June and was attached to the 1st Marine Division to assist with the final operations ashore. The 10th Army commander, Lieutenant General Buckner, was killed observing his troops' advance on the final organized resistance on 18 June 1945. Major General Roy Geiger assumed command of 10th Army, the only Marine officer to command a field army, while retaining command of IIIAC. The next day he was promoted to lieutenant general. General Buckner had expressly picked Geiger to assume command in the event of his death. Five days later Geiger was relieved by Army Lieutenant General Joseph W. Stilwell. The two final pockets on the island's south end as well as a large inland pocket was wiped out on 21 June. Okinawa Shito was declared secure at 1700 hours. Nakagusuku Wan was renamed Buckner Bay in honor of the deceased general. (It reverted to its original name when Japan regained control of the island.)

Kume Shima, fifty-five miles west of Okinawa, was secured by the Fleet Marine Force, Pacific Amphibious Reconnaissance Battalion on 26–30 June to establish a radar site and fighter direction center. Landing on the island's southeast coast, the force met no opposition from the estimated fifty-man garrison, which was later engaged. This was the final amphibious assault in World War II. VAC was scheduled to invade Miyako Shima in the Sakishima Gunto near Formosa after Okinawa was secured. VAC was badly mauled at Iwo Jima and the operation was canceled in April.

The cost of securing Okinawa Gunto was high. Over 100,000 Japanese troops and Okinawan *Boeitai* fought on Okinawa and other islands in the Ryukyus. Estimates of casualties are difficult to determine owing to the duration of the action, numbers of enemy forces, and the nature of combat on Okinawa. Approximately 66,000 combatants were killed and half of the survivors were wounded. A total of 7,400 combatants were taken prisoner during the campaign. Some 3,400 unarmed laborers—*Boeitai*, Koreans, and Chinese—were captured. Large numbers turned themselves in after Japan surrendered. Approximately 10,000 IJA and IJN personnel and 8,000 Okinawan *Boeitai* and conscripts survived the battle.

Island Command's military government and military police took change of 285,272 Okinawan and Japanese civilians. At the conclusion of the operation, 42,000–50,000 Okinawan civilians were estimated to have died owing to Japanese or American combat action, suicided, or were murdered by the Japanese (to prevent their surrender or to steal their food). Postwar studies found that over 122,000 civilians were killed, almost one-third of the indigenous population and a figure rivaling the combined death toll of over 120,000 at Hiroshima and Nagasaki, and a culture was shattered.

Large numbers of Japanese troops were killed in postoperation mop-ups and additional prisoners were taken, ultimately growing to 16,350 by the end of November 1945. It was the first time that large numbers of Japanese troops willingly surrendered.

The remainder of the Ryukyu Islands were formally surrendered on 7 September 1945 to Lieutenant General Joseph Stilwell by Admiral KATO Tadao. There were still approximately 105,000 IJA and IJN personnel on the other Ryukyu Islands. Small numbers of Japanese renegades and Okinawan rebels conducted a low-level guerrilla war against U.S. occupation forces into 1947.

American losses ashore were 3,250 Marine dead and missing and 15,700 wounded. The Army lost 4,700 dead and missing and 18,100 wounded. There were 26,200 non-battle casualties. The United States lost 763 aircraft, 458 in combat, and the Japanese lost 7,830: 4,155 in combat, 2,655 operationally, and 1,020 destroyed on the ground. U.S. Navy losses were inordinately high with thirty-six ships sunk and 368 damaged. These high rates were largely due to the suicide plane attacks on the fleet, which accounted for twenty-six sunk and 164 damaged. These attacks were also the cause of the Navy's high casuality rate of 4,900 dead and missing and 4,800 wounded. The Royal Navy suffered four ships damaged, 98 aircraft lost, 62 KIA, and 82 WIA.

The United States now possed a base just 320 miles southwest of Kyushu. A massive construction project began with 87,000 construction troops who would build a planned twenty-two airfields to accommodate the Eighth Air Force deploying from Europe as well as Navy and Marine aviation units. Only a portion of these fields were completed including six 10,000-foot bomber fields. Navy and Marine fields were established at Awase and Chimu on Okinawa and Plumb Field on Ie Shima. These fields were known collectively as Naval Air Stations, Okinawa.

Naval Operating Base, Okinawa was established at Baten Ko on the south end of Buckner Bay. It controlled port facilities at Naha, Chimu Wan, Nago Wan, and Katchin Hanto on the north end of Buckner Bay. The island developed into a major staging base for Army and Marine units destined fro the invasion of Japan. Two devastating typhoons in September and October caused major damage and forced the relocation of some naval base facilities. The main naval base was moved from Baten Ko to the southeast end of Katchin Peninsula to what is still known as WHITE Beach, the headquarters for Commander, Fleet Activities, Okinawa and Naval Air Facility, Okinawa. The 1950–53 Korean War made Okinawa an important Army logistics and Navy operating base as did Vietnam through the 1960s and into the 1970s.

The Army Air Forces maintained a major bomber bases at Kadena Air Base and the U.S. Air Force continued to do so when organized in 1947. B-29 and B-50 bombers flew long-range missions to bomb North Korea during the Korean War. B-52 bombers habitually flew missions to Vietnam from Okinawa and strategic reconnaissance aircraft operated from there on missions throughout Asia. In 1973 the Navy moved its facilities from Naha Air Base to Kadena Air Base to collocate with the Air Force.

As combat units departed for the States after the war the 44th Infantry, Philippine Scouts (a U.S. Army unit comprised of Filipino troops) garrisoned the island in January 1947 leading to racial disputes. The 44th Infantry left in May 1949 and was replaced by the U.S. Army's 29th Infantry to guard the air bases. The 29th was replaced by the 75th Infantry in June 1954, and itself inactivated in March 1956. The 173d Airborne Brigade (Separate) was activated on Okinawa in 1962 and remained there until departing for Vietnam in 1965. The Army's 1st Special Forces Group ("Green Berets") was based on the island from 1957 to 1974. In 1956 the 3d Marine Division was reassigned from Camp Gifu in Japan to Camp Courtney on Okinawa. It remained there until deployed to Vietnam in 1965, returning in 1969. The Division remains stationed there along with III Marine Expeditionary Force. Marine Corps installations on Okinawa today are collectively called Camp Smedley D. Butler, but are scattered about the island.

The military administration of Okinawa and the Ryukyu Islands was initially the Navy's responsibility, with assistance from the Army, but on 1 July 1946 the military government was turned over to the Army. Progressively more responsibility was given to Okinawans as the government developed. Surprisingly, many Okinawans, especially students and leftists, desired that Okinawa be returned to Japanese control and withdrawal of the U.S. armed forces, even if the armed forces furnished 70 percent of the island's income. Progressively violent protests were experienced through the 1960s and early into the 1970s. It was finally agreed between the governments of the United States and Japan that Okinawa would be returned to Japanese sovereignty on 15 May 1972. U.S. military bases would be allowed to remain and have to this day. Some of the thirty-nine separate U.S. military installations are shared with Japanese Self-Defense Force units, but problems still exist.

Today Okinawa is a thriving community with modern urbanization sprawling across the island, but the island group is still the poorest of Japan's prefectures. An array of war memorials, exhibit sites, and tours are available to visitors. The island's appearance has changed markedly since the war and little will appear familiar to visitors. Many of the town names have been changed with several towns merging and new arising. Shuri Castle was rebuilt and reopened in 1992.

The Cornerstone of Peace Park (*Heiwa No Ishi-Ji*) was opened at Mabumi on Okinawa's south end in 1995. Its walls are enscribed with almost 240,000 names of Okinawan, Americans, Japanese, Koreans, and Formosans who died on the island.

READING SUGGESTIONS

Alexander, Col. Joseph H. *Closing In: Marines in the Seizure of Iwo Jima.* Washington Navy Yard: History and Museums Division, Marine Corps Historical Center, 1994.

Alexander, Joseph H. *The Final Campaign: Marines in the Victory on Okinawa.* Washington Navy Yard: History and Museums Division. Marine Corps Historical Center. 1996.

Appleman, Roy E.; Burns, James M.; Gugeler. Russell A.; and Stevens, John. *The US Army In World War II. The War in the Pacific. Okinawa: The Last Battle.* Washington, DC: US Government Printing Office. 1948.

Astor, Gerald. *Operation Iceberg: The Invasion and Conquest of Okinawa in World War II—An Oral History.* New York: Dell Books, 1995.

Bartley, Lt. Col. Whitman S. *Iwo Jima: Amphibious Epic.* Washington, DC: US Government Printing Office, 1954.

Bureau of Yards and Docks. *Building the Navy's Bases in World War II, Vol. II.* Washington, DC: US Government Printing Office, 1947.

Coletta, Paolo E. and Bauer, K. Jack (Editors). *United States Navy and Marine Bases, Overseas.* Westport, CT: Greenwood Publishing Co., 1985.

Craven, Wesley F. and Cate, James L. *The Army Air Forces in World War II: The Pacific: Matterhorn to Nagasaki. June 1944 to August 1945. Vol. 5.* Chicago: University of Chicago Press, 1953.

Crowl, Philip A. and Love, Edmund G. *United States Army in World War II: Seizure of the Gilberts and Marshalls.* Washington, DC: US Government Printing Office, 1985.

Feifer, George. *Tennozan: The Battle for Okinawa and the Atomic Bomb.* New York: Ticknor & Fields. 1992.

Garand, George W. and Stonebridge, Turman R. *History of US Marine Corps Operations in World War II: Western Pacific Operations. Vol. IV.* Washington, DC: US Government Printing Office, 1966.

Huber, Tomas M. *Leavenworth Papers: Japan's Battle for Okinawa: April to June 1945.* Washington, DC: US Government Printing Office. 1990.

Leckie, Robert. *Okinawa: The Last Battle of World War II.* New York: Viking Press, 1995.

Morison, Samuel E. *History of US Navy Operations in World War II: Aleutians, Gilberts and Marshalls, March 1943–April 1944. Vol. VII.* Boston: Little, Brown and Company, 1951.

Morison. Samuel E. *History of United States Naval Operations in World War II. Victory in the Pacific. Vol. XIV*. Boston: Little, Brown and Company, 1960.

Nalty, Bernard C. and Crawford, Danny J. *The United States Marines on Iwo Jima: The Battle and the Flag Raisings*. Washington Navy Yard: History and Museums Division, Marine Corps Historical Center, 1995.

Nichols, Maj. Charles S., Jr. and Shaw, Henry I., Jr. *Okinawa: Victory in the Pacific*. Washington, DC: HQ, Marine Corps, 1955.

Spur, R. *A Glorious Way to Die: The Kamikaze Mission of the Battleship Yamato, April 1945*. Scranton, PA: Newmarket Press, 1981.

Wright, Derrick. *Battle for Iwo Jima, 1945*. Stroud, Gloucestershire: Sutton Publishing, 2000.

Yahara Hiromichi. *The Battle for Okinawa*. New York: John Wiley & Sons, 1995.

6

North Pacific Area

The North Pacific Area was the smallest of the three Pacific Ocean Areas, encompassed the fewest strategically important islands, and saw comparatively little action. The area's southern boundary was latitude 42° north running from the California/Oregon state line across the Pacific, clipping the south end of Hokkaido Island, the northernmost of the main Japanese Home Islands, and striking shore just to the south of the Korea/China border. It follows the coast of Russia northward, bridges the Bering Straits, follows mainland Alaska's coast, then Canada's, then the Washington and Oregon States' coasts. Alaska's Aleutian Islands were the most important in the area. It was in the western Aleutian Islands that the only land combat in North America would take place in World War II. The largest island in the area is Sakhalin, of which the south half was Japanese territory and the north Soviet territory, immediately off the coast of Russia and north of Hokkaido. A chain of islands, Kurile or Chrishima Islands, running from northeast Hokkaido to the south end of Russia's Kamchatka Peninsula is Japanese territory.

ALEUTIAN ISLANDS, ALASKA

The Aleutian Islands run in a 1,200-mile-long chain curving in a shallow arc westward from the end of the Alaska Peninsula toward Russia's Kamchatka Peninsula (see Map 105). The nearest significant Alaskan mainland city, Anchorage, is 2,000 miles from the chain's west end. Only 650 miles east-southeast was a Japanese base at Kataoka on Paramushiro Jima in the Kurile Islands (WRITING). The almost uninhabited Alaska Peninsula juts southwestward from mainland Alaska with the easternmost of the Aleutians, Unimak Island, situated at approximately 53° N 163° W to the westernmost, Attu Island, at 52° N 172° E. Longitude 180° (the nominal International Date Line) defines the western and eastern Aleutians running just to the east of Amchitka Island and west of Ulak. This places the western Aleutians, including those occupied by the Japanese, in the Eastern Hemisphere. The stated dateline, however, follows a different course running southwest from the Bering Straits, separating Alaska and Russia by fifty-seven miles, to the west end of Attu Island and then angles back to the southeast to longitude 180° at latitude

Map 105
Aleutian Islands, Alaska

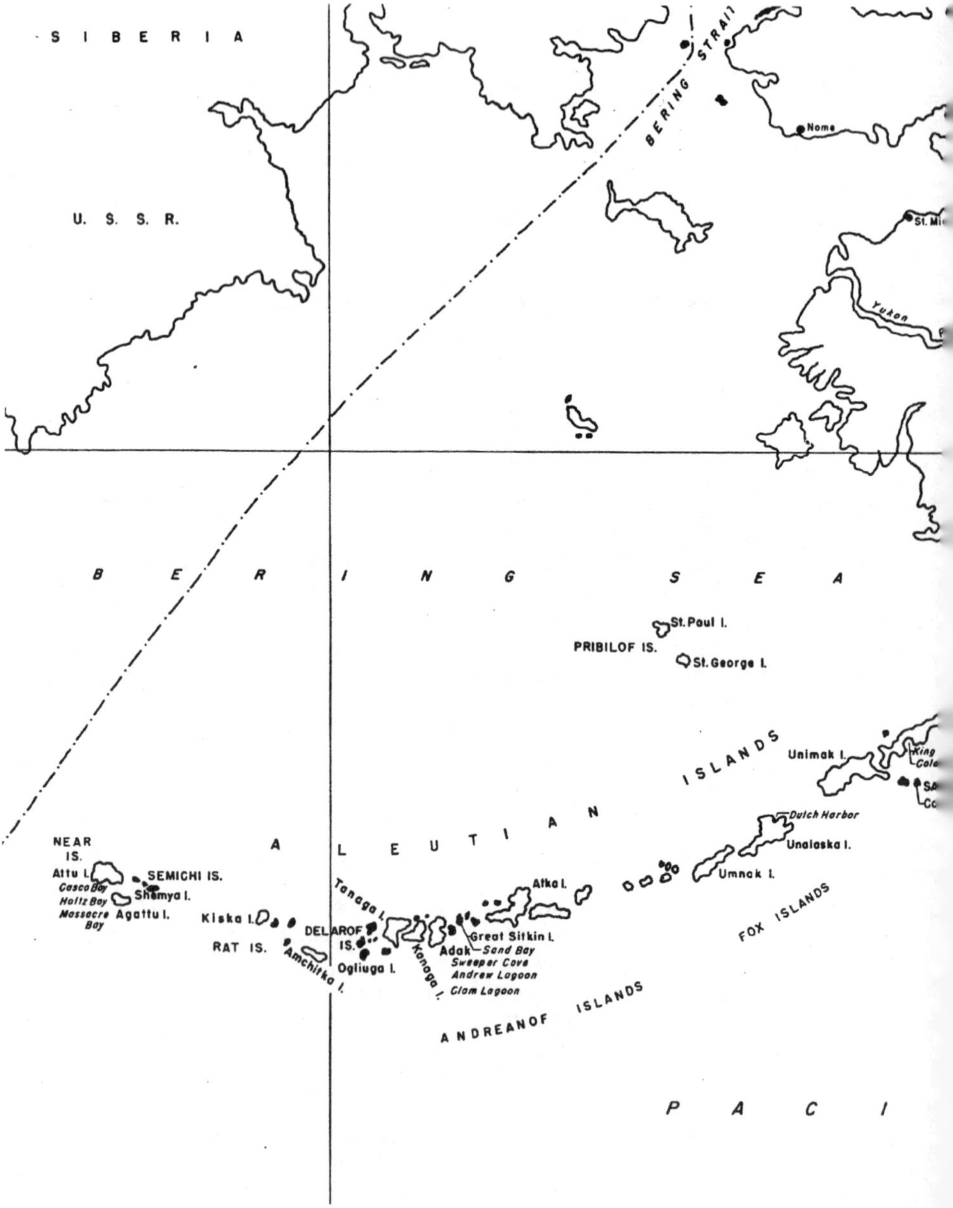

S I B E R I A

BERING STRAIT

Nome

U. S. S. R.

St. Mi

Yukon

B   E   R   I   N   G   S   E   A

St. Paul I.
PRIBILOF IS.
St. George I.

ISLANDS
Unimak I.
King
Cole

A   L   E   U   T   I   A   N   Dutch Harbor
Unalaska I.

NEAR
IS.
Attu I.   SEMICHI IS.   Atka I.   Umnak I.
Casco Bay
Holtz Bay   Shemya I.   FOX ISLANDS
Massacre Agattu I.   Kiska I.   Tanaga I.
Bay   DELAROF   Great Sitkin I.
RAT IS.   IS.   Adak Sand Bay
Amchitka I.   Ogliuga I.   Sweeper Cove
Kanaga   Andrew Lagoon
Clam Lagoon

A N D R E A N O F   I S L A N D S

P   A   C   I

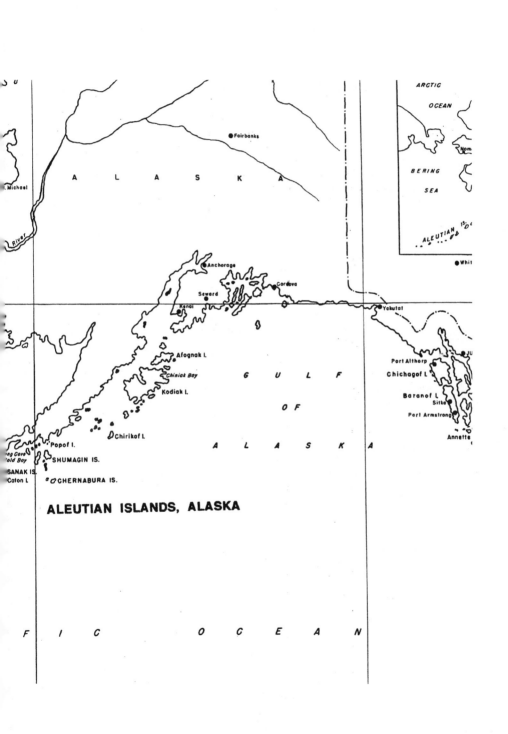

ALEUTIAN ISLANDS, ALASKA

45° north. This places all of the Aleutians and western mainland Alaska in time zone 1 (most of Alaska was in time zone 2). North of the Aleutians is the Bering Sea and to the south is the North Pacific.

The Aleutians possess from seventy to 120 islands, depending on one's criteria, but only fifteen are of strategically significant size. Total land area of the significant islands and islets is 6,821 square miles. It is the world's longest archipelago of small islands. The islands are mountainous, usually running along the islands' north sides, rugged, and of volcanic origin. There are over twenty volcanoes scattered through the islands. The highest elevation is 9,372 feet on Unimak Island. The islands were heavily eroded by Ice Age glaciers. They are rocky and largely barren of vegetation other than low, tough grasses and scrub brush. Inland valleys are covered with ferns, weeds, rye grass, and wildflowers in the summer. The hills and mountains generally remain covered or partly covered by snow throughout the year.

Many low, level areas are covered with tundra, rare on the Alaska mainland. This is an overlay of lichens, mosses, and weeds atop two to ten feet of dead and partly decayed, matted, water-sogged vegetation over muck-like volcanic ash on a permanently frozen subsoil. It could freeze solid or turn into a quicksand-like ooze making it impossible to construct buildings, permanent roads, or airfields. It had to be removed down to solid ground and then the area backfilled with sand or gravel before construction. In low and coastal areas muskeg is encountered covering sometimes many square miles up to twenty feet deep. These are bogs of water-sogged, decayed moss resembling peat. Interwoven tree trunks and limbs were often found buried in muskeg making it difficult to dig down to solid ground. It would freeze solid in the winter and turn into seemingly bottomless swamps in the summer. Unless frozen, the tundra and muskeg posed an obstacle to wheeled vehicles and even men on foot. While tracked vehicles might negotiate across some areas, repeated crossings only churned it into an impassable muck. There was one single tree in the Aleutians, a small tree that had been flown into Umnak Island, planted at the base headquarters and protected by a sign stating "Umnak National Forest." Trees could not take root because of the constant high winds.

The Aleutians are divided into several smaller island groups, although they were seldom recognized other than by geographers. Place names in the Aleutians are a rich mixture of native Aleut, Russian, and American. The most significant islands in the Aleutians and those that played a part in the war, from east to west, are:

Fox Islands	Rat Islands
Unimak	Amchitka*
Unalaska	Kiska*
Akum	Near Islands
Umnak*	Shemya*
Adreanof Islands	Agattu
Seguam	Attu*
Amila	
Atka*	
Great Sitkin*	
Adak*	
Kanga	
Tanaga*	

*Indicates islands on which U.S. bases were built.

Weather conditions are extremely harsh with subzero winter temperatures, frequent Arctic storms with high winds, up to 140 miles per hour lasting for days; snow, sleet, rain, *willowaws* (violent winter squalls) reaching gale proportions within thirty minutes between October and March, and blizzards, perpetual low overcast skies, and fog experienced day and night. There were only eight to ten clear days a year, no dry and no calm seasons. The islands average forty to fifty inches of rain a year with most falling in the fall and early winter. Because of the moderating effects of ocean currents, the temperature was usually higher than on the mainland in the summer months, but fell far below freezing in the winter. The weather extremes proved to be an unmerciful enemy to both sides and hindered land, air, and sea operations to an almost unimaginable extent. Countless examples of Aleutian weather extremes can be given, but one will suffice. Visibility was often so poor and the cloud ceiling so low that it was common practice for bombers attacking Japanese-held islands to fly in a column at twenty-five-foot altitude following the lead bomber's prop wash wake on the water. The Japanese occupying islands in the extreme western Aleutians had an advantage as the weather pattern moves from west to east providing them in advance of the American bases to the east on what conditions would be.

Health hazards include frostbite, hypothermia (lowering of core body temperature and little understood during the war), exposure, trenchfoot, immersion foot, pneumonia, upper respiratory illness, tuberculosis (from frosting of the lungs), and dehydration. Boredom in the remote outposts, enhanced by monotonous terrain and brutal weather conditions, was a serious psychological problem. The problem was magnified by fewer than eight hours of daylight between November and February. In the summer months swarms of mosquitoes posed a serious moral problem, but were nonmalarial.

The Territory of Alaska (TA) (GOOSEWING, PANTHEON, PHAETON) with 586,400 square miles, over twice the size of Texas, was purchased by the United States from Russia for $7,200,000 in 1867. Regardless of the territory's vastness it had a prewar population of only 72,600. Of these there were 39,200 whites and 32,500 Eskimos, Aleuts, and Indians. In the prewar summer months seasonal laborers from the States would increase the population up to another 20,000. During the war this increased to over 100,000 workers employed on extensive construction projects. There were also 230 Japanese residents in Alaska, half of whom were native-born American citizens. Even though the military commanders and the territorial governor opposed their internment, they were deported to Utah and Colorado and interned with over 110,000 others of Japanese ancestry (64 percent American citizens) as were 23,000 Japanese in Canada.

Alaska, along with the Territory of Hawaii, enjoyed a special status as an incorporated territory meaning it did not just belong to the United States, but was part of the United States, a status it was given by Congress in 1912. As such the Constitution and laws of the United States applied fully. The governor was appointed by the president. In World War II the governor was Ernest Gruening and the territorial capital was at Juneau (QUIVER). Alaska possesses invaluable resources, but many were untapped as development was limited by weather conditions, lack of infrastructure, and little manpower. Forestry products, furs, mining, oil, and fishing held great potential.

Alaska had long been considered to be strategically important. Fairbanks in the center of Alaska is 4,000 miles from Moscow, Berlin, and London and most other national capitals in the Northern Hemisphere are even closer. The most direct route between the United States and Tokyo is the "Great Circle Route" traversing southern Alaska and the Aleutians. In 1941 both Tokyo and New York City were fifteen hours' flying time from Fairbanks. It was considered at one point to use this route for the main bomber offensive on Japan. Successes in the Central Pacific, the brutal weather conditions, and an under-developed support infrastructure negated this role.

Chilkoot Barracks (TENSTRIKE) at Skagway was the only military installation in Alaska prior to 1940. That year construction began on Fort Richardson eight miles north of Anchorage and Elmendorf Air Base two miles east of Anchorage (GAMEKEEPER, PICKUP) near the landward end of the Alaska Peninsula. Ladd Field, the main air depot, was built twenty-five miles south of Fairbanks (HANDICAP) in 1939 and other future airfields were surveyed. The Cold Weather Aviation Laboratory was established at Ladd Field to test aircraft in the harsh conditions. Located 155 miles farther to the east was Fort Randall at Cold Bay (METAPHOR, SEAWASP) on the southwest end of the Alaska Peninsula where an Army airfield had been built. Naval Base, Kodiak Island is 372 miles northeast of Cold Bay. Kodiak Island (LIMEJUICE, OCEANBLUE), the largest of Alaska's islands, is off of the south coast near the base of the Alaska Peninsula and is not part of the Aleutians. Here too is located Fort Greeley (ACCLAIM), which shared an airfield with the Navy aviation facility. Operating airfields and staging fields were eventually constructed on the Alaska mainland at Metlakatla, Juneau, Yakutat, Cordova, Gulkana, Northway, Big Delta, Ruby, Nome, McGrath, Bethel, Naknek, and Port Heiden.

Regardless of these preparations, at the beginning of the war, Alaska for all practical purposes was defenseless. There were few troops, aircraft, and naval forces to man the still-developing bases. Alaska had one of the lowest defense priorities in the U.S. armed forces. This was to remain the case even as the Japanese were being driven from the western Aleutians.

The overall initial military command in Alaska was the Alaska Defense Command established on 28 March 1941 and headquartered at Fort Richardson on the mainland under Brigadier General (later Lieutenant General) Simon B. Buckner, Jr. The command was responsible for territorial defense planning, training the Alaska National Guard, and controlling the Alaskan Coastal Frontier. The command was reorganized as the Alaskan Department on 1 November 1943 and additionally tasked with supporting the Lend-Lease supply effort to the Soviet Union. A total of 6,430 Lend-Lease aircraft were transferred to the USSR via Alaskan airfields. Buckner was succeeded by Lieutenant General Delos C. Emmons in June 1944.

The Alaskan Air Force, under Brigadier General (later Major General) William O. Butler, was formed at Elmendorf Air Base in January 1941 and a month later was re-designated 11th Air Force. This command was later based on Adak Island. After the western Aleutians were recovered, the 11th Air Force flew covering missions for North Pacific Force ships attacking naval installations, airfields, and fish canneries in Japan's Kurile Islands as well as its own raids.

The Alaska Naval Sector and Naval District 17 Headquarters under Rear Admiral Robert A. Theobald was at Naval Base, Kodiak Island, as was a Marine barracks. An intermediate naval base and the Army's Fort Ray were located at Sitka (formerly New Archangel) on Baranof Island among the coastal Alexander Archipelago islands on Alaska's southeast arm running along Canada's west coast. Naval operating elements were assigned to the North Pacific Force (Task Force 8, later redesignated TF 16), also under Admiral Theobald, which never obtained fleet status.

Command of the North Pacific Area was cumbersome and divided between the Army and the Navy resulting in numerous conflicts and redundant effort. The North Pacific Force assumed command of all naval and air forces as well as Army ground forces. It was not to be a harmonious relationship. Even though Theobald was relieved by Rear

Admiral Thomas C. Kinkaid on 1 January 1943, because of his inability to cooperate with the Army, this situation continued until after the Japanese were driven from the Aleutians. December 1941 found the Alaska Defense Command with 21,800 Army troops, 2,200 Army Air Force, and just over 500 Navy personnel. The only naval vessels were the gunboat USS *Charleston* (PG-51) and a few Coast Guard cutters. The Navy had six seaplane patrol bombers and the Army Air Force had only two fighter and two light bomber squadrons. The air power was soon slightly increased to include some heavy bombers. Other than some antiaircraft units, most of the Army troops were engineers and service troops constructing the various bases and airfields. Military dependents were evacuated from the territory in December 1941. The Aleut people had lived in the islands for at least 9,000 years, but by World War II they were few in number and most of the islands were unpopulated.

The islands discussed here are those occupied by the Japanese in June 1942.

Kiska Island

Kiska is the westernmost of the Rat Islands and is sixty miles northwest of Amchitka, the nearest large island, thirteen miles west of Segula, and 165 miles southeast of Attu, the other major island occupied by the Japanese, and 610 miles west of Dutch Harbor. The nearest American air base was Fort Glenn on Umnak Island 536 miles to the east. Kiska is located at 52°07' N 177°36' E. It was code-named AMATEUR.

Kiska covers 110 square miles, has a maximum width of six miles, but averages three to four miles wide, and is twenty-two miles long from the northeast to the southwest (see Map 106). On the northeast end of the island is Kiska Volcano, 3,966 feet high and inert, although smoke was reported in 1907 and 1927. At the base of the volcano is a flat area of muskeg, lakes, ponds, and streams. Moving southward the ground again rises and then drops to a tableland on the east coast at North Head. Kiska Harbor is bounded by North and South Heads with its seaward eastward opening partly protected by Little Kiska Island, 1-½ by three miles. The U.S. Navy had established a small coaling station in the harbor, but this was long ago abandoned. The few beaches are narrow, steep, rocky, and backed by low bluffs. Much of the coast is faced with cliffs of varying height. A chain of barren ridges runs from the head of Kiska Harbor along the island's west shore. Behind the east coast is a tableland area of tundra, soft clay, and streams. The shores are rocky and steep with only a few small sandy beach areas. The island was unpopulated other than a Navy radio station manned by ten sailors.

Attu Island

Attu is the westernmost of the Aleutian Islands being only 700 miles east of the Russian mainland and 650 miles from Japan's Kuriles. Dutch Harbor is 740 miles to the east and Kiska is 165 miles to the southeast. The nearest large island is Agattu to the southeast. Attu is situated as 52°50' N 173°11' E. Its code name was JACKBOOT and later AMNESIA.

Attu is thirty-eight miles long east (Chirikof Point) to west (Cape Wrangell) and fourteen miles wide (see Map 107). It is mountainous and rugged with tundra-covered valleys. The few beaches are narrow and the ground behind them slopes steeply upward. Most of the shoreline and nearshore waters are rock studded and currents are difficult. The east end of the island, which the Japanese had occupied and where the action took place,

Map 106
Kiska Island, Aleutian Islands

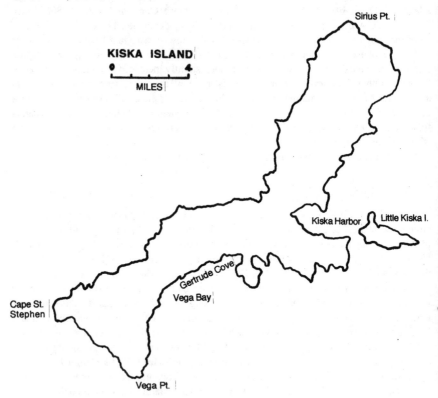

is indented by three large bays: Holtz on the northeast, Sarana in the center and separated from Holtz Bay by broad Cape Khiebnikof, and Massacre Bay on the southeast separated from Sarana Bay by a long, narrow peninsula. From the head of this bay runs a broad tundra and stream-covered valley known as Massacre Valley and overlooked by Cold Mountain. Massacre Bay and Valley derive their name from the frequent mass seal killings by hide hunters that took place there before the turn of the century. A spine of mountains runs down the island's center with ridges branching off to the south and north coasts. The highest elevation on Attu is 3,084 feet near the west end. On the island's northeast shoulder a small bay barely dips into the coast, Austin Cove. The south coast is indented by four more bays, from east to west: Temnac, Nevidiskov, Abraham, and Etienne. The island's only settlement was Chichagof Village at the end of the small Chichagof Harbor located on the northeast shoulder of the broad Cape Khiebnikof peninsula. It had a population of thirty-nine Aleuts and an elderly white couple, the village teachers. The peninsula itself is covered with ridges, valleys, lakes, and streams.

Map 107
Attu Island, Aleutian Islands

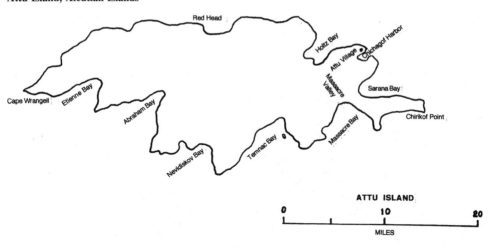

Shemya Island

The island of Shemya is the easternmost of the small Semichi Group, part of the Near Islands. The island was code-named FELSPAR and had been nicknamed "The Rock" and "The Black Pearl." It is 137 miles northwest of Kiska and thirty-five miles east-southeast of Attu. Shemya is located at 52°43' N 174°06' E.

It is unusual in the Aleutians being generally level, but does possess rolling terrain and some high ground with the highest point being 240 feet. Other than a few small ponds and patches of scrub it is featureless. It measures 2-¼ by 4-¼ miles. The island was uninhabited when 1,100 troops of the *303d Independent Infantry Battalion* occupied it shortly after Attu was seized in June 1942 as an outguard for the latter (see Map 108). The island remained occupied only a short time and the Japanese withdrew to Attu in August before the Americans secured it as a staging base for the assaults on Attu and Kiska.

Islands on which key U.S. bases were established are discussed briefly here. Additionally, small installations, minor facilities, emergency landing strips, radio stations, etc. were built on various other small islands.

Unalaska Island

This island is east of Unimak, itself off the east end of the Alaska Peninsula. It is twenty-three miles wide and sixty-seven miles long. On its northeast side is Unalaska Bay. In the bay is the small island of Amaknak on which Dutch Harbor is situated. It is one of the best anchorages in the Aleutians. Base construction began in 1940. Dutch Harbor (INCUBUS, PILLORY) included the Army's Fort Mears with antiaircraft guns, a small naval air base with submarine and seaplane bases, a Coast Guard station, and a Marine barracks with some coast defense guns. It had no airfield.

Map 108
Shemya Island, Aleutian Islands

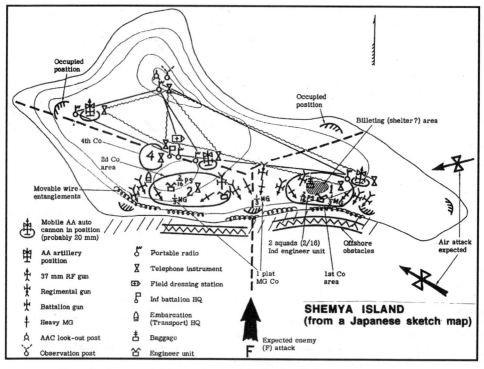

Copy of a Japanese sketch map showing defensive installations.

Umnak Island

A 3,000-foot airfield, Fort Glenn, was built under difficult conditions and great secrecy at Otter Point on the east end of Umnak Island (HAPPYLARK, WHIRLING). Its mission was to protect the only military base then in the Aleutians, Dutch Harbor sixty miles to the east. A small naval facility was built at Otter Point in late 1942. It later served as a staging field for aircraft en route to the central Aleutians.

Adak Island

In the central Aleutians Adak Island (CAREER) became an important staging base and the main forward headquarters for operations into the western Aleutians. It and Atka Island (PASQUINADE) to the east were occupied by the 2d Battalion, 134th Infantry on 30 August 1942 (Operation FIREPLACE). This move led the Japanese to believe that the Americans would use the Aleutions as a stepping stone to invade the Home Islands from the northeast and they reinforced Attu and Kiska. Development of a naval operating base soon began. It included a naval air station with two runways and two Army airstrips. Both Army and Navy air facilities were built on Atka (nicknamed "Atkatraz") and there was a Marine barracks. A Navy refueling base was built on Great Sitkin Island (LIPSTICK,

PLIMSOLL) to the northeast of Adak in 1943 and a naval auxiliary air facility was established on Tanaga Island (AMERLET) fifty miles west of Adak.

Amchitka Island

Amchitka (AFFECTION) is 178 miles west of Adak. An Army staging base and an airfield were built there in 1942. Previously the crew of a U.S. submarine (SS-127) that had run aground was marooned on the island in June 1842, but was recovered. A naval aviation facility including a seaplane base was built in 1943. In 1951 the Army began Project WINDSTORM on Adak. This saw the detonation of three underground nuclear weapons in 1965, 1969, and 1971, the last being the largest underground nuclear test ever conducted by the United States.

Regardless of the theoretical strategic value of the Aleutians, owing to the realities of the region's brutal weather conditions and difficult terrain, both sides of the conflict would probably have been better off avoiding the area, but then, that is not how wars are fought.

The Japanese occupation of the western Aleutians was mainly a diversion for the June 1942 Battle of Midway some 2,000 miles to the south. The goal was to draw U.S. Navy forces away from the main objective to protect American soil. There were other reasons though. While some Japanese officers felt that the American carrier-launched (USS *Hornet*, CV-8) B-25 bomber raid on Tokyo of 18 April may have been launched from an aircraft carrier, others thought that the raid had been flown from a "secret" base in the western Aleutian Islands. They also suspected an air base on Adak Island in the central Aleutians, where there was none until later. Once Midway had been seized along with the western Aleutians, Japanese seaplane bombers could patrol the ocean between the two areas to further protect the northeastern approaches to the Home Islands. The Japanese had no plans to use the Aleutians as a springboard to invade Alaska, Canada, or the northwest United States although this threat was greatly feared at the time.

Japanese naval operations in the North Pacific were the responsibility of the *Northern Area Fleet* headquartered at Kataoka on Paramushiro Jima in the Kurile Islands. Its main operating force was the *5th Fleet* based at Ominato on Honshu and under the command of Vice Admiral HOSOGAYA Boshiro. The senior IJA command was the *Northern Army* under Lieutenant General HIGUCHI Kiichiro at Sapporo on Hokkaido (this command was redesignated *5th Area Army* in the spring of 1944) and included the *27th Army*. The United States learned of the Japanese plans for the *AL Operation* on 21 May and the Task Force 8, the North Pacific Force, departed Pearl Harbor on the 25th. The Japanese *2d Mobile Force* with two carriers launched a weak air attack on Dutch Harbor on the morning of 3 June inflicting little damage. A second air raid was launched the next day, but damage was light. The Japanese carrier force soon retired, but reports of a Japanese fleet operating in the Bering Sea led to fears that Nome on the Alaska mainland near the Bering Straits or Saint Lawrence Island just to the south of the Bering Straits was in danger.

On 7 June the *Kiska Occupation Force* was assembled off of Kiska and 550 troops of the *Maizura 3d SNLF* with 700 laborers landed on the island to be the first foreign troops to set foot on American territory since 1814. Nine U.S. sailors manning the radio station were captured; the tenth surrendered after fifty days at large. Later in the day the *Adak-Attu Occupation Force* landed 1,200 troops of the *301st Independent Infantry Battalion* at Massacre Bay on Attu and descended on unsuspecting Chichagof Village. The white teacher committed suicide (some accounts claim the Japanese shot him, but this does not appear to be the case) and interned the Aleuts and the teacher's wife (who had also attempted to commit suicide). They were later sent to Japan. The U.S. command did not know of the landings until 10 June.

Army Air Force and Navy bombers attacked the Japanese ships in Kiska Harbor on 11 June and the air raids lasted until the 13th, what became known as the "Kiska Blitz." The Navy patrol bombers operated from Atak Island from a seaplane tender, but it withdrew on the 13th after depleting its bombs and fuel. While a number of Japanese ships were damaged, none was sunk and almost half of the U.S. aircraft were downed or damaged. The Japanese now controlled two islands they had little use for and the Americans would have to liberate them mainly because of public pressure; they had little military need for them as well. Most Aleuts were evacuated from the rest of the Aleutians to Admiralty Island near Juneau and some returned home after the war. The Japanese began construction of airfields and defenses on both islands while the Americans contin- ued to hit them with air raids. On 27 August the Japanese began shipping troops from Attu to Kiska until October when Attu was reoccupied.

The Battle of the Komandorskie Islands occurred on 23 March 1943 when a small U.S. task group intercepted a Japanese force attempting to reinforce Attu. The action took place 180 miles west of Attu and 100 miles south of the Komandorskie Islands, Soviet territory. The 2-½-hour daylight battle was reminiscent of a World War I gun battle with no aircraft or submarines involved. Only minimal damage was inflicted on both sides, but Vice Admiral HOSOGAYA was blamed for failing to defeat the American blockade of Attu and was relieved by Vice Admiral KAWASE Shiro on 26 March as commander of the *5th Fleet*.

At this time the only major amphibious operation the United States had conducted was Guadalcanal. The assault on Attu was also to be the Army's first amphibious operation. Approval for Operation LANDCRAB was given on 1 April 1943. Air and naval bombard- ment soon began. The only infantry in Alaska was the 138th Infantry Regiment deployed in scattered locations for security and the 4th Infantry retained as a mobile reserve on Unalaska and then Adak. The 7th Infantry Division (17th, 32d Infantry, -159th Infantry) under Major General Albert E. Brown departed California in late April. After a layover at Cold Bay, the division assaulted Kiska on 11 May. There were 2,650 troops defending Attu under Colonel YAMASAKI Yasuyo. Their main base was at Chichagof Harbor and they established defensive positions facing the inland approaches to the base. They had attempted to build an airstrip at the southwest end of Holtz Bay. Agattu Island, thirty- five miles southeast of Attu, had been used by the Japanese as an anchorage to avoid American aircraft. While small IJA elements had landed for security, no base was estab- lished there.

Attu was defended by the *301st* and *303d Independent Infantry Battalions*, and *North Chishima Coast Defense Infantry Unit*. These units had been reinforced by 1,570 men brought in ships and submarines between November 1942 and April 1943 for a total of about 4,000.

The division's Provisional Scout Battalion landed on Beach SCARLET in Austin Cove on the northeast coast. Two infantry battalions, the Northern Landing Force, then landed on Beach RED on the north shoulder of Holtz Bay, linked up with the Scout Battalion on the 14th, and advanced around the bay toward Chichagof Village. Also on the 11th three more battalions of the Southern Landing Force landed at the head of Massacre Bay on Beaches YELLOW and BLUE without opposition; all of the landings were covered by dense fog, which also concealed their movements ashore. The battalions moved up Massacre Valley and were engaged by the Japanese in the evening. Progress was slow, not only because of enemy action, but also owing to weather and terrain. The Northern Landing Force in the mountains suffered greatly from the weather while fighting a Japanese rearguard. It linked up with the Southern Landing Force on the 15th. As American progress was deemed too slow, the division commander was replaced by Major General Eugene M. Luandrum on 16 May. The 4th Infantry was committed on the 20th and the Japanese were gradually forced back to Chichagof Harbor. In the predawn hours of 29 May the Japanese killed all of their 400 wounded and the up to 1,000 remaining Japanese executed a *banzai* charge on American lines in Chichagof Valley only to be wiped out. The island was declared secure later in the morning. The Japanese reported to higher headquarters that the Americans ineffectively employed gas on 14 May, but this is not true.

As the battle on Attu raged, elements of the 4th Infantry landed on Shemya Island to the east on 28 May. Work soon began on a 10,000-foot B-29 runway. While the airfield was operational, it never launched B-29s at Japan. (After serving as a staging field through the Korean War the airfield was deactivated in 1954. It was reactivated in 1958 as Shemya Air Force Base and in 1993 was redesignated Eareckson Air Force Station. It remains the only operational military airfield in the Aleutians.) A Marine photo-reconnaissance detachment of three aircraft operated from the USS *Nassau* (ACV-16) in support of the Attu operation. It was the first Marine unit to fly combat missions from an aircraft carrier and the only Marine unit, other than Marine barracks, to operate in the North Pacific Area.

Only 28 Japanese were taken prisoner. Of the 15,000 U.S. troops ashore there were 550 KIA, 1,150 WIA, and 1,800 out of action because of cold weather injuries, disease, and nonbattle injuries.

An airfield was soon operational on Attu and on 10 July the first American air raid on the Japanese Home Islands since the Doolittle raid and the first from an American land base was launched successfully at Paramushiro. Other raids on the Kuriles followed. A naval operating base with a seaplane base and Marine barracks was also built on the island.

The bombardment of Kiska Island began long before the planned 15 August 1943 Operation COTTAGE. The island was also blockaded and the Japanese experienced great difficulty in supplying the garrison, which could only be accomplished by submarines. U.S. intelligence estimated there were 10,000 Japanese troops on Kiska, but there were actually only 6,000 who had built a massive underground base as well as an above-ground base on Gertrude Cove southwest of Kiska Harbor. Construction of a fighter strip was attempted and abandoned to the muskeg. A modest submarine base was constructed on the south side of Kiska Harbor.

On 21 May it was decided that the Japanese defense forces would be evacuated and employed to defend the Kurile Islands. The evacuation was begun by submarine, but this would require up to fifty round trips. By the end of June only 500 men had been evacuated while 300 were lost with three of the submarines. The Japanese took a gamble and decided to evacuate the remaining 5,183 men with fifteen surface ships. The *KE-GO Operation* was executed on 27/28 July with the evacuation ships departing Paramushiro on the 21st. An American task force shelling Kiska was diverted to intercept seven unidentified ships detected southwest of Attu. The force sped away to make the intercept. They fired on radar contacts, but no sign was ever found of any ships. In what has been called the "Battle of the Pips" (referring to radar contacts) the American ships may have engaged a group of surface-running submarines conducting a deception operation to cover the evacuation. By the time the task force returned to Kiska, after refueling, the Japanese had evacuated all troops, embarking them in one hour from the island, successfully returning to Paramushiro on 1 August.

While airmen reported the island deserted it was surmised that the Japanese had gone into the hills or were underground. Operation COTTAGE was executed on 15 August as planned. The force assigned the mission was designated Amphibious Training Force 9 (a cover designation for the Kiska Task Force) under Major General Charles H. Corlett. It consisted of the combined U.S./Canadian commando unit, the 1st Special Service Force (1st–3d Regiments), 53d Infantry Regiment, 87th Mountain Infantry Regiment, 17th and 184th Infantry Regiments detached from the 7th Infantry Division, and the 5,300-man 13th Canadian Infantry Brigade Group commanded by Brigadier H.W. Foster for a total of 34,400 troops. The units staged at Amchitka Island and the expeditionary force assembled at Adak where rehearsals were conducted. The force departed for Kiska on 13 August.

The landing force arrived off of the northwest coast of Kiska and the first troops went ashore by rubber boat at 0120 hours meeting no resistance. Beaches 9 and 10, on which the 1st Regiment, 1st Special Service Force landed in advance of the main body, were six miles east of and on the opposite side of the island from the abandoned Japanese base. The 13th Canadian Brigade and 184th Infantry conducted a demonstration off of the northwest coast. It was soon apparent that the Japanese had left, but the troops remained alert expecting a surprise attack. The 87th and 17th Infantry landed at 0630 hours on Beaches 9 and 10 and moved inland. Numerous casualties were caused by friendly fire in the fog. The 1st Special Service Force's 2d Regiment, on standby at Amchitka, was prepared to conduct a parachute assault to reinforce the landing force, but this was canceled. On the morning of the 16th the Force's 3d Regiment came ashore in the predawn hours on Beach 14 some seven miles north of the former Japanese base. They were followed by the 13th Canadian Brigade and 184th Infantry. The 53d Infantry remained afloat in reserve. Part of the 1st Service Force's 1st Regiment was landed on Little Kiska Island guarding the entrance to Kiska Harbor later on the 16th. Three British-made 5-inch guns were found there dated 1897, leading to speculation that they had been brought from Hong Kong. They were actually leftovers from the 1905 Russo-Japanese War, previously purchased from Great Britain. Kiska was searched until 22 August when there was no question that it was deserted.

Even though the Japanese had slipped off of Kiska, the landing proved to be an intelligence boom because of the vast amount of new weapons and equipment recovered including two submarines. There were Allied losses, however. The United States suffered twenty-four men killed by friendly fire and four by booby traps, fifty were wounded by the same causes, and there were 130 trenchfoot cases. The Canadians lost three dead and one wounded. On 18 August the USS *Abner Read* (DD-526) struck a mine near shore losing seventy men and forty-seven wounded. The last action in the Aleutians occurred on 13 October 1943 when Japanese bombers raided Attu, but caused little damage. The Canadian brigade remained to garrison Kiska for three months.

U.S. military bases remaining in Alaska today include Forts Richardson (new post built in 1950 east of Elmendorf Air Force Base, the original Fort Richardson), Wainwright (former Ladd Field renamed in 1961), and Greely (former Big Delta Air Force Base); Elmendorf (former Fort Richardson) and Eielson Air Force Bases (former 26-Mile Strip), all on the mainland; and Eareckson Air Station on Shemya Island. A Coast Guard base is located at the old Navy base on Kodiak Island. Adak Naval Air Facility was active until closed in January 1998. It was recently announced that a special early-

warning radar for the planned National Missile Defense system was to be emplaced on
the island, with little consideration given to the environment problems learned so long
ago by engineers. In 1985, the Department of the Interior designated the Attu Battlefield
and Airfields and Kiska Harbor as National Historical Landmarks. This designation provides protection of the sunken Japanese ships found in Kiska Harbor.

READING SUGGESTIONS

Bureau of Yards and Docks. *Building the Navy's Bases in World War II, Vol. II.* Washington, DC:
     US Government Printing Office, 1947.
Conn, Stetson; Engelman, Rose C.; and Fairchild, Byron. *The United States Army in World War
     II, The Western Hemisphere, Guarding the United States Outposts.* Washington, DC: US
     Government Printing Office, 1964.
Garfield, Brian. *The Thousand-Mile War: World War II in Alaska and the Aleutians.* New York:
     Doubleday, 1969.
Morison, Samuel E. *History of US Navy Operations in World War II: Aleutians, Gilberts and
     Marshalls, March 1943–April 1944, Vol. VII.* Boston: Little, Brown and Company, 1951.

Selected Bibliography

Alexander, Col. Joseph H. *Across the Reef: The Marine Assault of Tarawa*. Washington Navy Yard: History and Museums Division, Marine Corps Historical Center, 1993.
———. *Closing In: Marines in the Seizure of Iwo Jima*. Washington Navy Yard: History and Museums Division, Marine Corps Historical Center, 1994.
———. *The Final Campaign: Marines in the Victory on Okinawa*. Washington Navy Yard: History and Museums Division, Marine Corps Historical Center, 1996.
———. *Utmost Savagery: The Three Days of Tarawa*. Annapolis: Naval Institute Press, 1995.
American Historical Association. *G.I. Roundtable: What Future for the Islands of the Pacific?* (EM 45), Madison, WI: US Armed Forces Institute, 1944.
Ancell, R. Manning and Miller, Christine M. *The Biographical Dictionary of World War II Generals and Flag Officers: The U.S. Armed Forces*. Westport, CT: Greenwood Publishing Co., 1996.
Argyle, Christopher. *Chronology of World War II*. New York: Exeter Books, 1980.
Astor, Gerald. *Operation Iceberg: The Invasion and Conquest of Okinawa in World War II—An Oral History*. New York: Dell Books, 1995.
Averill, Gerald P. *Mustang: A Combat Marine*. Novato, CA: Presidio Press, 1987.
Bacon, Mary A. (Editor). *United States Army in World War II: A Pictorial Record, Vol. III, The War against Japan*. Washington, DC: US Government Printing Office, 1952.
Bartley, Lt. Col. Whitman S. *Iwo Jima: Amphibious Epic*. Washington, DC: US Government Printing Office, 1954.
Bergerud, Eric M. *Touched by Fire: The Land War in the South Pacific*. New York: Penguin Books USA, 1996.
Breuer, William B. *MacArthur's Undercover War: Spies, Saboteurs, Guerrillas, and Secret Missions*. New York: John Wiley and Sons, 1995.
Brown, David. *Warship Losses of World War II*, Revised Edition. Annapolis, MD: Naval Institute Press, 1990.
Bureau of Yards and Docks. *Building the Navy's Bases in World War II, Vol. II*. Washington, DC: US Government Printing Office, 1947.
Cannon, M. Hamlin. *United States Army in World War II: Leyte: The Return to the Philippines*. Washington, DC: US Government Printing Office, 1987.
Central Intelligence Agency. *The World Fact Book, 2000*. Washington, DC: CIA, 2000.

Chapin, Capt John C. . . . *And a Few Marines: Marines in the Liberation of the Philippines*. Washington Navy Yard: History and Museums Division, Marine Corps Historical Center, 1997.

―――. *Breaking the Outer Ring: Marine Landings in the Marshall Islands*. Washington Navy Yard: History and Museums Division, Marine Corps Historical Center, 1994.

―――. *Top of the Ladder: Marine Operations in the Northern Solomons*. Washington Navy Yard: History and Museums Division, Marine Corps Historical Center, 1997.

Cogan, Frances B. *Captured: The Japanese Internment of American Civilians in the Philippines, 1941–1945*. Athens, GA: University of Georgia Press, 2000.

Coggins, Jack. *The Campaign for Guadalcanal*. Garden City, NY: Doubleday and Co., 1972.

Coletta, Paolo E. and Bauer, K. Jack (Editors). *United States Navy and Marine Bases, Overseas*. Westport, CT: Greenwood Publishing Co., 1985.

Conn, Stetson; Engleman, Rose C.; and Fairchild, Byron. *The US Army in World War II: The Western Hemisphere, Guarding the United States and its Outposts*. Washington, DC: US Government Printing Office, 1964.

Controvich, James T. *The Central Pacific Campaign 1943–1944: A Bibliography*. Westport, CT: Greenwood Publishing Co., 1990.

Cowdrey, Albert E. *Fighting for Life: American Military Medicine in World War II*. New York: The Free Press, 1994.

Craven, Wesley F. and Cate, James L. *The Army Air Forces in World War II, Plans and Early Operations—January 1939 to August 1942, Vol. 1*. Chicago: The University of Chicago Press, 1948.

―――. *The Army Air Forces in World War II: The Pacific: Guadalcanal to Saipan, August 1942 to July 1944, Vol. 4*. Chicago: University of Chicago Press, 1950.

―――. *The Army Air Forces in World War II: The Pacific: Matterhorn to Nagasaki, June 1944 to August 1945, Vol. 5*. Chicago: University of Chicago Press, 1953.

Cressman, Robert J. *A Magnificent Fight: The Battle for Wake Island*. Washington Navy Yard: History and Museums Division, Marine Corps Historical Center, 1992.

―――. *Official Chronology of the US Navy in World War II*. Annapolis, MD: Naval Institute Press, 2000.

Crowl, Philip A. *United States Army in World War II: Campaign in the Marianas*. Washington, DC: US Government Printing Office, 1960.

Crowl, Philip A. and Love, Edmund G. *United States Army in World War II: Seizure of the Gilberts and Marshalls*. Washington, DC: US Government Printing Office, 1985.

Dear, I.C.B. (General Editor). *The Oxford Companion to World War II*. New York: Oxford University Press, 1995.

Dod, Karl C. *United States Army in World War II: The Corps of Engineers: The War against Japan*. Washington, DC: US Government Printing Office, 1987.

Doland, Ronald E. (Editor). *Area Handbook Series: Philippines: A Country Study*. Washington, DC: US Government Printing Office, 1993.

Drea, Edward J. *Defending the Driniumor: Covering Force Operations in New Guinea, 1944*. Ft Leavenworth, KS: Combat Studies Institute, 1984.

Dull, Paul. *Battle History of the Imperial Japanese Navy, 1941–1945*. Annapolis, MD: Naval Institute Press, 1996.

Dyer, George. *The Amphibians Came to Conquer: The Story of Admiral Richmond Kelly Turner, Vol. I and II*. Washington, DC: U.S. Navy. (Also published as FMFRP 12–109–1 and 2, 26 Sept 91.)

Ellis, John. *World War II: A Statistical Survey*, Corrected Edition. New York: Facts on File, 1993.

Ellis, Richard. *Encyclopedia of the Sea*. New York: Alfred A. Knopf, 2000.

Feifer, George. *Tennozan: The Battle for Okinawa and the Atomic Bomb*. New York: Ticknor & Fields, 1992.

Frank, Richard B. *Guadalcanal: The Definitive Account of the Landmark Battle*. London: Penguin, 1992.

Frederick, William H. and Worden, Robert L. *Area Handbook Series: Indonesia: A Country Study.* Washington, DC: US Government Printing Office, 1993.

Fuchida Mitsuo and Okumiya Masatake. *Midway: The Battle that Doomed Japan, the Japanese Navy's Story.* Annapolis, MD: Naval Institute Press, 1955, 1976.

Fuller, Richard. *Shokan: Hirohito's Samurai, Leaders of the Japanese Armed Forces, 1926–1945.* London: Arms & Armour Press, 1992.

Funk, Charles, E. (Editor). *The New International Year Book: A Compendium of the World's Progress for the Year 1944.* New York: Funk & Wagnalls Co., 1945.

Gailey, Harry A. *Bougainville: The Forgotten Campaign, 1943–1945.* Lexington: The University Press of Kentucky, 1991.

———. *Liberation of Guam, 21 July–10 August 1944.* Novato, CA: Presidio Press, 1988.

———. *Peleliu 1944.* Baltimore, MD: Nautical and Aviation Press, 1983.

Garand, George W. and Stonebridge, Turman R. *History of US Marine Corps Operations in World War II: Western Pacific Operations, Vol. IV.* Washington, DC: US Government Printing Office, 1966.

Garfield, Brian. *The Thousand-Mile War: World War II in Alaska and the Aleutians.* New York: Doubleday Publishing, 1969.

Gayle, Brig. Gen. Gordon D. *Bloody Beaches: The Marines at Peleliu.* Washington Navy Yard: History and Museums Division, Marine Corps Historical Center, 1996.

General Staff, GHQ, Southwest Pacific Area. *Reports of General MacArthur, the Campaigns of MacArthur in the Pacific, Vol. I.* Washington, DC: US Government Printing Office, 1966.

———. *Reports of General MacArthur, Japanese Operations in the Southwest Pacific Area, Vol. II.* Washington, DC: US Government Printing Office, 1966.

Gillespie, Oliver A. *The Pacific: Official History of New Zealand in the Second World War 1939–45.* Wellington, NZ: Department of Internal Affairs, 1952.

Graham, Michael B. *Mantle of Heroism: Tarawa and the Struggle for the Gilberts, November 1943.* Novato, CA: Presidio Press, 1997.

Greenfield, Kent R.; Palmer, Robert R.; and Wiley, Bell I. *United States Army in World War II: The Fall of the Philippines.* Washington, DC: US Government Printing Office, 1947.

Hammel, Eric M. *Guadalcanal: Starvation Island.* Pacifica, CA: Pacifica Press, 1992.

———. *Munda Trail: The New Georgia Campaign.* New York: Orion Books, 1989.

Harwood, Richard. *A Close Encounter: The Marine Landing on Tinian.* Washington Navy Yard: History and Museums Division, Marine Corps Historical Center, 1994.

Heinl, Lt. Col. Robert D., Jr. and Crown, Lt. Col. John A. *The Marshalls: Increasing the Tempo.* Washington, DC: HQ Marine Corps, 1954.

Hinz, Earl. *Pacific Battlegrounds of World War II: Then and Now.* Honolulu, HI: Bess Press, 1995.

Hixon, Carl K. *Guadalcanal: An American Story.* Annapolis, MD: Naval Institute Press, 1999.

Hough, Lt. Col. Frank O. and Crown, John A. *The Campaign on New Britain.* Washington, DC: US Government Printing Office, 1952.

Hough, Lt. Col. Frank O.; Ludwig, Maj. Verle E.; and Shaw, Henry I., Jr. *History of US Marine Corps Operations in World War II: Pearl Harbor to Guadalcanal, Vol. I.* Washington, DC: US Government Printing Office, 1958.

Hoyt, Edwin P. *Guadalcanal.* New York: Stein & Day, 1982.

———. *Storm over the Gilberts.* New York: Mason/Charter, 1978.

Huber, Tomas M. *Leavenworth Papers: Japan's Battle for Okinawa: April to June 1945.* Washington, DC: US Government Printing Office, 1990.

Isely, Jeter A. and Crowl, Philip A. *The U.S. Marines and Amphibious Warfare: Its Theory, and Its Practice in the Pacific.* Princeton, NJ: Princeton University Press, 1951.

King, Fleet Adm. Ernest J. *U.S. Navy at War 1941–1945: Official Reports to the Secretary of the Navy by Fleet Admiral Ernest J. King, U.S. Navy.* Washington, DC: US Navy Department, 1946.

Krancher, Jan A. (Editor). *The Defining Years of the Dutch East Indies, 1942–1949: Survivors'*

Accounts of Japanese Invasion and Enslavement of Europeans and the Revolution that Created Free Indonesia. New York: MacFarland and Co., 1996.

Lebra, Joyce C. *Japanese-Trained Armies in Southeast Asia*. New York: Columbia University Press, 1977.

Leckie, Robert. *Challenge for the Pacific: The Bloody Six-month Battle for Guadalcanal*. Cambridge, MA: Da Capo Press, 1999.

———. *Okinawa: The Last Battle of World War II*. New York: Viking Press, 1995.

Livingston, William S. and Louis, William R. (Editors). *Australia, New Zealand, and the Pacific Islands since the First World War*. Austin: University of Texas Press, 1979.

Lodge, Maj. O.R. *The Recapture of Guam*. Washington, DC: HQ Marine Corps, 1954.

Long, Gavin M. *The Six Years War: A Concise History of Australia in the 1939–1945 War*. Canberra: The Australian War Memorial and the Australian Government Publishing Service, 1973.

Maurer, Maurer (Editor). *Air Force Combat Units of World War II*. Washington, DC: US Government Printing Office, 1961.

Melson, Maj. Charles D. *Up the Slot: Marines in the Central Solomons*. Washington, DC: Marine Corps Historical Center, 1993.

Miller, John, Jr.. *United States Army in World War II: Cartwheel: The Reduction of Rabaul*. Washington, DC: US Government Printing Office, 1959.

———. *United States Army in World War II: Guadalcanal: The First Offensive*. Washington, DC: US Government Printing Office, 1949.

Millett, Allen R. *Semper Fidelis: The History of the U.S. Marine Corps*. New York: The Macmillan Company, 1991 (revised and updated edition).

Milner, Samuel. *United States Army in World War II: Victory in Papua*. Washington, DC: US Government Printing Office, 1957.

Morison, Samuel E. *History of US Navy Operations in World War II: The Rising Sun in the Pacific, 1931–April 1942, Vol. III*. Boston: Little, Brown and Company, 1948.

———. *History of US Navy Operations in World War II: The Coral Sea, Midway, and Submarine Actions, May 1942–August 1942, Vol. IV*. Boston: Little, Brown and Company, 1949.

———. *History of US Navy Operations in World War II: The Struggle for Guadalcanal, August 1942–February 1943, Vol. V*. Boston: Little, Brown and Company, 1949.

———. *History of US Navy Operations in World War II: Breaking the Bismarcks Barrier, 22 July 1942–1 May 1944, Vol. VI*. Boston: Little, Brown and Company, 1950.

———. *History of US Navy Operations in World War II: Aleutians, Gilberts and Marshalls, March 1943–April 1944, Vol. VII*. Boston: Little, Brown and Company, 1951.

———. *History of US Navy Operations in World War II: New Guinea and the Marianas, March 1944–August 1944, Vol. VIII*. Boston: Little, Brown and Company, 1953.

———. *History of US Navy Operations in World War II: Leyte, June 1944–January 1945, Vol. XII*. Boston: Little, Brown and Company, 1958.

———. *History of US Navy Operations in World War II: The Liberation of the Philippines, Luzon, Mindanao, the Visayas 1944–1945, Vol. XIII*. Boston: Little, Brown and Company, 1959.

———. *History of United States Naval Operations in World War II, Victory in the Pacific, Vol. XIV*. Boston: Little, Brown and Company, 1960.

Morton, Louis. *United States Army in World War II: Strategy and Command: The First Two Years*. Washington, DC: US Government Printing Office, 1962.

Nalty, Bernard C. *Cape Gloucester: The Green Inferno*. Washington Navy Yard: History and Museums Division, Marine Corps Historical Center, 1994.

Nalty, Bernard C. and Crawford, Danny J. *The United States Marines on Iwo Jima: The Battle and the Flag Raisings*. Washington Navy Yard: History and Museums Division, Marine Corps Historical Center, 1995.

Nichols, Maj. Charles S., Jr. and Shaw, Henry I., Jr. *Okinawa: Victory in the Pacific*. Washington, DC: HQ Marine Corps, 1955.

Nimmo, William F. *Stars and Stripes across the Pacific: The United States, Japan, and the Asia/ Pacific Region, 1895–1945*. Westport, CT: Praeger, 2001.

O'Brien, Cyril J. *Liberation: Marines in the Recapture of Guam*. Washington Navy Yard: History and Museums Division, Marine Corps Historical Center, 1994.

Philippine Army (no author). *Philippine Army: 100 Years*. www.army.mil.ph/pa100yrs.htm.

Prange, Gordon W.; Goldstein, Donald M.; and Dillon, Katherine V. *Miracle at Midway*. New York: McGraw-Hill Book Co., 1982.

Price, Willard. *Japan's Islands of Mystery*. New York: John Day Company, 1944.

Rand McNally. *World Atlas, Premier Edition*. Chicago: Rand McNally and Company, 1943.

Rasor, Eugene L. *The Solomon Islands Campaign, Guadalcanal to Rabaul: Historiography and Annotated Bibliography*. Westport, CT: Greenwood Publishing Co., 1997.

———. *The Southwest Pacific Campaign: Historiography and Annotated Bibliography*. Westport, CT: Greenwood Publishing Co., 1996.

Rentz, John R. *Bougainville and the Northern Solomons*. Washington, DC: HQ Marine Corps, 1948.

Rogers, Robert F. *Destiny's Landfall: A History of Guam*. Honolulu: University of Hawaii Press, 1995.

Rottman, Gordon L. *U. S. Marine Corps World War II Order of Battle*. Westport, CT: Greenwood Publishing Co., 2001.

Rowan, R.W. *The Pacific Islands Handbook, 1944*. New York: The Macmillan Company, 1945.

Ruffner, Frederick G. and Thomas, Robert C. *Code Names Dictionary*. Detroit: Gale Research Company, 1962.

Shaw, Henry I., Jr. *First Offensive: The Marine Campaign for Guadalcanal*. Washington Navy Yard: History and Museums Division, Marine Corps Historical Center, 1992.

Shaw, Henry I., Jr., and Kane, Maj. Douglas T. *History of US Marine Corps Operations in World War II: Isolation of Rabaul, Vol. II*. Washington, DC: US Government Printing Office, 1963.

Shaw, Henry I., Jr.; Nalty, Bernard C.; and Turnbladh, Edwin T. *History of US Marine Corps Operations in World War II: Central Pacific Drive, Vol. III*. Washington, DC: US Government Printing Office, 1966.

Sherrod, Robert. *History of Marine Corps Aviation in World War II*. San Rafael, CA: Presidio Press, 1952, updated edition 1980.

———. *Tarawa*. New York: Duell, Sloan, and Pearce, 1944. Reprinted by The Admiral Nimitz Foundation.

Smith, Myron J., Jr. *The Battles of the Coral Sea and Midway, 1942: A Selected Bibliography*. Westport, CT: Greenwood Publishing Co., 1991.

Smith, Robert R. *United States Army in World War II: The Approach to the Philippines*. Washington, DC: US Government Printing Office, 1984.

———. *United States Army in World War II: Triumph in the Philippines*. Washington, DC: US Government Printing Office, 1963.

Sommerville, Donald. *World War II Day by Day: An Illustrated Almanac 1939–1945*. Greenwich, CT: Brompton Books, 1989.

Spur, R. *A Glorious Way to Die: The Kamikaze Mission of the Battleship Yamato, April 1945*. Scranton, PA: Newmarket Press, 1981.

Stanton, Shelby L. *Order of Battle, U.S. Army, World War II*. Novato, CA: Presidio Press, 1984.

Stockman, James R. *The Battle for Tarawa*. Washington, DC: Historical Branch, G-3 Division, Headquarters, Marine Corps, 1954.

Taaffe, Stephen R. *MacArthur's Jungle Victory: The 1944 New Guinea Campaign*. Saint Lawrence: University of Kansas Press, 1997.

Tanaka Kengoro. *Operations of the Imperial Japanese Armed Forces in Papua New Guinea Theater during World War II*. Tokyo: Japan Papua New Guinea Goodwill Society, 1980.

Tyson, Carolyn A. *A Chronology of the United States Marine Corps, 1935–1946, Vol. II*. Washington, DC: Marine Corps Historical Center, 1971.

Urwin, Gregory J.W. *Facing Fearful Odds: The Siege of Wake Island*. Lincoln, NE: University of Nebraska Press, 1998.

U.S. Army. *Handbook on Japanese Military Forces* (TM-E 30-480). Washington, DC: US Government Printing Office, 1944.

U.S. Navy. *Glossary of U.S. Naval Abbreviations with Revisions* (OPNAV 29-P1000). Washington, DC: Office of Naval Records and History, Office of the Chief of Naval Operations, 1949.

———. *Glossary of U.S. Naval Code Words with Revisions* (NAVEXOS P-474). Washington, DC: Office of Naval History, 1948.

Whitman, John W. *Bataan: Our Last Ditch*. New York: Hippocrene Books, 1990.

Williams, Mary H. *United States Army in World War II: Chronology 1941–1945*, Washington, DC: US Government Printing Office, 1960.

Winters, Harold A. *Battling the Elements: Weather and Terrain in the Conduct of War*. Baltimore, MD: John Hopkins University Press, 1998.

Wukovits, John E. *The Final Campaign: Marines in the Victory on Okinawa*. Washington Navy Yard: History and Museums Division, Marine Corps Historical Center, 1996.

Wright, Derrick. *Battle for Iwo Jima, 1945*. Stroud, Gloucestershire: Sutton Publishing, 2000.

———. *A Hell of a Way to Die: Tarawa Atoll, 20–23 November 1943*. London: Windrow & Greene, 1996.

Yahara Hiromichi, Col. *The Battle for Okinawa*. New York: John Wiley & Sons, 1995.

Young, Donald J. *The Battle of Bataan: A History of the 90 Day Siege and Eventual Surrender of 75,000 Filipino and United States Troops to the Japanese in World War II*. Jefferson, NC: McFarland & Company, 1992.

Index

About the Author

GORDON L. ROTTMAN has served twenty-six years in the U.S. Army in Special Forces, airborne infantry, long-range reconnaissance patrol, and military intelligence assignments in the Regular Army, Army National Guard, and Army reserve. He began writing military history books in 1984. He is employed by TRW System and Information Technology Group as a special operations forces scenario writer at the Army's Joint Readiness Training Center, Fort Polk, LA.